THE U.S. ARMY AND WORLD WAR II

SELECTED PAPERS FROM THE ARMY'S COMMEMORATIVE CONFERENCES

Judith L. Bellafaire
General Editor

CENTER OF MILITARY HISTORY
UNITED STATES ARMY
WASHINGTON, D.C., 1998

Library of Congress Cataloging-in-Publication Data

The U. S. Army and World War II : selected papers from the Armys commemorative conferences / Judith L. Bellafaire, general editor.
    p.   cm.
    1. United States. Army—History—World War, 1939–1945—Congresses. 2. World War, 1939–1945—Campaigns—Europe—Congresses. 3. World War, 1939–1945—Campaigns—Pacific Area—Congresses. 4. United States. Army—Sources—Congresses.
I. Bellafaire, Judith Lawrence.
D769.2.U18   1998
940.54'21—dc21   97–38399
                                                                              CIP

First Printing—CMH Pub 68–4

For sale by the U.S. Government Printing Office
Superintendent of Documents, Mail Stop: SSOP, Washington, DC 20402-9328
ISBN 0-16-049589-X

Foreword

As part of the Department of Defense's efforts to commemorate the fiftieth anniversary of World War II, the U.S. Army Center of Military History sponsored three international conferences on the Army's role in the war. The first was held in 1990 and focused on "The U.S. Army in World War II Through the Summer of 1943." In 1992 the conference theme was "The U.S. Army During World War II: The Mediterranean and European Theaters, 1943–1945." During the 1994 conference on "The U.S. Army in the War Against Japan: 1943–1945," scholars and veterans discussed the Pacific and China-Burma-India theaters. This collection contains some of the best papers from those meetings.

Center historians have separated the various presentations into four general categories, or sections. One covers prewar planning, another the home front, and two the European and Pacific theaters of operations, reflecting the diversity of both the war and the interests of those seeking to understand its many facets. Here one will find the more conventional treatments of doctrine, strategy, and operations side by side with those focusing on military mobilization and procurement, race and gender, psychological warfare, and large-scale advice and assistance programs. And despite significant changes since those desperate times in military technology and the geopolitical landscape of the world, the human problems highlighted by the authors are not much different from many of those facing Army leaders today. Although the past can never provide the specific recipes needed for the future, experience has shown that both the basic ingredients and the manner in which they are processed and prepared have remained remarkably constant. For this reason I recommend highly this collection of readings to those grappling with the challenges of the present.

Washington, D.C.   JOHN W. MOUNTCASTLE
17 February 1998   Brigadier General, U.S. Army
                                              Chief of Military History

Contents

The views expressed in the papers collected in this volume are those of the authors and do not reflect the official policy or position of the Department of Defense, or the U.S. government.

Introduction

The following four papers examine the efforts of the United States Army to plan for a war everyone feared and no one wanted. Political, economic, and social forces as well as some of the Army's own traditions hindered the Army's attempts to prepare, train, and modernize its soldiers and equipment. Despite this often difficult environment, the Army managed to lay the critical foundation for the rapid mobilization which ultimately became necessary.

One of the traditional ways the U.S. Army has planned for war is by training its future leaders. Making use of archival materials ignored by previous researchers, Henry Gole examines the strategic planning studies conducted by students at the U.S. Army War College between 1934 and 1940. He concludes that the resulting analyses and reports, referred to as the color plans, were excellent "spade work" which the War Plans Division (WPD) of the War Department General Staff (WDGS) eventually used in developing the much vaunted "RAINBOW Plans" of 1939–1941.

Gole emphasizes the link between the work of War College students and that of the Army General Staff. Initially, instructors at the War College asked their colleagues on the General Staff to help them develop projects and assignments for the students. The result was that a number of student projects contributed to the development of a variety of strategic war plans—the color plans—applicable to different geographical regions. Some instructors sent student work to members of the General Staff for their comments, and many students were assigned to the General Staff after they left the War College. Gole concludes that the preliminary work of students at the War College paved the way for the development of the RAINBOW Plans devised by the General Staff between 1939 and 1941. The RAINBOW Plans provided overall American strategic direction for the war.

Historians have long been aware of the difficulties which Army leaders of the interwar years encountered as they sought to modernize weapons, equipment, and tactics to make the U.S. Army ready to engage modern enemy armed forces on the battlefield. Chronic budget shortages compounded by political isolationism kept the interwar Army small and encouraged it to use World War I surplus ammunition and weapons to train and equip its troops. Boyd Dastrup's paper, "Travails of Peace and War: Field Artillery in the 1930s and Early 1940s," describes the specific modernization problems faced by artillery officers. Dastrup identifies both forward-looking artillery officers who understood the importance of developing new concepts and those who tended to think traditionally. At issue were innovations such as the replacement of horse-drawn artillery with motor-towed and "self-propelled" artillery, air observation support, and centralized command and control. While some Army leaders believed these innovations would lead to the more efficient use of artillery, traditionalists felt that they were dangerous risks because they had not been proved in battle.

According to Dastrup, by 1935 most artillery officers had finally accepted the inevitability of motor-towed artillery pieces but continued to resist the idea of self-propelled artillery. Even after funds for modernization became more available, some leaders continued to balk. Horses always seemed more reliable than many of the primitive automotive vehicles then available, and larger artillery pieces always demanded larger crews and heavier ammunition. Other innovations—such as replacing the 75-mm. gun with the 105-mm. howitzer, directing fire from the fire direction center at the battalion level rather than from the battery, and using aerial observation to help direct artillery fire—faced similar hurdles.

The German offensives of 1939 and 1940 fully demonstrated to American artillerymen and others that efforts to modernize were essential. The War Department demanded that the Ordnance Department acquire self-propelled artillery pieces. In 1942 the War Department tasked the field artillery to test air observation techniques, experiments that resulted in the allotment of two small aircraft, two pilots, and one mechanic to each field artillery battalion. Dastrup believes that the combat experiences of the U.S. Army in North Africa, which included the employment of both self-propelled artillery and aerial observation, demonstrated that the Army had successfully pushed through enough doctrinal reforms to enable American artillery to perform well against the battle-hardened Germans.

In "'Through the Looking Glass': Bradford G. Chynoweth as United States Military Attache in Britain, 1939," Theodore Wilson describes how politics and personalities combined to render the astute observations of Army officer Col. Bradford Chynoweth near worthless. The habitually outspoken Chynoweth was assigned to the U.S. embassy in London against the wishes of the U.S. ambassador, Joseph P. Kennedy, "a prickly personality who was extremely protective of his prerogatives." Wilson demonstrates how Chynoweth's original orders from the War Department put him on an inevitable collision course with the redoubtable ambassador, who did not hesitate to make use of his political connections with Assistant Secretary of War Louis Johnson to seek Chynoweth's removal before he had been in London six months.

But the ambassador's gain was the nation's loss. Wilson's detailed account of the observations Chynoweth sent the War Department during his brief tenure reveal the efficacy of Chynoweth's thoughtful analyses. For example, Wilson stresses Chynoweth's emphasis on the capacity of the British people to resist invasion, in direct opposition to popular opinion in the United States that the British were an "effete race" who would not last long in a fight. At the same time, however, Chynoweth warned his superiors that British leaders were determined to avoid the mistakes of the Great War. This time they would do their best to make sure that their allies (the French, the Poles, and the Americans) fought alongside them and took just as many casualties. They would not back down and allow their allies to go it alone—but neither would they "get in the game until the other players were on the field."

Although Chynoweth found much to admire about the British Army, he complained in his letters that British military doctrine "gave undue emphasis to passive defence" and failed to understand the importance of teamwork among the various combat arms. Wilson reminds the reader that Chynoweth's observations are in tune with those of many recent military historians.

Unfortunately, Chynoweth's communications were treated cavalierly by those same officials who had originally dispatched him to London. Wilson concludes by comparing the misuse of Chynoweth's observations with those of Truman Smith, the U.S. military attache in Berlin from 1938 to 1939. No matter how prescient or on-target such information might be, it will not be used if it does not conform to what those in power want to hear.

During World War II U.S. troops engaged the enemy first on the Philippine Islands. Thomas Huber looks at their performance in "The U.S. Bataan Campaign, December 1941 to April 1942." Huber criticizes General Douglas MacArthur and Washington planners for failing to stockpile enough supplies of medicine, food, and ammunition for U.S. and Filipino troops to defend the islands adequately against the Japanese. MacArthur and his superiors had believed that the presence of air assets on the islands would be sufficient to deter attack.

When U.S. troops in the Philippines found themselves in the unenviable position of attempting to defend Bataan against a larger and better supplied invader, however, they did exceptionally well given an impossible situation. They established three lines of defense across the Bataan peninsula. This forced the attacking Japanese forces, starting at the top of the peninsula, to breach one defensive line at a time, giving U.S. and Filipino troops time to retreat and reinforce the next line. The defenders attempted to hold out as long as possible in the hope that reinforcements and supplies would arrive from the States.

Although Huber praises the overall defensive plan and commends the efforts of the U.S. and Filipino soldiers, who fought without enough food, medicine, and ammunition, he also identifies a mistake in the location of one of the defensive lines. The Abucay-Mauben line was bisected by Mount Natib, creating a gap which the Japanese easily exploited. Huber believes that had the defenders dug trenches and tunnels, they would have been able to avoid much of the enemy artillery fire. He admits, however, that this effort was probably too much to ask of troops weakened by disease and the scarcity of food and medicine and would have only postponed the inevitable for a few more weeks. Huber concludes that given their limited resources, the American forces on Bataan achieved far more than military policy makers are normally entitled to expect.

The above papers demonstrate that although the U.S. Army was far from prepared for World War II and experienced substantial difficulties attempting to plan, modernize, and equip for war, U.S. soldiers performed more than adequately during their first combat experiences.

War Planning at the U.S. Army War College, 1934–1940: The Road to Rainbow

Henry G. Gole

The case presented here revises an interpretation of United States war planning between the World Wars that has been the conventional wisdom on the subject since 1953. This conventional wisdom holds that the color plans of the 1920s and 1930s were not in touch with contemporary international events; that allegedly they were abstract, unreal, and not useful to the planners of 1939–1941 who devised the Rainbow Plans that provided strategic options to political authority and strategic direction for those who would fight World War II.

Examples of what has been found in previously unexploited archives illustrate three major points contradicting common belief: (1) Planning at the U.S. Army War College (AWC) from 1934 to 1940 was realistic and in touch with contemporary international developments; (2) the same planning was strikingly prescient in anticipating both friendly and enemy actions and the course of the conflict as the United States with allies fought a two-ocean war; and (3) the War Department General Staff (WDGS) was fully aware of the planning for coalition warfare at the AWC and often used the students to augment its own undermanned divisions.

Writing in 1953, Maurice Matloff gave high marks to the harried American military planners of 1939–1941 who designed the Rainbow Plans that realistically addressed the most likely threats to the security of their country, and he dismissed earlier war planning as simplistic and irrelevant. Referring to the color plans of the 1920s and 1930s, he wrote: "A characteristic of all these plans was their limited scope. Nothing in the way of a global or total war was envisaged. With the exception of Orange (signifying Japan), they bore little relation to contemporary developments in international affairs."[1]

Describing the activities of American military planners on the eve of war, he asserted that it was not until 1939–1941 that planning underwent a change from the "abstract exercises" of the color plan period "to reestablish contact with reality" by recognizing Germany and Japan as the likely foes.[2]

It is Matloff's observations that have become the conventional wisdom on American war planning between the two World Wars.[3] There has been no challenge to Matloff's interpretation to date, nor has he changed his mind.[4] A fresh look at war planning in the United States in the 1930s is needed, because the mainstream interpretation missed evidence that links work done at the AWC to the RAINBOW Plans.

A memorandum dated 14 March 1957 from Louis Morton (as Deputy Chief Historian) through Kent Roberts Greenfield (Chief Historian) to the Chief of Military History refers to "25 foot-lockers of Course Material in the AWC basement and attic." Morton wrote:

The collection at Carlisle, housed partly in the attic of the library of the present AWC is . . . probably only second in value to the General Staff [collection] of the period 1919–1941 . . . at the [National] Archives. The College during these years was primarily an educational institution, but its students for part of this period based their studies on the actual war plans developed by the joint and general staffs . . . and did important spade work [for the Joint and General Staffs]. [Emphasis added]

That "spade work" is the antecedent of the RAINBOW Plans and connects War College planning to General Staff work.[5]

Morton scanned the contents of the footlockers, recognized their value, and wanted them for the Center of Military History. There is no record that the materials ever got to Washington. It appears that the curricular materials in the archives of the U.S. Army Military History Institute (MHI), Carlisle Barracks, Pennsylvania, include the former contents of those footlockers. In any event, the course materials for the period 1919–1940 were not available to the authors of the relevant volumes in the series called the United States Army in World War II.[6] Had Matloff and coauthor Edwin M. Snell been aware of the war planning at the college, particularly that portion of the war plans period called "Participation with Allies" from 1934 to 1940, they would have known that there was a transition stage leading from the color plans to the RAINBOW Plans. Planning "Participation with Allies" was strategic planning for coalition warfare; it anticipated the United States fighting as a part of an allied coalition against an enemy two-ocean coalition.

Matloff knew that significant modifications to his interpretation of prewar plans and preparations would be made by future historians as new sources were inevitably uncovered. In 1953 he said: "The full story must be sought in the archives of the Service, Inter-Service, and British-American staff agencies, which are still in the very early stages of being mined by professional scholars."[7]

We now have access to the AWC course materials that apparently are those identified by Louis Morton in 1957. No one has gone through the 1919–1940 course materials specifically with war plans in mind, nor has anyone asked if what was done at the college mattered to the General Staff. The present study does both and reports findings that modify the way we should understand United States war planning between the World Wars. The RAINBOW Plans were neither a spontaneous combustion nor *deus ex machina*. War planning at AWC from 1934 to 1940 fed directly into the RAINBOW Plans.

War planning at AWC had always been taken very seriously. Assistant Commandant George S. Simonds said of the 1922–1923 curriculum: "The actual preparation of war plans had been given more prominence than any other feature of the course."[8] The class of 1925 was told:

It is essential that you keep in mind all during the year that all work done is pre-liminary to and preparatory for the preparation of actual war plans. Almost without exception everything undertaken during the year has its application, either direct or indirect, to the preparation of war plans.[9]

Emphasis on war planning in the AWC course continued right up to 1940.[10]

War plans based on GREEN (Mexico) and CRIMSON (Canada) were played routinely because it was prudent to have plans on file to cover war with contiguous foreign powers. ORANGE (Japan) was also played each year after 1906 when war planners—after the Russo-Japanese War—recognized that conflict between the United States and Japan was one of the more likely wars of the future. Indeed, the U.S. Navy was inclined to regard a future war with Japan as inevitable.[11] RED (Great Britain) was played frequently because it filled a pedagogical need of the school: RED provided the only enemy whose power could be projected to America's Atlantic backyard and, with the cooperation of Canada, to the American northeast.[12]

Until Germany, Italy, and Japan showed a willingness to use military force in the 1930s, one had to stretch one's imagination to find a direct military threat to the United States in the years between the two World Wars. Nevertheless, war planning at the AWC from 1934 began to show a good deal of imagination as students carefully monitored contemporary developments in international affairs and considered coalition warfare on a global scale.[13]

Review of the plans from 1934 to 1940 demonstrates that planners kept one eye on the region assigned for study by the faculty and one eye on the other side of the world, where events raised doubts in the minds of planners as to the location of the greater threat to the United States. There was an awareness that one might easily fall into the trap of committing forces or other resources to the wrong theater or to the wrong war. Students at the AWC were conditioned to think of simultaneous wars in the Pacific and in Europe.

As American involvement in war moved from the realm of possibility in the early 1930s to that of high probability in the late 1930s, planners turned their attention to the Western Hemisphere from 1938 through 1940. The modest resources immediately available to the nation, and especially to the nation's third-rate Army, suggested that only modest short-term strategies were possible initially. Defense of the so-called Alaska-Hawaii-Panama strategic triangle was about all the United States could manage until American potential was more fully realized.

The introduction of "Participation with Allies" to the War Plans portion of the course at the AWC in 1934 brought a new realism to war planning.[14] A U.S.-led coalition consisting of BLUE (the United States), PINK (the Soviet Union), RED (Britain), and YELLOW (China) confronted ORANGE (Japan) and CARNATION (Manchukuo). The backdrop to the scenario was the actual international situation in 1933–1934, except that in the war game PINK and ORANGE are actually fighting, and ORANGE has violated BLUE neutrality. The situation presented to the students can be summarized as follows. PINK and ORANGE come to blows without declaration of war. BLUE attempts to get the disputing parties to an international body for arbitration, but: "Orange would probably refuse to take part in, or would withdraw from this conference. . . . This action would be similar to the manner in which Orange withdrew from the League of Nations as a result of the Manchurian affair."[15] The prospective allies agree to a conference "to settle the terms on which they would deter the war and to decide on the contribution each would promise for its prosecution." This conference evolves into a "permanent Inter-Allied War Council." Ultimately, BLUE, RED, PINK, and YELLOW declare war on ORANGE and CARNATION.

One reality struck the committee immediately: the distances involved. From San Francisco to Manila via Hawaii is about 7,000 miles. ORANGE is a mere 400 to 600 miles from any port between Vladivostok and Shanghai. The distance to the U.S. naval base in the Philippines is significant, but there was even worse news about it: The United States had failed in all the years since 1898 to fortify a base in the Philippines. That meant that the United States would almost certainly be denied a base in the region shortly after the initiation of hostilities with Japan. It was assumed that Japan would enjoy local superiority and seize the Philippines at the war's outset.

The strategic choices became: (1) a risky bold stroke requiring the U.S. Navy to cover great distances to confront the Japanese fleet in decisive

Trafalgar-like battle close to Japan or (2) seizure of air and sea bases en route to the Far East as the fleet conducted a much slower and more deliberate strategy.

In the context of this scenario the British Fleet would take much of the pressure off the Americans. However, even with the overwhelmingly superior naval power of the two fleets available to them, in developing the scenario the allies were careful, too careful in the opinion of those uninitiated to naval combat.

Capt. William F. Halsey, U.S. Navy (USN)—a student in the class of 1934—was asked during the question and answer session why the naval operation took so long when the friendly coalition enjoyed such clear naval superiority. He responded with an analysis that was made the previous year at the Naval War College when he attended that course. In brief, the U.S. Navy response to a Japanese defensive strategy was the slower and more deliberate offensive. Since the United States would prevail in a long war of materiel, it would be foolish to risk all on the roll of the dice.[16]

Even before deciding on a specific course of action, it was clear that the United States would need a big troop buildup including mobilization and conscription.[17] The planners showed a realistic appreciation of public opinion and an understanding of American traditions and institutions. Their ruminations foreshadowed the contentious peacetime conscription of 1940 and the cautious course the president had to follow in dealing with the public, the press, and the Congress as the country edged toward war. The connection between foreign and domestic policy was also appreciated, and the psychological predisposition of the American people was understood, i.e., war would lead to economic recovery but: "American public opinion and sentiments are, in general, opposed to the conduct of war, and it would require flagrant enemy acts and properly handled propaganda to arouse the nation to the point of prosecuting a war effectively."[18]

The students displayed confidence in the potential of the United States to overwhelm any foe, but they expressed their concern for the short term. By 240M (240 days after mobilization) the BLUE coalition would be superior to ORANGE, but until then the situation was dangerous. The United States had to depend upon others and good luck while she built her armed forces for war. Speculation about what the Japanese would do concluded that they would go on the strategic defensive. "Orange will consider, but not adopt, a surprise submarine attack against the Blue Fleet, assembling in Hawaiian waters. . . . Orange Fleet will assume the strategic defensive and conduct a war of attrition with submarines."[19]

The American planners believed that the Imperial Japanese Navy would form an outer line of light forces to harass approaching enemy naval forces and subject them to attrition. The inner line of Japanese battleships, land-based aircraft, mines, and coastal defense guns would then engage the depleted enemy force in decisive battle that would determine the outcome of the war. The planners were convinced that control of the sea would lead to ultimate victory, because control of the sea was required to maintain land forces in the Pacific region.[20] One suspects that the Army students were attentive to Halsey on naval matters and that he applied the 1933 Naval War College solution to the AWC problem of 1934.

The committee concluded its presentation by saying that the degree of cooperation attained by the allies in the World War was about as much as one could expect. And then they added a remark that immediately brings Franklin D. Roosevelt and Winston Churchill to mind: "The most important factors in determining the degree of cooperation and unity of effort that an alliance can obtain are the personalities of its civil and military leaders." They unknowingly described Dwight D. Eisenhower when they said: "Tact and diplomatic skill are essential qualifications for an allied Commander-in-Chief."[21]

The "Participation with Allies" portion of the 1935 course demonstrates as well that the faculty was in touch with contemporary international affairs and that the students were sophisticated in their analyses of all instruments of state power as they wrestled with complex political-military issues handed to them by their faculty. The scenario presented the students with a problem in Europe, but Japan's readiness to exploit the European situation to her advantage in the Far East raised the real possibility of American involvement in a two-ocean war. The student briefer of the committee report was not engaging in hyperbole or buttering up the faculty on 17 April 1935 when he said:

This situation was conceived by the Faculty some months ago and events of today outside the walls of this institution, are in a fair way to substantiate the Faculty's flight of fancy to a degree most flattering to the perspicacity of that august body. Indeed the members of War Plans Group #4 have experienced some difficulty in keeping separate the developments of the problem from the news in the daily press.[22]

As the situation developed, a Nazi coup in Austria resulted in Italian occupation of Alpine passes with the approval of Britain and France. War followed as Italy confronted Germany and Austria; France occupied the Saar and sent troops to the Rhine, but—significantly—not beyond. The Nazi Confederation consists of Germany, Austria, Hungary, and Yugoslavia. A German-financed revolt broke out in the Ukraine; Czechoslovakia was overrun as France held the Rhine, but French public opinion, "while insisting on defense, was opposed at the outset of war to undertaking more than was essential for security—and the advance to the Rhine satisfied that."[23]

Russia closed her western frontier, suppressed the revolt in the Ukraine, and reinforced her Far East army. Japan, as a result of a secret understanding with Germany, mobilized and concentrated a large force in northwest Manchukuo, demanding a free hand in China and cessation of further fortification of Singapore and Hong Kong. She notified the United States that any movement of the U.S. Fleet west of the 180th meridian (roughly halfway between Hawaii and Wake Island) would be considered a hostile act; she asserted the right of sovereignty over mandated islands which she was fortifying. "Great Britain, urged on by Australia and New Zealand, sought cooperation of the United States in enforcement of a mutual policy in the Pacific and Far East. . . . In the fighting on the western front during February and March, German operations were characterized by unrestricted aerial warfare."[24]

In the United States:

the American people loudly demanded that the United States not enter the conflict no matter what the cost. Laws were passed withdrawing protection to nationals or property in the war zone and mindful of our World War debts forbidding the making of loans to belligerents . . . then came the Japanese ultimatum denying to our fleet movement west of the 180th meridian, which hurt the pride of Americans and opened their eyes to the real threat to our commercial future.[25]

Japan closed the Sea of Japan and the China Sea to all foreign ships not licensed by the Japanese Government, and the United States and Britain declared a state of armed neutrality in the Pacific, an action warmly received by the American public. Shortly thereafter, several American and British ships were destroyed in the ports of Le Havre and Cherbourg by Nazi aircraft. The United States and Britain declared war on the Nazi Confederation.

Proceeding from this scenario, the main decisions of the planning group were:

(1) . . . the United States is committed to the war in Europe but sooner or later will have to deal with Japan. (2) Our war aims are to prevent the Nazis or any other Confederation becoming supreme in Europe, and Japan becoming all powerful in the Far East. It will not suffice that our assistance be limited to money and supplies and it has been decided to send an expeditionary force to Europe . . . all we need to send to France is a respectable force—and we can save our main effort for Japan. . . . (3) it is essential that a strong naval force be stationed in the Pacific.[26]

Linking Germany and Japan in a military axis as early as 1935 correctly anticipated what happened in November 1936—a year and a half later. Once allied, close cooperation between these disturbers of the peace was expected, but Germany and Japan went their willful and independent ways before and during World War II—to their disadvantage. It was important to Japanese planning that the United States and Britain commit to Europe so that the Japanese would have a free hand in the Pacific—as they had during World War I. Hence, the German-Japanese connection in the 1935 scenario presented the problem of the two-ocean war to Britain and the United States. The committee decided to defeat the Germans before turning to the defeat of Japan. The defeat of Germany by the forces of Britain, France, Italy, and the United States did not appear to be a very difficult task, considering German unpreparedness for a major war in 1935.

The students clearly understood the contemporary international scene and the background to issues; their analysis also included an examination of cultural dictates and domestic constraints to policy in the United States and among possible belligerents on both sides.[27] One of the themes to emerge was suspicion of the Japanese among the American people and how this attitude might be used to enlist "wholehearted assistance to the prosecution of the war," particularly in the western states, where there was a sense of a "yellow peril."[28]

There was also an economic argument that might win support for an American war in the Pacific and the expectation that war would stimulate "idealism." "It is believed that the cynical attitude of the depression era would quickly disappear once the country was committed to war and that pre–World War idealism would reassert itself as a marked national characteristic."[29] The subcommittee was confident that the administration would be able to manage the support of the public.

Ever since the Civil War, the trend of our political system has been to increase the power of the Executive. Within recent years, and especially since 1932, this trend has been intensified. In event of war, this trend will enhance the power of the administration to control events and, probably to influence the public to support its policies.[30]

And the students looked to the other side of the Atlantic to assess the potential of propaganda:

The Nazi government of Germany has used all means of propaganda and advertising with telling effect. There is every reason to believe that these same means would be quite as effective in influencing American public opinion, especially in the emotional stress of impending or actual international conflict.[31]

In another flash of insight, the students anticipated a propaganda ploy by the Soviet Union. When the Japanese concentrated troops in Manchuria, the Soviets reinforced on the border. As it looked like war between Japan and the Soviet Union, "Communist agitation in the U.S.

was greatly reduced at once. . . . Several of the strongest peace organizations changed their peace-at-any-price attitude. Propaganda against Japan became more common. The Pacific attitude of Russia was emphasized."[32] This scenario fairly describes the new line of Communist propaganda taken when the Germans turned on the Soviet Union in 1941.

The students believed that there was a willingness on the part of France to take some symbolic action when the Nazi coalition invaded Czechoslovakia in the scenario, but there was no desire to engage in decisive combat with Germany. French aversion to war was so pronounced that she would convince herself that it would be enough to put French troops on the Rhine. This action by the French in the make-believe world of 1935 is strikingly like that actually taken in 1939 after the German invasion of Poland, when the so-called *Sitzkrieg* lasted from September 1939 to the spring of 1940.[33]

The committee also got right not only the prospective close cooperation between the Americans and the British but also the nuances of the relationship before and after the United States' entry into the Second World War. Movement toward intimate cooperation with Britain had to be paced with the perception of a threat to the United States by the American public. The development of the alliance with Britain in the 1935 scenario comes very close to the way that the president played his cards from 1939 until the American declaration of war in December 1941.

It was clear that if Britain were engaged in a European war while also fighting a war in the Pacific, priority would go to the European theater. Therefore, Australia and New Zealand would press the British to cooperate with the Americans. This estimate by the planners of 1935 proved sound when the United States dominated the Pacific in World War II and by degrees accepted former British responsibilities around the world.

After a thorough analysis of friendly and enemy ways, means, and ends, the committee decided: (1) to transport U.S. troops and supplies to Europe in order to assist in the defeat of the Nazi forces; and (2) to concentrate the U.S. Fleet in Hawaii in order to prepare for war with Japan. It was assumed that Britain, France, and Italy would be capable of defeating the Nazi Confederation, thus allowing the United States to withhold forces for possible use against Japan. Nowhere was anything like the *Blitzkrieg* of 1940 even suggested. The United States promised to send at least 250,000 troops to Europe but not more than 500,000. American troops would be started to France by 30M (30 days after U.S. mobilization) to complete training and to be ready to take over a section of the front by about 270M. The memory of the slow-moving Great War was evident, as it was expected that there would be time for a deliberate American buildup. And why not? The French Army was estimated to number some four and one-half million men, and it was allied to Britain and Italy. The German Army had been unilaterally increased from the Treaty Army of 100,000, but professional soldiers believed that it was not fully trained for protracted war against a first class foe.[34] Surely, the European allies were sufficiently superior to the enemy coalition that there would be no urgent need for United States troops, but the United States needed to take part in the war if it was to have a voice in peacemaking.

Strong American naval forces stationed in Hawaii would cooperate with the great British Navy operating out of its impregnable base in Singapore. There was no sense of great urgency.

[The Japanese] generally begin their wars by surprise attacks before there is any declaration of war. This must be guarded against, but with the strong forces allied against them it does not seem probable that they will detach any important force for distant operations away from their homeland.[35]

After all, the U.S. Navy was superior to the Japanese Fleet in battleships by a margin of 15 to 9. The Japanese advantage was in other types: cruisers, destroyers, submarines, and in land-based aviation in the mandated islands. But the U.S. Fleet combined with the British Mediterranean Fleet (the Italians and French would take up the slack in the Mediterranean) was estimated to enjoy a 2 to 1 advantage over the Japanese in the Pacific. The Japanese would be tough, but sheer allied weight would defeat them.

The 1936 alignment of contesting coalitions in "Participation with Allies" was like that of 1935, with one significant difference: Italy, an ally of the United States in the 1935 scheme, was moved to the German-led Central Coalition. This change indicated that Italian aggression in Abyssinia and Benito Mussolini's bombast removed Italy from the side of the angels. It also shows that the planners at the AWC were in touch with contemporary international developments.[36] The scenario of 1936 presented the student committee with a European threat to American security greater than the threat in the Pacific. The 1936 response to the question of where American interests were to be found anticipated the "Germany first" strategy. The students came very close to predicting how World War II would break out, how the contending coalitions would evolve, the course of the war, and its outcome.

Again in 1937 one of the war planning groups addressed the big war in Europe and a simultaneous threat from Japan.[37] This was the war that would become World War II—whose outcome would be determined by "economic and material factors."[38] The French Army was highly regarded for its morale, training, combat efficiency, supply, command and staff, but there were doubts regarding the will of the people and the stability of the government. France, it was thought, was in danger should a defeat occur. The committee warned: "Its future stability may falter in the face of a military defeat."[39]

The committee saw two courses of action available to the enemy coalition. The first was to go on the defensive in the west, to contain the French, while crushing Czechoslovakia, Yugoslavia, and Rumania and continuing east against Russia. Japan would strike Russia from the east. The rationale for this course was the early possession of the natural resources of the Soviet Union, Czech industry, and Rumanian oil.[40] The second course was the one that the Student Committee no. 6 expected the enemy to select: The Germans would make their first main effort in France and then turn east.[41]

Two friendly courses of action were considered. The first was to conduct offensive operations against Japan while on the strategic defensive in Europe. The object was to knock Japan out of the war while keeping Russia involved. A variation of this plan called for an offensive via Italy to the Balkans, the Mediterranean offensive to be conducted simultaneously with the Pacific offensive. The object was to isolate Turkey, menace the Coalition from the south, and to insure free passage of Allied shipping in the Mediterranean. Course two called for containing the Japanese by reinforcing the British Fleet in the Pacific and conducting the main offensive operations against Germany from France. This was the course chosen.[42]

The determining reason for the student choice would prove to be a later source of friction between the Americans and their British allies when actual hostilities began: "The heart of the Coalition is Germany." The students would send the American expeditionary force "with the armies of France and Britain directly against the heart of the Coalition."[43] The Americans were always ready to go for the jugular; the British preferred a strategy of nibbling at the edges to weaken Germany before risking the decisive battle.[44] In precisely this connection it is interesting to note the consideration and rejection of proposals to conduct landings in Africa, the Baltic, the North Sea, and Italy. The plans for landings were discarded because it was estimated they would have been too expensive in men and materiel and too peripheral. It was also thought that once ashore in Italy our forces would have faced formidable mountain barriers favorable to the defender.[45]

The 1937 version of "Participation with Allies" is the fourth consecutive consideration of the problems of coalition warfare at the AWC and is addressed from the perspective of the American concern with a two-ocean war as events heat up in Europe and Asia. It anticipates the basic considerations that would perplex leaders in their deliberations before the United States entry into World War II and after. They had to decide where to put their main effort—Atlantic or Pacific. Once they decided to defeat Germany first, they had to agree on whether the offensive would be direct or indirect. That is what the fifteen student officers of Committee no. 6 did in 1937.

However prescient the studies and war plans done at the AWC between the wars, they would be no more than a historical curiosity had they remained unknown to the war planners on the General Staff. Such was not the case. The Army's leadership knew about the planning and just about everything else that went on at the college and annually requested projects and plans to be prepared by the college for a General Staff that was always short of officers. Normally WPD consisted of twelve officers, including the Assistant Chief of Staff, WPD, a brigadier general. In the entire period from 21 September 1921 to 31 December 1940, only ninety-two officers served in WPD.[46] The AWC record of the connection between the college and the War Department in 1939–1940, says: "Close cooperation with the War Department was continued by the study of issues of special interest to the War Department."[47] This observation is supported by the contents of so-called "Zero" files and "Flat" files in the MHI curricular archives.[48] These files contain correspondence between the college and the various sections of the WDGS—G–1, G–2, G–3, G–4, and 16 WPD—regarding both general and specific projects that students might do, and did, for the staff sections. The relationship was characterized by a polite professionalism. The college was prepared to assist the General Staff, but the Commandant and faculty never forgot that the AWC mission was to educate. The General Staff, on the other hand, made it clear in the requests sent to the college that the Commandant would have the final word regarding student efforts.

Further evidence of a close and continuous relationship between the college and the General Staff can be found in assignment patterns as well as in direct written communication in which the Staff requested assistance from the college. The annual assignment of several AWC graduates to the War Plans Division of the General Staff was routine. For the AWC classes from 1934 to 1940, the following numbers of graduates, by year group, were assigned to the influential WPD: 1934, four; 1935, four; 1936, nine; 1937, three; 1938, six; 1939, four; and 1940, four. The six officers of the AWC class of 1938 were serving in WPD when the bombs fell on Pearl Harbor.[49] Other General Staff sections also received recent graduates on a regular basis.[50]

In addition, 436 generals spread around the Army had some influence on the institution. About two-thirds of the AWC classes that experienced "Participation with Allies" in the War Plans Period of the course from

1934 to 1940 served as generals in World War II. Many of them were famous commanders: Omar N. Bradley, Courtney H. Hodges, Jonathan M. Wainwright, and William F. Halsey, USN, 1934; Mark W. Clark and Matthew B. Ridgway, 1937; J. Lawton Collins, 1938; George E. Stratemeyer and Hoyt A. Vandenberg, 1939; and Maxwell D. Taylor and Lyman Lemnitzer, 1940. Far more served in faceless staff jobs where policy was made for the conduct of the war and the peace to follow. Despite attaining high rank, staff officers remain relatively unknown to the public.[51] A few examples of relatively unknown officers who were at AWC in the 1930s (later in key planning positions) make the point.

Thomas T. Handy (AWC 1935) provided unprecedented continuity in WPD (later OPD) from August 1936 until October 1944, except for one year with troops (June 1940–June 1941). He joined WPD for his first tour as a major after completing the Naval War College, and he left OPD as a lieutenant general in 1944. He succeeded Dwight D. Eisenhower as chief of the Operations Division when Eisenhower was sent to command troops in Europe, and he worked with George C. Marshall on an almost daily basis as the chief of Marshall's wartime command post.[52]

Thompson Lawrence (AWC 1933) was selected to teach at the War College in 1938. He previously had taught at both the United States Military Academy, West Point, New York, and at Leavenworth, Kansas, and would retire a major general. In 1940 he was one of that group of students and faculty directed to temporary duty with the War Plans Division. His specific assignment was to work on War Plan RAINBOW.[53] While a student at the AWC, Lawrence served on committees studying War Reserves and General Mobilization; Joint Operations Overseas, Expedition To Seize and Hold Halifax; War Plans–RED Coalition; and Southern Theater (GREEN).[54] It is just this kind of academic work that has been called unrealistic and out of touch with contemporary international affairs, but it is hard to imagine a better preparation for what Lawrence had to do in 1940 as he worked on RAINBOW 4.[55] The plan was concerned with command and control exercised by the General Headquarters (GHQ) established at AWC as of July 1940 and possible deployment of U.S. troops to Brazil (PURPLE). Lawrence's students had worked out Plan PURPLE in both 1938 and 1939. The work on RAINBOW 4 in 1940–1941 refined previous planning and took him to *terra cognita* as he wrestled with the problems of hemispheric defense from 1938 into 1941 at the AWC for WPD. Further, WPD's 1938 request that the college "specify by name and location . . . the critical points . . . which if occupied by U.S. naval or land forces would . . . delay the advance of enemy forces" had rehearsed both the college and WPD for a very similar planning exercise in 1940, this one "for real."[56]

Charles L. Bolte (AWC 1937)[57] clarifies the rationale for planning for the unlikely war with Britain and Canada, but Bolte says that Japan concerned his colleagues most:

Orange was the premier problem plan. We have to have a plan for the contiguous theater, in which you could have a war with Mexico or a war with Canada or Britain or something, just to get a scenario to set it up. But the Orange Plan was the one that got the most attention from the students and from the faculty who were guiding the course.[58]

Bolte said that even "after the basic decision was made by the political heads, Mr. Churchill and Mr. Roosevelt, that we would win in Europe first and then turn to the Pacific . . . our Navy was always reluctant as to Europe."[59] He joined the AWC faculty after he completed the course in 1937. He said that General Marshall closed the college in 1940 because "there were presumably good officers being students at the War College, and on the faculty, so he . . . scattered us around."[60] Bolte at first assisted the chief of Air Corps and then joined the War College Group before going to London as a member of the "special observer group" for the ABC conversations. He was close to the centers of power in the critical period before the United States entered the war and would end his career with four stars.

Bolte's recollections are confirmed by those of his friend, John E. Hull (AWC 1938),[61] who recalled that before the war everyone was looking to Japan when war was considered. It is not clear from the interviews if it was September 1939, or if it took the German successes in the Spring of 1940 to place Europe ahead of Japan as the chief concern of American war planners.[62] Hull said that it was generally assumed that in a war with Germany, Italy, and Japan, the United States would go on the strategic defensive in the Pacific and put the main effort in Europe to defeat Germany and Italy.[63] Hull succeeded Handy as ACS, OPD, when Handy became Deputy Chief of Staff, U.S. Army.

Russell Maxwell (AWC 1934), credited with coining the term "Hemisphere Defense," is another who found himself in the midst of planning for the defense of the Western Hemisphere at the end of the decade. He served as the special assistant to the Secretary of War in 1938 as an expert logistician.[64] Among the subjects attracting his professional interest in this period were American logistical support to Britain and the nations of the hemisphere; bases in Newfoundland and Bermuda; congressional authorization to the Secretaries of War and Navy "to assist the governments of American republics to increase their military and naval establishments"; and aviation capabilities in Latin America.[65] Clearly, he was well prepared for his responsibilities in war and in the transition to war.

His work from 1939 onward brought him into close contact with George Marshall, George Strong of WPD, and Assistant Secretary of War Louis A. Johnson. When the shooting war in Europe broke out, he was named Administrator of Export Control. Later he would ply his trade as a logistical planner by heading up the U.S. Military Mission to the Middle East. Two weeks before Pearl Harbor he was in Cairo, and he remained in the region until 1943.

In addition to the close and constant contact AWC had with the General Staff via correspondence and assignments, the Assistant Chief of Staff, War Plans Division, and his colleagues, the G–1, G–2, G–3, and G–4, addressed the students each year, informing the classes of staff missions and functions and indicating current problems of professional interest to the General Staff.[66] Key officers went from the college to General Staff assignments and back to teach there or to command the college. In the period under discussion, a former commandant and a deputy commandant went on to serve as the Chief of Staff of the Army and as the Deputy Chief of Staff, respectively.

The relatively unrestrained creativity of students was exploited by the more cautious General Staff. The clearest evidence of this exploitation is the tasking of the college by the Staff found in the so-called MHI-AWC-"O" and "Flat" files in the curricular archives.[67] Much of the student work was of interest to the Staff because it was done in response to the Staff. Student work, including the Individual Staff Memorandum (ISM), a written project required of each member of the class, was often assigned after consultation with the various sections of the War Department General Staff. The ISM done by students was "exactly like the form used in the War Department in preparing a Memorandum for the Chief of Staff."[68]

In 1932, among the ISMs sent to the War Department was one by George S. Patton, Jr., and another by Capt. Edward J. Foy, USN, who would later teach at AWC.[69] Students had the opportunity to deal with current issues of concern to those at the top of the military hierarchy and an opportunity to be "discovered" as bright fellows with a future. The small sections of the General Staff had the benefit of the thinking of those bright fellows and could take what was useful and toss out what was not.

But it was not just the students who came up with fascinating ideas. In 1931, while still ACS, WPD, Brig. Gen. George S. Simonds wrote a note proposing that one of the students examine a notion that would reappear almost a decade later in quite different circumstances. "An interesting study for Ind. Memo. next year—'Would it be worthwhile for England to cede [*sic*] her possessions in the Western Hemisphere to the U.S. in consideration of the cancellation of all debts?'"[70] Someone added in pencil: "If so what disposition should we make of them?"

Staff response to the studies done by students varied from simple acknowledgment of receipt to rather expansive commentary. One of the students failed to cover himself with glory in his ISM, but without apparent damage to a promising career. Future Admiral of the Fleet William Halsey addressed "Japan's Attitude at the Forthcoming Naval Conference." The comment on his paper is: "The study is not sufficiently extensive nor exhaustive to be of great value." His grade: satisfactory.[71]

A sense of the issues that were important to the General Staff is found in the list of topics staff sections asked the classes to study, and not only on the eve of World War II. In 1932, for example, WPD listed, among others: What war plans should be prepared by our war planning agencies? Was there a conflict between political and military strategy among the Allied Governments in the Great War? How should air forces be allotted to GHQ, Armies, Corps, Divisions? Is the policy of "Paramount Interest" the best that can be used to insure coordination and cooperation between the Army and the Navy in joint operations? G–3 was interested in motorization, mechanization, whether the tank was an infantry or cavalry weapon, antitank systems, air force issues, civil defense against bombs and gas, antiair capabilities in the division, mobilization, the reserve components and volunteers, organization of the War Department, and the need for a Department of National Defense. G–2 wanted the students to study the international objectives of the "Russian" government, if Alaska was an asset or a liability to national defense, subversion in the military and how to combat it, and the Nicaraguan Canal issue. The staff's proposed list of topics to be studied by War College students is a kind of barometer of security concerns by year throughout the 1930s.[72]

In 1935 Malin Craig, AWC commandant (and soon to be Army Chief of Staff), asked the War Department's G–2 for a "list of subjects on intelligence matters which in your opinion, would make worthwhile topics for a two weeks' individual study by students of this college." Within two days he had a promise to provide the list requested.[73]

The topics sent from WPD to the AWC in 1938 reflect an increasing sense of urgency as they became more specific than they had been earlier in the decade. For example, the staff shopping list for the college that year included requests for a study of hemispheric strategy and recommended troop deployments; it asked: "Are the economic and political advantages of sufficient importance for the U.S. Government to subsidize 30 percent of the U.S. Merchant Marine?" WPD also asked for analysis of the "Relative value of defensive war along the line Alaska-Hawaii-Panama [the so-called "strategic triangle"], or along the line Aleutians-Guam-Samoa, versus offensive war in the Western Pacific."[74] All of these WPD requests were honored. The center of gravity for planners shifted from Europe to the Western Hemisphere and to the "strategic triangle" in 1938 as war planners trimmed their sails to match modest plans to modest means. The reason for the shift in War College planning is these requests to the college from the General Staff's War Plans Division.[75]

In addition to the regular exchange of correspondence and student work in support of the staff, an officer working on a special project could call for help from the AWC. For example, John D. Reardon, Air Corps, was a member of a board at the War Department doing studies on a number of air force issues in 1934 when he asked that the college assist by assigning students to study the issues. George Simonds, commandant, was keenly aware of current issues being studied by the General Staff and he assigned students to the air force issues.[76]

It is not surprising that Commandant Simonds was so responsive. He was in his person a strong link between the college and WPD for much of the interwar period. He was a member of the first postwar class, graduated in 1920, and upon graduation he was assigned to the faculty. During 1922–1924 he was assistant commandant, and from 1932–1935 he was commandant.[77] His previous assignment on the General Staff enabled Simonds to keep the college in the mainstream of national security thinking. He had served as ACS, WPD, under General Douglas MacArthur, so he understood the thinking and desires of the Chief of Staff. As one of MacArthur's principal staff officers, Simonds produced plans to comply with MacArthur's insistence that mobilization plans be geared to war plans and that mobilization plans be flexible enough to support the color plans.

Simonds added two weeks to address mobilization as a part of the War Plans Course in his first year as commandant (1932–1933). In his second year he reestablished the college War Plans Division and ensured that the Navy and Air Corps faculty members were part of it. Just as joint operations meant coordination of the U.S. services, alliances meant that there was a need for a better understanding of the dynamics of coalition warfare. Therefore, it was on his watch as commandant that "Participation with Allies" was added to the usual color plans worked out by students each year. Simonds left the AWC in January 1935 to become Deputy Chief of Staff to MacArthur. Under Simonds the college was not an academic backwater out of touch with Army concerns; Simonds was an influential man in the Army, and his successor as commandant was no less influential.

Malin Craig served as commandant for less than a year (from February to October 1935) before he succeeded MacArthur as Chief of

Staff. Being the commandant of the AWC in the decade before World War II was obviously one of the most prestigious assignments in the Army and a stepping stone to higher perches in the military hierarchy. One can be sure that officers notice patterns of advancement and pay attention to men of achievement like Simonds and Craig. Staffs respond quickly and students take careful notes when the boss is a rising star. Craig, while Chief of Staff, turned to the bright men he left at the AWC to do special projects of interest to him. With Craig and Simonds running the Army, the college was well connected.[78]

The college had done its work well. The *data* produced in considering the strengths and weaknesses of potential friend and foe across the full spectrum of national power—political, economic, psychosociological and military—were voluminous and useful in real world planning. The *process* was also useful. Continuous reconsideration of the color plans between the World Wars (and of coalition warfare in a two-theater war from 1934) and the rationale for the plans was important in forming a habit of mind critical to a strategist. More important than the mechanics of planning, the elite of the U.S. Army made it a habit to think about war from the level of national strategy. That habit partially explains why American officers, whose command experience was at and below regimental level, were capable of stepping into key staff positions near the apex of political power and into high command with confidence and competence. They were self-conscious, elite, and well schooled. As General Handy put it, the AWC experience made graduates the Ph.Ds. of the Army.[79]

A careful comparison of Rainbow Plans 1 to 5 with the war planning done by at least one committee each year at the AWC from 1934 to 1940 under the title "Participation with Allies" reveals that all of the elements of Rainbow are to be found in the college planning. Further, some of the combinations of elements are also visible.

All the Rainbow Plans included defense of the hemisphere as the *sine qua non* of American war planning.[80] Defense of the Western Hemisphere south to the bulge of Brazil, 10 degrees south latitude, was Rainbow 1. Rainbows 2, 3, and 5 were also—among other things—to prevent violation of the Monroe Doctrine to 10 degrees south latitude. The AWC Purple plan exercised in 1938 and 1939 was just what the Army and Navy Rainbow planners needed. It finds its way into all Rainbow Plans. Rainbow 4 was more ambitious. It was to protect all the territory and the governments of the Western Hemisphere against external aggression. In fact, Rainbow 4 simply restated the Monroe Doctrine. Purple was useful in taking the entire hemisphere into account, and so were color plans Green, Red, and Crimson. Data compiled by War College planners from

Newfoundland to and including Brazil was current, comprehensive, and available to Rainbow planners, some of whom had been AWC planners.

The differences between Rainbow 2 and Rainbow 3 recall considerations made by students again and again from 1934 to 1937 in "Participation with Allies" and in the Orange Plans. Rainbow 3 called for getting to the United States possessions in the Western Pacific as rapidly as possible, as in the 1938 Orange Plan at AWC. Rainbow 2 was a more cautious and deliberate plan for war in the Pacific, like the Orange solution at AWC in 1939.[81]

Rainbow 2 assumed a United States alliance with Britain and France. It further assumed America's allies could manage quite well in Europe, requiring minimal American participation in Europe. No one imagined that Germany would crush France and chase Britain from the Continent mere weeks after the Joint Planning Committee delivered the Rainbow Plan courses of action to the Joint Board in April 1940. In any event, Rainbow 2 looked much like the AWC "Participation with Allies" of 1935.[82]

Similarly, Rainbow 5 was much like the plans of the AWC in the 1936 version of "Participation with Allies." Both saw a need to project American forces "to the Eastern Atlantic and to either or both the African and European continents as rapidly as possible" in order to defeat decisively Germany or Italy or both, in concert with France and Britain.[83] The AWC student plan of 1936[84] reacted to a scenario portraying a situation much more serious in Europe than that of 1935. The 1936 plan required 750,000 American troops in six months, and over two million within a year. (In 1938 it was believed that 250,000 to 500,000 United States troops in Europe in 9 to 12 months would be sufficient.) In the 1936 plan it was still assumed that the British and French Fleets in European waters would permit the United States Fleet to keep its major combatants in the Pacific.

Rainbow 5 also resembled the AWC work of 1937.[85] That year the scenario in "Participation with Allies" found the United States at war with Germany and Italy, but not with Japan. One of the early decisions was that the U.S. Fleet would assume responsibilities in the Mediterranean, thus releasing British ships to counter Japanese naval strength in the Pacific. This was a variation on a familiar theme: Since the Army needed to mobilize and the Navy was a force in being, the swiftest response the president could make was the naval response. Further, the students of 1937 anticipated the *Sitzkrieg* and the German decisive victory over the weak nations of Eastern Europe. They also decided for offensive operations against Germany from France, going for the jugular in the exercise just as the

United States Army would in the course of World War II. Landings in Africa and Italy were also considered by the students in 1937.

Planning at the AWC from 1934 to 1940 was realistic and prescient. AWC work was known to the General Staff whose officers had experienced the planning for coalition warfare while students at AWC. The steady stream of visits and correspondence between the college and the staff, officer assignment patterns, and the fact that the students and faculty of the 1930s were among the key planners of 1938–1945, connect the AWC and the General Staff. It is incorrect to suggest that the planners of 1939–1945 proceeded from a zero base to the RAINBOW Plans of 1939. Knowledge of the war planning done at AWC from 1934 to 1940 reveals that planning was neither simplistic nor irrelevant. Conventional wisdom on American war planning between the two World Wars needs to be modified. The AWC coalition plans rehearsed planners by providing them with the "spade work" mentioned by Louis Morton in 1957. The spade work was preparation for the RAINBOW Plans of 1939 and the strategy for World War II.

NOTES

1. Maurice Matloff, "Prewar Military Plans and Preparations, 1939–41," *United States Naval Institute Proceedings* 79 (July 1953): 741.

2. Ibid., pp. 743–44.

3. This interpretation appears also in the first pages of Maurice Matloff and Edwin H. Snell's *Strategic Planning for Coalition Warfare, 1941–1942*, U.S. Army in World War II (Washington, D.C.: U.S. Army Center of Military History, 1953). The authors say their book "is a product of cooperative effort" (ix) and an outgrowth of Ray S. Cline's *Washington Command Post: The Operations Division*, U.S. Army in World War II (Washington, D.C.: U.S. Army Center of Military History, 1951). They also express their great obligation to colleagues at the U.S. Army Center of Military History by name: Kent Roberts Greenfield, Stetson Conn, Louis Morton, Richard M. Leighton, and Robert W. Coakley, all writers of books in the United States Army in World War II series. Louis Morton, *Strategy and Command: The First Two Years*, U.S. Army in World War II (Washington, D.C.: U.S. Army Center of Military History, 1962), p. 22, uses almost the same language as Matloff and Snell in describing the pre-RAINBOW Plans: "the early war plans were little more than abstract exercises and bore little relation to actual events." Morton's book is in The War in the Pacific subseries of United States Army in World War II; Cline's book and the Matloff and Snell book are in The War Department subseries.

4. See Matloff's 1965 essay, "The American Approach to War, 1919–1945," in Michael Howard, ed., *The Theory and Practice of War* (Bloomington: Indiana University Press, 1965), pp. 229–35. He expands on some of the points he raised in 1953, but his position on pre-1939 war planning by the United States is unchanged.

5. File HRC 313.2, U.S. Army Center of Military History, Washington, D.C. (hereafter CMH).

6. Cline's *Washington Command Post* was published in 1951; Mark S. Watson's *Chief of Staff: Prewar Plans and Preparations* was published by CMH in 1950; Matloff and Snell published their *Strategic Planning for Coalition Warfare* in 1953.

7. Matloff, "Prewar Military Plans," pp. 741–48; see also Matloff, "The American Approach to War, 1919–1945," in Howard, ed., *The Theory and Practice of War*. Matloff had not changed his interpretation by 1965 (see especially p. 218: "Limited in scope, the plans envisaged neither global nor total war.")

8. Summary of the Courses at the Army War College since the World War, 1919–40, 1922–23 Course Summary, p. 7, file no. 1–105, Military History Institute (MHI), U.S. Army War College (USAWC), Carlisle Barracks, Pa.

9. Ibid., 1924–25 Course Summary, p. 10.

10. Ibid., 1939–40 Course Summary, p. 31.

11. Michael Vlahos, *The Blue Sword: The Naval War College and the American Mission, 1919–1941* (Newport, R.I.: Naval War College Press, 1980). The author says that from about 1919, war with Japan was an obsession of the U.S. Navy. The "mission" of the subtitle is ORANGE, war with Japan. Before the Russo-Japanese War, the Japanese were praised at the Naval War College (p. 122). By 1906 they were called "Japs" and were seen as the "inevitable" enemy (p. 123).

12. RED-ORANGE Planning, p. 2, file no. 1–105, MHI. Unlikely, but the most dangerous to the United States, would be war with a British-Japanese alliance.

13. Examination of the thinking that went into the plans year by year is possible because data, analyses, the plans, and the question and answer sessions that followed student presentations are well documented and readily available. See the files for records of the curriculum at the USAWC. The War Plans Period files, especially "Participation with Allies" from 1934 to 1940, provide the detailed plans.

14. Preparation for War Course at the Army War College, pt. 2, 1933–34, War Plans Period, War Plans Group no. 4, "Participation with Allies," MHI. See also "Participation with Allies" from 1935 to 1940, MHI.

15. Ibid. See tab 3.

16. Ibid. See question and answer period following the presentation by the committee. This is a fair summary of what Halsey's classmates at the Naval War College concluded in the 1933 Plan ORANGE. Earlier it was thought that BLUE was sufficiently superior to ORANGE to permit the fleet to go to the Philippines without delay en route. See 2261–BB, Joint Problem 1, 1926, p. 12, Naval Historical Collection (NHC), RG 4. In 1933 both students and faculty were very pessimistic. See 2261–1, enclosure "T" for summarized data regarding losses and damage and enclosure "P," NHC, RG 4, for how damage was inflicted. Reaching from Hawaii to Manila is just too risky. See 2261–AA, NHC, RG 4, for a faculty critique of Ops. Prob. 4–33. Without a forward fortified base—Manila was assumed to be lost in the opening days of the war—Japanese damage to the U.S. Fleet so far from Pearl Harbor made a bold offensive unacceptable. Bases had to be established. That would require a more deliberate strategy in the Pacific. At the Naval War College in 1933 were also Ernest J. King, student commander of BLUE, and Raymond A. Spruance. See also Vlahos, *The Blue Sword*, p. 93.

17. Course at the AWC, 1933–34, War Plans Period, Group no. 5, "Participation with Allies," tab 4, p. 2, MHI.

18. Ibid., tab 5, p. 17.

19. Ibid., tab 5, app. 2, p. 38.

20. Ibid.

21. Ibid., tab 7.

22. War Plans Course, 1934–35, Rpt of Group no. 4, "Participation with Allies," Oral Presentation, pp. 1–3, file no. 5–1935–20, MHI. Except where otherwise noted, this report is the source of the scenario presented to the committee and the committee's reaction to the situation.

23. Ibid., app. 1.

24. Ibid., app. 2.

25. Ibid., apps. 2–3.

26. Ibid., app. 1 to tab 4, 5–1935–20.

27. See the tabs attached to 5–1935–20, especially tab 7, for thorough summaries of U.S. treaty obligations, declarations, and policies.

28. Ibid., tab 12, Political Estimate of the U.S., in 5–1935–20.

29. Ibid.

30. Ibid.

31. Ibid.

32. Ibid.

33. Ibid., tab 4.

34. Ironies abound! General Thomas T. Handy, who succeeded Eisenhower as chief of the Operations Division (OPD) when Eisenhower was sent to command troops in Europe, said of the reports of the U.S. Military Attache in Berlin, Truman Smith: "He kind of missed the biggest picture of all. . . . After every one of these moves [by the Germans], like into Austria and so on, Truman indicated that was about the last thing they'd do because it would take them 4 or 5 years to digest what they had." (MHI, Thomas T. Handy Papers, debriefing by Edward H. Knoff, Jr., Section 3, 1–3.) Smith's sources were excellent. The problem was that German military professionals, his sources, were advising their leader that the *Wehrmacht* needed time to consolidate and to train and absorb masses of new soldiers into an army that had expanded too rapidly. This was neither the first nor the last time that Hitler would confound military professionals, German or others.

35. An Estimate of the Naval Situation, app. 2, file no. 5–1935–20, MHI.

36. Preparation for War Course, 1935–36, pt. 2, War Plans Period, Rpt of War Plans Group no. 4, "Participation with Allies," file no. 5–1936–21, MHI.

37. Summary of the Courses at the AWC Since the World War, 1919–1940, 1936–37, pp. 1–5, file no. 1–105, MHI.

38. Preparation for War Course, 1936–37, pt. 2, War Plans Period, 8 May 37, supl no. 3 to the Rpt of Comm. no. 6, sub: War Plan–Participation with Allies, Joint Plan with Appendices, pp. 2–3, file no. 5–1937–24B, MHI. See also Course at the AWC, 1936–37, oral presentation, 10 Apr 37, with supl nos. 1 and 2, Rpt of Comm. no. 6, sub: War Plan, Participation with Allies–European, file no. 5–1937–24A, MHI. Note that file no. 5–1937–24B contains a supplement no. 3 from the same Comm. no. 6 which contains the Joint Plan with appendices and is dated 8 May 37. It appears that a clean copy of the report including all supporting documents was submitted a month after the oral presentation. Unless specified otherwise, the page references that follow are to file no. 5–1937–24A.

39. Ibid., p. 45.

40. Ibid., p. 78.

41. Ibid., p. 79.

42. Ibid., p. 78.

43. Ibid., p. 80.

44. For the theory and practice of American strategy, see Russell F. Weigley, *The American Way of War* (New York: Macmillan Co., Inc.; London: Collier Macmillan Publishers, 1973), pp. 312–59. "An army strong enough to choose the strategy of annihilation should always choose it, because the most certain and probably the most rapid route to victory lay through the destruction of the enemy's armed forces," p. 313. The Army Air Forces also sought battle with the main enemy force in order to destroy it (see pp. 334–43, especially p. 342).

45. See the Oral Presentation and pp. 80–82 in file no. 5–1937–24A.

46. In the period 1 Jan–6 Dec 41, 66 officers were assigned to WPD. Late in the war as many as 310 officers served in WPD/OPD. War Plans Division, app. D, "Master Personnel List, Arrivals and Departures," HRC 321, CMH. For the heavy responsibilities carried by WPD between the World Wars, see Mark Skinner Watson, *Chief of Staff: Prewar Plans and Preparations,* U.S. Army in World War II (Washington, D.C.: U.S. Army Center of Military History, 1950), pp. 74–75.

47. Summary of the Courses at the AWC Since the World War, 1919–1940 (1939–40), p. 4, file no. 1–105, MHI.

48. File nos. 7–1935–0, 7–1936–0, 7–1938–0, 7–1939–0, 407 flat, 387 flat, and 397 flat, MHI.

49. War Plans Division, app. D, "Master Personnel List, Arrivals and Departures," HRC 321, CMH, and the *Directory, Present and Former Staff and Faculty. Graduates and Students By Class, 1905–1984,* USAWC, 1984, are the documents cross-referenced by name to determine when graduates of AWC, by year group, served in WPD. For a good example of WPD seeking and getting help from AWC, see "Correspondence re: ISMs," file no. 7–1938–0, MHI. WPD requested a "strategy of a BLUE–South American combine against a German-Italian challenge to the Monroe Doctrine." Plan PURPLE was done at AWC in direct and specific response to the WPD request. In a longer study the author of the current work illustrates the evolution of PURPLE to an approved RAINBOW Plan. See also file no. 111–41/20, tags 6–21–40 and 6–22–40, MHI, assigning Thompson Lawrence (AWC 1933) to work on RAINBOW. As senior man and the instructor who had directed PURPLE at AWC in 1938 and 1939, Lawrence headed up the War College Group (WCG) under the direction of WPD in 1940. His signature appears on the RAINBOW documents found in file nos. 111–41/16, 111–41/15, 111–41/13, and 111–41/14, MHI. See also file no. 5–1939–8/1, MHI, to note that PURPLE evolves into RAINBOW 4.

50. Among the AWC graduates of 1934–1939 who held key non-WPD jobs in the transition from peace to war were Orlando Ward (1936), Walter B. Smith (1937), and John R.

Deane (1939)—Secretaries of the General Staff in that order from 3 July 1939 to 3 September 1942; from the class of 1934 James A. Ulio was Adjutant General from 3 March 1942 to 31 January 1946, Dawson Olmstead was Chief Signal Officer from 1 October 1941 to 30 June 1943 and Courtney H. Hodges was Chief of Infantry from 31 May 1941 to 9 March 1942. Harry J. Malony (1936) was ACS, G–3, in the spring of 1941. Edmund B. Gregory (1937) was the Quartermaster General from 1 April 1940 to 31 January 1946 and William N. Porter (1938) was Chief of the Chemical Corps from 31 May 1941 to 28 November 1945. See James E. Hewes, Jr., *From Root to McNamara: Army Organization and Administration, 1900–1963*, Special Studies Series (Washington, D.C.: U.S. Army Center of Military History, 1975), app. B.

51.

	AWC Total	
Year Group	Graduates	Generals
1934	84	49
1935	92	60
1936	95	61
1937	96	61
1938	96	64
1939	92	69
1940	102	72

Source: Directory, Present & Former Staff & Faculty. Graduates & Students By Class, 1905–1982, USAWC, pp. 31–38. One "staff officer" whose name became a household word was Lewis B. Hershey (1934). He directed the U.S. conscription system through three wars. Ten World War II corps commanders came from AWC classes 1934–1938; 29 of 34 came from AWC classes 1926–1938. See Robert H. Berlin, "United States Army World War II Corps Commanders: A Composite Biography," *The Journal of Military History* 53 (April 1989): 152, 158. None of the officers in Eisenhower's OPD on 3 April 1942 would qualify as household names, but they were the brains of the Army. Five of the 6 brigadier generals are AWC 1935–1940 graduates; 13 of the 19 colonels are AWC 1935–1939 graduates; 9 of the 13 AWC 1935–1939 graduates listed as colonels were later generals. By any definition, these were key men. Their rather recent experience at AWC was fresh as they performed important duties. See "Officers, War Department General Staff, Operations Division," Biog. Rm., DOD Telephone Directories, Basement, MHI.

52. MHI, the Thomas T. Handy Papers including "Transcripts of the Debriefing of General Handy," by Lt Col Edward M. Knoff, Jr., 1973–1974; see also Oral History: Gen Thomas T. Handy, USA, Ret., Maj Floyd J. Davis, Summer 1981. He believed that the school system saved the Army (Knoff, p. 8) and was impressed by the breadth of knowledge found among the faculty and students at AWC. (Knoff, Section 2, pp. 30, 51–52). He also said that Japan was seen as the Navy's problem, but Hitler's "acting up in Europe" was recognized by the American people as a reason to pay for an Army (Knoff, Section 5, p. 16).

53. "Secretary of War dirs. folwg. off. rpt. to ACofS, WPD at AWC folg. temp. duty.(i/c/w/War Plan Rainbow)" file no. 111–41/20 tags 6–21–40 and 6–22–40, MHI; Memo for ACS G–l, G–2, G–3, G–4, 17 Jun 40, sub: Color Plans, RAINBOW, with encl. 1, 14 Jun 40, same sub, signed by George V. Strong, ACS, WPD, WDGS, a detailed directive to the staff, file no. 111–41/20, MHI.

54. Maj Gen Thompson Lawrence: 201 file, Lawrence Family Papers, MHI.

55. Lawrence's signature is on the "Covering Memorandum for the Draft of the War Department Operations and Concentration Plans for Rainbow 4," 23 Oct 40, file no. 111–41/17.

56. "Correspondence re: ISMs," WPD requests that the college examine "Strategy of a BLUE–South American combine against a German-Italian challenge to the Monroe

Doctrine," file no. 7–1938–0, MHI; Comments and Corrections re: WPD, WDOP–R–4–40 (RAINBOW 4), 17 Sep 40, Lawrence, file no. 111–41/16, MHI; "Reproduction of Strategic Studies," 23 Sep 40, Lawrence, file no. 111–41/15, MHI; Troop Strengths, Deployments in W. Hemisphere, Lawrence, file nos. 111–41/13 and /14, MHI; Priorities of Photos in Caribbean, 14 Sep 40, Lawrence file no. 111–41/15, MHI.

57. Interv, Bolte with Dr. Maclyn Burg, 17 Oct 73, p. 24, MHI.

58. Interv, Bolte with Arthur J. Zoebelin, AWC, 1971–1972, pp. 7–8, MHI.

59. Ibid., p. 8.

60. Burg Interv. This "scattering" resulted in 23 percent (127 of 555) of AWC graduates 1934–1939 being assigned in WDGS as of March 1940 and 33 percent (215 of 652) of AWC graduates 1934–1940 being assigned in WDGS as of November 1941. Cross-reference, *AWC Directory 1990* and War Department Telephone Directories, 1 Mar 40 and 15 Nov 41.

61. Intervs, Hull with Lt Col James W. Wurman, Oct–Apr 73, MHI.

62. Ibid., Sec. 3, p. 45.

63. Ibid., Sec. 3, p. 37.

64. The *Philadelphia Inquirer* gave him credit for coining the expression "Hemisphere Defense" in a February 1939 report. MHI, Russell Maxwell Papers (see *Inquirer,* 12 Aug 45). His papers include correspondence, official papers, and newspaper clippings showing his interest in German, Japanese, and Italian penetration of Latin America, 1938–1941.

65. His papers include a copy of President Roosevelt's 14 April 1939 speech on Pan-America Day before the Governing Board of the Pan-American Union. The president woos Latin America and warns that the nations of the hemisphere should stay out of European affairs. One suspects that Maxwell played some role in contributing to the speech, but that suspicion is circumstantial and based on a reading of the papers in his file.

66. See for example, WP no. 5, 1937, and WP no. 5, 1938, MHI, for the visits of Brig. Gen. Walter Krueger, ACS, WPD, to the college. The texts of his presentations are available in the AWC curricular archives, as are those of the other assistant chiefs of staff for the entire interwar period. In his 1938 lecture to the class, Krueger said: "Additional officers that may be needed [in WPD] will be drawn from the student body of the Army War College." He made the same statement in 1937. In fact, in 1940 WPD was augmented by officers of AWC in an organization called "the War College Group" (WCG). See note 49.

67. See MHI, 7–1935–0, 7–1936–0, 7–1938–0, 7–1939–0 and 407 flat, and 397 flat for correspondence between AWC and the General Staff regarding student work done for the staff. See MHI, USAWC file 1–105, Summary of the Courses at AWC Since the World War, for an outline and summary of what AWC considered significant by year from 1919 to 1940.

68. Orientation, 1936, ISM no. 1, flat no. 407, MHI.

69. Flat no. 387, MHI.

70. Red Pencil note attached to 1931 files in flat no. 387, MHI.

71. Correspondence, re: Individual Staff Memoranda, 1933–1934, flat no. 407, MHI. See memo, 20 Oct 34, AWC Studies from MID to AWC. Of course, the conference itself was unsatisfactory.

72. Ibid.; Ltr, 1 Oct 31, List of Subjects for Individual Studies Requested by WDGS to AWC. Similar shopping lists will be found in the correspondence in the "zero" and "flat" files in note 64 for the various years.

73. Ibid.; Ltrs, Craig to Lincoln, 5 Mar 35, and response, 7 Mar 35. This, and many similar examples of quick response, suggests that cooperation was excellent and that probably there was a daily courier service linking the college and the War Department. Person-to-person correspondence frequently resulted in a response within forty-eight hours. There are advantages to locating senior service colleges in the national capital. There are also advantages to faculty and students in having a commandant whose star was rising.

74. Correspondence, re: ISMs, file no. 7–1938–0, MHI.

75. File marked Misc. no. 3, 1938, MHI. See also note 56.

76. Ltrs, Reardon to Simonds, 8 Dec 34, and Simonds to Reardon, 10 Dec 34, file no. 7–1935–0, MHI.

77. *Directory*, AWC, 1905–1984, USAWC, 1984, pp. 1, 2, 43. See also Harry P. Ball, *Of Responsible Command* (Carlisle, Pa.: The Alumni Association of the United States Army War College, 1983), p. 228. "Simonds was not averse to having his students take on studies that the War Department General Staff needed."

78. Craig's successors were Walter S. Grant (1924), who retired as a major general; John L. DeWitt (AWC 1920), who had served in WPD (1921–1924) and been deputy commandant at AWC (1928–1930). DeWitt supervised the internment of Japanese and Japanese-Americans after war broke out (Obituary, the *New York Times*, 22 Jun 62) and was commandant of the Army and Navy Staff College for its entire wartime existence (1943–1945). He retired with four stars. Philip B. Peyton (AWC 1931), the last of the prewar commandants, retired a major general. Simonds, Craig, Grant, and DeWitt had also served on the faculty, as did Stanley D. Embick, Walter Krueger, William H. Simpson, Joseph T. McNarney, Charles L. Bolte, and J. Lawton Collins (Ball, p. 252), and the following officers served in the War Plans Division: Embick (twice), Krueger (twice), DeWitt, Simonds, and McNarney (HRC 321, WPD Master Personnel List).

79. Thomas T. Handy Papers, "Transcripts of the Debriefing of General Handy," by Lt Col Edward M. Knoff, Jr., 1973–1974, S1–S2. He also said, "anything that came up, there was some guy who just knew a hell of a lot about it. . . . [The Army War College] was the one place where you could sit down and think."

80. For a summary of RAINBOWS 1–5, see Matloff and Snell, *Strategic Planning*, pp. 5–9.

81. For student development of ORANGE in 1938 and 1939, see file no. 7–1938–0, MHI, for correspondence between WPD and AWC turning AWC attention to the Western Hemisphere and the strategic triangle. See file no. 1–105, 1937–1938, MHI, for rationale for AWC doing RED, GREEN, ORANGE, and PURPLE. See file nos. 5–1938–21 and 5–1939–6, MHI, for two variations of ORANGE: 1938 was a roll of the dice; 1939 was deliberate.

82. Oral Rpt of Group no. 4, file no. 5–1935–20, MHI.

83. Matloff and Snell, *Strategic Planning*, p. 8.

84. Rpt of the War Plans Group no. 4, file no. 5–1936–21, MHI.

85. File no. 5–1937–24A, MHI.

Travails of Peace and War
Field Artillery in the 1930s and Early 1940s

Boyd Dastrup

During the 1930s and early 1940s, the U.S. Army's field artillery experienced a profound change. Throughout these years limited budgets compounded by conservative thinking within the field artillery, especially after 1933, influenced the pace of modernization. Nevertheless, the field artillery motorized its field pieces, revamped fire direction, reorganized, and rearmed to improve close support for the other combat arms.

After a decade of limited progress in the 1920s with modernizing the field artillery, Maj. Gen. Harry G. Bishop, Chief of Field Artillery (1930–1934), took aggressive action to rearm and reequip. At the general's urging the War Department directed the Field Artillery Board in 1931 to test four M1897 75-mm. guns with carriages that had been adapted for high-speed movement by replacing their wooden wheels with steel wheels with pneumatic tires. After conducting trials between May 1932 and March 1933, the Board recommended employing trucks as prime movers for light artillery and testing a battalion of towed 75-mm. guns. Although the lack of funds caused by the Great Depression prevented the battalion trial, Bishop accepted the results of the battery test as evidence that light trucks were acceptable for towing light artillery for the division. Even though the specific type of vehicle to be used was unsettled in 1933, Bishop concluded that the War Department could not avoid adopting towed artillery as it had done since the late 1920s by using the rationale that suitable motor vehicles did not exist.[1]

General Bishop's prompting, a declining horse population in the United States, a grant from the Public Works Administration (PWA) to increase motorized equipment in the National Guard and Regular Army, and a modernization program initiated in 1933 by the Chief of Staff, General Douglas MacArthur (1930–1935), combined to encourage the War Department to motorize its light artillery. Still reluctant to depend totally on motor vehicles as prime movers, the War Department estab-

lished the goal of motorizing 50 percent of its light batteries to complement its medium and heavy batteries, which had been motorized in the
1920s. As an expedient, the War Department adapted old M1897 carriages
for towing behind a truck until a new carriage could be developed.
Supported by funds from the PWA, the War Department standardized a
new carriage with pneumatic tires, antifriction bearings, and springs in
1936 to give the 75-mm. gun two types of carriages—a modified M1897
carriage and a modern one. Even though lingering resistance from conservative field artillery officers slowed down progress, the War Department
motorized fifty-eight of its eighty-one M2 75-mm. (modernized French
M1897) gun batteries by 1939 and even produced an experimental towed
M2 105-mm. howitzer.[2]

In comparison, leadership within the field artillery continued to
oppose introducing self-propelled artillery. As they had done during the
1920s, many field artillery officers contended throughout the 1930s that
towed artillery was more maneuverable, less conspicuous, and less likely
to be deadlined for repairs than self-propelled artillery and could be pulled
by horses if necessary. Simply put, adopting self-propelled artillery represented an even more radical step than acquiring towed artillery and was
resisted.[3]

Just as World War II was beginning, Maj. Gen. Robert M. Danford,
Chief of Field Artillery (1938–1942), expressed the feelings and fears of
many field artillery officers about motorization. In a lecture in September
1939 to Army War College students, he explained that the motor surpassed the horse in some situations, while the horse was better in others.
He explained, "For light division artillery, the horse still remains superior
as the prime mover off roads, through the mud, the darkness and the rain.
. . . To discard him during peace in favor of the motor, 100 per cent, is
simply putting all our eggs in one basket, and is, in my judgment, an
unsound policy."[4]

Although Danford hesitatingly accepted motorization, he hoped to
preserve some horse-drawn light artillery. For the general, motorizing all
was too risky because motor vehicles were still unproved in combat and
because motorizing the field artillery meant abandoning tradition for the
unknown, and this was difficult to do.[5]

Caught in the middle of a technological revolution, many field
artillery officers reluctantly converted most of their light artillery to towed
by 1939 but did not want self-propelled artillery. Yet, as early as the mid-
1930s, most field artillery officers conceded that the appearance of reliable motor vehicles made horse-drawn artillery obsolete and that they had
to adopt motorized artillery. Even so, swayed by their apprehensions and

faced with the possibility of restructuring tactics, doctrine, and organization, they kept their horses even though the availability of suitable motor vehicles and money dedicated to motorization removed two of the three obstacles that had stood in the way of progress in the 1920s and first years of the 1930s. After 1933 only conservatism, the third obstacle, hindered motorization.[6]

Meanwhile, improvements in motor transportation, the development of a 155-mm. howitzer carriage suitable for towing behind a motor vehicle, pressure from eager reformers, and the desire to stay abreast of developments in foreign armies caused attitudes to change about the division's field artillery armament. Ever since the War Department's decision of the early 1920s to equip the division with new 75-mm. guns and 105-mm. howitzers, which meant dropping the 155-mm. howitzer, many field artillery officers pushed to replace the 75-mm. gun with the 105-mm. howitzer. They wanted to keep the 155-mm. howitzer because a 105-mm. and 155-mm. howitzer combination would give the division superior firepower and mobility. Besides being too light, the 75-mm. gun's flat trajectory limited its utility by preventing it from hitting targets on the reverse side of the slope, which discouraged employing the gun.[7]

In June 1938 General Danford directed the Field Artillery School at Fort Sill, Oklahoma, to determine the best weapons for the division to end the controversy that had been raging for almost two decades. The school emphatically rejected using 75-mm. guns and 105-mm. howitzers because they lacked sufficient firepower and only offered mobility. Rather, the school wanted to equip the division with 105-mm. and 155-mm. howitzers because of their mobility and firepower. Yet, the school realized that a surplus of 75-mm. guns and ammunition from the Great War would delay or even prevent scrapping the 75-mm. gun for the 105-mm. howitzer.[8]

Even though tests of the triangular division in 1937–1939 supported employing 105-mm. and 155-mm. howitzers, the War Department still resisted changing the division's artillery. In 1939–1940 the War Department noted that the M2 105-mm. howitzer's range of 12,500 yards was shorter than the M2 75-mm. gun's range of 13,600 yards, that it took longer for the howitzer to go into action, that the howitzer had not been proved in battle, that there was a surplus of 75-mm. guns and ammunition, and that replacing the 75-mm. gun with the 105-mm. howitzer would be expensive and difficult to justify in peacetime.[9] In fact, Chief of Staff George C. Marshall (1939–1945), pointed out in February 1940 that abandoning the 75-mm. gun and ammunition and spending vast sums of money to arm the division with 105-mm. howitzers was awkward to defend and that he was unwilling to convert to the 105-mm. and 155-mm. howitzer combination. Like many of his predecessors, Marshall hesitated spending money on new weapons in peacetime when a surplus from the Great War existed.[10]

Nevertheless, events of 1940 finally prodded the War Department to reshape the division's artillery. Reports by field artillery officers during maneuvers of April and May 1940 further validated the need for 105-mm. and 155-mm. howitzers. Moreover, the Germans' success with 105-mm. howitzers in their divisions encouraged the War Department to change its position. Influenced by overwhelming evidence in favor of abandoning the 75-mm. gun for the 105-mm. howitzer, in June 1940 the Organization and Training Division (G–3) of the General Staff announced its decision to arm the division with three battalions of 105-mm. howitzers (thirty-six) and one battalion of 155-mm. howitzers (twelve).[11]

Adopting new field pieces in the 1930s generally faced stiff challenges. The Field Artillery School commented in 1937, "It cannot be expected that this reserve [M1897, M1916, and M1917 75-mm. guns, M1918 155-mm. howitzers, M1918 155-mm. guns, and M1918 240-mm. howitzers] will be replaced, in peace, with more modern materiel, because of the great cost involved." Although the school acknowledged that new light, medium, and heavy field pieces were being developed, it lamented, "However so long a time is required for production, issue, and training with new types that it is safe to assume that any war fought by the United States during this generation will be begun and continued during a considerable period with modified World War materiel."[12]

Because of a war surplus, Congress', the War Department's, and the field artillery's hesitancy to purchase new weapons during peacetime and the lengthy time required to introduce new weapons, the Field Artillery School viewed the future pessimistically in 1937. Replacing old field pieces with new ones simply was not likely because Congress and the War Department would not provide money to produce new pieces that were in varying stages of development. As such, the field artillery was destined to continue equipping its batteries with old, worn out guns or modernized old models until a war broke out to force Congress to allocate the funds for manufacturing new weapons in the needed quantities.[13]

Motorization also caused reforms in fire direction to be made. Since the inception of indirect fire at the beginning of the twentieth century, the battery had been the firing unit.[14] Because of this practice, the field artillery had two methods of massing fire on a target from two or more batteries. First, if all of the battery forward observers could see the target, adjusting fire was easy. If the target was obscure, the other batteries would watch for the bursts of the adjusting battery and then try to engage the target. Second, when the target could be located on a map, the observers would pass its grid coordinates to the batteries to compute firing data. When a map was not available or when only one observer could see the target, massing fire was difficult and slow even for static warfare.[15]

Without a method of massing fire quickly on a battlefield that was becoming more mobile with the advent of motor vehicles, Maj. (later Maj. Gen.) Carlos Brewer, Director of the Gunnery Department at the Field Artillery School, and his instructors overhauled fire direction procedures in 1931. Inspired by a British artillery officer, Lt. Col. Neil Fraser-Tytler's book, *Field Guns in France,* that detailed the colonel's wartime experiences of shifting fire around the battlefield, they revised air and ground observation methods, created a firing chart, located the battery position through survey, and designated targets with reference to the base point on the firing chart. Yet, they did not centralize computing firing data at the battalion because they could not find a way that was not slow and laborious.[16]

Maj. (later Maj. Gen.) Orlando Ward, Brewer's successor, and his instructors developed a means for massing fire rapidly. In 1932–1934 they created the fire direction center in the battalion. The battalion commander would dispatch forward observers, while the center would compute firing data and synchronize fire on the most dangerous target. With accurate maps a battalion could mass fire within ten minutes after a call for fire, while a battery could provide fire within five minutes. Without maps massing fire was slower. Although the system could only handle observed fire, the fire direction center surpassed anything in Europe and made the battalion the firing unit.[17]

Even though the fire direction center improved the ability to mass fire, many senior field artillery officers of the late 1930s opposed placing the battalion commander in charge of directing fire. In emotionally charged articles they insisted that the battery commander was "king in his own right, and that no one but the battery commander could give orders" to fire. Influenced by such officers and the Chief of Field Artillery, Maj. Gen. Upton Birnie (1934–1938), the War Department refused to adopt the fire direction center and left the battery as the firing unit.[18]

During the latter years of the 1930s, Lt. Col. (later Maj. Gen.) H. L. C. Jones, who became the director of the Gunnery Department in 1939, and his staff made the fire direction center acceptable. They centralized all computation for observed and unobserved fire at the fire direction center and made the battery commander responsible for observed fire and the battalion commander for unobserved. Only after Colonel Jones demonstrated the ability of the fire direction center in 1941 to mass fire rapidly and effectively did the Field Artillery School commandant, the Chief of Field Artillery, and the War Department accept the center and break with the past.[19]

Unlike the fire direction center that improved the field artillery's capacity to perform its traditional role of supporting the other combat arms, using field pieces to fight tanks had the potential of forging a new and controversial mission. Even though field artillery officers of the 1920s and 1930s devised antitank tactics, they still clung tightly to those missions that predated tanks. Addressing student officers at the Army War College in September 1938, General Danford said, "The artillery should not be diverted from its primary role solely for antitank defense except in real emergencies."[20] Danford and most field artillery officers opposed antitank warfare as a primary mission because it would give the field artillery a defensive role and divert it from supporting the other combat arms. Therefore, they favored acquiring extremely mobile antitank weapons and attaching them to the division or corps.[21]

Literature at the Field Artillery School confirmed that field artillery officers knew about the tank's ability to alter tactics and organization dramatically. Nevertheless, they did not envision employing tanks, infantry, and artillery in formations as the Germans were developing with *Blitzkrieg* warfare or as B. H. Liddell Hart or J. F. C. Fuller were promoting in Great Britain. As far as the field artillery was concerned, the tank was still an infantry support weapon.[22]

Consequently, on the eve of World War II, a mix of the old and new uneasily coexisted in the field artillery. Antiquated weapons and conservative thinking certainly dominated the field artillery. Progressive people at the Field Artillery School and General Bishop tried to move the field artillery forward, but conservative thinking by most field artillery officers, to include Chiefs of Field Artillery after 1934, and limited funds hampered modernization.

German offensives of 1939 and 1940 dispelled any lingering American doubts about modernizing the field artillery.[23] Impressed with the mobility of German self-propelled 105-mm. howitzers, the War Department initiated action to acquire its own. Pressed by expediency, the Ordnance Department mounted an M2 105-mm. howitzer on a medium tank chassis, designated the weapon the M7 self-propelled 105-mm. howitzer, also known as the Priest because of its pulpit-like machine gun turret, and rushed it to the British in North Africa late in 1942. The adoption of self-propelled and towed artillery opened a new era. After depending on horses for years, field artillery officers finally came to terms with motor vehicles as prime movers for their field guns.[24]

Simultaneously, the war in Europe caused Congress to increase funding for defense. Contracts were let, and by late 1942 towed M2 105-mm. howitzers, self-propelled M7 105-mm. howitzers, towed M1 4.5-inch guns, towed M1 155-mm. guns, self-propelled M12 155-mm. guns, towed M1 8-inch howitzers, and towed M2 8-inch guns were beginning to replace World War I pieces and their modernized versions. Besides having more mobility and firepower than their predecessors, these new weapons fired high-explosive shell, chemical shell, steel shrapnel, and shot for piercing armor.[25]

The introduction of more powerful artillery, the growing use of camouflage, and deeply defiladed battery positions made ground observation more difficult. In some cases only air observation could detect targets. Because of this, field artillery officers set out to make aerial observation more responsive to their needs. As early as 1935, General Bishop openly opposed using air service personnel as observers in aircraft because they were not trained artillerymen and did not know the requirements of the field artillery. By doing this, the general challenged the decision made in 1926 to place aerial observation under the control of the Air Corps.[26]

Several years later, field artillery officers led by General Danford also agitated for better air observation. Influenced by this dissatisfaction, Aeronca, Piper, and Taylorcraft aircraft manufacturers offered their light aircraft complete with pilots to senior commanders participating in the Army maneuvers in Tennessee, Texas, Louisiana, and the Carolinas in 1941 for testing in artillery observation and liaison roles. Chief of the Air Corps Lt. Gen. Henry H. "Hap" Arnold accepted using the light planes and assigned them to squadrons of O–49 observation aircraft for employment in the maneuvers. Named "Grasshoppers" by Maj. Gen. Innis P. Swift, Commanding General, lst Cavalry Division, at Fort Bliss, Texas, the light aircraft flew over 400,000 miles during the maneuvers, completed more than 3,000 missions without losing an aircraft, and demonstrated their utility in air observation, courier, and reconnaissance missions.[27]

Notwithstanding the Grasshoppers' success, field artillery officers participating in the Louisiana Maneuvers complained about the quality of the Air Corps' air observation. They wrote that they never knew when air observation would be available, that the diversion of aircraft to other missions was disruptive, that coordination between the field artillery and the Air Corps was difficult, and that there was never enough aircraft for artillery missions. Unable to depend on the Air Corps, in 1941 the War Department saw the possibility of making air observation organic to field artillery units. After all, the Germans were employing this type of air observation successfully in the war, while the British were introducing it.[28]

In light of the requirement for better air observation and the precedent being established in Europe, the War Department tasked the field artillery to test organic air observation. Using various models of light aircraft, experiments conducted at Camp Blanding, Florida, and Fort Sam Houston, Texas, in February and March 1942 demonstrated the timeliness of organic air observation. After studying the after action reports, the War Department approved adopting organic air observation for the field artillery. Subsequently, a directive of 6 June 1942 allotted two small air-craft, two pilots, and one mechanic to each field artillery battalion and the same to each group, division, and corps artillery headquarters.[29]

The war years of 1939–1942 generated significant changes in the field artillery. The acceptance of motorized artillery as the prime mover even though vestiges of horse-drawn artillery were still hanging on, determined efforts to introduce new weapons, the adoption of organic air observation, and the decision to accept the fire direction center revolutionized the field artillery. Even so, field artillery officers could only speculate about how effectively they could mass fire and provide close support under combat conditions.

Early in 1943 in North Africa, American field artillery met one of its first combat tests. As Maj. Gen. Lloyd R. Fredendall's dispersed U.S. II Corps with a decentralized artillery command was struggling to hold the passes around Kasserine Pass, General Dwight D. Eisenhower, Supreme Allied Commander, dispatched reinforcements from Algeria to Tunisia. After several days of forced marches, Brig. Gen. S. LeRoy Irwin, Commander, 9th Infantry Division Artillery, moved his artillery of three bat-talions and two cannon companies into position at Thala to bolster sorely tested British defenses. During the night of 21–22 February, Irwin sited forty-eight American howitzers and thirty-six British pieces to enfilade the road from Kasserine Pass and massed fire on the Germans as they approached. Unable to continue forward under such destructive fire, the Germans finally retreated to Kasserine Pass. Meanwhile, Brig. Gen. Clift Andrus, Commander, 1st Infantry Division Artillery, massed barrages on the Germans and Italians as they drove towards Tebessa to cover the German advance on Thala and forced the Axis to retire back toward Kasserine Pass.[30]

Although American field artillery played an important role at Kasserine Pass by massing fire on the enemy, American participants expressed mixed observations about its effectiveness. Joseph B. Mittelman, a soldier in the 9th Division, complemented the field artillery's gallant stand. Yet, artillery commanders knew that they had to master the fire direction center and centralize command. After all, effective fire sup-port in North Africa came only after Irwin and Andrus had organized their command properly to mass fire.[31]

After pushing the Germans back, the Allies then drove the Axis out of North Africa. Taking advantage of the fire direction center, radio-equipped observers attached to infantry or armor units or sent aloft in organic spot-ter aircraft, and centralized command, field artillerymen repeatedly massed fire on German positions. During the Battle of El Guettar on 23 March 1943, for example, American field artillery with help from tank destroyers knocked out nearly thirty enemy tanks to help contain the attack early in the day. Later that same day, massed fire from American field artillery shattered another German attack led by thirty-eight tanks. Following El Guettar, an enthusiastic report recorded that American artillery had crucified the Germans with high explosive shell. Based on El Guettar and other battles, field artillerymen concluded that artillery was one of the dominating factors on the battlefield when it was employed en mass. As a result, corps and division commanders used as much field artillery as possible to support operations and often massed up to twelve battalions (144 guns) to attack enemy positions. This led the Field Artillery School to conclude in 1943 that massed fire was a necessity for successful operations.[32]

Besides this demonstration of firepower at El Guettar, other intense and accurate American artillery bombardments during the Allied push in Tunisia destroyed the Axis. Commenting on his field artillery's effective-ness, Maj. Gen. Manton Eddy, Commander, 9th Division, noted, "One Nazi who had served on almost every German front said that the American artillery fire was the most deadly that he had experienced."[33] After driving the Axis out of North Africa, Lt. Gen. Omar Bradley, Commanding General, II Corps, during the latter days of the North African campaign, explained that massed fire was a major factor in the Allied success at Gafsa and El Guettar.[34]

The fire direction center, organic air and ground observers, motorized light artillery, and the newly created field artillery group that had been organized for corps artillery made effective close support possible. With few exceptions the field artillery depended on observed fire because the hills and ridges of Tunisia provided excellent positions for observation. The commander of the 1st Armored Division's artillery indicated that any one of his observers could adjust fire for any of the division's batteries because of the fire direction center. Explaining the impact of the center further, the commander wrote, "On any important target I usually mass all the artillery of the division [forty-eight guns]."[35] At the conclusion of the fighting, Bradley reaffirmed the artillery commander's position. He point-ed out that the fire direction center was so flexible that any air or ground observer could adjust fire for any battery in his corps and bring fire from all the artillery in the corps (324 guns) onto a single target if it required such firepower.[36] As such, the fire direction center and radio-equipped

observers tied observers and battalions into an effective fire support network to crush enemy resistance and simultaneously united the field
artillery, armor, and infantry into a potent combined arms team.[37]

Despite being new, organic air observation also played a key role in
North Africa. In a brief article in *Field Artillery Journal* in 1944, Maj.
Edward A. Raymond, a field artillery officer, explained that air observation had "come into its own."[38] In fact, the battles of El Guettar, Mateur,
and Bizerte silenced detractors. Although the enemy was a master of camouflage, air observers repeatedly identified gun flashes from almost perfectly concealed positions for corps artillery to engage. Hostile antiaircraft
fire might have prevented air observers from flying behind enemy lines on
occasion, but they could still pick out enemy batteries to be neutralized or
adjust fire on targets over ten thousand yards away. In light of this, flying
behind the enemy lines was not critical for effective fire support. During
action near Hill 609 by Sidi Nsir late in April and early May 1943, for
example, organic air observers located so many targets that the 34th
Infantry Division's artillery "could hardly haul in ammo fast enough to
respond to the calls for fire."[39]

Aerial observation also had a side benefit. During the battles of El
Guettar, Mateur, and Bizerte, observation aircraft flying over enemy lines
often caused hostile batteries to cease firing to prevent them from disclosing
their positions, which allowed the Americans to mass fire with impunity.[40]

At the same time, towed and self-propelled pieces proved themselves.
In 1943 the War Department noted that towed pieces were highly mobile
and maneuverable but that self-propelled guns were even more so.
Although self-propelled artillery was not any faster than towed artillery on
the road, it had the ability to move into position faster to deliver fire, to
displace quickly to avoid counterbattery fire, and to follow armor over terrain that was impassable for towed artillery. As a result, self-propelled
artillery could be used aggressively on the offense and support fast-moving armor forces in North Africa.[41] An article in *Field Artillery Journal* in
March 1944 reported that the M7 was not only mobile but also offered the
crew protection from small arms fire and shell fragments so that the
weapon could be sited forward and closely support any action. Although
the M7 performed effectively, many field artillery officers still thought
that it was too slow and heavy to support fast-moving armor. Even so,
towed and self-propelled artillery silenced critics and had become an
acknowledged asset by mid-1943.[42]

Despite this, the M7 105-mm. self-propelled howitzer's inability to
shift its direction of fire by traversing only the tube created problems. With
the towed M2 105-mm. howitzer, the gun crew could change direction of

fire easily and quickly by moving the trails when the target was beyond the tube's range of traverse. This was impossible with the M7. Because of the short traverse of the M7's tube, the crew had to reposition the gun mount when calls for fire were outside of the tube's range of traverse. This was slow and required a high degree of skill and teamwork on the part of the driver, the gunner, and section chief. As such, early action in North Africa in 1943 reinforced the wisdom of 360-degree on-board traverse recommended by the Westervelt Board of 1919.[43]

Even though most Army officers agreed that American field artillery had performed effectively in North Africa, some saw the need for changes. General Irwin and Col. George B. Barth, Chief of Staff, 9th Division, wanted to expand the light battery from four to six pieces for more firepower. In a confidential review of combat action, the Field Artillery School pointed out that the U.S. II Corps' 324 field guns fired over 23,000 rounds a day in North Africa. Although this number of guns appeared to be impressive, it was not. Because of the failure of the Germans to mass their artillery and their lack of artillery and ammunition, II Corps had sufficient artillery. In light of this, the school then warned that the Army should not draw any false conclusions from the North African campaign concerning field artillery support. The school thought that the division's organic artillery of forty-eight guns was the bare minimum and that a corps required more than II Corps had in North Africa when the United States invaded Europe to overcome the vast concentrations of enemy artillery on the Continent.[44]

Even so, combat action in North Africa in 1943 vindicated the progressive reforms of the 1930s and dispelled the apprehensions of conservative field artillery officers. Towed and self-propelled artillery supplied unprecedented mobility without sacrificing firepower, while the fire direction center and organic air observation dramatically facilitated massing fires for close support. By improving firepower, mobility, and responsiveness, the new weapons and techniques introduced during the 1930s and early 1940s revolutionized the field artillery, while combat strengthened the requirement for firepower.

NOTES

1. Maj. Gen. Paul B. Malone, "The Significance of the Truck Drawn Battery of 75mm Guns," *Field Artillery Journal* (May–June 1933): 205–08; "Truck-Drawn 75mm Gun Battery and Battalion," *Field Artillery Journal* (July–August 1933): 293; Maj. J. H. Wallace, "Test of the Truck-Drawn 75mm Battery," *Field Artillery Journal* (July–August 1933): 301.

2. Maj. J. H. Wallace, "The New 75mm Gun Carriage, M2," *Field Artillery Journal* (March–April 1936): 146, 149; The Field Artillery School, *Field Artillery Materiel* (Fort Sill, Okla.: The Field Artillery School, 1932), pp. 18–19; Maj Gen Robert M. Danford, Lecture, Army War College, 23 Sep 39, p. 18, Morris Swett Library, Fort Sill; "Army Motorization Plan," *Field Artillery Journal* (January–February 1934): 94–95; Janice McKenney, "More Bang for the Buck in the Interwar Army: The 105mm Howitzer," *Military Affairs* (April 1978): 82–85.

3. "Forecast of Field Artillery Progress During Next Five Years," *Field Artillery Journal* (November–December 1933): 510.

4. Danford, Lecture, U.S. Army War College (USAWC), 23 Sep 39, p. 19.

5. Ibid.

6. "Forecast of Field Artillery Progress During the Next Five Years," p. 510.

7. The Field Artillery School, "A Study of the 105mm Howitzer with Particular Regard to the Practical Aspects of Certain Features of Design," Sep 38, pp. 1–2, Morris Swett Library, hereafter cited as Study of the 105mm Howitzer; McKenney, "More Bang for the Buck in the Interwar Army," pp. 84–85; Jonathan M. House, "Designing the Light Division: 1935–44," *Military Review* (May 1984): 41–47.

8. Study of the 105mm Howitzer, pp. 1–2, 19, 42.

9. House, "Designing the Light Division: 1935–44," pp. 41–47; McKenney, "More Bang for the Buck in the Interwar Army," pp. 84–85.

10. Mark S. Watson, *Chief of Staff Prewar Plans and Preparations* (Washington, D.C.: U.S. Army Center of Military History, 1950), pp. 39–40.

11. McKenney, "More Bang for the Buck in the Interwar Army," p. 85.

12. Field Artillery School, *Field Artillery Materiel*, 1937, p. 11.

13. Ibid.; Watson, *Chief of Staff Prewar Plans and Preparations*, pp. 31–40.

14. Field Artillery School, *Digest of Field Artillery Developments* (Fort Sill, Okla.: Field Artillery School, 1935), pp. 1–2; U.S. Forces, European Theater, General Board, Rpt on Study of Field Artillery Gunnery, no. 64, n.d., pp. 21–22, in Morris Swett Library.

15. Riley Sunderland, "Massed Fire and the FDC," *Army* (May 1958): 58; U.S. Forces, European Theater, General Board, Rpt on Study of Field Artillery Gunnery, pp. 21–22; Lt. Col. Frank G. Ratliff, "The Field Artillery Battalion Fire-Direction Center—Its Past, Present, and Future," *Field Artillery Journal* (May–June 1950): 117; Russell Gugeler, Fort Sill and the Golden Age of Field Artillery, p. 6, unpublished Ms, Morris Swett Library.

16. Field Artillery School, *Digest of Field Artillery Developments*, 1935, p. 2; U.S. Forces, European Theater, General Board, Rpt on Study of Field Artillery Gunnery, p. 22; Ltr, Brewer to Cmdt, The Field Artillery School, 5 Feb 44, correspondence on the Development of Fire Direction Center (FDC), Morris Swett Library; Ltr, Col Sidney F. Dunn, former instructor in Gunnery Department, to Cmdt, The Field Artillery School, sub: Development of the Field Artillery Fire Direction Center, 21 Feb 44, correspondence on the Development of the Field Artillery FDC, U.S. 401st Field Artillery Group Field, Morris Swett Library; Ltr, Field Artillery School to Col Dunn, 10 Mar 44, correspondence on the Development of the FDC, Morris Swett Library; Riley Sunderland, *History of the Field Artillery School*, vol. 1 (Fort Sill, Okla.: The Field Artillery School, 1942), pp. 129–30; Brig Gen R. G. Barkalow to Cmdt, The Field Artillery School, sub: Development of the Field Artillery FDC, 4 Feb 44, in correspondence on the Development of the FDC, Morris

Swett Library; Ratliff, "The Field Artillery Battalion Fire-Direction Center," p. 118; Gugeler, Fort Sill and the Golden Age of Field Artillery, pp. 8–l0.

17. Ltr, Dunn to Cmdt, The Field Artillery School, sub: Development of the Field Artillery Fire Direction Center, 21 Feb 44; Ltr, Maj Gen Orlando Ward to Cmdt, The Field Artillery School, 15 Jun 44, in correspondence on Development of FDC; Sunderland, *History of the Field Artillery School*, pp. 157–58; Ratliff, "The Field Artillery Battalion Fire-Direction Center," p. 116; Field Artillery School, *Digest of Field Artillery Developments*, 1935, pp. 1–2.

18. Ratliff, "The Field Artillery Battalion Fire-Direction Center," p. 118; Ltr, Ward to Cmdt, The Field Artillery School, 15 Jun 44; Ltr, Dunn to Cmdt, The Field Artillery School, sub: Development of the Field Artillery FDC, 21 Feb 44.

19. Ltr, H. L. C. Jones to Cmdt, The Field Artillery School, 23 Feb 44, pp. 1–4, in Development of FDC File; Ratliff, "The Field Artillery Battalion Fire-Direction Center," pp. 118–19; Sunderland, *History of the Field Artillery School*, pp. 210–11.

20. Danford, Lecture, USAWC, 28 Sep 38, p. 28, Morris Swett Library.

21. Ibid.

22. The Field Artillery School, *Tactical Employment of Field Artillery* (Fort Sill, Okla.: Field Artillery School, 1938), pp. 16, 289.

23. Frank E. Comparato, *Age of Great Guns: Cannon Kings and Cannoneers Who Forged the Firepower of Artillery* (Harrisburg, Pa.: The Stackpole Co., 1965), p. 226.

24. The Field Artillery School, *Field Artillery Materiel*, 1937, p. ll; Constance M. Green, Harry C. Thomson, and Peter C. Roots, *The Ordnance Department: Planning Munitions for War* (Washington, D.C.: U.S. Army Center of Military History, 1955), pp. 314–15.

25. War Department, *Field Manual 6–130, Field Artillery Field Manual, Reference Data* (Washington, D.C.: Government Printing Office, 1940), pp. 8–11; The Field Artillery School, Characteristics of Weapons Chart, 1 Mar 40, Morris Swett Library; Field Artillery School, *Field Artillery Fundamentals* (Fort Sill, OK: The Field Artillery School, 1942), pp. 177–78; Danford, "Message from the Chief of Field Artillery," *Field Artillery Journal* (December 1940): 410.

26. Harry G. Bishop, *Field Artillery: King of Battle* (Boston: Houghton Mifflin Co., 1935), pp. 130–35; Laurence B. Epstein, "Army Organic Light Aviation," *U.S. Army Aviation Digest* (June 1977): 11–16.

27. William W. Ford, "Grasshoppers," *U.S. Army Aviation Digest* (June 1982): 3–4; Epstein, "Army Organic Light Aviation," pp. 11–16. Ford's article is the first of a five-part series in *U.S. Army Aviation Digest* in 1982 on the history of Army aviation. Ford was also one of the founding fathers of organic air observation.

28. Ltr, Danford to Chief of Staff, Army, sub: Air Observation, 8 Oct 41, tab D, Memorandum to the Chief of Staff, War Department, Washington, D.C., sub: Air Observation, 8 Oct 41, Morris Swett Library; Bishop, *Field Artillery*, pp. 130–35; Ltr, Col Fred C. Wallace, Office, Chief of Field Artillery, to Adjutant General, sub: Air Observation for Field Artillery, 15 Jul 40, tab B, Memorandum to the Chief of Staff, War Department, sub: Air Observation, 8 Oct 41; Ltr, Department of Tactics and Communications to Cmdt, The Field Artillery School, sub: Air Observation for Field Artillery, 8 Aug 41, tab F, Memorandum to the Chief of Staff, War Department, sub: Air Observation, 8 Oct 41.

29. Maj. Delbert L. Bristol, "Air OP is Here to Stay," *Field Artillery Journal* (October 1946): 586; Lt. Col. Lowell M. Riley, "Organic Air Observation for Field Artillery," *Field Artillery Journal* (July 1942): 498; Capt. Angus Rutledge, "Organic Air Observation for Field Artillery," *Field Artillery Journal* (July 1942): 498.

30. Martin Blumenson, "Kasserine Pass, 30 January–22 February 1943," in Charles E. Heller and William A. Stofft, ed., *America's First Battles: 1775–1965* (Lawrence, Kans.: University Press of Kansas, 1986), pp. 255–62; George F. Howe, *Northwest Africa: Seizing*

the Initiative in the West (Washington, D.C.: U.S. Army Center of Military History, 1957), p. 466; David W. Hazen, Role of the Field Artillery in the Battle of Kasserine Pass, unpublished MA thesis, U.S. Army Command and General Staff College, 1978, pp. 97–111.

31. Joseph B. Mittelman, *Eight Stars to Victory: A History of the Veteran Ninth U.S. Infantry Division* (Columbus, Ohio: F. J. Heer Printing Co., 1948), p. 92; Blumenson, "Kasserine Pass, 30 January–22 February 1943," p. 262.

32. Col. Douglas J. Page, "El Guettar: March 25–Apr 8, 1943," *Field Artillery Journal* (September 1943): 646–47; Lt. Col. P. W. Thompson, "Close Support in Tunisia," *Field Artillery Journal* (July 1943): 836; Col. C. C. Benson, "Some Tunisian Details," *Field Artillery Journal* (January 1944): 482–84; Rpt, HQ II Corps, sub: Employment of Field Artillery of the II Corps in Northern Tunisian Campaign, n.d., pp. 1–10, Morris Swett Library; Rpt, HQ II Corps, sub: Employment of the Artillery of the II Corps during Gafsa–El Guettar–Maknassy Campaign, 1 May 43, p. 8, Morris Swett Library; Howe, *Northwest Africa*, pp. 560–62; Field Artillery School, Review of Confidential Information, 10 Aug 43, pp. 5, 50, Morris Swett Library.

33. Ltr, Eddy to CG, Allied Forces Headquarters, 21 Jun 43, in Rpt on Operations Conducted by 9th Infantry Division, 1943, Morris Swett Library.

34. "Official Commendation," *Field Artillery Journal* (September 1943): 652.

35. Rpt, Col Thomas B. Hedekin to Cmdt, The Field Artillery School, sub: Rpt of Observer to North African Theater, 5 Jul 43, app. C, p. 21, Morris Swett Library.

36. Ibid., p. 19.

37. Ltr, Eddy to CG, Allied Forces Headquarters, 21 Jun 43.

38. Maj. Edward A. Raymond, "Air OPs," *Field Artillery Journal* (May 1944): 274.

39. Lt Col P. W. Thompson, Lecture, Field Artillery School, 26 Jun 43, p. 22, Morris Swett Library; Capt. Woodrow M. Smith, "A Summary of Tunisia," *Field Artillery Journal* (November 1943): 836; Field Artillery School, Review of Confidential Information, 10 Aug 43, p. 8.

40. Thompson, Lecture, 26 Jun 43, p. 221; Lt. Col. William W. Ford, "Grasshoppers," *Field Artillery Journal* (September 1943): 651.

41. Col. Lowell M. Riley, "Armored Artillery Action," *Field Artillery Journal* (March 1944): 179.

42. War Department, *Lessons of the Tunisian Campaign*, pp. 17–18; Field Artillery School, "Artillery in Combat," Aug 44, p. 14; Lt Col. Douglas G. Dwyre, "The Field Artillery Puts on Armor," *Field Artillery Journal* (December 1943): 917; Field Artillery School, Review of Confidential Information, 19 Aug 43, p. 8, Morris Swett Library.

43. Dwyre, "The Field Artillery Puts on Armor," p. 918.

44. Field Artillery School, Review of Confidential Information, Nov 43, p. 4; and 10 May 43, p. 22.

"Through the Looking Glass"
Bradford G. Chynoweth as United States Military
Attache in Britain, 1939

Theodore Wilson

On 13 July 1939, the United States Military Attache, Lt. Col. Bradford G. Chynoweth, headed the first section in his weekly report from London, "Through the Looking Glass." Pursuing what would be a recurring metaphor during his brief, stormy tenure as the Army's designated observer of a British military establishment and people teetering at the brink of war, Chynoweth admitted:

When I crossed the Atlantic three months ago, I entered into the land of the March Hare. Every time I get the situation nicely rationalized and sit back for a breathing spell, I suddenly find, like Alice, that I drank out of the wrong bottle and things are growing screwy again. Then, before I have it all rationalized once more, somebody informs me that a pouch is going out at five o'clock. . . . "The time has come," the Walrus said, "to talk of many things.". . . I must sit down at my trusty machine and hammer it out.[1]

Chynoweth's frank acknowledgment of disorientation alternating with temporary glimmers of enlightenment reflected a world dramatically transformed from the leisurely minuet of three-hour lunches at the Army and Navy Club, embassy receptions, and long weekends in the country to an ever more frantic whirl of War Office briefings, post visits, and rumor swapping over awful coffee and excellent whiskey.

A chronicle of Chynoweth's efforts to peer down the rabbit hole and to make sense of Britain's political, psychological, and military response to the crisis of Spring–Summer 1939 is as much a description of how and to what effect official intelligence-gathering was done in those long ago days before the CIA and electronic intercepts as it is an objective assessment of what the U.S. War Department learned about British military capabilities as a result of Bradford Chynoweth's sacrifice of renal function. This brief commentary is also intended to introduce those who have not already encountered "Chen" Chynoweth as a peer of Eisenhower, Patton, and

Bradley, one who arguably would have attained high command in World War II had not a "brilliant albeit slightly poisonous" pen, a penchant for expressing opinions bluntly, and an explosive temper crippled his career.[2] These are not, admittedly, attributes customarily associated with the post of a diplomat (the central function of a military attache), but they seem to have cropped up regularly among those U.S. Army officers posted abroad during the first half of the present century. The combination of two such combative individuals as Bradford Chynoweth and his immediate superior, Ambassador Joseph Kennedy, ensured that the former's abbreviated tour in London produced personal and political fireworks—and, also, some remarkable insights about Britain on the eve of war.

Bradford G. Chynoweth was the son of a career Army officer. Upon graduation from West Point, he was commissioned a second lieutenant in the Corps of Engineers in July 1912. Chynoweth's career followed a familiar pattern in the pre–World War I Army: battalion posting, Engineer School, service with the Punitive Expedition, and promotion to captain after four years. During the next two years, Chynoweth moved from the Office of the Chief of Engineers in Washington to a staff assignment at the Fort Meade Overseas Replacement Depot, and from there to a stint as Assistant District Engineer in Detroit, while experiencing rapid—if temporary—advancement to the rank of lieutenant colonel.

In October 1919, discouraged about his future prospects in the postwar Army, Chynoweth resigned his commission and entered the "mystical world beyond the gate," first trying his hand as a mechanical engineer in New York City and then entering the "automobile business" in Detroit.[3] "I felt sure that in civil life there was no red tape, and that virtue was always promptly rewarded. I expected to find none of the personal relations difficulties that had so irritated me in the Army," Chynoweth later recalled. But, he admitted, "I picked a very poor year to hit U.S. Industry."[4]

In November 1920, perhaps influenced by his brother-in-law, George A. Lynch (later to serve as Chief of Infantry), Chynoweth reversed course, accepted a commission as captain (spurning the Engineers for the Infantry) and entered the Tank School at Fort Meade.[5]

Through the 1920s and early 1930s Chynoweth's assignments reflected a deep interest in mechanized infantry and the benefits of excellent connections. General Staff duty was followed by attendance at the Infantry School, Fort Benning, which was followed by another stint in Washington in the Office of the Chief of Infantry. This led to service with the 42d Infantry at Camp Gaillard, Panama Canal Zone, and to the command of a battalion of the 6th Infantry in 1926–1927. After graduating from the Command and General Staff School in 1928, Chynoweth served as a member of the Infantry Board at Fort Benning for three years. This was a plum assignment, but Chynoweth nearly wrecked himself professionally by filing a minority report to the Board's recommendations for reorganizing the Infantry Battalion.[6]

Chynoweth was tardily selected for the Army War College and, following graduation in June 1932, went to the Operations and Training Division (G–3) of the War Department for four years.[7] He was then appointed Senior Instructor of the New Jersey National Guard. He found the assignment generally interesting, except when he had to deal with politicians such as Governor Harold Hoffman and genial amateurs such as Maj. Gen. Clifford R. Powell, commanding general of the New Jersey Guard.[8]

In 1937, Chynoweth gently declined an invitation to take a staff assignment in Washington. He said in explanation:

I used to be quite ambitious, not so much for preferment as for an opportunity to accomplish things. During my four years on the GS this entirely left me. . . . I have found enough interest in this job . . . to work quite hard at it. . . . I have a job which does not entail spending all day, every day, in an office. All summer I live out of doors. The NG is pretty bad at times . . . but one doesn't expect the Guard to be perfect. . . . My attitude towards the Army . . . is about like my attitude towards my present job. I have told both the Division Commander and the State A.G. that I didn't ask for the job, I like it well enough, I am willing to leave it whenever necessary, but I do not feel constrained to make a single decision based on whether or not it might affect my tenure. . . . I don't want to go to Washington. Neither do I positively want not to go. I can't think of a job in Washington from the President on down that I want.[9]

Chynoweth's comfortable exile in Princeton was shattered on 16 May 1938, when a letter arrived from Col. E. R. W. McCabe, Assistant Chief of Staff, G–2, head of the Military Attache and Foreign Liaison Section of the War Department's Military Intelligence Division and an old friend and squash partner. McCabe informed Chynoweth that the post of Military Attache in London would become vacant on or about 1 May 1939.[10]

Initially, Chynoweth was "cool on it" [the post of Military Attache in London]; however, he admitted that "my family was wild to go." He inquired about the duties of an attache, expressing concern in particular about the social obligations and mentioning that, while briefly serving as a junior presidential aide, he had failed miserably to "keep up" with Franklin D. Roosevelt's confidant, Edwin "Pa" Watson, a talented diplomat and social butterfly. McCabe wrote back reassuringly that "the Military Attache is, of course, a part of the staff of the Ambassador and at times does perform the duties of a sort of social aide, but most certainly not to the extent of that required of an Aide at the White House. The main job is to obtain military information and to maintain contacts with the offices of the Army of the country to which the Attache is accredited. . . . The most important qualification for Attache is a thorough knowledge of the military profession; and the social graces are entirely secondary."[11] McCabe may be charged with disingenuousness if not dissimulation, but U.S. involvement in the business of intelligence-gathering was both relatively recent and modest in scope.

In 1885 the War Department established an intelligence division (one officer and one clerk "to collect information on foreign armies"), and four years later Congress was persuaded to authorize sending abroad Army officers for the purpose of collecting military information.[12] Prior to 1937, the Appropriation Act limited the number of officers detailed on duty as Military Attaches to thirty-two, and budgetary constraints had resulted in a number of these posts going unfilled. However, the War Department escaped from that particular straitjacket and by the outbreak of the European War in September 1939 had in place its full complement of thirty-two attaches keeping tabs on some forty countries.

McCabe's assurances sufficed for Chynoweth, who had a life long fascination with the British and their Empire and a wife who was "always after me to take a long leave and go abroad."[13] Orders were cut for Chynoweth to report for temporary duty in the War Department on 13 February 1939 and, following briefings and consultations, to proceed to London to relieve Col. Raymond E. Lee, who had been Military Attache to Great Britain and Eire for nearly four years.[14]

What assumptions about the "world crisis" and British military capabilities did Chynoweth take along to London? Insofar as can be established, they reflected the views of a progressive-minded Army officer with no special knowledge of world conditions but a habit of reading widely and an ingrained need to make sense of what was learned. Today, he probably would be categorized as a "unilateralist," one who was sharply aware of the swift evolution of military technology and of America's vulnerability to threats to cut world trade routes and deny access to vital strategic raw materials.[15] He described the belief that the United States could stay out of a future general war as an "empty dream" and, though horrified by the likely effects on American society, advocated total peacetime economic mobilization and universal military training.[16] Before Chynoweth could test these opinions, a crisis erupted that threatened to quash his appointment and, even though forestalled, left a legacy of antagonism in London.

When Chynoweth reported to G–2, McCabe confessed that he had erred in not realizing that the Assistant Attache for Air in London, Martin Scanlon, actually outranked Chynoweth and, according to standard operating procedure, should be named to the post. "What the hell," Chynoweth said, stunned. McCabe, who "despised Scanlon for some reason," decided to send Chynoweth and a new Assistant Air Attache to London and to designate Scanlon "an additional member, merely attached to the office." The peculiar arrangement reflected the War Department's desire to accommodate Ambassador Joseph Kennedy, a prickly personality who was exceedingly protective of his prerogatives. Not only was Kennedy unhappy that the War Department had chosen to send an unknown junior officer, fresh from service with the New Jersey National Guard, to *his* Embassy, but Colonel Scanlon was on close terms with the Kennedy children, and his wife served as Mrs. Kennedy's social secretary. The Ambassador had requested in February 1939 that Scanlon not be reassigned "for at least six months," and Assistant Secretary of War Louis Johnson had issued the necessary instructions. This posed award problems for the three officers concerned and particularly for the incoming military attache. Chynoweth later recalled that "Pink Bull [Col. Harold R. Bull, Secretary of the General Staff] . . . said that he and General Marshall thought this a huge mistake. It was! But off I went to London."[17]

Chynoweth's instructions were straightforward. He was to keep tabs on the British military and provide a general assessment of political and economic conditions. His predecessor, Raymond Lee, had not been able to submit specific data on various questions, a failure he attributed to the refusal of Ambassador Kennedy to make use of the attache's office. The War Department was dissatisfied with the quality of intelligence on such issues as aircraft production and British improvements in weapons design, though whether Lee was to blame or whether the fault lay with the War Office's obsessive reluctance to share information with their American cousins was not clear. The outgoing Chief of Staff, General Malin Craig, instructed Chynoweth "to persuade Mr. Kennedy that he ought to use his military attache—he isn't using him at all."[18] That was to prove an impossible demand.

Chynoweth reached London early in April 1939, just as the last whiff of Munich's euphoria evaporated and Britain and France set course for a joint strategy for conduct of a war that now, once again, appeared unlikely. He dutifully met with Lee, who had arranged introductions to prominent British officials and helped with such essential matters as membership in the Army and Navy Club. Lee reacted strongly when informed of Chynoweth's mission to establish a good working relationship with Ambassador Kennedy. "My God," he exclaimed, "Lay off it. The man is dynamite."[19]

In truth, Kennedy's tenure as Ambassador was stormy, though the lightning bolts of his outrage had been directed toward the "striped pants

boys" in the State Department, and increasingly, that unpredictable personality in the White House, President Franklin D. Roosevelt, rather than to
the British government. A wealthy banker who was prominent in the
Democratic Party, Kennedy had been an implausible choice as F.D.R.'s
envoy to the Court of St. James. D. C. Watt has written: "An Irish Catholic,
steeped in the murky dealings of Boston's Irish politics, . . . Kennedy had
been sent to London both to get him out of Washington where he was
anathema to Roosevelt's closest allies, and as a practical joke on the
British. Instead, Kennedy had taken to London's political society like a
duck to water and the British had equally taken to him."[20]

Kennedy embraced the viewpoint associated with the "Cliveden set"
that a general war was unlikely, that Britain had no business meddling with
such questions as the fate of Poland, but that if war did come a German victory was assured. Privately, Kennedy appears to have concluded that
Britain's "bulldog breed" was exhausted. He became a vocal advocate of
isolationism and an embarrassment to Roosevelt, who by Spring 1939 had
judged Kennedy an "inveterate defeatist."[21] Kennedy found himself trapped
in splendid seclusion in London, denied the opportunity to influence
American politics. Small wonder his proverbial temper grew still shorter.

The opportunity to test Ambassador Kennedy's volatility (and
Chynoweth's unexplored diplomatic skills) soon arose. Despite persistent
requests, the Ministry of Air had refused to release figures about British
aircraft production. In the aftermath of Charles Lindburgh's visit to
Germany and his paeans regarding German air superiority, Chynoweth
learned from Sir Cyrill Newall, Chief of Staff of the Royal Air Force, of
top-level discussions about the dispatch of "air-force figures" to President
Roosevelt via Ambassador Kennedy. Though British military representatives had opposed disclosure and the use of Kennedy as a conduit, the current figures had been given to the Ambassador "in absolute secrecy" by
the Air Minister, Sir Kingsley Wood.

One week later, Chynoweth and Assistant Air Attache George
McDonald met with Kingsley Wood. "Sir K. was just like the cat that has
swallowed the canary. Butter wouldn't melt in his mouth." After the meeting broke up, Kingsley Wood gave McDonald the official figures. Why go
to such trouble to keep the aircraft data from U.S. military representatives
and then, one week later, let them in on the secret? The only logical conclusion, Chynoweth and McDonald agreed, was that the British had given
Kennedy "padded figures" and, having gotten maximum political benefit
from the deception, had now decided to come clean.

Disturbed that the U.S. Ambassador was being used in a deception
operation, Chynoweth decided to bell the cat. He demanded an appoint-

ment with Ambassador Kennedy on 20 April. He spelled out his concerns about the air production figures and about the role of the Military Attache. "He was very considerate about it," Chynoweth reported to McCabe, "but says that he is committed to a policy of mutual trust with the Government. Says he and the P.M. have agreed to tell each other no lies, and that this transaction was on orders from the P.M." Since Kennedy obviously was convinced that the British government would not dare give him padded figures, Chynoweth shifted to the less awkward question of his eagerness to assist the Ambassador in the collection and interpretation of military information. Kennedy promised to use the Military Attache "when he could."[22]

Chynoweth noted presciently: "I came over here with the idea of playing ball with the Ambassador and I want to do it. At the same time, I owe primary loyalty to the War Department. This sort of thing puts me on the horns of a dilemma. I don't want to be cross checking on him. On the other hand, when he becomes an agency for transmission of military intelligence, I've got to consider letting you know about it." He concluded that the "sound thing" was to inform McCabe and to trust his judgment. Unfortunately, a garbled version of Chynoweth's comments (apparently leaked by G–2) got back to Kennedy and Chynoweth found his next conversation with the Ambassador decidedly less pleasant.[23]

For the next several weeks, Chynoweth worked hard to develop contacts with British officials and other military attaches in London. He wrote to Col. John Crane, Foreign Liaison Officer, G–2: "I am just beginning to feel a bit oriented here. Things have moved rapidly and the air is indeed full of tension." But, he had learned, no one seemed sufficiently concerned to change their peacetime routine. "This is the most amazing place for getting nothing done. The air is soporific. I sleep later than I ever could in the U.S. Offices open at 10:00. Very few come in before that. Some officials don't arrive until noon. At 1:00 PM all knock off for lunch which lasts until 3:00 PM. Of course, after lunch, all gather in the Club coffee room where they discuss the situation and do a lot of contact work. . . . At the embassy I find myself here at 6:30 to 7:00 PM at least half the days. We have many callers during the day. As a result, the day has gone by miraculously and one has done very little." On the other hand, he admitted, "I can't imagine a more fascinating post than this one *now*."[24] Chynoweth was slowly establishing a network of useful acquaintances. "I can talk more and more freely with them during that magic hour after lunch at the clubs," he boasted.[25]

At the same time, red tape and British mistrust of foreigners, especially if they spoke English with American accents, snarled progress. The official routine called for the submission of requests through the War Office Foreign Liaison section. It was not considered good form "to wander around looking for things without permission." But nothing ever seemed to get done. Follow-up letters to formal written requests elicited no reply. When "oral entreaties" were then made, "glowing promises" would emerge from the bowels of Whitehall but nothing more. Chynoweth concluded that the mania for secrecy resulted from the "natural" reluctance to tell anyone who wasn't British anything, a rigid system of laws and regulations governing dissemination of information, and a system of administration that "is bureaucratic to an unbelievable degree. The present crisis clogs the channels of communication because officials are engaged in making plans and doing things that one would expect them to have done a year ago." Finally, wartime controls over information were being proposed, and, as one who had studied Britain's policies in World War I at the Army War College, Chynoweth commented: "Their secrecy is the dumbest and most unreasoning on earth." He acknowledged that the going would be slow and that both Lee and the Naval Attache had emphasized that the "only way" to obtain information in Britain "is by contacts and gossip and inference." But he persisted in hoping for a more satisfactory arrangement.[26]

Chynoweth's efforts to obtain information for the study of Britain's aircraft industry led to a disastrous confrontation with Ambassador Kennedy. He admitted to the War Department on 5 May that he and McDonald were "running into a secrecy block." The natural tendency of the British to hold their cards close was exacerbated by the lack of a "working arrangement" with the Ambassador. Chynoweth offered the opinion that "the Ambassador does not have any great affection for the War Department. . . . My own opinion . . . is that the British are pulling his leg for all it's worth. They like him immensely. It seems to me that they like him *too much.* My observation is that they like those who will work their way."[27] Acutely aware of Malin Craig's guidance, he determined to press the Ambassador to make use of his military attaches.

This was the background to Chynoweth's discovery, a few days later, that the Air Ministry had been negotiating with Ambassador Kennedy for a reciprocal exchange of information about the technology concerning "radio detection" of aircraft. It seemed likely that the recent British generosity regarding aircraft production data had been the first move in a game designed to elicit information about U.S. military technology.

Chynoweth lost no time in taking his concerns to the Ambassador. During "quite a talk on the matter" on 9 May he set forth his frustrations and urged that Ambassador Kennedy keep his advisers informed about any and all issues of military import. Kennedy stressed that the matter of exchanging data about aircraft detection had been "taken up with him as a secret and that he therefore hadn't told us." Chynoweth reiterated, with some force, that "there should be no secrets between us in respect to military information." Kennedy exploded. "Wham bang slam!!! I never saw such a blow up," recalled Chynoweth many years later. The Ambassador angrily replied that Chynoweth had not done anything to earn his confidence and "doesn't think I ever will." Kennedy's heated words ignited Chynoweth's temper. He commented that the British government viewed Ambassador Kennedy as a "gift of the Gods," and that he was being used to the detriment of American interests and security. Kennedy made it abundantly clear that he wanted nothing further to do with his military attache. Indeed, until Chynoweth's departure three months later, he communicated with the Ambassador, at the latter's insistence, only by memo, and the two men saw each other only at formal receptions.[28]

Chynoweth found himself in an impossible situation. His efforts to persuade the Ambassador to cooperate were probably doomed from the outset. "I wouldn't be at all surprised if the Ambassador asks for my relief, without any further delay," Chynoweth admitted immediately after the ugly scene in Kennedy's office. "I recognized when I went in to see him that I was playing with the buzz-saw, but it seemed to me necessary at least to make one effort to protect the War Department interests."[29]

A story later surfaced that Kennedy got rid of Chynoweth because the Military Attache openly espoused American entry into the war, thereby undercutting the Ambassador's isolationist, "pro-German" stand. Chynoweth vehemently denied any such explanation, arguing that he supported a "pro-U.S." policy and advocated rearmament as a way to stay out of the war. The evidence suggests that a personality clash exacerbated by the Ambassador's *amour propore* and his manipulation by self-interested elements in the Chamberlain government was the root cause.[30]

Thus, by mid-May Chynoweth found himself *persona non grata* with his own Ambassador and almost totally frustrated in his primary mission of obtaining authoritative information from British Army and War Office representatives about their plans and state of readiness. Ironically, he had better luck with the British than with his alleged compatriots in the U.S. Embassy. Eventually, Chynoweth arranged visits to a number of British Army installations and even wangled an invitation to the maneuvers slated for 17–19 September.

Chynoweth had acted with characteristic directness. On 6 July he wrote to Brig. Gen. F. G. Beaumont-Nesbitt, the War Office liaison. Chynoweth informed his British opposite number that he was encountering difficulties "in doing my real job of getting to know something of the

British Army. In comparing notes with our military attaches in the various countries of Europe, one finds that considerable freedom prevails even in countries where one might expect to discover the reverse. The British Military Attache in Washington is given informal access to our posts and schools throughout the United States. Wouldn't it be to the ultimate advantage of both of our countries if freedom could become reciprocal?"[31] Chynoweth followed up with a frank discussion of his frustrations at the War Office, and Beaumont-Nesbitt promised to "try to get action." A jubilant Chynoweth reported to WD G–2 that, following his talk with Beaumont-Nesbitt, the "very next day my phone rang six times with arrangements being made from the War Office to do things for me."[32] Thenceforward until wartime security clamped down in the critical period prior to the German invasion of Poland, Chynoweth enjoyed reasonable access to British military officialdom.

Acknowledging all these qualifications, Chynoweth's impressions (conveyed through some thirty situation reports, numerous letters, and technical memoranda) of what was happening in and to Britain during the four months he was engaged in seeking to perform the job of military attache stand as a uniquely interesting body of testimony. Despite Chynoweth's often excited prose style, his reports embodied an attitude of detachment. Here are the opinions of an intelligent, educated officer, possessing a broad range of experience, and representing a nation which possessed almost no inkling that it would shortly be immersed in the widening conflict. They compare favorably with the self-interested partisanship of such later observers as Sherman Miles or the Emmons-Strong Mission of Fall 1940. Colonel Chynoweth's immediate and total conversion to the British cause was the partisanship of a fan or cheerleader, not a second-string quarterback yearning to take the field.

The Chynoweth commentary divides into four amorphous categories: specific information about British military capabilities; observations about the "state of play" (the intentions and actions of the government and its representatives); the political, economic, and social conditions affecting Britain's ability to wage war; and a mass of comments about institutions, attitudes, and national character.[33] Dominant themes were Britain's woeful state of military unpreparedness, the frantic and highly visible efforts to build an air force of "formidable dimensions" and the puzzling lack of urgency about readying the British Army for modern war. It almost seemed, Chynoweth concluded, that no one could take seriously the need for substantial ground forces.

In April 1939 the Territorial Army was doubled—on paper—to nearly 500,000 men, but Chynoweth's first impression of the Territorials was of "an amateur organization," less prepared than the National Guard. After tours of Aldershot and Sandhurst, he was unimpressed with the curricula and shocked by the adherence to peacetime routine. "The few troops that I have seen (regulars) were splendid looking men. I haven't a doubt that they would perform up to the full traditions of their history. But they are not making intensive preparations either for an expedition or for wartime expansion," he observed.

Why was this so? Chynoweth hazarded three tentative hypotheses for Britain's apparent sloth. First, the British were reluctant to mobilize a ground expeditionary force for a continental war unless "assured of complete support by Russia or the U.S. or both." Second, they were determined to "keep English boys out of trouble and to let other countries furnish the gun-fodder." Third, British policy was to subordinate all other arms to the expansion of the Royal Air Force, viewing the "air menace" as of overwhelming concern. Clearly, Britain was playing a dangerous game, "the greatest gamble of human history." She was determined to fight, if necessary, to protect the Empire and "if she can get enough help to make it a fair gamble." That meant, ideally, recruiting the United States to help.[34]

The British determination to avoid "another blood pudding in Flanders Field" formed a continuing strand in Chynoweth's assessment of British strategic policy. The Army was needed to repel an invasion or for use in the Mediterranean but "the blunder of 1914" must not be repeated. The letter (though not the spirit) of that pledge was violated by the dispatch of the British Expeditionary Force to France in September 1939, but after Dunkirk it was to be honored with zealous adherence for some four years. Chynoweth's reports were notable as well for their emphasis on the capacity for resistance of the British people if forced to fight (in contrast with the popular portrayal of the British as effete and "racially deteriorated"). These reports also offered a corrective to the view, derived from the perspective of Whitehall and certain offices in 10 Downing Street, that the Chamberlain government had totally discounted the potential military significance of the United States in any general war.[35]

A pragmatic reason for Britain's tardy mobilization was to be found in the government's reluctant, partial imposition of conscription in late April. Chynoweth was shocked by what he perceived to be the lack of forethought shown by the British. "Why mobilize great masses of men when there are no camps, uniforms, equipment, nor instructors for them? I seriously doubt if there is even a plan to provide for general mobilization." This comment reflected a hazy understanding of the mechanics of Britain's regimental system, the central element for housing and training inductees. On 28 April he reported a conversation with a member of the Army

Council, who expressed great interest in America's adoption of a draft in 1917. "His questions led me to assume that, in characteristic British fashion, having announced conscription, they would now study it up and make plans to promote it," Chynoweth commented.[36]

Two weeks later, passing along rumors of secret British-French staff conferences, Chynoweth returned to a football metaphor to describe Britain's posture regarding construction of an anti-Hitler entente. "I feel that they will play if they can play quarterback, and if they can sign up enough of a line to make it worth while," he stressed. "I don't believe that they intend to take one tiny bruise beyond what seems necessary to get the other fellows well into the game. Once the game begins, they can be counted upon to go to the limit, if it becomes necessary. But they aren't now organized to make it possible for them to go the limit in the first year of a war." He concluded prophetically, "the French, the Poles, and some others are going to have to take the first bruising shocks."[37]

Solid information about the British Army comprised Chynoweth's 25 May report, following an extended visit to a Territorial Army unit, the Queen's Westminster Rifles. He went expecting to be disappointed but returned with a greatly improved opinion of the Territorials. In particular, the affiliation of each Territorial regiment with a regular regiment which served as its "parent" was a decided plus. "There results a much more definite uniformity of standards in the two components than prevails in our own service." He noted that the Territorial Army was "far more national in character" than the National Guard—and far less politicized. Requirements for training nights and annual periods of field training were similar for the two armies, but periods of enlistment, turnover rates, officer selection procedures, and pay scales differed significantly. One notable difference was the importance the British gave to "snap," pride of unit and emphasis on swagger. While Chynoweth disavowed any desire to debate the merits of European and American traditions of close order drill, he admitted that "the precision and swank of these recruits, who have averaged some fifteen to twenty hours of training, considerably exceeds that of any similar National Guard units that I have seen." As one who had enjoyed a congenial association with the National Guard, he was amazed by the similarities between the two organizations ("who copied whom—somebody cribbed") and impressed by the benefits conferred by eliminating the "political element" in such matters as selection and promotion of officers.[38]

Chynoweth subsequently observed the Territorials in field training. He was, if anything, even more highly impressed by the quality of officers and the majority of enlisted men in the Territorial Army. The training regimen being followed elicited praise as well. As with all other aspects of British military organization, field training was grounded in decentralization of responsibility. In contrast with the highly centralized control and standardization of method in effect in the U.S. Army, the British practiced devolution of authority down to the regimental and even battalion level. Among the benefits were encouragement of initiative at the unit and individual level, control by rational discourse rather than "that stentorian bellowing which we seem to like" (with notable saving of time), and an almost total absence of the American tendency for higher commanders to micromanage. A serious negative effect of decentralization—repeatedly emphasized by Chynoweth—appeared to be the British inability to produce and implement quickly an overall plan of action.[39]

After a whirlwind automobile tour of the West Country and Wales over the June Bank Holiday, Chynoweth was bubbling with admiration for "these crazy English"—and tremendous anxiety that the United States put forth "OUR MAXIMUM EFFORT" not to be caught unprepared as Britain and France had been at the time of Munich.[40] The longest dispatch of his tenure sought to make sense of two months spent talking with the British and about the British with members of the foreign diplomatic community. His decision to work through a rat's nest of discordant impressions had been reinforced by an influx of U.S. military attaches and language students from all across Europe coming to London for annual physical examinations.

By behaving as "a simple-minded American with a penchant for free speech," Chynoweth had absorbed one painful lesson: the absolute importance of discretion to anyone watching or watched by the British. As he noted: "To be discreet is to be British. One can commit the rape of a continent, provided one does it with discretion. Good form!" Whether their mania for discretion was the result of a precarious perch atop "a great empire consisting of diametrically mixed races, colors, and religions" or derived from Britain's inbred insularity, he was unable to say. Equally impossible to explain were the incredible contrasts he found. How could "fabulous wealthy-magnificent poverty, civilization-backwardness, kindness-cruelty, freedom-restraint, democracy-monarchy, independence-aristocracy, community-caste, beauty-ugliness, civic honesty-social meanness, decency-scandal, high virtue bordered and patrolled by the world's largest army of prostitutes" coexist in one small island?

Everything, Chynoweth noted, linked to its opposite "contributes to make the life of the military attache a bewildering maze." Chynoweth was finding London a tough assignment in more ways than one. During earlier service in the Far East and European sections of the Military Intelligence

Division, he had concluded that the job of military attache, though "without honor in his own country," was certain to be "interesting and cushy." He had been forced to revise the latter part of that opinion.[41]

Momentarily losing all perspective, Chynoweth claimed to have discovered one certainty about the British—the power of tradition. After visiting the Grenadier Guards and the Queen's Westminsters, exchanging toasts at the annual banquet of the Royal Regiment of Artillery, watching the tattoo at the Royal Tournament and trooping the colors, Chynoweth cried "Eureka!" He believed that he had found the key to the British Army in its obsessive regard for ritual. "For twenty years I've been frothing at the mouth over the paint-and-polish crusade in our Army. *Now* to fall for a mob of red coats and bearskin hats," he groaned. "The heart and soul of the British Army have been exposed in these elaborate ceremonies—this magnificent pageant. The entire history of England, the blood of her fallen, and the beauty of her legend—[has been] compressed into a ritual—a spiritual essence distilled to intoxicate the people of Britain and *to sell her Empire to the World*." Chynoweth distrusted British motives and he was repelled by the British capacity for self-delusion, but he had to admire the democratic spirit that—for him—ultimately justified imperial rapacity, smugness, and hypocrisy.[42]

In light of current debate about the nature and direction of the German war economy, Chynoweth argued that modern warfare comprised "not tanks, or planes, or men advancing into action," but a struggle between competing systems of production. He claimed that Hitler invented this new style of war, based on superior organization, more numerous armament, and trained forces poised for action. Hitler had taken Mahan's concept of the fleet-in-being and recast it as armament-in-being. "Just as Napoleon won battles by swifter concentration of armies, so is Hitler winning wars by swifter concentration of *production*. And we, potentially the champions in such a game, are playing the role of Napoleon's old Austrian opponents—fighting this modern war of production by piecemeal efforts." He feared that America's traditional reliance on its ocean barriers and commitment to gradual mobilization would lead to disaster. "TO ARMS! NOW!" he pleaded to those placid readers back home.[43]

For the next six weeks, except for a fairly sober report on a visit to Eire, Chynoweth offered variations on this theme. Caught in that dizzying swing between love and revulsion which has infected innumerable Americans who come to live in Britain and among the British, he found himself mired in contradictions. "I would scarcely dare to write at all if it weren't for the comforting knowledge that nobody ever believes a military attache anyway," he observed in early July.[44] Not surprisingly, his moods swung with the ebb and flow of the diplomatic game being played out in eastern and southeastern Europe.

The one consistent portrayal remained Chynoweth's assessment of the British Army. He was impressed by what its best units demonstrated and by how few they were. "I think it is a fact that the British Navy considers itself ready for emergency. That the Air Force feels fairly cocky. The Army is on the make but not ready for serious effort for months to come," he wrote in mid-July.[45] So much had still to be done. Production of tanks was lagging and targets for Bren guns, originally set for early spring, would not be met until September, according to his sources. Noting that some of the Territorials were training with World War I–vintage 12-pounders, not having been supplied either with old 18-pounder field guns or any of the new 26-pounders, he concluded that artillery production too was lagging. The priority everywhere seemed to be antiaircraft defenses, with antiaircraft batteries "springing out over the English landscape, particularly along the lower Thames, like measles."[46] An inescapable conclusion was that the War Office was committed to a policy of passive defense, a view supported, Chynoweth believed, by the enthusiasm in official circles for Basil Liddell Hart's cleverly "doctrinaire" new book, *The Defence of Britain*.[47]

A claim that defense will win the next war as it had allegedly won the First World War was hardly surprising, Chynoweth noted, given the state of Britain's preparedness. On 31 July he estimated that "if war strikes soon" the British Army would be able to muster at most four regular divisions. The Territorials, while coming along quickly, still required "some months more of training before they could be used against the Germans with a fair chance for their lives." This assessment applied in particular to the infantry. Chynoweth quoted the Inspector General of the Home Forces as saying: "With intelligent men you can make artillerymen quite rapidly, but you just can't train an infantryman in a hurry."[48]

Ironically, longtime tank corps officer Chynoweth concluded that British Army doctrine and organization had swung too far in the direction of maneuver warfare. Their approach to mechanization had "built too much on speed and not enough on power and protection." That imbalance was being corrected with the newest generation of tanks. However, he worried about the British mania for "motorization." They appeared to have gone even farther than had the U.S. Army, in his opinion, in being "over-motorized." Chynoweth believed that units with little combined arms training, under many conditions, would actually be slowed by dependence on motor transport. But he acknowledged that the regulars—whom he had not yet seen in the field—might be able to muster the discipline and high level of staff work required to realize the desired standard of tactical mobility.

He was never given that opportunity, for on 26 August the maneuvers scheduled for mid-September were indefinitely postponed.[49]

Chynoweth's impressions conform quite closely to historians' assessment of the British Army on the eve of World War II. Brian Bond has written of this period: "The Army was in a profound state of disarray. . . . The doubling of the Territorial Army, by a proverbial stroke of the pen, the introduction of conscription, the expansion of anti-aircraft defenses, and the commitment of the Field Force to France created conditions of near chaos which could not be remedied within a few months."[50] While the problems of mobilization were eventually mastered, Chynoweth's characterization of British military doctrine as backward looking; giving undue emphasis to "passive defense," and failing to pay attention to the importance of "teamwork" in modern warfare, finds echoes in historical studies of the British Army written over the past decade. These works have faulted military leaders for preparing to fight a static war and for ignoring the combined arms dimension.[51] Though diffuse, fragmentary, and couched in colloquial language, Chynoweth's reports stand as a testimonial to what can be learned by shrewd observation, the persistent cultivation of contacts, and an efficient clippings service.

That these assessments were produced at all is a tribute either to Bradford Chynoweth's powers of concentration or to his astonishing naivete. Chynoweth only gradually realized that his status was precarious, given Ambassador Kennedy's violent antipathy. In a letter to Col. B. Q. Jones, Assistant Commandant of the War College, Chynoweth confessed: "This is the most interesting job imaginable. It is somewhat confusing for a beginner (and particularly one as undiplomatic as myself) to land on *such* a job at *such* a time and in *such* a place. But it is worth the show to me. I may be thrown out of here on my ear in short order, but they can't take away the interesting time I have already had."[52]

First reactions from Washington seemed to confirm that Chynoweth's tangle with Ambassador Kennedy was a teapot tempest. McCabe noted: "I quite agree with you in your assessment of the British, and I hope very much that we will not fall into their trap. . . . My reaction in regard to the Ambassador is that I would go a little farther than half way in my dealings with him but not much farther." If Chynoweth made "an honest effort to make him see the light of day" and Kennedy remained aloof, then he should be left "to play his own hand."[53]

A week later McCabe stated that there had been "no repercussions at this end of the line" to the confrontation but then raised doubts by urging Chynoweth to leave the Ambassador "severely alone," for "nothing could possibly be gained by trying to force the issue."[54] It appeared that some people in Washington were beginning to worry that Chynoweth's propensity to self-destruct might have wider effects. This interpretation is supported by a letter from Chynoweth's brother-in-law, General Lynch, warning that Chynoweth's "recent personal letter to G–2 relative to your interview with the Ambassador" was not being treated as a confidential document. He urged Chynoweth to "govern yourself accordingly," though he did affirm that "your position seems to be strongly supported in G–2." Chynoweth promised McCabe that he would "give the Ambassador a wide scope" and proceeded blissfully with gathering information by traditional means. After all, except for the residue of personal antipathy, his relations with the Ambassador differed little from the situation during Lee's tenure.[55]

In retrospect, one finds in subsequent communications from a War Department an increasingly distant tone. On 18 July McCabe dispatched a critique of the "Comments on Current Events" submitted during June. "They are delightful reading and contain information which is of real value to the War Department," McCabe acknowledged. But their discursive nature and Chynoweth's blunt characterizations of "politics and personalities" and such irrelevancies as his dissatisfaction with the maintenance allowance made impossible their dissemination to "other agencies" beyond M.I.D. McCabe urged that the "military bearing" of Chynoweth's general observations about "national economics, politics, and psychology" be spelled out, a task he undoubtedly realized was hopeless. The G–2 functionary noted that "hereafter" Chynoweth's reports would be evaluated according to established procedures of the Intelligence Branch.[56]

Another clue to maneuvering behind the scenes was the acknowledgment by British acquaintances and American visitors to the Embassy that Chynoweth was being labeled pro-British and pro-interventionist. Eugene Meyer, publisher of the *Washington Post*, admitted as much during a "fact-finding visit" to London for Secretary of War Henry H. Woodring. "You have been writing some alarmist reports, and I want to know why. Why are you talking as though a great war were impending? We don't think there will be a war!" When Chynoweth attempted to explain that his conviction "was instinctive rather than factual," Meyer berated him for possessing a "military mind" and claimed that everyone with whom he had talked insisted there would be no war.[57]

Most significant was a letter in early July from Ambassador Kennedy to Assistant Secretary of War Louis Johnson, requesting another six-month extension for Colonel Scanlon. As a principal justification for not transferring Scanlon, Kennedy asserted:

I do not at all like the present Military Attache, Col. Chynoweth. He may be the most efficient officer in the world . . ., but he and I will never be able to see eye to eye. I have had two personal conversations with him and both of them have ended up in a very heated argument, and all I can say is that if his attitude toward the British in his quest for information is at all similar to his attitude as I see it, I doubt if our relations would stay very friendly. After my conversations with him . . . I wouldn't tell him the right time, let alone give him any information. . . . The discussions between us are not particularly important. It is a question of personalities clashing, and I am frank to say that I do not look forward with any pleasure to working with him.

While the Ambassador stopped short of asking formally for Chynoweth's recall, he did observe that "if any acute trouble were to break out I would regard his being here as particularly unfortunate." That sufficed for Louis Johnson, who informed Kennedy on 15 July that "immediately upon receipt of your letter of July 3rd I worked the matter out as you desired." Scanlon was to remain in London and Chynoweth would be replaced as soon as possible, "although, of course, this has got to be arranged in a 'face-saving' manner."[58]

The ax fell in early August. McCabe informed Chynoweth that the Ambassador "has been in personal communication with the Secretary of War" about the "situation" in London. Kennedy had made it clear that he found Chynoweth unacceptable as Military Attache. McCabe stressed that "not . . . the slightest reflection" upon Chynoweth's abilities was involved and the Ambassador had presented his demand for Chynoweth's removal solely on a "persona non grata" basis. Knowing, McCabe said, that Chynoweth would not wish to continue in a position which would be embarrassing to him and "indirectly" to the War Department, he was therefore being relieved as of 15 October.[59]

Subsequently, Chynoweth learned that Ambassador Kennedy had proposed he be recalled almost immediately after their 9 May clash. The War Department at first had resisted, caving in only after Kennedy pulled political strings with Assistant Secretary of War Johnson. An agreement was struck to recall Chynoweth without staining his record with an "unsatisfactory" evaluation. It was explained as one of those unfortunate situations in which two strong personalities came into conflict. In fact, Chynoweth escaped with surprisingly little harm to his career.[60] Among the assignments offered as compensation, he chose the 1st Battalion, 66th Infantry, a light tank outfit stationed at Fort Meade. That job led to still further conflicts related to Chynoweth's crusading spirit and combative personality.[61]

Whether Bradford G. Chynoweth should have been appointed United States Military Attache, given his rough edged personality, is an open question. But his commentaries on the British military and musings about the British psyche were often penetrating and offered a useful corrective to the negativism emanating from the U.S. Embassy. His final dispatch, dated 5 September but written over the course of that breathtaking week in which Britain toppled into the abyss, embodied all of Chynoweth's virtues: empathy for a people suddenly transfixed by the arrival of war, incisive vignettes about the short-term effects on Britain, and the prophetic philosophizing of his very best communiques. "War fever—but not a happy fever. Very little of the hip-hip-hurray spirit of adventure. These people didn't *want* to fight. It wasn't their choice at all. But they felt it necessary—*something to be done.* As one observes this civilian population getting ready for the grim ordeal, one is impressed by two outstanding features of modern war: first, its three-dimensional aspects which bring 'the front' right into your own backyard; and, second corollary, that every man, woman and child is now a soldier, right in the war up to the neck."[62]

Acknowledging that he was forwarding his final report, Chynoweth waxed philosophical: "The future is in the balance and predictions are idle. My own task over here is ended. It has been my inestimable privilege to be attachéd (not to the American Embassy, because I have never yet been a real part of that), but to the British Army and with the British people. It has been a rare experience to be in contact with this great people during their transition from Peace to War." Confessing his own fondness and admiration for the British, Chynoweth emphasized: "I don't trust them fully. But I trust them as much as any people whom I know." He worried that Britain and France would fail to win a quick victory, for in "a long-drawn war" the United States inevitably must be pulled in. He therefore urged, as he had done since his arrival, that the War Department advocate "complete and unrestricted armament" for such a course alone made likely America's avoidance of war and made possible ultimate victory should American participation take place.[63]

Chynoweth departed London wondering if his warnings were being heeded—or if they were even being read. "To be of value, intelligence has got to be used," he subsequently observed. The difficulties experienced by Truman Smith, U.S. Military Attache in Berlin in 1938–1939, who "came home and gave a splendid picture of the juggernaut that Hitler was preparing to drive over a prostrate world," only to be blanketed by "a cloud of official disapproval," offered an object lesson. As well, the appointment of Sherman Miles as Chynoweth's successor as U.S. Military Attache was hardly encouraging, for Miles had assured him during the transition briefing that he worried too much, that the Allies "would wipe up" the Germans. Miles "later went home and became Chief of Military Intelligence," Chynoweth caustically observed.[64] Any such conclusion underestimates the cumulative effects of Chynoweth's messages much as a judgment derived from a perusal of final exams misconstrues an instructor's contribution to the education of the students in that course. The path of Anglo-American political and military cooperation followed the script roughed in by Bradford G. Chynoweth, even if this gifted yet self-destructive maverick never received any credit for his contribution.

NOTES

1. Rpt no. 37, Bradford G. Chynoweth (BGC), U.S. Military Attache, London, 13 Jul 39, "Comments on Current Situation," BGC Papers, box 3, U.S. Army Military History Institute (MHI), Carlisle Barracks, Pa.

2. The reference to Chynoweth's "brilliant albeit slightly poisonous" pen is in a letter from Edwin F. Harding, editor of *Infantry Journal*, to Chynoweth, 10 Mar 38, BGC Papers, MHI; Chynoweth once noted that "Georgie" Patton, himself no slouch, had castigated him for his "mean disposition," BGC, "Recollections," p. 16, BGC Papers, MHI.

3. Bradford G. Chynoweth "201 File," U.S. Army Center of Military History (CMH) Archives. The "mystical world" quotation is from Hamilton Howze Oral History Interview, MHI.

4. BGC, "Recollections," p. 16; a similar if more complete description is in Bradford G. Chynoweth's engaging memoir, *Bellamy Park* (Hicksville, N.Y.: Exposition Press, 1975), pp. 87–90. It should be noted that for some events dealt with in this study there are three versions (Chynoweth's correspondence at the time, his subsequent unpublished memoir, and the significantly modified published autobiography). I have, of course, placed reliance upon the contemporary record where it exists.

5. This decision was facilitated by a provision of the National Defense Act of 1920, authorizing the Army to offer former regular officers "a free return with the loss only of the time they were out," BGC, "Recollections," p. 16.

6. This incident is described in Chynoweth's "Recollections" and corroborated by letters to friends. After filing his report, Chynoweth was called into the presence of General Campbell King, who greeted him "with cold hostility" and asked: "Have you ever had combat experience?" Chynoweth replied: "No Sir." King observed caustically: "Then how do you dare to oppose General Summerall who won his great reputation as a warrior?" Chynoweth answered: "The duty prescribed for the Infantry Board imposed upon me the duty of recommending for the best interests of the Infantry." King said: "I'll not send your letter in." King was reacting to pressure from Maj. Gen. Stephen O. Fuqua, who had disapproved the publication of Chynoweth's article on infantry reorganization for *Infantry Journal* and had written King: "While I do not desire to restrict in any way the right of an officer to the free expression of his ideas on Infantry subjects, nevertheless, as this officer is an instructor at the Infantry School, I desire that such ideas as he has expressed be known to you as, perhaps, if not watched, may be included by him in his instruction." Soon thereafter Chynoweth was on his way to Fort Sam Houston and the 23d Infantry; Ltr, BGC to J. L. Bradley, 4 Sep 30, correspondence, 1930–38 folder, BGC Papers, MHI.

7. Chynoweth was by his own admission hopelessly inept at the bureaucratic gamesmanship required of officers assigned to the War Department General Staff. See "Recollections," pp. 32–35, and Chynoweth, *Bellamy Park*, pp. 136–40.

8. BGC, "Recollections," pp. 23–24, BGC Papers, MHI; Chynoweth, *Bellamy Park*, pp. 144–49.

9. Ltr, BGC to Maj Gen George A. Lynch, 18 Jul 37, correspondence, 1935–37 file, BGC Papers, MHI.

10. Ltr, E. R. W. McCabe to BGC, 16 May 38, BGC Papers, MHI. McCabe had sought in 1930 to get an Assistant Military Attache in Britain, Italy, or Belgium for Chynoweth but that had fallen through when Chynoweth did not make the Chief of Infantry's Army War College list for 1931, a prerequisite for this appointment. Ltr, E. R. W. McCabe to BGC, 22 Dec 30, 1930–38 correspondence, BGC Papers, MHI.

11. Ltr, E. R. W. McCabe to BGC, 25 May 38, 1930–38 correspondence, BGC Papers, MHI. Until 1935, when Congress authorized funds for "extraordinary expenses" of U.S. Army personnel assigned abroad, only officers with private incomes could afford to accept appointments as military attaches. That led to unfortunate perceptions of all attaches as

ineffectual, uppercrust "swells," Bruce W. Bidwell, *History of the Military Intelligence Division, Department of the Army General Staff: 1775–1941* (Washington, D.C.: University Publications of America, 1986), pp. 381, 384–85.

12. Lecture, "The Military Intelligence Division, War Department General Staff," by Col E. R. Warner McCabe, 3 Jan 40, USAWC G–2 Course, #4, 1939–40, CMH Archives; Ralph H. Van Deman, *The Final Memoranda*, ed. by Ralph Weber (Wilmington, Del.: Scholarly Resources, 1986), p. 4; see also Bidwell, *History of MID*, passim.

13. Ltr, BGC to Col Henry H. Pfeil, 3 Dec 38, correspondence, 1938–39, BGC Papers, MHI.

14. WDGS, G–2, "Special Orders for Lieutenant Colonel Bradford G. Chynoweth," 22 Oct 38, correspondence, 1938–39, BGC Papers, MHI; for Raymond "Boy" Lee's two tours as military attache (he returned to London in June 1940), see James Leutze, ed., *The London Journal of General Raymond E. Lee, 1940–1941* (Boston: Little, Brown, 1971).

15. For purposes of comparison, see the description of Albert C. Wedemeyer's views in Charles E. Kirkpatrick, *An Unknown Future and a Doubtful Present: Writing the Victory Plan of 1941* (Washington, D.C.: U.S. Army Center of Military History, 1990), and Mark A. Stoler, "From Continentalism to Globalism: General Stanley D. Embick, the Joint Strategic Survey Committee, and the Military View of National Policy during the Second World War," *Diplomatic History* 6 (Summer 1982): 303–21.

16. Ltr, BGC to Col C. L. Hall, 28 Dec 38, and note, BGC, 3 Jan 68, in Apr–Sep 39 correspondence, BGC Papers, MHI.

17. BGC, "Recollections," p. 38. Chynoweth acknowledged that Scanlon, who was on close terms with the Kennedy children and whose wife was Mrs. Kennedy's social secretary, performed his duties effectively and made the best of a most embarrassing situation.

18. BGC, "Recollections," p. 38; Chynoweth's memoir, *Bellamy Park*, which generally toned down rambunctious characterizations of people and events, recalled that General Craig said: "Chynoweth, I have noted that the Ambassador in London does nothing to help the M.A. Office. I want you to see that he gives you cooperation!" p. 150. Craig also asked Chynoweth to find out why the assistant military attache, Capt. Sam Greenwell, had not filed any reports. "He has been there a year or more without a peep." It turned out that Lee had been following the familiar bureaucratic procedure of requiring that all reports be submitted with his signature. The extended discussion in Chynoweth's papers of problems relating to the transfer of duties from Lee to himself form a marvelous case study of organizational dynamics.

19. Chynoweth added: "This was an understatement. He was TNT or, better a Nuclear Bomb," BGC, "Recollections," p. 38.

20. Donald C. Watt, *How War Came: The Immediate Origins of the Second World War, 1938–1939* (New York: Pantheon, 1989), p. 132.

21. For Kennedy's dispatches, see U.S. Department of State, *Foreign Relations of the United States, 1939* (Washington, D.C.: Government Printing Office, 1962), I, passim. An excellent portrayal of this period in Anglo-American relations is David Reynolds, *The Creation of the Anglo-American Alliance 1937–1941: A Study in Competitive Cooperation* (Chapel Hill, N.C.: University of North Carolina Press, 1982).

22. Ltr, BGC to Col E. R. W. McCabe, 20 Apr 39, correspondence, Apr–Sep 39, box 2, BGC Papers, MHI.

23. Ibid.

24. Ltr, BGC to Col John A. Crane, 21 Apr 39, correspondence, Apr–Sep 39, box 2, BGC Papers, MHI.

25. Ltr, BGC to E. R. W. McCabe, 5 May 39, correspondence, Apr–Sep 39, BGC Papers, MHI.

26. Ltr, BGC to Col John A. Crane, 5 May 39, correspondence, Apr–Sep 39, box 2, BGC Papers, MHI; Ltr, BGC to Col E. R. W. McCabe, 5 May 39, correspondence, Apr–Sep 39, box 2, BGC Papers, MHI.

27. Ltr, BGC to E. R. W. McCabe, 5 May 39, correspondence, Apr–Sep 39, BGC Papers, MHI.

28. BGC, "Recollections," pp. 38–39, 39a. A sidelight to this problem was the continuing uncertainty as to the status of Colonel Scanlon. While the War Department refused to authorize his appointment as a second assistant air attache, Scanlon remained on friendly terms with the Kennedy family and enjoyed better access to the ambassador than did Chynoweth. Although Chynoweth insisted repeatedly in reports and his subsequent memoir that Scanlon never demonstrated disloyalty (in contrast with Major McDonald) the suggestion of internal skulduggery is an important element in his view of these events. See BGC, "Recollections," and BGC to E. R. W. McCabe, 17 May 39, correspondence, Apr–Sep 39, BGC Papers, MHI.

29. Ltr, BGC to E. R. W. McCabe, 9 May 39, correspondence, Apr–Sep 39, BGC Papers, MHI.

30. Chynoweth later wrote that he had described the clash with Ambassador Kennedy in such great detail "because there was a story . . . that Mr. K. had fired me because I wanted to get the U.S. in the war. This story was erroneous. It is true that Mr. K. did not want us in the war . . . Mr. K. was aid to be an associate with the Cliveden set (Lady Astor etc.) who were pro-German. I don't know. But my stand was pro-U.S. I liked the British. But I also liked the Germans. My pleas were for us to arm, and get strong on land and on both oceans because only so, in my belief, did we have any chance of staying out of the war. . . . But, repeat, Mr. K. did *not* fire me because of my stand on this or any other war," BGC, "Recollections," p. 39a.

31. Ltr, BGC to F. G. Beaumont-Nesbitt, 6 Jul 39, correspondence, 1938–39, box 2, BGC Papers, MHI.

32. Ltr, BGC to Col John A. Crane, Foreign Liaison Section, G–2, WD, 18 Jul 39, correspondence, 1938–39, BGC Papers, MHI. One notable breakthrough was delivery of a new model Bren gun which had been promised to the Americans for many months.

33. As is often the case, these observations shed as much light upon values and beliefs then current among Americans of Chynoweth's background as they tell us about the society under the looking glass. Analysis of those ideas is, however, not within the purview of the current study.

34. Rpt no. 13, BGC, Apr 39, sub: "Great Britain: Comments on Current Events," box 3, BGC Papers, MHI.

35. See, for example, David Reynolds, *Competitive Cooperation: The Creation of the Anglo-American Alliance, 1937–1941* (Chapel Hill, N.C.: University of North Carolina Press, 1983); D. C. Watt, *How War Came* (New York: Pantheon, 1989); and Robert P. Shay, Jr., *British Rearmament in the Thirties: Politics and Profits* (Princeton, N.J.: Princeton University Press, 1977).

36. Rpt no. 40090, BGC, 28 Apr 39, sub: "Great Britain: Comments on Current Events," box 3, BGC Papers, MHI.

37. With regard to the likelihood of war, Chynoweth commented: "Of course, much depends upon Hitler's technique. If he is sufficiently clumsy, he will knock over the applecart. But if he leaves a loophole large enough for a mouse, I would rather expect to see the democracies crawl through. If they don't maybe I'll be looking for a hole myself." Rpt no. 40134, BGC, 17 May 39, sub: "Great Britain: Comments on Current Events," box 3, BGC Papers, MHI.

38. Rpt no. 40169, BGC, 26 May 39, sub: "Great Britain (Combat), Organization-Divisions, The Territorial Army", box 3, BGC Papers, MHI. Chynoweth impulsively sent a copy of this report to the War Office. "Since then for two weeks I have been suppressed, though not yet crushed, under the silence of the whole British Empire. All of the contacts disappeared from view. Not another gesture until yesterday when they popped out again. . . . Watch a colony of prairie dogs! Then make a sudden movement and you're alone in the desert. I have done the unusual—and that is *not BRITISH.*" Rpt no. 40200, BGC, 13 Jun 39, sub: "Great Britain: Comments on Current Events," box 3, BGC Papers, MHI.

39. These observations are to be found in three special "combat" reports written by BGC, Rpt no. 40265, 18 Jul 39, sub: "The Territorial Army," Rpt no. 40313, 4 Aug 39, sub: "British Army Training," and Rpt no. 40312, sub: "Training Conceptions," box 3, BGC Papers, MHI.

40. Rpt no. 40209, BGC, 13 Jun 39, sub: "Great Britain: Comments on Current Events," box 3, BGC Papers, MHI.

41. Rpt no. 40269, BGC, 20 Jul 39, sub: "Great Britain: Comments on Current Events," box 3, BGC Papers, MHI.

42. Ibid.; Rpt no. 40200, BGC, 13 Jun 39, sub: "Great Britain: Comments on Current Events," box 3, BGC Papers, MHI; Chynoweth had regained his sense of balance about the value of spectacle by the time he wrote his "Recollections." He commented: "My greatest criticism of the Army during the period . . . between World War I and World War II had to do with the philosophy of 'Eyewash.' The proponents of Eyewash claimed that in WWI the British restored the morale of their army by 'polishing the trace chains of the artillery.' Of course there is a point there, like the endless polishing that goes on aboard a battleship in peacetime. But I think that the idea was distorted, in that period, and that showmanship was in excess. It was the easiest way to get good reports. I could epitomize my view by reciting from Gilbert and Sullivan: 'When I was a boy I swept the floor and polished up the handle of the big front door; I polished it up so faithfully that now I am the ruler of the Queen's Navy.'" "Recollections" folder, box 3, BGC Papers, MHI.

43. Rpt no. 40227, BGC, 13 Jun 39, sub: "Great Britain: Comments on Current Events," box 3, BGC Papers, MHI.

44. Rpt no. 40231, BGC, 5 Jul 39, sub: "Great Britain: Comments on Current Events," and Rpt no. 40227, BGC, 13 Jun 39, box 3, BGC Papers, MHI. This may be an appropriate point to discuss the reception and possible influence of Chynoweth's reports. A perusal of relevant Military Intelligence Division files suggests that the colorful observations emanating from London were treated in a routine fashion. Not all of the commentaries were logged in and some originals are missing, circumstantial evidence of circulation to other offices within the War Department General Staff. Given the convoluted administrative arrangements within the WDGS in general and G–2 in particular, such casual handling was hardly surprising. McCabe made use of at least one of Chynoweth's reports in the preparation of a memorandum regarding the "vitality" of the British Empire (G–2 to CofS, 27 Jul 39, 2657–A–326, MID Files, RG 165, NARA), but evidence of direct influence is lacking. Though at least some of Chynoweth's reports were read by his fellow officers (because of their literacy merit and the "gossip factor" stemming from his clash with Ambassador Kennedy), they had little or no immediate influence. For a general assessment of G–2's performance in the period before Pearl Harbor, see Bidwell, *History of the Military Intelligence Division*.

45. Rpt no. 40258, BGC, 13 Jul 39, sub: "Great Britain: Comments on Current Events," box 3, BGC Papers, MHI.

46. Rpt no. 40269, BGC, 20 Jul 39, sub: "Great Britain: Comments on Current Events," box 3, BGC Papers, MHI.

47. Rpt no. 40291, BGC, 31 Jul 39, sub: "Great Britain: Comments on Current Events," box 3, BGC Papers, MHI; Basil Liddell Hart, *The Defence of Britain* (London: Faber, 1939), was generally acclaimed in Britain. See the hostile critique of Liddell Hart's influence by John J. Mearsheimer, *Liddell Hart and the Weight of History* (Ithaca, N.Y.: Cornell University Press, 1988), and the spirited rebuttal by Jay Luvaas, "Liddell Hart and the Mearsheimer Critique: A 'Pupil's' Retrospective," *Parameters* (March 1990): 9–19.

48. Rpt no. 40291, BGC, 31 Jul 39, sub: "Great Britain: Comments on Current Events," box 3, BGC Papers, MHI.

49. Rpt no. 40312, BGC, 4 Aug 39, sub: "Great Britain (Combat): Training Conceptions," box 3, BGC Papers, MHI.

50. Brian Bond, *British Military Policy Between the Two World Wars* (Oxford: Clarendon Press, 1980), pp. 326–27.

51. See Bond, *British Military Policy*; Mearsheimer, *Liddell Hart and the Weight of History*; Harold R. Winton, *To Change an Army: General Sir John Burnett-Stuart and British Armored Doctrine, 1927–1938* (Lawrence: University Press of Kansas, 1988); and Williamson Murray, *The Change in the European Balance of Power, 1938–1939: The Path to Ruin* (Princeton, N.J.: Princeton University Press, 1984).

52. Ltr, BGC to Col B. Q. Jones, 26 May 39, correspondence, 1938–39, box 2, BGC Papers, MHI.

53. Ltr, E. R. W. McCabe to BGC, 19 May 39, correspondence, 1938–39, box 2, BGC Papers, MHI.

54. Ltr, E. R. W. McCabe to BGC, 29 May 39, correspondence, 1938–39, box 2, BGC Papers, MHI.

55. Ltr, George Lynch to BGC, 24 May 39, correspondence, Apr–Sep 39, box 2, BGC Papers, MHI. Chynoweth summed up the situation on 24 August: "From the first day of my arrival on this post it was evident to me that neither the Ambassador nor the Counsellor [*sic*] of Embassy desired any contact whatever with myself or with my office. My efforts to reach a cooperative basis, made in compliance with oral orders given me by the then Chief of Staff . . . were not skillful, and resulted in a final explosion on May 9th. Since that date, there has not been a single contact between the Ambassador and myself, except at Court Presentations. This lack of contact does not represent a change in the situation, as I am informed there was no contact prior to my arrival. The sole result of my effort to change the situation was some personal friction." Ltr, BGC to Assistant Chief of Staff, G–2, 24 Aug 39, correspondence, Apr–Sep 39, box 2, BGC Papers, MHI.

56. Ltr, E. R. W. McCabe to BGC, 18 Jul 39, correspondence, Apr–Sep 39, box 2, BGC Papers, MHI.

57. BGC, "Recollections," pp. 39–40, BGC Papers, MHI.

58. Ltr, Joseph P. Kennedy to Louis Johnson, 3 Jul 39, and Ltr, Louis Johnson to Joseph P. Kennedy, 15 Jul 39, box 6, Johnson Papers, MHI.

59. Ltr, E. R. W. McCabe to BGC, 24 Jul 39, correspondence, Apr–Sep 39, box 2, BGC Papers, MHI.

60. The personal embarrassment and difficulties to himself and his family were, of course, great. In a letter to his brother-in-law on 4 August Chynoweth noted that both he and his wife were "in a bit of a daze still." His first thought was to ask for three months of leave to "do the continent" but events soon ruled out any such plan; Ltr, BGC to Maj Gen George Lynch, 4 Aug 39, correspondence, 1938–39, box 2, BGC Papers, MHI.

61. Over the next two years, Chynoweth had several highly visible clashes with superiors (one resulting in a general court-martial) and succeeded in alienating such old friends as George Patton and his brother-in-law, George Lynch. Sent in November 1941 to the Philippines, he was promoted to brigadier general on 18 December 1941 and to the command of the 61st Division (Philippine Army). Compelled to surrender in April 1942, he was held as a prisoner of war for more than three years. He retired in 1947 and died 8 February 1985.

62. Rpt no. 40383, BGC, 5 Sep 39, sub: "Great Britain: Comments on Current Events," box 3, BGC Papers, MHI.

63. Ibid.; Chynoweth had observed in late July: "If we are going to cooperate" with the Allies and make known that policy, the U.S. fleet and "a very limited potential military strength" will suffice for a time. However, "if we really choose isolated neutrality," U.S. national defense policy must comprise the following: a two-ocean navy "equal to any two other navies on earth"; air strength "second to none"; a "fully equipped" army of at least 500,000 effectives; universal military training in peacetime; and "moral rearmament" of the American people. Rpt no. 40287, BGC, 27 Jul 39, sub: "Great Britain: Comments on Current Events," box 3, BGC Papers, MHI.

64. BGC, "A More Perfect Union" folder, box 5, BGC Papers, MHI.

The U.S. Bataan Campaign
December 1941 to April 1942

Thomas M. Huber

During the first eight months of the Pacific War, the Philippine Islands were the only place the United States was able to engage its adversaries in ground warfare. U.S. and Philippine forces faced special challenges in the Philippines, since their contact with the United States as a source of supply and reinforcement was almost completely cut off. What methods did U.S. forces rely on to cope with this set of circumstances, and how effective were they?

Background and Planning

The only resistance offered by U.S. ground forces early in the Pacific War was on the Bataan Peninsula in the Philippine Islands. Two weeks elapsed, however, between the main Japanese landings at Lingayen Gulf on 22–24 December 1941 and the establishment of a defense line on Bataan by American and Philippine forces. Moreover, conditions elsewhere during these two weeks (but also on Bataan) were greatly influenced by planning decisions made earlier in the Philippines and Washington.

Before 1935 the defense of the Philippine Islands had rested on the American 10,000-man garrison, half of which consisted of Philippine Scout units, that is, units where the enlisted men were Filipinos and almost all of the officers were Americans. There was also a native Philippine Constabulary created in 1901 to maintain "law and order."[1] But when the Philippines became a commonwealth in 1935 with full independence slated for 1946, all parties expected the native Philippine government to take over responsibility for the islands' defense. President-elect Manuel Quezon prevailed on Douglas MacArthur, then retiring as U.S. Army Chief of Staff, to become military adviser to the commonwealth government. MacArthur formed a small committee at the U.S. Army War College that included Maj. Dwight D. Eisenhower and Maj. James B. Ord to prepare a plan that would assure Philippine defense by 1946, the date for independence. Their plan called for a small regular army, a system of conscription, and a ten-year training program of two classes per year, as well as some air and naval elements. The plan was enacted into law as the National Defense Act by the new Philippine National Assembly in December 1935.[2]

The act specified a standing force of 10,000 troops and reserves of 400,000 by 1946. The regular force was to include the 6,000-man Philippine Constabulary so there would be some continuity of training and tradition. The act also provided for a conscription system and created an academy to train officers at Baguio. Under the new system 20,000 men were called to the colors in 1937, and the authorities were thus able to create a reserve of 4,800 officers and 104,000 men by the end of 1939. Philippine Scouts were used for instruction of the new troops. Some of these were promoted to noncommissioned officers (NCOs) and later to junior officers. A Philippine Reserve Officer Training Corps (ROTC) program also provided some native Philippine officers while the Baguio academy was still preparing its first class.[3]

While attention was paid to fashioning a new force structure, the Americans also gave some thought to how those forces would be used. MacArthur, in his capacity as military adviser, drew up comprehensive plans for the autonomous defense of all the islands and the seven straits, with no reliance on U.S. forces, to be implemented by 1946 when the Philippines became independent. This was the *terminus ad quem* at which the establishment of the Philippine Army was aimed. Meanwhile, however, the Philippines fell within the sphere of American war planning, especially the RAINBOW plans which were prepared by the War Department beginning in 1939. These incorporated the older color plans, including War Plan ORANGE, which covered the Philippine area, and assumed that in case of attack, U.S. forces would only attempt to control Manila Bay by withdrawing to Bataan and holding there until reinforcements could arrive.[4]

This status quo, with a gradually developing national army and a passive defense plan, obtained until early 1941, when tensions in the region stirred MacArthur to seek both more ambitious plans and a more ambitious force structure. Maj. Gen. George Grunert was named commander of the Philippine Department in June 1940, and in the course of requesting more assets, sent a succession of warning reports to Washington in the latter months of 1940. These were disregarded by the War Department, however, which believed that such resources as were available had to go first to strengthen Alaska, Hawaii, and Panama.[5]

The War Department's concern was already growing, however, when MacArthur wrote to Army Chief of Staff George C. Marshall on 1

February 1941 asking for a rapid buildup of Philippine forces. MacArthur worked from the premise of comprehensive defense by native forces of the Philippines, including Luzon, the Visayas, and the waters between. Thus he asked Marshall to sanction the organization of 30 reserve divisions, for a total ground force of 250,000, to be complete by the end of 1941. He also asked for naval and air elements and coastal defense guns. Grunert, meanwhile, who was asking only for more modest resources for the U.S. garrison, still thought in terms of a limited defense of Manila Bay only. Marshall promised MacArthur his defense material and reassured Grunert it would not be at his expense.[6]

By summer the sense of crisis in the area had deepened further. MacArthur on 7 July 1941 sent a letter to the War Plans Division requesting formation of a Far East Command. On 17 July 1941 the War Plans Division Chief, Brig. Gen. Leonard T. Gerow, recommended to Marshall (among other measures) that all Philippine Commonwealth forces be brought into the U.S. service for the duration of the perceived emergency; that a regional command, U.S. Army Forces Far East (USAFFE), be established; and that MacArthur be brought back to active duty as a major general (his permanent rank) to head it. These steps were approved by Secretary of War Henry L. Stimson on 26 July 1941.[7]

These actions represented a major, if tardy, increase in the War Department's commitment to the Philippines. U.S. Army forces in the Philippines at that time totaled 22,532 troops, of which 10,473 were in the Philippine Division and 2,073 in other combat units. The remaining 10,000 troops were devoted to harbor defense, air, and service activities. Of the 22,532 total, approximately 10,500 were Americans and 12,000 were Philippine Scouts. Authorities in the Philippines and Washington now cooperated to expand these numbers rapidly.[8]

MacArthur ordered in mid-August that the first regiment from each of the ten reserve divisions report for duty by 1 November. In mid-November he ordered the second regiment of each to report by 1 January. The Philippine Commonwealth divisions were to keep their own uniforms, scale of pay, promotion lists, and so on, but were to be paid by the U.S. Army. The Philippine Commonwealth's Regular Army and the Philippine Constabulary, however, were not to be brought into the American forces immediately. To each of the reserve divisions being activated forty American officers and twenty American or Philippine Scout noncommissioned officers were assigned as instructors.[9]

The ten reserve divisions would have about 7,500 troops each by mid-December, some 75,000 men, to which would be added a few thousand more in nondivisional organizations. The Philippine units were hampered somewhat by their lack of a common language and by the fact that many of their troops, including NCOs and clerks, were illiterate. In mid-December the Philippine units also suffered from being minimally clothed and equipped.[10]

While Philippine forces were being mobilized beginning in August, so too were American forces being augmented, especially air forces. There had been a gradual buildup before August, including an increase in the Philippine Scouts from 6,415 to 12,000 troops, eighty-one P–40 fighter planes, nine B–17 bombers, a tank battalion, fifty-four M–4 tanks, and fifty 75-mm. antitank guns. The pace of augmentation quickened in November. The War Department sent 10 pack howitzers, 178 75-mm. guns, 123 .30-caliber machine guns, 100 flamethrowers, and 15,000 land mines. The department also sent more planes, for a total of 194 aircraft by early December, including 35 B–17s, 107 P–40s, and 52 P–35s.[11]

The number of American troops also increased from 22,532 (31 July 1941), of whom 10,500 were Americans, to 31,095 (30 November 1941), of whom 19,000 were Americans. These were in addition to the approximately 80,000 Philippine Commonwealth troops that had been raised by December, so that the total USAFFE ground forces came to about 111,700 troops—still less than the 200,000 troops MacArthur estimated on 1 October were necessary for defense. As it happened, 19,000 more American troops plus military equipment were embarked for the Philippines in early December, but had to turn back after the Japanese attack.[12]

At the same time that the Philippine and U.S. force structure was expanding—from September through November—so too were the goals of the Philippine defense planners. The ORANGE Plans for the defense of the Philippines had existed for many years. The latest revision of these MacArthur inherited was War Plan ORANGE–3 (WPO–3), completed in April 1941. In WPO–3 the planners assumed the Japanese would attack with less than forty-eight hours warning from U.S. intelligence, that they would employ a force of about 100,000 troops, and land in many places simultaneously. WPO–3 provided that American forces would resist on the beaches, resist inland, and if that failed, withdraw to the Bataan Peninsula to retain control of Manila Bay.[13]

WPO–3 divided Luzon into six sectors, each of which was to fashion its own detailed defense and be independently provisioned. In the event of withdrawal to Bataan, each sector was to transport its own supplies to the peninsula. The beach forces were required to delay the Japanese advance long enough for stores to be moved to Bataan and Corregidor from depots around Manila. The Bataan forces were then to hold out for six months, by which time the U.S. Navy was to have fought its way back to the Philippines with reinforcements. Some U.S. planners in the Philippines in early 1941 doubted that a Bataan garrison could be relieved after six months, and instead felt that the garrison would exhaust its supplies and be defeated. Nonetheless, the official policy was that the Bataan force would survive until communications were reopened.[14]

The buildup of forces in the fall of 1941, however, led both MacArthur and planners in Washington to aspire to operational objectives far grander than those of WPO–3. On receiving a recent version of the RAINBOW 5 comprehensive war plans, which essentially confirmed WPO–3 in the Philippine area, MacArthur wrote to Marshall on 1 October 1941 asking for a more comprehensive plan. He wanted the "citadel-type defense" of WPO–3 to be abandoned in favor of an active defense of all the Philippine Islands and adjoining waters. MacArthur, of course, probably had been thinking in these terms ever since he—as military adviser to the Philippine president—was charged with developing plans for Philippine national defense.[15]

Marshall and the personnel in the War Plans Division (WPD) by the fall of 1941 agreed with MacArthur that the material in or on its way to the Philippines justified grander aspirations for its use. Brig. Gen. Leonard T. Gerow of the WPD sent a memo to Marshall on 8 October outlining the WPD's position on the Philippines. He asserted that the new force levels should be enough to discourage the Japanese from attacking, given Japan's involvement in China, Soviet resistance to Germany, and the economic embargoes against Japan. He especially felt that strong air forces placed in the Philippines would provide offensive powers that would deter the Japanese from acting. Gerow's view was that reinforcement of the Philippines meant the Japanese were unlikely to move against the U.S. presence there, which would allow concentration of Allied resources on the struggle against Germany.[16]

Based on this newly optimistic and confident consensus in Washington, Marshall dispatched a memorandum to MacArthur on 18 October giving him greatly enlarged operational goals. MacArthur was to defend not only all of the Philippine Islands and adjacent waters but also to cooperate with the Navy to raid Japanese sea communications, conduct air raids, and help defend the territories of the Associated Powers.[17]

Marshall's note to this effect apparently was hand-delivered to MacArthur on 3 November by Maj. Gen. Lewis H. Brereton. Marshall also had written that a new plan comprehending the points in his memo already had been drafted and would soon be considered by the Joint Board of Army and Navy planners, who actually would approve it on 21 November.

But MacArthur had begun already on 4 November to carry out a force reorganization compatible with the intent of the new plan.[18]

The extraordinary efforts of the American military leaders to strengthen the Philippines in the autumn of 1941 in the end made them confident that their forces were adequate. Their confidence rested largely on the premise that sea and ground attack could be deterred by the modest presence of air forces. This confidence, however, proved unwarranted. The optimistic mood of mid-November gave way by the end of the month to the conviction that the Japanese might soon attack the Philippines because of the failure of the Hull-Nomura talks. The American ambassador to Tokyo, Joseph Grew, cabled to Washington on 17 November that there might be a sudden Japanese attack outside the current China theater. On 24 November U.S. Navy Chief of Staff Admiral Harold R. Stark sent his Pacific commanders a communication to be shared with their Army colleagues in which he warned of the possibility of a surprise aggressive act against either the Philippines or Guam. On 27 November the War Department sent a "final alert" to MacArthur, noting that negotiations with Japan had broken down and, that in the event of hostilities, MacArthur should execute the RAINBOW strategy.[19]

MacArthur called a conference of his commanders after the 27 November message and advised them of the tense situation. He ordered the North Luzon Force (one of the four commands into which American forces in the islands were divided) to be ready to move to assigned positions of beach defense. It was not long thereafter before USAFFE had the opportunity to test whether its preparations were adequate and its plans realistic.[20]

The Approach to Bataan (24 December 1941 to 7 January 1942)

The Japanese Pacific offensives that began on 7 December 1941 (8 December in the Philippines) had two devastating features that USAFFE planners did not anticipate: the Japanese struck American rear naval bases at the same time that they attacked advanced bases, and they used their air power offensively to neutralize completely American air and naval assets in the Philippine area. The upshot was that the Philippines suddenly had to be defended with the ground assets on hand, because USAFFE had no supply line and few air resources left.

Japanese naval and air forces crippled the U.S. Pacific Fleet at Pearl Harbor on 7 December and on 8 December bombed Clark Field on Luzon and other points, destroying half of the American aircraft on the islands in one day. The Japanese used large fleets of bombers and fighter bombers based on Taiwan. The Japanese air fleets came again on 10 and 12–13 December, pounding U.S. air and naval assets and bases.[21]

American forces responded in the only way they could. The remainder of the Philippine-based U.S. Asiatic Fleet departed for Australia on 10 December rather than be needlessly destroyed. Most remaining American aircraft did the same. On 17 December the B–17s still able to fly lifted off Del Monte Field in the Visayas for Darwin. Exclusion of U.S. air and naval power from the western Pacific was then assured by Japanese landings on Guam on 10 December and on Wake on 23 December. These seizures meant that Midway, 4,500 miles away, was now the nearest American base to the Philippine Islands—the Philippines could expect no early relief.[22]

The bold knockout blows of early December put the Japanese in a position to devote their attention to land invasion of the Philippines. Japanese forces seized advanced bases in the archipelago on Bataan and Camiguin Islands, just north of Luzon, on 8 and 10 December. They captured key points on the north Luzon coast (Sparri and Vigan) on 10 December, on far south Luzon (Legaspi) on 12 December, and on Mindanao (Davao) on 20 December.[23]

The main Japanese invasion force, the *Imperial Japanese Army 14th Army* under Lt. Gen. Masaharu Homma, landed on Luzon on the east shore of Lingayen Gulf on 22 December. USAFFE failed to resist these landings, with the exception of the headquarters battalion of the 12th Infantry, Philippine Army (PA), which directed some machine-gun fire at the Japanese landing party. The enemy put ashore a secondary force at Tamon Bay, southeast of Manila, on Christmas Eve, with the objective of having the northern and southern forces converge on Manila.[24]

From their landing area, the Japanese advanced easily on 23 December about ten miles southeastward, into the Luzon interior, toward Manila. MacArthur thus realized on 23 December that his Philippine forces could not contain the Japanese on the beaches as he had previously hoped. During the period 12–22 December he had ordered his line units to stand fast, but also made hasty preparations to withdraw to Bataan if need be. By the twenty-third, however, MacArthur made up his mind and notified all his commanders that WPO–3 was now effective, that is, the operational plan now was to withdraw all USAFFE forces to Bataan. Ironically, MacArthur had deliberately discarded WPO–3 in November in favor of an active defense. Fortunately for him, WPO–3 was still familiar to all participants, so that it could be carried out quickly despite its earlier abandonment as policy.[25]

USAFFE headquarters moved from Manila to Corregidor on the night of 24–25 December, and the effort began to transport supplies to Bataan and Corregidor as rapidly as possible. Using a flotilla of small boats, USAFFE G–4 placed supplies for 10,000 troops for six months on Corregidor within twenty-four hours. Supplies were then directed toward Bataan, using water, truck, and rail. Small craft were essential for the supply movement to the peninsula, where ammunition, gasoline, and 3,000 tons of canned meat and fish previously had been stored.[26]

For the Bataan plan to work, the commander of the North Luzon Force, Maj. Gen. Jonathan M. Wainwright, had to hold the Japanese north of San Fernando, where Route 3 coming up from the south meets Route 7 going into Bataan. Wainwright had to hold the intersection long enough for the South Luzon Force to pass through it and enter the peninsula. The South Luzon Force was to withdraw northward toward San Fernando, then turn southwest into the peninsula. It was crucial that the South Luzon Force hold the Calumpit bridges over the Pampanga River until its assets had crossed.[27]

On 24 December, meanwhile, the Bataan Defense Force was established to prepare a defensive line on the peninsula to be manned by the main forces when they arrived. Maj. Gen. George M. Parker temporarily was removed from command of the South Luzon Force to supervise this work. The U.S. Army's Philippine Division (US) was already in Bataan, and the Philippine 31st and 41st Divisions (PA) soon arrived to help with the construction work. The defensive positions were surveyed and marked out by the 14th Engineers (Philippine Scouts [PS]), and the actual digging of foxholes and laying of wire was done by troops from the various divisions as they arrived.[28]

MacArthur ordered Wainwright and the North Luzon Force to hold the San Fernando intersection until 8 January. He was to do this by deploying five successive defense lines. After forming a line and forcing the advancing Japanese to halt in preparation for an attack, he was immediately to withdraw to a line farther to the rear and force the Japanese to halt again. This exercise was to be repeated five times. Wainwright's object was to achieve a maximum of delay with a minimum of casualties and enter Bataan intact.[29]

Each defense line was to be held during the day, then evacuated at night for the next line, which was to be established before dawn. A shell force was to remain behind to hold the old line until just before dawn. The defense lines were too long to be continuous and in practice they often covered only the most likely avenues of enemy approach.[30]

The North Luzon Force had reconnoitered the five defense lines in peacetime and arrayed them one day's march apart, making use of natural defensive features such as rivers, high ground, and swamps. They blocked

Routes 3 and 5, the main roads southward. The first line was sited where the North Luzon Force found itself on Christmas Eve, about ten miles behind the Lingayen beaches.[31]

The principal North Luzon Force units holding the five lines were, from west to east, the 21st, 11th, and 91st Divisions (PA), and the 26th Cavalry (PS). Commanders sought to have mutually supporting infantry and artillery elements on the line, but in practice this could not always be done. It was difficult to move supplies for North Luzon Force units, which were in almost constant motion. They were supposed to carry what supplies they could to Bataan and destroy the rest, but this goal was not achieved completely. Supply problems were complicated by the shortage of motor vehicles in which supplies arrived and the tendency of commanders to appropriate the vehicles in which the supplies arrived, thereby removing the vehicle from the logistics net.[32]

By Christmas Day the North Luzon Force had fallen back to the second line, where Japanese forces managed to attack them, breaking through at Carmen. The American forces retired to the third line by 27 December, but were not engaged there because the Japanese stopped at the Agno River to re-form. By 29 December the North Luzon Force had withdrawn to the fourth line. Wainwright was alarmed that the South Luzon Force had not yet cleared the Calumpit bridges and therefore ordered his units to stand at all costs at their present positions, the Tarlac line. In the original plan, however, only the fifth line—not the fourth—was organized for a protracted defense.[33]

Japanese forces attacked the Tarlac line, which held until 30 December, largely because of a firm stand by the 3d Battalion of the 21st Division (PA). On 30 December elements of the Tarlac line were ordered back to the fifth line, which was established by the morning of 31 December. Over seven days the North Luzon Force had withdrawn about fifty miles.[34]

Meanwhile the South Luzon Force also was withdrawing toward Bataan. Since General Parker had left to organize Bataan on Christmas Eve, Maj. Gen. Albert M. Jones was the force's commander. Smaller than the North Luzon Force, the South Luzon Force consisted only of the 1st and 51st Divisions (PA) with some attached artillery and armor assets. The South Luzon Force was not hard pressed by the Japanese in the way the northern force was, however, and its withdrawal northward toward Bataan was for the most part smooth and orderly. Most of the South Luzon Force crossed the Calumpit bridges and arrived at San Fernando by 31 December.[35]

By this time (indeed, on 30 December) General Homma had dispatched a force toward Plaridel. This movement lay to the east of the main

Japanese axis of advance and threatened to prevent the last arriving of the South Luzon Force units from crossing the Calumpit bridges. MacArthur, therefore, assembled a force to defend Plaridel, consisting of the retreating 71st Division (PA) and elements of the South Luzon Force passing near Plaridel on their way north. These units successfully delayed the advance of the enemy force. The last of the troops at Plaridel withdrew northwest across the Calumpit bridges at 0500 on 1 January 1942. The bridges immediately were destroyed at Wainwright's order at 0615. American observers were relieved that Japanese air power, apparently unaware of the bridges' importance to the American operational plan, had not attacked the bridges in force.[36]

Once it was clear the South Luzon Force would reach San Fernando, the North Luzon Force began evacuating their fifth defense line and moving through San Fernando for Bataan. The last U.S. forces moved through the town for Bataan at 0200 on 2 January, pressed by the *Kanno Detachment*, which attacked to the west of the main Japanese axis. Again, Japanese planes, perhaps occupied with the *Imperial Japanese Army*'s drive for Manila, did not attack the crowded roads.[37]

American commanders still sought to delay a Japanese advance in order to give troops in Bataan time to enter and prepare their lines. To this end, the 21st and 11th Divisions (PA) took up positions, where they soon were pressured by two reinforced Japanese regiments, the *Takabashi* and *Tanaka Detachments*. The 21st and 11th Divisions were forced back, but still kept the Japanese north of the Culo River until 6 January. The last of the American rear guard force crossed the Culo River at 0200 on 6 January, and the 91st Engineer Battalion blew up the bridge behind them. The 11th and 21st Divisions formed still another line near the Culo River, from which they withdrew on the morning of 7 January. This delay of the Japanese at Bataan's base went according to WPO–3 and was successfully executed, giving U.S. engineers additional time to prepare the Abucay-Mauban defense line on the peninsula.[38]

The fighting around Layac junction marked the end of the American forces' long withdrawal to the peninsula that began on 23 December. Subsequent fighting on Bataan would no longer have the quality of a maneuver withdrawal.

The Abucay-Mauban Line (7–26 January 1942)

The next phase of the Philippine campaign would take place entirely within the confined area of the Bataan Peninsula. Bataan is about twenty-five miles long and twenty miles wide, jungled and mountainous, scored by several streams and deep ravines. Two extinct volcanoes mark the center of the peninsula, Mt. Natib toward the north and Mt. Bataan in the south. There are numerous overgrown trails on the peninsula, but only two roads—Route 110 along the coast and the Pilar-Bagac road bisecting the peninsula from east to west.[39]

The American forces were relieved finally to be in a position they did not have to abandon immediately. They established a line about a third of the way down the peninsula, bisected by Mt. Natib, which left a gap in the line. The sector from Mt. Natib west to Mauban was commanded by General Wainwright and designated the I Philippine Corps, altogether about 22,500 troops. The corps consisted of the 1st, 31st, and 91st Divisions (PA), and the 26th Cavalry Regiment (PS), and a battery each of field artillery and self-propelled 75-mm. guns.[40]

The sector from Mt. Natib eastward was designated the II Philippine Corps and placed under General Parker. About 25,000 men, it consisted of the 11th, 21st, 41st, and 51st Divisions (PA), plus the 57th Infantry (PS) from the Philippine Division (US).[41]

Between the two corps was Mt. Natib, 4,222 feet high, jungled, and impenetrable. Mt. Natib prevented mutual reinforcement by the two corps, and also left the interior flanks of both corps somewhat up in the air—a major tactical flaw in the line. U.S. commanders believed they could not put the line south of Mt. Natib and still protect the only road bisecting the peninsula from east to west. They may have avoided the terrain north of Mt. Natib because of the absence of roads.[42]

South of the Abucay line and also bisecting the peninsula was a second defense line which roughly paralleled the east-west road from Pilar to Bagac. This line was not complete as of 7 January, so the Abucay line was to hold until this Pilar-Bagac line was finished. Part of the Philippine Division (US) and other units were kept at work on the second line through January. Corps and USAFFE artillery also were placed in this vicinity so as to cover both the Abucay line and any possible Japanese landings on the peninsula's southern coasts.[43]

At the southern end of Bataan a Service Command Area was established under Brig. Gen. Allan C. McBride to help provide effective supply. Within this area were the 2d Division, made up of the former Philippine Constabulary (PC), elements of the 71st Division (PA), and provisional infantry units consisting of air troops, sailors, and Marines. On 5 January MacArthur also established in the south a command echelon between his own USAFFE headquarters on Corregidor and the force on Bataan. Its commander was Brig. Gen. Richard J. Marshall, and its main function was to direct the combat activities of the two line corps and to provide services for them. American combat units also were posted along the coast in the south to oppose attempts at amphibious envelopment.[44]

The Abucay-Mauban line, the main battle position as on 7 January, had an outpost line flung out to its front and a regimental line in its rear. The eastern half of the line boasted a double apron of barbed wire, cleared fields of fire, foxholes, trenches, gun emplacements, and overhead camouflage. The western half of the line had some of these features, but was less developed.[45]

Supplies for the Bataan force had been moved to the peninsula with miraculous speed after 23 December but still were woefully inadequate.[46] Once Corregidor's stockage was complete, the supplying of Bataan began in earnest. Only one method of transportation, small watercraft, proved effective. There were no railroads on Bataan, and the roads into the peninsula were jammed with troop traffic. Moreover, few trucks were available. Large vessels were on hand in Manila harbor, but quartermasters preferred smaller vessels, launches, tugs, and barges, because only these could easily be unloaded on the three primitive piers on Bataan. Manila was the main source of supply. About 30,000 tons were moved from the supply concentrations at Manila before Japanese forces occupied the city on 2 January. In theory supplies were supposed to be brought into Bataan by the North and South Luzon Forces. Both were expected to roll up military stocks in outlying depots and either transport them to Bataan or destroy them completely. In practice, however, these forces suffered from "withdrawal fever," and in their haste they failed to do so.[47]

The biggest supply problem on Bataan proved to be food for the 80,000 USAFFE troops. MacArthur had put the Bataan force on half rations on 5 January, even before all the troops had arrived. The 2,000 calories was about what active soldiers required, so individuals and units resorted to local supply. Units harvested rice in the fields, set up a slaughter house for carabao, built a rice mill, purchased fish from Filipino fishermen, and made salt by boiling sea water. Individuals used their rifles for hunting carabao and other game.[48]

Clothing was also scarce, especially for Philippine troops who had received little issued clothing when they were mobilized. The PA soldiers' blue denim fatigue suits and rubber-soled shoes wore through quickly in the jungle. All PA troops had quality rifles, but not all had steel helmets. Shelter halves, blankets, sun helmets, and mosquito netting were also in short supply. The resultant exposure to jungle weather, combined with the deficient diet, produced a high rate of malaria, hookworm, and other diseases, made all the more serious by inadequate medical supplies, especially quinine.[49]

Gasoline stocks were moderately adequate. Uncontrolled use during the first few weeks led to rapid depletion, so consumption was limited thereafter by rationing to 4,000 gallons daily. Motor vehicles were not easily available, so units commandeered them and sometimes hijacked both vehicles and their loads. The Bataan Service Command tried to counter this practice by ordering all nonorganic vehicles into motor pools. Military police searched for illicit vehicles, but commandeered vehicles were often well hidden. Many vehicles were reclaimed by the Bataan Service Command's motor pools when gasoline rationing was imposed. Unable to get fuel for their unofficial vehicles, units turned them in.

Engineering equipment moved to Bataan also was moderately adequate. The 10,000 tons delivered included 350 tons of explosives, 800 tons of barbed wire, 200 tons of burlap sacks, and large quantities of construction material. The supply situation, especially food, proved an important factor in the outcome of the Bataan fighting.[50]

Combat engagement on the Abucay-Mauban line began at 1500 hours, 9 January, when the Japanese laid a concentrated barrage on the eastern half of the line, then advanced their infantry at both ends of the line. The *Imperial Japanese Army* continued to press attacks along the American line on 10–15 January, but with little success.[51]

On 15 January, however, the *141st Infantry* penetrated the American line and lodged themselves on a small hill between the 51st and 41st Infantry Divisions (PA). This modest lodgment led to the collapse of the left flank of the Abucay line within a few days, largely because of confusion. At dawn on 16 January, the 51st Division (PA) counterattacked, its 51st Infantry making far more progress than its 53d Infantry, thus creating an exposed salient. The Japanese *9th Infantry* threatened the left, while the *141st Infantry* attacked and broke through on the right shoulder. The 51st Infantry (PA), thus threatened with double envelopment, fled far to the rear.[52]

The *141st Infantry* turned left to attack the 43d Infantry (PA), which held its position and refused its flank, while the Japanese *9th Infantry* halted to regroup. The 53d Infantry (PA), nonetheless, feared attack and fell back. The chief of staff of the 51st Division (PA) also feared that the 53d Infantry (PA) would be overrun and, therefore, ordered its commander, Col. John R. Boatwright, to move westward across Mt. Natib and link up with the right flank of I Corps. This relocation was a harrowing experience for the 53d Infantry, which became separated and dispersed in the impenetrable jungle.[53]

These events of 16 January left the west flank of the Abucay line wide open. Nothing happened immediately because the *9th Infantry*, ordered to infiltrate around the II Corps left flank, then east across the II Corps rear, also became lost in the jungle and so, like the 53d Infantry (PA), removed itself from the battle.[54]

To restore II Corps' left flank, General Parker ordered an attack by his reserve, the Philippine Division (US), at dawn on 17 January. The Philippine Division and other elements advanced repeatedly against Japanese positions newly set up in the gap where the 51st Division (PA) had been, but as of 21 January still were unable to dislodge *Imperial Japanese Army* units from their salient above the Abucay Hacienda.[55]

Meanwhile General Wainwright in the I Corps sector was also hard pressed by the Japanese advance. On 15 January enemy forces engaged U.S. advanced units, pushing them back to the main lines at Mauban by the eighteenth. The whole American outpost line was driven in by nightfall on 19 January. Lt. Col. Hiroshi Nakanishi's *3d Battalion, 20th Infantry,* infiltrated around the east flank of I Corps, on the slopes of Mt. Natib, and on 21 January established a roadblock behind the 1st Division (PA), across the only road south capable of handling heavy equipment. Like the original lodgment of the *141st Infantry* in the II Corps sector, this battalion-size roadblock would lead to the collapse of the whole I Corps position.[56]

Wainwright himself encountered the block on his way to the front and commandeered a platoon of the 92d Infantry Division (PA) headquarters to attack it. After a two-hour assault with no results, Wainwright directed a larger force against the position, led by the 92d Infantry commander, Col. John H. Rodman, and consisting of elements of the 91st and 92d Infantry (PA), the 26th Cavalry (PS), and other units. Rodman's attacks on 22–23 January had no effect, however, perhaps because his numerous troops had little food and few automatic weapons.[57]

Because of the continuing road blockage, by the evening of 24 January the U.S. main battle line was short of food and ammunition. Col. Kearie L. Berry, commanding the 1st Division (PA) on the I Corps line, without authorization ordered the division to withdraw on the morning of the twenty-fifth. Since the road was blocked, the division had to move along the coast, which meant destroying all immobile guns and heavy equipment on the beaches. The evacuation of the Mauban line was completed successfully by the evening of 25 January.[58]

With both the I Corps and II Corps lines in disarray, Maj. Gen. Richard K. Sutherland, MacArthur's chief of staff, on 22 January already had given written orders to Wainwright and Parker to withdraw the whole force southward from the Abucay-Mauban line into the Pilar-Bagac line. Heavy artillery and service elements were to go first, beginning after nightfall on 23 January. Combat elements were to depart the next day, leaving one company per battalion in place as a covering force. This shell was to retire starting at 0300, 25 January. All elements were to be behind the new line by dawn of the following day.[59]

The evacuation went smoothly in the I Corps sector because it was underway already, but in the II Corps sector the withdrawal did not go as well.[60] The artillery and service elements pulled back without incident on the night of 23–24 January. In the evacuation of the main combat units, however, there was considerable confusion, especially at the intersection of the Y-shaped intersection of the east-west road between Abucay and Abucay Hacienda and the so-called Back Road running south. Traffic became extremely congested and often stopped completely. No military police were on hand to regulate it, and whole units became dispersed just trying to cross. Officers just trying to move the whole confused mass south were thankful that Japanese artillery did not apply interdictive fire to the spot.[61]

II Corps troops were fortunate not to be bombed at the Back Road junction, but at other points they were not so lucky. *Imperial Japanese Army* air elements were aware of the retreat and bombed and strafed the crowded roads in force. Nevertheless, the American covering force held firm, keeping retreating forces from being overrun. The last U.S. troops to depart the Abucay line were the 31st Infantry (PS) at 0300, 25 January. On the morning of 26 January the 194th Tank Battalion (US) still held a line across the Back Road, until they were flanked from the west and Japanese artillery was brought to bear. The retreat of the 194th Tank Battalion marked the successful completion of the American withdrawal by both corps sectors into the Pilar-Bagac line, which was well manned, well engineered, and still unattrited by combat.[62]

The operational flaw that pushed the U.S. forces back lay in their planning. Failure to resolve the gap in the Abucay-Mauban line created by Mt. Natib allowed the Japanese to isolate and destroy the left flank of the USAFFE II Corps more easily and to envelop the right flank of I Corps with a roadblock.

The Pilar-Bagac Line (26 January to 9 April)

USAFFE divided the Pilar-Bagac line between I and II Corps sectors at the Pantingan River. At least in this position the two sectors were in contact, forming a continuous line. The length of the coastline was reduced, making it easier to defend against amphibious envelopment. Mt. Samat on the II Corps side permitted good observation of the field, and II Corps placed its artillery there. In front of the line the Pilar-Bagac road could not be used for lateral movement, but American engineers linked a network of east-west trails for this purpose by mid-February.[63]

The II Corps area, east of the Pantingan River, was divided into four sectors (A, B, C, and D, numbered from the coast), and the I Corps area west of the river was divided into left and right sectors. The Japanese, still in pursuit of the retreating Americans, attacked Sector C on 27 January, but Brig. Gen. Clifford Bluemel stood firm with the 51st Division (PA) and the 32d Infantry (PA) against three concerted enemy attacks. Japanese units also attacked in the I Corps area on 30 January and 3 February, intruding elements behind the 1st Division (PA) lines and forming isolated pockets in the American area that were not eliminated until 17 February. Japanese attempts at amphibious envelopment by battalion-size units on 22 and 26 January and 1 February were contained and suppressed.[64]

The new American line held at all points, to the surprise of the Japanese who had just pushed through the Abucay line. On 8 February, therefore, General Homma pulled all of the *14th Army* forces back for a major force reorganization, while the morale of U.S. forces soared. Wainwright believed that morale on Bataan was higher after beating back the numerous attacks in early February than at any other time. USAFFE forces felt a sense of confidence and pride at this point. With experience they had begun to master the skills of jungle survival and jungle combat, and they were enjoying success. American patrols roamed boldly in front of the line, one as far north as the old Abucay defense line.[65]

General Bluemel and some other II Corps officers began to favor a counteroffensive to retake the Abucay line. II Corps headquarters staff rejected this proposal, however, on the grounds that a general offensive would exhaust the resources needed to carry out the main mission—to hold Manila Bay as long as possible. Moreover, forces on the move would be exposed to Japanese air and sea superiority, and troops taking the offensive need more food, gasoline, and ammunition than those on the defensive. Even if U.S. forces successfully retook the Abucay line, that would only mean longer lines of communications and a longer coastal perimeter to defend. II Corps headquarters believed that instead of thinking about an offensive, units should use the lull to strengthen their portions of the current defense line.[66]

Although American morale was high in early February, the logistical predicament of the encircled USAFFE force would cause its fighting power to be weakened critically in the next two months, even though it was almost free of contact with the enemy. There was a chronic food shortage from the moment the forces entered the peninsula, as well as shortages of clothing and shelter halves and the like. Troops became extremely resourceful at foraging jungle flora and fauna, but nonetheless, a severe shortage persisted.[67]

In part because of these deprivations and in part because of the jungle environment, physical deterioration and illness affected the whole force. By March virtually all troops suffered serious malnutrition. This meant chronic fatigue, reduced immunity to illness, and avitaminotic diseases themselves: beriberi, scurvy, and amoebic dysentery. Beriberi, caused by a shortage of vitamin B, was common. Malnutrition also caused night blindness and edema.[68]

Troops suffered from dengue fever and hookworm. But the most devastating disease troops faced was malaria. By March 35 percent of the force actually had malaria, and many of the rest were infected. The situation was aggravated by the location of the Pilar-Bagac line in the malaria-infested lowland between Mt. Natib and the Mariveles Mountains.[69]

In January all infected troops were given quinine, but by March there was not an adequate supply even for the actual sufferers. Dysentery serum, gangrene gas antitoxin (to avoid amputations), and some sulfa drugs, also ran low, although some other drugs lasted to the end of the campaign. Surgical hospitals functioned efficiently to the cessation of hostilities, though they were increasingly overburdened. Although it is not clear why, there were almost no hospitalizations because of psychological disorders.[70]

By the end of March American fighting power was badly eroded by the cumulative effect of hunger and illness. In many units half or more of the troops were incapacitated by malaria and dysentery. Of those left, officers commonly reported 50 percent combat efficiency—sometimes as low as 20 percent. Many troops were able merely to fire a rifle from a trench, but no more. They could not do physical labor, such as carrying a pack while retreating. These conditions contributed to a cumulative psychological fatigue in the force. At an earlier stage, stragglers often could be rallied just by an officer's encouragement to go back into battle. Later in the campaign, however, stragglers discarded their equipment and ignored such pleas as they became physically exhausted and mentally unequal to combat duty.[71]

Meanwhile, General Homma's *14th Army* was preparing for a major assault against the deteriorating U.S. line. The American troops were aware that the *14th Army* was moving men and supplies into Bataan, and also discovered that Homma had put a counter-reconnaissance screen in front of his line during the second week of March to obstruct U.S. patrols. This screen was moved to within 1,000 yards of the American positions, i.e., the coming attack's line of departure, by the last week of March. In this final week Japanese artillery and aerial bombardment, previously desultory, became intense and fell at all hours.[72]

The long-anticipated Japanese offensive finally came on 3 April, after a heavy aerial and artillery bombardment from 1000 to 1500. The bombardment and the following infantry assault were both focused on the left front of II Corps, Sector D, commanded by Brig. Gen. Maxon S. Lough. In this sector were the 21st and 41st Divisions (PA), each with three regiments on the line. Against this force General Homma sent forward the *4th Division* and the *65th Brigade*, both heavily reinforced.[73]

The five-hour preparatory bombardment had driven out the malnourished and weakened Filipino troops. They were disheartened, choked by the dust, and harassed by shell-ignited brush fires. They fled south in disarray. The burden of living in the jungle without resources for two months had almost destroyed U.S. forces on the Pilar-Bagac line even without further intervention by the Japanese. One wonders, however, whether moving the U.S. force underground into a trench and tunnel system might not have allowed the line to survive the heavy 3 April bombardment.[74]

General Lough felt that the 42d Infantry (PA) was a total loss, but tried to put the 41st, 43d, and 33d Infantries (PA) in position to block the Japanese advance. On 4 April the Japanese attacked farther into their breakthrough on the west side of Sector D and also attacked with tanks on the east side. The result was that Sector D disintegrated, and the 21st Division (PA) was driven back to its reserve position northeast of Mt. Samat, with its left flank exposed because of the 41st Division's disappearance.[75]

In this emergency, General Parker, II Corps commander, gave Lough the 31st and 45th Infantries (PA and PS) and other reinforcements and instructed him to counterattack on the morning of 6 April. The 45th Infantry (PS) was to advance along with the 31st and 33d up three jungle trails, while General Bluemel, commander of Sector C, was to support the attack with artillery and a simultaneous assault by the 51st Combat Team on Sector C's left flank.[76]

On the same day the Japanese launched a major attack in this same area. The *65th Brigade* was to make a holding attack on the west flank of U.S. Sector D, while the *4th Division* attacked on the east flank and tried to break through. The result was that on 6 April the *4th Division* met the Philippine Army units on the trails, driving them back, breaking through the American position, isolating II Corps from I Corps, overrunning Mt. Samat (II Corps' artillery position), and capturing critical trail junctions in the II Corps rear.[77]

The American San Vicente line proved to be ineffectual. General Homma resolved to strike through to the east coast, then move southward.

Although General Bluemel hurriedly sought to set up three defense lines along a succession of rivers, these were unable to obstruct the Japanese southward advance.[78]

As the Japanese *8th Infantry* and the *Nagano Detachment* continued rapidly south, Bluemel's resistance failed and American II Corps units fled in great confusion. Commanders of combat regiments had no idea where their units were. Command and control in the II Corps sector evaporated after 6 April, as *Imperial Japanese Army* air power strafed the refugee-clogged trails.[79]

Maj. Gen. Edward P. King, commander of Luzon Force, was forced to cope with the sudden collapse of II Corps. General MacArthur had left Corregidor for Australia with the USAFFE headquarters staff on 12 March. Wainwright had been promoted on Corregidor to commander of what nominally was a new organization, the U.S. Forces in the Philippines (USFIP). Wainwright chose General King as chief of Luzon Force, making him Wainwright's operational commander on Bataan.[80]

King's I Corps was still holding as of 8 April, though his forces dropped southward to avoid being flanked by the deep Japanese penetration of 6 April. This withdrawal did not alleviate King's dilemma, however, since the Japanese forces continued moving rapidly toward his headquarters. King therefore finally ordered the Provisional Coastal Artillery Brigade (PA) to turn away from the coast and form as infantry just north of Cabcaben.[81]

Wainwright had standing orders from MacArthur not to surrender, and in fact late on 8 April Wainwright ordered King to attack with I Corps north toward Olongapo. Nevertheless, King determined at a conference of his staff officers that evening that the Japanese would soon be in artillery range not only of the U.S. hospitals and service areas near Mariveles on the coast, but also of Corregidor itself. This would be the case whether the Americans continued to resist or not, so there was no tactical reason to further endanger hospital patients, service troops, or combat forces. Although he had no authorization from Wainwright, King announced to his staff at midnight that he intended to surrender.[82]

King met with the advancing Maj. Gen. Kameichiro Nagano on 9 April and attempted to negotiate surrender terms for all of Luzon Force. Nagano took King prisoner but did not give any terms or recognize any surrender of the whole force. American units were still obliged to surrender individually and unconditionally to whatever enemy units they encountered, an arrangement that led to the unhappy events of the Bataan Death March.[83]

There would be more travail for U.S. troops on Bataan, and more combat on Corregidor, but as of 9 April the American operational campaign on Bataan was over.

Conclusion

The sudden disintegration of USFIP forces after 3 April 1942 suggests that the American Bataan campaign was a failure. Despite this impression, the Bataan operation was a substantial success in many respects. Facing an opposing force that was greater in numbers, reinforceable, dramatically better supplied, and supported by complete air and sea dominance, U.S. ground units resisted effectively for three and a half months. Their efforts tied down a corps-size contingent of the *Imperial Japanese Army,* preventing its use elsewhere, and distracted higher-echelon Japanese planners who were forced to continue devoting their finite energies to the recalcitrant Philippine problem. The rugged resistance on Bataan also increased the confidence of the gathering Allied war effort in a way that combat actions in Malaya and elsewhere had not done.

Perhaps the most significant factor in the Bataan achievement was the overall operational plan of retiring to an area of such strategic importance that an adversary had to attack it, yet an area that was extremely favorable to the defender. Bataan was just such a terrain. It controlled the international port of Manila, which the Japanese needed. But it presented such a narrow land front to an attacker that advantages of numbers, equipment, and mobility could not easily be brought to bear. Moreover, the mountainous, jungled terrain on Bataan offered limited fields of fire, which mitigated the effect of an adversary's superior firepower. Once the U.S. forces put a line across the peninsula, it was difficult for the Japanese to advance regardless of how many units they had in the area. The credit for this method must go to the operational planners who devised WPO–3. Resourceful staff officers designed the Bataan solution before war in the Philippines even seemed likely.

The Bataan plan was not perfectly executed, however, in several respects. Supply on Bataan was disastrously inadequate, and the reason for this was that MacArthur, beginning in October 1941, abandoned the modest defensive Bataan solution in favor of an active defense of the whole Philippine archipelago. Moreover, both he and his superiors in the War Department believed that introducing moderate air assets into the Philippines would make defense of all the islands possible, and perhaps deter attack altogether. MacArthur failed to appreciate that moderate air assets could be overcome by an enemy's air assets, and did not in themselves provide any decisive advantage to the defender.

Only on 23 December 1941 did MacArthur turn to WPO–3, even though the plan had no official standing at the time. It was only a former plan, though fortunately one discarded recently enough that officers still remembered it. Failure to retain WPO–3 throughout 1941 meant that supplies were not stockpiled adequately on Bataan, that no permanent fortifications were built, and that fifteen days passed after Pearl Harbor before significant transport to the peninsula began. The consequent shortages meant disease casualties, hardship, and premature disintegration of the combat line after 3 April. The operational plan was sound, but weak logistics partially undermined it.

The Bataan operational plan itself was not flawless, of course. Placing the Abucay-Mauban line astride Mt. Natib made it much easier for the position to be turned. On the Pilar-Bagac line, the operational dispositions were better, but defensive tactics were not. Given the two-month lull in combat, and the Japanese predominance in artillery and air power, it behooved USFIP troops to move as much of their line as possible into trenches and tunnels. Food shortages would have made such labor difficult, but such action would have shielded troops from the destruction of massive bombardment. This omission also was a major factor in the early dissolution of the American lines after 3 April.

The U.S. Bataan campaign was far from perfect. Still, by shrewd employment of limited combat resources, American forces on Bataan achieved far more than military policy makers are normally entitled to expect.

NOTES

1. Maj Carlos J. Herrera, Philippine Army (PA), "The Philippine Constabulary in the Battle of the Philippines," unpublished Ms, Ft. Leavenworth, Kans., U.S. Army-Command and General Staff College (USA-CGSC), 1947, p. 70; Louis Morton, *The Fall of the Philippines*, The War in the Pacific, U.S. Army in World War II (Washington, D.C.: U.S. Army Center of Military History, 1953), pp. 8–9.

2. Maj Alfredo M. Santos, PA, "The First Regular Division in the Battle of the Philippines," unpublished Ms, Ft. Leavenworth, Kans., USA-CGSC, 1947, p. 20; Morton, *Fall of the Philippines*, pp. 9–10.

3. Morton, *Fall of the Philippines*, pp. 10, 12.

4. Ibid., p. 10; Mark S. Watson, *Chief of Staff: Prewar Plans and Preparations*, The War Department, U.S. Army in World War II (Washington, D.C.: U.S. Army Center of Military History, 1950), pp. 103–04, 413, 426.

5. Watson, *Chief of Staff*, pp. 414, 424–25.

6. Ibid., pp. 426, 431–32.

7. Morton, *Fall of the Philippines*, pp. 15, 17; Watson, *Chief of Staff*, pp. 436–37.

8. Morton, *Fall of the Philippines*, p. 24.

9. Ibid., p. 26.

10. Ibid., pp. 26–28.

11. Watson, *Chief of Staff*, pp. 441, 447–49.

12. Morton, *Fall of the Philippines,* p. 24; Watson, *Chief of Staff*, pp. 448–49.

13. Morton, *Fall of the Philippines*, pp. 61–62.

14. Ibid., pp. 62–64.

15. Ibid., p. 64; Watson, *Chief of Staff*, p. 445.

16. Watson, *Chief of Staff*, p. 445.

17. Ibid., pp. 445–46.

18. Morton, *Fall of the Philippines*, pp. 65, 67.

19. Watson, *Chief of Staff*, pp. 446, 505; Morton, *Fall of the Philippines*, p. 71.

20. Morton, *Fall of the Philippines*, p. 72.

21. Ibid., pp. 85–87, 94; Lt. Gen. Lewis H. Brereton, *The Brereton Diaries* (New York: William Morrow, 1946), pp. 38–44, 46; Wesley F. Craven and James L. Cate, eds., *Plans and Early Operations, January 1939 to August 1942*, vol. 1, The Army Air Forces in World War II (Chicago: University of Chicago Press, 1948), pp. 201–20.

22. Morton, *Fall of the Philippines*, pp. 79, 90, 107.

23. Ibid., p. 99.

24. Ibid., pp. 124, 125, 131, 140; Lt. Gen. Jonathan M. Wainwright, *Report of Operations of USAFFE and USFIP in the Philippines, 1941–1942* [hereafter *USFIP*] (Ft. Sam Houston, Tex.: Headquarters, Fourth Army, 1946), p. 32.

25. Morton, *Fall of the Philippines*, pp. 162–63; Wainwright, *USFIP*, p. 33.

26. Morton, *Fall of the Philippines*, pp. 164–65; and see Wainwright, *USFIP*, ann. 13, "Report of Operations of Quartermaster Corps."

27. Morton, *Fall of the Philippines*, p. 165.

28. Ibid., pp. 165–66; Wainwright, *USFIP*, p. 33.

29. Morton, *Fall of the Philippines*, p. 165; Wainwright, *USFIP*, p. 28a; Lt. Gen. Jonathan M. Wainwright, *General Wainwright's Story* (Garden City, N.Y.: Doubleday, 1946), p. 41.

30. Morton, *Fall of the Philippines*, p. 168.

31. Ibid., pp. 166–67.

32. Ibid., pp. 168, 169, 180.

33. Ibid., pp. 168, 180; and see Wainwright, *USFIP*, ann. 4, "Report of Operations of North Luzon Force," pp. 6–15.

34. Morton, *Fall of the Philippines*, pp. 187–88.

35. Ibid., pp. 190, 210; Wainwright, *USFIP*, ann. 4, p. 16.
36. Morton, *Fall of the Philippines*, pp. 203–05, 208; Wainwright, *USFIP*, p. 39; Wainwright, *Wainwright's Story*, p. 44.
37. Morton, *Fall of the Philippines*, pp. 211, 215.
38. Ibid., pp. 216–17, 223, 225, 230; Wainwright, *USFIP*, p. 43.
39. Morton, *Fall of the Philippines*, p. 245.
40. Ibid., p. 247; Wainwright, *USFIP*, pp. 43–44.
41. Ibid.
42. Morton, *Fall of the Philippines*, p. 248.
43. Ibid., pp. 247, 248.
44. Ibid.
45. Ibid., p. 252.
46. Ibid., pp. 255–56.
47. Ibid., p. 255; and see Wainwright, *USFIP*, ann. 13.
48. Morton, *Fall of the Philippines*, pp. 256–57; Wainwright, *USFIP*, p. 42.
49. Morton, *Fall of the Philippines*, pp. 28, 258.
50. Ibid., pp. 258–59.
51. Ibid., pp. 264, 266.
52. Ibid., p. 275.
53. Ibid., p. 276.
54. Ibid., p. 277.
55. Ibid., pp. 285–87; Wainwright, *USFIP*, p. 47.
56. Ibid., pp. 280–81; Wainwright, *USFIP*, ann. 4, pp. 19–20.
57. Morton, *Fall of the Philippines*, pp. 282, 283.
58. Ibid., p. 284.
59. Ibid., pp. 290–91, 293; Wainwright, *USFIP*, p. 48.
60. Morton, *Fall of the Philippines*, pp. 294, 295.
61. Ibid., p. 293.
62. Ibid., pp. 293, 294.
63. Ibid., pp. 325, 326, 327.
64. Ibid., pp. 297, 330–31, 335–36, 346; Wainwright, *USFIP*, p. 49; Wainwright, *Wainwright's Story*, pp. 61–62.
65. Morton, *Fall of the Philippines,* pp. 347, 350–52; Wainwright, *USFIP*, p. 53.
66. Morton, *Fall of the Philippines*, pp. 351–52.
67. Ibid., pp. 367, 373.
68. Ibid., pp. 376–77, 383; and see Wainwright, *USFIP*, ann. 14, "Medical Department Activities."
69. Morton, *Fall of the Philippines*, pp. 376, 378, 379.
70. Ibid., pp. 378, 380–83.
71. Ibid., pp. 380, 384.
72. Ibid., pp. 417, 418.
73. Ibid., pp. 421–22, 424; Wainwright, *USFIP*, p. 57.
74. Morton, *Fall of the Philippines,* pp. 424–25; Wainwright, *USFIP*, p. 58.
75. Morton, *Fall of the Philippines*, pp. 425, 427–29.
76. Ibid., pp. 432, 433.
77. Ibid., p. 440.
78. Ibid., pp. 447–49; Wainwright, *USFIP*, pp. 60–61; ann. 5, "Report of Operations of South Luzon Force," p. 50.
79. Morton, *Fall of the Philippines*, pp. 448–50.
80. Ibid., pp. 359, 365; Wainwright, *Wainwright's Story*, pp. 65–67.
81. Morton, *Fall of the Philippines*, pp. 451, 454.
82. Ibid., pp. 452, 455, 457, 458.
83. Ibid., pp. 462, 466–67; Wainwright, *USFIP*, p. 61.

PART II

The U.S. Army on the Home Front 1940–1945

Introduction

Large numbers of U.S. Army troops served in the continental United States (CONUS) rather than overseas during World War II. The following group of papers describes the efforts of the home-based Army to mobilize the U.S. economy for war and to train and equip soldiers for overseas duty.

In "The Development of the Ammunition Industrial Base: 1940–1942," Robert Bouilly explains the origins of the government-owned, contractor-operated (GOCO) ammunition plants built during the early years of the war. Bouilly demonstrates how the geographical location, operating methods, and production contracts of these plants all reflected the fact that Army planners were attempting to avoid the mistakes of planners during the previous war.

The new ammunition plants remained government owned and contractor operated because no commercial use could be projected for them in peacetime. But the government avoided using the cost-plus-percentage-of-the-cost (CPPC) contracts of World War I because Congress and the American public erroneously believed that such contracts were expensive. Instead, Washington relied on cost-plus-fixed-fee (CPFF) contracts throughout World War II.

New ammunition plants were constructed in the Great Lakes and Midwest regions because the East Coast facilities built during the Great War had overloaded and strangled important transportation and communication networks. Centrally located factories could ship goods to ports in every region of the country. Planners also believed that those industries situated in the Midwest would be less vulnerable to air attack.

The Army Ordnance Department controlled eighty-three GOCO ammunition facilities by 1943, when the Joint Chiefs of Staff halted construction in favor of ammunition production. Bouilly concludes that the great expansion of ammunition production facilities between 1940 and 1943 was successful and that these plants were a critical part of the "Arsenal of Democracy."

Frances Martin describes the job assignments, working conditions, and experiences of women who worked in Army Chemical Warfare Service (CWS) plants during World War II in "Women Workers at Chemical

Warfare Service Plants During World War II." Female workers at these plants produced a variety of items, from gas masks and protective clothing to chemical mortars, shells, grenades, and incendiary bombs. Martin examines in detail four plants located in different areas of the country: Edgewood Arsenal, Maryland; Pine Bluff Arsenal, Arkansas; Huntsville Arsenal, Alabama; and Rocky Mountain Arsenal, Colorado.

The typical woman employed at a CWS arsenal worked as a munitions handler in a munitions assembly plant with about 150 fellow employees, most female, both white and black. Munitions handlers performed jobs they could learn quickly and received little on-the-job training. Although few women worked in traditionally male jobs that required skill and experience—such as electricians, linemen, and carpenters—before World War II all munitions work had been an exclusively male occupation.

The role-breaking opportunities in munitions work exposed women to risks they had never faced before. Safety was a constant source of concern, especially in the production of white phosphorus grenades and in incendiary-filling operations. Fires broke out frequently at the Pine Bluff and Rocky Mountain Arsenals. The worst accident occurred at Edgewood just before the end of the war in May 1945 when twelve women were killed and over fifty injured in an explosion involving the manufacture of white phosphorus grenades.

According to Martin, the majority of female munitions workers were laid off at the end of the war, often at the same time as the munitions factories were hiring men under different job titles. Women who did not continue to work for the government after the war discovered later that they would not receive social security credits for their wartime jobs with the CWS because the government had its own retirement program. For some women, says Martin, "credit for war work meant the difference between having or not having enough work over a lifetime to get Social Security retirement benefits based on their own work record." Although this regulation did not apply just to women, they felt the greatest impact because they were the most likely to be laid off from government employment after the war.

In "Training Linguists for the Pacific War, 1941–1942," James McNaughton describes how the Army tapped the nation's Japanese-Americans to serve as translators, interpreters, and interrogators in the Pacific. McNaughton emphasizes the difficulty of locating sufficient numbers of Japanese-speaking Americans for military duty and how essential trained linguists were in conducting intelligence efforts against the enemy. The Army eventually was forced to start a school for the sole purpose of training such linguists, an effort which marked the Army's first large-scale language training program.

A logical source for Japanese linguists was the Nisei, second generation Japanese-Americans living on the West Coast. However, in response
to widespread prejudice against these citizens, the government forced most
into internment camps during much of the war. Nisei males of military age
residing in internment camps were understandably bitter about the treatment accorded them and their families, and some avoided military service
even when it was offered. Those willing to enter the Army usually preferred to demonstrate their loyalty more dramatically than attending a language school and opted to join combat units.

The Army discovered also that the majority of those Nisei already in
uniform had only rudimentary knowledge of Japanese, with less than 10
percent possessing any linguistic skills. Paradoxically, the Army saw those
young men who had been sent to Japan for schooling and were familiar
with the language as "security risks."

McNaughton traces the founding of the Army's Japanese language
school and describes the difficulties the school faced due to racial prejudice and the general scarcity of resources: space, furniture, teaching supplies, teachers, and students. At one point the War Department ruled that
Nisei soldiers could not be sent overseas, thus rendering the few Nisei
Japanese language students the school had managed to recruit ineligible
for overseas service. Although this ruling was eventually rescinded, many
Army commanders in the field were initially suspicious of Nisei interpreters, and placed them under guard in rear echelon areas. Nevertheless,
once commanders realized the potential value of these translators and
interpreters at the operational and tactical levels, they were able to make
significant contributions to the Pacific war effort.

In "The San Francisco Port of Embarkation in World War II: A Study
in Command and Control," Mason Schaefer explores the workings of the
San Francisco Port of Embarkation (SFPE), which supplied the Army in
the Pacific on its assorted and ever-changing island battlefronts with
troops, supplies, equipment, weapons, and ammunition. Although the port
command performed adequately, its relationship with Army leaders at the
Office of the Chief of Transportation and the Army Service Forces in
Washington was far from satisfactory, and Washington eventually fired
two of the port's commanding generals.

Misunderstandings were common. The Army staffs in Washington frequently criticized the SFPE for "refusing" to send proper estimates of the
number of ships it would need at a given time in the future. The estimates
were needed to properly allocate shipping resources to ports around the
world. Schaefer demonstrates how difficult it was for the SFPE to provide
the required information. In 1944 the Southwest Pacific theater requested

massive amounts of supplies from the SFPE. But when the port command sent the requested supplies, it sometimes discovered that the island ports did not have the capacity to unload and store all the supplies they had asked for. As loaded ships sat idle at these overseas locations for weeks, the SFPE's original estimates of the number of ships available for transporting supplies became invalid. Washington blamed San Francisco for the discrepancy.

According to Schaefer, the SFPE was caught between the constantly changing needs of the Pacific commanders it was attempting to serve and the needs of planners in Washington. In response, the SFPE adopted a crisis management technique that focused on solving problems in the field but failed to deal with those involving its superiors in Washington. More serious, as it devoted increasing efforts to solving short-term problems, the command began neglecting prosaic fundamentals such as keeping records, standardizing personnel management, and streamlining interdepartmental communications. Schaefer concludes that more attention to detail and less emphasis on crisis management would have allowed the SFPE to serve Army leadership in Washington and eventually the Pacific theater more efficiently.

In the last paper in this section, "Race Relations and the Contributions of African-American Troops in Alaska," Charles Hendricks reminds us of the critical logistical work of African-American engineer units in Alaska. Hendricks points out that despite assignment to an isolated geographical location with an extremely harsh climate, a minimum of heavy equipment, and less than optimal working conditions, African-American soldiers assigned to Alaska and the Aleutian Islands successfully completed roads, port facilities, runways, and bridges with few racial incidents and none of the mass disaffections or rebellions which occurred in CONUS and other theaters. Hendricks attributes this to the strong, fair-minded leadership that the troops experienced while in the Alaskan theater.

The Development of the Ammunition Industrial Base 1940–1942

Robert H. Bouilly

The development of an adequate ammunition base was an integral part of America's mobilization effort during World War II. Today, some fifty years later, a significant portion of the ammunition production base built between 1940 and 1943 forms the core of the present ammunition production base for mobilization. Although less than half of the twenty-five existing ammunition plants are presently active, the remaining plants represent a reserve. The basic managerial, contractual, and ownership system used to produce ammunition in World War II continues relatively unchanged to this day. In this system munitions and munitions components are manufactured by private contractors who run ammunition manufacturing facilities owned by the U.S. government. These facilities are usually referred to as GOCO (government-owned, contractor-operated) plants.

These ammunition plants are distinctive because of their GOCO status. Only the Department of Energy (DOE) nuclear plants and a few U.S. Air Force facilities share the same arrangement of ownership and management. These DOE and Air Force facilities also have their origins in World War II, and most share the same type of contractual arrangement with the government known as the cost-plus-fixed-fee (CPFF) contract. Variants have appeared over the years, but the cost-plus type persists and predominates. This too is a product of the mobilization effort.

The ammunition plants are spread across the interior of the United States in a curious arrangement. There is little centralization of production. Metal parts plants produce shells and propellant casings which usually have to be shipped hundreds of miles to load, assemble, and pack (LAP) plants. Similarly, explosive and propellant plants have to ship their chemical products to the LAP plants. Decentralization of production predominates. There is little hint of the River Rouge type of vertical integration of manufacturing that Henry Ford helped pioneer. Only the troubled Army Ammunition Plant (AAP) at Picayune, Mississippi, is vertically integrated with its combination of metal parts production with the LAP of projectiles. It is also one of the few Army ammunition facilities built since World War II. The present dispersion and specialization of plants obviously has its origins in World War II. Less obvious is the fact that the system is older and a product of the World War I experience.

This article is a brief examination of the origins of the present production system. It discusses the removal of control over the construction of these facilities from the Ordnance Department to the Quartermaster Corps and ultimately to the Corps of Engineers, where it remains today—a shift which is still bemoaned in the ammunition procurement community as it struggles with post–World War II production facilities built for the Army. They include a black powder plant in Indiana which does not work and nitroguanidine facilities in Kansas which required substantial modification before meeting designed production rates. Other Vietnam War–era projects such as the continuous TNT (trinitrotoluene) lines at Newport Army Ammunition Plant and the acid facilities at the Badger Plant in Wisconsin also have never worked or did not meet design specifications after being constructed.

This paper also notes the long tradition of Army production of ammunition for other services and allies. The tradition tends to be ignored in peacetime mobilization planning because powerful political considerations encourage a narrow view of requirements. Idle plants in peacetime are expensive and therefore unpopular. Yet the United States has found itself supplying ammunition to others not only in World War I and World War II but also in the Korean and Vietnam conflicts. It will most likely be required to do so again in the future.

The story ends with the sharp decrease in plant construction which followed resolution of the "sufficiency" debate during the latter part of 1942. At that time the Army found its construction program constrained as the War Production Board forced a review of the program by the Joint Chiefs of Staff. Subsequently, the Joint Chiefs trimmed both the Army's requirements and its construction goals.

The material examined here is not new. The literature on mobilization in World War II is considerable. A number of mobilization studies which consider ammunition production in World War II also look at interwar planning.[1] Some more recent mobilization studies refer to the Army's World War II experience, but none look at the present ammunition complex and try to locate the sources of its configuration.[2] This study is an attempt to examine more broadly the roots of the present ammunition complex which lie in the mobilization effort of World War II and beyond.

Before examining the creation of an ammunition production base at the beginning of World War II, it is necessary to revisit the World War I mobilization experience because there is a significant link between the two efforts. The mobilization planners in World War II studied the World War I experience and in a number of ways copied it.

Mobilization in 1917–1918 has been characterized as "pure improvisation. There was no prearranged plan, no carefully designed administrative machinery."[3] Even so, the ordnance departments of the War Department and the Navy made similar choices as they developed their ammunition production bases. Both depended on the private sector to provide metal parts for ammunition.[4] Both prevailed on the du Pont de Nemours Company to provide the bulk of the explosives and propellants they needed because du Pont stood as the colossus of American explosives and propellant production. Du Pont had retained its dominance in the industry despite an antitrust suit that forced it to divest a portion of its facilities in 1912 for the creation of the Hercules and Atlas Powder Companies.[5] In the end, fully 20 percent of the total explosives and propellant production for the Allies throughout World War I came from du Pont factories.[6]

Shortly after the start of the European War, British and French purchasing commissions contracted with American companies, especially du Pont, for the production of ammunition. This fostered a large increase in production and in production facilities even before the United States declared war in 1917.[7]

When the United States entered the war, the Allies noted the large American production of propellants and explosives in comparison to the long lead time required for the United States to manufacture a significant number of heavy guns. As a result, the United States agreed that it should concentrate on expanding its powder and explosives production for itself and Allied troops while France and Great Britain would equip the American Expeditionary Force with their artillery.[8]

The Ordnance Department's effort to increase the production of propellants and explosives concentrated on expanding propellant facilities and on providing the raw materials for explosives. Faced with a dearth of private capital, the government found it necessary to finance many of these projects. In all, the Ordnance Department financed and owned 53 ammunition production or raw materials facilities at a cost of $360 million.[9]

At the heart of the Ordnance Department's efforts was the creation of two huge smokeless powder plants: one at Nitro, West Virginia, and the other, called Old Hickory, just outside Nashville, Tennessee. The new plants would supply the requirements of the U.S. Army and allow the existing production to go to the Allies.[10] As in World War II, the government built facilities that allowed the country to produce explosives and propellants for foreign governments as well as for its own armed forces. The two plants were so large that they absorbed $150 million of the $360 million wartime facility program for ammunition.[11]

Chief of Ordnance Maj. Gen. William Crozier approached du Pont early in December 1917 with a proposal that the firm build and run the smokeless powder plants.[12] After months of negotiation,[13] du Pont accepted, only to have the War Industries Board reject the contract.[14] Bernard Baruch, the head of the War Industries Board, then contacted Daniel C. Jackling, who was a prominent mining engineer, and persuaded him to oversee the construction of the factories.[15] However, Jackling soon found that help from the du Pont company was indispensable. Eventually du Pont received a contract through Jackling to build the Old Hickory plant and run it for eighteen months under a cost-plus-a-percentage-of-cost (CPPC) contract. Both plants were in production by the close of the war, although not at full capacity. In the end du Pont built a larger plant, more quickly, at Old Hickory than did Jackling at Nitro. Du Pont's performance was not lost on the Ordnance Department and was a major reason why the company built fifty-four plants at thirty-two locations for the government in World War II.[16]

Du Pont's CPPC contract to run the Old Hickory Plant was typical of wartime Ordnance contracts. It differed little from the contract Hercules received to run the Nitro plant. The essential feature of the contracts was the cost section. The percentage-of-cost portion constituted the company's profit. The dollar amounts were determined after completion of the contract.[17]

Within two months of the armistice in November 1918, all production of powder and explosives came to a halt. A swift dismantling of the ammunition production base followed.[18] The Ordnance Department tried to hold on to some production capacity at the arsenals and even kept Old Hickory in reserve for a brief period. However, the pressure to reduce government facilities was so great that little was saved.[19] The Nitro plant had cost $60 million to build, but it brought only $8.5 million in salvage.[20] In another typical conversion from wartime production, the Amatol Plant at Amatol, New Jersey, became the site of the Atlantic City Speedway.[21] Old Hickory underwent a period of salvage before du Pont returned to a portion of the site in 1923 and built a rayon factory.[22] Finally, its large powder storage area experienced a devastating fire in 1924[23] which finished the plant as an ordnance facility. The only propellant facilities left in the United States were at the Army's Picatinny Arsenal at Dover, New Jersey, and the Navy's Indian Head Powder Factory at Indian Head, Maryland. A single du Pont TNT factory at Barksdale, Wisconsin, also survived. The productive capacity of the three remaining facilities was not large enough to sustain a war effort.

In the years after the war, a public reaction set in. Charges of war profiteering brought the CPPC type of contract into disrepute. Congress eventually outlawed its use because it believed that these contracts provided no incentive for the contractor to contain costs and actually encouraged the contractor to increase costs as a means of earning larger profits.[24] Congress was misguided. Contrary to popular belief, the fees were subject to a ceiling in both construction contracts and production contracts. Construction contracts were known as cost-plus-with-sliding-scale-and-fixed-maximum-fee contracts. These contracts were quite a mouthful to say which probably helped doom them in the eyes of legislators. As the contract type said, they had fixed maximum fees. Perhaps the fixed maximum fees could be judged too high, but there was no legerdemain here. Production contracts also had a variety of limits. Most were based on the modern "should cost" concept which calculated the cost of an item and established a maximum price per item based on that calculation. Furthermore, many of these contracts were renegotiated to provide lower percentages of profit after production experience indicated that lower production risks and costs were achievable.[25]

Planners in the War Department also reflected on the war experience and realized that the bulk of the wartime munitions production had been confined chiefly to a geographical triangle connecting Boston, Massachusetts; Pittsburgh, Pennsylvania; and Wilmington, Delaware. This concentration resulted in a slow strangulation of the industrial program during World War I caused by breakdowns in the power and transportation systems.[26]

In contrast to the pre–World War I period, much more planning occurred during the interwar period because the National Defense Act of 1920 gave the Army responsibility for mobilization planning. The Army's effort resulted in a series of plans which appeared in 1931, 1933, 1936, and 1939.[27]

As the planning process went forward, the Army made several decisions that shaped the mobilization effort of World War II. First, during 1934 the Ordnance Department went on record that the siting (the location) of future plants would be in the interior of the country. This recognized the military threat posed by aerial warfare. It also acknowledged the need to disperse industrial activity as a means of relieving strains on the transportation system.[28]

Another decision which came out of interwar planning concerned who would produce the ammunition. The services decided that the Army would provide the bulk of the explosives and propellants needed in a future conflict.[29] In 1940 the services further integrated their production efforts through the Joint Aeronautical Board, which standardized bomb types.[30] Later, in 1943, when the Army's load, assemble, and pack plant system had become established, the Army took over the loading of Navy bombs, except aerial depth charges.[31] For its part, the Navy occasionally produced heavy ammunition for the Army.[32]

Perhaps most striking about the interwar planning was its tentative approach toward requirements. Much of the early planning during the 1920s was unrealistic.[33] A Signal Corps planner went so far as to call these early mobilization plans "in the safe mirages."[34] Only in 1936 did the planners begin to associate industrial mobilization plans with a particular size and configuration of the Army. The result of this effort was the Protective Mobilization Plan (PMP) of 1939,[35] which became the basis of the June 1940 mobilization program.[36]

Development of the plan proved informative. The planners began to realize that the size of the mobilized Army would have to be cut back over the near term to accommodate industrial limitations, and mobilization began to be seen as a time-phased process. Plans for a four-million-man Army had to be cut back to an initial expansion of a two-million-man Army.

Even with a cutback in the proposed size of the Army, the amount of materiel required for a two-million-man force made the Army change its expectations. Previous assumptions that industry would provide the requisite plant expansions and new plants gave way to the realization that the government would have to finance the creation of a munitions industry. Realization became reality in mid-1940 when "construction emerged as the controlling factor in preparedness."[37] Even though the Army had begun systematic plant surveys in 1923 and had completed its ammunition procurement plans in 1934, it took industrial surveys keyed to the requirements of the Protective Mobilization Plan to show the Ordnance Department the need for building and financing numerous ammunition plants.[38]

Once the Army realized the need for new plants, government financing and ownership of these contractor-operated plants seemed natural. This approach had been used in capitalist countries before. The United States and Great Britain had both taken this approach in World War I. Britain had called its approach the "national factory system."[39] Again, at the start of World War II the British constructed a very similar system made up of "agency factories."[40] In a like manner, Canada created a number of munitions facilities during World War II which were government owned and contractor operated.[41]

Mobilization in the United States began with passage of the Munitions Program of 30 June 1940. As the Low Countries were overrun and France fell, President Franklin D. Roosevelt asked Congress for funding to start mobilization. William S. Knudsen of the National Defense Advisory Commission (NDAC) then asked each of the services to provide estimates of its industrial and materiel needs. A portion of the Ordnance Department's response contained a request for the funding of a number of ammunition facilities which became known as "first wave" plants. They were to be of substantial construction and would be retained after the war. Within the next two months construction began on forty-two ordnance plants—most of them ammunition production facilities.[42]

The new ammunition plants were to be government owned and contractor operated because no commercial use could be projected for them in peacetime. Most were to be completely financed by the War Department.[43] Exceptions included most toluene (a petroleum-based feedstock chemical for the production of TNT) plants and several ammonia facilities such as the Lake Charles (Louisiana) and the Muscle Shoals (Alabama) plants which were financed by the Defense Plant Corporation and the TVA (Tennessee Valley Authority), respectively. These facilities could produce gasoline or fertilizers in peacetime.[44]

Planning for this system of facilities preceded the crisis of 1940 as the Ordnance Department decided to copy much of the World War I system. That system featured three types of plants. As was the case in World War I metal parts would be provided by private industry because a capacity for their production already existed. Government-owned facilities would produce the propellant powder and explosives. The assembly of ammunition would be accomplished in facilities separate from the chemical plants, and would also be government owned.[45]

In 1936 Ordnance Department representatives met with two small arms ammunition manufacturers, Remington (a subsidiary of du Pont) and Western Cartridge, to establish a basis for wartime expansion. Out of this planning came the unit plan system which standardized the productive capacity and machinery for small-caliber lines.[46] In the spring of 1937, the Ordnance Department developed a similar initiative for large-caliber ammunition production planning as it established a small planning and liaison office in Wilmington, Delaware, close to the headquarters of du Pont and Hercules. This office formulated plans, selected tentative sites, and began to purchase a limited amount of equipment which required a considerable lead time before delivery.[47] Most construction of new ammunition plants came in three successive "waves." Congress authorized the first wave in the June 1940 appropriation. The second came in response to creation of the Lend-Lease program in March 1941, and a third followed Pearl Harbor. Two smaller waves followed, but they involved minor adjustments to the requirements program, and few new plants resulted from the last two waves. Instead, most of the money went for plant expansions at established sites and for additional machinery.[48]

The cost of the ammunition plants was high. The 25 load, assemble, and pack plants; 21 explosives and propellants works; 12 chemical works; and 13 small arms ammunition manufacturing plants cost more than $3 billion for the initial waves.[49] Total facilities expenditures for the war came to $4.3 billion out of the Army wartime construction program of $10.6 billion.[50]

Of the great wartime, government-sponsored, industrial plant construction programs, the ammunition program was the first to be substantially completed and the most expensive except for the aircraft plant program. Because it preceded the rubber, aviation gas, aluminum, and carbon steel programs, it enjoyed relatively few delays due to construction material shortages. Plants and works built in the first two waves were in production by mid-1943—in time to contribute to the peak in wartime ammunition production.[51]

The contractual arrangement for both building and operating the plants was a revival of the cost-plus instruments used in World War I. Stripped of the percentage of cost features that had been found objectionable, the new CPFF form worked reasonably well in World War II. Congress legalized its use in the June 1940 legislation as a means of financing plant construction. These CPFF contracts guaranteed construction firms their costs and made it possible for the government to advance up to 30 percent of the contract price so contractors could obtain materials. Moreover, the arrangement provided flexibility and safety in operating the plants. Government ownership under this arrangement allowed plants to remain relatively idle in low demand periods without the necessity of changing to other forms of production, as the search for profits would dictate in private industry. Removal of the profit incentive also discouraged cutting corners with safety—a factor which helped build an enviable safety record during the war. The Ordnance Department's early success with this contract form allowed the Department to keep using it throughout the war when the Army Service Forces put extensive pressure on other departments to switch to fixed price contracting.[52]

When the construction period began in earnest during the latter part of 1940, a number of conflicts arose. Basically, the Ordnance Department wanted autonomy in developing its program. The Ordnance Department clashed with both the War Department and civilian plant site review boards over the siting of plants. Despite its commitments to geographic dispersion in the interior of the country, the Ordnance Department wanted access to industrial centers such as Detroit and to western New York State locations such as Buffalo. These lay outside the Georgian Bay–Lake Ontario defense line—a line which made up part of the 200–250–mile protective strip inside the U.S. border. Within this strip new plant construction was discouraged. Often the War Department honored the limitation of the defense line and vetoed the proposed Ordnance Department sites outside the boundary.[53] As a result, the department located most ammunition plants in the middle of the country, in conformance with the prewar plans.

The June 1940 legislation and subsequent appropriations stipulated that all "non-command" (industrial facilities) construction would be subject to the approval of civilian boards. The agendas of these boards occasionally differed from that of the Ordnance Department. Before his War Production Board days, Donald Nelson headed the Plant Site Committee in the Office of Production Management. Nelson was proud of his committee's efforts to interject labor supply and postwar industrial development considerations into the process. His committee also enjoyed a measure of success in protecting prime farmland from being used for ammunition plants.[54] Even so, the Ordnance Department's insistence on a logical location of its chemical plants in relation to the loading plants and shipping points usually prevailed.[55]

The Ordnance Department preferred to build its plants in conjunction with large, established concerns as it had in World War I through contracts with firms such as du Pont. This desire brought Ordnance into conflict with the construction branches of the Army. (Prior to December 1941 the Construction Division of the Quartermaster Corps held this responsibility. Then, in December the responsibility transferred to the Corps of Engineers.) In the spring of 1940 the rising head of the Army's construction program, Col. Brehon B. Somervell, insisted that the Quartermaster Corps (and later the Corps of Engineers) should control the construction of the ammunition plants. He and the Ordnance Department conducted a running battle for control of Ordnance facility construction.[56]

In the end, Somervell won much of the battle. Initially, Ordnance retained more control of the selection of architects and contractors for the complicated propellants, explosives, and chemical plants than it did on the simpler load, assemble, and pack plants.[57] When the Construction Division of the Quartermaster Corps obtained responsibility for building the plants, it went further and split a number of architectural engineering contracts between firms in order to spread out the workload.[58] When planning began for the second wave of plants Somervell prevailed in his demands for advanced planning and for the development of standardized plans for each of the several plant types. At Somervell's insistence, the second-wave plants were quite austere and designed for a mere five-year life span.[59]

Ultimate control over the size of the ammunition plant program eventually developed outside the War Department. In the wake of a series of preliminary organizations, President Roosevelt created the War Production Board (WPB) just weeks after Pearl Harbor. This civilian super agency was responsible for coordinating the wartime economy and asked fundamental questions such as those Knudsen had asked earlier in June 1940. "How much production of war material is necessary to win the war?" It also asked another question not generally asked by the War Department: "Can the economy meet the requirements set forth by the military?" By mid-1942 the statisticians in the WPB concluded that the Army was demanding more than the economy could provide. What ensued was the famous "sufficiency" debate. The Army was not used to thinking in terms of an entire economy and had an inadequately integrated requirements program. The battle between Donald Nelson, who now headed the WPB, and Somervell, who now headed the Army Service Forces, over the size of the 1943 program eventually resulted in its referral to the Joint Chiefs of Staff for judicious pruning.[60]

Resolution of the debate signaled an important change in the course of the war effort because it marked the end of the early construction efforts in favor of an emphasis on production.[61] The Joint Chiefs of Staff did prune a number of construction programs from the 1943 budget—an action that was probably overdue, because most ammunition plants had proved to be more productive than projected, and not all anticipated Lend-Lease demands materialized. The result was a surplus of productive capacity. For example, the Gopher Ordnance Works in Rosemount, Minnesota, had been built to meet Russian Lend-Lease requirements. It cost $110,000 and stood unused during 1943 and 1944.[62]

Bureaucratic confusion also contributed to the excess in productive capacity. The Navy had contributed money to finance Army plants which provided ammunition for the Navy, but this was discontinued in 1943 after Congress uncovered a number of instances where the two services had been provided with duplicate funding.

Duplication also took another form. During 1942 the Navy objected to the low priority the Army had assigned the construction of plants designated to make Explosive D (ammonium picrate) used in large-caliber naval guns. In compensation for this apparent oversight, the Navy Ordnance Department began to finance its own facilities—especially the Lansing Paint and Color Company in Lansing, Michigan. At the same time the

Army Ordnance Department began construction of the New York Ordnance Works near Syracuse, New York, on "a misunderstanding of the requirements of the Navy Department."[63]

It was time to stop building new plants. The War Production Board's Facilities Bureau, for its part, recognized the excess capacity and halted construction at several incomplete plants including Vigo, Erie, and Pennsylvania.[64]

At its peak the Army Ordnance Department controlled about eighty-three GOCO ammunition and related facilities. Seventy-one came under the jurisdiction of the Field Director of Ammunition Plants at St. Louis while the Small Arms Ammunition Suboffice at Frankford Arsenal in Philadelphia controlled twelve others.[65]

Their contribution to the war effort was significant. The plants manufactured just under 10 percent of all munitions produced in the United States during World War II. The figures are so large as to be hard to comprehend. They produced approximately 1,177 million rounds of small arms ammunition, 57,476 short tons of ground artillery ammunition, and 45,000 short tons of aircraft bombs. This was supplemented by the production of considerable amounts of bulk explosives and propellants for other uses.[66] In more graphic terms this productive output would have filled a train of boxcars that stretched from coast to coast several times over. Just the production of steel for the U.S. requirement of large caliber projectiles required 600 rail cars a week at the peak of the war effort.[67]

In sum, mobilization of ammunition production facilities at the start of World War II was a success. As mobilization planners borrowed heavily from the World War I mobilization experience they helped create an "Arsenal of Democracy," as Donald Nelson so proudly described the American effort. The system of production worked so well that important elements of it remain in use today.

NOTES

1. R. Elberton Smith, *The Army and Economic Mobilization*, United States Army in World War II (Washington, D.C.: U.S. Army Center of Military History, 1959); Harry C. Thomson and Lida Mayo, *The Ordnance Department: Procurement and Supply*, United States Army in World War II (Washington, D.C.: U.S. Army Center of Military History, 1960).

2. Harry F. Ennis, *Peacetime Industrial Preparedness for Wartime Ammunition Production* (Washington, D.C.: National Defense University, 1980).

3. Harold W. Thatcher, *Planning for Industrial Mobilization, 1920–1940* (Washington, D.C.: Office of the Quartermaster General, 1943), p. 2.

4. Benedict Crowell and Robert Wilson, *Demobilization: Our Industrial and Military Demobilization After the Armistice, 1918– 1920* (New Haven: Yale University Press, 1923), pp. 121, 124; Bureau of Ordnance, *Navy Ordnance Activities: World War 1917–1918* (Washington, D.C.: Government Printing Office, 1920), pp. 74–75.

5. William S. Dutton, *Du Pont: One Hundred and Forty Years* (New York: Charles Scribner's Sons, 1949), pp. 177–79.

6. E. I. Du Pont de Nemours and Co., *Du Pont: The Autobiography of an American Enterprise* (New York: Charles Scribner's Sons, 1952), p. 115.

7. Grosvenor Clarkson, *Industrial America in the World War: The Strategy Behind the Line, 1917–1918* (New York: Houghton Mifflin Co., 1923), p. 407.

8. Harvey A. DeWeerd, "Production Lag in the American Ordnance Program: 1917–1918" (University of Michigan Dissertation, 1927), pp. 130–33, Military History Institute, Carlisle Barracks, Pa.

9. Benedict Crowell, *America's Munitions, 1917–1918* (Washington, D.C.: Government Printing Office, 1919), p. 105; J. Franklin Crowell, *Government War Contracts* (New York: Oxford University Press, 1920), p. 106; Lt. Comdr. Carleton H. Wright, "American Production of Military High Explosives and their Raw Materials," *United States Naval Institute Proceedings* 46 (October 1920): 1561–97.

10. Bernard M. Baruch, *American Industry in the War: A Report of the War Industries Board* (Washington, D.C.: Government Printing Office, 1921), pp. 176–77.

11. Crowell, America's Munitions, p. 105; Maj. Gen. William Crozier, *Ordnance and the World War* (New York: Charles Scribner's Sons, 1920), pp. 260–61.

12. Crozier, *Ordnance and the World War*, pp. 244–68.

13. Wright, "American Production of Military High Explosives and their Raw Materials," p. 125.

14. DeWeerd, "Production Lag in the American Ordnance Program," p. 134.

15. Dutton, *Du Pont: One Hundred and Forty Years*, pp. 109–11; Bernard M. Baruch, *Baruch: My Own Story* (New York: Holt and Co., 1957), p. 228; Crozier, *Ordnance and the World War*, pp. 245–68.

16. E. I. Du Pont de Nemours and Co., *Du Pont: The Autobiography of an American Enterprise*, p. 113; W. S. Carpenter, Jr., "Industry in World War II: The Record of E. I. du Pont de Nemours and Co.," *Army Ordnance* 30 (May–June 1946): 313–15.

17. Crozier, *Ordnance and the World War*, pp. 263–65.

18. Crowell and Wilson, *Demobilization: Our Industrial and Military Demobilization After the Armistice*, pp. 181–88.

19. Constance McLaughlin Green, Harry C. Thomson, and Peter C. Roots, *The Ordnance Department: Planning Munitions for War*, United States Army in World War II (Washington, D.C.: U.S. Army Center of Military History, 1955), p. 61.

20. Ordnance Corps, *The Ordnance Corps: 1812–1956*, n.p., n.d., p. 165.

21. "From War to Peace—Amatol Arsenal Becomes a Race Track," *Army Ordnance* 6 (May–June 1926): 448.

22. Margaret M. Tootle, "A History of Old Hickory, Tennessee" (MA Thesis, George Peabody College for Teachers, 1953), pp. 14–15, 21–22.

23. F. H. Miles, Jr., "The Old Hickory Fire," *Army Ordnance* 5 (September–October 1924): 518–20.

24. C. M. Culver, "Federal Government Procurement—An Uncharted Course Through Turbulent Waters, Part 2—World War I to World War II," *Contract Management* (July 1984): 9.

25. Crowell and Wilson, *Demobilization: Our Industrial and Military Demobilization After the Armistice*, pp. 115–20, 124–25.

26. Margaret L. Coit, *Mr. Baruch* (Boston: Houghton Mifflin Co., 1957), pp. 182–83; Douglas M. Considine, "From the Ground Up: Our Chemical Industry Had the War-Time Advantage of Starting Practically from Scratch," *Scientific American* 166 (June 1942): 278.

27. Marvin A. Kreidberg and Merton G. Henry, *History of Military Mobilization in the United States Army: 1775–1945* (Washington, D.C.: Department of the Army, 1955), pp. 503–08; Thatcher, *Planning for Industrial Mobilization*; Harry B. Yoshpe, "Economic Mobilization Planning Between the Two World Wars," *Military Affairs* 16 (Summer 1952): 71–83; Robert H. Connery, *The Navy and the Industrial Mobilization in World War II* (Princeton, N.J.: Princeton University Press, 1951), pp. 31–52.

28. Industrial College of the Armed Forces, *Study of Experience in Industrial Mobilization in World War II: Construction of New Facilities* (Washington, D.C.: Industrial College of the Armed Forces, 1947), pp. 139–40.

29. Berkeley R. Lewis, *History of the Ordnance Department in World War II, Monograph No. 4, Ammunition, 1 July 1940–31 August 1945* (Washington, D.C.: Office of the Chief of Ordnance, 1945), pp. 16–17; Bureau of Ordnance, Rockets, Explosives and Propellants, Pyrotechnics, n.d., unpublished Ms, Navy Library, Washington Navy Yard, Washington, D.C., p. 299; Smith, *The Army and Economic Mobilization*, p. 144.

30. Lewis, *History of the Ordnance Department in World War II, Monograph No. 4, Ammunition, 1 July 1940–31 August 1945*, p. 70.

31. Bureau of Ordnance, Rockets, Explosives and Propellants, Pyrotechnics, pp. 393–94.

32. John D. Millett, *The Organization and Role of the Army Service Forces*, United States Army in World War II (Washington, D.C.: U.S. Army Center of Military History, 1954), p. 273.

33. Thatcher, *Planning for Industrial Mobilization, 1920–1940*, pp. 61–62.

34. Irving Brinton Holley, Jr., *Buying Aircraft: Materiel Procurement for the Army Air Forces*, United States Army in World War II (Washington, D.C.: U.S. Army Center of Military History, 1964), p. 166.

35. Kreidberg and Henry, *History of Military Mobilization in the United States Army: 1775–1945*, pp. 476, 618.

36. Lenore Fine and Jesse A. Remington, *The Corps of Engineers: Construction in the United States*, United States Army in World War II (Washington, D.C.: U.S. Army Center of Military History, 1972), p. 309.

37. Ibid., pp. 11, 66, 114.

38. Ibid., p. 66; Smith, *The Army and Economic Mobilization*, p. 66; Holley, *Buying Aircraft*, p. 166.

39. William Hornby, *Factories and Plants, United Kingdom Civil Series* (London: Her Majesty's Stationary Office and Longmans, Green, and Co., 1958), p. 107.

40. M. M. Postan, *British War Production, History of the Second World War, United Kingdom Civil Series* (London: Her Majesty's Stationary Office and Longmans, Green, and Co., 1952), pp. 423–24, 432–34, 444–50; Hornby, *Factories and Plants, United Kingdom Civil Series*, pp. 155–66.

41. J. de M. Kennedy, *History of the Department of Munitions and Supply: Canada in the Second World War, Vol. I, Production Branches and Crown Companies* (Quebec: King's Printer and Controller of Stationary, 1950), pp. 34–52, 103–45.

42. Henry F. Pringle, Weapons Win War, n.d., p. 24, unpublished Ms, U.S. Army Center of Military History, Washington, D.C.

43. Lt. Gen. Levin H. Campbell, *The Industry Ordnance Team* (New York: Whittlesey House, 1946), pp. 112–14.

44. "Surplus Property Administration Reports on Chemical Plants," *Chemical and Engineering News* 24 (10 January 1946): 48; Maj. P. G. Slackman, "Procurement of Raw Materials for High Explosives: Ammonia, Oleum and Toluene," *Chemical and Metallurgical Engineering* 52 (October 1945): 113–15.

45. Lewis, *History of the Ordnance Department*, p. 90; E. B. Yancey, "Military Explosives: Ordnance and Industry Were Ready for World War II," *Army Ordnance* 26 (May–June 1944): 499–500; Crowell and Wilson, *The Armies of Industry I: Our Nation's Manufacture of Munitions for a World in Arms, 1917–1918*, pp. 158, 164, 181, 183.

46. Ordnance Department, Small Arms Ammunition: A History of an Industry. Vol. I, Narration, unpublished Ms, c. 1945, p. 65.

47. Henry M. Nash, "Smokeless Powder Production of Small Arms Cannon Propellants," *Army Ordnance* 22 (Jan–February 1942): 559.

48. Ordnance Department, Small Arms Ammunition: A History of an Industry. Vol. I, Narration, pp. 143, 145, 154–79; Thomson and Mayo, *Procurement and Supply*, pp. 108–14; Smith, *The Army and Economic Mobilization*, p. 499; Fine and Remington, *Construction in the United States*, p. 339; FDAP, app. 2–4.

49. Lewis, *History of the Ordnance Department*, p. 14.

50. Smith, *The Army and Economic Mobilization*, p. 499; Millett, *The Organization and Role of the Army Service Forces*, p. 98.

51. Reginald C. McGrane, *Facilities and Construction Program of the War Production Board and Predecessor Agencies, May 1940–May 1945* (Washington, D.C.: War Production Board, 1945), p. 174; Fine and Remington, *Construction in the United States*, pp. 328–32.

52. Smith, *The Army and Economic Mobilization*, pp. 283–84, 289–302; Holley, *Buying Aircraft*, pp. 334–35, 372–75, 410–11.

53. Industrial College of the Armed Forces, *Study of Experience in Industrial Mobilization in World War II: Construction of New Facilities* (Washington, D.C.: Industrial College of the Armed Forces, 1947), pp. 7–8; Smith, *The Army and Economic Mobilization*, pp. 498–99.

54. Donald M. Nelson, *Arsenal of Democracy: The Story of American War Production* (New York: Decapo Press, 1973), pp. 149–52; Fine and Remington, *Construction in the United States*, pp. 134–37; Byron Fairchild and Jonathan Grossman, *The Army and Industrial Manpower* (Washington, D.C.: U.S. Army Center of Military History, 1959), pp. 102–05, 107.

55. Lewis, *History of the Ordnance Department*, p. 7.

56. Fine and Remington, *Construction in the United States*, pp. 71, 185–87, 270–71, 460–73; Erna Risch, *The Quartermaster Corps: Organization, Supply and Services*, vol. 1, United States Army in World War II (Washington, D.C.: U.S. Army Center of Military History, 1953), pp. 16–18.

57. Fine and Remington, *Construction in the United States*, pp. 71–72, 185–87, 191.

58. Ibid., pp. 355–63.

59. Ibid., p. 359.

60. Nelson, *Arsenal of Democracy*, pp. 380–88; Civilian Production Administration, Bureau of Demobilization, *Industrial Mobilization for War: History of the War Production Board and Predecessor Agencies, 1940–1945*, vol. 1, *Program Administration* (Washington, D.C.: Government Printing Office, 1947), pp. 386–95; Millett, *The Organization and Role of the Army Service Forces*, pp. 218–19.

61. Civilian Production Administration, *Program Administration*, p. 652.

62. Francis Walton, *Miracle of World War II: How American Industry Made Victory*

Possible (New York: MacMillan Co., 1956), pp. 48, 269–70.

63. Bureau of Ordnance, Rockets, Explosives and Propellants, Pyrotechnics, n.d., unpublished Ms, Navy Library, Washington Navy Yard, Washington, D.C., pp. 298–99, 305–06; Thomson and Mayo, *Procurement and Supply,* p. 112; Millett, *The Organization and Role of the Army Service Forces,* p. 277; FDAP, app. 2–4.

64. Industrial College of the Armed Forces, *Construction of New Facilities,* pp. 87, 89.

65. FDAP, Basic, 1945; Thomson and Mayo, *Procurement and Supply,* p. 201.

66. Civilian Production Administration, *Program Administration,* pp. 170, 962.

67. Harold J. Babcock, Steel for Forged Shell, unpublished Ms, c. 1955, p.1, in author's files. Babcock was chief metallurgist of the Ammunition Engineering Group in Frankford Arsenal, Philadelphia, Pa.

Women Workers at Chemical Warfare Service Plants During World War II

Frances Martin

Women played a very important role in supporting the Chemical Warfare Service (CWS) during World War II.[1] They not only manufactured gas masks and protective clothing, but they also produced munitions such as 4.2-inch chemical mortars, shells, and incendiary bombs.

In the years between World War I and U.S. entrance in World War II, Edgewood Arsenal in Harford County, Maryland, was the only CWS arsenal. Edgewood regularly employed women to assemble gas masks, which were produced for all the services. Although the troop buildup resulted in a greater demand for gas masks, the factory at Edgewood was closed in 1942, and the work turned over to private industry.

Many former gas mask assemblers stayed on at Edgewood in other capacities. The shortage of manpower caused by enlistments and the draft brought about a conscious decision by the War Department to employ women wherever possible. Edgewood hired women to work packaging finished items and filling munitions. Smaller numbers of women were hired to work as laboratory technicians. The Technical Service even hired a few female chemists. Women also worked in traditional office jobs such as clerk-typist and stenographer, and increasingly as personnel administrators. Even so, the war was almost over before the Civil Service Commission held its first class for female supervisors.[2]

Responding to the perceived need for additional chemical munitions, the CWS built three new arsenals during World War II. The new arsenals were located in places that did not have critical labor shortages. Two of the new sites, Pine Bluff, Arkansas, and Huntsville, Alabama, were located in agricultural areas. The third and last to be on line was the Rocky Mountain Arsenal, located just ten miles from Denver, Colorado. All three arsenals began employing women. In fact, the Rocky Mountain Arsenal advertised jobs for both men and women even before the plant was operational.[3] In addition, CWS contractors located from

Massachusetts to California and from Wisconsin to Texas recruited women workers.

The four CWS arsenals were set in areas with different economic and demographic situations. Edgewood was over twenty miles from Baltimore, a large industrial city. Labor rates were high, but the available work force consisted of skilled industrial workers. Women, however, had been involved only in light industries, such as product assembly and canning. The greater Baltimore labor force was literate and mostly urban. Edgewood was an extremely small village with little available housing for workers. Therefore, few workers lived locally. Most commuted by bus, train, or car from Baltimore or other points. While private companies were unable to provide transportation to and from Baltimore, the Army supplied buses, or rather remodeled trucks made into buses. The bus ride cost 40–50 cents round trip. Some 700 workers rode the Army buses to and from work.

The train station was just outside the Arsenal's main gate. Approximately 370 day shift workers took the Philadelphia Local, which left Pennsylvania Station in Baltimore at 7:05 AM and left the Arsenal at 4:22 PM.

Other workers used private cars and car pools. Car pools were run a little differently then due to gas rationing. As one plant worker described it, "We would ride with one party until their ration stamps for gas were gone and then ride with someone else and use up their ration stamps." Another problem for car poolers was the scarcity of rubber tires.

Although 500 Edgewood employees lived in civilian dormitories on post, the conditions were such that only those satisfied with a low standard of living were interested in them. The rates were $15.00 a month for a single female and $10.00 a month for a double room. Men could bunk six to a room for $6.00 a month. There was an elementary school and nursery provided on post, with the nursery costing $3.00 a week.

At Edgewood 40 percent of all civilian employees were Afro-American. Nearly everybody willing to take a job was hired. It was late in 1941 when the first women began working in the manufacturing and filling branch, but later in the war, 52 percent of the manufacturing and filling branch employees were women. At the Edgewood Ordnance Assembly Plant, 70 percent of the workers were women by early 1945. To accommodate women workers, Edgewood and other arsenals made engineering changes and "split" certain jobs.

Pine Bluff Arsenal, Arkansas, was about twelve miles from the small town of Pine Bluff. The terrain was open and the roads easily accommodated vehicular travel. Although the Pine Bluff workforce was not as well educated as their counterparts in Edgewood, they were able to perform the required work assembling and filling shells and preparing mortars quite capably. The arsenal provided economic advantages to a rural area which to this day has few industrial assets.

The preliminary groundbreaking for the Pine Bluff Arsenal began on 2 December 1941. Originally planned as the foremost arsenal for making incendiary bombs of the thermite and magnesium type, Pine Bluff's role was soon extended to serve as a chemical manufacturing and filling plant. The plant first made four-pound magnesium bombs and later incendiary hand grenades. A white phosphorus incendiary filling plant was added in October 1942, and the assembly of 4.2-inch mortar shells began in November 1942. The loading of 100-pound bombs with incendiary oil started in March 1943, and hexachloroethane mixture (HC) smoke canisters were loaded beginning in April 1943.

The Pine Bluff Arsenal was located in an agricultural area, and the wages at the arsenal were far in excess to what many of the workers had ever earned. According to conclusions reached by the arsenal's personnel management division, this was one of the factors that led to higher than average absenteeism. The cost of living in the area went up significantly. Some of the workers were making twice as much as they had earned as farm laborers. Civilian employment reached its high-water mark in February 1944. The lack of skilled workers forced management to bring people in and train them.

Pine Bluff provided dormitories on post for 337 men, and eventually set aside one dormitory and recreation hall exclusively for women. Pine Bluff Arsenal was unique in that it put up workers in "floating dormitories." Because it drew in large numbers of new workers, Pine Bluff also had a government-sponsored housing development.

Pine Bluff had a sizable proportion of both male and female Afro-American workers.[4] Although there was little objection to the men of both races working side by side, the arsenal found it advisable to separate white and Afro-American women, perhaps because they were not used to working together. Although white workers were unwilling to have a black supervisor, the concept of equal pay for equal work did not appear to bother them.

Some work units which had all black employees were less willing to work for a black supervisor than for a white man, as they believed a black supervisor would be harder on them than a white supervisor would be.[5]

Huntsville was a small southern town before the onset of construction of the CWS arsenal and the adjoining Redstone Arsenal. The arsenals brought an increase in population to the area, which at first had a hard time coping with the large numbers of job seekers who, hearing of the arsenal, came looking for work and a place to stay prior to its opening.

The Huntsville labor market was primarily agricultural. Of the total population of 101,959 in the two-county labor area, just 33,544 were considered to be part of the labor force. Of these, 27,223 were already employed. That left a surplus of some 6,321 people, 1,022 of whom were women.[6]

Arsenal officials soon found out that skilled workers were migrating out of the area to higher paying war jobs in coastal cities, and that construction contractors were paying higher wages than the arsenal could offer. Skilled workers were scarce, as were clerical personnel, as the local business base had little need for clerical help. In addition, the Civil Service Commission reached out to Huntsville and other communities to recruit women for clerical jobs in Washington, D.C. In the beginning, Huntsville had to request trained clerical personnel from the Office of the Chief Chemical Officer. Later, the arsenal recruited promising employees from the plant workers for clerical jobs and provided them with the needed training.[7]

Such jobs as tool-crib operators, inspectors, clerks, forklift operators, guards, truck drivers, checkers, and press operators were done by women at the Huntsville Arsenal. Both men and women at the arsenal had a low average level of education. The median level of education was 7.6 years, with 30.4 percent of the employees having a 6th grade or lower level of education. Most employees had not held a previous industrial job. Women represented 37 percent of the workforce (white females 25 percent, colored females 12 percent). The arsenal received an infusion of more highly educated personnel when 100 women of color, students at Atlanta University, were recruited to work at the Arsenal.

Rocky Mountain Arsenal, the youngest of the arsenals, had the smallest number of employees during World War II. Peak civilian employment for the CWS was 2,841 people, plus 173 inspection division employees and over 100 Seventh Service Command employees.

Rocky Mountain Arsenal was distinct from the other arsenals in that women were encouraged to apply for jobs from day one. Prior to the plant's opening, the CWS said that only men would be used in manufacturing. Nevertheless, the arsenal began recruiting both men and women. The workforce was both urban and rural. Male workers were predominantly white, with a few Hispanics. Although the arsenal was not located far from Denver, transportation difficulties encouraged workers who could readily find alternative work in closer to Denver to do so.

The arsenal had no trouble finding unskilled female workers. There was a surplus of Negro and Hispanic women, but neither group had factory experience. A plus side of the personnel picture was that illiteracy was very low, and the average level of formal education was high.[8]

Prior to construction, it was estimated that 10 percent of the employees at Rocky Mountain would be women. Readily available records do not give the total actual hire figure, but it was certainly more than the original estimate. Employment records show that the arsenal accepted 35 percent of referred job seekers in March 1943; however, by June 1943, when the job market was tighter, the arsenal was forced to take in those workers whom it may not have normally taken, and the percentage jumped to 72.5.

Termination figures rose as well, however. Absenteeism at Rocky Mountain, while a problem, was not as bad as it was at other arsenals. Because workers were forbidden to take vacations, they saw little reason to accumulate leave. Nevertheless, personnel/employee relations representatives assiduously counseled absentees, and nurses were sent out to check on those using sick leave.[9]

The CWS tried to encourage employee morale by reexamining wage rates. The Edgewood and Rocky Mountain Arsenals, which were within larger metropolitan areas, attempted to be sensitive to wage rates. The Baltimore area arsenal in particular competed with shipyards and steel mills, which boasted rapidly rising wages. Civil Service wage rates, however, could not change without careful comparisons and wage surveys. It took three years to effect a change in pay for certain wage grade rates. It became harder and harder for government workplaces to keep workers when private industry had better pay and incentives, like free lunches.

Edgewood did not have lunchroom facilities or cafeterias until almost the end of the war. Workers who lived in rooming houses found it difficult to get lunch. Other workers would make up lunches not only for themselves, but for those who did not have cooking facilities at home. These problems were common with many hastily built or converted industrial/war plants. The newer arsenals included eating facilities in their initial construction.

During World War II, female arsenal employees worked in occupations which were previously unheard of for women. The typical woman employed at a CWS arsenal worked as a munitions handler in a munitions assembly plant with about 150 fellow employees, most of them women, both white and black. Munitions handlers finished off filled items, such as white phosphorus grenades. At Edgewood the water filtration plant was for a time totally manned by women. Some women worked as crane operators, but relatively few worked in traditionally male jobs that required skill and experience such as electricians, linemen, and carpenters. Although arsenal work provided some women with role-breaking opportunities, the work concurrently exposed them to greater risk. Women chemical workers were subjected to risks similar to those found in more prosaic areas, such as dry cleaning. At Edgewood, the impregnating of clothing with CC2 to make it impervious to a necessary mustard agent involved a laundering process which used tetrachloroethane as a solvent. As the clothes were dried, toxic fumes were emitted by the solvent, forcing the women to wear gas masks when they went near the dryers.

Despite improvements to the plant's ventilation system, several women reported becoming ill due to the fumes, and one individual died after working there only a few weeks. It was discovered that women were more affected by the fumes, possibly because women tend to breathe more rapidly and shallowly. Investigators believed that this breathing difference meant that women actually tended to inhale more fumes than men would in similar circumstances. Fortunately, the plant was closed down after less than a year's operation.

Accidents at Edgewood numbered about 1,500 a month; sickness occurred 625 times a month. Safety was also a problem at Pine Bluff, especially in the production of white phosphorus grenades and in incendiary filling operations. In 1943 there were 23 fires in September, 31 in October, and 13 in November, with four of the fires resulting in fatalities. Rocky Mountain also had problems with fires in the incendiary plant and tried different means to quickly quench them. Fortunately, the safety record of all the arsenals improved in 1944.[10]

Tragically, one of the worst accidents involving a CWS arsenal occurred at Edgewood shortly before the end of the war. On 25 May 1945, twelve women were killed and over fifty men and women injured in an explosion in a white phosphorus grenade filling plant. According to one of the survivors, "One minute it was quiet, everybody working with a little joyful laughter [in the background]. Then there was a loud explosion and pop pop pop—and people screaming—you couldn't see anything because of the smoke."[11]

A month later, a woman was killed and two others seriously injured in a second filling plant explosion. Because operations were conducted in one large open area, damage from the first explosion was more extensive. The recommendations from the investigation of the May explosion resulted in safer operations with separate cubicles and a limited number of workers allowed in each area.[12]

Although many female CWS workers accepted greater risks than they would have experienced in alternative forms of employment, their standard of pay did not reflect this. Before the war, female gas mask assemblers received lower pay than just about any other CWS worker. Discrimination in pay was not unique to the chemical warfare arsenals. It was found in private industry as well. If a woman held a specific job it would bear a certain title. If a man held a job with the same duties, he would have a different job title and higher pay.

The 1945 history of Rocky Mountain Arsenal notes that there was evidence that equal pay for equal work was not quite prevalent, and that some slight discrimination was apparent between the wages paid to women as opposed to those paid to men for the same work. Histories of the other arsenals do not address the pay issue in this manner.

During World War II many women workers received valuable training; and some women were able to utilize this training after the war. For most women at the CWS arsenals, however, new employee orientation, safety training, and on-the-job training appear to be the most training they received. Women recruited as civilian guards were the exception. These women, ranging in age from twenty-five to forty, received a twenty-week training course which included first aid, fire-fighting, military courtesy, guarding, patrolling, and protection against injury from chemical agents.[13]

Racial discrimination existed at all the arsenals as it did elsewhere in workplaces across the United States, including both civil service and military installations. At Edgewood, there were separate toilet facilities in some, but not all, areas. One black woman remembered that she had been told that she would be fired if she used the facilities reserved for whites. At that plant (the Ordnance Assembly Plant), the various stalls had black figures and white figures painted on them. The bathroom issue was substantial enough for an article in the *Afro-American*, a Baltimore newspaper. The problem, according to an ordnance assembly plant officer, was actually that the number of restroom facilities were not expanded as quickly as the number of women employees.

Also at issue were charges of discrimination in job placement and promotion. To be more objective, Edgewood went so far as to administer a trades test. The results were that more white than colored women passed the test which personnel administrators said tested education and manual dexterity.

Absenteeism among women workers was relatively high, which was not surprising considering that grocery stores closed no later than 6:00 PM and most workers had at least a half-hour commute to work. There was almost no way to get to work and back and also shop for food and necessary clothing and to take care of routine business.

In May 1945 the first large reduction-in-force at Edgewood involved 450 women munitions handlers. At the same time some departments were letting women workers go, other departments were hiring workers, usually men. The personnel office changed the job identification title of the female workers being let go from "munitions handler" to "protective equipment worker." The job of munitions handler was traditionally filled by a man, and was unlikely to be open to women after the war. The job of "protective equipment worker" was a traditionally female job.[14]

Most of the women who worked in the government-run plants would have been better off financially had they worked in plants managed by private industry. Although Social Security was in effect by World War II, government work was not covered because the government had its own retirement system. Most of the female CWS arsenal workers did not continue to work for the government after the war, so they received no retirement credit for their work. For some women, credit for war work meant the difference between having or not having enough work over a lifetime to get Social Security retirement benefits based on their own work record. Three full years of work represented twelve credits. A woman who turned sixty-two in 1975 needed only twenty-four credits to receive a minimum benefit. Thus, credit for the war years made a significant difference. A number of women found out to their regret that their wartime work counted for nothing when it came to retirement.[15]

Women workers were a tremendous asset in CWS plants. They helped the country produce the ammunition and other supplies needed by soldiers around the world. Their morale was high, and despite the less than glamorous types of jobs they did, the physical risks they accepted, and the racial and economic discrimination they experienced, the women arsenal workers persevered until the job was done.

For most of these women, their work during the war was the only work outside of the home they would ever have. However, a number of women would work again in plants during the Korean War and again in still fewer numbers during the Vietnam War.

NOTES

1. The term "Army chemical plants" refers to both government-owned and privately operated chemical plants which produced chemical items for the Army Chemical Warfare Service (CWS).

2. Interviews with two retired personnel management employees, Harford County, Md., 1989.

3. Chemical Warfare Service, *History of Rocky Mountain Arsenal*, Figure 5–13, "Notice to All Unemployed," p. 1877.

4. Material written during World War II referred to people of color as "colored," sometimes as Negro. The term "black" was not used nor was Afro-American or African-American. This paper will use the terms "Afro-American," and "black," unless the reference is a direct quote.

5. CWS, *Pine Bluff History 1941–1945*, vol. 1, sec. 4, "Personnel and Personnel Management," pp. 68–73; CWS, "Pine Bluff Arsenal: Pine Bluff Preliminary History," 30 Oct 43, pp. 1–10.

6. CWS, *History of Huntsville Arsenal, From July 1941 to August 1945*, vol. 1, table 8.

7. Ibid., pp. 87–89.

8. CWS, *History of Rocky Mountain Arsenal, 1945*, pt. 3, Personnel and Personnel Management, "General Requirements and Motivating Directive," p. 1781.

9. Ibid., pt. 3, sec. 3, "Classification and Assignment Policies and Procedures," p. 1733; Ibid., pt. 3, sec. 6, "Employee Relations," pp. 1764–1777; Ibid., pt. 3, sec. 2, "Procurement of Civilian Personnel," p. 1726.

10. *History of Edgewood Arsenal During World War II*, "Safety"; Ltr, Brig Gen A. M. Prentiss, Commanding Officer, HQ, Pine Bluff Arsenal, to Chief, CWS, War Department, ASF, ATTN: Chief, Civilian Personnel Branch, 3 Dec 43, sub: Internal Job Alignment Pine Bluff Arsenal, retired CWS record 231, Pine Bluff Arsenal 43; Memo, Wm. A. Hughes, Dir., Ind. Pers. Div., for Chief, CWS, 20 May 44, sub: Inspection of Civ Pers Administration at Pine Bluff Arsenal, Pine Bluff, Ark., CWS Archives 33, Pine Bluff Arsenal 44.

11. Interview with Charlotte Johnson Chase, Edgewood, Md., May 92.

12. CWS, Edgewood Arsenal file, "Explosion and Fire in Building 509, 1945."

13. "From Edgewood: Women Guards," *Chemical Warfare Service Newsletter* (May 1943): 11.

14. Based on *History of Edgewood Arsenal*, ch. on Personnel Administration; Intervs with retired employees of Edgewood Personnel, 1989.

15. Author was a claims representative for the Social Security Administration for over eight years (1967–1976) and saw several claims for benefits denied for lack of insured status because the claimants worked for the government rather than private industry during World War II.

Training Linguists for the Pacific War, 1941–1942

James McNaughton

The Pacific War forced the American Army and Navy to innovate in ways quite different from the war in Europe. Training military linguists in Japanese was one of the most unusual of these innovations, and one that cast a long shadow. The languages needed to defeat the European adversaries of the United States were widespread in American society and readily available in Europe, but Japanese was far less common and far more difficult for Westerners to acquire. The story of how the Army recruited and trained military linguists for the Pacific War, the first large-scale language training program in its history, is an inspiring but cautionary tale. The countless difficulties the program had to overcome to get off the ground and the sheer length of training time required for soldiers to reach the necessary proficiency level led the Army after the war to establish a permanent language training facility, which later evolved into the Defense Language Institute Foreign Language Center. The process of producing military linguists at the right time, in the right languages, and in the right numbers proved too difficult and time consuming to be left to crash programs in an hour of crisis.

Before World War II the United States relied on traditional methods for collecting information about Imperial Japan and its military forces, for which language proficiency was of minor importance. American diplomats, a few Western journalists, and other Western diplomats in Tokyo provided the bulk of the information flowing to Washington. Detailed information about current trends in the Japanese military was provided by American military attaches. Since 1907 the U.S. Army and Navy had each sent two officers a year to Japan to learn the language and serve as military observers. In the 1930s some of these attaches accompanied Japanese armies on campaign in China and reported on their organization, tactics, and equipment. Before the war these attaches formed the American military's only pool of Japanese linguists.[1]

Between the wars the small intelligence arms of the Army and Navy also made tentative steps toward using new technologies for intelligence collection. The Navy had used radio direction finding and traffic analysis against the Japanese Navy since the 1920s, and cryptographers from both services worked for years on breaking Japanese secret codes. In the summer of 1940 Army cryptographers met with their greatest success when they managed to break the most important Japanese diplomatic code. Beginning in the fall of 1940 the president and his top aides received daily a summary of the Japanese government's most secret diplomatic communications, codenamed MAGIC. This process kept a dozen or so Navy and War Department civilian translators busy full time. "Translation was the bottleneck of the Magic production line," according to one historian. "Interpreters of Japanese were even scarcer than expert cryptanalysts."[2]

Heavy reliance on this single source of intelligence gave America's leaders a false sense of security. For one thing, it revealed little about Japan's military. For another, it obscured the service's larger intelligence gap, their basic inability to gather wartime information about the Japanese armed forces in other ways. The Army and Navy were in fact ill prepared from the standpoint of intelligence to do battle with the forces of Japan. Without a full range of military intelligence, modern military forces are truly "ignorant armies" that "clash by night," in the words of a famous poet. Despite the possession of MAGIC, in 1941 America came close to clashing with Japan in just this way.

Once the war began the United States eventually developed a vast intelligence machinery in the Pacific theater, staffed by "hollow-eyed, unshaven cryptologists or photo-reconnaissance analysts deep in a basement or windowless room, surrounded by the clack of IBM sorters and tabulator machines or the stench of darkroom chemicals." Closer to the action on the front lines were thousands of tactical intelligence specialists interrogating prisoners, translating captured documents, and piecing together the Japanese order of battle.[3]

Linguists were crucial to this effort at all levels, but they were in critically short supply. "Linguist requirements for the European theater of war could have been met without leaving the sidewalks of New York City," MacArthur's chief of intelligence later testified, "but there was a vastly different story in the Far East."[4] Furthermore, Americans of Japanese ancestry were widely suspected of harboring secret loyalty to their home country.

The Army eventually took up the challenge of training Japanese linguists to support the Pacific War, but it had to overcome many obstacles in the process. For students the Army turned to a small number of these scorned Japanese-Americans. Their training was long and hard, for the Japanese language was notoriously difficult for Westerners to learn—even those of Japanese descent.

America's intelligence agencies were experiencing a rapid transformation in the year before Pearl Harbor as they sought to create the manpower, technology, and organizations they would need to fight a global war. The disastrous lack of intelligence coordination between the Army and Navy in this period was later revealed by the attack on Pearl Harbor, and no one had foreseen the sheer scale of the intelligence effort that the war would require. According to an official history, manpower problems "were pervasive throughout Army intelligence. The vast expansion of the Army's intelligence apparatus threatened to outstrip the supply of qualified people."[5]

The nation's top civilian leadership was clearly dissatisfied with the service intelligence agencies even before the war, and in the autumn of 1940 Republican lawyer William J. Donovan began to lobby for the creation of an independent civilian intelligence agency. This organization, authorized by Roosevelt the following summer as the Office of the Coordinator of Information (OCI), grew into the Office of Strategic Services (OSS), the predecessor of the postwar Central Intelligence Agency (CIA).[6]

Meanwhile, Brig. Gen. Sherman Miles, War Department G–2, had begun in 1940 to expand and modernize the Army's tiny peacetime intelligence establishment. In April of 1941 he was still complaining that "the work being done by the Division is still far below what should be expected of the military intelligence of a great power in our present situation."[7]

That same spring the problem of Japanese language training was frequently discussed by a small group of officers in the G–2's Far Eastern Branch. Their chief, Col. Rufus S. Bratton, had served two tours in Japan as an attache and was keenly aware of the threat posed by Japanese military power. In June one of his subordinates, Maj. Carlisle C. Dusenbury, another former Japanese language attache, proposed that the Army turn to the Japanese-American population on the West Coast and Hawaii. Among the hundreds of thousands of young men put into uniform the previous fall with the mobilization of the National Guard and the beginning of conscription were several thousand Nisei (second-generation Japanese-Americans). These men, argued Dusenbury, represented a likely pool of potential linguists. Together with a fellow G–2 staff officer, Lt. Col. Wallace Moore (the son of American missionaries stationed in Japan), Dusenbury developed a plan to select a small number of these soldiers and give them a short course in military Japanese. According to one participant, the planners hoped that "only a few weeks' review in general Japanese vocabulary and minimum instruction in military Japanese terminology and combat intelligence would be required to prepare the selectees for field duty."[8]

Bratton and Miles approved the plan and persuaded the rest of the War Department staff to allow G–2 to set up a new school for this purpose. The Army still lacked a unified training command at this time, but the G–3 staff was attempting to bring all training under centralized control and was reluctant to allow other branches of the General Staff to set up their own schools. Nevertheless, G–2 was already operating two small schools, one in Chicago for counterintelligence and one in Fort Monmouth for signals intelligence. Miles and his staff convinced the G–3 staff and secured approval to establish a third intelligence school for training Japanese linguists. Because the G–2 staff had neither the personnel nor the funding to start a field operating agency on its own, it directed Fourth Army on the West Coast to establish the school close to the source of potential students and instructors.[9]

These enterprising officers had hardly begun their plans when they were almost halted by the first of many obstacles the school was to encounter. That summer several American intelligence officers visited the British Interrogators' School and later recommended that the Army establish a similar institution. The proposal would have divided the Japanese language training program before it even began. "It was fortunate," one of the officers later wrote, "that the War Department approved a separate school for interrogation of Japanese prisoners under the control of officers familiar with Japanese psychology who had actually served short attachments with the Japanese Army."[10] The principle was thus established early on of keeping all Japanese language training in one school.

The Fourth Army commanding general, Lt. Gen. John L. DeWitt, was not particularly concerned about Japanese language training. Like all other continental U.S. armies at that time, Fourth Army was reorganizing for hemispheric defense. DeWitt's headquarters, located at the Presidio of San Francisco, was redesignated the Western Defense Command and assumed operational control of all tactical and coastal defense forces in its area. DeWitt was under pressure from the Department of Justice and the Army Provost Marshal General. Of special concern was sabotage and subversion, particularly in light of the European fifth-column activities which had contributed to the overthrow of several governments since 1938.[11]

These heightened anxieties about internal security joined in a fateful combination with long-standing anti-Asian prejudice in the region. California's early statehood had been marred by anti-Chinese rioting and exclusion laws. When Japanese immigration began in the 1880s these new immigrants also faced stiff resistance and hostility from white settlers. Congress halted immigration from the Far East in the 1920s, but not before over one hundred thousand Japanese had put down their roots on the American mainland. Like other immigrant groups, Japanese-

Americans had one foot in each world. In many ways they quickly assimi-
lated, although first-generation immigrants were forbidden to apply for cit-
izenship or own property. The men learned to make their way in the
American business world as farmers, gardeners, shopkeepers, and fishermen. Their sons and daughters, the Nisei, were citizens by birth and
became thoroughly Americanized through their schooling. Their parents
tried to keep their heritage alive through observing Buddhist religious
practices and sending their children to local Japanese martial arts and language classes. Some sent their sons back to Japan for schooling. But in
spite of these efforts, the Nisei grew up more American than Japanese. As
the international rivalry between the United States and Japan intensified,
the Nisei faced increasingly overt discrimination by white Americans living on the West Coast.

The U.S. War Department was more concerned with protecting national security than with the feelings and prejudices of Californians. The G–2
chose an unusually able officer, Lt. Col. John W. Weckerling, to launch
their Japanese language school. Weckerling had entered the Army for officer's training during World War I at age twenty, but spent the war in stateside training camps. After the armistice he elected to make the Army a
career, and in 1928 he was sent to Tokyo as a language attache. He
returned in 1934 as assistant military attache, where he witnessed first-
hand the rise of Japanese militarism during his five-year tour. He was then
transferred to the Panama Canal Zone for troop duty. In August 1941 his
knowledge of Japanese was put back to work when he was reassigned as
the Western Defense Command's G–2 with the mission of establishing
what became known as the Fourth Army Intelligence School.[12]

At the Presidio of San Francisco Weckerling found another former
language attache, Capt. Kai E. Rasmussen, a coast artillery officer then
commanding the batteries guarding San Francisco Bay. Together they set
about building a school. Weckerling found in Rasmussen a remarkable
leader who was to serve as the school's commandant throughout the war.
Rasmussen had sailed from his native Denmark for America in 1922 as an
adventuresome nineteen-year-old. After several months studying English
and working at odd jobs, he enlisted in the Army for service in the
Hawaiian Islands. Within two years he had won an appointment to the U.S.
Military Academy. In 1936 he was sent to Japan as a language attache,
where he spent four years studying the Japanese language and observing
their army, including six months with the Japanese army in China. In 1940
he returned to San Francisco, where Weckerling found him.[13]

The first task for the two men was to visit every Army post and camp
on the West Coast where Nisei soldiers were stationed. They found that

Army commanders were unsure of what to do with such soldiers, often assigning them to the most unpleasant and boring duties on post. As Weckerling later recalled, the two "personally interviewed each Nisei soldier in service" on the West Coast, some 3,700 in all, to find out "if the Army had sufficient skill to satisfy our intelligence requirements."[14]

They were sorely disappointed. To their surprise few of the Nisei knew much Japanese. As the school's official history commented dryly at the end of the war, "foreign ancestry per se is no guarantee of proficiency in a foreign language." After weeks of driving up and down the coast and conducting interviews in one hot, dusty camp after another they rated only 3 percent as "accomplished" in Japanese, 4 percent as "proficient," and another 3 percent as "fair." That meant that in all perhaps 10 percent had any hopes of becoming linguists. Those Nisei who knew Japanese best were usually either too old for military service or, if they had returned to Japan for schooling, security risks. Most of the rest knew only a few words of "kitchen Japanese."[15]

One of the Nisei they interviewed, Seattle-born Bill Hosokawa, later recalled his embarrassing encounter that summer with Rasmussen. "I thought I could boast a fair speaking knowledge of the language, but he quickly proved me completely inadequate in other respects," he wrote. "'Hosokawa,'" Colonel Rasmussen rasped with ill-concealed disgust, "'you'd make a helluva Jap.'" He was not selected.[16]

Rasmussen had better luck when he discovered 31-year-old Pfc. John F. Aiso, then working as a repair parts clerk for a quartermaster company. The son of a humble gardener in Southern California, Aiso was an able student. After graduating from Hollywood High School as valedictorian, he attended Brown University on a scholarship and then Harvard Law School. From 1936 to 1940, at the same time Weckerling and Rasmussen were attaches in Japan, Aiso was working in Japan and in Japanese-occupied Manchuria for British and American companies and improving his knowledge of Japanese. When he came down with hepatitis in the fall of 1940 he returned home to California, and while he was recuperating he received his draft notice. Rasmussen at once spotted his skill in Japanese, but that summer the Army announced that draftees over age twenty-eight were to be discharged, and Aiso was hoping to return to civilian life as soon as possible, marry, and start his own law practice in Los Angeles. Several weeks after his interview with Rasmussen, Aiso received orders to report to the Presidio of San Francisco, where Weckerling asked him to join the new school. Aiso hesitated at first, but the lanky Army lieutenant colonel placed a firm hand on his shoulder. "John, your country needs you." Aiso was startled—no one had ever called America "his country" before. "Okay, sir," he replied. "I'll do it." In short order he became chief instructor and put his permanent stamp on the school throughout the war.[17]

Searching for more students, Weckerling and Rasmussen screened thousands of personnel records for any other soldiers who claimed any knowledge of Japanese. But in this effort they were even less fortunate. Of the few they found, most had overstated their abilities by a wide margin.

Weckerling and Rasmussen also visited the campuses of several West Coast universities looking for instructors, but with little luck. Diplomatic relations between the United States and Japan had deteriorated steadily as the year went on. In the increasingly tense atmosphere, the Japanese-American community was split over Washington's handling of the crisis, and many Japanese-American intellectuals, including faculty members and graduate students, were reluctant to cooperate with Army authorities. By the end of October, Weckerling and Rasmussen had identified only four potential teachers, including Aiso. One, Oakland-born Shigeya Kihara, had recently completed a master's degree in international relations at the University of California at Berkeley. None of the four had ever taught Japanese before.[18]

In October students and instructors began to arrive at Fourth Army headquarters. Facilities on the Presidio were already overcrowded by the feverish mobilization. Weckerling secured an empty hangar at the recently closed Army airfield, Crissy Field, not far from the Golden Gate Bridge, to double as classroom and barracks. The Fourth Army quartermaster granted an initial allocation of $2,000. Furniture was almost nonexistent, so the first classes sat on orange crates until the Presidio's carpenter shop was prevailed upon to fabricate some primitive tables and chairs.

Textbooks were even harder to obtain. The new staff combed bookstores in San Francisco, Stanford, and Berkeley for dictionaries and readers. Print shops had to be found that could reprint Japanese dictionaries. Rasmussen spent weeks writing out course materials, based on the notes and textbooks he had saved from his own language tutoring, and these materials were laboriously mimeographed.

On 1 November 1941, after three months of intensive work selecting students and recruiting instructors and six months after the school was initially conceived, the Army school for Japanese linguists opened its doors. Of the original four instructors and sixty students, all but two were Japanese-Americans. Aiso was discharged to the Enlisted Reserve Corps and rehired as a War Department civilian to become chief instructor. The instructors improvised as the first weeks rolled on. A few more were hired, and some were relieved for lack of ability. Classes lasted six hours each day, and the students studied until late each night. Several students faltered under the demanding program. It soon became clear that even after the painstaking selection process, simple review was insufficient for most of the students, who had to begin from the very beginning. A quarter of them eventually failed to complete the course. But at last the War Department had a training program underway for Japanese linguists.[19]

One Sunday morning in early December Aiso was returning by cable car to the Presidio from the main telegraph office in downtown San Francisco when a hysterical woman began to berate him loudly and taunted the other men on the car shouting, "Kill him! He's a Jap! Kill him!" The first reports of the Japanese Navy's attack on the Pacific Fleet lying at anchor at Pearl Harbor had just reached the mainland. Aiso reached the main gate unscathed but shaken.[20]

The moment of crisis had arrived sooner than anyone had suspected. The Japanese attack almost spelled the end of the fledgling school. Aiso's nerve-wracking experience on the cable car was the harbinger of a wave of anti-Japanese hysteria that swept the West Coast. New civil defense measures were hurriedly put into effect as protection against anticipated air raids, submarine attacks, and sabotage. Rasmussen was briefly called away to resume command of the Bay Area's coast artillery before the War Department reversed the move. Several weeks later public passions were further inflamed when the results of the initial investigation of the Pearl Harbor disaster were released. The report alleged that the attack had been aided by widespread espionage by Japanese residents on the Hawaiian Islands.

In February 1942 Roosevelt signed Executive Order 9066 authorizing the evacuation of all persons of Japanese descent, citizen and noncitizen alike, from broadly defined restricted areas on the West Coast. From his position as Fourth Army G–2, Weckerling argued against the evacuation as unnecessary, but to no avail. In March the Army began the removal of over one hundred thousand innocent civilians, including women, children, and the elderly, in California, Oregon, and Washington, to temporary assembly areas, from which they were later moved to specially constructed War Relocation Centers in remote inland areas. Among their numbers were the families and friends of the students, who were powerless to help. On other Army posts Nisei soldiers were disarmed, confined to their barracks, and relegated to menial duties while their white officers and the military police watched them for signs of disaffection or subversive intent. The new school, so recently begun, was at risk of being closed.[21]

The Army had originally established the school on the assumption that Nisei would make the best students. If all Nisei were placed in detention camps, the Army would have to find others who could fill their shoes. The school's experience with non-Nisei students in the first few months was not encouraging. According to the official history, eighteen Reserve and National Guard officers who claimed some knowledge of Japanese "drifted in at odd times" during the first few months. Most spoke very little Japanese, despite a class or two at the university or, in one case, having been an overseer for Japanese laborers on a Hawaiian sugar plantation. Only two were sent directly to the field.[22]

Weckerling and Rasmussen worked to keep the school from going under. The students were cautioned against visiting downtown San Francisco, even on weekend passes. Many were unable to see their families before they were packed off to the war relocation centers. Back in Washington, the War Department G–1 staff issued a new policy in January 1942, reclassifying all Nisei as "enemy aliens" and thus no longer eligible for the draft. Some local commanders began to discharge Nisei already in uniform, and Weckerling and Rasmussen watched their pool of future students slip away. The War Department then further ruled that no Nisei could be sent overseas. "The implementation of this policy," Weckerling later wrote, "would have vitiated the only feasible plan to provide qualified interpreters and translators for the Pacific theater and would have thoroughly frustrated the efforts of the field intelligence agencies." The chief of the G–2's Far Eastern Branch managed to have this policy reversed. The Federal Bureau of Investigation and Army personnel security investigators began to refuse to clear Nisei through "loyalty checks," so Weckerling had to win the authority to make his own independent determinations. Under these discouraging conditions they continued to interview Nisei soldiers for a second class scheduled to begin that spring.[23]

In these crucial early months of the war America's military leaders were occupied with larger problems than the fate of a single Army training program. In Washington and the Pacific, commanders and their staffs worked feverishly to stave off disaster. The intelligence community itself was subjected to major reorganizations. In January 1942 Marshall relieved Miles as the War Department G–2, and in March the G–2 staff was reorganized, as was the rest of the General Staff. A separate Military Intelligence Service was established apart from the Military Intelligence Division staff. In May Marshall named as G–2 Maj. Gen. George V. Strong, "a senior officer possessed of a keen mind, a driving energy, and ruthless determination," as Eisenhower later described him. Strong had served as a language attache in Japan before the First World War. At the same time the Office of the Coordinator of Information was transformed into the Office of Strategic Services under the Joint Chiefs of Staff.[24]

Several other intelligence training programs were underway by then. In the summer of 1941 the Navy had enrolled a few officers in Japanese language classes at Harvard and the University of California at Berkeley, but in the spring of 1942 they launched a larger Japanese training program at the University of Colorado at Boulder. The Counterintelligence Corps Advanced Training School was moved to Chicago in November 1941. In January 1942 G–2 established a school for prisoner of war interrogation at Camp Blanding, Florida. In February the Army Air Forces opened their own intelligence school at the University of Maryland. The Military Intelligence Training Center was established at Camp Ritchie, Maryland, in June, and the Signal Intelligence Service moved into Arlington Hall and Vint Hill Farms, Virginia, that spring.[25]

These reorganizations and training efforts were conducted against a global backdrop that was as dire as could be imagined. Many feared that their efforts would be too late. Most prewar assumptions about intelligence requirements and capabilities were rapidly proved wrong. Within a few months the entire structure of American and allied forward-deployed forces in the Pacific, and with them their intelligence assets, were swept away. "The Dutch had a goodly number of Japanese linguists who had been lifetime residents of the islands of the Japanese empire," one intelligence officer later wrote. "Some of the best cryptanalysts in the world were subjects of Queen Wilhelmina and living in the Indies." Very few of them escaped to join the Allies. The Navy evacuated the only U.S. military decoding team in the Pacific theater from Corregidor by submarine. The valuable support given by Navy code-breakers and translators in Hawaii in the Battle of Midway in June was a clear demonstration of the need for just such assets. But the desperate first six months of the war were fought with the few linguists on hand.[26]

In San Francisco Weckerling and Rasmussen continued to struggle with the problems of the school. The evacuation of all Japanese-Americans from the West Coast made it difficult to keep the small school, with its Japanese-American students and instructors, in the heart of a major metropolitan area. Space on the Presidio was also at a premium, and the school needed room to expand. In March Rasmussen set out to find a new location. While touring the Midwest he secured an appointment with Minnesota's dynamic young governor, Harold E. Stassen. At that time Stassen was searching for ways to contribute to the war effort (that same spring, for example, he accepted a commission in the Naval Reserve). The two, so similar in many ways (Stassen was of partial Scandinavian ancestry), came to an immediate agreement. Stassen suggested an unused state home for indigent old men situated on 132 acres on the outskirts of the small town of Savage, not far from Minneapolis and Fort Snelling. Rasmussen accepted at once. The camp had few classrooms, but it had several sets of family quarters that would allow the school's permanent staff to bring their families. Rasmussen had the "Homeless Men's Camp" sign removed from the main entrance.[27]

On 1 May 1942, in a small ceremony on the Presidio of San Francisco, forty-five enlisted men and two officers graduated from the six-month Japanese course, a few days before the fall of Corregidor and the Battle of Coral Sea. By this time the Army and Marine Corps were shipping a division a month to the Pacific, and the intelligence services were straining to support them. At the theater level, Army and Navy intelligence managers were laying the groundwork for a massive strategic intelligence infrastructure. In April MacArthur established the Central Bureau in Australia (later expanded to form the Allied Translator and Interpreter Section), and in July the Navy established the Intelligence Center, Pacific Ocean Areas, in Hawaii. After graduation half of the group was sent to join the Marines for the Guadalcanal invasion in August and the other half was attached to the 7th Infantry Division, then on its way to the Aleutian Islands.[28]

Despite the urgent requirements in the field, the school could not afford to release all its graduates at once. The number of instructors had risen to eight, but this was not enough to expand the school's output to any appreciable degree, and the evacuation of Japanese-Americans had put a temporary stop to further recruiting from civilian sources. Weckerling and Rasmussen decided to hold back the ten best students to serve as instructors for the next class. A full year after the school was conceived, and six months after it began operation, only thirty-five linguists had been sent to the field.[29]

Following graduation the staff and the few remaining students packed up for the trip to Minnesota, where a few weeks later they were ready for the next input of about 180 students, three times the size of the first class. The school, renamed the Military Intelligence Service Language School, was also moved out from under Fourth Army control and became a field operating agency reporting directly to the War Department G–2. Rasmussen (now promoted to lieutenant colonel) became school commandant. Weckerling stayed behind in San Francisco.[30]

Shortly after the school arrived at Camp Savage, a Minneapolis newspaper published a glowing article about the school, to the despair of Army security officers: "Army School at Savage to Teach Jap Language; Only Classes of Kind for U.S. Troops." But there was no indication that the Japanese ever discovered that the Army was operating such a school. Rasmussen later praised local authorities for their support, saying that he had picked Minnesota "because the area selected not only had to have room physically, but room in the people's hearts."[31]

The students followed the course of study originally laid out at Crissy Field, studying a combination of basic Japanese and military intelligence subjects. The specific objectives remained vague. "A definite written directive was never issued to the commandant telling the exact mission of the school, entrance requirements, required subjects, standards for graduations, or the field requirements of the graduates," the official history later reported. "In the absence of such a directive it was assumed that the school was to train translators, interpreters and interrogators for the field forces." The pace of instruction was intense: "Duty officers found it necessary to stop the illicit burning of lights after 2300. Cramming by flashlight was the habit of many." And, according to the official history, there was "a rise in the need for eyeglasses." Fourteen of the best students were rushed through an accelerated three-month course and sent to the field in August. On 1 December 149 soldiers and 22 officers (including 20 Caucasian and 2 Chinese-American) were graduated and sent to the field.[32]

Two new manpower dilemmas confronted the school in its new home. First, the school needed a source of new students to keep going. By the summer of 1942 most potential students were either in war relocation centers or in the Nisei combat units the Army was organizing. That spring the Nisei from the Hawaiian National Guard were shipped to Camp McCoy, Wisconsin, eventually to form the 100th Infantry Battalion (Separate). There the school staff interviewed large numbers and selected many for subsequent classes, but many more preferred to prove their loyalty in combat, not in what they scorned as some rear-echelon desk job. Recruiting in the relocation camps was even harder. Many in the camps were bitter about their evacuation, and would-be volunteers were often subjected to harassment and beatings. One young man, Roy T. Takai, vividly remembered being spirited out of one camp after dark to avoid possible threats. Many volunteers faced the objections of their parents, a strong deterrent in Japanese-American families. Nevertheless Rasmussen and his officers visited each of the relocation camps and gathered up six new instructors and over four hundred students for the next class that began at Camp Savage on 15 December.[33]

Second, initial reports came back from the Pacific that many commanders were suspicious of the Nisei, who looked like their adversaries. Many of the school's best graduates were held under guard in rear areas and not allowed access to prisoners or sensitive intelligence information. Because the Army as yet had no system for granting field commissions (Nisei remained ineligible for commissioning until 1944), the Nisei linguists remained low-ranking enlisted men in a rank-conscious Army. The answer the school devised was to recruit Caucasian college men with language aptitude and train them in a special course, the path the Navy had elected from the outset. Ever ingenious, Rasmussen contacted the national head-quarters of Phi Beta Kappa, the scholastic honor society, for a list of members who might have a high aptitude for learning Japanese and asked the University of Michigan to establish a special twelve-month Japanese language program for these officer candidates. This contract training began in January 1943 for 150 students.[34]

Long before the first officer linguists reached the Pacific the enlisted Nisei linguists had proved their worth and were in great demand. By the time the third class began at Camp Savage in December 1942, American ground forces were engaged in heavy combat in the Solomons and New Guinea and in urgent need of translators and interrogators. Farther to the rear, signals intelligence was producing a mountain of intercepts to be translated. At the same time the Military Intelligence Service Language School had finally matured to the point where it could turn out graduates by the hundreds. The pattern of training had been set, and the Nisei had proved their value to field commanders. In fact, their skill and bravery encouraged the Army to organize two all-Nisei combat units for use in Europe. By war's end nearly three thousand Nisei linguists were serving throughout the theater. An equal number were still in training, many of whom would participate in the occupation of Japan. MacArthur's intelligence chief later claimed that "the Nisei saved countless allied lives and shortened the war by two years."[35]

The prewar leaders of the American intelligence community failed to provide for an adequate pool of Japanese linguists. They were encouraged in this neglect by several assumptions, among them that U.S. allies could supply linguists, that enough Japanese linguists could be easily found in the United States, and that any deficit could be easily made up through a crash training program. In this last assumption they were not completely wrong. A tiny staff of former language attaches and a handful of civilians built a language training program from scratch that managed to produce two hundred graduates by the end of the first year. Students and instructors alike proved to be an exceptionally able group of young men, despite their initial lack of language skills. Reflecting back on these achievements after the war, Rasmussen concluded that "we must establish the study of languages as a total career, military as well as civilian. . . . Linguists do not appear automatically. You cannot create language experts overnight."[36] After the war was concluded the Army heeded his advice and turned the school into a broader Army Language School for over two dozen languages. For each of the succeeding postwar crises since then, from Korea to the Persian Gulf, the Department of Defense has been able to draw upon a pool of pretrained military linguists and a strong language training base.

NOTES

1. For general information about American intelligence directed against Japan on the eve of war, see John Patrick Finnegan, *Military Intelligence: An Overview, 1885–1987* (Arlington Hall, Va.: U.S. Army Intelligence and Security Command, 1988), pp. 5'–72; David Kahn, "The United States Views Germany and Japan in 1941," in *Knowing One's Enemies: Intelligence Assessment Before the Two World Wars*, ed. Ernest R. May (Princeton, N.J.: Princeton University Press, 1984), pp. 476–501; and Roberta Wohlstetter, *Pearl Harbor: Warning and Decision* (Stanford, Calif.: Stanford University Press, 1962). For naval language attaches, see Ronald Lewin, *The American Magic: Codes, Ciphers and the Defeat of Japan* (New York: Farrar, Straus, Giroux, 1982), pp. 29–31. British historian Peter Lowe downplays the capabilities of British intelligence in the Far East in the same period: "Great Britain's Assessment of Japan Before the Outbreak of the Pacific War," in *Knowing One's Enemies*, pp. 456–75.

2. For the discovery and early exploitation of MAGIC, see Lewin, pp. 16–80; Wohlstetter, pp. 171–75; and David Kahn, *The Codebreakers: The Story of Secret Writing*, rev. ed. (New York: Signet, 1973), pp. 1–68, 298–322. "Bottleneck," Kahn, *Codebreakers*, p. 27.

3. Ronald H. Spector, *Eagle Against the Sun: The American War With Japan* (New York: Free Press, 1985), p. 445. Spector is the first historian of the Pacific War to give an extended account of allied intelligence efforts in the overall context of the war.

4. Maj. Gen. Charles A. Willoughby, *Congressional Record*, 90th Cong., 1st sess., vol. 113, no. 22 (15 Feb 67).

5. Finnegan, p. 61.

6. John Ranelagh, *The Agency: The Rise and Decline of the CIA*, rev. ed. (New York: Touchstone, 1987), pp. 37–56.

7. Finnegan, p. 59.

8. Details about the organization of the school are generally drawn from several sources, including Training History of the Military Intelligence Service Language School (n.d. [1946]); MISLS Training History, an. no. 1, Academic Training (20 Feb 46); MISLS Album (Minneapolis, Minn.: 1946); John Weckerling (Brig Gen, USA), "Japanese Americans Play Vital Role in United States Intelligence Service in World War II" (written in 1946, first published in 1971 in eight parts by Hokubei Mainichi, San Francisco, Calif., from 27 Oct to 5 Nov 71, reprinted in pamphlet form without pagination in Nov 71 for the fortieth anniversary of the founding of MISLS); and John F. Aiso, Interv, 30 Oct 87. Dusenbury: Weckerling, sec. 2. "Only a few weeks' review:" Weckerling, sec. 3.

Shigeya Kihara provided invaluable assistance in preparing the original version of this paper. Aiso and Kihara were both members of the original faculty and served throughout the war, Aiso as director of academic training.

Secondary sources include Masaharu Ano, "Loyal Linguists: Nisei of World War II Learned Japanese in Minnesota," *Minnesota History* (Fall 1977): 273–87, the best scholarly overview; Joseph D. Harrington, *Yankee Samurai: The Secret Role of Nisei in America's Pacific Victory* (Detroit, Mich.: Pettigrew Enterprises, 1979), based on numerous interviews with Nisei veterans; Bill Hosokawa, "Our Own Japanese in the Pacific War," *American Legion Magazine* (July 1964): 15–17, 44–47; and Tad Ichinokuchi, ed., John Aiso and the M.I.S.: Japanese-American Soldiers in the Military Intelligence Service, World War II (Military Intelligence Service Club of Southern California, 1988), a collection of valuable information and photographs published as a tribute to Aiso.

9. Other intelligence schools: Finnegan, p. 61, who comments that "G–3 stubbornly refused to give MID [Military Intelligence Division] any authority over intelligence training in general."

10. Weckerling, sec. 2.

11. For general background, see Stetson Conn et al., *Guarding the United States and Its Outposts*, United States Army in World War II (Washington, D.C.: U.S. Army Center of Military History, 1964).

12. For details on Weckerling's career, see Weckerling, "Japanese Americans Play Vital Role."

3. For details on Rasmussen's life and career, see "In Memoriam: Kai E. Rasmussen, 190?–1988" (Washington, D.C.: March 1988), and USMA *Register of Graduates* (1965).

14. "Personally Interviewed," Weckerling, sec. 3; "Sufficient Skill," Rasmussen, quoted in Ano, p. 276; see also Kai E. Rasmussen (Col, USA, Ret.), speech given at the Defense Language Institute, Presidio of Monterey, California, 25 Jun 77, reprinted in "In Memoriam." Training History, pt. 4, gives the number of Nisei interviewed as 1,200, and Academic Training puts it at 1,300, which may represent the numbers interviewed prior to 1 November. Other sources agree on the total number interviewed as 3,700.

15. "Foreign Ancestry," Training History, p. 7; percentages: Album, p. 8; Weckerling, sec. 3; and Rasmussen, 1977 speech.

16. Hosokawa, p. 45.

17. This incident is variously related in John Aiso and the M.I.S., p. 15; John F. Aiso, Interv, 30 Oct 87; Weckerling, sec. 3; and Harrington, pp. 20–21.

18. Reluctant to cooperate: Kihara, Interv, 15 Mar 90.

19. Training History, pp. 4–9, and Academic Training, pp. 3–9. Weckerling and the Album give eight as the initial number of instructors. Four had been hired by 1 November and the other four were hired as the term progressed. Thomas T. Sakamoto (Col., USA, Ret.), Interv, 16 Nov 87 (Sakamoto was one of the first sixty students).

20. Harrington, p. 29; Aiso Interv.

21. The story of the anti-Japanese hysteria on the West Coast is told in Bill Hosokawa, *Nisei: The Quiet Americans* (New York: William Morrow, 1969); the official Army history of the evacuation decision is told by Stetson Conn in Kent Roberts Greenfield, ed., *Command Decisions* (New York: Harcourt, Brace and Co., 1959), pp. 88–109, and in revised form as a chapter in Conn, *Guarding the United States*, pp. 115–49. For a more recent telling, see John Hershey, "A Mistake of Terrifically Horrible Proportions," in *Manzanar*, ed. by John Armor and Peter Wright (New York: Times Books, 1988), pp. 1–66.

22. "Drifted in at Odd Times," Academic Training, pp. 3–5.

23. Discharge policy: Weckerling, sec. 2. "Loyalty Checks," Training History, p. 9.

24. For the March 1942 reorganization of the G–2 Division, see Forrest C. Pogue, *George C. Marshall*, vol. 2, *Ordeal and Hope 1939–1942* (New York: Viking, 1966), pp. 200–201; Eisenhower's critical assessment in his *Crusade in Europe* (Garden City, N.Y.: Doubleday, 1948), pp. 32–34; and Finnegan, pp. 68–70. For the origins of the OSS in the context of the "bureaucratic battles" within the U.S. intelligence community, see Ranelagh, pp. 57–64.

25. Intelligence schools, Finnegan, p. 71. For related information on other Army training programs, see Robert R. Palmer et al., *The Army Ground Forces: The Procurement and Training of Ground Combat Troops*, United States Army in World War II (Washington, D.C.: U.S. Army Center of Military History, 1948), especially pp. 259–64 for the school expansions in 1940–1942.

26. PURPLE machine: Lewin, p. 148. Dutch East Indies: Brig. Gen. Elliott R. Thorpe (USA, Ret.), *East Wind, Rain: An Intimate Account of an Intelligence Officer in The Pacific, 1939–1949* (Boston: Gambit, 1969), pp. 57–58.

27. Move: Training History, pp. 9–11, and Rasmussen, 1977 speech. Stassen: *Current Biography 1948* (New York: Wilson, 1949), pp. 597–600. The following spring Stassen resigned as governor and entered active duty to serve as an aide to Admiral Halsey.

28. Spector, pp. 445–77. For ATIS, see General Headquarters, Far East Command, Military Intelligence Section, General Staff, Operations of the Allied Translator and

Interpreter Section, GHQ, SWPA, vol. 5, Intelligence Series (12 Jul 48). Some works by former naval intelligence officers, such as W. J. Holmes (Capt., USN, Ret.), *Double-Edged Secrets: U.S. Naval Intelligence Operations in the Pacific During World War II* (Annapolis, Md.: Naval Institute, 1979), gloss over the role of the Army Nisei linguists, hundreds of whom were supporting naval intelligence efforts by the end of the war. Guadalcanal and the Aleutians: Training History, p. 28, and Album, pp. 106–07. For some stories of the school's earliest graduates to reach the Pacific, see Harrington, pp. 83–148, and Loni Ding (producer), "The Color of Honor" (San Francisco, 1987), a documentary film containing extensive interviews with MISLS graduates.

29. Honor graduates held back as instructors: Academic Training, p. 14, and Sakamoto Interv, 16 Nov 87 (Sakamoto was one of the students held back).

30. June 1942 input: Academic Training, pp. 29–30, and Lt Col Roy T. Uyehata (USA, Ret.), Interv, 16 Nov 87 (Uyehata began as a student at Camp Savage in June 1942).

31. "Army School at Savage," n.d., unidentified news clipping (Minneapolis?: June 1942?). "Room in the People's Hearts," *Minneapolis Morning Tribune*, 23 Oct 45.

32. "Directive," Training History, p. 7; "Duty officers," Album, p. 48; "Eyeglasses," Academic Training, p. 27; Graduates: Training History, p. 23, and Academic Training, p. 30.

33. Recruiting: Academic Training, pp. 30–31; Hostility encountered in camps: Weckerling, sec. 4; Lt Col Roy T. Takai (USA, Ret.), Interv, 30 Oct 87. Hosokawa describes Kibei violence against those in the camps who cooperated with the government in his *Nisei: The Quiet Americans*, in a chapter entitled "A Time of Bitterness, Valor, and Confusion," pp. 359–78.

34. Joseph K. Yamagiwa, The Army Japanese Language School: A Preliminary Report on the Academic Program (Ann Arbor, Mich.: unpublished Ms, Oct 45), pp. 2–3, and Training History, pp. 13–17. See also Donald M. Richardson, ed., "Random Recollections of the Second Class, AIJLS, aka the Second OCS Class, MISLS, Fort Snelling, Minn." (unpublished Ms., Sep 88). Nisei under suspicion in the field: see, for example, Uyehata and Takai Intervs, and Col Bob Hoichi Kubo/Ben Hazard (USA, Ret.), Interv, 30 Oct 87 (Hazard was a member of the first OCS class at the University of Michigan; his first combat assignment was as linguist detachment commander with the 27th Division on Saipan in 1944, where Kubo was serving as an interrogator.

35. Maj Gen Charles A. Willoughby, quoted in "America's Secret Weapon in World War II" (Presidio of San Francisco: Presidio Army Museum, 1981).

36. Hosokawa, "Our Own Japanese," p. 47.

The San Francisco Port of Embarkation in World War II: A Study in Command and Control

Mason Schaefer

Two great oceans lay between the United States and the fighting fronts during World War II. The major American seaports, "Gateways to Battle," dispatched the U.S. Army's supplies and men. The San Francisco Port of Embarkation (SFPE) backed up the far-flung battlefronts of the Pacific Theaters of Operation. Although the SFPE shipped the Army the supplies and men needed for victory in the Pacific, the port's fragmented logistical command and control system denied the Army truly efficient support. This paper will attempt to trace the origins of the SFPE command and control problems, explain the impact of these problems on shipping, and postulate on why they remained unsolved at the end of the war.[1]

Although the comprehensive U.S. Army in World War II series touches on port operations, Chester Wardlow's Transportation Corps volumes do not discuss the SFPE's activities in detail. Wardlow addresses several important San Francisco issues (port congestion, divided command and control), but misses some of the complex factors behind them.[2] *Gateway to Victory*, Capt. James W. Hamilton and Lt. William J. Bolce's official SFPE history, avoids many of the more divisive issues. Popular war narratives tend to concentrate on grand strategy rather than logistics.[3]

As the Pacific Theaters' major Port of Embarkation (POE), San Francisco dispatched 23,589,472 measurement tons of military cargo, or one-half of all Army cargo destined for the theaters' rudimentary overseas ports scattered throughout the Pacific on continents, atolls, and jungled islands. Separated from battlefronts by thousands of nautical miles, the San Francisco Port of Embarkation needed effective command, control, and traffic management to support the theater.[4] As will be seen, the SFPE's individual parts worked well. However, despite the efforts of three military commanders during World War II, the port lacked the overall command strategy that would have made it a truly efficient theater supporter.[5]

The SFPE Organization

At the beginning of the war, the SFPE reported to the Quartermaster Corps, but in July 1942 the port was placed under the Office of the Chief of Transportation (OCT). The OCT established a standard layout for all POEs, which included a half-dozen major sections and many subdivisions. The SFPE's six major organizational groups each filled well-specified functions. These bodies included the Commanding General's Office, the General Staff, the Operating Divisions, Administrative Services, Technical Services, and Special Commands. Each subgroup contained several divisions, which varied in size from 10 to 7,000 persons.[6]

The Overseas Supply Division (OSD), a part of the General Staff, arranged all port shipments to the Pacific theaters. More than any other branch, OSD expedited the SFPE's supply outflow. The Division received requisitions from the theaters, checked them against War Department policies, and weighed operational concerns. After prioritizing the shipments, OSD then decided which supplies would go to what theater and arranged their overseas movements with the port's Water and Transportation Divisions. By 1945 OSD employed 1,134 soldiers and civilians.[7]

As the war escalated, the OCT and the Army Service Forces (ASF) criticized SFPE-OSD's supply management. These Washington-based organizations complained that the division did not prioritize supply outflow efficiently enough. By mid-1944, this shortcoming helped create the feared Pacific port congestion and shipping shortages. Largely because of OSD's inefficiencies, the OCT relieved Maj. Gen. Frederick Gilbreath, the SFPE's first wartime commander. Despite further reorganizations and two other command changes, the OSD remained a problem.[8]

There were three Operating Divisions by war's end—the Water Division, Transportation Division, and Postal Division. By August 1945 these three agencies employed the greatest number of port personnel— 11,121 civilians and soldiers. In tandem with the OSD, the Water and Transportation Divisions handled the most important port functions. The Transportation Division arranged cargo movements to the docks, while the Water Division loaded, manned, repaired, and converted ships.[9]

The port's traffic management chain started with the Overseas Supply Division. After setting supply priorities, OSD informed the port Transportation Division of cargo inflow. That agency moved incoming goods to port facilities or diverted them to holding points. "All phases of freight come within its functions," explained an official report. The 2,353-person Transportation Division directed motor and rail traffic within the port and managed personal property storage and movement.[10]

The traffic management chain's third and final link, the 7,651-person Water Division, loaded ships and worked all dockside facilities. These operations ranged from procuring and maintaining small watercraft to repairing and converting large transports. The Division also supplied crews for merchant vessels and hired stevedores and other pier personnel. Through liaison with Navy and War Shipping Administration (WSA) officials, Water Division officers leased berthing spaces. Because the Division grew out of the autonomous Army Transport Service,[11] its superintendents retained an independent outlook. As will be seen, this factor reduced efficiency when the number of operations increased during 1944–1945.[12]

The SFPE's well-administered facilities awed visitors; one important British official praised the "magnificent port organization at San Francisco and Oakland." "I have never seen warehousing more efficiently handled," exclaimed another investigator in 1944. Lt. Gen. Brehon B. Somervell, head of the Army Service Forces, found the SFPE a pleasure to inspect.[13] Clearly, the port did not possess an inherently inefficient structure.

With San Francisco's structural organization and facilities equal to other ports, its deeper problems lay elsewhere. Although OCT tried to model the SFPE after East Coast ports, the vast Pacific distances faced by the SFPE impacted on that port's operations and demanded a different approach. Where Atlantic POEs serviced a few well-developed European ports, San Francisco handled ninety-three destinations by January 1945. Ships spent weeks sailing to Pacific bases, with the appropriate lag in turn-around times.[14]

San Francisco's commanders, from General Gilbreath to Maj. Gen. Homer N. Groninger, drew on their vast transportation experience in their attempts to make SFPE more efficient. Too often, however, the port's individual parts worked at the expense of the overall organization. Investigations by the ASF and the OCT came to the same conclusion: the SFPE did not work as a single weapon with an overall strategy. The fault did not lie in the port's official organization but rather in an overall lack of coordination and cooperation between its various divisions.

General Gilbreath and the 1942 Surge

As the military reinforced Hawaii and Australia in 1942, SFPE rail traffic increased to "several hundred times normal peacetime flow." Washington officials changed priorities frequently, which further confused harried port personnel. SFPE traffic managers could not determine the consignee or destination of many poorly marked shipments. The port lacked both the warehouse space and labor to accommodate the massive influx. "These conditions soon produced a terrific overcrowding of the port," stated an SFPE history. "Decisive action was needed."[15]

The SFPE's commander, General Gilbreath, did not shrink from decisive action.[16] A native of Dayton, Washington, the 53-year-old Gilbreath took over the SFPE a month before Pearl Harbor. His varied background included a great deal of transportation and logistics experience. After graduating from West Point, Gilbreath served in World War I as a disbursing officer in Britain and then as the Army Transport Service (ATS) superintendent in St. Nazaire, France. By war's end, the strong-willed Gilbreath's organizing abilities had won him respect throughout the Army. "He knew what he wanted and went after it regardless of obstacles that might be placed in the way," stated Hamilton and Bolce. Gilbreath's stubborn determination served him well as he expanded the port and streamlined operations.[17]

To function effectively, the SFPE needed to master three challenges: freight processing, labor, and infrastructure. Overall, the port managed actual cargo loading well; its successful vehicle-handling efforts, which represented 16.8 percent of its workload and which strongly tested its cargo maintenance and preparation skills, bear this out.

Shortly after Pearl Harbor, the SFPE faced a flood of vehicles from several directions. Most task forces arrived by rail from field organizations and other new vehicles surged into port from various manufacturers. First and foremost, San Francisco required a centralized facility for the continuous flow of trucks and tanks. As the massive 1942 surge continued, Gilbreath took action. Clearly, he decided, all vehicles should go to a central dispatch point where trained technicians could inspect and prepare them for overseas shipments. To avoid fragmenting operations, the SFPE chose a single location for all vehicle-processing activities in 1942.

After some study, SFPE officials selected Oakland's Emeryville neighborhood, where they remodeled a large building at 52d and Green Streets, the Emeryville Motor Depot. By April 1942 the depot featured a production line for every phase of vehicle processing. Its parking lots and rail facilities completed, in 1942 Emeryville shipped out 1,906 vehicles and processed 3,681. As the war escalated, Emeryville handled 100 conveyances per day on average, sometimes 360. Its 1,181,115-square-foot parking space could accommodate 3,000 wheeled machines.[18]

General Somervell, commander of ASF, gave Emeryville high marks when he inspected the facility on 5 August 1943. During that year, the facility received and dispatched its greatest number of vehicles. Unsurprisingly, the motor depot soon became an SFPE showplace. Throughout the war, many distinguished visitors visited the clamorous machine shops. L. H. Williams, a British War Office official, found himself "greatly impressed" by the highly efficient preparation process: "Yours is a model from which we can learn a great deal . . . it has made a big contribution to the shipment of vehicles."[19]

By creating a single processing and staging point for vehicles, the SFPE aided in their efficient shipment. From December 1941 to August 1945, the port dispatched 3,956,645 measurement tons of tanks, tractors, trucks, and other machines, for a total of 100,054 vehicles processed and 99,731 shipped out.[20] But did this achievement ensure fully coordinated theater support, with the SFPE deciding the priority and quantity of shipments? As the war continued, the higher echelons of the OCT and ASF would find that question increasingly elusive and frustrating.

The SFPE's shipments of ammunition, vehicles, and aircraft represented 30 percent of its total output. As the port dispatched this cargo, it adapted quickly to rapidly changing theater requirements and volume. When huge numbers of vehicles poured into San Francisco after Pearl Harbor, the SFPE quickly established a central location for processing and shipping them out. In addition, the Port of San Francisco soon learned how to prepare, stage, and ship whole squadrons of warplanes to Pacific battlefronts. SFPE staffers also expanded and enhanced specific facilities at Benicia and Richmond for ammunition loading, and established rigorous and effective safety procedures. The port responded well to specific emergencies. However, as subsequent investigations would show, its command still did not reveal a unified concept of operations. At times its authority would seem too centralized, yet too unfocused.

A junction for several rail lines prior to World War II, San Francisco did not lack train facilities. Indeed, rolling stock delivered some 80 percent of the Bay Area's cargo. "All in all, it can be said that railroads provide the most feasible and efficient method of transporting freight," stated a Transportation Division cargo analysis. However, only the Southern Pacific Railroad offered direct connections with San Francisco itself. The Western Pacific and Atchison, Topeka, and Santa Fe lines both barged cars to the Embarcadero. Indeed, the port's rail holding-yards stood seven miles from the docks. After Pearl Harbor, the SFPE built thirty-seven warehouses on both sides of the bay. However, the port needed to truck in much cargo. Most rail lines did not lead directly from the warehouses to San Francisco or Oakland piers.[21]

World War II inspired major port improvements. Since Army planners found Fort Mason a "constricted area with no room for expansion," they looked to Oakland, a large suburb across the bay. As port officers noted even before Pearl Harbor, that city's dock area and Army base boasted ample land for warehouses, offices, and piers. Armed with such information, Brig. Gen. John C. H. Lee, the prewar SFPE commander, aggressively built up Army facilities at Oakland.[22] General Gilbreath expanded Lee's efforts by leasing and finally building more warehouses, piers, and office space.

Directly after Pearl Harbor, General Gilbreath won support from local civilian transportation executives, who formed a coordinating committee to help him run the port.[23] His actions came none too soon, for the port's freight traffic soon exploded. On 2 January 1942, for example, Gilbreath reported 2,987 loaded cars in the Bay Area, with 1,056 more expected the next day. "Such a condition cannot go on much longer without danger of clogging the rails to such an extent as to interfere with the offshore movement of troops," warned the port commander.[24]

To meet this emergency, Gilbreath directed the SFPE to unload and store overflow shipments. If necessary, he could use additional piers for temporary storage. The port commander also wanted to store excess cargo in holding points outside the SFPE. A few months later, the OCT established such holding stations at Tracy, Lathrop, and Yermo, California; and Pasco, Washington.[25]

During early January, troops and freight swamped San Francisco. "Supply services were being pressed to make shipments and gave little heed to conditions at the port," explains historian Chester Wardlow. On 12 January alone, for example, 3,208 loaded railcars entered the Bay Area marshaling yards.[26]

Gilbreath needed to stem this deluge at once. As supplies piled up on San Francisco docks in mid-January, he recommended that Washington embargo the port. Under an embargo, no supply services would ship cargo to Pacific terminals[27] without the SFPE commander's release. As for shipments already en route, Gilbreath wanted the services to hold them at regulating stations until he gave the word.[28]

The next day, 17 January 1942, the Army's adjutant general took official action. "Serious rail congestion now exists in the San Francisco Bay Area," he informed all corps areas, and directed that no factory or depot should dispatch supplies to the SFPE without a release from the Quartermaster General. Brig. Gen. Brehon B. Somervell, a War Department General Staff officer, seconded the adjutant general. Somervell officially diverted military supplies from San Francisco; only cargo specifically earmarked for the SFPE should continue there. A few months later, Somervell headed the Army Service Forces, which oversaw the Quartermaster and Transportation Corps.[29]

These actions effectively embargoed San Francisco. "The port's rail terminals were jammed with boxcars and overflowing with piles of shipments; a 'breather' . . . was needed to catch up with the sudden flood of supplies," wrote Hamilton and Bolce. All available employees now cleared the port. The SFPE first hauled 900 cars to interior locations until its staff could prepare additional port facilities. Stevedores then unloaded remaining cars and placed their contents into warehouses "irrespective of contents, consignee or destination."[30]

These quick actions cleared the port in two days. After one week, General Gilbreath ended the embargo and permitted railcars to enter the San Francisco port. Thanks to the cargo cutoff, the SFPE survived its first major surge. However, the port now needed expanded port facilities, improved traffic control, and extensive reorganization.[31]

General Gilbreath expanded the SFPE in the midst of the 1942 surge. In early January he proposed marine repair shops, transit sheds, dockage for eight transports, and three general warehouses totaling 702,000 square feet. By the spring of 1942 the port had constructed a vast new building for new port divisions and seven additional warehouses. Lured by additional office space, the Overseas Supply Division and Technical Services moved to Oakland in mid-1942. The OCT named the suburb an official SFPE branch on 29 June 1942.[32]

During the 1942 surge, the port controlled local railroad shipments by establishing the Port Rail Traffic Control Office (RTCO). The RTCO directed all depot-to-port freight movements within the War Department regulating system. To prevent congestion in 1942, no agency or company could move cargo to the docks or warehouses without first notifying the rail office. At all times, the RTCO would note the capacity of terminal yards, general operating conditions, and number of cars already inventoried.[33]

According to most observers, including historian Chester Wardlow, movement control in World War II avoided World War I's serious rail congestion. Shippers could not move cargo without block permits from the OCT, which coordinated closely with the ports of embarkation. As the port historians concluded, however, "this shipping release mechanism did not do the whole job and supervision was maintained even after shipments from inland points had been released."[34]

As ever-larger rail shipments poured into port, the SFPE's movement control efforts bore fruit. Over a period of five months, for example, the Transportation Division's cargo control section evaluated 79,000 loaded freight cars for port clearance. On any given day, the port could handle 2,500 cars without loss of efficiency. The Southern Pacific Railroad, for instance, could manage 600 cars at San Francisco and 700 at Oakland before congestion set in.[35]

Since it meshed well with the OCT, the SFPE's traffic system kept large railcar shipments from congesting the port. By evaluating shippers' requests and shuffling carloads to the docks or inland depots, the port Transportation Division avoided logistical chaos. To improve rail traffic control, the port expanded marshaling yards and built additional trackage in Oakland. Bolstered by this infrastructure, the SFPE then established an elaborate monitoring system by creating a rail traffic control office to direct movements of SFPE-bound east-to-west freight.[36]

After the surge, civilian rail company representatives monitored movement schedules and priorities for the RTCO. The RTCO in turn communicated with Army-manned "regulating sections" located at nationwide strategic rail terminals. "This system controlled and eventually eliminated the causes which had produced the freight congestion in January, 1942," stated an official report.[37]

Thanks to General Gilbreath's firm direction and the port staff's inventiveness, the SFPE survived the 1942 cargo surge. As Chester Wardlow has observed, lack of central control over supply movements caused congestion at most American terminals. However, the SFPE and other ports quickly mastered the flood of cargo through embargoes and movement direction. In turn, the War Department and Quartermaster Corps Transportation Branch (later OCT) provided overall supervision.[38]

The SFPE's crisis management skills brought the 1942 surge under control. However, as will be seen, the domestic ports' effective traffic management often merely pushed congestion into theater ports. As U.S. terminals dispatched mountains of supplies without carefully worked-out priorities, overseas bases faced an embarrassment of riches.

After the 1942 surge, the War Department created the Army Service Forces, which in turn directed the Office of the Chief of Transportation. Once outranked by General Gilbreath, Maj. Gen. Charles P. Gross became Transportation Chief and the port commander's superior officer. The two enjoyed a usually cordial but increasingly volatile relationship as the Pacific War escalated.

For now, at least, San Francisco basked in triumph. With its organizational and operational systems in place by September 1942, the port streamlined recordkeeping and cargo processing. In autumn 1942 the SFPE's improved cargo manifesting system won effusive praise from the OCT. Not long afterwards, however, tension rose between Washington and the Bay Area.[39]

Labor and Infrastructure Problems Confound General Gilbreath

In early 1943 Gilbreath proposed a broadly expanded San Francisco Port of Embarkation. He wanted the SFPE to function as "Headquarters,

Pacific Ports of Embarkation," a nexus which would closely control its subports at Los Angeles and Portland. An overall Pacific command could also quell western port rivalries and prevent misdirections of shipments.[40]

Gross found Gilbreath's logic unconvincing. "The trend of our organization has been in the opposite direction . . . than the one you suggest," he informed the port commander. He planned to make Los Angeles a separate POE in the near future, which would grant it more independence than Gilbreath wished. General Gross then rejected the port commander's audacious proposal.[41]

With or without subports, the SFPE's jurisdiction already covered a broad arena that stretched from Oakland to Humboldt Bay in the north. The other Pacific ports' expanded operations made their autonomy desirable in any case. Not for the first time, Gilbreath had overreached himself.

In addition to freight traffic management issues, labor and personnel management also concerned the San Francisco Port of Embarkation. During early 1942 the SFPE's personnel roster ballooned from 2,268 to 24,689. By August 1945, 29,979 persons worked the POE's facilities. However, San Francisco always needed more workers.[42]

Unfortunately, however, the SFPE never quite mastered the labor problem. The port's command launched massive recruiting campaigns which drew in both men and women. However, the port tended to react to short-term emergencies and did not plan adequately for labor shortfalls. As Gross concluded, such ad hoc measures hampered long-term success.

"One of the most serious problems that confronts this port is the enormous turnover of personnel," reported one division in November 1942. The SFPE constantly struggled to procure more stevedores, mechanics, drivers, clerks, supervisors, guards, inspectors, and other useful persons. "The Army of workers in the port is not yet big enough," wrote a *New York Times* reporter two months before Hiroshima. In his view, the labor shortfall added to operational "strain and excitement." To harassed port officials, the former probably outweighed the latter when labor issues came up.[43]

World War II's boom economy meant a buyers' market for workers, who could choose from many promising wartime contractors. Selective Service consumed many of the young men who would normally take port jobs. "It is too bad the government allowed [the] draft and enlistment of so many railroad, stevedore and steamship men," lamented a Lend-Lease official. Commercial companies could frequently offer workers higher wages than could a cost-conscious federal facility. Consequently, the port kept retraining untried personnel.[44]

Labor shortages affected every port department and branch. According to a 1945 OCT report, consistent OSD labor shortages reduced that divi-

sion's efficiency. Even the Medical Supply Branch experienced a 45 percent turnover rate in part-time employees.[45] Because most military officers
served overseas, port divisions could not maintain enough high-level supervisors. In mid-1944, for example, the Water Division listed a shortage of
experienced and competent officers as its most important problem.[46]

The SFPE's working conditions and hiring practices also shrank its
labor pool. When hiring, port divisions needed to refer labor requirements
to the OCT in Washington. Not surprisingly, this time-consuming process
slowed recruitment. Frequently, divisions spurred civilian resignations by
not classifying jobs highly enough to match actual responsibilities. Since
SFPE pay rarely matched that of the private sector, high turnover continued in low-paying, low-level positions. Unless the port increased the rate
per hour of dock seamen, complained Col. Clarence H. Kells of the
Quartermaster Corps in 1942, "We cannot hope to attract skilled men or
improve the efficiency of this organization." Eventually promoted to major
general, Kells took command of the SFPE in mid-1944. However, he
found labor problems as intractable as did his predecessor.[47]

With the fighting fronts diverting male workers, the SFPE turned to a
previously untapped source—women. Throughout the war, the port conducted all-out recruiting drives for both male and female employees. As
operations surged in early 1945, for instance, the SFPE sent teams of
recruiters to Chicago, Milwaukee, Minneapolis, St. Paul, and Des Moines,
and Davenport, Iowa. These groups signed 200 women to six-month clerical work contracts. In addition to typing and filing, women also repaired
ships, drove trucks, fixed military vehicles, took pictures, painted buildings, and served as job analysts and security guards. By war's end, 6,000
women worked the port.[48]

The SFPE also used women in uniform, usually as clerks. On 22
February 1943, a vanguard of 159 officers and enlisted women of the
Women's Army Corps arrived at San Francisco and occupied a barracks on
a Funston Park playground. As these newcomers quickly showed, "there
was practically no job at the Port which could not be handled by a
woman." WACs filled positions as drivers, stenographers, and code and
mail clerks and prepared morning reports and service records. Army nurses served at Camp Stoneman, where they labored under "extremely
demanding conditions."[49]

Although women broke many barriers during 1943–1945 at the SFPE,
still more remained. The port kept women out of certain jobs and gave
only a few supervisory positions. A large proportion worked at clerical
tasks, a traditionally "pink collar" area. As a contemporary report reveals,
port officials sometimes condescended to women: "Their attitude toward

their work is born of a desire to keep busy, and to learn and accomplish their tasks with the same fervor that a good housewife uses in keeping her home polished and shining."[50]

As the war with Japan reached a climax in 1945, the OCT pressed the SFPE to improve its labor policies. After an April 1945 inspection, Maj. Gen. William M. Goodman, the New York OSD chief and troubleshooter for General Gross, noted the SFPE OSD's serious personnel shortages. The current SFPE commander, General Kells, belatedly beefed up that Division. Nonetheless, Gross criticized his lateness in building up manpower. Surprisingly, the port also lacked a regular training program for new employees. Gross also noted that Kells and his predecessor, General Gilbreath, had failed to draw up contingency plans for workload increases. Despite the OCT commander's fatherly tone, he clearly found the SFPE's situation troubling, so troubling that he transferred Kells to the New York Port of Embarkation and replaced him at the SFPE with Maj. Gen. Homer Groninger.[51]

The Port of San Francisco managed to support the Pacific Theaters of Operation despite its continual personnel shortage. However, as Gross pointed out, crisis management would not be enough. In the victory surge against Japan, the SFPE could not bluff its way out of a personnel shortage.

As the labor shortage took its toll, the SFPE also scrambled for shipping. All ports of embarkation competed for cargo vessels to move masses of battlefront supplies. To obtain adequate shipping at the needed time, the ports submitted their tonnage requirements to the OCT. The latter then checked these submissions off against its own priorities and submitted the vessel request to the War Shipping Administration (WSA).[52]

Composed of WSA, Army, and Navy members, the SFPE's Local Committee invariably sent in tonnage requirements without specifying types of ships. Such an approach distorted the OCT's calculations, complained Brig. Gen. Robert G. Wylie, the Assistant Chief of Transportation. The SFPE's unstandardized ship requests had caused "a good deal of embarrassment" in Washington, he informed General Gilbreath.

For the past three months, Wylie continued, the SFPE had presented incomplete ship information to the OCT. The port's Water Division prepared requirements only six weeks in advance, and these forecasts greatly exceeded the OCT Planning Division's own predictions. "SFPE's estimates cannot be reconciled with the long range estimates nor with the six-week period estimate," Wylie observed. Worse still, San Francisco did not respond to frequent information requests. The port also expected the WSA to act directly on its tonnage requirements, when the OCT actually approved and submitted shipping requests from all ports.

"The great danger in this system is that no one in this headquarters knows at any given time the number of ships the West Coast will require," continued Wylie. The SFPE did not greatly heed his criticisms. In a fateful 7 July meeting, the West Coast Committee refused to standardize requirement procedures with eastern POEs. This move merely solidified the SFPE's maverick stance and ensured further conflicts with the Transportation Chief. The 1943 shipping imbroglio sparked further disputes that eventually caused Gilbreath's relief.[53]

With the Allies advancing in New Guinea and New Georgia, the Army Service Forces and Transportation Corps mounted more port inspections. In August 1943, for example, General Somervell spent three days at the port. "I am delighted with the operations of the San Francisco Port of Embarkation," the ASF chief informed Gilbreath. "Your command is certainly in fine shape." Outwardly, the port's operations looked flawless. Beneath the surface, however, lay the SFPE's more serious problems.[54]

The OCT began digging not long after General Somervell's visit. Some theater commanders complained of the SFPE's inadequate support and its OSD's misplaced priorities. Increasingly concerned, General Gross probed West Coast conditions. In November 1943 Col. Norman H. Vissering of the OCT's Operations Division inspected San Francisco facilities and met with important SFPE officers. He did not speak with General Gilbreath, who toured Pacific bases during the inspection visit.

Accompanied by OSD and Water Division representatives, Vissering first toured the port's warehouses and docks. "It is believed that these facilities are sufficient, generally speaking, to handle the projected movements of cargo," he concluded. "The general job of warehousing and pier storage was excellent in all cases." Vissering then tried to standardize port procedures, a much more difficult job.[55]

He discussed new methods of prioritizing cargo with several port officers, among them the SFPE's transportation chief.[56] General Gross wanted POEs to use cargo charts and time priorities to manage scarce West Coast shipping, Vissering explained. To distribute freight equitably between theaters, the ASF would need to know both the composition and quantity of cargo in port. Impressed, the port officers promised to implement the idea.[57]

Unwilling to let up, the OCT pressured the SFPE on this issue. Gross next sent Maj. Gen. William Goodman, his unofficial troubleshooter, to instruct the port on cargo charts and other issues. Another emissary, Maj. L. S. Smith, also visited San Francisco on a similar errand. Now back from his Pacific tour, Gilbreath objected to these probes. "As you know, many of the ports are rather suspicious of 'visiting firemen' and do not particularly appreciate being told that their way of doing business is not wholly satisfactory," observed Vissering wryly.[58]

Though displeased at first, Gilbreath relented somewhat when he learned that Smith would be merely observing the SFPE's use of cargo charts. Goodman, however, not only instructed the port in such charts but also investigated the Overseas Supply Division. His visit maintained OCT pressure on the port.

Though Gilbreath returned from the Pacific praising port/theater relations, he did not convince Gross. More immediate concerns troubled the OCT chief, who wanted Gilbreath to focus on the larger issues. As theater commanders had suggested, Gross wanted equipment to arrive at the same time as the troops, and on the fewest numbers of ships. Unimpressed with Gilbreath's optimism, he asked the port commander to improve the timing of shipments. When asked by Gross on 25 November 1943 about possible improvements, Gilbreath put him off. With two top officers absent, he needed more time. For now, Gross backed off.[59]

Gilbreath counterattacked shortly thereafter. In a December 1943 letter he objected to Gross' overseas reassignments of SFPE officers. The New York Port of Embarkation enjoyed a disproportionate share of personnel, he protested, so the OCT should not be raiding San Francisco. This argument did not convince Gross. "I don't know the basis of comparison you use," he retorted.

Indeed, he argued, the SFPE held on to officers better than most, not least because of Gilbreath's forceful character. "I have a feeling that your technique of screaming has resulted in a more tender treatment of you by my Personnel Division than of other ports," he chided. All commands contributed to the common effort, and ports should have the resources to deal with personnel transfers. "We cannot play the part of a lone wolf," Gross concluded significantly.[60]

The scramble for shipping intensified as Southwest Pacific operations increased. Determined to integrate maritime policy, the War Department abolished the Pacific coast's autonomous maritime board in June 1943. "It was found that the West Coast committee's figure on estimates of cargo as well as shipping were at great variance with the War Department's estimates," reported Lt. Col. Arthur G. Syran of the OCT's Water Division. In January 1944, for example, the West Coast projected a requirement of 447,313 long tons for the Southwest Pacific, which contradicted a 387,313-ton OCT estimate.[61]

This divergence, which had earlier displeased General Wylie, widened until the War Department, Navy Department, and War Shipping Administration formed a new central committee in Washington. In addi-

tion to setting policy, this group examined West Coast shipping requirements in detail. After six months of labor, the committee established systematic control over worldwide shipping. The Washington group shifted
vessels to the West Coast when the East Coast reported a shipping surplus
and otherwise expedited ship priorities.

Unimpressed by Washington's innovations, Pacific officials tried to
revive their independent shipping board in February 1944. "Such a division
of authority would cause confusion," complained Colonel Syran. "It would
at one stroke destroy flexibility of shipping." To avoid further fragmenta-
tion, the OCT quelled the projected West Coast shipping committee.[62]

Increasing ASF and OCT scrutiny revealed further SFPE command
problems. Gilbreath allowed his senior officers fairly free rein, and some
valued their independence over other considerations. As in most areas, the
port commander practiced a "crisis management" approach. If his subordinates would not cooperate with other divisions, he would take direct
action, but often after the situation had seriously deteriorated. In early
1944, for example, the Water Division's rickety command structure almost
collapsed.

Once the Army Transportation Service branch, the WD remained
somewhat insular within the port structure. Though all port divisions
pooled their efforts, the Water Division functioned autonomously as its
thousands of employees loaded ships and leased berth space. However, by
1944 the Allies advanced against Japan on all fronts. Division commanders could no longer place their own priorities ahead of the port's.

When theater commanders complained of slow cooperation with the
SFPE, other port division heads blamed the Water Division. Col. John H.
Mellom, the long-time superintendent, now became the focus of discord.
An experienced transporter, Mellom had so far conducted operations
acceptably. As ATS and Water Division head since Pearl Harbor, Mellom
enjoyed cordial relations with local shipping people and theater representatives. Both Gross and Gilbreath thought highly of him.[63]

However, the SFPE's growing workload required all port divisions to
cooperate closely. Despite a mountainous inflow, New York's OSD and
WD interacted smoothly enough to dispatch supplies efficiently. Sadly,
Mellom proved less than adept at such coordination. He frequently ignored
divisions' requests for information and would not meet with other superintendents. "In my opinion he is not an operator. Neither is he an organizer
or a planner," stated Lt. Col. J. R. Messersmith, head of the Transportation
Division. "It seems to me that Colonel Mellom procrastinates in everything that we try to get done," complained Col. M. L. Craig, director of the
Troop Movement and Equipment Division. Almost all other division direc-

tors scored his (Mellom's) uncooperativeness and poor organizational skills.[64]

Once supportive of Mellom, Gilbreath now condemned him, frequently berating him for his uncooperativeness and ill temper. For a short time in early 1944, Mellom's performance improved. However, he clearly could not adapt to the port's changing priorities. In May 1944 Gilbreath asked General Wylie for permission to relieve the officer. Wylie, who had served with Mellom early in the war, declined the request. Gross expressed "real alarm" at the thought of losing such an experienced transporter. In Washington, the OCT chose to see only Mellom's past as a veteran port officer.

At first unwilling to act, Gross relented when Gilbreath detailed Mellom's failings in several lengthy affidavits. With Gross' permission, Gilbreath sent the colonel packing. Ironically, he soon followed Mellom into exile.[65]

The Water Division crisis pointed up both the SFPE's growing command problems and divergences with the OCT. Gilbreath's own loose control of his senior subordinates backfired with Mellom, and the OCT failed to understand SFPE conditions and priorities. Two of the most important SFPE directorates—the OSD and Water Division—clearly needed reshuffling. Until those two worked as one unit with the Transportation Division, the SFPE's operations would suffer.

General Goodman's November 1943 probe now bore fruit. According to his investigation, Gilbreath had not effectively defined Overseas Supply Division functions. The Division also did not receive communications directly from the theaters. To Gross, Gilbreath simply did not give the OSD enough emphasis. Not long after the Water Division imbroglio, Gross relieved Gilbreath and sent him westward to head the South Pacific Base Command (SBPC). This body closed out now-dormant facilities in the Pacific theater.[66]

On 1 June 1944, Brig. Gen. Clarence H. Kells replaced Gilbreath.[67] Bespectacled and balding, the scholarly, 52-year-old Kells promised a less stormy reign. For the past two years he had successfully commanded the Boston Port of Embarkation. A native of Michigan, the veteran transporter had enlisted at San Francisco before World War I. Before commanding the Boston POE he headed the Transportation Corps' Water Division.[68]

Kells now needed to revamp the San Francisco Port of Embarkation. He faced a difficult task, for the POE bore Gilbreath's stamp from top to bottom. He had expanded the facilities, added thousands of new personnel, revamped the organization, and innovated new loading procedures. As most observers agreed, Gilbreath thoroughly understood port operations. Thanks to him, all the SFPE's individual parts functioned. However, Gross wanted and needed something more.

General Kells and the 1944 Surge

As Kells took command, the surge for victory soon tested the port. In mid-1944 the Allies conducted major operations in New Guinea and the Marianas, followed by an all-out drive to the Philippines. During the summer, however, the port managed the growing influx well. Kells sponsored new improvements in ship and freight car loading, which sparked praise from Gross.[69]

"I have a real satisfaction in the splendid preparations we have made for the big push in the Pacific," Gross informed Kells on 1 August. "I am particularly gratified in the new spirit that pervades your Port of Embarkation." Indeed, Kells' assumption of command restored peace to a once-fractious port. With the troubled Water Division under new command, the port looked ripe for real improvement. Unfortunately, this honeymoon did not last very long. The push to the Philippines reached mammoth proportions, which quickly revealed how little Kells had changed the SFPE's concept of command—not least because the port resisted central control.[70]

The San Francisco Port of Embarkation's relationships with theater commanders now took center stage. These crucial liaisons largely defined the growing Pacific supply crisis during late 1944. Theaters often abruptly changed requirements and canceled requisitions, then reordered supplies. Faced with such confusion, the port slowed its operations.

During fall 1944 operations in the Southwest Pacific, for example, that theater first curtailed requisitioned supply shipments and shipping requirements, then demanded fresh vessels and large quantities of engineering, signal, and ammunition equipment.[71]

Toward the end of October, as American forces landed at Leyte, large numbers of loaded ships backed up in the Southwest Pacific. Upon request from the SFPE, the ASF froze all shipments to Leyte in October. General MacArthur also halted requisitions to New Guinea, which faced severe port congestion.

Though the SFPE wanted to cancel theater requisitions outright, the Southwest Pacific theater preferred to keep them open. "So long as this condition prevailed the currently delinquent requisitions were bound to become even more delinquent," noted the port quarterly history.[72]

The SFPE could not plan loads properly or phase requisitions as long as it received information at the last moment. During the 1942 surge, the port had also failed to receive proper manifests and other notice of incoming shipments. In late 1944 the theaters sent requisitions that matched SFPE capacities, then requested supplies that exceeded those capacities. San Francisco could not guarantee shipping space for these added requisitions. As an OCT report later revealed, however, the port had also failed to keep timely control records. In addition, the SFPE lacked a direct theater liaison.[73]

At the theater level, supplies pushed into battlefronts choked all available facilities. As port battalions struggled to make warehouse space available, dozens of ships sat offshore at Leyte. "Perhaps the best parallel I can give of the situation here [in the Southwest Pacific] is that of someone trying to save water with all barrels and buckets full, and the taps still running," reported Herbert Schage, Regional Director, Forward Areas, Southwest Pacific, in late November 1944.[74]

Though advised to hold back shipping, military authorities would not do so. Unfortunately, Leyte's makeshift facilities could hold only a fraction of the tonnage estimated for them. By early December 66 vessels swung at anchor in port, with 78 more to come. At Hollandia, New Guinea, the troops had filled all warehouses and then all outside storage space. Some 133 ships sat offshore, waiting weeks for unloading. At Leyte, Schage complained of "such a chaotic and overlapping system of authority, or lack of it, that the right hand has no idea of what the left hand is doing."

Virtually pressed to the wall by mid-January 1945, General MacArthur's command canceled all resupply shipments for February. The SFPE then managed to release a "great number" of frozen requisitions. By March 1945, however, 100,000 measurement tons of New Guinea and Leyte supplies remained in limbo at the Lathrop Holding and Reconsignment Point. "This constant accumulation coupled with difficulties in procurement and in retention of adequate personnel added to the complexity of the problem," stated the port's first 1945 quarterly report.[75]

Instructed to give the Overseas Supply Division his first priority, General Kells did not quite meet General Gross' requirements.[76] Like General Gilbreath before him, he enmeshed himself in crisis management. When the theaters or Gross complained or suggested improvements, he rushed to implement them—after the fact.

Increasingly dissatisfied with SFPE operations, Gross again dispatched General William Goodman to the port in April 1945. As before, he found the OSD's authority inadequate and its office short of labor. He laid down a detailed list of recommendations, which included more personnel and a requisition control unit for the division. Kells dutifully implemented the suggestions by adding thirty-four officers and sixty-four clerks to the OSD. He also greatly expedited the port's editing process for requisitions. Though mildly pleased, Gross stressed quality rather than quantity of editing, especially with engineering requisitions.[77]

After a detailed June 1945 investigation, the OCT's Control Division strongly criticized the SFPE's Overseas Supply Division. Like General Goodman, the Control Division found the OSD undermanned, with low-ranked officers handling heavy responsibilities. The OSD also faced excessive or conflicting battlefront requirements: "The Southwest Pacific theater has consistently requisitioned tonnages in excess of ability to receive and unload." Despite the heavy workload and constantly changing requests, however, the "port has been doing a remarkable job of loading in accordance with theater priorities."

Nonetheless, the OSD processed follow-up documentation too slowly. According to a port headquarters survey, the paperwork backlog resulted from "inadequate supervision, insufficient personnel, lack of control records and late receipt of shipping documents." The OSD also maintained few progress statistics. In addition, that Division overextended its responsibilities by covering warehousing, ammunition inspections, and other technical duties.

Despite General Gilbreath's alleged plan for twice-weekly liaisons, the OSD failed to retain contact with theater officers. The Division controlled cargo only "tenuously," and failed to monitor freight status as closely as the New York POE. Follow-up deficiencies compounded the OSD's shortcomings. The port repeatedly failed to prioritize cargo or promptly answer theater inquiries.

In 1942 the SFPE's improved manifests set an example for other ports. Now San Francisco stood dead last in the important follow-up category. Its onetime subport, Los Angeles, rated "excellent" in that area, as did New York, Boston (General Kells' former port), and Hampton Roads. Seattle rated "satisfactory," as did Charleston and New Orleans (which shipped out much material to the Pacific). The SFPE lagged behind most West Coast POEs, as well as the East Coast terminals. Overall, San Francisco's unstandardized recordkeeping procedures and follow-up hurt its position.

Backlogs of follow-up records now required seventy-hour work weeks at the OSD. The engineer branch, for example, faced 30,000 man-hours of makeup work. Repeatedly, OSD subdivisions failed to maintain permanent control records. In sum, the report scored the SFPE's crisis management approach to operations. General Goodman's investigation and the OCT report both strongly indicted General Kells' port management. With the Pacific War reaching high gear, the SFPE needed to unite its efforts.

Clearly, Kells reacted to events rather than directing them. General Gross wanted a different sort of leader for the SFPE.[78]

General Groninger and the End of the War

In mid-June the Chief of Transportation selected the capable and experienced New York port commander, Maj. Gen. Homer M. Groninger, to be the SFPE director. Still confident of Kells' abilities on the East Coast, Gross assigned him to the New York POE. Once head of the New York OSD, Goodman arrived in San Francisco as deputy port commander in July 1945. He could now put his major recommendations into effect. Both Groninger and Goodman intended a major port reorganization, as the SFPE would be supporting an invasion of Japan herself.[79]

Indeed, operations increased dramatically through the summer of 1945. In August, for example, 93,987 passengers passed through the SFPE en route to the battlefields, the war's all-time high. During that month, the Emeryville Motor Depot processed 3,889 vehicles, its greatest wartime total. However, the expected invasion of Japan did not happen. Two mushroom-shaped clouds over Hiroshima and Nagasaki ended the war at one stroke. The San Francisco Port of Embarkation never faced its final test.

In essence, the San Francisco Port of Embarkation supported the Pacific Theater more than adequately. The port definitely dispatched enough supplies to "get the job done," and American operations did not collapse for lack of beans and bullets. Despite this achievement, Transportation Corps planners and theater commanders remained unsatisfied. The SFPE, OCT, and ASF fought a continuous battle for command and control. As ports struggled for autonomy, the overall command in Washington pushed for uniform procedures. Theater demands for immediate supplies, a consistent shortage of labor, and the much lengthier Pacific lines of communication also affected this struggle. Given these myriad factors, the OCT, Army Service Forces, and SFPE never quite resolved the command and control issue.

The SFPE's wartime performance thus involved factors more complex than simply dispatching supplies. On several fronts, the port command succeeded brilliantly. Despite often conflicting instructions, the SFPE invariably dispatched the amount of supplies requested—on time. Beset by daily emergencies, port officers quickly obtained scarce equipment and packed the difficult cargo on ships.

Though he expanded facilities and halted the 1942 congestion, General Gilbreath did not establish full command and control over the port. He allowed SFPE divisions to operate in isolation, without a unified system; the

Water Division crisis of 1944 brought this situation to a head. Gilbreath's successor, General Kells, did not significantly alter this "crisis management" approach. Japan's early surrender in August prevented General Groninger from placing his own stamp on SFPE wartime operations.

As mentioned, the port faced a number of difficulties beyond its control. The SFPE supplied dozens of distant Pacific ports thousands of miles apart. Its widely spaced supply depots lay farther from the port than those on the East Coast. SFPE labor recruiters competed with the draft, other government agencies, and civilian contractors offering boomtown wages. The theaters often swallowed up the best military transporters. These local factors made it difficult for port commanders to duplicate the efficient organizations of New York and Boston.

However, the SFPE failed to correct certain organizational shortcomings within its control. Despite constant urgings from General Gross, Generals Gilbreath and Kells lagged in setting up effective training programs for employees. They did not grant enough authority or status to the Overseas Supply Division, the vital body that decided the rhythm and efficiency of cargo outflow. The OCT constantly prodded the port to establish a cargo planning system. Clearly, crisis management could take the SFPE only so far.

Agencies in Washington did not perform flawlessly. The OCT and ASF only sporadically monitored the SFPE. As at San Francisco, the Office of the Chief of Transportation paid attention when the theaters complained, then moved on to other things. Somervell and Gross would alternate effusive praise with sharp criticism. For much of Gilbreath's tenure, the Washington agencies did not carefully analyze SFPE operations.

As the United States poured an unlimited volume of ordnance, ammunition, and vehicles onto battlefronts, "brute logistics" prevailed. Transportation formed only one part of the Army distribution system. Pressure from Washington might have disrupted the SFPE's orderly traffic management procedures in any case.

Any major foreign deployment, from the Spanish-American War to Operation DESERT SHIELD, immediately tests American ports of embarkation. As military cargo floods once sleepy terminals, deploying units pressure port commands to ship all their gear immediately. Endless trainloads of supplies strain rail facilities meant for one-tenth the volume. Shipments of rations, aircraft, vehicles, and ammunition pour in from all directions simultaneously. A port command must master traffic control immediately or face paralyzing congestion.

During the recent Operation DESERT SHIELD deployment to Southwest Asia, the United States again "oversupplied" the fighting front. Thousands of cargo containers reportedly traveled from the United States to Saudi Arabia and back again without being opened or otherwise utilized. Clearly, the logistics system lacked a certain quality of command and control. Unfortunately, the United States may not always have the largess to sustain such extravagance. America's Army may still need to relearn the lessons of San Francisco in World War II.

NOTES

1. This paper will focus on cargo operations rather than troop staging. Passenger traffic is a paper in itself and would dilute this paper's overall emphasis on freight transportation and supply issues.

2. Chester Wardlow, *The Transportation Corps: Responsibilities, Organization, and Operations*, U.S. Army in World War II (Washington, D.C.: U.S. Army Center of Military History, 1951); Chester Wardlow, *The Transportation Corps: Movements, Training, and Supply*, U.S. Army in World War II (Washington, D.C.: U.S. Army Center of Military History, 1956).

3. Capt. James W. Hamilton and Lt. William J. Bolce, *Gateway to Victory: The Wartime Story of the San Francisco Army Port of Embarkation* (Stanford, Calif.: Stanford University Press, 1946).

4. "San Francisco Port of Embarkation Statistical Study—December 1941–August 1945," Record Group (RG) 336, Records of the Office of the Chief of Transportation (hereafter known as RG 336), Suitland Federal Records Center (SFRC), Suitland, Md.

5. Ibid.

6. Ibid., pp. 25, 29.

7. Hamilton and Bolce, *Gateway to Victory*, pp. 53–54; Memo no. 54, "Assignment of Responsibilities for Overseas Supply," 2 May 44, RG 336, SFRC.

8. Maj Gen Clarence H. Kells replaced General Gilbreath in May 1944. A year later, the OCT replaced him with Maj Gen Homer Groninger, former head of the New York Port of Embarkation.

9. SFPE Statistical Study. Water Division figures are c. 1945; Hamilton and Bolce, *Gateway to Victory*, p. 31.

10. "Port Transportation Office," Functions Rpt, 25 Nov 42, RG 336, SFRC; SFPE Statistical Study. Transportation Division figures c. 1945.

11. Until mid-1943 the Water Division acted as the local branch of the Army Transport Service. At that time, General Gross renamed it the WD and officially tied it to the local port command structure.

12. Hamilton and Bolce, *Gateway to Victory*, pp. 76–77.

13. "Survey of Pacific Supply," Rpt, 15 Jun 45, by the Control Division of the Office of the Chief of Transportation; Ltr, William Jeffers [president of the Union Pacific Railroad] to James Patterson [Under Secretary of War], 17 Apr 44. Ltr, L. H. Williams to Gilbreath, 23 Jun 43. Williams served in the Controller of Ordnance Service, British Army Staff; Special Bulletin from General Gilbreath, 7 Aug 43, RG 336, SFRC.

14. Hamilton and Bolce, *Gateway to Victory*, p. 77.

15. "Historical Record, San Francisco Port of Embarkation, 1941–2," RG 336, SFRC.

16. Colonel Gilbreath became a major general in 1942. General Gross, Chief of Transportation during World War II, was also a colonel until mid-1942.

17. Hamilton and Bolce, *Gateway to Victory*, pp. 197–98.

18. San Francisco Port of Embarkation Report, 25 Nov 42, "Improvements of Methods," Section; SFPE Statistical Study; Hamilton and Bolce, *Gateway to Victory*, p. 72; "A Description of the Objectives and of the Functioning of the Emeryville Motor Depot," 19 Feb 43, RG 336, SFRC.

19. Ltr, Williams to Gilbreath, 23 Jun 43, RG 336, SFRC.

20. SFPE Statistical Study; Hamilton and Bolce, *Gateway to Victory*.

21. Hamilton and Bolce, *Gateway to Victory*, pp. 65–67; "Analysis of Army Freight Arriving in 1943 at San Francisco Port of Embarkation," Port Transportation Office File, RG 336, SFRC.

22. Memo, Reybold to Chief of Staff, 7 Jan 41, RG 336, SFRC.

23. Ibid., pp. 5–6.

24. Memo, Wardlow to Superintendent, Army Transport Service, SFPE, 12 Nov 41; Memo, Gilbreath to Assistant Chief of Staff, G–4, Washington, D.C., 4 Jan 42, RG 336, SFRC.

25. Ibid.

26. Wardlow, *The Transportation Corps: Movements, Training, and Supply*, p. 269.

27. In early January 1942, San Francisco controlled all Pacific ports, including Seattle, Washington; Los Angeles, California; and Portland, Oregon. Seattle became an official port of embarkation on 17 January 1942, while Los Angeles remained an SFPE subport until mid-1943.

28. Memo, Gilbreath to Supply Service Commanders, 16 Jan 42, RG 336, SFRC.

29. Memo, Adams to Commanding Generals of All Corps Areas, 17 Jan 42; Memo, Somervell to Adjutant General, 18 Jan 42, RG 336, SFRC. Large quantities of supplies for Western Defense Command (WDC) installations had also arrived at the SFPE for storage and/or shipment. These were now to be sent directly to those installations and not the port.

30. "SFPE Report as of 25 Nov 42," RG 336, SFRC.

31. Ibid.

32. Memo, Gilbreath to Adjutant General, 9 Jan 42; Hamilton and Bolce, *Gateway to Victory*, p. 17; "Special Report, 3 Nov 42"; RG 336, SFRC. Each warehouse stretched three city blocks in length.

33. Memo no. 6, Col E. C. Johnston, Chief of Staff, to Port Subordinate Commanders, RG 336, SFRC.

34. Hamilton and Bolce, *Gateway to Victory*, p. 65.

35. Ibid.; Ltr, Wardlow to Gilbreath, 16 Sep 42; Minutes of Weekly Meeting of Port Traffic Control Board, 7 Sep 42; RTCO Report of 20 Jun 43, RG 336, SFRC.

36. Memo, Oliver to Gilbreath, 26 Jan 42; "SFPE Report as of 25 Nov 42"; RG 336, SFRC.

37. Ibid.

38. "Report of the Chief of Transportation," p. 31. Other congested ports included New Orleans and New York.

39. Memo, Wylie to Commanding Generals of POEs, 26 Sep 42; Memo, Vissering to Wylie, 5 Oct 42; Memo, Gilbreath to Gross, 25 Sep 42, RG 336, SFRC.

40. Memo, Gilbreath to Gross, 14 Apr 43, RG 336, SFRC.

41. Memo, Gross to Gilbreath, 19 Apr 43, RG 336, SFRC.

42. SFPE Statistical Survey, RG 336, SFRC. In 1939 the SFPE employed a mere 613 persons.

43. SFPE Report, 25 Nov 42, sec. V–IX; R. L. Duffus, "Port of Men Going to War," 21 Jun 45, *New York Times Magazine*; RG 336, SFRC.

44. "SFPE Report for Jul 42"; Memo, Howland to Watson, 22 Feb 43; RG 336, SFRC.

45. "Historical Record, San Francisco Port of Embarkation, 1943"; "Overseas Supply Division," Feb 43 Rpt; "Control Division, Jul 43 Report"; "Report of the SFPE, 25 Nov 42," RG 336, SFRC.

46. "SFPE First Quarterly Report, 1944," 24 Apr 44, sec. IV, "Problems"; RG 336, SFRC.

47. "Overseas Supply Division," Feb 43 Rpt; Memo, Gross to Kells, 11 May 45; Memo, Kells to Executive, OCT Water Division, 19 Jul 42; RG 336, SFRC.

48. Hamilton and Bolce, *Gateway to Victory*, p. 135.

49. Ibid., pp. 123–25.

50. Rpt, "Women as Laborers," RG 336, SFRC.

51. Memo, Gross to Kells, 11 May 45, RG 336, SFRC.

52. Memo, Wylie to Commanding General, SFPE, 27 Jul 43.

53. Ibid.

54. "Special Bulletin from General Gilbreath," 7 Aug 43, RG 336, SFRC.

55. Memo, Vissering to Chief, Water Division, of OCT, RG 336, SFRC.

56. Colonel Vissering also spoke to Col. John Mellom, the Water Division head, and Col. Edward C. Johnston, General Gilbreath's Chief of Staff.

57. Ibid.

58. Memo, Vissering to Maj L. S. Smith, 1 Dec 43, RG 335, SFRC.

59. Gross' comments on 19 Nov Ltr from General Gilbreath, RG 336, SFRC.

60. Ltr, Gross to Gilbreath, 7 Dec 43.

61. Memo, Syran to Hicks, 7 Feb 44, RG 336, SFRC.

62. Ibid.

63. Memo, Gross to Gilbreath, 15 May 44; Memo, Gilbreath to Gross, 21 May 44, with affidavits from SFPE division heads; RG 336, SFRC.

64. Memo, Gilbreath to Gross, 21 May 44, with affidavits from SFPE division heads; RG 336, SFRC; Wardlow, p. 356. Colonel Messersmith later became an important officer in the OCT.

65. Memo, Gilbreath to Gross, 22 May 44; Memo, Gross to Gilbreath, 15 May 44, RG 336, SFRC.

66. Wardlow, p. 356. Among other activities, Gilbreath shut down bases in New Zealand, the Russell Islands, and Bora Bora.

67. General Kells quickly became a major general after taking over the port command.

68. Hamilton and Bolce, *Gateway to Victory*, p. 197.

69. Ibid.

70. Memo, Gross to Kells, 1 Aug 44, RG 336, SFRC.

71. "SFPE, First Quarterly Report, 1945," RG 336, SFRC.

72. Ibid.

73. Ibid.; "Survey of Pacific Supply," 15 Jun 45 Rpt by Control Division of OCOFT; RG 336, SFRC.

74. Memo, Schage to F. W. Isherwood, Executive Assistant, War Shipping Administration, SFPE, 27 Nov 44, RG 336, SFRC.

75. "Quarterly Historical Report, 1945," RG 336, SFRC.

76. Wardlow, p. 356.

77. Memo, Gross to Kells, 11 May 45, RG 336, SFRC.

78. "Survey of Pacific Supply."

79. Ibid., p. 200.

Race Relations and the Contributions of African-American Troops in Alaska

Charles Hendricks

At the end of April 1942, nearly a month before the African-American soldiers of the 97th Engineer General Service Regiment arrived in Valdez, Alaska, Brig. Gen. Clarence Sturdevant, the Assistant Chief of Engineers charged with overseeing the construction of a military highway to Alaska, wrote apologetically to Maj. Gen. Simon Bolivar Buckner, the senior Army officer in Alaska and a West Point classmate, "I have heard that you object to having colored troops in Alaska and we have attempted to avoid sending them."

Sturdevant had arranged the assignment of the African-American 93d and 97th Engineers to the project in mid-March when his planners determined that the four white engineer regiments initially selected to work on the road could not open it in the single year desired by the War Department. In mid-April he sought and obtained a third African-American unit for the project, the 95th Engineers. Sturdevant explained to Buckner that the black troops would be "hard at work in two reliefs on a 20-hour schedule in out-of-the-way places," and that plans called for them to return below the 49th Parallel in the fall.[1]

General Buckner, who was planning to retire to Alaska after the war, seemed to have some trouble sorting out his professional responsibility for defending American territory from his personal disdain for African-Americans and his vision of Alaska's future as he responded to Sturdevant:

I appreciate your consideration of my views concerning negro troops in Alaska. The thing which I have opposed principally has been their establishment as port troops for the unloading of transports at our docks. The very high wages offered to unskilled labor here would attract a large number of them and cause them to remain and settle after the war, with the natural result that they would interbreed with the Indians and Eskimos and produce an astonishingly objectionable race of mongrels which would be a problem here from now on. We have enough racial problems here and elsewhere already.

However, Buckner did not object to employing black troops on the highway "if they are kept far enough away from the settlements and kept busy."[2]

Buckner's vivid words have been quoted repeatedly since I inserted them, somewhat stretching my topic, in an article on "Eskimos and the Defense of Alaska" published in 1985, but they do not tell the whole story.[3] In light of the racial attitudes which the Buckner-Sturdevant correspondence evinces, the significant contributions made by African-American troops in Alaska and northwestern Canada during World War II were surprisingly large. Given the stridency with which Buckner expressed his antipathy toward blacks, I find it particularly remarkable that his Alaska Defense Command and its successor, the Alaskan Department, managed, as the war progressed, to provide an atmosphere comparatively conducive to the success of African-American soldiers.

Buckner was initially unwilling to assume the burden of supplying the 97th through Valdez or Fairbanks. This forced the regiment to haul most of its own supplies and led Sturdevant to instruct his on-site highway commander, Brig. Gen. William Hoge, to ask "for *white* handling detachments, and additional transportation" for the unit. The 97th started its work slowly, as its heavy equipment operators gained experience on road-building machinery that had not been made available to the unit during most of its training in Florida. But the unit picked up speed as it headed toward the Canadian border. A race for the border developed between the 97th and 18th Engineers, a white engineer combat regiment building the highway west from Whitehorse. The two regiments met near Beaver Creek, some twenty miles inside Canada, on 25 October 1942. The black troops had won the race.[4]

The 93d and 95th Engineers, working on Canadian sections of the highway, obtained less opportunity for such achievement. The 93d built some one hundred miles of road in the southern Yukon by 10 August. Despite the rapid early progress, achieved while all Alaska Highway units were still enhancing their speed, the regiment was then assigned follow-up and maintenance duties behind the white 340th Engineers.[5]

The 95th was never given a chance to open new sections of the highway. Upon its arrival at the highway's southern terminus, it was stripped of most of its heavy equipment, which was turned over to the white 341st Engineers. The 95th was assigned to build bridges and to widen and improve the roadway largely by hand behind the 341st. The African-American regiment thus took great pride in its construction in just seventy-two hours of the 300-foot-long Sikanni Chief River bridge. Similarly handicapped was the 388th Engineer Battalion (Separate), an African-American unit formed from the 93d Engineers in Louisiana which began work on the Canadian oil, or Canol project, in June 1942 without ever obtaining the equipment of a general service regiment. The men of the 388th worked as stevedores on the long river supply route from Waterways, Alberta, to Norman Wells in the Northwest Territories.[6]

Under the War Department's chaplain assignment policies, each of the African-American units working on the Alaska Highway and Canol projects was assigned a black chaplain, but all of their other officers were white. Brig. Gen. James O'Connor, who during 1942 took over on-site supervision of both projects, wanted to keep it that way. In January of 1943 he rebuffed a War Department offer to provide some secular black officers for the units, arguing that there were no towns with Negro communities along the highway to provide them with social outlets. O'Connor's command also spurned offers made at various times by General Sturdevant for three black engineer dump truck companies and up to four black engineer general service regiments to relieve, or in the case of the companies to supplement, units already on the highway.[7]

As the sole African-American officers in these units, the chaplains bore a heavy morale burden. Capt. Edward Carroll, chaplain of the 95th, traveled with a Victrola which he employed both at religious services and in evening relaxation. Sometimes the chaplains had to step in to protect their men. Chaplain Carroll recalls having done so in the case of a soldier who dated a white woman who had also received the attentions of a white officer. The officer accused the soldier of raping the woman. Reverend Carroll observed that she was a prostitute and assisted the soldier in getting the charges dropped. Chaplain A. J. Smith of the 97th was less successful in protecting his soldiers' interests. Fairbanks was placed off limits to the 97th after some white residents became aroused because black soldiers were openly accepted at the town's restaurants, theaters, bars, and night clubs.[8]

Reverend Carroll, who subsequently became bishop of Boston in the United Methodist Church, was but one of a number of African-American Alaska Highway veterans to pursue noteworthy careers after the war. M. Sgt. George Owens, who served in the Yukon with the 93d Engineers, pursued a career in higher education and served as president of Tougaloo College from 1964 to 1984. Sgt. Herbert Tucker of the 95th became head of the District of Columbia's Department of Environmental Services.[9]

While the officers in charge of the Alaska Highway project did not always adequately equip their black regiments nor fully utilize their members' talents, they did manage to obtain excellent publicity for their use of African-American troops. An August 1942 *Time* magazine article on the highway observed that "more than 40% of the engineer workers are Negro."

The article included a photo of "a cold Alaska river: bridged in two days by U.S. Negro engineers." Newspapers across the United States and Canada published the wire-service photograph of black Cpl. Refines Sims, Jr., shaking hands with white Pfc. Alfred Jalufka atop their bulldozers at the Beaver Creek meeting of the 97th and 18th Engineers. General O'Connor's aide, Lt. Richard Neuberger, a future United States Senator from Oregon, made sure that newspapers serving the black community obtained the stories as well. He sent Walter White, head of the National Association for the Advancement of Colored People, news releases on the final breakthrough and on the formal highway opening ceremony in which two African-American and two white enlisted men held the ribbon cut by Canadian and Alaskan officials.[10]

The Army did not meet Sturdevant's goal of returning the African-American Alaska Highway regiments to the United States during the fall of 1942. It was able, however, to release the white 18th and black 93d Engineers to Buckner's Alaska Defense Command in January 1943. As he began building air bases and troop cantonments west through the Aleutians after the Japanese attack on Dutch Harbor, Buckner became eager to obtain more engineer troops, black or white. He sent the 93d's first battalion to the important naval base at Cold Bay on the Alaska Peninsula and its second battalion to Fort Glenn on Umnak Island in the Aleutians.[11]

Col. Walter Hodge, the 93d's commander, became chief Army engineer at Cold Bay, and he was assigned several white infantry and engineer companies to assist the African-American companies in his 1st Battalion. At Cold Bay the 93d built warehouses, installed water and fuel pipelines and a sewage system, expanded the airfield and the base's road net, added an ambulance entrance to the base hospital, built Pacific huts, and relaxed in its own NCO club. Nine of the 93d's heavy equipment operators were selected in July 1943 to work with white engineer units in Adak, where more men with their skills were needed. Other members of the unit had trouble at Cold Bay. One private was sent to the station hospital in Anchorage as a "mental case." Another, already a prisoner in the guardhouse, was charged with assaulting a commissioned officer.[12]

The 2d Battalion of the 93d worked at Fort Glenn along with and sometimes under the direction of the white 802d Engineer Aviation Battalion. The African-American battalion surfaced airfield runways and a road and built hangars, warehouses, and Pacific huts to live in. By late April 1943 the battalion diary recorded with considerable satisfaction:

The change in living conditions this organization has undergone the past few months is amazing. But four months ago we were living in poorly heated tents in temperatures from 30 to 60 degrees below zero. The present conditions of weather proof, well-insulated buildings, and electricity seems to be the heigth [sic] of luxury.

Ah, life in the balmy Aleutians.[13]

The African-American port troops, whose service in Alaska's towns Buckner had earlier dreaded, arrived in the Alaska Peninsula and the Aleutians soon after the 93d Engineers. The 383d Port Battalion sailed to Alaska in April and May 1943, with most of the unit going first to Adak. Company A of the 383d and detachments from other companies, however, sailed with the Attu task force. Company A landed at Massacre Bay on 13 May, D+2. The black port troops worked eighteen-hour shifts unloading cargo onto beaches initially just a mile behind the combat zone on the island. About 100 soldiers from these African-American companies served as litter bearers during the later stages of combat there. Although they came under sniper fire, none were killed or wounded.[14]

Elements of two African-American port battalions, the 372d and the 383d, unloaded ships on most of the western Aleutian Islands for the base-building projects undertaken there in 1943–1945. They did their work well. Brig. Gen. Harry Thompson, who commanded at Adak, reported that his "Negro troops were nearly as efficient in tons per day as the white troops but were definitely more careful in handling cargo." At another island, Thompson observed, "white Port troops were removed from ships work and put on other jobs because of a lack of efficiency compared to the Negro troops." These official reports were a far cry from information the War Department received from Milne Bay, New Guinea, where white officers expressed fears of hostile secret organizations among black port troops and reported substantial quantities of mishandled cargo floating around the bay.[15]

Confrontations between African-American soldiers and white military or civilian authorities occurred frequently during World War II, both in the southern United States and elsewhere. In July 1943 General George Marshall pointed to six "riots of racial character" that had occurred in "recent weeks" and concluded that "Disaffection among negro soldiers continues to constitute an immediately serious problem." Sometimes these clashes became violent and claimed the lives of participants. Even if they did not, they could lead to charges of mutiny against black soldiers. For example, seventy-four African-Americans in Company E, 1320th Engineer General Service Regiment, in Hawaii were tried by court-martial for mutiny in 1944 and convicted. The men had failed to report to work after all of their black officers were summarily transferred from the unit. Thurgood Marshall would participate in the appeals of these cases. Two black units that served in Alaska during World War II also experienced mass disobedience, but neither had these problems while in Alaska.[16]

The 483d Port Battalion came to Excursion Inlet at the northern end of Alaska's Inside Passage in the spring of 1943, after working the previous winter in New Orleans. Assigned not to Buckner's command but to the Seattle Port of Embarkation, the 483d transshipped lumber and petroleum products to ocean-going vessels heading to the Aleutians. They were a talented group. In their spare time they published a weekly newspaper, improved their living areas, and built a post theater where a number of noted artists, including film star Ingrid Bergman, came to perform.

The unit returned to the states in January 1944 and the men were given twenty-day furloughs. When the battalion sailed for England on 7 May 1944, however, it was missing some 200 men who had gone AWOL shortly before departure.[17]

The unauthorized absences occurred when Lt. Col. Peter Miller, who had commanded the battalion in New Orleans and initially in Alaska, returned to the unit after an absence of several months. First Sgt. Ernest Cain of one of the battalion's port companies, while subsequently confined in a military stockade, presented a long list of complaints against Miller, many of which involved charges of racial prejudice. Among these was his refusal to allow any enlisted men to attend officer candidate school, his instructions to a captain in the company "that the only way he could get a promotion was to work the 'niggers' hard and keep them working," the racially segregated seating he ordered in the theater built by the battalion, and his refusal to allow his soldiers to play softball with teams from white units.[18]

These grievances came from a unit that had served in Alaska, but not under the command of General Buckner or his mid-1944 successor, Lt. Gen. Delos Emmons. Respecting the spirit of newly formulated War Department policies opposing discrimination in the use of recreational and other facilities, the Alaskan Department managed to avoid large-scale racial conflict despite the arrival there in February 1944 of the 364th Infantry, an African-American regiment that had been involved in some of the more noteworthy racial clashes of the war.[19]

While stationed near Phoenix, Arizona, in November 1942 some 100 men of the 364th had engaged in a shooting match with a group of African-American military policemen in which a soldier and a civilian had been killed and twelve soldiers seriously wounded. Another soldier had been killed in 1943 by a local sheriff outside the unit's new station, Camp Van Dorn, Mississippi. Some soldiers involved in the Phoenix disorder had tattooed on their bodies the phrase "Double V," standing for victory over both the Axis powers and American racism, a popular slogan in the contemporary African-American press.[20]

By the time the 364th arrived in Alaska, it had been purged of its most troublesome soldiers and of officers who had failed to demonstrate the ability to lead African-American troops. Over 250 changes had been made in officer personnel in the year and a half after Col. John Goodman, a native of Waco, Texas, was given command of the regiment in the aftermath of the Phoenix melee. Goodman issued a policy that "there shall be no discrimination based on race, color, or creed. All officers of the regiment," he explained, "use the same messes, sleeping accommodations, and bath houses." Despite Goodman's policies, some separation of accommodations for white and black officers persisted even in Alaska and at least one black officer complained to the War Department of discriminatory treatment and sought a transfer to a unit with all African-American officers.[21]

In response to this complaint, Goodman observed that the mixing of white and black junior officers created unnecessary friction and proposed, with General Buckner's approval, that his junior officers be all of one race. The War Department had just issued a new policy under which African-American officers would be assigned to Army units in company- or battalion-size groups. In May 1944 the War Department authorized the Alaskan Department to replace the white lieutenants in the 364th with black officers that the department would provide.[22]

The 364th, meanwhile, performed well. In the summer of 1944 it removed pierced-steel plank from runways on Adak "in a highly efficient manner [and] in an exceptionally short period of time," in the words of General Thompson. By June 1945 Goodman, by then a brigadier general and commander of all U.S. troops on Shemya, could see no difference between units with all, some, or no white officers. Goodman expressed his support for racial equality in the Army unambiguously: "I am firmly convinced that a man in uniform is a soldier and should be treated the same as any other soldier without regard to color, race or creed."[23]

The youthful African-American artist Don Miller was among those who benefited from the racial tolerance which had developed in the Alaskan Department by the end of the war. Miller and African-American printer Alba Morris joined the ten-man staff of Adak's Army daily, *The Adakian*, at the invitation of its editor, mystery writer Dashiell Hammett, who in 1944 was a corporal. Thompson, a fan of Hammett's popular detective stories, had placed the author in charge of this paper, apparently unconcerned about Hammett's ties to the Communist Party. Future newsmen Bernard Kalb of NBC and Bill Glackin of the *Sacramento Bee* also served on *The Adakian*. The African-American Miller saw his work as a cartoonist on this distinguished staff as a turning point in his very successful career as an artist and illustrator. He would later paint the Martin Luther King, Jr., mural in the main public library of Washington, D.C.[24]

While some senior commanders in the Aleutians criticized the leadership skills of newly commissioned African-American officers, all agreed that the policy of equal privileges in athletics, theaters, clubs, stores, and buses had greatly enhanced racial harmony, despite some passive white disapproval. By the end of the war, senior officers in Alaska understood, in the words of the commander of the 383d Port Battalion, that the "Efficiency of Negro troops reaches a low level under conditions where ignorant, uneducated, and thoughtless white officers use terms such as 'Nigger, black so-and-so, etc.'" That commander recalled a specific instance where delays had followed the use of such terms by Navy officers, who likely had less experience working with African-American troops.[25]

African-American soldiers did a wide range of significant work on the Alaska Highway, on the Alaska Peninsula, and in the Aleutians during World War II. Willing workers when given respect, the African-American troops made known their needs as well as their capabilities. Over the course of four years of war, American military leaders in Alaska came increasingly to understand those needs and to provide a surprisingly egalitarian environment for American soldiers, black and white. To a considerable degree, the challenges those military leaders faced in a demanding war led them to implement much more tolerant racial policies than the highly prejudiced statements made just a few years earlier would have led one to predict.

NOTES

1. Sturdevant to Buckner, 2 Apr 42, containing the quotations; Sturdevant to Col William Hoge, 3 Mar 42; Sturdevant to Lt Gen Brehon Somervell, Comdr, Services of Supply, 14 Mar 42, all in file 611, Alcan Highway, box 14; annotated copy of Hoge to Sturdevant, 17 Apr 42, file 50–15, box 15, all in Accession 72A3173, Office of History, U.S. Army Corps of Engineers, Alexandria, Va.; Heath Twichell, *Northwest Epic: The Building of the Alaska Highway* (New York: St. Martin's Press, 1992), p. 121; George W. Cullum, *Biographical Register of the Officers and Graduates of the United States Military Academy,* 9 vols., 3d ed. (Boston, 1891–1950), vol. 9, pp. 121–22, 125–26.

2. Buckner to Lt Gen John DeWitt, Comdr, Western Defense Command, 3 Nov 41; Buckner to Sturdevant, 20 Apr 42, containing the quotations, copies of both in Corresp of Lt Gen Buckner, box 14, Records of the Alaskan Department, Record Group (RG) 338 (Records of U.S. Army Commands), National Archives and Records Administration (NARA); the undated original of the latter in the Sturdevant file, Office of History, U.S. Army Corps of Engineers. Brig. Gen. Dwight Eisenhower, then Army assistant chief staff, War Plans Division, reported that Governor Ernest Gruening also opposed assigning black troops to Alaska, arguing, as Eisenhower paraphrased him, "that the mixture of the colored race with the native Indian and Eskimo stock is highly undesirable." See Eisenhower to Army Chief of Staff George Marshall, 25 Mar 42, case no. 4, file 291.21, Operations Division Classified General Correspondence (Class Gen Corresp), box 472, RG 165 (Records of the Army Staff), NARA.

3. Hendricks, "The Eskimos and the Defense of Alaska," *Pacific Historical Review* 44 (August 1985): 271–95, with the quotation on p. 280; Everett Louis Overstreet, *Black on a Background of White: A Chronicle of Afro-Americans' Involvement in America's Last Frontier, Alaska* (Fairbanks: That New Publishing Co., 1988), pp. 42–43; Twichell, *Northwest Epic,* pp. 144–45; and Bill Gifford, "The Great Black North," *Washington City Paper* 13, no. 40 (October 1993): 24.

4. Sturdevant to Hoge, 11 May 42, containing the quotation, file 50–15, box 15, Accession 72A3173; Twichell, *Northwest Epic,* pp. 122, 211–12, 335; Blanch Coll, Jean Keith, and Herbert Rosenthal, *The Corps of Engineers: Troops and Equipment,* United States Army in World War II (Washington, D.C.: U.S. Army Center of Military History, 1958), pp. 16, 139–40; Shelby L. Stanton, *Order of Battle: U.S. Army, World War II* (Novato, Calif.: Presidio Press, 1984), pp. 542, 570.

5. "History of the Whitehorse Sector of the Alcan Highway," 10 Jun 43, pp. 6, 9, with the mileage figure taken from John T. Greenwood, "Building the Road to Alaska," in Barry W. Fowle, ed., *Builders and Fighters: U.S. Army Engineers in World War II* (Fort Belvoir, Va.: Office of History, U.S. Army Corps of Engineers, 1992), p. 134.

6. Twichell, *Northwest Epic,* pp. 130–32, 143, 188–91; "The History of the Ninety-Third Engineer Regiment (GS) prior to 1 Jan 43," file ENRG–93–0.1, box 19549, World War II Operations Rpts, RG 407 (Records of the Adjutant General's Office), NARA. While Brig. Gen. James O'Connor, who assumed command of the southern sector of the highway in May 1942, made the decision to turn the 95th's equipment over to the 341st, Sturdevant and Hoge had already decided in April that the seventh regiment assigned to the project, ultimately the 95th, would be used "in the rear of the 341st." See Hoge to Sturdevant, 17 Apr 42.

7. Ulysses Lee, *The Employment of Negro Troops,* United States Army in World War II (Washington D.C.: U.S. Army Center of Military History, 1966), pp. 208–13; Telg, Col Joseph Gorlinski (a Sturdevant subordinate) to O'Connor, 20 Aug 42, and Ltr, Sturdevant to Somervell, 4 Feb 43, with 2d Ind, Col H. A. Montgomery, commanding, Northwest Service Command, to Somervell, 28 Feb 43, all in file 370.5 (Alcan Highway), Class Gen Corresp, box 130, entry 52A41, RG 77 (Records of the Office of the Chief of Engineers), NARA.

8. Gifford, "The Great Black North," p. 28; An. 3 (Psychological) to G–2 Periodic Rpt no. 50, 1–8 May 43, file 91–DC1–2.1, box 7, American Theater, World War II Operations Rpts, RG 407, NARA; Lt Col J. A. Day, Inspector General, Northwest Service Command, to O'Connor, 29 Jun 43, file 333.1 (97th Engineers), Class Gen Corresp, box 344, entry 52A41, RG 77, NARA.

9. Information received by phone from the Information Service of the United Methodist Church and from the Office of the President, Tougaloo College; Twichell, *Northwest Epic*, p. 144; Gifford, "The Great Black North," pp. 28, 34.

10. Twichell, *Northwest Epic*, pp. 181, 213–14; *Time* 40, no. 9 (August 1942): 78–79, containing the quotations; Neuberger to White, 4 Nov 42, and 26 Nov 42, box 2–A–642, Papers of the National Association for the Advancement of Colored People (NAACP), Manuscript Division, Library of Congress.

11. Sturdevant to Hoge, 16 Aug 42, file 50–15, box 15, Accession 72A3173; Buckner to Dewitt, 25 Nov 42, Corresp of Lt Gen Buckner, box 14, Alaskan Department, RG 338, NARA; Unit Diary, 93d Engineer General Service Regiment, 1943, containing the quotation, in file ENRG–93–0.7, and "History of the Ninety-Third Engineer Regiment (GS) for 1943," file ENRG–93–0.1, both in box 19549, World War II Operations Rpts, RG 407, NARA; Stetson Conn, Rose Engleman, and Byron Fairchild, *Guarding the United States and Its Outposts*, United States Army in World War II (Washington, D.C.: U.S. Army Center of Military History, 1964), p. 284.

12. Unit Diary, 93d Engineer General Service Rgt, 1943, and "Diary of Regimental Headquarters, Ninety-Third Engineer Regiment (GS) for Period 1 Jan 44 to 22 Jun 44," both in file ENRG–93–0.7.

13. "Diary of Second Battalion, Ninety Third Engineer Regiment (GS) for Period 1943," file ENRG–93–0.7.

14. Cards of Headquarters and Headquarters Detachment, 383d Port Bn TC, and the 881st and the 884th Transportation Corps Stevedore Companies, microfilm box 106, microfilmed unit history cards of the Operations and Directory Section, WDOB [1947]; former Stf Sgt Benjamin Woods (of Co A, 383d Port Bn) to the Army Center of Military History, 5 May 88, 383d Transportation Port Bn File, all in the Organizational History Branch, CMH; Brig Gen Harry F. Thompson, Comdr, U.S. Troops, Adak, to Lt Gen Delos Emmons, Comdr, Alaskan Department, 28 Jun 45, p. 6, file 291.2, box 53, Class Gen Corresp, Alaskan Department, RG 338, NARA.

15. Unit history card of the 372d Port Bn, Organizational History Branch, CMH; "Military Strength of the Alaskan Department, 31 Dec 43," file 320.2 (Alaskan Dept.), pt. 1, Class Gen Corresp, box 126, entry 52A41, RG 77, NARA; Thompson to Emmons, 28 Jun 45, with the quotations in pt. 2; Maj Fred Gustorf, Ninth Service Command, to Somervell, Aug 44, case 44, file 322.97 OPD, box 831, Operations Div Class Gen Corresp, RG 165, NARA.

16. Lee, *The Employment of Negro Troops*, pp. 348–79; Memo, Marshall for Commanding General, Army Service Forces, et al., 13 Jul 43, containing the quotations, file 291.2, box 2, Northwest Service Command, RG 338, NARA; Court Martial, 1320th Engineers, files, boxes 2–B–18 to 20, Papers of the NAACP, Manuscript Division, Library of Congress.

17. History, 483d Port Bn, Transportation Corps, 3 Apr 44; Historical Rpt, 656th Port Co, 15 Dec 44; Historical Rpt of Co C, 483d Port Bn, now 658th Port Co, 15 Dec 44; Historical Record of the 659th Port Co, (Co D), 483d Port Bn, all in file TCBN–483–0.1, box 23320, World War II Operations Rpts, RG 407, NARA; Isadore Zack, "CIC in Zone of Interior: The Case of the Mass AWOL of the 483d Port Battalion," *Golden Sphinx: The Voice of Intelligence* (Fall 1993): 1, 4, 18, copy in 483d Port Bn File, Organizational History Branch, CMH.

18. Zack, "The Case of the Mass AWOL," with the quotation on p. 4.

19. Lee, *The Employment of Negro Troops*, pp. 308–09; Journal, 364th Infantry, Mar

41–May 46, entries for 14 Jan–1 Mar 44, file INRG–364–0.7, box 21241, World War II Operations Rpts, RG 407, NARA.

20. Lee, *The Employment of Negro Troops*, pp. 366–70; Gustorf to Somervell, 3 Aug 44.

21. Lee, *The Employment of Negro Troops*, pp. 222–23, 367; John F. Goodman biography file, Historical Resources Branch, CMH; 2d Lt Robert E. Jackson, HQ Co, 2d Bn, 364th Inf, to Maj Gen J. A. Ulio, the Adjutant General, 4 Apr 44, with 1st Ind, Goodman to Ulio, 25 Apr 44, containing the quotation; Lt Col B. C. Kennon, Comdr, 2d Bn, 364th Inf, to Goodman, 21 Apr 44; Capt Paul Little, Comdr, Co K, 364th Inf, to Lt Col Earl Keiso, Comdr, 3d Bn, 364th Inf, 23 Apr 44, all in case 40, file 322.97 OPD, box 831, Operations Division Decimal File, RG 165, NARA.

22. 1st Ind, Goodman to Ulio, 25 Apr 44; 3d Ind, Buckner to Ulio, 28 Apr 44; Telg, Maj Gen Thomas Handy, War Department Asst Chief of Staff, G–1, to Buckner, 27 May 44, all in case 40; Ulio to Major Army Commanders, 7 Jan 44, case 27, both in file 322.97 OPD.

23. Thompson to Emmons, 28 Jun 45, pp. 17–18, containing the first quotation, and 1st Ind, Goodman to Emmons, 30 Jun 45, with the second quotation on p. 6, on Lt Col W. R. Coleman, Asst Adjutant General, Alaskan Department, to Goodman, 7 Jun 45, all in file 291.2, box 53, Class Gen Corresp, Alaskan Department, RG 338, NARA; Journal, 364th Infantry, Mar 41–May 46, entry for 21 Sep 44; and Cullum, *Biographical Register*, vol. 9, p. 219.

24. Richard Layman, *Shadow Man: The Life of Dashiell Hammett* (New York: Harcourt Brace Jovanovich, 1981), pp. 173–95; Diane Brenner, Anchorage Museum of History and Art, to Hendricks, 2 Dec 93; and Interv, Hendricks with Julia Miller, Don Miller's widow, on 19 Apr 94.

25. Thompson to Emmons, 28 Jun 45, pp. 2 (containing the quotation), 4, 5, 8–12, 15; Brig Gen Maxwell O'Brien, Comdr, U.S. Troops, Amchitka, to Emmons, 22 Jun 45, pp. 2–3; "Consolidation of Rpts: Participation of Negro Troops in the Post-War Military Establishment," pp. 6–8, 10, all in file 291.2, box 53, Class Gen Corresp, Alaskan Department, RG 338, NARA.

PART III

The U.S. Army at War
The War in Europe, 1944–1945

Introduction

In "Eisenhower Versus Montgomery: Postwar Memoirs as Primary Sources," Patrick Murray examines perhaps the chief historiographical debate surrounding Allied performance in the European Theater of Operations. While many military historians believe that General Dwight Eisenhower correctly insisted on a broad front of operations against the German Army, others maintain that General Bernard Montgomery should have been allowed to push forward against the Germans in late 1944 in a single, northern line of attack.

As Murray demonstrates, the debate began in late 1944, fueled by newspaper reports (particularly in English papers such as the *Daily Telegraph*, the *Daily Mail*, the *News Chronicle*, and the *Daily Express*) attempting to chronicle the planning and decision-making process at Allied Headquarters and criticizing Eisenhower's command and strategic abilities. American observers attacked Montgomery in their turn, and the war of words continued following the publication of the memoirs of key participants and their aides throughout the late 1940s and 1950s.

At the heart of the debate lie several extremely sensitive issues, including the command of U.S. troops by a foreign officer, and the contention, first made famous by journalist Chester Wilmot in *The Struggle for Europe*, that had Eisenhower allowed one of his generals to attack the German heartland in a "single knife-like thrust" in the fall of 1944, the war would have ended that year. According to this view, the Allies could have avoided the Battle of the Bulge and its massive casualties as well as the division of Germany, for then the Red Army would not have had the opportunity to move so far west.

Murray disputes this contention, reminding us that it took eight more months of devastating air attacks and the approach of 160 Russian divisions from the east at the same time that the Allies were entering Germany from the west to force a Nazi capitulation. The Germans would certainly have mounted a ferocious counterattack to any Allied incursion into their territory in 1944.

The importance of the broad- vs. narrow-front controversy in military history can be clearly understood when one reads James Huston's

"Normandy to the German Border: Third Army Logistics." Huston challenges the prevailing agreement among historians that insoluble logistical problems forced Allied military leaders to curtail their pursuit of their disorganized foes beyond the Siegfried Line and across the Rhine River in the late summer and early fall of 1944. Huston believes that the Allies had a variety of logistical options available to them that they simply failed to address. Had they acted more forcibly to remedy their supply difficulties in the fall of 1944, Huston argues, the Allies could have entered Germany then, avoiding the Battle of the Bulge and hastening the end of the war.

Huston believes that the Army's major logistical problem was not in landing enough supplies at the port towns, but rather in moving them great distances inland. The French railways had been severely damaged and needed great investments of labor, time, and equipment to make them operational. Although the famous Red Ball Express did much to alleviate some of the logistical backlog on the roads, Huston believes that this organization could have been much more productive had the Army provided it with more experienced truck drivers, mechanics, and soldiers to act as "traffic cops." Huston argues that the U.S. Army put too many of the wrong types of soldiers on the Continent and then used them poorly. Why did traditional combat divisions continue to arrive on the Continent when engineer companies were needed to repair roadways, railroads, and airstrips and truck companies were needed to transport supplies?

The author also maintains that Allied leaders also fumbled in not making greater use of their existing air transportation capabilities. He argues that strategic bombing should have ended with the invasion of Normandy, and that the bombers of the Eighth Air Force could have been better used to carry gasoline and other necessary supplies. Rather than ferrying over 2,000 tons of bombs each day to Germany, the Air Forces should have been carrying 2,000 tons of supplies—enough for ten divisions a day—to France. If Patton's Third Army had kept moving rather than grinding to a halt for lack of fuel, argues Huston, the Germans' Ardennes offensive would not have taken place, and Allied commanders would have been able to end the war much sooner.

According to the next author, American military leaders had at their disposal professional experts to advise them on the handling of logistical backups. In "American Geographers and the OSS During World War II," Keir Sterling describes how William J. Donovan created a new central intelligence-gathering agency to "collect and analyze all information and data which may bear upon international security." The new organization, initially called the Coordinator of Information (COI), became the Office of Strategic Services (OSS) in June 1942.

The Research and Analysis Branch of the OSS contained large numbers of geographers charged with collecting, digesting, and analyzing geographic intelligence. One section made maps of areas for which few maps existed—the Pacific Islands, Japan, Burma, and China. OSS geographers stationed in Washington also prepared technical studies and daily situation reports for the Operations Division of the War Department and the Joint Chiefs of Staff.

Sterling describes how top geographers were recruited for COI along with their most promising graduate students. Of the 2,000 professional geographers in the United States in 1941, 500 were in Washington (350 in uniform) working for government agencies, and another 60 ultimately worked in Europe during 1944 and 1945. To produce detailed maps of key transportation systems and to analyze their logistical potential, they conducted studies of major port cities and the routes leading inland, estimating railroad capacity. Their efforts proved critical to the easing of logistical problems at Antwerp and Marseille.

In "To Hurdle the Last Barrier: The U.S. Army Engineers and the Crossing of the Rhine River, 1944–1945," John Greenwood calls the Rhine crossings one of the "largest and most meticulously planned operations in military history." The river was the last significant natural barrier protecting the Nazi heartland, and its breaching was vital to the final offensive of the western Allies.

The Office of ETOUSA's Chief Engineer was responsible for planning the crossings. That office assembled a mass of detailed topographical information, including the depth, width, and current of the river at various points, as well as riverbed conditions and the height of the banks on which defenders might be stationed. The chief engineer and his staff also had to obtain aerial photo-mapping information, select the crossing sites, and define the bridging requirements. These requirements included supplies, equipment, and personnel necessary for each corps of each army to construct first floating and later fixed bridges. Great care also went into the selection of routes wide enough to accommodate the size of certain necessary amphibious vehicles and equipment.

One major concern was the enemy's ability to deliberately flood the Rhine by destroying the upstream dams, since the floating bridges which the Army planned to use were vulnerable to major changes in the Rhine's water level. However, the anticipated flooding never materialized, and during March, April, and May U.S. Army engineers built sixty-two bridges faster than the most optimistic of estimates. The Rhine River crossings benefited from good weather, low water, and feeble German resistance.

Christopher Gabel's "Tank Destroyers in the European Theater of Operations" describes the difficulties encountered by the newly created tank destroyer units during their first experiences on the battlefield. Initially created to deal with Germany's vaunted panzer units, the tank destroyer battalions failed to fulfill that critical task. Much of America's early tank doctrine was in fact erroneously based on contemporary American tactics which envisioned tank formations operating in isolation on the battlefield. In contrast, American tank destroyer crews in Tunisia found that German tanks fought in close coordination with other arms as part of the blitzkrieg concept. The German tanks refused to play the part laid out for them in U.S. tank destroyer doctrine.

The American commanders, however, were quick to revise their tactics and adapt their tools to field exigencies. In both Italy and France, tank destroyers, fully tracked armored vehicles, well armed and fast but with extremely thin armor, were quickly integrated into a variety of combat arms teams. They provided, for example, direct-fire support to infantry units, muscle to cavalry patrols, and mobile artillery for other task groups. In Europe, tank destroyer units helped engineers and infantry to break through Normandy hedgerows and helped the infantry destroy German pillboxes along the Siegfried Line.

In "'The Very Model of a Modern Major General': Background of World War II American Generals in V Corps," Charles Kirkpatrick attempts to draw a career profile of the average American general officer. Army officers appointed to division command during World War II had spent the majority of their careers in the austere interwar Army, small in size and short on money. Promotions were agonizingly slow—officers spent many tours at the same rank, and majors were expected to have gray hair. The structure and size of the Army allowed officers few opportunities to work with troops in a command capacity, making practical experience with real units a rare commodity. Seeking to discover the impact of this environment on the wartime command abilities of senior U.S. officers, the author analyzes the careers of V Corps generals. Surprisingly, he concludes that the minimal amount of "troop time" experienced by many of these officers had little adverse effect on their ability to command. He also found no evidence that battlefield experience attained in World War I, including the acquisition of medals for combat or valor, aided later careers.

Kirkpatrick concludes that it was the many years spent in the Army "schoolhouse"—that is, the courses in military theory, strategy, and tactics offered at the Command and General Staff School, the Army War College, and the branch schools—that enabled the generals of V Corps to perform competently on the battlefield. Few failed in their missions or were relieved of command. These men may not have been military geniuses, states Kirkpatrick, but they "stood up and hit the ball" when called upon.

Eisenhower Versus Montgomery
Postwar Memoirs as Primary Sources

Patrick Murray

Military historians will recall the debate between General Dwight D. Eisenhower, the Supreme Allied Commander, and Field Marshal Sir Bernard Law Montgomery, commanding general of the British 21st Army Group. The two men disagreed over the invasion of Southern France in August 1944, opening Antwerp to ship traffic in the fall and leaving Berlin to the Soviets in the spring of 1945. Their best known argument concerned the direction and command of the Allied advance on the Rhine, beginning in September 1944. Eisenhower favored advancing on the Ruhr, the industrial heart of western Germany, on what has come to be called a broad front, both north and south of the Ardennes plateau, while Montgomery favored a single, northern line of attack.

Reading the memoirs of the participants in the debate over strategy and command in northwest Europe in 1944–1945 in their order of publication and comparing them to their unpublished sources leads to the following conclusions: (1) the postwar memoirs picked up where the British newspapers left off; (2) each memoir affected subsequent memoirs, but the Cold War prevented a totally frank retelling; (3) most memoirs were written in haste without much research by people who needed the money, which guaranteed controversy; (4) by 1948 and the Berlin Crisis the tone of the postwar debate had been set; and (5) the postwar memoirs need to be considered in relation to the lack of documentation of high-level decision making brought about by Eisenhower's style as Supreme Commander.

During the war most American headquarters read the British papers on the same day they were printed, especially the *Daily Mail*, which had a Paris edition. Its slant often infuriated American soldiers. For example, Lt. Col. Chester Hansen, who kept the headquarters' diary in General Omar N. Bradley's 12th Army Group, referred to it as "anti-American."[1] Both Hansen and Ralph Ingersoll, the Anglophobic intelligence officer at 12th Army Group and author of the 1946 *Top Secret*, believed that the British government sanctioned a Fleet Street campaign to have Montgomery named either ground forces commander or deputy supreme commander.[2] However, editorial opinion in Britain was not monolithic, witness the *Daily Telegraph* editorial in November 1944, favoring Eisenhower's broad-front strategy.[3]

On 20 December 1944, the German Ardennes counteroffensive formed the backdrop for the biggest press controversy of the campaign when Eisenhower divided the front on a line—Givet, France–Houffalize, Belgium–Pruem, Germany—giving Montgomery command of both the United States First and Ninth Armies and leaving Bradley the Third United States Army. Columns such as A. J. Cummings' "Monty Should Be Deputy C-in-C" in the *News Chronicle* and Alan Moorehead's "A 1914 General Asks Me How Rundstedt Did It" in the *Daily Express* criticized both the broad-front strategy and the lack of a ground forces commander. Writing just before Montgomery's expanded role became public knowledge, Cummings argued that Eisenhower did not have enough time to devote to running the ground war; only a deputy ground commander could do the requisite amount of thinking and planning. The day after Eisenhower secretly put Montgomery in command of the northern half of the salient, Moorehead said that there had been no subtlety to Allied grand strategy and recommended either a British or American ground forces commander as well as concentration on one locus of attack to penetrate the German front.[4]

On 7 January 1945, Field Marshal Montgomery held a press conference, ostensibly to allay public criticism of Eisenhower, but in the process he referred to the Bulge as the trickiest battle that he had ever handled. Montgomery's remarks appeared condescending to Americans, especially so at 12th Army Group's advanced headquarters where Hansen and Ingersoll, the resident Anglophobes, had little trouble convincing Bradley to hold his own press conference, during which Bradley announced that the field marshal's enlarged command was "temporary." Subsequently the *Daily Mail* took offense and called Bradley's statement "A Slur on Monty."[5]

The contradictory press conferences and *Daily Mail* editorial led the British War Cabinet to conclude "that public statements by High Allied Commanders during the conduct of campaigns might lead to embarrassment, and possibly even some impairment of friendly relations between the Allies." Britain's Minister of Information, Brenden Bracken, called the editor of the *Daily Mail* to his office, and the paper agreed to drop the issue.[6]

For the next two decades Montgomery's command of two American armies during the Battle of the Bulge would remain perhaps the most controversial aspect of the campaign. It was certainly the sharpest wound of the war as far as Omar Bradley was concerned. Interestingly enough, the depth of feeling on the issue can be traced on the map. If a memoir is a product of a headquarters south of the line Givet-Houffalize-Pruem, it can be counted upon to be irrational on the subject of Montgomery's command of the First and Ninth Armies.

One year after the Battle of the Bulge, in the first winter of the Cold War, former Prime Minister Winston Churchill, on an American tour, stopped by the Pentagon to talk with the newly appointed American Ambassador to the Soviet Union, Lt. Gen. Walter Bedell Smith, Eisenhower's wartime Chief of Staff. Churchill was worried that memoirs of the recent conflict might damage relations between their two countries. Anticipating the theme of his "Iron Curtain" speech, which he would deliver in Fulton, Missouri, in March, Churchill maintained that the present situation of "crisis and hazard" in Europe required continuation of the wartime Anglo-American alliance and its sense of common purpose. Churchill also worried that a completely frank retelling of the wartime controversies was counterproductive to Anglo-American relations in light of postwar realities.[7]

The need for continued good relations among wartime Allies influenced the first round of memoirs by major players. Eisenhower had come to the same conclusion as Churchill when he warned his former wartime aide, Capt. Harry C. Butcher, USNR, not to cite confidential memoranda in Butcher's upcoming memoir, *My Three Years With Eisenhower.* In late December 1945 the two men went over Butcher's manuscript, and Eisenhower told Butcher to tone down descriptions of Charles de Gaulle and Montgomery for the sake of continued good relations with their respective countries.[8]

In 1946 Montgomery, then Chief of the Imperial General Staff (CIGS), sent much the same message to his former Operations Officer at 21st Army Group, Col. David Belchem. Belchem was ghost writing a history of the 21st Army Group, *Normandy to the Baltic,* and the field marshal told him to avoid politics. Montgomery wanted "[A] plain tale of facts, unembellished by any controversial or unsavory details."[9] Six years later, in 1953, Churchill, once again Prime Minister and Minister of Defense, assured then President Eisenhower that *Triumph and Tragedy* contained nothing that could imply there had been any "controversy or lack of confidence between us."[10]

Efforts to maintain good relations between the wartime Allies on the memoir front were never entirely successful, however. Some controversy was bound to occur with nearly each new memoir. For example, when the British serialization of Butcher's *My Three Years With Eisenhower*

revealed impatience with Montgomery's handling of the battle for Caen—
"Eisenhower Aide: General Almost Sacked Montgomery"—Montgomery
reacted at once, writing Eisenhower: "This is a terrible pity. And the reper-
cussion is bound to be that some British author will retaliate by getting at
you."[11]

In late October 1947 General George S. Patton, Jr.'s posthumous *War
as I Knew It* was serialized in the *Saturday Evening Post.* Implicit in
Patton's criticism of SHAEF (Supreme Headquarters Allied Expeditionary
Force), which did not mention Eisenhower by name, was that SHAEF
lengthened the war by restricting gasoline deliveries to Third Army in
September 1944 when, according to Patton, Third Army could have
crossed the Rhine in ten days, thus bringing the war to an earlier end.
Patton's single thrust theme repeated claims that had first appeared in
Ingersoll's 1946 *Top Secret* and led Eisenhower to complain to Bedell
Smith in Moscow: "I am beginning to think that crackpot history is going
to guide the future student of the late conflict."[12]

Eisenhower's 1948 *Crusade in Europe* contained the following generic
refutation of the single thrust without mentioning Patton by name: "In the
late summer days of 1944 it was known to us that the German still had dis-
posable reserves within his own country. Any ideas of attempting to thrust
forward a small force, bridge the Rhine, and continue on into the heart of
Germany was completely fantastic."[13] *Crusade in Europe* went from the
general to the specific, refuting Montgomery's single thrust by describing
their famous meeting at Brussels airport of 10 September 1944, using language that has influenced the debate ever since:

I explained to Montgomery the condition of our supply system and our need for
early use at Antwerp. I pointed out that, without railway bridges over the Rhine
and ample stockages of supplies on hand, there was no possibility of maintaining
a force in Germany capable of penetrating to its capital. There was still a considerable reserve in the middle of the enemy country and I knew that any *pencillike*
[italics added] thrust into the heart of Germany such as he proposed would meet
nothing but certain destruction. This was true, no matter on what part of the front
it might be attempted. I would not consider it.[14]

After reading *Crusade in Europe*, the still-serving Montgomery wrote
the recently retired Eisenhower that he was saddened by being made the
center of speculation in the press when he could not defend himself.
However, when the *Sunday Times*, of 21 November 1948, printed "EISEN-
HOWER'S BOOK: THE FACTS," Montgomery had in fact begun his own
counterattack. Collaborating with Sir Dennis Hamilton, the unnamed military correspondent, the review borrowed several stock phrases from the
field marshal's wartime papers:

Eisenhower's consistent refusal to have an overall Army Commander-in-Chief will always be a matter for discussion and criticism. He insisted on commanding the land armies himself; he is not in any way a battle commander, and he had no previous experience, in fact, he did not understand how to command *in the field*. . . . [A] Supreme Commander sits on a lofty perch, he exercises command in a great strategical sphere and he cannot exercise tactical command at the same time. Eisenhower did attempt to do so, with results disastrous in their postwar setting.[15]

When Montgomery wondered why Eisenhower had written so soon after the war he concluded that it must have been for the money: nearly all the professional soldiers faced rather modest retirements. Eisenhower's deal with Doubleday saw him sell the copyright, which the IRS took as a onetime sale of property, and he made over half a million dollars. Montgomery's chief of staff for three years, Maj. Gen. Sir Francis de Guingand, faced retirement as a substantive colonel, and only a letter from Eisenhower moved Whitehall to advance him to the rank he had held for three years. De Guingand went off to France and within three months had published *Operation Victory* but unfortunately took a lump sum payment instead of royalties. Field Marshal Lord Alan Brooke, the wartime Chief of the Imperial General Staff, had to sell his house and his prized works on bird watching before several directorships came his way; he and Sir Arthur Bryant split fifty-fifty the royalties from the two volumes of his edited diaries, *The Turn of the Tide* and *Triumph in the West*. In 1954 Montgomery sold his papers to the Kemsley Group, which would later serialize his memoirs in the *Sunday Times,* and he also arranged to become its military correspondent.[16]

Ralph Ingersoll and Harry Butcher both needed money for second marriages and new businesses. Butcher informed Eisenhower that Kay Summersby, Eisenhower's wartime driver and receptionist, had written *Eisenhower Was My Boss* (1948) partly out of pique, but also a need for money. Churchill needed a syndicate to save his beloved Chartwell, which was purchased by wealthy friends and reverted to Britain's National Trust upon his death. Churchill's memoirs of the Second World War earned the Nobel Prize for literature in 1953 and made him independently wealthy; he received one million dollars for their syndication alone.[17]

By June 1948 the Cold War congealed around Berlin, which was again the focus of round-the-clock American and British flights. As a result of the Berlin Crisis and the Cold War, the initial military criticism of the single thrusters began to take on an added political dimension. More than any other work, Chester Wilmot's 1952 *The Struggle for Europe* fashioned the public's Cold War perception of the debate over strategy and command in northwest Europe. Explicit in Wilmot's criticism was that a handful of

American decisions led to the Soviets' winning the "struggle for Europe" because they had liberated Prague, Vienna, Budapest, and Berlin.

Unlike earlier works, Wilmot conducted research over a six-year period and in the process interviewed Montgomery several times. Wilmot's papers contain twelve typed pages titled "The Conduct of the Campaign After the Change In Command." Based on Montgomery's papers from 4 September to 28 October 1944, all the documents cited dealt with strategy rather than command. Reaching 14 October 1944, Wilmot noted: "There was an exchange of letters about this time on the subject of command (letters not on file)."[18]

Tremendously influential and still in print, *The Struggle for Europe* cast the debate between Eisenhower and Montgomery almost exclusively in strategic terms. To Wilmot's readers the field marshal appeared most concerned with Eisenhower's failure to concentrate on one thrust line. Wilmot elevated the debate to an ethereal level it did not deserve, and it was nowhere close to Montgomery's 1944–1945 criticism of what he regarded as Eisenhower's most persistent failure, that of battlefield commander. In his chapter "The Great Argument" Wilmot quoted Montgomery's call for "a solid mass of forty divisions, which would be so strong that it need fear nothing."[19] However, Wilmot neglected to point out that when Montgomery wrote that paper on 17 August 1944, Eisenhower's entire command did not contain forty divisions. Neither did the journalist print Montgomery's conclusion on Operation MARKET-GARDEN from their interview in 1949, when he said:

I hoped that [Eisenhower] would reinforce my success but I knew that we could not hope to get much more than a bridgehead beyond the Rhine before the winter, and be nicely poised to break out in the New Year. By the time MARKET GARDEN was undertaken its significance was more tactical than strategic.[20]

Wilmot's 1952 arguments are more applicable to Eisenhower's 1948 "pencillike" reference than to August–September 1944. If his point was to prove that Montgomery's single-thrust plan had not been "pencillike," then only Montgomery's plans to employ forty divisions need be cited. If, however, the point was to prove a negative, i.e., that broad front prevented a September single thrust from ending the war, then the field marshal's 1949 comments about the tactical significance of MARKET-GARDEN could not be printed in 1952.

The Memoirs of Field-Marshal the Viscount Montgomery of Alamein in 1958 continued in the Churchillian style of reprinting documents, and again the student of the debate was led to believe that strategy superseded command.[21] Montgomery's *Memoirs* omit his cable to Bedell Smith of 21 September 1944 recommending that Eisenhower relinquish command of the ground forces and operational control of the First United States Army, which numbered eight divisions at the time.[22]

Montgomery's greatest rival during the campaign, Omar Bradley, had predicted in his own ghost-written memoir, *A Soldier's Story*, in 1951 that historians would have difficulty determining responsibility for strategic decisions owing to the numerous personal and telephone conversations between himself and Eisenhower.[23] During the height of the German counterattack in the Ardennes, SHAEF's Deputy Chief of Staff for Air, Air Marshal James Robb, had observed that Eisenhower and Bradley were in daily phone contact, while the Supreme Commander almost never talked to Montgomery.[24]

Further complicating the task of the historian of the debate was the asymmetric contact between SHAEF and American and British army groups. Examination of Eisenhower's calendar between mid-August 1944 and the end of the war in 1945 shows that Eisenhower and Bradley met 47 times as opposed to 16 meetings between Eisenhower and Montgomery, nearly a 3 to 1 ratio. In fact, Montgomery traveled to SHAEF once during the war, on 5 October 1944, because his superior, Field Marshal Sir Alan Brooke, the Chief of the Imperial General Staff, was in attendance.[25]

Bradley visited SHAEF headquarters 21 times and stayed overnight 9 times. Montgomery visited SHAEF once and never stayed overnight. Eisenhower traveled to see Montgomery 15 times and once stayed overnight at 21st Army Group in 1944. The Supreme Commander met with Bradley at 12th Army Group or a third location 26 times and stayed overnight with Bradley 19 times. Including their vacation in Cannes over 20–22 March in 1945, Eisenhower and Bradley had the potential of 30 late-night conversations.[26]

Eisenhower spent the night at Montgomery's headquarters only once during the war, on the night of 28–29 November 1944. Alanbrooke's published diary, *Triumph in the West*, reprinted the message he received from Montgomery after that evening's conversation. Montgomery's message claims that Eisenhower had agreed to adopt the single-thrust strategy:

Ike visited me today and we have had a very long talk. I put the following points to him. 1st. That the plan contained in his last directive had failed and we had in fact suffered a strategic defeat. He agreed. 2nd. That we must now prepare a new plan and in that plan we must get away from the doctrine of attacking all along the front and must concentrate our resources on the selected vital thrust. He agreed.[27]

In 1985 Montgomery's Military Assistant, Lt. Col. Christopher P. "Kit" Dawnay wrote an essay, "Inside Monty's Headquarters: Recollections of the Man." Dawnay described accompanying Eisenhower to his room on the night of 28–29 November 1944 and then returning to take down Montgomery's nightly message to Brooke:

"Get this message sent to the CIGS." I wrote it down at his direction and was astonished to discover that he was claiming that Ike had agreed in principle with the single-thrust strategy. I read the message back and asked if it was correct. He assented. I said "May I say something, sir?" "Yes, certainly." "Ike does not agree, sir." His only comment was "Send that message, Kit." And so I did. But Ike had not agreed.[28]

Bradley was right in 1951 when he said that the telephone would complicate the writing of the history of the recent war; he could have added personal animus. The paucity of personal contact between Eisenhower and Montgomery was consensual on both their parts, and it has skewed historians' interpretation of the campaign. Precisely because they avoided one another, Montgomery and Eisenhower generated the written documentation that dominates the historical literature. What contact there was between SHAEF and 21st Army Group was left to de Guingand, Bedell Smith, or Maj. Gen. John M. "Jock" Whiteley, Eisenhower's British Deputy G–3, Plans and Operations Officer.

Lack of supervision and visitation from Eisenhower led Montgomery to conclude in 1958: "We did not advance to the Rhine on a *broad* front; we advanced to the Rhine on *several* fronts, which were un-coordinated."[29] On the other hand, the collaboration between Eisenhower and Bradley must have been just as important to the conduct of operations across northwest Europe; however, it is overlooked because of the plethora of documentation concerning the debate between Eisenhower and Montgomery.

The debate over the potential of the single thrust continues fifty years after the events because both participants and students of the war want to believe in a magic bullet that would have ended the war before Christmas 1944. Ending the war six months early would have avoided tens of thousands of casualties, the division of Germany, the bankruptcy of Britain, and, presumably, the Allied disadvantages in the Cold War with the Russians. Somehow, single thrust would have changed the past, the present, and the future.

The former chief of staff of the 21st Army Group doubted claims that the war could have been ended for the want of a nail in September 1944. Sir Francis de Guingand's *Operation Victory* in 1947 pointed out that: "It took a Russian offensive using about 160 divisions, massive offensives on our part, as well as eight more months of devastating air attack, to force the Germans to capitulate, and even then Hitler and his gang never gave up."[30]

Despite de Guingand's admonition, single-thrusters attach almost biblical significance to Montgomery's "forty divisions." In 1958 Samuel Eliot

Morison cautioned against the type of fallacy perpetuated by the single-thrust school. Morison believed that critics fallaciously assumed that if the Allies had done something different then the Germans would have done the same thing that they did; however, Morison pointed out that the Germans would have counteracted any change in Allied strategy.[31]

Single thrust is alive and well, the most famous nonevent in history, fashioned by men with books to sell and axes to grind. However, the postwar memoirs were as much about the previous book as they were about the war, and the only magic bullet was the one Hitler put into his brain on 30 April 1945 when the Russians were less than a quarter of a mile from his bunker.

NOTES

1. The Hansen Diary, 6 Jan 45, Chester B. Hansen Papers, U.S. Army Military History Institute (MHI), Carlisle Barracks, Pa.

2. Ralph Ingersoll, *Top Secret* (New York: Harcourt, Brace, and Co., 1946), pp. 276–80; Hansen Diary, 8 Jan 45, MHI.

3. London *Daily Telegraph*, 17 Nov 44, p. 4, British Newspaper Library, Colindale, London.

4. London *Daily Express*, 4 Jan 45, p. 3, and London *News Chronicle*, 6 Jan 45,: 2, the British Newspaper Library.

5. London *Daily Mail*, 11 Jan 45, p. 2, British Newspaper Library.

6. Public Record Office (PRO): CAB 65/49, War Cabinet Conclusions, 11 Jan 45, PRO, Kew, London.

7. Walter Bedell Smith, *Eisenhower's Six Great Decisions: Europe 1944–1945* (New York and London: Longmans, Green, and Co., 1956).

8. Louis Galambos, et al., eds., *The Papers of Dwight D. Eisenhower: The Chief of Staff*, 9 vols. (Baltimore and London: Johns Hopkins University Press, 1978), vol. 7, p. 685.

9. Charles Richardson, *Send for Freddie: The Story of Monty's Chief of Staff, Major-General Sir Francis de Guingand, KBE, CB, DSO* (London: William Kimber, 1987), p. 189.

10. Martin Gilbert, *Winston Churchill: Never Despair, 1945–1965*, vol. 2 (Boston: Houghton Mifflin, 1988), pp. 810–11.

11. Nigel Hamilton, *Monty: Final Years of the Field Marshal, 1944–1976* (New York: McGraw-Hill Book Co., 1986), p. 606.

12. Galambos, et al., eds., *The Papers of Dwight D. Eisenhower: The Chief of Staff*, vol. 9, pp. 2014–25. The published edition of Patton's memoirs, *War as I Knew It* (Boston: Houghton Mifflin, 1947), was prepared for publication by Patton's widow and by his former deputy chief of staff, Col. Paul Harkins. For Patton's original comments the reader may compare the second volume of Martin Blumenson's *The Patton Papers* (Boston: Houghton Mifflin, 1974) to *War as I Knew It*.

13. Dwight D. Eisenhower, *Crusade in Europe* (Garden City, N.Y.: Doubleday and Co., 1948), p. 292.

14. Eisenhower, *Crusade in Europe*, p. 306.

15. "Eisenhower's Book: The Facts," *Sunday Times*, 21 Nov 48, p. 4.

16. G. E. Patrick Murray, *Eisenhower and Montgomery: Broad Front vs. Single Thrust, The Historiography of the Debate Over Strategy and Command* (Philadelphia: Temple University Press, 1991).

17. Ibid.

18. 15/15/127, Montgomery, the Chester Wilmot Papers, the Liddell Hart Collection, the Liddell Hart Centre for Military Archives (LHCMA), Kings College, University of London.

19. Chester Wilmot, *The Struggle for Europe* (London: Collins, 1952; also London: The Reprint Society, 1954), p. 511.

20. Wilmot-Montgomery Interv, 23 Mar 49, p. 5, 15/15/127, Montgomery, Chester Wilmot Papers, Liddell Hart Collection, LHCMA.

21. *The Memoirs of Field-Marshal the Viscount Montgomery of Alamein* (London: Collins, 1958), pp. 265–98.

22. Richard Lamb, *Montgomery in Europe, 1943–1945: Success or Failure?* (London: Buchan and Enright, Publishers, 1984), p. 27.

23. Omar N. Bradley, *A Soldier's Story* (New York: Holt, 1951), pp. 354–55.

24. Diary of Air Marshal Robb, 12 Jan 45, The Papers of Air Chief Marshal Sir James Robb, AC 71/9/26, Royal Air Force Museum, Hendon, London.

25. Alfred D. Chandler, Jr., ed., and Stephen E. Ambrose, associate ed., *The Papers of Dwight D. Eisenhower: The War Years,* 5 vols. (Baltimore and London: Johns Hopkins University Press, 1970), vol. 5, pp. 164–89.

26. Ibid.

27. Arthur Bryant, *The Triumph in the West: A History of the War Years Based on the Diaries of Field-Marshal Lord Alanbrooke, Chief of the Imperial General Staff* (Garden City, N.Y.: Doubleday and Co., 1959), p. 258.

28. E. B. Howarth, ed., *Monty at Close Quarters: Recollection of the Man* (London: Leo Cooper in Association with Martin Secker and Warburg, 1985; reprint, Bath: Chivers Press, 1987), p. 21.

29. *Memoirs of Field-Marshal the Viscount Montgomery,* p. 286.

30. Francis de Guingand, *Operation Victory* (London: Hodder and Stoughton, 1947), p. 412.

31. Samuel Eliot Morison, *Strategy and Compromise* (Boston: Little, Brown, and Co., An Atlantic Monthly Press Book, 1958), p. 9.

Normandy to the German Border
Third Army Logistics

James A. Huston

After a discouraging start in Normandy where progress originally fell far behind schedule, the breakout exceeded all expectations. Allied planners had hoped for the fall of Cherbourg by D+7 to D+15; that city was not taken until D+20 (26 June). The V Corps was to have taken St. Lô by D+9; however, St. Lô was not occupied until D+42 (18 July).[1] After the breakout in the last week of July, however, the armies not only made up for lost time, but plunged far ahead of all schedules. The original plan had assumed a halt at the Seine of about a month to permit a more or less orderly buildup before the next phase. The advancing columns reached the Seine only eleven days ahead of schedule, but in the preceding thirty days they had covered a distance expected to take seventy. By D+90, when it was planned that they should close to the Seine, spearheads of the Third Army were already 200 miles beyond.[2]

The OVERLORD plan had anticipated that by D+30 the port of Cherbourg and six smaller ports would be added to Mulberry A (an artificial harbor) and over-the-beach supply operations for a total of 27,000 long tons a day—sufficient to support the combat operations of twelve divisions on the Continent. But Brittany was supposed to become the main U.S. base area. Brest, as in World War I, was to be the main port for the landing of troops and their individual and organizational equipment. Quiberon Bay was to be developed into the principal supply port with a capacity of 10,000 tons a day (as compared to 8,000 to 9,000 at Cherbourg). Brest, Quiberon Bay, and Lorient were intended to be in operation with total capacity for all ports of 37,000 tons a day, by D+60.[3]

However, Cherbourg was not captured until nineteen days behind the original schedule, and it was so badly wrecked that supply operations could not begin until nearly a month later. Although the target for Cherbourg was the landing of 150,000 tons by 25 July, less than 18,000 tons had been landed there by that date. Mulberry A was demolished by storms only three days after it came into operation on 16 June and was never rebuilt. Continuation of large-scale, over-the-beach operations made up the difference. Of 447,000 tons landed between 1 and 25 July, i.e., in the twenty-five days before the breakthrough, 88 percent came over the beaches.[4]

Actually, top commanders and logistics officers had agreed in mid-July that the specific plans for the buildup of supplies would be disregarded. Instead, they would take the more pragmatic approach of delivering supplies to the Continent by utilizing available Normandy ports to their maximum capacity.[5]

It turned out that delays in Brittany were much greater than in the Cotentin. By mid-July it was accepted that the Brittany ports probably would not be in American hands until a month later than planned. After the Third Army became operational, its 6th Armored Division, in one of the most spectacular divisional operations of the war, sped 200 miles through central Brittany to arrive in the vicinity of Brest on 6 August, only to find the city too well fortified and defended to be captured. Indeed, the German defenders at Brest held out until 18 September. At a tremendous cost in resources—particularly in the expenditure of artillery ammunition—the Americans with great determination thereby gained an empty prize. The port, almost completely destroyed, never was put to use.

Another task force swept along the northern coast of Brittany, but the 83d Division faced a long and costly battle before it was able to reduce St. Malo on 17 August—another port never put to use.

To the south, the 4th Armored Division raced past Quiberon Bay and Lorient, leaving them in the hands of German garrisons as it impatiently turned back to the east. The division paused long enough to take Nantes, and then hurried on to get out in front in the race to the east. None of the major Brittany ports ever came into use (the German garrison at Lorient, as well as at St. Nazaire, held out until the end of the war). Some minor ports on the northern coast were used to some extent, but they brought in far less supplies than had been expended on the peninsula.[6]

Some logisticians and historians consider the failure to take the Quiberon Bay area one of the great mistakes of the war. They suggest that with Quiberon Bay in operation as a port and major supply base, there would have been no shortage of fuel and other supplies for the Third Army and no need for that army's infamous disappointing halts. It is difficult to understand why no effort was made for Quiberon Bay comparable to those made for the ports of Brest and St. Malo, or indeed why Quiberon Bay did not receive priority over the above ports. Quiberon Bay's defenses were weaker than those of the other ports, and its planned capacity was greater.

Still, its capture probably would not have made a great deal of difference, for the problem was not in landing sufficient supplies, but in moving them great distances inland.

Instead of a base of support, Brittany proved to be a serious drain on the Third Army as it tried to maintain its headlong pursuit beyond the Seine.

Of course, another major port, Marseille, did come into operation. After the landings of U.S. and French forces in southern France on 15 August, both Toulon and Marseille fell to the French on 28 August. After extreme repairs to the harbor, the first Liberty ship discharged at Marseille on 15 September, the same day that the forces driving up the Rhône valley came under General Eisenhower's command. Marseille provided ample support for the 6th Army Group, but this gave little support at that time to the Third Army.[7] On 22 September Lt. Gen. Jacob L. Devers, Commander of the 6th Army Group, reported that the Line of Communications (LOC) from Marseille could support two more divisions. Instead of sending supplies from this source to the Third Army, Eisenhower's response was to take the XV Corps from the Third Army and give it to the Seventh.[8]

In Normandy there was an anticipated shortage of refrigerated storage for perishable food. The obvious solution, suggested by the Theater Quartermaster, was to use 10,000 tons of small, slow reefers from the United States as floating storage. The Communications Zone (COMZ) commander agreed with this, but the New York Port of Embarkation, wedded to the notion that ships should not be used for storage, vetoed the idea.[9] The only solution available was to send more bologna, salami, and Spam.

The big question was how to move supplies away from the beach area up to the armies. Railways had been so badly damaged by Allied bombing and by enemy action that it took considerable time and a large labor force to get them into operation. By the end of August 18,000 men, including 5,000 prisoners of war, were engaged in railway construction. French railway workers began to appear with tools and missing parts that had been hidden from the enemy—even some American-made parts brought to France during World War I appeared. New pieces of rolling stock were brought in on Landing Ship Tanks (LSTs) that had been fitted with rails.[10]

One railway line from Avranches to LeMans opened, but the single track prohibited two-way traffic, and congestion and a shortage of cars quickly presented a problem. Operators there might have taken a lesson from General Hermann Haupt during the Battle of Gettysburg. The general sent trains out of Alexandria, Virginia, in convoys over the single-track Western Maryland Railroad. After the trains unloaded, they went backward to Alexandria while another convoy prepared to depart. On a track that previously carried only 5 trains a day, Haupt was sending forward 30 trains a day and delivering 15,000 tons of supplies.[11] In the absence of regular signals, trainmen at night flagged trains with flashlights, cigarette lighters, and even lighted cigarettes.[12]

Between 24 August and 2 September 70 trains carried 30,000 tons of supplies from LeMans to Chartres. By that time the trains were averaging 5,000 tons a day.[13] Clearly, the railroads were not yet adequate to carry the necessary supplies to the front. Yet traditional combat divisions continued to pour in, while only 94 of 130 scheduled truck companies had arrived by the end of July.[14]

After the breakthrough, the big question was what to do about long-distance hauling. The answer came in improvising the Red Ball Express. Organized under the provisional Motor Transport Brigade of the Advanced Section (ADSEC), COMZ, the Express began operations on 25 August with 67 truck companies, carrying 4,482 long tons of supplies, on a one-way return loop highway system in which roads were reserved for its traffic. Regarded as a temporary expedient, its mission was to deliver 80,000 tons of supplies from St. Lô to Chartres by 1 September. Just four days after the Red Ball Express began operations, it achieved a record haul of 12,342 tons delivered by 132 truck companies with 5,958 vehicles. All kinds of trucks were used, from the common 2 ½-ton truck to 4-ton tractors with 2,000-gallon gasoline tank semitrailers; 1 ½-ton tractors with 3 ½-ton stake and platform semitrailers; and 12-ton trucks with 45-ton trailers (tank transporters, pressed into service to carry rations and other supplies). It was possible to get many more trucks than had been planned for by diverting vehicles to Europe which had been intended for use on the Ledo Road in Burma.[15]

As extended, the second phase of the Red Ball Express began on 10 September, with a route from St. Lô to Versailles. From there a northern fork went to Soissons for support of the First Army while a southern fork continued eastward to Sommesous for support of the Third Army, with return route via Fontainebleau and Chartres.[16]

The Red Ball Express had a record of remarkable accomplishment; yet there was disappointment that it was not better. One problem was a shortage of trained drivers. Infantry replacements were pressed into service. A newly arrived rifleman might be taken to an assembly area where he was shown a vehicle. If he could identify it as a truck he was told to climb aboard and see if he could drive it. Three times around the orchard, and he was "qualified."

There was also a chronic shortage of military police to control the routes. Often there was poor convoy discipline and drivers frequently traveled at double the 25-mile-an-hour speed limit. A British officer was reported to have said, "If you are to avoid one of those Yank convoys, you must not only scamper off the road, but also climb a tree." Beyond a certain carelessness in driving, there was some malingering, some sabotage, and some diversion of cargoes into the black markets. Often vehicles were loaded to less than capacity, and there were frequent delays in loading and unloading. Poor maintenance led to loss of additional time. (At one time eighty-one loaded vehicles were found unserviceable between Vire and Dreux.) Poor documentation, poor supply information, and poor maintenance records made it especially difficult to control these conditions. A further complication was in the administrative organization—the old problem of functional vs. regional control. While the Motor Transport Brigade of ADSEC was charged with the mission, some five sections controlled the roads and other activities through which the system passed.[17]

The OVERLORD plan had included a provision for supply by air, mainly as an emergency expedient. A Combined Air Transport Operations Room (CATOR), organized originally under the Allied Expeditionary Air Force and later under control of the First Allied Airborne Army, served as a regulating station for supply by air. But the determination of priorities remained with a Priorities Board at Supreme Headquarters. This usually took the form of a compromise among various claimants, including 21st Army Group (British), the U.S. 12th Army Group, the civil relief of Paris, and Airborne Army demands for withholding troop carriers to prepare for planned airborne operations.[18]

On 15 August, as Third Army was requesting 1,500 tons by air delivered to the LeMans area, SHAEF authorized 2,000 tons a day for ten days. The first delivery, consisting of rations, arrived on the nineteenth and continued for several days, but at a level of only 600 tons a day, which gave only little relief.[19]

By 1 September the supply lines were about played out. Each additional mile of advance multiplied the difficulties of bringing up supplies to sustain it. At this time the Third Army's allocation of supplies was 2,000 tons a day. By 27 August (one day after infantrymen of the 35th Division watched Germans by the thousands walking away from the Joigny area), the Third Army's supply of gasoline was exhausted. Against a requirement of about 380,000 gallons a day, the army received 173,500 gallons on the twenty-ninth and a total of 107,000 gallons over the next four days. The capture of 500,000 gallons of enemy stocks brought only temporary relief.[20]

Patton was becoming desperate. He sent out colonels to divert convoys bound for other destinations into Third Army dumps. He sent Red Ball trucks on forward to deliver fuel to forward units, and he commandeered fuel from trucks that they were carrying for their return trips. Every available method was being used to deliver motor fuel *except* for railway tank cars, which were being used mainly to carry aviation gasoline for the Ninth Air Force. C–47 aircraft delivered 100,000 gallons of gasoline in jerricans to an airstrip near Orleans between 27 and 29 August, but the aircraft were then withdrawn for tactical airborne operations. Engineer troops were trying to keep up with the advance by laying pipeline. A pipeline did reach Chartres on 8 September, but by that time truck companies had to travel a minimum of 250 miles to deliver fuel to forward units. The Red Ball Express itself was consuming 300,000 gallons of gasoline a day in making its deliveries.[21]

Between 26 August and 8 September major units of the Third Army ground to a halt. For ten to fourteen days, men engaged in the "care and cleaning of equipment," while German units prepared to receive them on the Moselle.[22]

Again, the big problem was not in getting supplies to the Continent, even with the lack of any good ports other than Cherbourg, but in getting them forward over longer and longer supply lines. By the end of August, 90 to 95 percent of all supplies on the Continent lay in base depots near the beaches. No intermediate depots were to be found between Normandy and the Army dumps 300 miles away.[23]

During the very height of the crisis in gasoline supply, COMZ displaced its vast entourage first to the Cotentin peninsula and then to Paris. In mid-August the central headquarters of COMZ in England moved to join its forward echelon at Valognes, south of Cherbourg. Engineer troops set up tented quarters for 11,000 people and built huts to provide 560,000 square feet of office space. Within days, the capture of Paris became imminent, and Lt. Gen. J. C. H. Lee immediately made plans to move to that city. Between 1 and 15 September the entire COMZ headquarters, including additional elements from London, pressed precious motor (and 25,000 gallons of gasoline) and air transport into service to move to Paris. There that organization ultimately took over 90 percent of the hotel space. COMZ headquarters occupied 167 hotels, Seine Base Section, 129, and SHAEF, 25.[24]

Even as the supply situation was deteriorating, Patton, Bradley, and Montgomery each had been formulating plans for a rapid thrust into Germany that might end the war. On 21 August Patton was forming in his mind a plan so bold that he trembled even to think about it. He called it a "sure thing."[25] He wrote in his diary:

We have, at this time, the greatest chance to win the war ever presented. If they will let me move on with three corps, two up and one back, on the line Metz–

Nancy-Epinal, we can be in Germany in ten days. There are plenty of roads and railroads to support the operation. It can be done with three armored and six infantry divisions. . . . It is such a sure thing that I fear that these blind moles don't see it.[26]

On a visit to Third Army headquarters, General Alphonse Juin, French Army Chief of Staff, agreed that the weakest spot in the Siegfried Line was east of Nancy, and pronounced Patton's plan truly "Napoleonic."[27]

For his part, Bradley was developing his own "blueprint for victory." It was similar to Patton's in that it aimed for the heart of Germany through Frankfurt; but of course Bradley wanted to use both the First and the Third Armies.[28] Meanwhile, Montgomery was pushing his own proposal on Eisenhower for a single thrust into Germany. The British Field Marshal put it as follows:

My own view, which I presented to the Supreme Commander, was that one powerful full-blooded thrust across the Rhine and into the heart of Germany, backed by the whole of the resources of the Allied Armies, would be likely to achieve decisive results. . . . There appeared to be two feasible axes along which such a thrust into Germany could be mounted. The first was the northern axis through Belgium to the Rhine, crossing the river north of the Ruhr industrial region; once over the Rhine, this route led to the open plains of northern Germany. The alternative axis was through Metz and the Saar area, leading into central Germany.[29]

Eisenhower's response to all this was to assign priority to Montgomery's Northern Army Group to make the main effort, but to avoid any single thrust beyond. As he put it: "I knew that any pencillike thrust into the heart of Germany such as proposed would meet nothing but certain destruction. This was true, no matter on what part of the front it might be attempted. I would not consider it."[30]

Patton was disheartened, but he still tried to push on. He told a corps commander to run until his engines stopped and then go on, on foot (but there is no record that anybody walked very far). Determined to get across the Meuse River, Patton noted in his diary (30 August), "In the last war I drained three-quarters of my tanks to keep the other quarter going. Eddy [another corps commander] can do the same." He went on to note, "It is terrible to halt, even on the Meuse. We should cross the Rhine in the vicinity of Worms, and the faster we do it, the less lives and munitions it will take. No one realizes the terrible value of the 'unforgiving minute' except for me." The same day he wrote to his wife, "If I could only steal some gas, I could win this war." On 23 September Patton was directed to go over to the defensive. He called the failure to rush the Siegfried Line "before it could be manned" the "momentous error of the war."[31]

The Third Army resumed the offensive on 8 November. But no longer was it in rapid pursuit. It was now slow, bitter fighting, through rain and snow and mud. Tanks were as often held up by the mud and by swollen streams as they were by enemy guns. Infantrymen became foot soldiers again. But they were not on long-range strategic marches; they were advancing by fire and movement all the way across Lorraine. Patton still held to an objective across the Rhine. But long before he could get there he would have to turn his army northward to strike at the enemy counteroffensive around Bastogne.[32]

How could the result in 1944 have been otherwise? Why was it that in September it appeared that the war might be won in a matter of weeks when in fact it took another eight months?

Taking a leaf from Einstein, who sought to bring the laws of the physical universe together in a "unified field theory," and from Stephen B. Jones, who adapted this notion to form a "Unified Field Theory of Physical Geography,"[33] one might think of military operations in terms of a "unified field theory."

In this case, the elements of military operations may be thought of in terms of a chain of five interconnected lakes, where the level and the content of one spreads to all the others. This might represent: Area–Mission–Situation–Decision–Movement. Taken all together, these would create a field in which each element would affect all the others.

The term *area* refers to a zone of operations, a sector or the terrain. The *mission* would be that of any command in the area. The *situation* refers to the nature and disposition of friendly and enemy forces and civilian populations in the area. The *decision* is dependent upon and related to the area, the mission, and the situation and puts the military operation into action. This action leads to *movement*. Just as physical bodies in motion create a field, military movement on or over the terrain creates a *field* in which all the other elements are joined and in turn are influenced by it.[34]

Let us see how the unified field theory might apply to the Third Army in July and August 1944. The area was a zone of operations in north central France, from Normandy and Brittany eastward, between the Loire River on the south and the First Army on the north. The terrain was gently rolling in the west and mostly flat toward the east, a mostly agricultural land dotted with towns and villages. The mission was to destroy the enemy and liberate France within that zone; the initial objectives were to clear the ports of Brittany and to reach the upper Seine River between Paris and Orleans. The enemy situation was fluid, with strong defenses in the west but little to the east; the civilian population was numerous and friendly. Air superiority was almost total. The decision was to send one corps into

Brittany and two eastward toward the Seine. The movement was composed of the movement of armored divisions and motorized infantry divisions toward their assigned objectives accompanied by the movement of aircraft for air support; of men, vehicles, and supplies for logistic support; and of bands of French Forces of the Interior (FFI), or the Resistance, for local tactical support. On the other side there was the movement of German forces, some in retreat, some in stubborn defense at the ports, and some in counterattack toward Avranches and the sea.

All of this created a field where all these elements came together in a situation that changed from hour to hour. Out of this field came new decisions—to divert a corps to meet the German counterattack, to persist in the capture of Brest and St. Malo, to give up on the other ports in favor of concentrating forces for the race to the east, and to drive beyond the Seine River to the German border and then into Germany itself.

These decisions caused a sweeping extension of the area, and the movement over that terrain modified the field where all came together. The new field was composed of overextended supply lines. The movement of supplies, especially gasoline, dwindled at the front. This modification of the field brought a halt of some units for twelve days at the end of August and early September. Then, after another two weeks of forward movement, a new mission came out of that field, to go over to the defensive. This period of immobility (except for some local battles around Metz) lasted for over six weeks. It was a period when movement on the German side was not only shoring up defenses, but was concentrating forces for the great Ardennes counteroffensive.

Movement is critical in developing and maintaining a favorable field in military operations. Descartes developed a model of the universe based on just two ingredients—matter and motion. Traditionally, the essence of military tactics has been expressed as fire and movement; grand strategy being policy and movement, and logistics being supply and movement.

While speeding across France, the Third Army was a scourge for enemy defenders and a specter for the High Command. At rest in eastern France, however, it had little effect as the Germans went about preparing their defenses to the front and their Ardennes counteroffensive to the north. Now it was left to the enemy, by his movement, to define the field.

Might it have been possible to keep the Third Army moving? Might it have been possible to create a field in which the Ardennes counteroffensive could not have taken place?

Traditionally, historians prefer to avoid questions of what might have been. Yet military experience may have significant applicability in new situations, and it may be useful to speculate on other possible courses of action.

The infantry rifleman as main battle force was obsolete by the Battle of Verdun in World War I, and the introduction of the tank at Cambrai confirmed this, though nobody seemed to recognize it. The infantry rifleman was rendered obsolete by modern artillery, the machine gun, and the tank. The modern armor of World War II should have reinforced this fact. However, there could have been a more decisive role for infantry in 1944.

Actually, the roles of infantry and armor should have been reversed. Armored units were seen as being able to exploit a breakthrough and maintain a rapid pursuit. And so they had. But the greatest use of the foot soldier might have been in continuing the pursuit—to get out and walk when the tanks ran out of gas, to keep moving before the enemy could reorganize an effective defense.

Was there any way that the Third Army might have kept moving in the summer and fall of 1944? Yes: by walking instead of halting at the end of August through September and October and (b) by a series of strategic-logistic decisions that might have been taken earlier.

During the summer of 1944 German units were streaming out of central and northern France. How were they moving? Mostly by walking, accompanied by horse-drawn artillery. Instead of sitting idle those 10–12 days in late August and early September, and then sitting on the defensive for 6 weeks from September to November, why were infantry units of the Third Army not walking too? True, the Germans were walking toward their supplies, while the Americans would be walking away from theirs. Still, the Americans considered their biggest problem to be the shortage of gasoline. Other supplies probably could have been kept up for a force moving on foot. In those 12 days it should have been possible to walk 180 miles along the level roads of eastern France. That would have taken some units beyond Nancy to Aix-en-Othe. In the additional 6 weeks given over to defense, it should have been possible to walk all the way to Berlin!

Aside from the immediate expedient of walking, a series of different strategic-logistic decisions might have made all the difference.

The stabilized warfare of World War I, with its daily requisitions and daily supply trains moving up to fixed positions, was a logistician's dream. The race across France in 1944 was a logistician's nightmare. The breakthrough—presumably the aim of all major offensive action—was the one contingency against which he could not prepare. But does this not point to a deficiency in planning? Should not the pursuit be perceived as the *main effort*?

The trouble with wrong decisions and wrong assumptions was not necessarily in making them initially, but rather in persisting in them in the face of rapidly changing situations.

On the question of the broad front vs. the single main thrust, it might have been wiser to choose the single thrust on which Montgomery, Bradley, and Patton all agreed. R. G. Ruppenthal, the official historian, has justified Eisenhower's decision for a "broad front" strategy largely on the basis of logistic limitations.[35] But those very logistic limitations argued for concentrating available resources behind a single decisive thrust, as Montgomery maintained.

Then, in the last half of September, a better decision might have been to make the main effort with the Third Army, rather than with the northern army group in Operation MARKET GARDEN. It was unfortunate that the Third Army was immobilized at a time when it was on the move against light resistance.

Finally, the assumption that it was going to be a long war, i.e., that it would continue through the winter, should have been amended at the time of the breakthrough in Operation COBRA to an assumption that the war in Europe could be ended within another four months.

All this would have carried important implications, including the following:

(1) Forget the Brittany ports after 3 August, and leave only a holding operation there to protect the Third Army's rear as it drives eastward. Brittany might have been a major base area, but its ports turned out to be of no value. Instead of granting priority of supplies to VIII Corps in its battles for St. Malo and Brest, the priority should have been in the opposite direction. In any case, the only need for those ports would have been on the assumption of a long war. One staff officer, frustrated with endless calculations on port capacities and plans for capture in the original OVERLORD plan, put down a "law" that he called "Operation OVERBOARD." He wrote: "The general principle is that the number of divisions required to capture the number of ports required to maintain those divisions is always greater than the number of divisions those ports can maintain."[36]

(2) Forget strategic bombing and divert the heavy bombers to carrying supplies. The impact of strategic bombing would be greatest in a long war. Strategic bombing should have ended with the Normandy landings. Throughout July, August, and September B–17s and B–24s of the Eighth Air Force were carrying over 2,000 tons of bombs each day to Germany. Indeed, total tonnage dropped by the strategic air forces during those three months was 403,808 tons.[37] Put to better use, they could have been carrying 2,000 to 3,000 tons of supplies (enough for ten divisions) a day to France, while bombers of the Fifteenth Air Force in Italy could have been bringing in another thousand tons a day.

(3) Forget further airborne operations and put the troop carrier aircraft to work carrying supplies for the main effort on the ground. The First Allied Airborne Army planned at least a half-dozen major airborne operations before it finally launched Operation MARKET in Holland. For these proposed operations troops were moved around, and up to 1,500 aircraft were held out of other action. In each case, as ground forces overran the planned objective, the operation was canceled.[38] During the period between 11 June and 16 September, the IX Troop Carrier Command carried 33,421 tons of freight and 48,767 passengers, and evacuated 42,139 casualties.[39] Without the planning of additional airborne operations, those figures might have been three or four times that great. Aerial delivery was a very expensive way of moving supplies, but when the critical limitation was not in the quantity of supplies already on the Continent, but rather in transportation, this method could have bypassed broken bridges, destroyed railroads, and rough highways. It was a source that should have been used. Admittedly, large-scale supply by air would have involved serious problems in the construction or repair and the operation of airstrips. But that is where a good many of the men in those idle divisions should have been assigned. The Berlin airlift, with World War II–type C–47, C–46, and C–54 aircraft, in the spring of 1949 delivered an average of 8,000 tons of freight (enough tonnage for the equivalent of twenty-six divisions) a day. It achieved a single-day record of nearly 13,000 tons.[40]

(4) Forget the landing of additional infantry divisions in France and instead bring in additional truck companies, aviation engineers for building airstrips, and highway and railway construction engineers. The hoped-for capture of Brest and the possible use of Bordeaux were planned with the idea of bringing in additional combat divisions. Those would be needed only if the war were prolonged.[41]

(5) Move up DRAGOON, the invasion of southern France, to April 1944, but use only half as many men accompanied by twice as many supplies and transport vehicles, with the surplus going to the support of the Third Army.

(6) Put the soldiers of the extra three divisions (other than those already diverted to the Red Ball Express) that had landed in France but were being held immobile for want of supplies to work on the lines of communication. Here were 45,000 men that should have been put to work on the Red Ball Express as drivers, auxiliary MPs, and road maintenance crews; assigned to railway repair tasks; and put to use even as carrying parties to carry supplies from Red Ball Express terminals up to the forward units.

(7) Mules. Planners should have brought in pack animals from Italy and France to carry supplies forward. Patton used 4,000 mules, horses, and

donkeys to deliver ammunition, rations, signal equipment, and water during Seventh Army's sweep around Sicily. Seven thousand animals were sent to Italy for use by the 10th Mountain Division.[42] It is common to think of using pack animals in rough terrain, where there are few good roads and the use of motor vehicles is limited. The use of motor vehicles was limited across the plains of France for want of gasoline just as surely as they were limited by the terrain in Italy. An old soldier knows it always is better to walk with his mule than to sit on his ass!

(8) Inland waterways. France had numerous rivers and canals which could have been used in supporting Allied operations across France. Water transportation is more economical in fuel consumption, and maintenance is far less, than for highways or railways, and France had a great number of barges on its rivers and canals. In World War I, American planners had given little thought to the use of water transportation, but the American Expeditionary Forces (AEF) did put into service 307 barges and 13 tugs. (Tugs were ordinarily used on rivers, while horses usually towed the barges on the canals.) Most of these were used on the Seine, and some barge traffic went as far as Montargis and Dijon. American tonnage at that time reached only 47,000 tons a month, but that was helpful. At the same time, the British were shipping 250,000 tons a month on rivers and canals in their sector.[43] The OVERLORD planners did not consider the inland waterways to be of sufficient military value to warrant a major effort at restoring them. Only in November did the theater Chief of Transportation establish an Inland Waterways Division. That month the Seine was cleared to Paris, and then the Oise and the Rhône-Saône.[44] Had more been done sooner, the use of inland waterways could have helped relieve the supply crisis of September.

(9) Narrow-gauge railroads. With greater foresight and planning, provision might have been made for laying some light, narrow-gauge track in some areas for the forwarding of supplies. In some places this might have been done much more rapidly than repairing standard railroads or even rebuilding torn-up highways. Light traction engines could have been used; alternatively even mules might have been used to pull cars.[45]

One further observation might be in order. The logistic squeeze became tighter with the arrival of each new division. Ruppenthal has suggested that no more than 20 divisions could have been supported as far forward as the Rhine, when in October Bradley's 12th Group had 29 divisions.[46] But why did all 29 have to go to the Rhine? Why not use the other 9 to help support the first 20? If a dozen or fewer divisions were enough to cross the English Channel and take Normandy against strong, well-organized defenses, why were 20 divisions not sufficient to cross the Rhine against an enemy on the run? Patton insisted that with 9 divisions he could cross the Rhine and strike at the heart of Germany. Furthermore, although Ruppenthal reports that only about one-half of the normal requirements were being met, it should be noted that the requirements for a division in pursuit were only about one-half of those needed for "normal" attack situations. Requirements were based upon an assumed daily need of about 650 tons of supplies for each division, but experience showed the daily average requirement of an armored division in pursuit and exploitation to be 328 tons, and for an infantry division, 296 tons.[47]

Could the war in Europe have ended in the fall of 1944? Might the great losses in the Ardennes have been avoided? If things had been done differently, this may have been possible. Had the Third Army kept moving on foot, supplied by mule and by air, how far could it have gone?

Some analysts have maintained that German military strength was such that even had gasoline been available, no continuation of the pursuit and exploitation by the Third or even by the First and Third Armies could have been decisive.[48] In support of this contention, these scholars point to the strength that the Germans were able to muster for their counteroffensive in the Ardennes.

However, if we look at the whole "field," and see the difference between a force in motion and a force at rest, we can also see the difference between a force well organized and supplied and a disorganized force on the run. The Germans had about as great a force in the Ruhr in April 1945 (21 divisions, 325,000 men) as in the Ardennes in December 1944 (24 divisions).[49] Yet these forces were almost helpless against the double envelopment by the First and Ninth U.S. Armies.

The words of George W. Cecil echo out of that lost opportunity: "On the plains of hesitation bleach the bones of countless thousands who, on the eve of victory, rested, and resting, died."

NOTES

1. First U.S. Army, Rpt of Operations, 20 Oct 43—1 Aug 44, pp. 56–63; Gordon A. Harrison, *Cross-Channel Attack*, United States Army in World War II (Washington, D.C.: U.S. Army Center of Military History, 1951), pp. 187–88; Martin Blumenson, *Breakout and Pursuit*, United States Army in World War II (Washington, D.C.: U.S. Army Center of Military History, 1961), pp. 146, 172–73.

2. R. G. Ruppenthal, "Logistic Planning for OVERLORD in Retrospect," in the Eisenhower Foundation, *D-Day: The Normandy Invasion in Retrospect* (Lawrence: University Press of Kansas, 1971), pp. 89–94.

3. Roland G. Ruppenthal, *Logistical Support of the Armies*, 2 vols., United States Army in World War II (Washington, D.C.: U.S. Army Center of Military History, 1953, 1959), vol. 1, pp. 292–97, 464–71.

4. Ibid., pp. 464–66.

5. Ibid., p. 473.

6. Blumenson, *Breakout and Pursuit*, pp. 357–415; Ruppenthal, *Logistical Support of the Armies*, vol. 1, pp. 475–79.

7. Ruppenthal, *Logistical Support of the Armies*, vol. 1, pp. 475–79.

8. Ibid., vol. 2, p. 16.

9. William F. Ross and Charles F. Romanus, *The Quartermaster Corps: Operations in the War Against Germany*, United States Army in World War II (Washington, D.C.: U.S. Army Center of Military History, 1965), pp. 504–06.

10. Ruppenthal, *Logistical Support of the Armies*, vol. 1, pp. 545–51.

11. James Huston, *The Sinews of War: Army Logistics, 1775–1953*, (Washington, D.C.: U.S. Army Center of Military History, 1966), pp. 206–07.

12. Ruppenthal, *Logistical Support of the Armies*, vol. 1, pp. 546–47.

13. Ibid., pp. 550–51.

14. Ibid., pp. 557–58.

15. Ibid., p. 560; Joseph Bykofsky and Harold Larson, *The Transportation Corps: Operations Overseas*, United States Army in World War II (Washington, D.C.: U.S. Army Center of Military History, 1957), pp. 331–34.

16. Ruppenthal, *Logistical Support of the Armies*, vol. 1, pp. 567–68; Bykofsky and Larson, *The Transportation Corps*, pp. 334–35.

17. Ruppenthal, *Logistical Support of the Armies*, vol. 1, pp. 559–72.

18. Ibid., pp. 572–76; James Huston, *Out of the Blue: U.S. Army Airborne Operations in World War II* (Lafayette: Purdue University Studies, 1972), pp. 201–04.

19. Ruppenthal, *Logistical Support of the Armies*, vol. 1, pp. 576–78.

20. Ibid., p. 504; George S. Patton, Jr., *War as I Knew It* (Boston: Houghton Mifflin, 1947), pp. 119–30; Blumenson, *Breakout and Pursuit*, pp. 666–70; Lalislas Farago, *Patton: Ordeal and Triumph* (New York: Dell, 1963), pp. 561–70.

21. Ruppenthal, *Logistical Support of the Armies*, vol. 1, pp. 565, 576–83; First U.S. Army, Rpt of Operations, 1 Aug 44—22 Feb 45, anns. 9–14; Blumenson, *Breakout and Pursuit*, p. 691.

22. Blumenson, *Breakout and Pursuit*, pp. 668–70.

23. Ibid., pp. 689–90; Ruppenthal, *Logistical Support of the Armies*, vol. 1, p. 496; Farago, *Patton*, p. 560; First U.S. Army Rpt of Operations, 1 Aug 44–22 Feb 45, anns. 9–14; Logistics in World War II, Final Rpt of the Army Service Forces, 1947, p. 162.

24. Forrest C. Pogue, *The Supreme Command*, United States Army in World War II (Washington, D.C.: U.S. Army Center of Military History, 1954), pp. 322–23; Huston, *Sinews of War*, p. 531.

25. Farago, *Patton*, pp. 538–41.

26. Martin Blumenson, *The Patton Papers* (Boston: Houghton Mifflin, 1974), p. 523.

27. Farago, *Patton*, p. 540.

28. Omar N. Bradley, *A Soldier's Story* (New York: Henry Holt, 1951), p. 398; Ralph Ingersoll, *Top Secret* (New York: Harcourt, Brace, 1946), pp. 211–13.

29. Field Marshal the Viscount Montgomery of Alamein, *Normandy to the Baltic* (Boston: Houghton Mifflin, 1948), p. 193.

30. Dwight D. Eisenhower, *Crusade in Europe* (New York: Doubleday, 1948), p. 306.

31. Patton, *War as I Knew It*, p. 120.

32. See Hugh Cole, *The Lorraine Campaign*, United States Army in World War II (Washington, D.C.: U.S. Army Center of Military History, 1950).

33. Stephen B. Jones, "A Unified Theory of Political Geography," *Annals of the Association of American Geographers* 64 (1954): 111–23.

34. See James Huston, "A Unified Field Theory of Military Operations," *Defense Analysis* (1989): 369–72.

35. Ruppenthal, *Logistical Support of the Armies*, vol. 2, pp. 8–15; Ruppenthal, "Logistics and the Broad Front Strategy," in Kent Roberts Greenfield, ed., *Command Decisions* (New York: Harcourt, Brace, 1959), pp. 419–27.

36. Quoted in Ruppenthal, *Logistical Support of the Armies*, vol. 1, p. 46.

37. U.S. Strategic Bombing Survey, The Effects of Strategic Bombing on the German War Economy (1945), p. 5.

38. Huston, *Out of the Blue*, pp. 193–98.

39. Ibid., pp. 198–210.

40. James Huston, *Outposts and Allies: U.S. Army Logistics in the Cold War, 1945–1953* (Selinsgrove: Susquehanna University Press, 1988), pp. 89–90.

41. By D+90 (4 September), 20 U.S. divisions had landed on the Continent; during the next month another 10 arrived; and during the two months after that (to 3 November) another 9 arrived. Ruppenthal, *Logistical Support of the Armies*, vol. 2, p. 281.

42. Bykofsky and Larson, *The Transportation Corps*, pp. 184–222; Ruppenthal, *Logistical Support of the Armies*, vol. 1, pp. 331–34.

43. William J. Wilgus, *Transporting the A.E.F. in Western Europe* (New York: Columbia University Press, 1931), pp. 456–65; Rpt of the Military Board of Allied Supply, 2 vols. (Washington, D.C.: 1925), vol. 2, p. 1054; Paul S. Bond, "Use of Inland Waterways in World War I," unpublished Ms, U.S. Army Center of Military History, Washington, D.C.

44. Bykofsky and Larson, *The Transportation Corps*, pp. 354–55.

45. Rpt of Military Board of Allied Supply, vol. 1, pp. 206–20; vol. 2, pp. 985–88; Huston, *Sinews of War*, pp. 378–83.

46. Ruppenthal, *Logistical Support of the Armies*, vol. 2, pp. 6–7; Ruppenthal, "Logistic Planning for OVERLORD in Retrospect," p. 96.

47. FM 101–10, Staff Officers' Field Manual, Organization, Technical and Logistical Data (Aug 49), pp. 308–12.

48. Blumenson, *Breakout and Pursuit*, pp. 668–69; Ruppenthal, "Logistic Planning for OVERLORD in Retrospect," pp. 94–99.

49. Rpt by the Supreme Comdr to the Combined Chiefs of Staff on the Operations in Europe of the Allied Expeditionary Force, 6 Jun 44–8 May 45, pp. 76, 105.

American Geographers and the OSS During World War II

Keir B. Sterling

As the international situation worsened during the summer of 1940, Col. Frank Knox, President Franklin Roosevelt's newly appointed Secretary of the Navy, asked his friend William J. Donovan, a successful New York corporate attorney, to undertake what became the first of several fact-finding missions to Europe. The two men met with Roosevelt, and Donovan specifically was asked to assess British defensive capabilities and the effects of German subversive activities, in addition to securing a variety of other information. In contrast to the pessimistic views of certain other observers, Donovan came back from Europe convinced that Britain could withstand the Nazi onslaught, provided that she received some substantial aid from the United States.[1]

The 57-year-old Donovan, a graduate of Columbia College and also its law school, had won the Distinguished Service Medal, the Distinguished Service Cross, and the Medal of Honor as a colonel with the New York 69th Regiment during World War I, together with a chestful of foreign decorations. During the 1920s he served as U.S. Attorney for Western New York and held several positions in the U.S. Department of Justice. In 1932 he was an unsuccessful Republican candidate for Governor of New York. Donovan was a contemporary of Roosevelt's and had been a classmate of the President's in law school. He was not, however, close to F.D.R., and had in fact often been critical of New Deal policies.[2]

During the 1930s, Donovan had made several trips abroad to assess several aspects of the international situation for himself. These drew attention to his capacity for collecting and synthesizing intelligence information. By the later part of 1940, when Roosevelt asked Donovan to take another fact-finding trip to Europe, Donovan had become convinced that, because of the worsening world crisis, America needed to develop some kind of central intelligence-gathering agency. Roosevelt agreed, and the following summer Donovan was asked to direct it. On 11 July 1941,

Donovan was named Coordinator of Information (COI). His prescribed task was to "collect and analyze all information and data which may bear upon international security; to correlate such information and data, and to make such information and data available to the President and to such departments and official of the government as the President may determine."[3]

During his first six months as Coordinator of Information, Donovan was primarily concerned not only with the gathering and analysis of information, but with radio propaganda. On the eve of Pearl Harbor, he began turning his attention to cloak-and-dagger activity and to a variety of other projects. Much of his time, however, was spent squabbling with the heads of various other federal agencies, some new, some of long standing, over matters of jurisdiction. COI, the Office of Facts and Figures, and the Coordinator of Inter-American Affairs, among others, quarreled with each other and also with Army and Navy Intelligence, the State Department, and the Federal Bureau of Investigation (FBI) about which ones were to control the collection, analysis, and dispensing of various kinds of intelligence and which were to handle propaganda work. Naturally, the old line players resented the COI and the other new boys on the block and fought to protect what they regarded as their proper turf. The personalities of the principal players frequently played an important role in these disputes.[4]

It also must be stressed that Donovan "had no base of power except for his friendship with Knox and his access to the President," and this last proved to be both a blessing and a curse. Donovan had arranged matters such that COI would report directly to Roosevelt. This generally involved hand-carrying documents, which in the early months of COI's existence, at least, was often done by Colonel Donovan himself. Donovan had to be responsive to F.D.R.'s moods and whims in order to retain the President's favor and keep his post. Donovan was a brilliant and intuitive person, but he was given to shifting enthusiasms, and was generally regarded as a poor administrator. This was reflected in the somewhat chaotic early history of the Research and Analysis Branch of the COI.[5]

With the charter of his new agency in hand, and naturally eager to prove his mettle to F.D.R., Donovan immediately began to get in touch with friends and colleagues in and out of government for the names of suitable people who could help him get his operation under way. Donovan recognized that many of the people with the skills he required could be found in the many academic and research institutions scattered across the nation.[6]

What was to become the Research and Analysis Branch, the heart of Donovan's organization, was put together with the aid of Archibald

MacLeish, a well-known poet and, since 1939, Librarian of Congress. During the months of June and July 1940, MacLeish met with representatives of the American Council of Learned Societies, the Social Science Research Council, other government agencies, and leading academics at some of the eastern universities to secure names for a board of advisers who would assist Donovan. James Phinney Baxter, President of Williams College and a student of diplomatic and military history, was selected by Donovan to come to Washington to head up Research and Analysis (R&A), and Baxter in turn invited William Langer, a leading European historian at Harvard and a colleague of long standing, to serve as his director of research.[7]

Together they assembled a Board of Analysts, who were to help set tasks for and oversee the work of the R&A staff. Of the half-dozen men originally represented on this board, three were historians, two were economists, and one was a political scientist. None were geographers, but that omission soon would be rectified.[8]

As originally (and rather hastily) organized, R&A was subdivided into both functional and geographic divisions. A Division of Special Information (DSI), housed in the annex of the Library of Congress, contained eight geographic subdivisions, each concerned with a different part of the world. There were also four other units located elsewhere in the city of Washington, including an Economic Division, a Psychology Division, a Geography Division, and a Central Information Division, which essentially performed certain necessary service tasks. DSI was created at Donovan's request with monies transferred to the Library of Congress for the purpose.[9]

The Geography Division consisted of a Map Information Section, which supplied the best available maps for particular foreign areas; the Cartographic Section, which prepared maps and other cartographic aids not already available; and the Geographic Reports Section, which prepared technical studies concerning various parts of the world and on problems which overlapped the regional divisions, such as detailed studies of the Pacific Ocean islands.[10]

By the middle of August Preston E. James, a 41-year-old professor of geography at the University of Michigan, and one of the nation's leading Latin-Americanists, was invited to Washington to head up the Latin-American Division. James was a captain in the Army Reserve whose long standard text on the geography of Latin America first made its appearance in 1942. At his suggestion, Baxter got in touch with Richard Hartshorne, an almost exact contemporary of James', and a professor of geography at the University of Wisconsin, who was the author of the *Nature of*

Geography (1939), a seminal assessment of the discipline, now considered a classic text. Hartshorne was invited to join the Board of Analysts, soon to become known to R&A insiders as the "College of Cardinals." Hartshorne was also named Chief of the Geography Division. Both men were on the job before the end of August.[11]

Together, Hartshorne and James selected many of the original group of geographers who came to work for COI, and set up the regional units within the branch. Hartshorne spent much of his time establishing research priorities, passing on finished research projects, and resolving personal squabbles. He played a vital role in assuring geographers a voice within R&A, and ended the war as de facto chief of staff to William Langer, who succeeded Baxter as Chief of R&A in September 1942.[12]

The Board of Analysts proved unable to perform the critical task of giving direction to the work of R&A. There were three principal reasons for this. One had to do with Donovan's hands-on style of direction. For some months, until early 1942, when he turned much of his attention to the work of other COI divisions, Donovan called daily morning staff meetings at R&A, where members of the Board of Analysts were told what they were to do. Donovan's priorities changed constantly, which made a hash of the board's preference for decisions made in an atmosphere of calm deliberation. Further, the people "nominally in charge of research" were often taken up with "purely administrative tasks for which they had little experience and less time." Finally, R&A "had no administrative staff of any consequence for the first year of its existence, and no effective staff in that [area] until well beyond the end of its second year." Donovan gradually lost interest in R&A's day-to-day operations and became more interested in derring-do. He did, however, continue to look for the products of R&A research.[13]

As the authors of one unpublished history of R&A put it at the end of the war, the lack of "any clear definition of function" between DSI and non-DSI units "resulted in the most unhappy sort of lack of coordination of [R&A] Branch activity, and sowed seeds of jealousy and mistrust, of outraged sense of jurisdiction and heated personal relationships which were to plague the Branch for at least two years after its establishment, and long after a more rational scheme of organization had been evolved." Another complicating factor was that government personnel rules governing job titles and pay were often in conflict with the realities of this struggling wartime agency made up largely of non–civil-service academics.[14]

Fortunately, a reorganization of functions within R&A in the spring of 1943 improved its effectiveness. The Division of Special Information at the Library of Congress was discontinued, and its staff were absorbed in other parts of R&A. The old Geography, Economics, and Psychology Divisions were abolished, and their personnel were assigned to one of the regional divisions, which were amalgamated and reduced from eight to four. Geographers continued to perform their tasks of collecting, digesting, and analyzing geographic intelligence. All cartographic functions were placed in a new Map Division, which embraced map collection, map intelligence work, the compilation of new maps and cartographic devices, and the establishment of a vast new map library.[15]

Richard Hartshorne and Preston James were among the stars of the outstanding newer generation of American geographers, a profession which embraced some 2,000 scholars in 1941. By 1945 perhaps as many as 500 of these individuals had taken up posts in Washington and overseas, working for half-a-dozen government agencies. Most of them, recruited by Hartshorne and James, wound up in COI, which became the Office of Strategic Services (OSS) in June 1942. Between 300 and 350 of the geographers who ultimately came to Washington ended up in uniform as officers and enlisted personnel. Roughly half ended up in the Army and half in the Navy, with a scattering in the Marines. Most began as lieutenants or ensigns and received one or two promotions during the war. Many found that wearing a uniform made it easier for them to deal with various military offices, particularly because civilians were no longer as welcome once jurisdictional jealousies developed between OSS and some military agencies. Interestingly, however, OSS geographers in the enlisted ranks working in London found that their words and work carried more weight with senior military and civilian officials when they wore civilian clothes on duty, a privilege which was accorded to them early on.[16]

The overwhelming majority of geographers in military ranks were men (in one sample the figure was 98 percent), whereas women in the profession were outnumbered only about two to one. The 4,002 women in R&A played a critical role, although the preponderance of them were librarians and typists. Only about 25 percent of the researchers in R&A were female. One woman was Chief of Station in Ceylon, with a staff of seventy women. Lois Olson, another contemporary of James and Hartshorne, who had studied at Chicago and the London School of Economics, had long prewar federal service in the Labor and Agriculture Departments. She was Assistant Chief of the R&A Geography Division in London in 1944.[17]

One OSS geographer described World War II as the "best thing that [had] happened to geography since the birth of Strabo," the ancient Greek savant generally regarded as the father of the field. This is because the discipline in this country before 1941 was 90 percent academic, half high school and college instructors, the other half in primary school classrooms.

About a third held doctorates, another third had completed their M.A.s and the remainder had no graduate degrees. Before the war "practitioners were largely small scale . . . in approach but afterward they were more [broad gauged] and international in scope." There were few foreign specialists in 1941, whereas after 1945 their numbers had grown considerably.[18]

The pool of professionals who were deemed suitably qualified for employment with OSS therefore numbered about a thousand. From this pool, it was of course necessary to deduct those already in government service, together with a substantial number who remained in academia. Government agencies showed little interest in hiring high school and grade school geography teachers during the war on the theory that these people, most of them female, were "less well equipped."

Recruiting in the "small, close academic family" of those who remained progressed very quickly. Unfortunately, very few American geographers "had developed any specialized competence in Europe." Most of those who had were "unsuited for employment in OSS because of age or scholarly status, or were assigned in the agency to higher administrative posts." The staff of the Geography Division had to be built utilizing "a research staff at a relatively lower level for the collection and organization of so-called topographic intelligence—that is, of detailed information concerning specific areas." Most geographers brought into the Division were relatively young college instructors and junior assistant professors, many of them recent Ph.D.s, doctoral candidates whose studies had been interrupted by the war, and a few young but promising college graduates who had had little time to pursue graduate study. Most of the young Ph.D.s were paid salaries which were lower than they might have received had they worked elsewhere in Washington, but many felt that they could make a better geographic contribution in R&A.[19]

R&A geographers constituted one of the finest faculties ever assembled. Consequently, morale was high. Some critics, however, snapped that Ph.D. merely stood for piled higher and deeper, and others noted that invidious distinctions within R&A were sometimes felt between those who held the terminal degree and those who did not.[20]

Early in the war, an advisory committee of geographers employed in non–defense-related federal agencies was convened to help determine what the geographers assigned to COI might accomplish for the agency and what contributions they might make to the work of other government departments. This was because during the first year or more of R&A's existence, its people had to prove what they were capable of doing for the military. Many in government questioned whether the so-called "bad eyes brigade" (also known as the "Professor Farm," and the "Chairborne

Division," by critics) could come up with information of use to the military. The Advisory Committee managed to help the Geography Branch avoid most of the "serious problems of potential duplication" of work with long-standing agencies such as the Division of Maps at the Library of Congress and the Office of the Geographer of the State Department. Certainly the "longstanding professional relations of the persons involved" helped considerably.[21]

Many R&A personnel were hired from elite academic institutions. Among the geographers, the securing of personnel was sometimes serendipitous. While driving to Washington from Madison, Wisconsin, for example, Richard Hartshorne stopped for the night with a colleague at Ohio State University in Columbus. Did his host know of any young map makers who might be available, Hartshorne inquired? His host proposed the name of a 26-year-old doctoral candidate, a student of his named Arthur Robinson, who was soon invited to join the geographical hegira to Washington. Robinson grabbed his T-square and drawing board and soon found himself head of the Cartographic Section of the Geography Division, and later after the January 1943 reorganization of R&A as Chief of the Map Division.[22]

Robinson's section was housed for the duration of the war in one of several structures at 25th and E streets in Washington which had formerly been occupied by the National Institutes of Health (NIH). COI gradually moved into this complex as the various subdivisions of NIH moved out. The site today is shared by the E Street Expressway, the Saudi Arabian Embassy, and parts of the J.F.K. Center for the Performing Arts and the Watergate Complex. Donovan and his people faced a never-ending problem of finding sufficient space for their operations in the wartime capital. Other buildings pressed into service included the old Washington Auditorium, on the site of the present State Department Building, and an old skating rink nearby, which was hastily enclosed and winterized.[23]

One OSS staffer who worked there for a time later related that some floor space in one of the NIH buildings Donovan needed had been occupied for some time by a colony of syphilitic monkeys. German intelligence was evidently quite good, because within days after the unhappy monkeys were moved elsewhere, German radio announced that they had been displaced by an OSS contingent. The German commentator added some pointed remarks concerning the juxtaposition of these two events.[24]

In June 1942 COI was renamed the Office of Strategic Services, or OSS, and was transferred to the jurisdiction of the newly formed Joint Chiefs of Staff. This was done so that senior military professionals would be better able to utilize the information Donovan's people were producing at earlier stages in the decision-making process. It also gave Donovan and the OSS some protection from certain outspoken critics in the military who might otherwise have dismembered OSS and distributed its assets to various military departments and to the State Department.[25]

By March of 1942 the Geographic Reports Section was devoting two-thirds of its time to the compilation of new maps. An increasingly large cartographic staff was required. Robinson, who later completed his doctoral dissertation on the "Foundation of Cartographic Methodology," and who today is the dean of American cartographers, has pointed out that modern map making was in many ways in its infancy in 1941. The few courses in cartography offered by American graduate schools were very traditional in nature. Most prewar maps were prepared by "engineers or draftsmen." They had "at best a high school education," as did their supervisors. They had artistic talent, but had no background in either geography or cartography. The National Geographic Society, which was based in Washington, "refused to allow others to use their excellent, patented photographic system" of making maps. Many R&A section heads who needed maps prepared for their reports had no idea how to present their ideas. Robinson and his rapidly growing staff had to teach themselves how to mass produce maps, and slowly worked their way through a bewildering array of conceptual and technical problems. Before they were finished, they had developed several new machines which facilitated the map-making process.[26]

Some R&A people and others tended to be a bit patronizing about the cartographic function, believing that map making was a relatively simple process. Robinson later admitted that the Map Division was a pick-up operation at first, since most geographers did not know how to make proper maps. There was much learning by doing during the first several years of the war, but Robinson and his staff proved to be quick studies, and before too many months had passed were producing daily situation maps for the Operations Division of the War Department. When people with some training as geographers or cartographers could be found or pressed into service as map makers, Robinson sought help where he could get it. He found that piano players, for example, had greater finger flexibility than other people, and that he could often make decent cartographers out of them. The Map Division soon "functioned as the map maker for the strategic planners of the Joint Chiefs of Staff and provided the cartographic support for the United States' participation at the Quebec and Cairo Conferences of the Allied Powers." Sophisticated topographic models were made of most of the Eurasian landmass. By 1945, in the words of Robin Winks, they had produced thousands of "elegant, meticulous maps, some of them works of art, giving dramatic point to the intelligence data embedded in the prose" of OSS reports. Among other things, Robinson's people learned to make thematic maps which in many instances "carried the major communication load" in OSS reports.[27]

After the war, the Cartographic and Map Intelligence sections would be incorporated in the nascent Central Intelligence Agency, (CIA) while the modeling section wound up in the Army Map Service.

OSS map makers spent considerable time collecting or copying existing maps in American libraries and research institutions such as the American Geographical Society Library in New York. Washington agencies were "utterly deficient" in maps in 1941, save for the Map Division of the Library of Congress. Virtually all military map work was essentially handled by the Army Corps of Engineers. The Army's map budget in 1941 allowed for two draftsmen assigned to Army G–2. Cartographic information for most portions of Europe and Latin America was reasonably accurate. For those concerned with Asia and the Pacific, the situation was very different. There were two complete sets of maps of Japan in this country before Pearl Harbor. One belonged to a geographer who was a Japanese specialist at the University of Wisconsin, while the other was held by the Department of Agriculture. There was little material on some parts of the Far East such as Manchuria. There were few maps of the Philippines, which had been an American possession for over forty years. For many parts of the Pacific, R&A researchers at the Library of Congress had to depend upon old British Admiralty charts, or maps made by the Wilkes Expedition, which had returned from its four-year exploration of the Pacific in 1842. Most military planners soon were made aware of the vital importance of good maps.[28]

At one point during the war, Floyd Masten, a red-headed OSS operative, was sent to China for the express purpose of bringing back a complete set of maps of that country made some years before by the Chinese government. Masten was obliged to grow a luxuriant beard and work under cover. Masten played the role well. Donovan met him at Chungking on one of his junkets and sent a cable back to Washington stating that he had just met a fine and knowledgeable young man whom OSS ought to hire immediately. Only later did Donovan discover that Masten was already on the payroll. The Chinese maps were secured only after Masten assured his Chinese counterparts that British intelligence would not be allowed to see them. A special safe was constructed at OSS Headquarters in Washington, and the maps were promptly deposited there. British intelligence operatives showed up a day after they arrived, asking to see them.[29]

Preston James later recalled the pervasive common ignorance in this country in the 1940s about Latin America even among educated persons.

Latin America was nevertheless considered quite important to the OSS during the early war years, because of the danger of Axis activity there. The Germans had many options in 1941, and F.D.R. was very concerned about the security of both South America's east and west coasts. One R&A geographer was put to work trying to figure out which points along the western coast of Mexico could be used by the Japanese as places to post their submarines. Others made studies of political and economic conditions and the availability of quinine, rubber, and other essential raw materials. The Latin American Division of OSS became less important following the invasion of North Africa late in 1943, and after a few holdout nations south of the border had declared war against the Axis Powers in 1943.[30]

When in 1942 an OSS outpost was set up in London, it was initially thought that R&A and other sections might have to lean on the British for assistance because the American organization was less operational and more familial. The British considered their intelligence organizations more sophisticated, and geographers in R&A at first depended upon their British colleagues for aid in learning the ropes. R&A geographers at first worked closely with their British opposite numbers, but these close relationships became less necessary after 1943, especially as Langer became convinced that his geographers were at least as effective in doing their job as were the British. Additionally, Donovan was less interested in cooperating with the British after 1943.[31]

Robin Winks has observed that OSS was "large, divisive, and incoherent," but that it was "more united" than comparable British agencies such as MI 6, Special Operations Executive (SOE), and the Foreign Office Research Department.[32]

During 1944 most R&A activities in London were geared to preparation for the invasion of France, and increasing numbers of people were sent there to perform a variety of pre– and post–D-Day research tasks.

Preston James and a number of other Latin-Americanists were transferred to the new Europe-Africa Division following the OSS reorganization early in 1943, and James was named Chief of the Geographic Section of Europe-Africa. James, who has been described as an abrasive but highly efficient administrator, was considered "rude and unhousebroken," but a "superb scholar." It was said of him that he repeatedly "restored the tensions" relieved by others. James had about sixty geographers working for him in Europe, each with a jeep, an ex–Hollywood photographer, and a driver. Their principal task was to produce detailed maps of key transportation systems, and to analyze their logistical potentialities. This work was known as the Intelligence Photographic Documentation Projects (IPDP), soon known to participants as "Ippy-Dippy." Each team would study the major highways leading from port cities inland, looking at the capacities of these roads, how goods could be taken across beaches onto docks and into the hinterland, how road networks were to be mapped, and so forth. Such studies of the port systems of Antwerp and Marseille, for example, enabled Army logisticians to overcome critical supply bottlenecks late in 1944 and early in 1945. In preparation for this work, the Army Corps of Engineers gave each R&A man a quick course on how to figure the volume of goods that can be funneled into and out of a port. It was decided to study the facilities of the port of Baltimore as a test case without telling the Baltimore authorities. Unfortunately, as a result the man in charge of port security lost his job, which had not been the intention of those who planned the operation.[33]

Another task undertaken was a "detailed survey of the location of millions of displaced persons on the European continent, the routes likely to be followed by them upon the collapse of German control, useful river crossings or other points where their trek could best be controlled by military government authorities, and billeting capacities in cities enroute, which were estimated with the help of prewar and captured wartime statistics, Allied bomb damage estimates and other data."

The chief job subsequently done on the Continent was the initiation of an extensive project calling for the analysis, description, and photographing of strategic aspects of the terrain, transportation, industrial, and urban centers of much of western Europe. This project in the field of military geography engaged the services of over a dozen geographers for almost a year and was based upon experimentation leading to the development of new criteria and techniques of field and photographic appraisal.[34]

OSS geographers had to learn to work within very tight deadlines, as did other R&A personnel. One morning in London in 1944, the late Felix Gilbert, for many years a leading authority on European history, together with a geographer attached to R&A London (one who had until recently been assigned to the Latin-American Division) and a British colleague, received instructions to sit down and come up with a plan for the projected Allied occupation zones of Berlin for the Joint Chiefs. They began work at nine in the morning, and were to complete it within three hours. They met the deadline and, with one modification, their recommendations were followed by the four Allied powers.[35]

The requirements for meeting tight military deadlines, often with very short notice, could be extremely suspenseful for many academic perfectionists within R&A. In addition, most projects had to be completed anonymously on a team basis, which again ran counter to most traditional academic research and writing practices. Unfortunately, the editorial section of R&A tended to impose a certain simplicity on the prose of all reports, which some authors found deflating.[36]

The Morgenthau Plan, named for F.D.R.'s Secretary of the Treasury, tentatively called for the destruction of Germany's heavy industry in the Ruhr Basin after the war and for its separation from the rest of Germany. The objective was to permanently weaken future German war-making capacity. One R&A geographer was obliged to look into the practicality of this proposal. In addition to field trips and interviews with local and regional German officials, this individual had to spend many hours over several days making notes in the cramped Plexiglas nose of a B–26 Marauder borrowed from the Army Air Forces, as it lumbered up and down the Rhine. Simultaneously, a photographer shot pictures of land and water features on his instructions as the plane sped along. Normally, this was done at an elevation of 300 feet, though sometimes it was necessary to descend to half that height. The R&A man concluded that Morgenthau's plan, though fraught with many geographic, economic, and political difficulties, was technically possible. By war's end, however, political and other considerations had rendered the plan and the project moot.[37]

Several R&A geographers were sent to Germany to scout out repositories of German topographic and other maps, including map publishers, for detailed information concerning German map-making techniques and map makers. One objective here was to seize this information and material before the Russians could do so.[38]

It has been said that knowledge often surges in times of stress. "Extraordinary science" alternated with ordinary science during World War II. Geography and medicine were two fields which seemed to surge most after 1945 because of wartime exigencies. This is the more remarkable in the case of geography, whose ranks within R&A, according to one OSS veteran, consisted of a group of glorious amateurs.[39]

Historians, economists, and to a lesser extent political scientists were among the more visible R&A personnel during and after the war. On the other hand, geographers were remembered as having been less troublesome than the economists. One OSS veteran recalls that geographers were usually called research analysts, intelligence analysts, map librarians, or editors, but very rarely geographers. Unfortunately, geographers were not as successful as other social scientists in establishing the autonomy of their discipline, in part, perhaps, because of the manner in which R&A reports and other products were put together. Nevertheless, the dramatic expansion of geography as a field of inquiry after the war, and growing public awareness of its importance, owed much to the efforts of the geographers who labored for OSS and other federal agencies between 1941 and 1945.[40]

NOTES

1. Thomas F. Troy, *Donovan and the CIA: A History of the Establishment of the Central Intelligence Agency* (Washington, D.C.: Central Intelligence Agency, Center for the Study of Intelligence, 1981), pp. 27–42; Robin W. Winks, *Cloak and Gown, 1939–1961: Scholars in the Secret War* (New York: William Morrow, 1987), pp. 64–65. There are several published biographies of General Donovan. They include Corey Ford, *Donovan: Of OSS* (Boston: Little, Brown, 1970); Richard Dunlop, *Donovan: America's Master Spy* (Chicago: Rand McNally, 1982); and Anthony Cave Brown, *Wild Bill Donovan: The Last Hero* (New York: Times Books, 1982).

2. There appears to be much disagreement as to the nature of Donovan's relationship with President Roosevelt (FDR) prior to 1940. Dunlop, *Donovan*, p. 25, and Brown, *Wild Bill*, pp. 20–21, state that Donovan did not know FDR in law school, although he was aware of who he was. The implication is that the two young men did not move in the same circles. G. J. A. O'Toole, *Honorable Treachery: A History of U.S. Intelligence, Espionage, and Covert Action From the American Revolution to the CIA* (New York: Atlantic Monthly Press, 1991), p. 357, states that friendship between the two men went "back more than thirty years." Bradley F. Smith, *The Shadow Warriors: OSS and the Origins of the CIA* (New York: Basic Books, 1983), an extremely valuable work, points out that the "long association" of the two men was based on their having "crossed paths frequently in New York and Washington politics," but emphasizes that any alleged closeness between them has been "exaggerated." He suggests that they did share "comparable personalities." O'Toole, in *Honorable Treachery*, pp. 359–62, suggests that Donovan was reluctant to head COI, but this does not square with what was known about Donovan's personality. According to Smith, *Shadow Warriors*, p. 31, General Donovan was an activist, an enthusiast, and a doer. Smith also points out (see page 66) that Donovan "waxed so eloquent" about establishing COI that he persuaded FDR to give it a try. Also see Rhoda Jeffries-Jones, *The CIA and American Democracy* (New Haven: Yale University Press, 1989), p. 16, in which Donovan is characterized as "an incorrigible activist." Tom Braden, "The Birth of the CIA," *American Heritage* (February 1977): 5, remarks of Donovan, "He went over people's heads; he ignored channels and organization charts. And he would try anything. The more insane the idea, the more likely it seemed that Donovan would wave his hand and say 'Let's give it a try.'" Braden quotes Dean Acheson, later Harry Truman's Secretary of State and no great fan of Donovan's, as saying of the general, "Donovan would have surprised no one if . . . he left one morning and returned the previous afternoon."

3. Smith, *Shadow Warriors*, pp. 64–65, 70–72.

4. Ibid.

5. Ibid., p. 72; Winks, *Cloak and Gown*, pp. 66–68.

6. Smith, *Shadow Warriors*, p. 74.

7. MacLeish's and the Library of Congress' participation in the genesis of the COI is well documented in the records of the Library of Congress: the Central File, MacLeish-Evans, box 748, housed in the Manuscript Division, Library of Congress (LC), hereafter MacLeish. See, for example, MacLeish to Donovan, 29 Jun 41, outlining what he and the LC staff were prepared to do to help COI; Telg, MacLeish to Verner Clapp, LC, 6 Jul 41, concerning needed budget details for the proposal; MacLeish to Donovan, 29 Jul 41, concerning a day-long conference of university, foundation, National Archives, and LC officials who met to recommend academic personnel who would initially staff R&A; Donovan to MacLeish, 30 Jul 41, outlining his understanding of what LC will do for COI; all in MacLeish. Smith, *Shadow Warriors*, p. 73; O'Toole, *Honorable Treachery*, pp. 413–15; Kermit Roosevelt, ed., *War Report of the OSS (Office of Strategic Services)* (New York: Walker and Co., 1976), pp. 9, 11. Donovan's COI activities were the subject of a piece in

the *Washington Times Herald*, "New U.S. Bureau Created to Lead 'War of Words,'" by Guy Richards, on 20 Sep 41.

8. Roosevelt, *War Report*, p. 50.

9. Ibid., pp. 11, 14, 49, 50; "Division of Special Information" in the Library of Congress; Relations of the Division to the Office of the Coordinator of Information, n.d.; "Functioning of the Reference Section of the Division of Special Information," 11 Oct 41; Ernest S. Griffith, Director, Legislative Reference Service, to MacLeish, 21 Oct 41, concerning progress in acquiring and servicing materials for DSI; List of DSI Personnel, 1 Nov 41, all in MacLeish.

10. Richard Hartshorne, "The Organizations and Functions of the Sections of the Geography Division," Internal COI Memorandum, 11 Aug 42, Record Group (RG) 226, entry 145, box 5, National Archives and Records Administration (NARA); Roosevelt, *War Report*, pp. 58–59, 169–70; Arthur H. Robinson, wartime Chief of OSS's Map Division, discussed with the author the daunting challenges entailed in developing and organizing his agency beginning in 1941, Interv with Arthur H. Robinson, Madison, Wis., 2 Oct 88. In brief, the United States faced a serious shortage of cartographers in 1941, and quickly had to develop "cartographic methods that would permit the utilization, with a minimum amount of training, of large numbers of inexperienced persons." Preston E. James and Clarence F. Jones, *American Geography; Inventory and Prospect* (Syracuse, N.Y.: Syracuse University Press, 1954), p. 559. Some 300 or more geographers were employed in Washington in 1943. The government affiliations of 217 of them are listed in P. E. James and G. Martin, *The Association of American Geographers: The First Seventy-Five Years, 1904–1979* (New York: Association of American Geographers [AAG], 1978), p. 90. The Research and Analysis Division of OSS employed 75 of these people. An earlier list by name and government agency as of 23 June 1942 will be found in David J. Robinson, ed., *Studying Latin America: Essays in Honor of Preston E. James* (Ann Arbor, Mich.: University Microfilms, 1980), p. 74.

11. James later recalled that he was teaching a summer session class at Harvard, his alma mater, one day in July 1941. "I was lecturing, when suddenly the door opened, in came the departmental secretary, and she said 'Professor, I have Washington on the line.'" Much to the admiration of the students present, James calmly replied "Tell them to wait, I'll be through at 10 o'clock." James, who had anticipated a call to join COI, was a well-known authority on Latin America. He has been an Army Reserve officer since 1921 and was then a captain. He has been in Washington some months earlier consulting with the State Department on a variety of issues. Robinson, *P. E. James*, pp. 60–63. James was profiled by Inga Arvad in the *Washington Times Herald* on 24 Oct 41.

12. Interv with Richard Hartshorne, Madison, Wis., 30 Sep 88; Interv with Kirk Stone, Madison, Wis., 1 Oct 88. Stone was a doctoral candidate at Michigan in 1941, came to Washington as Dr. Hartshorne's personal assistant, and later took a commission in the Navy. His was one of twenty-five military positions assigned to Research and Analysis. He later taught at the Universities of Wisconsin and Georgia. See also William L. Langer, *In and Out of the Ivory Tower* (New York: Neale Watson Academic Publications, 1977), ch. 9.

13. Smith, *Shadow Warriors*, pp. 76–77; Roosevelt, *War Report*, pp. 50–51; Robin W. Winks, "Getting the Right Stuff: FDR, Donovan, and the Quest for Professional Intelligence," in George C. Chalou, ed., *The Secrets War: The Office of Strategic Services in World War II* (Washington, D.C.: National Archives and Records Administration, 1992), p. 28.

14. The quotation is taken from an incomplete unpublished history of R&A in RG 226, entry 99, box 76, folder 45, NARA. From internal evidence, much of this manuscript, which is in several sections, was probably written by Dr. Stone and reviewed by Dr. Hartshorne. It is not known who else may have had a hand in its composition. Langer points out that Donovan had to get a special exception from FDR from Civil Service regu-

lations concerning salaries for some of his OSS people. "Even so [Langer later wrote] I and my colleagues were to receive only what we had been earning at the universities, and during the war the highest civil service grade was usually excluded from federal pay raises voted by Congress. For us government service was no gold mine." Langer, *Ivory Tower*, p. 182. On the other hand, an examination of OSS payroll information at several stages during the war and discussions with several OSS veterans suggest that many of the more junior personnel were paid salaries in excess of what they had been earning in academia before the war. Robinson Interv; Henry S. Sterling personal files and wartime OSS personnel records, secured from CIA through FOIA, Ltr, John H. Wright, Information and Privacy Coordinator, CIA, to author, 1 Jun 93.

15. Roosevelt, *War Report*, pp. 58–59, 167; Robinson Interv; Hartshorne and Stone Intervs; Interv with George Beishlag, Towson, Maryland, 12 Apr 90. Dr. Beishlag was with the Latin American Division of R&A and later the Map Division. He later chaired the Geography Department at Towson State University. He points out that the R&A staff were constantly moving from office to office around Washington.

16. Stone Interv. Stone points out that as jurisdictional jealousies developed, some roadblocks were thrown up by the military against men in civilian clothes. Civilians, for example, were no longer welcome to come in through the back door of the old Navy Department building in Washington. When in uniform, however, one could go through the back door, which saved one walking many blocks. Robinson Interv; Kirk Stone, "Geography's Wartime Service," *Annals of the AAG* (March 1979): 89–96; Arthur H. Robinson, "Geography and Cartography Then and Now," *Annals of the AAG* (March 1979): 97–102; Roosevelt, *War Report*, p. 168; "Lessons From the Wartime Experience for Improving Graduate Training for Geographic Research," Rpt of the Committee on Training and Standards in the Geographic Profession, National Research Council, *Annals of the AAG* (September 1946): 195–214; Robinson, *P. E. James*, p. 74; Roosevelt, *War Report*, p. 168; Hartshorne Interv.

17. G. F. Deasy, "Training, Professional Work, and Military Experience of Geographers, 1942–1947," *Professional Geographer* 6 (1947): 7; Winks, "Right Stuff," pp. 24–25; Henry S. Sterling personal files.

18. Stone, "Wartime Service," p. 89.

19. G. F. Deasy, "Wartime Changes in the Occupation of Geographers," *Professional Geographer* 7 (1948): 36–37; Deasy, "Training," pp. 3–7.

20. Beishlag Interv. Beishlag, who was invited to join COI in the spring of 1942, was a civilian in 1943, when he was drafted into the Army. He remained with OSS as an enlisted man, and rose to the grade of Technician, 4th Class (equivalent of sergeant), but worked in civilian clothes.

21. Beishlag Interv; Winks, "Right Stuff," p. 20; Barry M. Katz, *Foreign Intelligence: Research and Analysis in the Office of Strategic Services, 1942–1945* (Cambridge: Harvard University Press, 1989), p. 46.

22. Katz, *Foreign Intelligence*, p. 44; Winks, "Right Stuff," pp. 20, 22; Robinson Interv; Hartshorne Interv. The Ohio State professor who recommended Robinson to Hartshorne was Roderick Peattie.

23. Robinson Interv; see also "Coordinator of Information–Office of Strategic Services, D.C. Building and Areas Occupied–July 1941 to Dec. 1944," together with a number of periodic "Bureau [later "Organization"] Space Records," entry 132, box 9, RG 226, NARA. This lists no fewer than twenty-six different buildings which were utilized by COI/OSS at various times, nineteen of which were in use in December 1944.

24. Beishlag Interv.

25. O'Toole, *Honorable Treachery*, pp. 404–05; Smith, *Shadow Warriors*, pp. 118–21.

26. Robinson Interv. Robinson has noted that enlisted men ordinarily could not be recruited for map-making assignments, because their physical training toughened their hands too much.

27. Robinson Interv; Robinson, "Geography Then and Now." Preston James and Arthur Robinson were two of the five geographers involved in a videotaped symposium entitled "Geographers, Cartographers, and the Second World War," held as part of the annual AAG meetings in Washington on 23 April 1983. This will be cited hereafter as Geographer's Symposium. Roosevelt, *War Report*, pp. 169–70; Winks, *Cloak and Gown*, p. 90. James and Jones note, in *American Geography*, p. 558, that "probably more maps were made and printed during the five years from 1941 to 1946" than previously had been produced. Troy notes that the Joint Chiefs of Staff generally had very high praise for the quality of research and cartographic work coming out of R&A during the war. Troy, *Donovan and the C.I.A.*, p. 133. See also Roosevelt, *War Report*, pp. 104, 113.

28. Robinson Interv; Robinson, Geographer's Symposium.

29. Beishlag Interv.

30. James, Geographer's Symposium; undated Memorandum in files of Henry S. Sterling; Robinson, *P. E. James*, pp. 67, 79.

31. Winks, "Right Stuff," pp. 26–28.

32. Ibid., p. 26.

33. James, Geographer's Symposium; Stone Interv; Henry S. Sterling personal files; Winks, *Cloak and Gown*, pp. 89–90. Guido Wegend, a geographer long on the faculties of Rutgers and Arizona State, remarked in a videotaped interview that he worked under Preston James in France and Germany during 1944 and 1945. He was one of the first American geographers (if not *the* first) to become a specialist on port studies, an expertise he developed while with OSS. This field entails the study of patterns of cargo and ship movements and the functions of port facilities. Wegend subsequently became a political geographer. The interview was conducted in April 1988 by Maynard Dow of Plymouth State University in New Hampshire as part of his "Geographers on Film" series.

34. Undated Memorandum, Sterling files.

35. Beishlag Interv; Felix Gilbert, *A European Past: Memoirs, 1905–1945* (New York: W. W. Norton, 1988), pp. 188–89; Ltr, Felix Gilbert to author, 16 Apr 90; Henry S. Sterling personal files. Sterling, a geographer and Latin-Americanist long on the faculty of the University of Wisconsin, chaired the three-man team. The name of the British representative is not known, but historian Harold Deutsch, who for some time headed the R&A office in Paris, has suggested in personal conversation that it may have been David Balfour. Balfour, who was with the Political Warfare Executive and later became a distinguished historian, at one time may have been on the faculty of the University of East Anglia in Norwich. Arthur Schlesinger, "The London Operation: Recollections of a Historian," in Chalou, *The Secrets War*, somewhat overstates the case when he suggests (page 65), that Gilbert was "evidently responsible for the zonal division of Berlin." As a former resident of the city, Gilbert unquestionably played a vital role, but the evidence suggests that the decisions made by the team were joint efforts. See also Katz, *Foreign Intelligence*, pp. 83–84.

36. Beishlag Interv.

37. Undated Memorandum in the files of Henry S. Sterling, the geographer who did this study. The results, mimeographed in an internal R&A study (no. 3371) were entitled "The Ruhr: Problems of Boundary Delimitation," 11 Dec 45. OSS having been disbanded several months previously by direction of President Truman, this study was published under the aegis of the Interim Research and Intelligence Service of the Department of State. Many of the aerial photographs are in the possession of the author.

38. Interv with Clarence Olmstead, Madison, Wis., 22 Sep 89. Olmstead is another OSS geographer who was for many years on the faculty of the University of Wisconsin.

39. Stone Interv.

40. Beishlag Interv; Stone, "Wartime Service," pp. 95–96; Winks, *Cloak and Gown*, p. 90. Edward Ackerman, an R&A operative later on the faculty of Harvard, made a valuable assessment of the wartime contributions of OSS geographers and their prewar preparation.

He argued that "geography's wartime achievements [were] based more on individual ingenuity than on thorough, farsighted training [in the prewar period]." Most young geographers were "unfamiliar with foreign geographic literature," had an "almost universal ignorance of foreign languages," were at a disadvantage because of their "general lack of sys-
temic specialties [having emphasized regionalism in graduate school]," and suffered somewhat because of the "strangeness of the problems [with which they dealt] and [from the]
pressure under which [they] worked" during the war. He contended that a better systematic
grounding was needed for all work in geography, including regional studies. Edward A.
Ackerman, "Geographic Training, Wartime Research, and Immediate Professional
Objectives," *Annals of the AAG* (December 1945): 122, 125. James and Jones add to this
by noting the "almost complete lack of cartographic training in the United States" in 1941.
James and Jones, *American Geography*, p. 559. Arthur Robinson has several times noted
that World War II provided cartography with a substantial boost which helped make it a
discrete academic discipline after the war. Robinson Interv; Robinson, Geographer's
Symposium.

To Hurdle the Last Barrier
The U.S. Army Engineers and the Crossing of the Rhine River, 1944–1945

John T. Greenwood

The assault crossings and subsequent bridging of the Rhine River by the Allied forces in March 1945 is one of the largest and most meticulously planned operations in military history. This paper will focus on how the U.S. Army engineers in the European Theater of Operations (ETO) planned their crossing and bridging operations.

Strategic Setting

The Anglo-American strategy for the war against Germany called for a cross-Channel invasion, a massive buildup of forces on the Continent, and then decisive offensive operations that would defeat Germany within one year (by D+360 days). Allied planners focused on the destruction of the German Armed Forces in the field and of Germany's industrial war-making capacity at home. Hence, the major emphasis in postinvasion ground operations fell to the British and Canadian armies of Field Marshal B. L. Montgomery's 21st Army Group. Driving to the northeast across France and Belgium, they were to thrust north of the Ardennes onto the North German Plain to encircle the Ruhr, Germany's foremost industrial area, from the north and east.[1]

The First, Third, and Ninth U.S. Armies of Lt. Gen. Omar N. Bradley's 12th Army Group would mount a secondary drive eastward through France, Luxembourg, and Belgium. Advancing on a broad front toward the Rhine River to bring more Allied divisions to bear on the Germans, Bradley's forces would cover Monty and also link up with the U.S. and French forces of Lt. Gen. Jake Devers' 6th Army Group that would move up the Rhône River valley after landing in southern France. The 12th Army Group would breach the Siegfried Line, seize the Saar to neutralize another major German industrial area, cross the Rhine near Mainz, and move on to Frankfurt and beyond. From there, the American armies would swing to the north and northeast to join up with Monty to envelop the Ruhr, thus effectively destroying Hitler's ability to continue fighting.[2]

General Dwight D. Eisenhower, Supreme Allied Commander, and his planners realized that adopting this strategy for the ground war in Europe required U.S. Army forces to hurdle two great water obstacles—the English Channel and the Rhine River. The last significant natural barrier protecting the Nazi heartland, the Rhine had to be jumped to complete the destruction of Nazi Germany and its capacity to wage war. Thus, even as they prepared to take the first barrier during Operation OVERLORD in 1944, the engineers of European Theater of Operations, U.S. Army (ETOUSA), were already looking east to that last barrier.[3]

ETOUSA Engineer Planning

Planning and coordination for theaterwide engineer operations such as the Rhine crossings fell largely to Maj. Gen. Cecil Ray Moore, ETOUSA's Chief Engineer, who doubled as the Chief Engineer of the Communications Zone (COMZ) once American forces were firmly established on the Continent. Engineers from the Office of the Chief Engineer (ETOUSA/OCE) down to the divisions had to weigh many complex factors in planning to get the American armies over the historic Rhine barrier and on to Berlin. An assault crossing over a river the size of the Rhine against a defended shore is one of the most complicated and dangerous operations in modern mobile warfare, and also one of the most critical to its success. From the very start, then, Moore viewed the proposed multiple assault crossings and bridging operations on the Rhine River as second only in importance to the D-Day invasion.[4]

The Rhine River[5]

The physical characteristics of the Rhine River and its entire basin dictated much of the engineer planning. The 820-mile-long Rhine River, the most important river of Germany and western Europe, begins in southeastern Switzerland, flows through Lake Constance, and then runs west for 100 miles to Basle where it turns north for its 420-mile-long journey through Germany to the Netherlands and the North Sea.

The Rhine in Germany is divided into three sections, each with its own particular geologic and topographic features that present military engineers with greatly varying challenges. From Basel to Mainz and the confluence of the Main River, known as the Upper Rhine, the river runs through a broad valley, 20–30 miles wide, between the Vosges Mountains to the west and the Black Forest in the east. The river's current is about 12–13 feet per second, its depth ranges up to 25 feet, and its bottom and banks are largely gravel, sand, and mud.

From Worms to Bingen, the Rhine heads north through the Hessian Plain that extends eastward to Frankfurt. In this historic gateway to central Germany, the river adds the Main River to its waters as it turns westward at Mainz before bending north again just beyond Bingen to enter the Middle Rhine, or Gorge Section, that stretches north to Bonn, just south of Cologne. This is the Rhine of Germanic legend, the setting for many an epic Wagnerian opera, and the home of the Lorelei and the scenic castles of medieval robber-barons. Here the river is compressed between rugged 500-foot-high cliffs. From excellent observation posts and positions high on the eastern cliffs, German defenders could easily dominate the few available approaches from the west to crossing points.

In this section, the current reaches 16 feet per second, the depths vary up to 100 feet, and the bottom is rock. On both sides of the river rugged approaches and limited road nets make this an extremely unattractive crossing zone, except for the brief opening around Koblenz where the Moselle River enters the Rhine. To ETOUSA's engineers in 1944, this scenic Gorge Section was most unattractive for any river-crossing and bridging operations. It should be no surprise, then, that Allied leaders orig-inally envisioned no American crossings in this sector.[6]

On the Lower Rhine, from Bonn to the Dutch border, the river enters the flat Cologne Plain, the southwestern extension of the North German Plain, where it widens out and slows down to 4–8 feet per second as it sweeps by Cologne, Düsseldorf, Duisburg, and the Ruhr basin. The river is as much as 25 feet deep, and the bottom, banks, and floodplains are main-ly silt, sand, clay, and gravel. To the west of Emmerich, the Rhine enters the Netherlands, where it splits into the Neder Rjin and the Waal.

From Basel to the Dutch border the Rhine's width varies from 700–1,200 feet, but at places, especially around Mainz, it widens to 2,000 feet. Throughout its length, it is unfordable, even at low water, and thus is a major obstacle to military operations.

Although a sophisticated system of dikes and levees, often 15–25 feet high, canalizes the river throughout most of its length, the Rhine is subject to frequent floods and high water periods. During floods the river level can rise 25 or more feet and overflow extensive lowland areas along the river, creating a very serious obstacle. The Rhine was also vulnerable to artifi-cially created floods should the Germans destroy the dams on the river's upper reaches and eastern tributaries and breach its levees and dikes.

Planning Options

As Allied planners knew, the Rhine and the terrain on either side of it present a formidable series of natural obstacles to the conduct of military operations. The Allies had already decided on two main avenues of approach to Germany—north and south of the Ardennes. These avenues yielded six main corridors of approach to the river—across the Lower Rhine north of the Ruhr; down the Meuse River valley and then turning east across the Roer and Erft rivers to Cologne; down the Moselle River to Koblenz; through Kaiserslautern toward Worms, Mainz, and Frankfurt; through the Saverne gap in Alsace; and through the Belfort-Mulhouse gap in the south. Once east of the Rhine, the flat North German Plain offered the best terrain for mobile operations, while the heavily wooded and more difficult terrain in the middle and southern sections restricted an attacker.

Combined with the overall Allied plans and the progress of operations in the summer and fall of 1944, these natural avenues of approach to and exit from the Rhine limited the Allies to three good crossing areas—between Emmerich and Orsoy north of the Ruhr, between Cologne and Coblenz, and between Bingen and Worms. Bradley's 12th Army Group had three principal corridors of advance to the Rhine—the Meuse and Moselle rivers and Kaiserslautern gap to Mainz and Worms. To the north Montgomery had the lowland corridor and to the south Devers had the Saverne and Belfort gaps, which led only down the Rhine or into the forests of Baden and Württemberg. Allied emphasis lay with Montgomery in the north.[7]

Detailed Engineer Planning Proceeds

While general planning for the Rhine crossings started before the invasion, especially with detailed aerial photo-mapping, serious preparations began only in August 1944. American commanders believed then they could push through the Low Countries, Luxembourg, Lorraine, and Alsace, to the Rhine before Thanksgiving and end the war before Christmas. The Engineer Sections of First and Third Armies began studying potential crossing sites and bridging requirements in August and September 1944. Col. John F. Conklin, Third Army Engineer, established a special planning staff to prepare for the crossings and order necessary bridging materials.[8]

In October and early November 1944, General Moore and his staff participated in a series of meetings of engineers from every Allied army and army group, ETOUSA, and SHAEF at First Army, 12th Army Group, and SHAEF headquarters to discuss the crossing operations. Although it was too early to pinpoint specific crossing sites, continuation of the broad-front approach projected Lt. Gen. William Simpson's Ninth Army to cross around Wesel, north of the Ruhr; Lt. Gen. Courtney Hodges' First Army to cross in the Cologne area; Lt. Gen. George S. Patton's Third Army to cross at Mainz to drive on Frankfurt and Darmstadt; and Lt. Gen. Alexander Patch's Seventh Army of 6th Army Group to cross between Mannheim and Karlsruhe. After an exhaustive review of the Rhine's current, width, banks, bottom conditions, and potential crossing sites, the engineers concluded the following: naval landing craft were needed; ferries, amphibious trucks (DUKWs), and amphibious tanks (Duplex Drive, DD Tanks) would need aerial cableways; special designs and construction equipment were required for fixed-pile COMZ bridges; and that floating bridges would need heavier anchors and special nets and booms to protect them from debris, enemy mines, and swimmers coming downstream.[9]

The U.S. Navy, Europe, quickly agreed to provide 72 Landing Craft, Vehicle and Personnel (LCVPs), 45 Landing Craft, Mechanized (LCMs), and 100 armored amphibious tractors—Landing Vehicles, Tracked (LVTs), or "Alligators," along with 867 officers and men in three Naval Landing Detachments assigned to the First, Third, and Ninth Armies. The Seventh Army on the upper Rhine had no naval support for its crossings. Each army was assigned 24 LCVPs, while 6 LCMs went to First Army, 15 to Third Army, and 24 to Ninth Army. ETOUSA provided Army DUKWs to support the crossings. In addition, the Army's Transportation Corps provided "Sea Mule" tugs which were primarily for use in the construction of the semipermanent highway and railroad bridges.[10]

The U.S. Navy delivered the LCVPs, LCMs, and LVTs in December 1944 and January 1945, but then they had to be moved to the front. The 36-foot LCVPs could be hauled from the Channel on standard engineer M19 heavy ponton trailers, but special cradles had to be designed for M25 tank transporters to move the 50-foot by 14-foot 22-ton LCMs to training and assembly areas and then up to the Rhine. Their size and weight limited these loads to carefully chosen routes. The opening of the Albert Canal eased the transportation problems for the naval craft destined for the First and Ninth Armies, but Third Army's craft had to go overland from the Channel to the Toul, France, depot and then to forward assembly areas.[11]

Many Army engineer units were unfamiliar with the naval landing craft, so extensive training was conducted in the First, Third, and Ninth Armies to familiarize the assault engineers and infantry with landing craft operation, loading, and landing characteristics. For example, the Ninth Army's XVI Corps, which had the assignment of crossing the Rhine at

Rheinberg as part of Montgomery's assault, set up training centers on the Meuse for its two assault divisions: for the 30th Infantry Division at Echt and at Sittard for the 79th Infantry Division.[12]

Engineer Concept of Operations

Overall engineer planning was based on the Allied concept of a broad-front advance and the seizure of the entire west bank of the Rhine before each army crossed as well as on current Army doctrine and theater SOP. Each corps of each army would secure one bridgehead and develop the crossing site to support the buildup. Using storm and then assault boats, often under cover of smoke, army engineer units would carry a division's infantry and engineer assault troops to the far shore where they would secure and hold a bridgehead with artillery and air support. Corps and army engineer units would then come forward to install and operate Treadway and heavy ponton ferries and DUKWs that, along with the Navy's LCVPs, LCMs, and LVTs, would begin to carry troops, tanks, trucks, field pieces, food, and ammunition, etc., across the river.[13]

Once the bridgehead was firmly established and observed artillery fire no longer fell on the bridging sites, at approximately H+2 days, army and corps engineer combat groups would bring up bridging trains and begin building tactical floating bridges. These were either Class 40 M2 Treadway or Class 40 reinforced 25-ton heavy ponton bridges that could carry most standard U.S. Army vehicles, including M4 Sherman medium tanks. Only the new 90-mm. gun Pershing M-26 tank, which was just arriving in numbers in the theater, was too wide and heavy for the Treadway assault bridge and would have to be ferried across. As the fighting moved away from the secured crossing sites, corps and army engineers would put in two-way Class 40 floating Bailey bridges. The engineer construction units of the Advanced Section, Communications Zone (ADSEC/COMZ), would begin building semipermanent, fixed-pile railway bridges and two-way Class 40/one-way Class 70 highway bridges that could carry fully loaded M25 tank transporters.[14]

This crossing and bridging sequence was standard procedure in the ETO and conformed to prevailing engineer doctrine. The theater had only a limited amount of tactical floating bridging, and it could not be left pinned to the Rhine when it was urgently needed for more pressing uses at the front. However, the tactical bridges could not be lifted and moved forward until suitable replacement bridges, usually floating Bailey bridges, were installed. Secure fixed bridging had to be built quickly, not only to free the tactical bridges but also to carry the heavier traffic of the road and rail lines and the petroleum pipelines lines of communication (LOCs) to the frontline fighting units.[15]

Accurate information on the river's condition was required for the detailed planning of the assault crossings and ferry operations, and the construction of tactical, floating Bailey, and fixed COMZ bridges. During operations, timely information on the changes in the stages and flow in the main river and its tributaries would be critical to getting combat troops across the river and then safeguarding their supply lines. Floating bridges were very vulnerable to sudden rises in the river levels or to currents over seven feet per second, which restricted their load-carrying capacity. In floods, they had to be removed or they would be washed away, thus severing the lifeline to the front. Just in case their worst fears were realized and significant amounts of tactical bridging were lost to floods and enemy action, General Moore and 12th Army Group built up comfortable safety margins with a 50 percent reserve for the three heavy ponton bridges and a 100 percent reserve for the ten Treadway bridges planned for the initial bridging phase.[16]

Advantage of Civil Works' Experience

General Moore also organized the Rhine Flood Prediction Service (RFPS) in December 1944 to determine the flow rates and flood stages of the river, to monitor any changes, and to develop predictions for favorable crossing times. By January 1945 gauging stations on the Rhine's major tributaries in Allied hands were feeding data back to hydrologists, hydrometeorologists, and engineers at the RFPS office near Paris. Combined with forecasts and weather reconnaissance data from the Army Air Forces' 21st Weather Squadron, this information allowed reliable predictions to be made of river stages for the following 12, 24, and 48 hours. Such information was crucial for the engineers who would actually make the crossings, operate ferries, and build the floating bridges.[17]

In this area, as in so many others, the U.S. Army engineers profited greatly from their unique blend of military and civil engineering expertise that came from their extensive experience in the peacetime Civil Works program of the Corps of Engineers. The planning of large Civil Works projects such as Bonneville Lock and Dam or Fort Peck Dam provided engineer officers with a knowledge of all aspects of hydrology, river hydraulics, and the eccentricities of river basin systems like the Rhine. They had extensive prewar experience in the engineering design and construction of large, complex projects; the acquisition and movement of large quantities of construction materials; the mobilization and direction of large manpower resources; and the use of modern heavy construction machinery and power tools. Thus, U.S. Army engineer officers and their units possessed capabilities far superior to any other military engineers in the world, and these advantages paid huge dividends during the war.[18]

Locating Crossing Sites/Planning Bridges

Drawing on this knowledge and experience, the Chief Engineer's staff accumulated every scrap of historical information available on the Rhine and meticulously charted the known hydrologic history, topography, and geologic conditions of the river and river basin. In close cooperation with the Engineer Sections of the 6th and 12th Army Groups, they determined heights and widths of the dikes and levees to pinpoint the best assault crossing and bridging sites. Engineers were especially concerned because the best construction sites for the critical fixed bridging were usually located near bridges on existing road and rail networks in built-up areas. These locations, however, were not always tactically suitable for assault crossings.[19]

Close scrutiny was given to possible crossing sites in the flat floodplain areas along the river where the cross-country movement of armored and other heavy vehicles after rains or flooding would be severely restricted without additional roadwork. Extensive "trafficability" analyses were done and new maps drawn up and distributed. Road and rail nets on both sides of the river were examined to determine the best crossing and bridging points from an operational standpoint and the best locations for the communications zone (COMZ) bridges. They had to tie easily into the rebuilt road and rail LOCs that carried the Allies' main logistical lifelines. All existing bridges were carefully studied to estimate the bridging materials, manpower, and time that would be required to put in an entirely new bridge or to repair a damaged one.[20]

Once the planners at all levels reached their conclusions, the stockpiling of the crossing and bridging materials required for the tactical assaults and COMZ bridges began. The bill of materials ran into the many hundreds of items. For the tactical bridges alone, the list included 2,500 outboard motors and 3,000 assault boats, 679,850 feet of steel cable, 525 inflatable pneumatic rubber floats, 500 25-ton heavy pontons, 28 complete Treadway bridges with pneumatic floats, 86 complete 25-ton heavy ponton bridges with reinforcing heavy pneumatic floats, and 170 Bailey bridge sets with 90 heavy ponton sets.[21]

The COMZ bridges presented special problems because of the widely varying characteristics of the river bottom and the lack of sufficiently long timber piles from the forests of the Ardennes and Vosges. The ADSEC engineer standardized designs for road and rail bridges to use pile bents and light steel trestles to achieve sufficient height above the river. For structural steel girders, 3,145 German-designed steel "meter" beams in lengths of 22 to 82 feet were manufactured for the Allies at the former German plant in Differdange, Belgium. Other construction materials, especially timber, spikes, nails, cement, gravel, sand, stone, etc., were either procured locally or manufactured by engineer units. Indeed, most of the 6,720 40–70-foot timber piles and 3,713,000 boardfeet of lumber for these bridges came from sawmills operated by nondivisional engineer units and forestry companies.[22]

Every boardfoot of timber, ton of gravel, pound of nails, and light steel trestle framework that came from France, Belgium, or Luxembourg reduced the strain on the engineer supply system as well as on the entire Allied logistical structure. The innovative procurement and manufacture of numerous critical items relieved bottlenecks in the engineer supply system all the way back to the United States, assured the availability of needed supplies, and permitted more reliable planning. By early March 1945 engineer depots and storage areas in 6th and 12th Army Groups were filled with over 100,000 tons of engineer supplies and equipment in readiness for the assault on the Rhine barrier.[23]

Hurdling the Rhine

After the diversion to deal with the German Ardennes offensive, the Allies resumed operations to close up to and cross the Rhine by late March 1945, with Monty leading the way in the north. These carefully laid plans were thrown off schedule when the Combat Command B, 9th Armored Division, unexpectedly captured the Ludendorff railway bridge over the Rhine at Remagen on 7 March 1945. As a result, the Allies shifted gears. Without an assault crossing, the First Army quickly put in its planned floating bridges and built a substantial bridgehead east of the Rhine.[24]

On 22–23 March Patton's Third Army jumped the Rhine on the run at Nierstein and Oppenheim and pushed on toward Frankfurt, and later also crossed in the Gorge Section and at Mainz. The Ninth Army crossed on 23–24 March at Rheinberg as part of Monty's massive Operation PLUNDER. Two divisions of Seventh Army crossed at Worms on a 9-mile front on 25–26 March. The initial tactical and floating Bailey bridges went in largely as scheduled—8 bridges in First Army, 12 in Ninth Army, 9 in Third Army, and 4 in Seventh Army. The armies quickly built 7 fixed-pile highway bridges, and the ADSEC engineers then added 5 highway and 5 railroad bridges and 4 petroleum pipelines over the Rhine.[25]

The Rhine River crossings were one of the largest military operations in history, involving 1,250,000 men in the 21st Army Group, another 1,200,000 in 12th Army Group, and over 350,000 more American troops in 6th Army Group. From early March to early May 1945 Army and COMZ engineers built 52 tactical and floating bridges and 10 Communications Zone bridges to carry the gasoline, oil, food, ammunition, men, and material that doomed Hitler's Third Reich.[26]

Summary

The American engineers succeeded at the Rhine for a number of reasons. Engineers at every echelon in ETOUSA devoted thousands of hours to careful study, planning, coordination, and preparation to every tactical and engineering aspect. Most foreseeable tactical and technical problems were considered and provided for, from Navy LCVPs to overcome the swift river current to extra heavy anchors for floating bridges and protective booms. In the Communications Zone, standardized designs were developed to speed construction of the critical LOC railway and highway bridges and to maximize the use of locally procured construction materials. Thousands of tons of engineer equipment and supplies were collected in depots and then moved to the forward staging areas and on to the crossing points according to precisely worked-out movement plans. Bridges were then built quickly, far faster than even the most optimistic estimates. For example, the 2,200–foot-long railway bridge at Wesel was completed in ten days rather than the 45 estimated, and the 2,815-foot Duisburg railway bridge was completed in just 6 1/2 days in early May.[27]

The crossings also benefited from good weather, which kept the water level unusually low, and from generally feeble German resistance. The Germans blew few dams on the tributaries, so no sudden surge of high water prevented or interrupted the crossings. Although the Germans had good defensive positions on the eastern shore, few German units offered serious resistance once the assault units established their footholds. This lack of resistance was a consequence of the crushing losses suffered west of the river from December through March when the Germans threw away the troops and equipment needed to hold the long Rhine barrier.[28]

By the Spring of 1945 the Army's combat and construction engineers who planned and executed the crossings and built the bridges were trained, experienced, and technically proficient. Engineer units were plentifully equipped with excellent military bridging equipment, such as the M2 Treadway bridge and the Bailey bridge, and the finest heavy construction equipment and power tools in the world. Their men were trained to use this vast array of material in innovative and effective ways. At all levels in their planning and operations to hurdle the Rhine, the Army engineers fully demonstrated the imagination, initiative, technical engineering competence, courage, and soldierly skills that marked their many other contributions to the U.S. Army's role in the final Allied victory in Europe.

NOTES

1. Dwight D. Eisenhower, *Crusade in Europe* (Garden City, N.Y.: Doubleday and Co., Inc., 1948), ch. 13, "Planning Overlord," pp. 220–52 *passim.*
2. Eisenhower, *Crusade in Europe,* pp. 225–29; Forrest C. Pogue, *The Supreme Command* (Washington, D.C.: U.S. Army Center of Military History, 1954), pp. 244–56 *passim.*
3. Intervs, Maj Gen Cecil R. Moore (USA Ret.) with Dr. John T. Greenwood, 12–14 Dec 78, 29 Sep 79, 17 Oct 80, and 14 Oct 81, in Office of History, U.S. Army Corps of Engineers, Fort Belvoir, Va.; Office of the Chief Engineer, European Theater of Operations, U.S. Army (OCE/ETOUSA), "Forced Crossing of the Rhine, 1945," OCE/ETOUSA Historical Rpt 20, 1 Dec 45, pp. 1–3; OCE/ETOUSA, *Final Report of the Chief Engineer, European Theater of Operations, 1942–1945* (OCE/U.S. Forces European Theater, 1946), p. 170; Alfred M. Beck et al., *The Corps of Engineers: The War Against Germany* (Washington, D.C.: U.S. Army Center of Military History, 1985), pp. 277–98.
4. Ibid.
5. Unless otherwise noted, this section is based largely on Brig. Gen. Patrick H. Timothy, *The Rhine Crossing: Twelfth Army Group Engineer Operations* (Office of the Engineer, 12th Army Group, 1945); and Kenneth Paterson, "The Construction of Semi-Permanent Bridges over the River Rhine by the American Armies in the European Theater," 1945, app. 13, OCE/ETOUSA, "Railroad Reconstruction and Bridging," OCE/ETOUSA Historical Rpt 12, apps., 1 Dec 45; also Rpt, Office of the Chief Engineer, ETOUSA, "Rhine River Crossings: March 1945," in Record Group (RG) 332, ETO Engineer Section, National Archives and Records Administration (NARA).
6. Eisenhower, *Crusade in Europe,* pp. 366–78; Timothy, *The Rhine Crossing,* pp. 4, 5, 39.
7. Eisenhower, *Crusade in Europe,* pp. 366–78; Pogue, *The Supreme Command,* pp. 420–33 *passim;* Timothy, *The Rhine Crossing,* pp. 4–5.
8. Timothy, *The Rhine Crossing,* pp. 13–20; Maj. Gen. Cecil R. Moore, "Rhine River Railroad Bridges," *Military Engineer* 37, no. 239 (September 1945): 337; Brig Gen John F. Conklin, Engineer, Third U.S. Army, "After-Action Rpt of the Engineer Section," in *After-Action Report of the Third U.S. Army* (Third U.S. Army, 1945), pt. 12, p. 29; Col. Francis X. Purcell, "A Design for Bridging," *Military Engineer* 37, no. 241 (November 1945): 440–45.
9. OCE/ETOUSA, *Final Report,* pp. 300–301; Timothy, *The Rhine Crossing;* Moore, "Rhine River Railroad Bridges"; OCE/ETOUSA, "Forced Crossing," pp. 5–6; and Minutes of Meeting at HQ First Army, "Engineer Problems in Crossing the Rhine," 9 Oct 44; Minutes of Conference of ETO Army Group and Armies, "Engineer Participation in the Impending Crossing of the Rhine River," 19 Oct 44; Minutes of Conference at SHAEF Engineer Division, "Naval Equipment Required for Rhine Crossings," 23 Oct 44; Ltr, Col B. C. Dunn, Dep Chief Engr, SHAEF, to Chief Engr, COMZ, "Special Equipment for Crossing Rhine," 23 Oct 44; "Notes of Conference on River Crossing Equipment Held at Headquarters Twelfth Army Group on 8 November 1944," 9 Nov 44, all apps. in OCE/ETOUSA, "Forced Crossing of the Rhine," apps. to Rpt 20 (OCE/ETOUSA, 1945).
10. Timothy, *The Rhine Crossing,* pp. 11–12; Lt. Col. Marvin C. Ellison, "Landing Craft in River Crossings," *Military Engineer* 37 no. 241 (November 1945): 447–49.
11. Timothy, *The Rhine Crossing,* p. 20; "Forced Crossing," pp. 46–48.
12. "Forced Crossing," pp. 10–13; Brig. Gen. Richard U. Nicholas, Engineer, Ninth U.S. Army, *Ninth Army Engineer Operations in Rhine River Crossing* (Ninth U.S. Army, 30 Jun 45), pp. 11–12.
13. Timothy, *The Rhine Crossing,* pp. 7–10; Third Army, "Engineer Outline Plan for Assault Crossing of Rhine River," app. w/Incl, "Analysis of Requirements for Equipment

and Troops," n.d.; "Forced Crossing," pp. 5–8; War Department Field Manual (FM) 5–6, *Engineer Field Manual: Operations of Engineer Field Units* (Washington, D.C.: Government Printing Office, 1943), 23 Apr 43, see especially ch. 5, "River Crossing Operations," pp. 85–125.

14. See note above; War Department FM 5–10, *Construction and Routes of Communication* (Washington, D.C.: Government Printing Office, 1944), 28 Jan 44; Timothy, *The Rhine Crossing*, pp. 7–12; Roland G. Ruppenthal, *Logistical Support of the Armies: September 1944–May 1945*, vol. 2 (Washington, D.C.: U.S. Army Center of Military History, 1959), pp. 367–78, 405–24.

15. See note above; OCE/ETOUSA, *Final Report*, pp. 170, 300–306.

16. Timothy, *The Rhine Crossing*; Memo, Col L. W. Prentiss, Acting Chief, Supply Div, OCE/ETOUSA, for Dep Chief Engr, sub: Certain Materials and Equipment for 12th Army Group (1st, 3d, and 9th Armies) Required for the Rhine Operation, 12 Feb 45, w/Incl, same sub, 12 Feb 45, in "Forced Crossing—Appendices."

17. Timothy, *The Rhine Crossing*, pp. 16–19; OCE/ETOUSA, *Final Report*, pp. 92–94; Lt. Col. Stanley Dziuban, "Rhine River Flood Prediction Service," *Military Engineer* 37, no. 239 (September 1945): 348–53; Interv, Mr. Franklin F. Snyder, hydrologist with Rhine River Flood Prediction Service, with Dr. John T. Greenwood, 6 Jun 95, pp. 39–70; Franklin F. Snyder, "The Rhine River Flood Prediction Service," 93d Annual Meeting, American Society of Civil Engineers, New York, 17 Jan 46.

18. Interv, General Moore.

19. Timothy, *The Rhine Crossing*, pp. 4, 13–16; Moore, "Rhine River Railroad Bridges," pp. 337–38; Nicholas, *Ninth Army*, pp. 6–7.

20. Timothy, *The Rhine Crossing*, pp. 13–14; Moore, "Rhine River Railroad Bridges," pp. 337–39; Interv, General Moore, Dec 78, pp. 131–32, 227–32; 29 Sep 79, pp. 52–54; Nicholas, *Ninth Army*.

21. Timothy *The Rhine Crossing*; Moore, "Rhine River Railroad Bridges"; Prentiss Memo, 12 Feb 45; Memo, Col L. W. Prentiss, Acting Chief, Supply Div, OCE/ETOUSA, for Dep Chief Engr, sub: Certain Materials and Equipment for 12th Army Group (1st, 3d, and 9th Armies) Required for the Rhine Operation, 11 Mar 45, w/Incl, same sub, 9 Mar 45; Rpt, Maj R. H. Wood, Engr Supply Ofcr, "Status of Stream Crossing Equipment, Sixth Army Group and Base Depots," 24 Feb 45, in "Forced Crossing—Appendices."

22. See above, especially Prentiss Memorandums, 12 Feb and 11 Mar 45; Ltr, Maj R. J. Schomer, OCE/ETOUSA, to Col J. S. Seybold, Ch, Supply Div, OCE/ETOUSA, "Status of Supply for Railway Bridges for the Rhine River Crossing," 5 Mar 45; Ltr, Col P. D. Berrigan, Ch, Const Div, OCE/ETOUSA, to All Allied Engrs, Rhine River—Pile Driving, 30 Jan 45, w/Incl Memo, Summary of Pile Driving for Fixed Trestle Rhine River Bridges, 27 Jan 45, in apps., "Forced Crossing—Appendices"; Moore, "Rhine River Railroad Bridges," pp. 338–40; OCE/ETOUSA, *Final Report*, pp. 222–25, 300–304; Paterson, "Construction."

23. Ibid.

24. Eisenhower, *Crusade in Europe*, pp. 378–86; Omar N. Bradley, *A Soldier's Story* (New York: Henry Holt and Co., 1951), pp. 509–22; Rpt, Col W. A. Carter, Engr, First U.S. Army, *Report of the Rhine River Crossings, First United States Army* (Office of the Engineer, First U.S. Army, May 1945), pp. 1–15; Charles B. MacDonald, *The Last Offensive* (Washington, D.C.: U.S. Army Center of Military History, 1973), pp. 208–35.

25. For accounts of the assault crossings, see Barry W. Fowle, "The Rhine River Crossings," in Barry W. Fowle, ed., *Builders and Fighters: U.S. Army Corps of Engineers in World War II* (Fort Belvoir, Va.: Office of History, U.S. Army Corps of Engineers, 1992), pp. 463–75, and MacDonald, *The Last Offensive*, ch. 13, "The Rhine Crossings in the South," pp. 266–93, and ch. 14, "The Rhine Crossings in the North," pp. 294–320; Beck, *The War Against Germany*, ch. 23, "The Assault Crossings of the Rhine," pp. 499–536; OCE/ETOUSA, "Forced Crossing," pp. 15–41.

26. OCE/ETOUSA, "Forced Crossing"; Timothy, *The Rhine Crossing.*

27. OCE/ETOUSA, "Forced Crossing," pp. 42–45; OCE/ETOUSA, "Railroad Reconstruction and Bridging," pp. 74–95; Ruppenthal, *Logistical Support of the Armies,* vol. 2, pp. 405–41.

28. Eisenhower, *Crusade in Europe,* pp. 377–91.

Tank Destroyers in the European Theater of Operations

Christopher Gabel

The central mission of the U.S. Army in World War II was to invade the continent of Europe and destroy the military might of Nazi Germany. The cutting edge of German military power was a doctrine of mechanized war known popularly as *Blitzkrieg*. To defeat the *Blitzkrieg*, the U.S. Army pursued two initiatives. One was to develop the Army's own capability to wage mechanized warfare, a program that eventually placed 16 armored divisions in the field. The second was to create an "antidote to *Blitzkrieg*." This initiative led to the creation of the tank destroyer quasi-arm, a force which ultimately fielded 71 battalions, 61 of which served in the war against Germany. The mission of these tank destroyer battalions was to stop and defeat enemy armor, thus allowing our own mechanized forces to take the war to the enemy.

Tank destroyers proved to be a valuable asset in combat. They participated effectively in many of the key operations that culminated in the liberation of Europe. Paradoxically, though, the tank destroyers never truly accomplished the mission for which they were created—the defeat and destruction of Germany's mechanized forces.

At the root of this tank destroyer paradox was a flawed conception of armored warfare that emerged within the Army during the period 1939–1941. Specifically, the American military did not fully appreciate the combined arms characteristics of German mechanized operations. Under German doctrine, tanks habitually enjoyed the close and effective support of tactical air, motorized infantry, artillery, engineer, antitank, and antiaircraft elements. To the U.S. Army of the pre–Pearl Harbor period, however, armored warfare meant, first and foremost, massed tanks, with the other combat arms only minimally represented. In American minds, the closest analogy, perhaps, was Napoleonic heavy cavalry, with steeds of steel rather than horseflesh charging across the battlefield to strike decisive blows. Accordingly, when the Army set about creating an armored force in 1940, it established a division table of organization that possessed eight tank battalions, two infantry battalions, and an awkwardly composed artillery contingent.[1] And when the Army formulated its antidote to *Blitzkrieg*, it operated under the misconception that defeating a panzer force was simply a problem of stopping a charge by massed tanks. The answer—massed antitank guns that possessed the mobility to intercept intruding armor and the firepower to destroy it.

On 24 June 1941, the War Department directed that each infantry division activate an antitank battalion out of assets that already existed within the division.[2] This battalion was to constitute a mobile divisional antitank reserve, capable of intervening in mass against armored attacks anywhere in the division sector. The idea of a mobile reserve of massed antitank guns remained the cornerstone of official tank destroyer doctrine throughout the war.

At this juncture, however, the Army high command introduced a doctrinal flaw of major proportions. General George C. Marshall, the Army Chief of Staff, directed that the antitank battalions would possess an "offensive weapon and organization" and would employ "offensive tactics."[3] Lt. Gen. Lesley J. McNair, head of General Headquarters (GHQ) and a major player in antitank developments, stated, "Defensive action against a tank calls for a counterattack in the same general manner as against older forms of attack."[4] At other times, however, McNair advocated a much more passive form of antitank action, suggesting that antitank forces would "emplace and camouflage themselves" when in the presence of hostile tanks.[5]

This ambiguity created considerable confusion among the new antitank forces and within the Army at large. Nobody was sure whether antitank combat was to be offensive or defensive. And if antitank forces were to fight offensively, exactly how should an antitank gun go about attacking and defeating a tank? Most significantly, however, the call for offensive antitank action suggested that antitank units were expected to defeat enemy armor more or less on their own, without the close and effective support of the other combat arms.

Organizational ambiguity compounded the doctrinal confusion. On 3 December 1941, Marshall directed that the antitank battalions be withdrawn from the divisions and be placed directly under GHQ.[6] The antitank battalions were redesignated "tank destroyers," to emphasize the aggressive fighting expected of them. In combat, these tank destroyer battalions were to be pooled at corps and higher levels, forming a general antitank reserve capable of responding in mass to hostile armored incursions anywhere along the front. Thus the tank destroyers were deprived of a permanent higher tactical headquarters capable of combining their actions with those of the other combat arms.

Some of these developments, which seem so troubling in retrospect, might possibly have been uncovered and corrected before the tank destroyers went to war. The Army had a golden opportunity to do so during the famous 1941 maneuvers. Instead, the deficiencies of the emerging tank destroyer doctrine were actually reinforced. One incident in particular stands out. During the Carolinas phase of the great maneuvers, the 69th Armored Regiment, 1st Armored Division, found itself isolated behind enemy lines in the vicinity of Albemarle, North Carolina. Two regiment-size antitank groups, operating as a mobile antitank reserve, trapped the armored regiment in its bivouac and essentially destroyed it. Encouraging as this was to tank destroyer advocates, it should be noted the 69th Armored Regiment lacked infantry and artillery, and was beyond the assistance of any friendly force.[7] A German panzer regiment would not have been caught in such a situation. This engagement, and many others like it that occurred during the maneuvers, indicated only that U.S. armor doctrine needed fixing[8] (which, incidentally, the Armored Force proceeded to do). Maj. Gen. Jacob L. Devers, chief of the Armored Force, felt strongly that the maneuvers were rigged in favor of the antitank forces. He told *Time* magazine that "we were licked by a set of umpire rules."[9]

Such protests fell on deaf ears. The 93d Tank Destroyer Battalion, which participated in the annihilation of the armored regiment at Albemarle, went on to become the school troops for a new Tank Destroyer Center. Its book of standing operating procedures became the foundation for a tank destroyer field manual. The tank destroyer concept, complete with misconceptions, ambiguities, and confusion, coalesced into formal doctrine.

A year after the battle of Albemarle, tank destroyers got their initiation into combat. A total of seven battalions participated in the Tunisian campaign that lasted from November 1942 to May 1943. Each of these battalions possessed thirty-six self-propelled guns and a total complement of 842 officers and men. According to Field Manual (FM) 18–5, the tank destroyer bible, battalions were to be held in reserve and were to respond separately or in groups to enemy armored attacks. They were to act offensively. The tank destroyer motto, "Seek, Strike, and Destroy," accurately represents the spirit of tank destroyer doctrine.[10]

Unfortunately, the German panzer forces in Tunisia refused to play the part laid out for them in FM 18–5. They did not attack in tank-pure formations. Nor did they charge impetuously across the battlefield, as had American armored forces in the 1941 maneuvers. Instead, German panzers almost invariably operated as part of a combined arms team, complete with artillery preparations, air support, accompanying infantry, and their own antitank weapons sited in overwatch positions.[11] The tank destroyer battalion had no organic means of dealing with enemy infantry, artillery, or antitank forces. German antitank weapons proved particularly devastating—any tank destroyer that tried to "Seek, Strike, and Destroy" the panzers was likely to receive an armor-piercing round for its efforts.

In the course of the Tunisian campaign, tank destroyers had one clear-cut opportunity to execute their doctrine as written. At the battle of El Guettar, fought on 23 March 1943, the 601st Tank Destroyer Battalion (reinforced) had the mission of defending the artillery and communications of the 1st Infantry Division. Except for the friendly artillery, it was unsupported by other troops. When fifty tanks of the *10th Panzer Division* attacked, the tank destroyers utilized the aggressive fire and movement tactics prescribed by doctrine to turn back the assault and destroy an estimated 30 enemy tanks. Unfortunately, the battalion lost 27 of the 40 tank destroyers engaged.[12]

This, to the best of my knowledge, was the only instance from the entire war in which a tank destroyer battalion operated as a unit against enemy armor. When American higher commanders in Tunisia realized that tank destroyer doctrine bore little resemblance to the realities of armored warfare, they were quick to improvise. Instead of holding tank destroyer battalions in reserve, awaiting the infrequent appearance of enemy armor in mass, they broke up the battalions and distributed tank destroyers by companies and platoons among the frontline positions. There the tank destroyers acquired a secondary mission as assault guns. Higher commanders also found that tank destroyers with their three-inch guns were serviceable as indirect-fire artillery. These patterns of tank destroyer employment continued for the duration of the war in the Mediterranean theater.

Participants and observers of the campaign in Tunisia were generally critical of the entire tank destroyer concept. Allied Forces Headquarters felt compelled to issue a training memo that sharply curtailed the aggressive tendencies of the tank destroyers: "While it is true that tank destroyer battalions constitute a mobile reserve of antimechanized fire power with which to meet a hostile tank attack, numerous encounters have shown that their characteristics are such as to prohibit their use offensively, either to seek out the hostile tanks in advance of our lines or to meet and shoot it out with them in the open. . . . The statement in FM 18–5 that they are designed for offensive action will not be construed to the contrary."[13] Maj. Allerton Cushman, an Army Ground Forces (AGF) observer, wrote: "Troops in Africa have found that the best way to meet a German tank attack is from concealed, dug-in positions."[14]

Commentary such as this forced the Tank Destroyer Center to rewrite doctrine. A new version of FM 18–5 that appeared in 1944 continued to insist that tank destroyers should be held in reserve for commitment in mass against major armored attacks. However, it also acknowledged for the first time that close cooperation with the other arms was a prerequisite for success in combat. Most significantly, the writers of the new field manual deleted all references to offensive action on the part of tank destroyer forces.

However, the greatest change in tank destroyer doctrine following the North Africa campaign was imposed from above. McNair, by now head of AGF and thus in charge of all Army doctrine, had never liked the idea of self-propelled tank destroyer weapons, thinking them too clumsy and difficult to conceal. In 1943 he directed that half of all tank destroyer battalions be converted to towed weapons—essentially light field guns drawn by half-tracks. The Tank Destroyer Center protested to no avail.

Although the tank destroyers had proved something of a disappointment in North Africa, their greatest challenge lay before them. The invasion of Normandy promised an opportunity for the tank destroyers to prove their worth. Whereas German panzers had seldom appeared in strength during the fighting in Tunisia and Italy, planners for Operation OVERLORD expected plenty of armored action in Normandy. They accurately identified ten panzer divisions in the theater, all of which could reach Normandy within five days of the Allied invasion. The Germans could be expected to mass these forces for concentrated blows against the beachhead. Thirty tank destroyer battalions (11 towed, 19 self-propelled) were to absorb and defeat the blows directed against the American sector[15] while Allied armor launched spoiling attacks to keep the enemy off balance.

The actual campaign in Normandy followed a different course altogether. The Germans resorted to a cordon defense, with armor generally employed piecemeal. The U.S. First Army was not called upon to defeat massed panzer counterattacks. Rather, its main task was to root out a stubbornly defending foe. With relatively few exceptions, this pattern prevailed throughout the European campaign.

It is just as well that the tank destroyers were denied the opportunity to face massed German armor in Normandy, for they quickly discovered that their weapons were inadequate for the task. The Ordnance Department had somehow come to believe that the 3-inch weapon that equipped both towed and self-propelled tank destroyer battalions could defeat even the heaviest German tanks at a comfortable 2,000 yards.[16] Moreover, the towed tank destroyer proved to be of little use to an army in the attack. Fortuitously, the Ordnance Department on its own initiative had developed a 90-mm.

self-propelled tank destroyer that proved effective against all German panzers, but this weapon did not begin to reach the theater until the autumn of 1944.

Thus it is fortunate that tank destroyers in Europe found most of their combat to involve the secondary missions pioneered in Tunisia. During the fighting in Normandy, self-propelled tank destroyers provided a source of mobile firepower for the infantrymen struggling to carve their way through the hedgerows. In the course of heavy fighting around St. Lô, the 654th Tank Destroyer Battalion and the 35th Infantry Division to which it was attached developed an especially effective technique for penetrating hedgerow defenses. First, engineers blew gaps in the hedgerows to bring the tank destroyers, operating in platoons of four, up to the front line of infantry. Tank destroyer observers, on foot with the infantry, guided the self-propelled weapons into position and directed their fire onto enemy machine gun nests in the hedgerow to the front. With enemy fire thus suppressed, the infantry attacked and cleared the enemy hedgerow. Engineers then opened paths to bring the tank destroyers forward again to repeat the process against the next enemy-held hedgerow.[17]

That autumn when the Allies reached the Westwall, or Siegfried Line, tank destroyers proved to be equally useful against concrete fortifications. For example, the 803d Tank Destroyer Battalion supported infantry in the reduction of pillboxes by assigning a platoon of four self-propelled tank destroyers to each infantry assault battalion, and providing the tank destroyers with infantry radios so they could be controlled by the infantry company commanders. The tank destroyer platoon then engaged a pair of pillboxes at a time, with one gun firing at the embrasure of each pillbox and with two guns standing by in an overwatch role. The three-inch rounds did not usually penetrate the fortifications, but they did prevent the enemy from manning his weapons, thus enabling the American infantry to reach the blind side of the fortifications. On a radio signal from the infantry company, the tank destroyers ceased fire and the infantry assaulted the pillboxes from behind.[18]

Tank destroyers also served effectively as indirect-fire artillery. An outstanding example of this occurred in February 1945 when XIX Corps mounted a deliberate assault crossing of the Roer River. Two tank destroyer battalions, one towed and one self-propelled, added seventy-two guns to the fires of division and corps artillery. At H-hour the towed battalion placed neutralization fires on all known German positions in the assault sector, and three of the self-propelled platoons delivered interdiction fire at the rate of 100 rounds per platoon per hour on three highways leading to the assault area. Meanwhile, the other six self-propelled platoons provided direct fire on call from tank destroyer observers who crossed the river with the infantry. When the assault elements passed beyond effective direct fire range, these platoons also shifted to indirect fire. After three and one-half hours of planned fires, the tank destroyers became available for on-call fire missions designated by a tank destroyer fire direction center. Missions included interdiction, harassment, and neutralization fires. The tank destroyers were even prepared (but not called upon) to execute "time on target" fires.[19]

The widespread use of tank destroyers in secondary missions effectively destroyed the coherence of tank destroyer battalions. There were, nonetheless, a few occasions in which tank destroyers were called upon to execute their primary mission of defeating massed enemy armor in the attack.

One of these occurred in late September near Arracourt, where Combat Command A, 4th Armored Division, held off repeated assaults by German panzers in brigade strength. On the morning of 19 September CCA's outpost line detected panzers approaching through the fog and rain. Company C of the 704th Tank Destroyer Battalion utilized the mobility of its self-propelled weapons to maneuver platoons from point to point along the perimeter and help defeat the attack. Capt. James Leach, commander of Company B, 37th Tank Battalion, confirmed that one tank destroyer platoon alone destroyed fifteen German tanks that day. Undoubtedly, the weather contributed significantly to the happy outcome of this engagement. The heavy fog offered concealment to the defenders, allowing the tank destroyers to maneuver freely and neutralizing the superior range of the German armament.[20]

What should have been the supreme test of the tank destroyer forces in Europe came in December 1944 when ten German panzer divisions spearheaded a major counteroffensive that shattered the U.S. First Army's line in the Ardennes. Some two dozen tank destroyer battalions ultimately participated in the efforts to halt and then reduce the German penetration. Had tank destroyer doctrine been observed, these battalions would have formed up into regiment-size groups and fallen upon the intruding armor in mass. By this point in the war, however, official tank destroyer doctrine had been largely forgotten, and the battalions themselves were fragmented and dispersed beyond recall. Self-propelled tank destroyers, fighting in platoon strength, performed with distinction at Elsenborn Ridge, St. Vith, and Bastogne. Tank destroyers received credit for destroying a total of 306 enemy tanks during the entire Ardennes campaign, most of these falling victim to self-propelled units. The hapless towed units, on the other hand, difficult to displace and maneuver, accounted for the overwhelming majority of tank destroyer casualties.[21]

The Ardennes campaign reinforced a growing conviction within the Army that the tank destroyer quasi-arm was not an essential element of the combined arms team. A theater general board that convened after Victory in Europe (V–E) Day recommended that the independent tank destroyer battalions be eliminated and that the self-propelled tank destroyer weapons be incorporated within the infantry division. General Jacob Devers, who became the head of Army Ground Forces in June 1945, had never believed in the tank destroyer concept. For years he had insisted that "defensive antitank weapons are essentially artillery. Offensively the weapon to beat a tank is a better tank."[22] Late in 1945 the War Department commenced the mass inactivation of tank destroyer units. By the end of 1946 the tank destroyers had ceased to exist.

The tank destroyer concept of World War II can only be judged a doctrinal failure. The problems began early on when the Army mistakenly assumed that armored warfare equated with charging massed tanks, failing to appreciate the sophisticated combined arms aspects of German panzer operations. Thus tank destroyers were created as a single-arm force, lacking the capability of dealing with combined arms opponents. Marshall and McNair compounded this problem by attempting to impose an offensive orientation upon what was inherently a defensive mission. In any event, the course of operations in Tunisia, Italy, and western Europe involved relatively few instances of German armor operating offensively and in strength. Finally, shortcomings in weaponry meant that tank destroyers were frequently outgunned by their intended quarry.

Despite all this, tank destroyer units found ways to contribute significantly to the "crusade in Europe." Soldiers in the field redeemed the failure of doctrine through their ingenuity, resolve, and courage.

NOTES

1. Army Ground Forces (AGF) Study no. 27, "The Armored Force, Command and Center" (Historical Section, AGF, 1946), p. 15.
2. U.S. Army Tank Destroyer Center, "Tank Destroyer History" (Camp Hood, Tex., c. 1945), pt. 1, chs. 7–8.
3. Memo, Chief of Staff for Assistant Chief of Staff G–3, 14 May 41, sub: Defense Against Armored Forces, George C. Marshall Papers, George C. Marshall Library, Lexington, Va.
4. Quoted in Tank Destroyer Center, "History," pt. 1, ch. 1, p. 13.
5. Conference in the Office of the Chief of Staff, 7 Oct 41, George C. Marshall Papers, Marshall Library.
6. Tank Destroyer Center, "History," pt. 1, ch. 1, p. 16.
7. See Christopher R. Gabel, *The U.S. Army GHQ Maneuvers of 1941* (Washington, D.C.: U.S. Army Center of Military History, 1991), ch. 8.
8. See, for example, "Matters To Be Covered in Critique, Maj B. P. Purdue, Performance of Antitank," records of Headquarters, Army Ground Forces, GHQ, National Archives, Washington, D.C.
9. "Second Battle of the Carolinas," *Time* (8 December 1941): 66.
10. "New Tank Destroyer Battalions," *Infantry Journal* (January 1942): 56–59.
11. For German tactics in Tunisia, see Allied Forces G–3 Training Section, "Training Notes From Recent Fighting In Tunisia: Experiences, Observations, and Opinions Collected From Officers and Men of Front Line Units, 18–30 Mar 43," Combined Arms Research Library (CARL), Fort Leavenworth, Kans.; Great Britain, War Office, General Staff, "German Armored Tactics in Libya," Periodical Notes on the German Army no. 37, Feb 42, CARL.
12. George F. Howe, *Northwest Africa: Seizing the Initiative in the West,* United States Army in World War II (Washington, D.C.: U.S. Army Center of Military History, 1957), pp. 559–60; U.S. Army Tank Destroyer School, "Tank Destroyer Combat," Camp Hood, Tex.; Andrew D. Bruce Papers, Military History Institute (MHI), Carlisle Barracks, Pa.; Maj Allerton Cushman [Army Ground Forces] Observer Rpt, 29 Mar 43, CARL.
13. Allied Forces Headquarters Training Memorandum no. 23, Employment of Tank Destroyer Units, 21 Mar 43, CARL.
14. Cushman, Observer Rpt, 3 May 43, CARL.
15. U.S. Forces, European Theater, General Board, "Report on Study of Organization, Equipment, and Tactical Employment of Tank Destroyer Units" (1946), CARL.
16. Charles M. Baily, *Faint Praise: American Tanks and Tank Destroyers During World War II* (Hamden, Conn.: Archon, 1983).
17. First U.S. Army, "Artillery Information Service," Dec 44, p. 57.
18. Ibid., p. 62.
19. Paul B. Bell, "Tank Destroyers in the Roer River Crossing," *Field Artillery Journal* (August 1945): 497–98.
20. U.S. Army, Armored School, "The Employment of Four Tank Destroyer Battalions in the ETO" (Ft. Knox, Ky.: 1950), pp. 64–80.
21. First U.S. Army, "Artillery Information Service," May 45, p. 81.
22. Extract of Gen Devers' Rpt, 9 Feb 43, Bruce Papers, MHI.

"The Very Model of a Modern Major General" Background of World War II American Generals in V Corps

Charles E. Kirkpatrick

What was the average American general officer in World War II like? Of course, no general is self-critical in his *Who's Who* entry, and wartime propaganda dubbed even the most mediocre commander a "military genius." Still, the traditional view is generally a favorable one. A few prominent men—MacArthur, Eisenhower, Bradley, Patton, for example—led a general officer corps that was composed of superior, but not necessarily well known, leaders, and some solid, but average, performers. Time and a sense of proportion have moderated that picture somewhat.

So far from elevating the more famous World War II leaders to the ranks of Hannibal, Gustavus Adolphus, Turenne, Marlborough, Frederick the Great, Napoleon, Wellington, Grant, and the elder von Moltke, more recent scholarship tends instead toward a biting criticism of their competence and attainments. Indeed, Patton's pursuit of the Germans across France in the summer of 1944 may not compare favorably with Grant's pursuit of Lee in 1864; Montgomery's victory at Alamein may not actually have been another Cannae; and Zhukov's drive to Berlin may not have been a victory as sweeping as Wellington's at Waterloo.

British historian John Ellis presents an extreme view that none of the Allied generals deserve much praise. He castigates not only the average officer but also those customarily considered to have been gifted. Ellis describes Patton's operations in France in August and September of 1944 as "following," rather than "pursuing," the Germans, and dismisses Patton as "one of the best traffic policemen in the history of warfare." He characterizes Soviet operations as using a sledgehammer to crack a walnut. It is probably sufficient to note that, in appraising Montgomery's sense of maneuver, he writes that the Field Marshal "lumbered into action" with the "majestic deliberation of a pachyderm." Ellis concludes that, given the caliber of field commander available, Eisenhower's determination to pursue his broad front of attack against Germany only made sense; none of his generals could have succeeded in a "knife-like thrust" toward Berlin.[1]

Other historians, while less provocative in their criticisms and more generous in their judgments, still erect no monuments to Allied generals' battlefield performance. This is especially true when Americans evaluate American generals. In Russell Weigley's opinion, "unimaginative caution" characterized American generalship during the western European campaign. He concludes that American leadership "by and large was competent but addicted to playing it safe," and hazards the suggestion that the enormous Allied materiel superiority justified taking risks that might well have ended the war more quickly.[2] Reflecting on the same question, Allan R. Millett nonetheless remarks on those officers' adaptability and overall competence, despite their lack of experience.[3] That is not to say that men were not relieved of command. Six corps and twelve division commanders were among the most prominent cases of relief from command in the European Theater.[4] The vast majority of American generals, however, did what was expected of them, and some of those relieved of their commands later ran training centers and commanded other units both in the United States and in overseas theaters.

How good were American generals in World War II? The available evidence buttresses expert opinion that is, on the whole, not particularly complimentary. But the search for tactical genius among that group of officers misses the point. Their most remarkable characteristic was not how ordinary they might have been, or how undistinguished in command. The astonishing thing, given their collective background, is that the average officers reared in the interwar period could manage the fundamental tasks of higher command: to organize, train, supply, feed, equip, and move a formation with which they had no experience, at a level of command to which they had probably never aspired, under the stress of war, and then to perform competently in battle in command of brigades and divisions.

Agreeing with the points that Weigley and Millett have made, I have previously suggested that, in understanding how the United States Army fulfilled its mission in the war, it is more important to study what West Point once called the "undistinguished middle" than to focus on the few generals who caught the attention of the press.[5] The average officers whose leadership made the Army's vast expansion possible had their abilities shaped by the atmosphere that prevailed within the interwar service. How did that shared experience of two austere decades prepare them to be wartime commanders? In trying to answer that question, I have begun by studying the careers of the generals who led U.S. V Corps and its divisions in the European Theater between 1943 and 1945.

Generals in V Corps: A Collective Portrait

Twenty-two generals commanded the corps, the corps artillery, divisions assigned for a reasonable length of time, and ran the corps staff.[6] (*Table 1*)

TABLE 1—GENERALS IN V CORPS	
Maj. Gen. Leonard T. Gerow	V Corps
Maj. Gen. Clarence R. Huebner	V Corps
	1st Infantry Division
Maj. Gen. Clift Andrus	1st Infantry Division
Maj. Gen. Edward H. Brooks	2d Armored Division
Maj. Gen. Walter M. Robertson	2d Infantry Division
Maj. Gen. Raymond O. Barton	4th Infantry Division
Maj. Gen. Stafford L. Irwin	5th Infantry Division
Maj. Gen. Lunsford E. Oliver	5th Armored Division
Maj. Gen. Robert W. Hasbrouck	7th Armored Division
Maj. Gen. Donald A. Stroh	8th Infantry Division
Maj. Gen. Louis A. Craig	9th Infantry Division
Maj. Gen. John W. Leonard	9th Armored Division
Maj. Gen. Norman D. Cota	28th Infantry Division
Maj. Gen. Charles H. Gerhardt	29th Infantry Division
Maj. Gen. Leland S. Hobbs	30th Infantry Division
Maj. Gen. Paul W. Baade	35th Infantry Division
Maj. Gen. William W. Eagles	45th Infantry Division
Maj. Gen. Emil F. Reinhardt	69th Infantry Division
Maj. Gen. Walter Lauer	99th Infantry Division
Maj. Gen. William C. Lee	101st Airborne Division
Brig. Gen. Charles G. Helmick	V Corps Artillery
Brig. Gen. Henry J. Matchett	Corps Chief of Staff[7]

All of these men were commissioned after the turn of the century, half before World War I and the remainder in 1917, and reached their professional maturity in the interwar Army.[8] Their careers were similar in many ways. All were born in the decade between 1888 and 1898, most before 1894. In 1944, during their active combat commands, the oldest was fifty-six and the youngest forty-six. Thirteen graduated from the U.S. Military Academy, but 3 more came from other military schools: Virginia Military Institute, Norwich, and the Naval Academy. (*Table 2*) The remaining 6 obtained direct appointments to the Regular Army by a variety of routes. The majority (14) were Infantrymen, while 6 were Artillery officers and the remaining 2 represented the Cavalry and Corps of Engineers.

TABLE 2—CLASSMATES AT USMA		
Officer	*Graduation Year*	*Branch*
Reinhardt	1910	Infantry
Baade	1911	Infantry
Barton	1912	Infantry
Robertson	1912	Infantry
Craig	1913	Cavalry/Artillery
Oliver	1913	Engineers
Hobbs	1915	Infantry
Leonard	1915	Infantry
Irwin	1915	Cavalry/Artillery
Cota	1917	Infantry
Eagles	1917	Infantry
Gerhardt	1917	Cavalry
Hasbrouck	1917	Artillery

Their military schooling ran along predictable lines. Sixteen attended some form of basic course for their branch, including such pre–World War I instruction as the School of Arms at Fort Leavenworth. Seventeen definitely attended their branch advanced course.[9] Seven of these officers served at the Infantry School, as student or instructor or both, during the "Benning Renaissance" of June 1927 through November 1932, when George C. Marshall was assistant commandant. Hobbs, Cota, Stroh, and Eagles studied under Marshall's revised curriculum, and Huebner, Matchett, Lee, Cota, and Eagles worked directly for Marshall as instructors. Omar Bradley arrived in the summer of 1929 and was thus in a position to observe Matchett, Lee, and Cota as instructors, and Eagles as both student and instructor. (*Tables 3, 4, and 5*)

TABLE 3—RESIDENCE AT THE INFANTRY SCHOOL																							
Officer	1918	1919	1920	1921	1922	1923	1924	1925	1926	1927	1928	1929	1930	1931	1932	1933	1934	1935	1936	1937	1938	1939	1940
Huebner				└—F		—└A┘																	
Barton		└B┘				└A┘																	
Matchett						└A┘						└—	—F—		—┘								
Gerow							└A┘																
Robertson							└A┘																
Cota								└B┘		└A┘						└——	F——	┘					
Stroh					└B┘					└A┘										└F┘			
Eagles			└B┘											└A┘									
Lee			└B┘												└A┘								
Lauer									└A┘														
Hobbs										└A┘													

F=Faculty   B=Basic Course   A=Advanced Course

TABLE 4—RESIDENCE AT THE FIELD ARTILLERY SCHOOL

Officer	1920	1921	1922	1923	1924	1925	1926	1927	1928	1929	1930	1931	1932	1933
Andrus						AAAAAA								
Brooks		BBBB												
Craig			AAAAA											
Hasbrouck		BBBFFFFFFFFFFF												
Helmick					AAAAA		FFFFFFFFFFFFFFF							
Irwin	BBBBB				AAAAAA			FFFFFFFFFFFFFFFFFFF						

F=Faculty   B=Basic Course   A=Advanced Course

TABLE 5—STUDENTS AND FACULTY AT FORT BENNING
DURING GEORGE C. MARSHALL'S TENURE (JUNE 1927–NOVEMBER 1932)

Officer	1925	1926	1927	1928	1929	1930	1931	1932	1933	1934	1935
Hobbs			└─S─┘								
Cota				└─S─┘				└─F─┘			
Stroh			└─S─┘								
Lee								└─S─┘			
Eagles					└─S─┴──────F──────┘						
Huebner	└──────F───────┘										
Matchett					└──────────F──────────┘						

S=Student   F=Faculty

Every officer in the group graduated from the Command and General Staff School at Fort Leavenworth, 9 of them attending the two-year curriculum that ran from 1929 through 1938. Gerow, Huebner, Baade, and Robertson were honor graduates of their one-year classes, and Irwin was a distinguished graduate of his. (*Tables 6 and 7*) Sixteen graduated from the Army War College in Washington, D.C. (*Table 8*) War came before the junior members of the group had the opportunity to attend that school. Various officers attended other schools. Two graduated from the Naval War College, 2 from the field officer course at the Chemical Warfare School, 1 from the Air Corps Tactical School, 2 from the short staff course taught in France at Langres during World War I, 2 from the Staff Course taught at the Army War College before World War I, and 1 from the British Combat Intelligence School. William C. Lee, the only member of the group who attended the Tank School during its existence at Fort Meade, and who also graduated from the French Tank School at Saumur, instead made his mark as the pioneer of American airborne forces. None of the armored division commanders in this group attended either school.

TABLE 6—LEAVENWORTH COURSE

Officer	Course
Andrus	Two Year
Craig	Two Year
Hobbs	Two Year
Brooks	Two Year
Cota	Two Year
Gerhardt	Two Year
Hasbrouck	Two Year
Matchett	Two Year
Stroh	Two Year
Reinhardt	One Year
Baade	One Year
Gerow	One Year
Barton	One Year
Robertson	One Year
Helmick	One Year
Oliver	One Year
Irwin	One Year
Eagles	One Year
Huebner	One Year
Lauer	One Year
Lee	One Year

TABLE 7—RESIDENCE AT FORT LEAVENWORTH

Officer	1922	1923	1924	1925	1926	1927	1928	1929	1930	1931	1932	1933	1934	1935	1936	1937	1938	1939	1940
Andrus*							└	S	┘										
Baade		└	S┘					└		F	┘								
Barton	└	S┘						└		F	┘								
Brooks*												└	S	┘					
Cota*							└	S	┘								└	F	┘
Craig*							└	S	┘										
Eagles														└	S┘				
Gerhardt*										└	S	┘							
Gerow				└	S┘														
Hasbrouck*												└	S	┘					
Helmick				└	S┘														
Hobbs*												└	S	┘					
Huebner			└	S┘				└		F	┘								
Irwin					└	S┘													
Lauer																	└	S┘	
Lee																	└	S┘	
Matchett*							└	S	┘										
Oliver					└	S┘													
Reinhardt	└	S┘																	
Robertson				└	S┘														
Stroh*										└	S	┘							

S=Student   F=Faculty   *Attended two-year curriculum

TABLE 8—RESIDENCE AT ARMY WAR COLLEGE

Officer	1928	1929	1930	1931	1932	1933	1934	1935	1936	1937	1938	1939	1940
Huebner	S	S											
Baade	S	S											
Robertson		S	S	F	F								
Reinhardt			S	S									
Gerow			S	S									
Helmick					S	S							
Barton					S	S							
Andrus						S	S						
Hobbs							S	S					
Cota								S	S				
Hasbrouck									S	S			
Irwin									S	S			
Stroh									S	S			
Brooks									S	S			
Craig										S	S		
Matchett												S	S

S=Student F=Faculty

Many of these officers already knew each other. In schools, the network of acquaintances broadened. The Corps of Cadets at the Military Academy was fairly small in the World War I era, averaging between 100 and 150 men per class. The men in the classes of 1910 through 1913 were in a position to know one another, as were the men in 1912 through 1915. Likewise, those commissioned in 1915 were at West Point at the same time as those commissioned in 1917.[10] Attendance at branch schools, Command and General Staff School, and the Army War College broadened acquaintances and allowed men commissioned from different sources to meet. They also met other men with whom they would later serve. Helmick, for example, was a Leavenworth classmate of Dwight Eisenhower, and had met Gerow during the 1930s.[11]

Their military experience varied greatly. Thirteen served in the landings or occupation of Vera Cruz in 1914, on the Mexican border, or with Pershing's Punitive Expedition into Mexico in 1916 and 1917. The same number, although not necessarily the same men, served in France during World War I, and all were promoted to higher ranks in the National Army. Relative seniority had little to do with the temporary grades the officers attained during that war. Every man commissioned before 1917 became a major or lieutenant colonel. Those entering the service in 1917 attained temporary ranks from first lieutenant (Lauer and Lee) through major (Cota) and lieutenant colonel (Huebner), with most serving as captains. (*Table 9*)

TABLE 9—PROMOTION EXPERIENCE

Officer	Commission	WWI Rank	Capt.	Maj.	Lt. Col.	Col.	BG
Reinhardt	1910	Maj.	1920	1920	'35	'39	'41
Baade	1911	Lt.Col.	1920	1920	'35	'40	'41
Gerow	1911	Lt.Col.	1920	1920	'35	'40	'40
Andrus	1912	Lt.Col.	1920	1920	'35	'40	'42
Barton	1912	Maj.	1920	1920	'35	'41	'42
Robertson	1912	Maj.	1920	1920	'35	'40	'41
Craig	1913	Lt. Col.	1920	1920	'35	'41	'42
Helmick	1913	Lt. Col.	1920	1920	'35	'41	'42
Oliver	1913	Lt. Col.	1920	1920	'35	'41	'42
Hobbs	1915	Maj.	1920	1920	'36	'41	'42
Irwin	1915	Maj.	1920	1920	'36	'41	'42
Brooks	1917	Capt.	1920	1935	'40	–	'41
Cota	1917	Maj.	1919	1932	'40	'41	'43
Eagles	1917	Capt.	1919	1932	'40	'41	'42
Gerhardt	1917	Capt.	1920	1932	'40	–	'41
Hasbrouck	1917	Capt.	1920	1936	'40	'42	'42
Huebner	1917	Lt. Col.	1920	1927	'38	'41	'42
Lauer	1917	1st Lt.	1920	1935	'40	'41	'43
Lee	1917	1st Lt.	1920	1935	'40	'41	'42
Matchett	1917	Capt.	1920	1934	'40	'41	'44
Stroh	1917	Capt.	1920	1934	'40	'41	'43

Of those who served in France, only a handful stood out as combat leaders. Huebner had far and away the most distinguished record. He commanded a company and then a battalion of the 28th Infantry in the 1st Infantry Division, and was at the front from November 1917 through the end of the war. He won a Distinguished Service Cross at Cantigny and another near Soissons, was recognized with a Distinguished Service Medal for his leadership, and was wounded twice in action. A temporary lieutenant colonel at the end of the war, Huebner outranked all of his contemporaries commissioned in 1917 and almost half of those commissioned between 1910 and 1915. Leonard Gerow, six years Huebner's senior, served on staff with the Signal Corps in France, thus lacking the same chance for distinction. Nonetheless, he also reached the temporary rank of lieutenant colonel.

John Leonard's record approximated Huebner's. During the Punitive Expedition of 1916, he marched into Mexico with the 6th Infantry. In France, he commanded the 3d Battalion of that regiment at Frapelle, St. Mihiel, and in the Meuse-Argonne battles, earning the Distinguished Service Cross and being wounded in action. Edward Brooks won a Distinguished Service Cross while serving with the 76th Field Artillery.

Louis Craig, serving both in the line and on division, corps, and army staffs, took part in four campaigns and earned foreign awards that included the British Distinguished Service Order, the French Chevalier of the Legion of Honor and Croix de Guerre with Palm, and the Belgian Order of the Crown of Leopold and Croix de Guerre. Charles Helmick, commanding Battery B, 15th Field Artillery, and later regimental executive officer, fought on the Marne and the Soissons and won two Silver Stars.

Others who got to the war zone had much more ordinary experiences. Paul Baade was a company commander in the 332d Infantry of the 81st Infantry Division in the last months of the war. William Lee was in the 81st Infantry Division in October and November of 1918, including the Meuse-Argonne offensive. Charles Gerhardt, who went to France with the 3d Cavalry, was at the front as aide de camp to Maj. Gen. William M. Wright in V Corps, VII Corps, and in the 89th Infantry Division. Robert Hasbrouck went overseas with the 62d Coast Artillery and became executive officer of a military prison at the end of the war. Leland Hobbs arrived with the 11th Infantry Division just in time for the armistice, and Walter Lauer was adjutant for III Corps Schools.

With the swift decrease in the size of the active Army after 1919, command opportunities—indeed, even opportunities to serve with troops at all—diminished dramatically. Instead, these officers typically spent many years in the Army school system or on higher level staffs. Three taught at the Military Academy, 10 were Professors of Military Science in the Reserve Officer Training Corps at various colleges and universities, generally on tours that lasted four to five years; 15 taught at branch schools; 7 taught at the Command and General Staff School; 1 taught at the Army War College; and 4 served as instructors with the National Guard or Organized Reserves. Every officer in this group was an instructor at one time or another, and 16 of them were instructors more than once. Nine spent years as staff officers in the War Department General Staff, the office of their chief of branch, in the Office of the Assistant Secretary of War, the National Guard Bureau, as finance officers or inspectors general, or as attaches. Four served for a time with the Civilian Conservation Corps. (*Table 10*)

While every one of these officers served his time in troop assignments and commanded a company, battery, or troop, many of them had to wait years for the opportunity to command a battalion. The lucky few commanded during or immediately after World War I. Huebner and Leonard commanded battalions in combat, and Leonard had a second command in the 6th Infantry during the 1930s. Just before the great demobilization in 1919, Hobbs commanded a battalion of the 63d Infantry and Oliver briefly commanded the 2d Engineers. Commands were scarce in the next ten years. In 1924 Helmick succeeded to the 1st Battalion, 3d Field Artillery, a command that only lasted through the summer months;[12] Matchett to a battalion of the 27th Infantry; and, in 1928, Oliver to the 29th Engineers. In 1930 Andrus commanded a battalion of the 13th Field Artillery. Helmick commanded the 2d Battalion, 8th Field Artillery, in Hawaii in 1930; Robertson commanded the 31st Infantry between 1933 and 1935. Gerhardt was named to a squadron of the 11th Cavalry in 1936. Craig finally had the chance to command in 1939, in a battalion of the 77th Field Artillery. Baade, Hobbs, and Reinhardt commanded at battalion or regimental level only on the eve of World War II. The remaining officers, including Brooks, Cota, Eagles, Hasbrouck, Irwin, Lauer, Lee, and Stroh, either commanded only very briefly or never commanded at the battalion level until after the war started. Almost without exception, service in regularly organized divisions came in 1940 or afterwards, during the chaos of mobilization and training. Even at the outbreak of war, the Army had only three regularly organized divisions, and they were at half strength or less.[13]

TABLE 10—SUMMARY OF ASSIGNMENTS					
Officer	Troop Time	Student	Instructor	Total School	Higher Staff
Huebner	7	3	9	12	7
Andrus	10	7	4.75	11.75	9
Gerow	11	4	2	6	12.5
Baade	11	2	8	10	8
Barton	10.5	3	10	13	6.5
Brooks	10	4	8	12	2
Cota	8	6	8	14	4
Craig	11	4	7.5	11.5	6
Eagles	5.5	3	10.5	13.5	6
Gerhardt	8	4	7	11	5
Hasbrouck	9.5	3.5	8	11.5	4
Helmick	10.5	4.5	4	8.5	9
Hobbs	10.5	5	3.5	8.5	8
Irwin	6	4	12	16	4
Lauer	9	2	5	7	7.5
Lee	8.5	5	6	11	3
Matchett	13	4	4	8	4
Oliver	5.5	3.5	5	8.5	8
Reinhardt	18.5	2.5	9	11.5	0
Robertson	8.5	3	6	9	13
Stroh	14.5	5	3	8	2
Averages	9.8	3.9	6.68	10.58	6.12

The importance of battalion command to an officer's career went without saying. But the significance of that command to his professional development was less certain. Thomas T. Handy, later Chief of Operations Division and Deputy Chief of Staff under Marshall, explained the essential arithmetic of the problem, estimating that, because of the few battalions and the number of officers competing for the positions, only about one in five in his branch would ever have the chance to command a battalion at all. Even so, he emphasized, the command might not be terribly significant because the battalion might not be more than a glorified company in strength.[14] Few units were like the war-strength 29th Infantry at Fort Benning, and most of these officers commanded battalions that were far below their authorized strength.[15]

Troop time of any sort, whether in command or on staff, ranged from an atypical high of 18.5 years, in the case of Reinhardt, to an atypical low of 5.5 years, in the cases of Eagles and Oliver. More significant than the number of years with troops was the currency of that experience as war loomed. That, too, varied widely. In 1940 sixteen had served with troops within the previous 5 years, although these tours might have been as short as 6 months. Huebner, the future corps commander, had last been in a troop unit in 1924. The rest had last been in a troop unit, perhaps only as a staff officer, sometime between 1925 and 1935. (*Table 11*)

TABLE 11—MOST RECENT TROOP DUTY AS OF 1940

Officer	1924	1925	1926	1927	1928	1929	1930	1931	1932	1933	1934	1935	1936	1937	1938	1939
Huebner	X															
Eagles		X														
Hobbs			X													
Oliver				X												
Brooks						X										
Andrus							X									
Robertson									X							
Gerow									X							
Stroh										X						
Hasbrouck										X						
Irwin											X					
Matchett											X					
Barton												X				
Cota												X				
Helmick												X				
Reinhardt												X				
Baade													X			
Craig													X			
Gerhardt													X			
Lauer													X			
Lee													X			

Promotion was slow, sharply limiting the opportunities for professional growth that went with increased responsibility. General Lucius D. Clay, recalling the glacial pace of promotion, remarked that performance had nothing to do with promotion,[16] and General Williston Palmer's observation that he was "getting pretty gray haired" by the time he became a captain encapsulated the experience of the group of men who later served in V Corps.[17] Every one of them was forty or older when promoted to lieutenant colonel. Those commissioned before World War I had the good fortune to be promoted to the permanent grade of major by 1920. Those commissioned in 1917 became permanent captains in 1920. In all cases, however, the next promotion came between 12 and 16 years later. Most of these men became general officers in 1941 and 1942. Those commissioned before World War I had more experience to prepare them for their next new rank, since they had all been lieutenant colonels since 1935 or 1936. But for the group commissioned in 1917, promotion to lieutenant colonel came only in 1940 (except Huebner, who was promoted in 1939), and the transition to weightier responsibilities was more abrupt. Brooks and Gerhardt became brigadier generals the next year; Eagles, Hasbrouck, Huebner, and Lee in 1942; Cota, Lauer, and Stroh in the first half of 1943; and Matchett in 1944.

Taking all of the extremes into account, it is possible to describe the median officer of this group. The general commanding within U.S. V Corps in 1944 was 52 years old and had been in the Army for 29 years. He was a combat arms officer who had commanded a battalion but had very limited experience in larger tactical organizations. Including the World War, he had worked with troops for almost 10 years, been 4 years a student officer, and served 7 years as some sort of instructor. In all, he had spent between a third and one-half of his career in the Army schools system. He had been assigned to higher level staff for 6 years, most often in one of the War Department General Staff sections. He had served in the field during time of war, but had not necessarily ever been under fire.

He was a graduate of all of the Army schools, and particularly the prestigious Command and General Staff School, which he attended roughly at the same time as his contemporaries in rank. Leavenworth taught a common tactical language and procedure for solving tactical problems, and the typical officer did well there. Because of the small size of the officer corps and the amount of time he spent in schools, he personally knew most of the other generals who had come from the same branch, and was acquainted with those who had served in other branches. He was not a military intellectual, did not write extensively about his profession in the service journals, ponder new and innovative weapons, or peer into the future with any particular prescience.[18]

On the whole, these officers' careers were ordinary and undistinguished, and no single aspect of their experience in the interwar years seems to have been especially formative, in view of their subsequent performance in World War II. World War I achievements, as recognized by the temporary rank they earned between 1917 and 1919, made no difference in their subsequent promotion or assignments. Nor was World War I combat duty predictive of future attainments. Huebner was a dynamic tactical commander in France, but probably a poorer corps commander than Gerow, who did not fight in the earlier war. Leonard, whose combat record equaled Huebner's, did not rise beyond a division command. Brooks and Craig, who were also highly decorated, likewise remained at division level. Helmick, twice decorated for heroism, remained a brigadier general throughout the war. Those officers who did not command in battle, or who did not get to France during the fighting, were promoted to division command in World War II at the same time as their battle-tested contemporaries.

The number of years spent in troop assignments, or number of command tours, had equally little bearing on these officers' eventual assignments. Eagles, with only 5 years' troop duty, became a general a year before Lauer, who had roughly twice his time in line units. Reinhardt, with 18 ½ years in troop assignments, was promoted to general the same year as Robertson, 7 years his junior, who had been with troops only 8 ½ years. Oliver, who commanded an armored division successfully, spent most of his interwar years in Corps of Engineers' civil works. Senior staff assignments offer much the same picture. Those known as successful staff officers (men such as Gerow, Robertson, Andrus, Baade, and Lauer) and who spent many years in such duty, were promoted no faster and assigned no differently than those (including Brooks, Cota, Hasbrouck, Lee, Matchett, Reinhardt, and Stroh) whose duties denied them extensive staff experience.

Since all attended the same schools, there is little to distinguish among them except their individual class standing. There too, no clear-cut pointers emerge. Irwin, distinguished graduate of his Leavenworth class, and Gerow, Huebner, Baade, and Robertson, honor graduates of their classes, did not perform in command significantly better than their peers who graduated without distinction. There is likewise little to choose between the demonstrated abilities of those officers who graduated from the much-vaunted two-year Leavenworth curriculum, as opposed to those who graduated from the one-year course. It is also worth remembering that the generals who were relieved from command during the war were also Leavenworth graduates with similar academic records. Nor did the

"Benning Renaissance" seem to have much impact. Huebner, Hobbs, Cota, Stroh, Eagles, Matchett, and Lee, who studied and taught at Fort Benning while Marshall was there, did not outperform the men who missed that experience.

The sum total of their training and experience was ordinary performance in war. Even the corps commanders did not stand out. When he had a particularly difficult task in mind, Omar Bradley thought first of J. Lawton Collins, whom he clearly considered his star performer and whom he ranked tops among his five corps commanders, or of James A. Van Fleet, whom he promoted from regimental to corps command in a period of only nine months.[19] He ranked Leonard Gerow only eighth among senior American generals, and Huebner twenty-ninth. Near the end of the war, Eisenhower also ranked Gerow eighth among a group that included Army commanders. That Mark Clark stood fifth in Eisenhower's listing may help give some perspective to Gerow's relative position.[20] Gerow's promotion to 15th Army was clearly not a bid to employ his tactical gifts in a larger organization. He had only six divisions in his army, was initially relegated to training missions, and ultimately consigned to occupation of the west bank of the Rhine during the final campaign in Central Europe in March and April of 1945. Years later, in a nomination to the Fort Leavenworth Hall of Fame, the most expansive claim the anonymous author could make for Gerow was that Bradley considered him trustworthy.[21] Contemporaries were less kind to Huebner. Courtney Hodges complained about his handling of V Corps and James Gavin had only contempt for his plan of attack on the Roer Dams in February 1945.[22]

Some of the division commanders, especially Robert Hasbrouck, developed minor reputations as tacticians, but it is difficult, except in obituaries, citations for awards, and public relations releases, to find even much faint praise. In one of the most fulsome measures of acclaim I have found, and that in an obituary, Ernie Pyle is quoted as saying of Raymond (Tubby) Barton, commanding the 4th Infantry Division, that he was "a fatherly, kindly, thoughtful good soldier." This is not the stuff of which legends are made. By any objective standard, these were average men who diligently and capably accomplished the missions they were assigned, but without particular distinction. In describing them, the term "workmanlike" seems far more apt than "great." But that was enough.

The operations of V Corps challenged the abilities of these average generals assigned to it. The senior American tactical headquarters in the United Kingdom in 1943, V Corps superintended the organization and training of troops for the invasion of Europe. The Corps subsequently participated in the largest amphibious landing in the history of Normandy, helped secure the beachhead, and captured the key terrain that made possible the breakout from St. Lô. In a junction with British forces it closed the Falaise-Argentan pocket on 21 August 1944 (albeit too late to capture the bulk of retreating German forces). The Corps then moved rapidly to capture Paris, Sedan, and the city of Luxembourg by 9 September and was attacking through the Siegfried Line into Germany shortly thereafter. The V Corps' divisions held the northern shoulder of the German breakthrough in the Ardennes, and, in January 1945, launched an offensive that took them through Leipzig and into Czechoslovakia. By V–E Day, V Corps had fought continuously for 338 days, advanced 1,300 miles, and taken part in nearly every important operation from 6 June 1944 through 22 May 1945. Aside from the casualties it inflicted, the Corps took a total of 352,523 prisoners of war.[23]

Every one of those operations—and especially the amphibious landing—was a difficult and demanding one in which the opportunities to fail were much more numerous than the opportunities for distinction. Endless complexities attended even the smallest movement, as opposed to tactical maneuver, of a fighting corps. On the whole, the generals who commanded the Corps and its divisions measured up to the task. Only one, Lloyd D. Brown, was relieved of command.

In accepting the assessment that these officers were competent, rather than exceptional, it still remains to be decided what in their backgrounds made that sustained competence possible. On the basis of this small sample, the question must remain an open one. None of the factors usually mentioned seems a sufficient answer. The source of commissioning, previous combat experience, amount of time spent in command versus staff or schools, the schools themselves, personal relationships among men who had known each other professionally and personally for years, and the pace of promotion are all suggestive, but not conclusive. The only thing about the interwar period that offers any explanation for these officers' performance during World War II is that their average of ten years in schools gave them a thorough grounding in the technical aspects of command. Even that is a purely subjective judgment. The single conclusion that does emerge from a review of the generals who commanded V Corps is that there is probably some substance to the idea that the "undistinguished middle" group of officers was far more important than is usually acknowledged; that they had a thorough, albeit orthodox, knowledge of their profession; and that Weigley's and Millett's conclusions about their conservative habits of command have merit. The next step is obviously to continue this study by reviewing the careers of generals who commanded in other corps and in other theaters, and particularly those who were relieved of command, for their careers seem in every way similar to those who succeeded.

In the interim, a contemporary's judgment seems most accurate. General Williston B. Palmer, a member of that group of officers commissioned right after World War I and promoted from captain to brigadier general in the course of only seven years, noted of his peers that "the number that stood right up and hit the ball was very high."[24] General Palmer's point is an important one, and it is important to understand it correctly. The significance of the interwar experience was that, to extend Palmer's baseball metaphor, those were years of continuous batting practice that enabled average hitters to perfect their swings. When it came to war, the generals who ran V Corps rarely hit home runs, but they reliably hit singles, the accumulation of which won the game.

NOTES

1. John Ellis, *Brute Force: Allied Strategy and Tactics in the Second World War* (New York: Viking, 1990), pp. 299, 386–87, 420, 436.

2. Russell F. Weigley, *Eisenhower's Lieutenants: The Campaign of France and Germany 1944–1945* (Bloomington: Indiana University Press, 1981), p. 729.

3. Allan R. Millett, "The United States Armed Forces in the Second World War," in Millett and Williamson Murray, eds., *Military Effectiveness*, vol. 3, *The Second World War* (Boston: Allen and Unwin, 1988), pp. 45–89.

4. This is a subject in itself. Among the corps commanders, Gilbert R. Cook was relieved purely for medical reasons. The same cause was cited in the reliefs of Charles H. (Cowboy Pete) Cortlett and John P. Lucas, although a more important cause in each case was probably Bradley's dissatisfaction with Cortlett's "lack of fire" and Clark's willingness to go along with Devers' and Alexander's conclusion that Lucas was beaten at Anzio. Clark also fired Ernest J. Dawley after almost incessant meddling in the operations of his corps at Salerno. Eisenhower relieved Lloyd R. Fredendall from II Corps after Kasserine and Hodges relieved John Milliken from III Corps after Remagen (although he immediately went on to command 13th Armored Division successfully to the end of the war). The division commanders relieved of duty included: Terry Allen (1st Infantry Division), John Bohn, Lloyd D. Brown, Jay W. MacKelvie, Lindsay McD. Silvester, Ralph C. Smith, Eugene M. Landrum, Horace H. Fuller, Edwin F. Harding, William C. McMahon, Orlando Ward, Leroy H. Watson, and John S. Wood. Allen and Ward returned to the ETO in command of divisions later in the war. Wood was relieved "without prejudice" as being worn out. The necessity for some of the reliefs, including Harding's, Smith's, and Watson's, remain disputed. See Martin Blumenson, "Relieved of Command," *Army* (August 1971): 30–37; DAMH-RA Information Paper, 14 Aug 91, sub: Relief of Commanders Before and During World War II, on file in the U.S. Army Center of Military History (CMH); and DAMH-RA Information Paper, 1 Nov 90, sub: Historical Circumstances Surrounding the Relief of National Guard Commanders in World War II Mobilization, on file in CMH.

5. "Filling the Gaps: Reevaluating Officer Professional Education in the Inter-War Army, 1920–1940," a paper read at the conference of the American Military Institute at Lexington, Virginia, 14–15 Apr 89; and "Orthodox Soldiers: Army Formal Schools Between the Two World Wars," a paper read at the meeting of the Organization of American Historians in Washington, D.C., 23–25 Mar 90.

6. I arbitrarily chose to include those divisions assigned to V Corps for more than one month during the battles in western Europe. Thus, I excluded 78th Infantry Division (less than three weeks), 80th Infantry Division (less than two weeks), 82d Airborne Division (two days), and 90th Infantry Division (less than ten days). Unit assignment data drawn from *V Corps Operations in the ETO*; [Office of the Theater Historian, European Theater], "Order of Battle United States Army World War II: European Theater of Operations, Divisions" (unpublished Ms, Paris, 1945), copy in CMH; and [Historical Division, Department of the Army], "Combat Chronicle: An Outline History of U.S. Army Divisions" (unpublished Ms, Washington, D.C., Jul 48), copy in CMH.

7. Command tenure information drawn from staff paper, General Officers–World War II Assigned Command of Higher Units (Army Groups, Armies, Corps, Divisions), Personnel and Administrative Div, War Department General Staff, 1 Apr 47, copy in CMH. I have included Maj. Gen. John W. Leonard although I lacked detailed information about him. I included William C. Lee as a reference point, although he did not command his division on the Continent. Similarly, I have not included the conspicuous combat failure, Maj. Gen. Lloyd D. Brown, relieved of command of the 28th Infantry Division in Normandy, because I lacked even the most basic data about his career.

8. Biographical data on these officers have been drawn from: [Association of Graduates, U.S.M.A.], *Register of Graduates and Former Cadets of the United States Military Academy* (West Point, N.Y.: Association of Graduates, annually); Files HRC201, extracts from personnel files, CMH; *Army Register* (Washington, D.C.: Government Printing Office, annually through World War II); obituaries from *Assembly*, magazine of the Association of Graduates, USMA, monthly; and T. M. Dunleavy, ed., *Generals of the Army* (Washington, D.C.: 1953–1955).

9. Seventeen 201 summaries specifically mention the advanced course. The biographical sketches available are occasionally vague about schools junior to the Command and General Staff School. Since, however, the branch advanced course was a virtual prerequisite for Leavenworth, it is almost certain that every officer attended it.

10. *Register of Graduates, USMA.* Graduating totals for these classes were: 95 in 1912, 93 in 1913, 164 in 1915, and 151 in 1917.

11. Eisenhower did not particularly impress Helmick as a man of the future, although he "knew that he stood pretty high in the class." Interv, Maj Gen Charles G. Helmick by Lt Col Joseph W. A. Whitehorne, Mt. Vernon, Va., 3 Feb 83, pp. 49, 62, copy in CMH.

12. Helmick Interv, p. 24.

13. Ronald Spector, "The Military Effectiveness of the U.S. Armed Forces, 1919–1939," in Allan R. Millett and Williamson Murray, eds., *Military Effectiveness*, vol. 2, *The Interwar Period* (Boston: Allen and Unwin, 1988), comments on this and related issues, p. 80.

14. Conversations between Gen Thomas T. Handy and Lt Col Edward M. Knoff, Jr. (Senior Officer Debriefing Program, U.S. Army Military History Institute [MHI], Carlisle Barracks, Pa., 1976), sec. 2, pp. 8, 10.

15. See *Army Station List* (Washington, D.C.: Government Printing Office, annually for these years), which indicates the size of units as well as their station.

16. Conversations between Gen Lucius D. Clay and Col R. Joe Rogers (Senior Officer Debriefing Program, MHI, 1973), secs. 1, 3. Also see conversations between Gen Clyde D. Eddleman, Lt Col L. G. Smith, and Lt Col M. G. Swindler (Senior Officer Debriefing Program, MHI, 1975), secs. 1, 17, for similar comments.

17. Palmer MHI Interview, p. 28.

18. Even Aubrey S. Newman, a thoughtful commentator on military affairs today, envisioned neither the armored division nor airborne assaults, although he observed both the Christie tank and a parachute demonstration while serving at Fort Benning in the 1920s. A. S. Newman, "Mutual Good Faith: A Key to Change," *Army* 32: 6; Coffman and Herrly, "The American Regular Army Officer Corps Between the World Wars: A Collective Biography," *Armed Forces and Society* (November 1977): 55–73.

19. Omar N. Bradley with Clay Blair, *A General's Life* (New York: Simon and Schuster, 1983), pp. 400, 408.

20. Documents cited in Weigley, *Eisenhower's Lieutenants*, p. 758.

21. Leonard T. Gerow 201 file extract: "Nomination to Fort Leavenworth Hall of Fame," unpublished Ms, CMH file.

22. Bradley and Blair, *A General's Life*, p. 395. The 82d Airborne Division was briefly deployed to help in the Roer Dam attacks. See James M. Gavin, *On To Berlin* (New York: Viking, 1978), p. 295.

23. HQ V Corps, G–3 Historical Sub–Section, *V Corps Operations in the ETO: 6 Jan 1942–9 May 1945* (Germany: V Corps Headquarters Printing, 1945), especially summaries on p. 13 and in ch. 25.

24. Conversations between Gen Williston B. Palmer and Lt Col H. L. Hunter (Senior Officer Debriefing Program, MHI, 1972), p. 29.

PART IV

The U.S. Army at War
The War in the Pacific, 1943–1945

Introduction

A majority of the papers in this section deal with the theme of combined, or coalition, warfare: the ability of the U.S. Army to plan and conduct military operations in conjunction with Great Britain and Australia, our Allies in the Pacific. In "Combined Operations in the Southwest Pacific Area: The Australian Army in MacArthur's Operations," David Horner details General Douglas MacArthur's inability to work closely with the Australian Army. Horner believes that MacArthur preferred to use Australian troops in nonessential military operations and ultimately refused to employ them at all.

Initially, the Australian Army provided a majority of MacArthur's forces in the Southwest Pacific Area (SWPA) and thus played a majority role in the land campaigns which the military forces conducted under MacArthur's control. This situation lasted until early 1944, when U.S. troops began arriving in large numbers in the Pacific. MacArthur continually sought ways to prevent American troops from fighting under Australian commanders, even when Australian troops outnumbered American troops. By setting up special "task forces," MacArthur arranged for U.S. Army commanders to report directly to him rather than to the commander of the Allied Land Forces in the Southwest Pacific Theater, General Sir Thomas Blamey.

In describing those instances in which American troops did come under Australian control, such as at Salamaua and Lae in September 1943, Horner emphasizes that the two armies usually worked well together with a minimum of difficulty at lower levels of command. Problems, such as those evident during the Finschhafen operation, occurred only when MacArthur's headquarters involved itself directly in an ongoing campaign.

By 1944 fresh U.S. troops began replacing the exhausted Australian divisions, which withdrew for rest and refitting. Horner believes that after the Australians were again ready for action, MacArthur avoided using them. For example, rather than employing Australian troops in the Philippine campaign, MacArthur ordered them to garrison islands already captured. When Australian commanders complained, MacArthur found a series of smaller actions on Bougainville, Aitape, Tarakan, and Borneo to keep them busy. Horner questions the strategic necessity of these operations, conducted with minimum notice by the press, and emphasizes the number of lives lost during these forgotten operations.

In conclusion, Horner reiterates that it should have been possible to manage combined operations more efficiently at the theater level of command. Although separating national military components at the operational level has many advantages, such a policy sacrifices the synergy sometimes possible in combined operations and can result in an overly rigid employment of scarce resources. In sum, MacArthur's headquarters failed to intelligently manage combined military operations in the Southwest Pacific Theater, to the detriment of the Allied war effort.

Harry Gailey attacks MacArthur from another perspective in "MacArthur, Fuller, and the Biak Episode." Gailey examines the general's decision to capture the island of Biak, 350 miles northwest of Hollandia, which contained three operational airfields constructed by the Japanese. MacArthur wanted control of the Biak airfields in time to put them to use during the campaign to capture the Marianas, scheduled for mid-June 1944. The capture of Biak's airfields would allow Maj. Gen. George Kenney's Fifth Air Force to strike at Palau during the Marianas operation.

The mission was assigned to the 162d and 186th Regimental Combat Teams of the 41st Division, commanded by Maj. Gen. Horace Fuller. The island was attacked on 27 May; according to plan, the three airfields were to be in U.S. hands by 10 June. MacArthur's chief intelligence officer, Maj. Gen. Charles Willoughby, had assured him that there were few Japanese troops on the island and that victory should be relatively easy. Given this information, MacArthur could not understand why Fuller failed to adhere to the tight but theoretically achievable schedule. Unfortunately, Willoughby's estimate was wrong, and Fuller paid the price for the error.

To deny the Allies the airfields as long as possible, the Japanese defenders built a series of elaborate interconnecting trenches and tunnels, and placed antiaircraft guns, mortars, and automatic weapons overlooking the landing beaches. They also reinforced the natural ridges above the coveted airfields with bunkers and pillboxes.

The American attack proceeded slowly from day one, and Fuller requested reinforcements almost immediately. His superior, Lt. Gen. Walter Krueger, sent him two battalions of the 163d Regiment and the message to "hurry up and get it done." Krueger was under significant pressure from MacArthur, who could not understand what the problem was and had already announced to the press the imminent capture of the island.

Meanwhile, the Japanese reinforced Biak by barging in 1,000 men from a neighboring island. They attempted to send more reinforcements, but were discouraged by U.S. scout planes. Krueger, by now better apprised of the situation on Biak, attempted to defend Fuller to MacArthur on 7 June. MacArthur was unappeased. Reluctantly, Krueger sent Lt. Gen. Robert Eichelberger to Biak to take the command from an outraged Fuller. Upon his arrival, Eichelberger realized that Fuller had been doing everything correctly. Biak eventually fell, but not until 27 June.

Gailey believes that Fuller was unfairly treated by MacArthur's headquarters and simply lacked the troops to capture the airfields in the requisite amount of time. The real reason the attack proceeded so slowly was not faulty command, but rather poor intelligence and poor planning by MacArthur and his headquarters.

Richard Stewart's "The Office of Strategic Services (OSS) Operational Group Burma: The 'Arakan Group'" is the first of three papers which focus on the China-Burma-India (CBI) Theater. Stewart describes how the U.S. Office of Strategic Services formed the Arakan Group to help the British regain control of the coast of Burma and the islands and peninsulas of Malaya and Indonesia.

Stewart sees the Arakan Group as an example of successful combined warfare: a U.S. intelligence unit under British command helping British naval forces reoccupy lost territory. In this paper, the author traces the formation of the unit, the selection and training of the men, their arrival in Ceylon, and a subsequent change of mission. Originally, the unit members had been told they would operate out of British submarines. When these vessels were transferred out of the area, the Arakan Group was directed to conduct short reconnaissance missions for possible amphibious operations along the Arakan coast and to collect intelligence on the possible whereabouts of Japanese. Stewart details the eleven missions conducted between December 1944 and February 1945 that made it possible for British forces to reoccupy the Burmese coast with minimal losses.

Monroe Horn's "Everything Old Is New Again: The American Military Effort in China, 1941–1945," examines the faulty relationship between the United States and China during the war. Horn believes that a "theme of failure" permeated American-Chinese relations during World War II and seeks to explain the reasons for this failure in the context of America's traditional relationship with China. The author holds that "the American failure in China during World War II was not caused by choosing the wrong strategy, . . . by the collisions of prickly personalities, . . . [or] by the often inexplicable policies of Franklin Roosevelt . . . [but by] the very nature of traditional American policy toward China, with its intensity, ignorance, amateurism, and moralism."

According to Horn, the United States and China had incompatible goals during World War II. The Nationalist Chinese government, specifically Marshal Chiang Kai-shek, wanted to defeat Japan while using the Chinese Army as little as possible. The generalissimo hoped to save the bulk of his army for a more important fight against the Communists. He also needed to keep his best troops available to intimidate rival warlords. Chiang planned to achieve this seemingly impossible task by using as much American aid and air power as he could coax out of the U.S. government. The Flying Tigers, a group of former U.S. military pilots flying planes purchased with Lend-Lease funds, serve as a good example of how the marshal preferred to fight the war.

U.S. strategists preferred to ignore Chinese realities. They wanted the Chinese Army to keep Japanese troops engaged in China so they could not be sent elsewhere in the Pacific. To "help China help itself," they dispatched military advisers to train the Chinese Army and Lend-Lease aid to equip it. The U.S. government also used Lend-Lease aid as a bribe to keep China from seeking a separate peace with Japan.

Horn describes how the first U.S. commander of the CBI Theater, Lt. Gen. Joseph Stilwell, fought with Chiang over the conflicting strategies of the two nations. The Chinese leader in turn lobbied Washington to have Stilwell removed and did all he could to limit Stilwell's influence in the CBI.

The author points out that a major Japanese offensive in China during 1944 finally panicked Washington into demanding that Stilwell be given authority over the Chinese Army. Chiang insisted that he be given personal control over Lend-Lease supplies in return. Washington leaders decided instead to replace Stilwell with Lt. Gen. Albert Wedemeyer.

Ironically, Chiang Kai-shek was unable to maintain power in China after the war. After Chiang's forces were ignominiously defeated by Mao Tse-tung's Red Army, American politicians blamed one another for "losing" China to the Communists. But Horn believes that the U.S. "mistake" in China was in ignoring the ongoing civil war and offering all its support to Chiang. Such generous support made Chiang less inclined to cooperate with the Communists or, more importantly, to put his own house in order. Lend-Lease aid, often provided with little administrative support, overwhelmed the Nationalist government and encouraged corruption and inflation in Chiang's government, weakening it even further.

Horn traces America's uncritical support of Chiang and the Nationalists to idealistic hopes that China would eventually become the leading country of Asia, a democratized, Christianized country. The only group in China remotely western, says Horn, was the Nationalists. For ideological reasons, Washington policy makers would never have considered working with the Chinese Communists, even had their true strength been recognized, and in the end this obdurance doomed U.S. military policy to failure.

Mark Gallicchio's perspective of the U.S.–China alliance is extremely different. In "Army Advisers and Liaison Officers and the 'Lessons' of America's Wartime Experience in China," Gallicchio attempts to prove that the U.S. military's experience in China was not a total failure, particularly when looked at from a field perspective rather than from that of the "political machinations occurring in Chung-King and Washington." In the field, he points out, American officers and their Chinese counterparts "worked together on a daily basis to create a modern military force."

The author focuses on the efforts of two individuals, Brig. Gen. Haydon Boatner, who commanded the training center at Ramgarh, India, and Brig. Gen. Frank Dorn, who headed a similar center in Yunan, China. Both of these men were familiar with and respected Chinese culture. Boatner had served as assistant military attache during the 1920s and 1930s and had a master's degree in Chinese history. Dorn was an assistant attache to General Stilwell in the 1930s and was extremely interested in Chinese art. Naturally sympathetic toward the Chinese, both attempted to impress on their subordinates the need to respect their Chinese counterparts and avoid adopting condescending attitudes toward them.

Working under Boatner and Dorn, many American advisers were impressed with the quality of the Chinese junior officers and their willingness to learn. Under the tutelage of the Americans, the training and capabilities of the Chinese enlisted men also began to improve. By 1944, after those units trained by Boatner's and Dorn's officers began to see success, "the Chinese," says Gallicchio, "were at last beginning to retake ground and gain confidence in themselves."

After Stilwell was recalled and replaced by Wedemeyer, Wedemeyer continued the liaison work in the field begun by his predecessor. During the Japanese offensive in late 1944, called *ICHIGO*, Nationalist forces were severely damaged. But by July 1945 they had rebounded and begun a series of successful operations against the Japanese armies in Burma and China. At the end of the war, Wedemeyer and his staff believed that the liaison and training missions had been successful. According to Gallicchio, it was the State Department which insisted on scaling back training efforts in China after the war, and the State Department, rather than a particular political party or president, should be blamed for "losing" China.

In "Nisei Linguists and New Perspectives on the Pacific War: Intelligence, Race, and Continuity," James McNaughton continues the saga of Nisei linguists started in Part I. This time, McNaughton describes the experiences of these soldiers in the field with Army and Marine units. He traces the significant contributions these men made to Allied intelligence as they interrogated prisoners and translated captured documents.

McNaughton also points out that after the war many Nisei linguists served in the Army of Occupation as War Department civilians. Many continued their service throughout the Korean and Vietnam Wars. The author believes that a study of the careers of some of these linguists would help historians to trace the continuity of U.S. security policy in the Pacific from the end of World War II through the Vietnam War.

In "The Ultimate Dilemma of Psychological Warfare in the Pacific: Enemies Who Don't Surrender and GI's Who Don't Take Prisoners," Clayton Laurie traces the difficulties faced by psychological warfare units in the Pacific. Their mission was to convince enemy soldiers to surrender through use of the spoken and written word, but their work was burdened by factors beyond the dedicated, often fanatical mentality of the average Japanese soldier.

Military commanders in the Pacific, says Laurie, were suspicious of psychological warfare. In addition, U.S. psychological warfare units found it difficult to coordinate their propaganda efforts with those of their Allies, especially British military propagandists working hard to remind their colonies that they would return to their former status after the war. The geographical nature of the Pacific also made psychological warfare arduous. It was expensive and logistically complicated to use leaflets and radio broadcasts to reach the many scattered small islands garrisoned by enemy troops. Islanders spoke innumerable varieties of native languages, many were illiterate, and the military lacked linguists capable of communicating with many native peoples.

But a significant problem, according to Laurie, was the accepted notion that all Japanese soldiers would fight to the death. The legendary discipline of the Japanese soldier was founded on deep social conditioning, rigid military discipline, and a thorough indoctrination as to what to expect if captured by Allied troops. The latter, well aware of Japanese attitudes, did not expect to take prisoners and acted accordingly. Furthermore, many soldiers were suspicious of any enemy surrender attempts, as Japanese soldiers had been known to deceive U.S. troops with false surrender claims. As a result, there were very few Japanese military prisoners of war, a condition that also made it impossible for psychological warfare units to prove their value to their commanders.

Robert Maddox's "Generals, Admirals, and Atomic Bombs: Ending the War With Japan" wades into the current historiographical controversy over the necessity of dropping the atomic bomb. The author discusses the writings of several influential historians who question President Harry S. Truman's motives for using the bomb. He castigates them for attributing to Truman knowledge that was unavailable to the president at the time he made his decision. Maddox seeks to explore Truman's motives by examining only that information in the president's possession in August 1945. He concludes that Truman honestly believed the use of the bomb might alleviate some of a vast number of anticipated military and civilian casualties in the planned Allied invasion of the Japanese island of Kyushu.

According to Maddox, the diplomatic information available to Truman indicated that the Japanese were not considering surrender along any terms acceptable to the United States. Japan was controlled by military leaders "blind to defeat and bending all remaining national energy to smash an invasion of the home islands."

Unlike historians writing years later, Truman lacked access to the Strategic Bombing Survey of 1946, which determined that the atomic bombs were unnecessary because of the damage already done by B–29s. However, Truman was well aware of the increasing desperation of Japanese military actions. The number of kamikazes was increasing as was the number of Japanese troops stationed in defensive positions on Kyushu, where the Japanese Army leaders believed U.S. troops would land during the eventual attack.

Maddox also points out that Truman's military advisers, the Joint Chiefs of Staff, did not anticipate that the bomb would negate the necessity of an invasion. Rather, they assumed the invasion would go on as scheduled regardless of the bomb, and they hoped that the invasion coupled with the atomic bomb would provide the pressure necessary for a total capitulation.

In reality, says Maddox, the Joint Chiefs were right. Even after the atomic bombs were dropped on Hiroshima and Nagasaki, the Japanese cabinet was reluctant to surrender. Only the action of the emperor himself, who finally broke a tied cabinet vote, resulted in capitulation before the Allied invasion could take place. Neither Truman nor anyone else could have foreseen when the Japanese would surrender, or what action would finally be decisive in that regard.

Combined Operations in the Southwest Pacific
The Australian Army in MacArthur's Operations

David Horner

In the Allied composition of its forces, the Southwest Pacific Area, commanded by General Douglas MacArthur, was unique among the theater commands set up in the Second World War.[1] Some commands, such as the Pacific Ocean Area, commanded by Admiral Chester Nimitz, were almost completely American. Other commands were Allied in nature but the main forces came from the two major Allies—Britain and the United States. For example, Southeast Asia Command, commanded by Britain's Admiral Lord Louis Mountbatten, included a majority of British or British-Indian forces with smaller, but still significant American forces. Mediterranean Command under General Dwight Eisenhower had large numbers of American and British forces, and later included Canadians, French, New Zealanders, and Poles. Similarly, Eisenhower's Allied Expeditionary Force in Europe included many nationalities, but the principal forces came from the United States and Britain.

By contrast, the Southwest Pacific Area was a coalition of forces from the United States and Australia with only very small numbers from the Netherlands and New Zealand. The Australian Army provided the majority of MacArthur's forces and played the largest part in his land campaigns for a period of two years, from the time the command was set up until the early months of 1944.

The management of this coalition of unequal Allies posed particular problems. In 1942 Australia had a population of a little over 7 million people while the United States numbered some 135 million. The U.S. President, Franklin D. Roosevelt, and the British Prime Minister, Winston Churchill, together decided the shape of the Allied war effort and this was refined by the Combined Chiefs of Staff, consisting of the chiefs of staffs of the two great powers. Australia had no role in this strategic decision-making.

As a major world power in the 1940s, the United States was loath to place its forces under an Allied commander, but in certain circumstances was willing to do so. For example, in North Africa U.S. Army forces were placed under the Allied Land Commander, General Harold Alexander. Later, at Normandy, U.S. land forces came under General Bernard Montgomery during the early stages of the campaign.

But in the Southwest Pacific Area it rankled to place American land forces under a commander from a small country such as Australia, and from the beginning MacArthur tried to find ways of ensuring that Americans did not serve under Australian command. Yet, until sufficient American land forces had arrived and been trained, MacArthur had to rely on the Australians for his offensives. Before discussing these offensives, it is important to set out the command arrangements in Australia.

At the top was General Douglas MacArthur, the Commander-in-Chief, Southwest Pacific Area. His headquarters, known as General Headquarters, or GHQ, was located in Melbourne and later in Brisbane. Despite the fact that it was supposed to be an Allied headquarters, it was staffed almost completely with American officers. When the U.S. Army Chief of Staff, General George C. Marshall, urged MacArthur to include Australian officers MacArthur replied that no qualified officers were available.[2] This was clearly untrue, since three Australian divisions had already fought several major campaigns in the Middle East and many officers had recent command and staff experience in operations; but MacArthur had his way.

Below this level MacArthur's forces included the Allied Naval, Land, and Air Forces. MacArthur's naval forces were more powerful than those of the Royal Australian Navy and an American, Vice Admiral Herbert Leary, became Commander, Allied Naval Forces. This arrangement caused few command problems and the Chief of the Australian Naval Staff became responsible for the close defense of Australia.

The Royal Australian Air Force had few modern aircraft, but was expanding rapidly. Similarly, the U.S. air forces in Australia were expanding rapidly as men and machines arrived from America. Lt. Gen. George Brett became Commander, Allied Air Forces, an organization with an unhappy history. MacArthur and other senior Americans resented the placing of U.S. air units under Australian commanders, and in August Maj. Gen. George C. Kenney replaced Brett. He separated the Allied Air Forces and directly commanded the U.S. Fifth Air Force. The Australian operational air units were placed under an Australian commander who reported to Kenney. The numerous problems with the command arrangements for the Australian air units will not be discussed in this paper. From an Allied point of view, the air offensive was in American hands, and before long the Americans provided the largest part of the available air forces.

Command of the Allied Land Forces went to the Commander-in-Chief of the Australian Army, General Sir Thomas Blamey. That an Australian should command these forces seemed unchallengeable. After all, in mid-1942 the Australian Army consisted of 10 infantry divisions, 2 motor divisions, and 1 armored division. One of these divisions was still in the Middle East but the remainder were in Australia with some units in New Guinea.[3] Admittedly some divisions were poorly trained as the 8 divisions of the militia had only recently been called up for full-time service, but the 6th and 7th Divisions had fought in the Middle East. By contrast there were only 2 under-trained U.S. divisions in Australia.

Just as there were few Australians on MacArthur's GHQ staff, there were few Americans assigned to Blamey's Land Headquarters. When Blamey asked MacArthur for U.S. officers he received little encouragement. Indeed MacArthur realized that the senior Australian staff officers had vastly more experience than their American counterparts and he warned Washington that the dispatch to Australia of poor officers would result in what he called a "black eye for U.S. when placed with experienced and capable Australian officers."[4]

The feeling at the time is shown when Maj. Gen. Robert C. Richardson visited Australia in June 1942 on behalf of the U.S. Chief of Staff. MacArthur offered Richardson the command of the U.S. I Corps, then being formed in Australia. He declined because he did not want to serve under Blamey's command. MacArthur wanted a U.S. corps headquarters so that when it came to operations he could set up an American task force which would come directly under his, rather than Blamey's, command. The U.S. War Department was sympathetic to MacArthur's request, but had to acknowledge that they had to play the game of coalition warfare; as Maj. Gen. Thomas Handy, an Assistant Chief of Staff at the War Department, put it, "the Australians have 350,000 troops and a little break for them seems to be necessary."[5]

Inevitably, when the Japanese began their offensive in Papua in July 1942, they were met by Australians of New Guinea Force rather than American troops. But as the Japanese advanced over the rugged Owen Stanley Ranges towards Port Moresby, it was clear that New Guinea needed to be reinforced. MacArthur's first reaction was to send the U.S. 32d Division to New Guinea to operate directly under GHQ in Brisbane. This would have produced an impossible command structure, with two separate superior headquarters in Australia commanding separate national forces in the one operational area.[6] Apparently Blamey talked him out of that folly, and instead the commander of the 1st Australian Corps, Lt. Gen. Sydney Rowell, was ordered to Port Moresby to command the New Guinea Force.

With him went the 7th Australian Division. Gradually the force in New Guinea was built up so that there were two infantry brigades at Milne Bay and three in the Port Moresby–Kokoda Track area.

In late August the Japanese mounted major offensives at both Milne Bay and on the Kokoda Track, and MacArthur and GHQ reacted badly to the news of Australian reverses. The tense atmosphere in Brisbane is shown by a letter written by Blamey's chief of staff, Maj. Gen. George Vasey, in Brisbane to Rowell in Port Moresby:

You possibly do not realize that for GHQ this is their first battle and they are therefore, like many others, nervous and dwelling on the receipt of frequent messages. . . . It boils down to the question of who is commanding the army—MacArthur or TAB [Blamey], and it seems the sooner that is settled the better.[7]

In signal messages to Washington MacArthur began to blame the reverses not on faulty strategy or the superior numbers of the Japanese but on the poor quality of the Australian troops and commanders. As he said, "the Australians have proven themselves unable to match the enemy in jungle fighting."[8] Rowell in New Guinea, who the previous year had been chief of staff of the 1st Australian Corps in the Greek and Syrian campaigns, resented these criticisms, commenting at the time: "I do hope that there is a show-down [between Blamey and MacArthur]. Taking it by and large, we do know something about war after three small campaigns."[9]

Eventually, at the height of the crisis MacArthur suggested to the Australian Prime Minister, John Curtin, that Blamey go to New Guinea to take personal command there. Blamey had full confidence in Rowell's handling of the battles, but had to obey. Unfortunately, Rowell took Blamey's arrival as showing a lack of confidence in his command. There was an intense clash of personalities, and Blamey relieved Rowell of command of New Guinea Force. Lt. Gen. Edmund Herring soon arrived to succeed Rowell, but Blamey also remained at Port Moresby. In effect, he was now a task force commander—the very command arrangement which MacArthur had told Washington he wanted to institute several months earlier.

Blamey reaped the result of Rowell's careful planning, and at the beginning of October the counteroffensive began, back over the Owen Stanley Ranges towards the northern beachheads at Buna, Gona, and Sanananda. It was a grim battle against stubborn Japanese resistance, on short rations, and with troops suffering from malaria.

The U.S. 32d Division was brought forward from Australia, and the final battles to clear the Japanese beachheads at Buna, Gona, and Sanananda on the north coast of Papua were to be conducted by the 7th Australian and the U.S. 32d Divisions, all under Herring, the Commander of the 1st Australian Corps. Herring took his headquarters forward, across the Owen Stanley Ranges, while Blamey remained in command of New Guinea Force at Port Moresby. Meanwhile, MacArthur also journeyed north to Port Moresby.

The U.S. 32d Division, under Maj. Gen. Edwin F. Harding, was a National Guard division which had not previously been in action and was not fully trained for jungle warfare. Its initial attack on Buna was a disaster, and MacArthur immediately bypassed the chain of command and ordered Harding to "take Buna at all costs."[10] A week later there had still been no action from the Americans.

Blamey used reports of the American inactivity to counter MacArthur's earlier criticism of the Australians. According to Blamey's chief of staff, when the Australians were being driven back along the Kokoda Track, "the jokes of the American officers in Australia, making fun of the Australian Army, were told all over Australia." He thought that MacArthur, his chief of staff, Maj. Gen. Richard Sutherland, and Kenney were "not guiltless" among those who had made disparaging remarks.[11] On 25 November MacArthur suggested bringing the U.S. 41st Division up from Australia to reinforce the 7th Division, and Blamey objected. Kenney, who was present, recorded: "Blamey frankly said he would rather put in more Australians, as he knew they would fight. . . . I think it was a bitter pill for General MacArthur to swallow."[12]

Upset and humiliated at reports that American soldiers had dropped their weapons and run, MacArthur called his American corps commander, Maj. Gen. Robert Eichelberger, to Port Moresby. On 30 November MacArthur told Eichelberger "to take Buna, or not come back alive."[13] Eichelberger later wrote: "At the time I did not realize General MacArthur was being gloated over by the Australia high command who had been criticized by him previously."[14]

By the time the Japanese were annihilated in late January 1943, the Australians had deployed six infantry brigades to the area and the Americans four infantry regiments. Both the Australians and the Americans had come to terms with the jungle. Furthermore, on a working level there had been close cooperation between the two armies. For example, when in early January MacArthur and Blamey returned to Australia, Herring took over as commander of New Guinea Force and Eichelberger assumed command of the 1st Australian Corps. Earlier, the 18th Australian Brigade had fought at Buna under the command of the U.S. 32d Division, while an American regiment fought under the 7th Australian Division.

The Papuan campaign lasted exactly six months. The Japanese committed a little over 20,000 troops, 13,000 of whom were killed. The

Australians and Americans together suffered 8,546 battle casualties. Casualties from malaria exceeded 27,000; those suffering from tropical diseases numbered over 37,000. In the break up of these casualties, the Australians lost more than 2,000 killed; the Americans 600. By comparison, in the Guadalcanal campaign, which took place at about the same time, about 1,600 Americans were killed.

This account of the arguments between the Australians and the Americans in the Papuan campaign is essential background to explain what happened in following months. For example, even before the end of the campaign, MacArthur took steps to remove Blamey from command of American troops. On 11 January 1943, he asked Marshall to send Lt. Gen. Walter Krueger from America "to give the U.S. Army the next ranking officer below General Blamey in the Allied Land Forces which is not now the case and is most necessary."[15] Soon after Krueger's arrival MacArthur formed Alamo Force to conduct the operations of the Sixth Army, which was to be commanded by Krueger. There were not yet enough troops to form a U.S. Army in Australia, but Krueger, who also commanded Alamo Force, "realized that this arrangement would obviate placing Sixth Army under the operational control of the Allied Land Forces."[16]

Krueger's deputy chief of staff commented later that Alamo Force was created "to keep control of Sixth Army units away from General Blamey."[17] This new command system was, in the words of the Australian official historian, Gavin Long, achieved "by stealth and by the employment of subterfuges that were undignified, and at times absurd."[18]

Much as MacArthur would have preferred to use American troops for the 1943 offensive, he would have to again rely on the Australians. After a major strategy conference in Washington, on 28 March 1943, the Joint Chiefs of Staff issued MacArthur a directive which listed the following tasks: (1) the establishment of airfields on Kiriwina and Woodlark; (2) the seizure of Lae, Salamaua, Finschhafen, Madang, and western New Britain (Cape Gloucester); and (3) the seizure of the Solomon Islands to include the southern portion of Bougainville. The third task was to be given to the forces of the South Pacific Area operating under MacArthur's strategic direction.[19]

To implement this plan, MacArthur divided his force into four task forces, not counting the South Pacific Forces. The first task force was New Guinea Force, under Blamey. This was composed mainly of Australian Army units, but included some Americans, and had the task of seizing Lae, Salamaua, and the Huon Peninsula up to Madang. The second task force was New Britain Force under Krueger. This was an American task force based on the newly formed Sixth Army, and had the task of seizing the islands of Kiriwina and Woodlark and the western end of New Britain. The third task force was the Allied Naval Forces, under Admiral Arthur Carpenter. Its task was to support the operations of the preceding two task forces, defend forward bases, protect the lines of communication, and transport the land forces to their amphibious landings. The forth task force was the Allied Air Forces under Kenney. Its task was to destroy enemy aircraft and shipping, support the two land task forces, support the defense of the forward bases, and provide air transport for the land forces.

While planning for this offensive went ahead, the 3d Australian Division was advancing along jungle and mountain trails from Wau towards Salamaua, on the north coast of New Guinea. By advancing towards Salamaua, Blamey intended to draw the Japanese away from Lae. He intended to land the 7th Australian Division by air at Nadzab, inland from Lae in the Markham Valley, while at the same time landing the 9th Australian Division by sea east of Lae.

The subsequent operations became the largest and most complex in the Southwest Pacific to that time. In the advance on Salamaua the 3d Division, later relieved by the 5th Australian Division, was supported by a regiment of the U.S. 41st Division, which landed by sea at Nassau Bay and advanced along the coast. This regiment came under Australian command, but at times there was some confusion about the command arrangements.

As at Sanananda six months earlier, there was intermingling of units. For example, one American battalion supported an Australian infantry brigade. Because of the terrain, almost all the artillery was grouped along the coast. This included two American field artillery battalions and about half of the Australian field regiment. An American colonel was appointed commander of the 3d Division artillery, with an Australian assistant. Since the armies had different fire control procedures, forward observers were deployed in pairs, an Australian to direct Australian guns and an American to direct American guns.

The low point in cooperation came early in the campaign when an American battalion commander refused to obey orders from Maj. Gen. Stanley Savige, the commander of the 3d Division. The battalion commander then wrote directly to MacArthur to complain that the intermingling of the two armies had produced a situation which, as he said, would "steadily become worse to the detriment of the American Army." He wrote, "God knows, we have as bad failings as theirs, but we are accustomed to our failings and are better able to deal with and correct them." In the end the Australian division commander removed the U.S. battalion commander from his position. MacArthur supported this action, but was determined to never allow such a situation to develop again.[20]

Nevertheless, there were to be more combined operations. The landing of the 7th Australian Division at Nadzab was preceded by a parachute drop by a U.S. Paratroop Regiment operating under the command of the Australian division commander, Maj. Gen. Vasey. The operation involved detailed cooperation with the Advanced Echelon of the U.S. Fifth Air Force. The operation went satisfactorily, although the U.S. Paratroop Regiment saw little action since there were no Japanese at the landing zone.

The 9th Australian Division was transported to its landing beaches by the American amphibious force, under Admiral Daniel Barbey, and American engineer units went ashore to assist the landing. The amphibious landing took place on 4 September, the air landing began on 5 September, and Salamaua was captured on 11 September and Lae on 16 September. It was a brilliant orchestration of sea, air, and land resources involving the three services of both countries.

Yet there were tensions during the planning phase. It will be recalled that MacArthur had appointed Blamey as commander of New Guinea Force. Prior to the operation, GHQ was critical of Blamey's planning, claiming that he had delegated responsibilities that he was not entitled to delegate. Blamey's staff quickly pointed out that the Australian Army worked on a more decentralized basis. The Australian official historian wrote:

This misunderstanding underlined the weakness whereby since April 1942 an American general headquarters on which there was quite an inadequate Australian representation reigned from afar over a field army that was, for present purposes, almost entirely Australian, and whose doctrines and methods differed from those of GHQ. It was evidence of the detachment of GHQ that, after sixteen months, its senior general staff officers had little knowledge of the doctrine and methods of its principal army in the field.[21]

General Sir Ivan Mackay, who in late September assumed command of the New Guinea Force from Blamey, noted that there was "a certain impatience to hurry on, or vary, arrangements entered into with the Americans, or agreed to at pre-operational conferences." The result was "a tendency to try and 'wangle' things," which reacted to the discredit of the Australians.[22]

On 22 September another Australian amphibious landing took place at Finschhafen, along the coast from Lae, and this time the Australian 9th Division had a hard fight, facing determined Japanese counterattacks. There was a major dispute between Rear Admiral Daniel Barbey, commanding the U.S. Navy's Seventh Amphibious Fleet, and Lt. Gen. Herring, commanding the 1st Australian Corps, over the reinforcement of

Finschhafen. Herring requested Barbey to transport another brigade but Barbey claimed that GHQ had told him not to move in more troops. The problem was that both MacArthur and Blamey had returned to Australia. Yet Blamey was still nominally the task force commander, and Mackay, acting in his stead in New Guinea, did not have the authority to order Barbey to act. Blamey approached MacArthur and permission was given to reinforce Finschhafen—just in time to repulse a Japanese counter-attack. As Herring commented later: "We damn nearly lost Finschhafen."[23] Eventually, four Australian brigades were brought in before the high point of Sattelberg was captured in November. The Australians then advanced along the coast.

Meanwhile, the 7th Australian Division had advanced up the Markham Valley and into the Ramu Valley. This advance was facilitated by moving troops forward by air, and was designed to protect airfields which were to be established in the open valleys. The Australians fought their way into the rugged Finisterre mountains and by March 1944 were closing on the town of Madang on the northern coast.

During this series of campaigns, which began with the defense of Wau in March 1943, and ended a year later with Australian forces advancing along the coast to Madang, occurred an outstanding achievement by the Australian Army, supported by Australian and American Air Forces and the U.S. Navy. The Australians deployed five infantry divisions, rotating the troops to maintain pressure on the enemy. During these operations the Australians lost 1,231 killed and 2,867 wounded. In the last half of the campaign 10,000 men were evacuated with malaria.

During this period the American Army played only a minor role in the Southwest Pacific Area's operations. The troops of Alamo Force who stormed ashore on Kiriwina and Woodlark Islands in July 1943 were met by the Australian coastwatchers who had been there for many months. There was no fighting. One American infantry regiment fought at Nassau Bay and suffered 81 killed and 396 wounded. In December 1943 the U.S. 1st Marine Division landed at Cape Gloucester at the western end of the island of New Britain. The campaign lasted about three weeks and the Marines lost 248 killed.

It must be remembered that during 1943 troops of the South Pacific Area under MacArthur's general strategic direction fought hard campaigns in the Solomon Islands, but within the Southwest Pacific Area proper the bulk of the fighting was carried out by the Australians.

However, in 1944 all this was to change. The Australian divisions, exhausted by their months of hard campaigning, were withdrawn to Australia. By early 1944 the Australian Army had been reduced considerably from the 13 divisions available in mid-1942 to 8 divisions. The 5th and 11th Divisions were still serving in New Guinea; the 12th was defending the Northern Territory; the 3d and the 6th were ready for action at short notice; and the 1st, 7th, and 9th were in training. By contrast, the American forces had expanded dramatically. Whereas in mid-1942 there had been only 2 U.S. infantry divisions in the Southwest Pacific Area, there were now 7 infantry divisions, 3 separate regimental combat teams, and 3 engineer special brigades. By the third quarter of 1944, when MacArthur had assumed responsibility for the forces in the Solomons, he had eighteen American divisions.

Beginning with the landing on Los Negros in February 1944, MacArthur's American Army units conducted the overwhelming majority of the operations throughout that year; including the landings at Aitape and Hollandia in April, Wakde and Biak in May, Noemfoor and Sansapor in July, Morotai in September, and Leyte in the Philippines in October. The Australian Army played no part in this series of remarkable amphibious operations, which saw the Allied line advance over 2,000 miles in eight months. The landings were commanded by the Alamo Task Force, and as Commander of Allied Land Forces, Blamey had no role.

MacArthur's rapid advance, the buildup of American divisions— which continued throughout the year—and manpower shortages in Australia presented the Australian strategic planners with severe problems. The crucial question was whether MacArthur would use any of the Australian divisions in the Philippines. In March 1944 MacArthur told the Australian Prime Minister, John Curtin, that the spearhead of his advance would be three Australian divisions and an American paratroop division. He said that the Australians would be commanded by an Australian Corps commander and that Blamey would have less of a role in the future.[24] It is difficult to believe that MacArthur was completely frank with Curtin, for his outline plan for the capture of the Philippines made no mention of Australian units and the previous month he had told his staff that plans to use the Australians would probably not come off.[25]

The following month, Curtin and Blamey left for a visit to the United States and Britain, and while they were away they received news from Australia that MacArthur intended to use Australian troops on garrison duties. Blamey was therefore interested in a proposal then being developed by the British Chiefs of Staff for an advance from either northern Australia or western New Guinea into the Netherlands East Indies.

When MacArthur heard of this plan, he said that it would therefore not be possible to use Australians in the Philippines. However, this was only an excuse, for the plan to advance into the Netherlands East Indies from northern Australia or West New Guinea was never approved. MacArthur never had any intention of using Australians in what he perceived as a purely American operation.

When MacArthur ordered Blamey to relieve the six American divisions engaged in garrison or holding operations in the Solomons and New Guinea, Blamey produced plans to use seven Australian brigades. MacArthur insisted that Blamey use twelve brigades—or four Australian divisions—thus making less divisions available for use in the Philippines.

The Australian divisions were not used for the invasion of the Philippines, but at various times during the latter months of 1944 and the early months of 1945 plans were floated to use two Australian divisions in the northern Philippines. None came to pass.

By the beginning of 1945 Australia had one division (the 6th) in action advancing from Aitape to eliminate a large, but poorly supplied, Japanese army around Wewak on the north coast of New Guinea. Another division (the 5th) was on the island of New Britain where, although it dominated most of the island, it largely had a static role, bottling up the Japanese on the Gazelle Peninsula. The Australian 2d Corps with four brigades was on the island of Bougainville where it had begun an offensive to destroy the Japanese garrison. In all, twelve Australian brigades from the 3d, 5th, 6th, and 11th Divisions were deployed in the New Guinea area under the 1st Australian Army.

Some critics have described these campaigns as unnecessary. Blamey argued that MacArthur had insisted that they use more brigades than were necessary to garrison the islands and that the Australians were doing no more than the Americans were doing on the southern islands of the Philippines. Two cases can be made for continuing these operations. First, the Japanese were occupying Australian territories and had control of a population for whom Australia had a League of Nations Mandate. It was Australia's responsibility to liberate these people. Second, Blamey could not know that the war would end as soon as it did. If Australia were to have a role in the invasion of Japan, it had to clear up the Japanese enclaves so that sufficient troops could be released. No doubt MacArthur would have made similar arguments for continuing the clear-up operations in the Philippines.

From a tactical point of view, the Americans had little to do with these campaigns, which were supported mainly with Australian and New Zealand aircraft and by ships of the Royal Australian Navy. By the end of the war, about 1,000 Australians had been killed in the Aitape and Bougainville operations. The U.S. Eighth Army, conducting similar operations in the southern Philippines, lost 454 killed. By contrast, 12,520 Americans were killed in Okinawa alone.

One point of dissatisfaction was the lack of news about these campaigns in the press. MacArthur and his staff still retained the prerogative to decide what was to be released in the official communiques. The Australian official historian wrote: "probably never in the history of modern war had so large a force, although in action, been hidden from public knowledge for so long."[26] When questioned at the time, MacArthur replied that it was incongruous for the press to criticize him for failing "to aggrandize their current minor operations to make them appear to be of major importance."[27]

Blamey and the Australian government were becoming increasingly dissatisfied at the role of their forces within the Southwest Pacific. As Blamey observed in February 1945, a "feeling that we are being sidetracked is growing strong throughout the country."[28] Blamey also began, belatedly, to complain to the Prime Minister, Curtin, that he had been maneuvered out of his role as Commander, Allied Land Forces. When Curtin wrote to MacArthur on this issue, MacArthur merely replied that he had operated through task forces for the previous eighteen months and made no mention of the position of Commander, Allied Land Forces.[29]

By this time, MacArthur had his headquarters in Manila. When GHQ moved forward to Hollandia in mid-1944, elements of Blamey's Advanced Land Headquarters had moved forward also, but when GHQ moved to the Philippines, Blamey's headquarters was excluded. Eventually, a small liaison staff was established in Manila under Blamey's chief of staff, while Blamey's Advanced Land Headquarters was located on the island of Morotai.

In response to agitation from the Australians for some indication of what he had in mind for them, MacArthur in March 1945 outlined plans to use the 7th and 9th Australian Divisions for operations in Borneo. Blamey approved the plans to capture Tarakan. The oil fields and refinery there would be useful for the Allies, and it would be a good base to build an airfield for later operations in Borneo. Troops of the 9th Division, supported by American and Australian planes and ships, landed on Tarakan on 1 May 1945. During the fighting, 215 Australians lost their lives. Afterwards, it was discovered that the airfield could not be repaired in time to be used for future operations and that the oil facilities were too damaged to be used before the end of the war.

The rest of the division landed at Brunei Bay on 10 June, and 114 Australians lost their lives. Later research has shown that MacArthur's and the Joint Chiefs' arguments that the British wanted a naval base at Brunei were hardly truthful.[30]

By this time, Blamey and his senior commanders were more wary of MacArthur's proposed final landing by the 7th Australian Division at

Balikpapan in southeastern Borneo. Neither Blamey, Moreshead, the commander of the 1st Australian Corps controlling operations in Borneo, nor the commander of the 7th Division could see any strategic purpose for that operation. In response to a query from the Australian Prime Minister, MacArthur told him that to cancel the operation "would disorganize completely not only the immediate campaign but also the strategic plan of the Joint Chiefs of Staff."[31] The Australian government therefore approved the operation. What the Australians did not know was that MacArthur had told the Joint Chiefs that the Balikpapan operation was necessary because not to carry it out would "produce grave repercussions with the Australian government and people."[32] When the landing took place on 1 July, a total of 229 Australians were killed and 634 wounded. Japan did not surrender one minute earlier as a result of this action.

In the last year of the war, the Australian Army had six divisions in action. This was a very large contribution; there was only one division (the 1st) left in Australia, all others had either been disbanded or were in action. Australia was the only Allied country to have more Army units in action after May 1945, when the Germans surrendered in Europe, than before. Nevertheless, this substantial Australian contribution should be compared with that of the Americans. By 1945 there were nineteen American divisions and four separate regimental combat teams in the Southwest Pacific Area, and American casualties in the Philippines were 10,380 killed and 36,550 wounded.

By this time, the notion that the Southwest Pacific Area was a combined Australian-American Allied command had disappeared. For the planned invasion of Japan, Australia was to provide only one division, and that was for one of the later as opposed to the initial landings.

In many respects, this marginalization of Australia was inevitable. Indeed, it was only force of circumstances that had allowed the Australian Army to play such a large role in an Allied command in the period between mid-1942 and mid-1944. The Australian military leaders were, of course, present when MacArthur accepted the Japanese surrender in Tokyo Bay in September, and Blamey had his moment of victory when on Morotai he accepted the surrender of all the Japanese in the southern area.

It would be a mistake to allow this discussion of the arguments over strategy and command to obscure the fact that at a working level the Australians and Americans fought well together. This was more evident in the naval and air forces than in the army. It was not the purpose of this paper to discuss the other services, but we should note, in passing, that the naval forces worked together in combined task forces, and at times Australian officers commanded task groups that included U.S. Navy ships.

For much of the war in New Guinea an Australian air force operational group, later known as the 1st Tactical Air Force, operated as part of the U.S. Fifth Air Force. Meanwhile, U.S. bombers flying out of northern Australia came under the Australian air officer in charge of that area.

By their nature, army formations are given specific areas of operations, and there is little scope for the intermingling of units. In any case, even with the best of intentions, such intermingling does not produce a more effective force than one of the same nationality. It is at a higher level that it is necessary to manage combined operations. In many respects, the conduct of combined operations in New Guinea in 1942 and 1943 was an outstanding achievement, with both sides providing resources in which the other was lacking. The Australians lacked naval and air forces; for the first two years the Americans lacked well-trained and combat-hardened army formations. Together, the forces of the two nations halted the Japanese advance, drove them back in hard, slogging battles, and set up the situation which allowed the successful campaigns of 1944 and 1945.

NOTES

1. For a detailed discussion of the issues covered in this paper see D. M. Horner, *High Command: Australia and Allied Strategy, 1939–1945* (Sydney: George, Allen and Unwin, 1982).

2. Signal, MacArthur to Marshall, 15 Jun 42, OPD Exec 10, item 7D, Record Group (RG) 165, National Archives and Records Administration (NARA).

3. The militia divisions in Australia were the 1st, 2d, 3d, 4th, 5th, 10th, 1st Motor, and 2d Motor. Northern Territory Force was a division-size formation with both AIF and militia units and was later to become the 12th Division. The AIF divisions in Australia were the 7th and the 1st Armored. Of the three other AIF Divisions, the 6th was moving from Ceylon to Australia, the 8th had been captured at Singapore, and the 9th was still in the Middle East.

4. Signal AG 152, MacArthur to Adjutant General War, 8 Apr 42, Sutherland Papers, Correspondence with War Department, NARA.

5. Minutes of Conference, 26 Jul 42, OPD 333, item 17, RG 165, NARA.

6. S. F. Rowell, *Full Circle* (Melbourne: Melbourne University Press, 1974), p. 110.

7. Ltr, Vasey to Rowell, morning and afternoon 28 Aug 42, Rowell Papers, Australian War Memorial (AWM).

8. Signal, MacArthur to Marshall, 30 Aug 42, OPD Exec 10, item 23a, RG 165, NARA.

9. Ltr, Rowell to Vasey, 30 Aug 42, item 225/2/5, AWM 54.

10. Lida Mayo, *Bloody Buna* (Garden City, N.Y.: Doubleday, 1974), p. 120.

11. Berryman, quoted in *Eichelberger Dictations*, bk. 2, ch. 7, pp. 122–23, copy from Jay Luvaas.

12. George C. Kenney, *General Kenney Reports* (New York: Duell, Sloan, and Pearce, 1949), p. 151.

13. Robert L. Eichelberger, *Our Jungle Road to Tokyo* (London: Oldhams, 1951), p. 42.

14. Jay Luvaas, ed., *Dear Miss Em, General Eichelberger's War in the Pacific, 1942–1945* (Westport, Conn.: Greenwood Press, 1972), p. 33.

15. Signal, MacArthur to Marshall, 11 Jan 43, RG 4, MacArthur Memorial Military Archives (MMMA).

16. Walter Krueger, *From Down Under to Nippon* (Washington, D.C.: Combat Forces Press, 1953), p. 10.

17. Interv tapes, Papers of General George H. Decker, U.S. Army Military History Institute, Carlisle Barracks, Pa.

18. Gavin Long, *The Final Campaigns* (Canberra: Australian War Memorial, 1963), p. 599.

19. Louis Morton, *Strategy and Command: The First Two Years*, United States Army in World War II (Washington, D.C.: U.S. Army Center of Military History, 1962), p. 641.

20. Maj Archibald Roosevelt to MacArthur, 26 Jul 43, Sutherland Papers, Miscellaneous, NARA.

21. David Dexter, *The New Guinea Offensives* (Canberra: Australian War Memorial, 1961), p. 283.

22. Ltr, Mackay to Blamey, 6 and 7 Oct 43, Blamey Papers 170.3, AWM.

23. Ivan Chapman, *Iven G. Mackay, Citizen and Soldier* (Melbourne: Melway, 1975), p. 279.

24. Notes of Discussions with the Commander-in-Chief, Southwest Pacific Area, Canberra, 17 Mar 44, CRS A5954, box 3, Australian Archives (AA).

25. Record of Conversation, Maj Gen Chamberlin, Brigadier White, 1500 hrs, 25 Feb 44, Blamey Papers 43.5, pt. 1.

26. Long, *The Final Campaigns*, p. 37.

27. Ltr, MacArthur to Shedden, 12 Feb 45, CRS A5954, box 75, AA.

28. Signal, Blamey to Berryman, 17 Feb 45, Blamey Papers, 43.68, AWM.

29. MacArthur to Curtin, 5 Mar 45, RG 4, MMMA.

30. Horner, *High Command*, p. 396.

31. Quoted in Teleprinter Msg 1238, Shedden to Fraser and Blamey, Blamey Papers 23.11, AWM.

32. Signal CA 51543, MacArthur to Marshall, 12 Apr 45, CCS 381, POA (6–10–43), Sec 11, RG 218, NARA.

MacArthur, Fuller, and the Biak Episode

Harry A. Gailey

More than fifty years have passed since some of the key events of the Pacific war transpired. Yet many areas of that conflict remain unexplored. While some campaigns have drawn the attention of numerous historians and journalists, others have remained obscure and unreported. In previous works, my primary concern was to explore some of these. While researching these monographs, I became very interested in one of the dominant figures of World War II—General Douglas MacArthur. I wondered, as did many of his biographers, how it was possible for him to have escaped the stigma attached to Admiral Kimmel and General Short, especially since his plans for the defense of Bataan have been called into question. One can explain MacArthur's survival and the adulation heaped upon him early in the war by noting that the nation was in desperate need of heroes. However, the carefully orchestrated government and media program creating the MacArthur myth was so successful that it continued to obscure very questionable decisions by MacArthur and his headquarters throughout much of the war.

MacArthur's handling of the Buna-Gona-Sanananda operations, the removal of Maj. Gen. Edwin Harding, and his unjust criticisms of the Australians have drawn the attention of some historians, although more detailed monographic studies would be welcomed. Lesser known is the way that MacArthur's and Lt. Gen. Walter Krueger's headquarters bungled the Biak operation and passed off the blame to the assault commander, Maj. Gen. Horace Fuller—in many respects a reprise of Buna.

By the spring of 1944 MacArthur's policy of bypassing major Japanese strongholds and utilizing his amphibious capability to seize air and staging bases had brought his forces close to Wewak. Wewak was the headquarters of General Hatazo Adachi's *18th Army,* comprising more than 20,000 troops. In one of his finest strategic moves of the New Guinea campaign, MacArthur decided against assaulting Wewak; instead, Maj. Gen. Robert Eichelberger's I Corps landed in two places on Humboldt

Bay, 200 miles to the west of Wewak. Caught by surprise, the Japanese at Hollandia and Tanahmerah put up only slight resistance, and by 26 April the airfields and port facilities had been captured.

At the same time, the 163d Regimental Combat Team (RCT) of the 41st Division landed at Aitape, 125 miles to the east, and quickly overcame the Japanese defenders of the airstrip there. Buoyed by these successes and the need for larger functioning heavy bomber fields, MacArthur ordered Krueger to seize Arare on the mainland, 130 miles farther up the coast, as well as the air base on Wakde Island. Brig. Gen. Jens Doe's 163d RCT had accomplished these goals by 17 May. All had gone well during the spring offensive until Krueger decided to capture Sarmi, a town sixteen miles east of Aitape. This was the headquarters of the Japanese *36th Division*, a majority of whom were first class troops, well dug in in a series of strong positions. The 158th RCT, which was given this task, had been hastily assembled at Finschhafen, relieving the 163d. The 158th was halted short of the objective at "Lone Tree Hill." At one time there were twenty-two different U.S. enclaves defending the hard-won gains in this drive up the coast.

Eventually, on 22 June, the 6th Division would capture Lone Tree Hill, but the Japanese held Sarmi until the end of the war. A further disconcerting set of events that modified MacArthur's and Krueger's plans was General Adachi's decision to recapture Aitape. Moving west from Wewak, the bulk of his *18th Army* struggled through the ninety miles of jungle for more than a month. Adachi would not be in a position to attack until July, but MacArthur, informed as to the approximate size of the force, had to keep the reinforced 32d Division at Aitape.[1]

While many of these complex mainland offensives were still not complete, MacArthur decided to capture Biak. From a theoretical strategic viewpoint, the capture of Biak seemed to be an important step for the ultimate success of MacArthur's Reno V plan for advancement to the Philippines. The island, the largest of the Schouten group, lay 350 miles northwest of Hollandia and 100 miles east of the Vogelkop. It was known that the Japanese had constructed three operational airfields on the narrow coastal plain inland from the three villages of Sorido, Barokoe, and Mokmer. The capture of these would allow Maj. Gen. George Kenney's Fifth Air Force planes to dominate Geelvinck Bay and the Vogelkop Peninsula, as well as to extend the range of heavy bomber operations northward toward the Carolines. This was not the only reason for MacArthur's haste in pressing for the occupation of Biak. The relative ease by which Toem and Wakde had been taken underscored the belief that the seizure of the Biak airfields could be accomplished in time for planes operating from there to aid the proposed Marianas campaign scheduled for mid-June.

MacArthur's optimism was further strengthened by the successful submarine attacks in early May on a convoy from China containing an estimated 20,000 soldiers scheduled to reinforce the Japanese *2d Army*. Four transports were sunk, and the Japanese lost half of the troop complement.[2]

Planning for the Biak invasion followed the usual pattern for operations in the Southwest Pacific. The general strategic goals and time frame would be set by MacArthur's headquarters. In all such operations, this meant that MacArthur was deeply involved not only in establishing strategic goals, but was also concerned with all phases of an operation. Prior to issuing an operations instruction, he normally listened carefully to all his senior advisers and then made the final decision himself. He would then keep in touch with the tactical operation to a greater extent than was the practice in either Europe or the Central Pacific. Subordinate headquarters would be responsible for making the tactical plans and for coordinating efforts between land, air, and naval forces. Once they had agreed upon the specific plans, these would be referred to MacArthur's headquarters for final approval.[3] Thus, one can assume that nothing of importance was done during an operation without MacArthur's knowledge.

The planning for the Biak operation, because of the need for bases for Kenney's planes to provide air cover, was closely tied to that of the capture of Wakde Island. MacArthur's first operations order for the occupation of Sarmi on the mainland and Wakde was issued on 27 April and called for the assault to begin on 15 May. Objections by Rear Adm. Daniel Barbey, Amphibious Force commander, and Kenney caused MacArthur to order that the plans be recast to target Wakde first; then, within ten days Biak would be assaulted under cover of Wakde-based planes. After much high-level discussion, D-day for the Wakde operation was set for 17 May and Z-day for Biak on 27 May.[4] The Wakde assault would be made by the 163d RCT of the 41st Division, commanded by General Doe. The remaining regiments, the 162d and 186th RCTs of the 41st Division, were given the responsibility for Biak. General Fuller, commanding the division, was also designated as HURRICANE Task Force commander. Fuller and his division had performed well during the Hollandia operation, and MacArthur had promised Fuller a corps command as soon as the expansion of his force would allow for the creation of more large units.[5] MacArthur, with little knowledge of Biak, fully expected that two RCTs would be sufficient to capture the airfields by 10 June. The plan called for Fuller's troops to land from LVTs and DUKWs on three beaches in the vicinity of the village of Rosnek, six miles east of Mokmer airfield. Then the 186th was to secure the lodgment and move inland toward the plateau, while the 162d drove west along the narrow coastal shelf to secure the airfields.

One reason for the later problems on Biak was the faulty intelligence provided to MacArthur. His chief intelligence officer, Maj. Gen. Charles Willoughby, had assured him that there were between five to seven thousand Japanese on the island, of whom only 2,300 were combat troops. According to Willoughby, the invasion would encounter "stubborn but not serious" resistance.[6] Willoughby's optimism was in contrast to the estimates given to MacArthur's headquarters by ULTRA. Although ULTRA missed the fact that there were elements of the Japanese *36th* and *14th Divisions* and a number of service units on the island, it had warned of twice as many troops as Willoughby projected. MacArthur accepted ULTRA's reports of the location of the major Japanese fleet units that might interfere with the invasion, but he chose to accept Willoughby's conclusion that the only real resistance the 41st Division would encounter would be the Japanese *222d Infantry Regiment*. Thus, he believed the intelligence information that confirmed his predetermined position.

The capture of Biak, while not absolutely necessary, did fit into MacArthur's long-term plans. Not only would the possession of the airfields make it possible to strike at Palau during the planned Marianas operation, but it would provide air cover for his projected July invasion of the Vogelkop, that of Halmahera in September, and the Philippines in November. Willoughby's suggestion that Z-day be postponed was quickly dismissed.[7] Willoughby's concern had nothing to do with fears of the Japanese on Biak. Rather, he felt that the landings could cause Admiral Soemu Toyoda, commander of the Japanese *Combined Fleet*, to order main elements southward and thus be in a position to destroy the weak American Seventh Fleet. MacArthur refused to wait until a major fleet action had eliminated this very real naval threat. He was willing to gamble on a quick favorable conclusion to the Biak operation.[8]

In the months preceding the invasion, Biak had become a source of debate between Japanese naval and army leaders. Originally, the island was included within the empire's main defense line. Not until 9 May did the *High Command* redefine the southernmost line to exclude Biak. Col. Naoyuku Kuzume, the Japanese commander on Biak, was informed that he could not expect reinforcements. He had earlier expected considerable numbers of troops from the *3d Division* then located at Geelvinck Bay. The *High Command* reiterated his initial mission—to deny the enemy the use of the airfields for as long as possible. The means for this goal were considerable. The main unit in Kuzume's plans was the *222d Imperial Infantry Regiment,* a veteran unit with a great deal of combat experience in China, which had reached Biak in December 1943. The *222d* was supported by Rear Adm. Sadotoshi Senda's 1,500-man *Special Naval Landing Force.* There were also a number of specialized units, including heavy artillery units, an antiaircraft battalion, and a tank battalion. Kuzume also had at his disposal a large number of mortars and automatic weapons of all calibers.[9] Most important, Kuzume (and later Lt. Gen. Takezo Numata) would prove masters of defense. They knew where the Americans would probably land and that the terrain adjacent to that southwest shore was perfect for defense.

The beaches along the southern shore of Biak were paralleled by a high, narrow ridge line. Northward there was a series of limestone caves, some of which were large enough to shelter a thousand men. Kuzume placed his large-caliber guns in positions to dominate the beach areas. Beginning in the previous December, he had his troops construct a series of interconnecting trenches, tunnels, and fortified positions. He dug in his antiaircraft guns, mortars, and automatic weapons along the ridge lines. There were three strong points in the terraces behind Mokmer airfield. One, the West Caves, consisted of three large sinks surrounded by bunkers, pillboxes, and interconnected trenches. In the center area was the Ibdi Pocket, and controlling the eastern part of the airfield were the East Caves. Each of these had bunkers and were covered by mortars and mobile artillery. Kuzume had no intention of wasting troops in futile charges, but was going to exact a heavy price for each strong point.[10]

Operation HURRICANE began early in the morning on 27 May with a major foul-up for the landing forces. After softening up barrages by the navy and air force, advance elements of the 186th RCT landed on four beaches around Bosnek. The currents, swifter than imagined, carried the landing craft one and a half miles west and landed the first waves in a mangrove swamp. Later waves compensated for the currents, and by evening more than 12,000 infantry, a tank company, a battalion of medium artillery, and a battery of heavy artillery had been landed. After landing, elements of the 162d quickly advanced northwest toward the airfields as the 186th consolidated the beachhead and moved east of Bosnek. This relatively successful start was slowed by only a thin screen of Japanese defenders south of the ridge and by some heavy weapons fire from higher elevations. One reason for the apparent quick success of the 162d was that many of the Japanese troops were out of position. This error was quickly rectified by General Numata, chief of staff of the *2d Area Army*, who was on an inspection trip to Biak. He assumed command and directed the defenses of the island until he left on 15 June.

Fuller's plan was to have the 162d quickly capture the airfields while the 186th advanced westward along the high ridges parallel to the coast, destroying the Japanese positions there. By the twenty-ninth, both regiments had been halted by well-placed enemy fire, and the 162d had been forced out of the Mokmer village area which they had taken the previous day. It was obvious to Fuller that the airfields could not be used, even if captured, until the Japanese had been cleared from the ridges. Even at this early stage, the high temperatures and humidity were taking their toll on the 41st Division troops. There was little water on the island, and for the first few days many front-line units operated without it. After the initial setback, Fuller established a defensive perimeter and requested more troops before resuming the offensive. Krueger reluctantly sent two battalions of the 163d from Sarmi, which arrived on 1 June.[11] He also informed Fuller that he expected him to move forward and carry out the assigned mission quickly.

Krueger's attitude toward Fuller was conditioned largely by the pressure he was receiving from MacArthur's headquarters for a speedy capture of the airfields. On the day following the invasion, MacArthur announced the impending capture of the island and noted that this would represent "the practical end of the New Guinea campaign."[12] On that same day he radioed General Krueger, "My heartiest congratulations to you, General Fuller, General Doe and all officers and men of your command concerned upon the brilliant success attained at Wakde and Biak."[13] Located in Brisbane, out of touch with the reality of the fighting on Biak, he announced on 1 June that Japanese resistance was "collapsing" and two days later that "mopping up" was proceeding.[14] The tendency to claim premature victory was a problem at MacArthur's headquarters. They had been guilty of such posturing before and would be again throughout the Philippine campaign.

On 5 June MacArthur, aware that more than "mopping up" was needed, sent Krueger a query. He radioed: "I am becoming concerned at the failure to secure the Biak airfields. . . . Is the advance being pushed with sufficient determination? Our negligible ground losses would seem to indicate a failure to do so."[15] Krueger's reply indicated he was dissatisfied also and had repeatedly directed Fuller "to push his attack with the utmost vigor." He indicated that he had contemplated removing Fuller, but delayed until he had reports from his G–3, Colonel Eddleman. Finally, spurred on by MacArthur's query, he sent his chief of staff, Brig. Gen. George Decker, to investigate the situation.[16]

Meanwhile, on Biak, Fuller had fed the reinforcements into the line. After heavy artillery concentration, he moved the 186th north to try to flank the Japanese positions. Because of the very rugged terrain along the main ridge, that drive slowed down and resolved itself into a number of small unit actions. Supply continued to be a problem, and the Japanese remained firmly in control of their major defenses. Fuller was then ordered by Krueger to shift his assault once again in the direction of the airfields. On 7 June elements of the 186th finally took the Mokmer airfield. Engineers were brought in and the field was repaired by the fifteenth but, as Fuller had known, it could not be used since the Japanese still controlled the heights. Heavy counter battery fire from the 105-mm. howitzers managed to knock out many of the Japanese mobile guns, and most of Numata's tanks were destroyed in futile attacks against the heavier, more powerful Shermans. However, from 7–10 June all attempts to gain total control of the low dominating ridge north of the airfield were unsuccessful. The 162d began a drive along the coast on the eleventh, captured Borokoe airfield, and gained positions a mile beyond at Sorido. Two of the regiment's battalions then moved north to the low ridge line and the West Caves. Fuller's troops were too few and too exhausted to clear the Japanese from their strongholds along the high ground and in the West Caves.

Fuller had qualms from the beginning about the number of men assigned to him for the operation when he met with General Eichelberger at corps headquarters at Lake Sentani before the invasion. Eichelberger recalled that Fuller told him at that time that he had led a full-scale amphibious operation against Hollandia and now, five weeks later, was being asked to prepare for another. Fuller had been very concerned that he would have only two regiments assigned to him.[17] Even the arrival of the bulk of the division's third regiment on 1 June did not give him the force he believed he needed to assure that the airfields could be used. Repeated attempts to dislodge the Japanese convinced him of the need for more troops, and on 13 June he formally requested that Krueger send another regiment to Biak. His front-line troops were fatigued—many by this time had been in combat continuously for seventeen days in very hot, humid weather. It is difficult to know how many men had become ill by this time, but some sense of this problem can be seen in the fact that there were 6,811 medical casualties for the entire campaign.[18]

Krueger reluctantly approved the request for more troops while discounting Fuller's report that the Japanese were being reinforced. Fuller was correct. By this time the Japanese had barged in under cover of darkness at least one thousand troops from the mainland and Noemfoor Island. The unit belatedly chosen by Krueger to reinforce the 41st Division, the 34th Infantry Regiment of the 24th Division, did not arrive from Hollandia until the eighteenth, too late to be of any help to Fuller.

Fuller's fears of massive Japanese reinforcements paralleled Willoughby's earlier warnings to MacArthur. The Japanese were trying to reinforce Biak. In May, aware of the probability of attacks on the Marianas, Admiral Toyoda planned for the long-hoped-for final showdown with the American fleet and began to mass the *Combined Fleet* in preparation for it. Nevertheless, he planned to use a part of the fleet to support the reinforcement of Biak.

In an operation code-named *KON*, the Japanese gathered an amphibious force of 4,000 men, the transports of which were guarded by a battleship, three cruisers, and six destroyers. The convoy was scheduled to arrive at Biak on 4 June. MacArthur continued to discount all reports of reinforcements even after the convoy was sighted. He believed that the Japanese ships were headed instead for Halmahera. Fortunately for MacArthur and the 41st Division troops on Biak, planes from the Japanese scouting force erroneously reported a large Allied naval force, which included carriers, just off Biak. Fearing a confrontation with such a large force, the convoy commander ordered a return to base. The Japanese would make two other major attempts at reinforcing the Biak garrison. The second *KON* operation was even larger than the first, but it was intercepted by American planes that sank two destroyers and damaged three other ships. The Japanese commander, once again fearful of encountering a major Allied naval force, aborted the mission. The last relief expedition was canceled, because all major ships were needed to counter the 15 June invasion of Saipan.[19] Had any of these plans been successfully carried out, the entire Biak operation would have been in jeopardy, since MacArthur's weak naval force could not have halted any of the Japanese convoys.

On 8 June Krueger sent a long letter to MacArthur, explaining in detail the development of the situation on Biak. This recapitulation was a masterpiece of brevity and accuracy. He defended Fuller, noting that he had been faced with a most difficult task and that a possible alternate plan for the capture of the airfields was "judgment after the event and presupposes that there were enough troops on the spot to permit it, which is debatable since the 163d RCT (less 1 Bn) did not arrive until 31 May." Krueger closed his communication by pointing out that he had earlier considered removing Fuller but now gave him a full vote of confidence by noting, "I am glad I did not do so then, and feel that it would be unwarranted now when, I am sure, he is about to accomplish his mission successfully."[20] Yet, despite the positive support indicated in the dispatch, within less than a week, Krueger had reversed his position and removed Fuller from command of the HURRICANE Task Force.

The reason for this turnabout was the continuing pressure which MacArthur put on Krueger to make sure that at least one airfield would be operational by 15 June. Although Krueger was concerned about Fuller's inability to quickly eradicate Japanese resistance, he understood the difficulty of reducing the main points of resistance without which the airfields could not be used.

On Biak, one of Fuller's main goals was to isolate the Japanese in the Ibdi Pocket. After repeated attacks by the 162d and 163d RCTs, the pocket was cut off from all reinforcements by 10 June. Infantrymen, supported by tanks, were engaged in the time-consuming process of either neutralizing or sealing off the many caves there, a task which would not be completed until 22 July. Japanese resistance was even more determined in the West Caves and the Mokmer Caves areas. It was not until 21 June that the West Caves were neutralized. The Japanese still continued to resist in the Mokmer Caves until 4 July.

MacArthur did not appreciate the situation on Biak, and on 14 June he communicated his displeasure in an eyes-only dispatch to Krueger, flatly stating, "The strategic purpose of the operation is being jeopardized by the failure to establish without delay an operating field for aircraft."[21] After receiving this, Krueger decided he had to act. He informed MacArthur that he had ordered General Eichelberger and his entire I Corps staff to Biak to take command of the operation. Fuller would remain only as the 41st Division commander.[22]

Eichelberger later reported that he was shocked with the suddenness of Krueger's decision. He had been busy supervising the work entailed in making Hollandia into a large functioning Allied base. He claimed that at the time he was ordered to meet with Krueger prior to leaving for Biak, he "had received no information of the progress of the fighting at Biak. . . . General Byers [I Corps chief of staff] and I were old hands at this game and particularly remembered the time we were ordered to Buna with no warning of any kind…working as we were at Hollandia we received absolutely no reports from Sixth Army or GHQ about how things were going at Biak. This would seem unbelievable that a force in the field wouldn't be kept informed about what was going on in adjacent combat units, but it was typical, even into Japan."[23]

Such a situation might have been typical, but I Corps was not totally unaware of the situation on Biak. Byers did not want a repeat of the Buna situation when Eichelberger, without warning, was ordered in to relieve Harding. He ordered the corps signal officer to intercept messages between Alamo Force and GHQ. Byers later related that he caught "the dickens from Mac's Chief Signal Officer for this but it was the only way we could keep aware of the trouble on Biak."[24] This breach of protocol proved fortunate, since the corps staff was not totally unprepared when called upon to deal with Biak.

Eichelberger stated that he and his chief of staff had only "a few maps with us but almost no knowledge of what we would find at Biak."[25] What he found when he arrived on the morning of the fifteenth was a very angry General Fuller. Fuller deeply resented his demotion and believed that it was Krueger who had been unjustly critical of his handling of the operation. Eichelberger's assumption of command of HURRICANE Task Force only confirmed that his superiors believed that he had failed. He had concluded even before Eichelberger had arrived that Krueger was the man most responsible, and he had already posted a letter to the Alamo Force commander requesting to be relieved of command of the 41st Division and to be reassigned outside the South West Pacific area.

Eichelberger and Fuller were friends (they had been classmates at West Point), and Eichelberger tried to dissuade Fuller from leaving Biak. Undoubtedly one of the reasons, aside from friendship, was the fact that Fuller understood more of the Biak situation than anyone—lessons that Eichelberger would be forced to master quickly. Fuller was adamant, despite assurances from Eichelberger that Fuller would probably soon receive a corps command if he continued with a lesser role on Biak; he had assigned to Krueger the role of the villain and would not serve under him any further. Fuller insisted that a radio message be sent to speed up his relief. Krueger approved the request and also suggested that General Doe be named acting division commander.[26]

Before leaving Biak, Fuller addressed a letter to the men of the 41st in which he exonerated them of any part in the failures to live up to the expectations of higher authority. He left Biak on 18 June, the day before Eichelberger's first offensive. He would later serve with distinction as deputy chief of staff to Lord Louis Mountbatten in the Southeast Area Command. Ironically, MacArthur praised Fuller for not complaining about his treatment, and when the two met later there appeared to be no rancor. Fuller was later awarded the Distinguished Service Medal for his actions at Hollandia and Biak.[27] It is doubtful whether Fuller would have been so well disposed toward MacArthur had he been aware that it was MacArthur and not Krueger who caused his relief.

Fuller's overreaction and his assumption of Krueger's primary responsibility may have been incorrect, but his belief that he had not been treated fairly was quite accurate. Two of the 41st regimental commanders agreed with their commander that the Biak operation was well in hand. The airfields had been captured, and it was only a matter of time before the low ridge line and the West Caves would be secured. Col. Oliver Newman, commanding the 186th, recalled that he was not aware of a time factor. He wrote, "I was never informed that there had been a deadline set for the capture of the Biak airfields, nor that there was any pressure being applied on General Fuller from higher headquarters. I only learned this after his relief. As far as I know the operation was proceeding with satisfactory speed. Had I known of the need for speed in supporting the Marianas attack I might have acted differently on several occasions."[28]

Eichelberger, MacArthur's "fireman," was later supportive of Fuller's handling of the operation. He pointed out that the invasion was begun with only two regiments and that meant only a rough parity with Kuzume's forces. Military textbooks stated that the invader should have a three-to-one advantage. Two days before the offensive was renewed, Eichelberger, after personally surveying the front lines, wrote, "This is the toughest terrain I have seen yet to fight in except at Buna. The interior is a series of coral cliffs with numerous natural caves. It has been and will continue to be a rough fight."[29] He further noted that the "Japanese defense of Biak was based on brilliant appreciation and use of terrain."[30] Considering all the facts, he concluded that the 41st Division had not done badly.[31] Such statements by the I Corps commander pose the question: Did Fuller's relief hasten the collapse of Japanese resistance and the use of the airfields?

As was the case in many instances where a commander was removed, there was no appreciable gain on Biak. After studying the situation for three days, Eichelberger ordered an offensive beginning on 19 June. He brought nothing tactically new to the offensive; rather his attack plans were roughly the same as Fuller's had been. The major difference was that he could attack with four regiments supported by a stronger force of tanks and tank destroyers. The West Caves were taken, and the 34th Infantry secured the high ground overlooking the Sorido and Borokoe airfields on 22 June. On that same day P–40s began to operate from Mokmer. Severe fighting continued to reduce the Japanese in the Ibdi Pocket and East Caves, and this was accomplished by 27 June. Scouring the inland areas for the remaining Japanese would continue through 20 August.

It appears obvious that Eichelberger's presence did not cause the operation to be ended any faster than if Fuller had retained command. MacArthur's headquarters initially had been at fault in underestimating the number of the enemy on the island and the defensive possibilities offered by the terrain. By committing only two regiments and prematurely announcing victory, MacArthur had created a situation which could be rectified only by more men and equipment and time. Instead of understanding this fully, a great injustice was done to a fully competent commander whose record, despite later supportive statements by MacArthur, was tarnished by an unwarranted relief.

NOTES

1. Details of the earlier campaigns are from Samuel Milner, *Victory in Papua,* United States Army in World War II (Washington, D.C.: U.S. Army Center of Military History, 1957) and Robert Ross Smith, *The Approach to the Philippines,* United States Army in World War II (Washington, D.C.: U.S. Army Center of Military History, 1953), pp. 13–83.

2. Samuel Eliot Morison, *History of United States Naval Operations in World War II,* vol. 8, *New Guinea and the Marianas* (Boston: Atlantic, Little Brown, 1962), p. 21.

3. Paul P. Rogers, *The Bitter Years: MacArthur and Sutherland* (New York: Praeger, 1991), p. 72.

4. General Headquarters, Southwest Pacific Headquarters, Operating Instructions No. 51/1, 10 May 44, box 175, folder no. 4, RG 3, MacArthur Memorial Military Archives (MMMA), Norfolk, Va.

5. Jay Luvaas, ed., *Dear Miss Em, General Eichelberger's War in the Pacific, 1942–1945* (Westport, Conn.: Greenwood Press, Inc., 1972), p. 130.

6. Edward J. Drea, *MacArthur's Ultra: Code Breaking and the War Against Japan, 1942–1945* (Lawrence: University Press of Kansas, 1992), p. 135.

7. Ibid.

8. Ibid., p. 136.

9. Ibid.

10. Detailed information on the Biak operation taken from Alamo Force Operations Rpt, Wakde-Biak, and HURRICANE Task Force Operations Rpts, Biak, 17 May–20 Aug 44, National Archives, Suitland, Md., and Smith, *The Approach to the Philippines,* pp. 280–396.

11. General Walter Krueger, *From Down Under to Nippon* (Washington, D.C.: Zenger Publishing Co., 1979), p. 95.

12. Clayton D. James, *The Years of MacArthur,* vol. 2 (Boston: Houghton Mifflin Co., 1975), p. 459.

13. Radio Msg, MacArthur to Krueger, 28 May 44, box 14, folder no. 3, RG 4, MMMA.

14. James, *The Years of MacArthur,* p. 459.

15. MacArthur to Comdr of Alamo Force, 5 Jun 44, box 14, folder no. 3, RG 4, MMMA.

16. CG Alamo to CINC SWPA, 5 Jun 44, box 14, folder no. 3, RG 4, MMMA.

17. General Robert Eichelberger, *Our Jungle Road to Tokyo* (New York: Viking Press, 1950), p. 136.

18. Smith, *The Approach to the Philippines,* p. 392.

19. Morison, *New Guinea and the Marianas,* pp. 118–33.

20. Ltr, Krueger to MacArthur, 8 Jun 44, box 14, folder no. 3, RG 4, MMMA.

21. Eyes-alone dispatch, MacArthur to CG Alamo Force, 14 Jun 44, box 14, folder no. 3, RG 4, MMMA.

22. Comdr Alamo Force to CINC SWPA, 14 Jun 44, box 14, folder no. 3, RG 4, MMMA.

23. Luvaas, *Dear Miss Em,* p. 126.

24. Ibid., p. 143.

25. Eichelberger, *Our Jungle Road,* p. 138.

26. CG Alamo Force to GHQ SWPA, 16 Jun 44, and MacArthur to CG Alamo Force, 16 Jun 44, box 14, folder no. 3, RG 4, MMMA; Ibid.

27. James, *The Years of MacArthur,* p. 460.

28. Smith, *The Approach to the Philippines,* p. 345.

29. Luvaas, *Dear Miss Em,* pp. 129–30.

30. Department of the Army, *Reports of General MacArthur,* 4 vols. (Washington, D.C.: U.S. Army Center of Military History, 1966), vol. 1, pt. 2, p. 152.

31. Eichelberger, *Our Jungle Road,* p. 144.

The Office of Strategic Services (OSS) Operational Group Burma: The "Arakan Group"

Richard W. Stewart

There is little question that the European and Mediterranean theaters had their share of successful Office of Strategic Services (OSS) operations. Operations in support of Tito in Yugoslavia, in support of the British and partisan efforts in Italy, and numerous operations in Greece which helped drive out the Germans in 1944 were notable triumphs. One cannot overlook, however, the successes of the OSS in the China-Burma-India Theater. OSS Detachment 101 in Burma was the first operational OSS unit to be activated in 1942. Before its disbanding late in 1944, it had trained, equipped, and led over 10,000 Kachin, Shan, Naga, and other Burmese nationals against the Japanese. As the war drew to a close, hundreds of combat-experienced Operational Group (OG) soldiers moved into China and trained twenty Commando units, six of them as parachute infantry—a new dimension for the Chinese Army. Many of these Operational Group veterans came from the Mediterranean and European Theaters. However, no small number of them came from Detachment 101 and from a hitherto overlooked unit, the only Operational Group formed in the CBI or Pacific theaters: the Arakan Group.

The Arakan Group was formed because of mission requirements and chance rather than by OSS planning or design. In mid-1944, a young major by the name of Lloyd Peddicord working in the office of intelligence in the Headquarters of the Southeast Asia Command (SEAC) was approached by an American naval officer who worked for the OSS. The officer asked Peddicord whether he would like to go to work for the OSS if he could obtain his release from his present assignment. Major Peddicord was interested in working for the OSS although, like virtually everyone else, he knew little about it. The naval officer wanted Major Peddicord to put together a special OSS Operational Group that would work out of submarines launched from Ceylon against the Japanese-held coast of Burma and the islands and peninsulas of Malaya and Indonesia.

The first target, however, was to be the Arakan coast, which was the scene of major fighting between the Japanese *28th Army* and the British XV Corps. After having been summarily ejected from Burma in 1942, the British were attempting two years later to advance down the coast and outflank Japanese positions in Central Burma. The advance had bogged down. Major Peddicord and his men were to conduct a series of intelligence-gathering and destructive raids along the coastline to help the offensive along.

Peddicord was a natural for the mission. Before the war started, he had helped put together the Amphibious Corps Atlantic Fleet reconnaissance training program at Norfolk, Virginia, and Fort Pierce, Florida. As part of that process, Peddicord and a number of young Marine Corps and Army officers worked on hundreds of schemes to improve the movement of troops and materiel ashore for intelligence reconnaissance. Some worked and others did not. Trial and error was the main scientific method used.

For example, one of the group was an engineering officer who had formerly worked for Firestone rubber. This led to a number of experiments on rubberized products including a large rubber bag with a jeep inside. In theory, the bag would be pushed off a destroyer and towed ashore for vehicle reconnaissance. As Peddicord later recounted, "That didn't work at all."[1]

Other experiments included ten-man rubber boats, seven-man boats, two-man double-pointed boats, individual flotation devices, submarine photography methods using periscopes, and direction-finding techniques for homing in on raider parties with walkie-talkies returning to the submarine after a mission. Many of these innovations, perfected in the North African landings, were used later in the Pacific.

With this background in amphibious raider training and the use of submarines as part of that concept, Peddicord returned to the States to begin recruiting for his new amphibious Operational Group. He started by finding officers and senior noncommissioned officers from his Fort Pierce days to serve as the leaders of his Operational Group. He then turned to the 87th Division, training at Fort Jackson, South Carolina, to obtain additional volunteers. Peddicord needed only twenty-five men, but on at least one occasion, one of the regiments of the 87th Division responded to the call for volunteers by marching up an entire battalion to the screening location. During the screening process, Peddicord focused on finding men with experience living out of doors and in survival techniques; one of his favorite questions was, "Were you a Boy Scout?" He wanted men used to leading and to operating independently.

After assembling his volunteers, Peddicord moved them to the OSS training center at the former Congressional Country Club, impressed into wartime service and given to the OSS. While the men received their basic OSS training in stealth, weapons, survival, and close-quarters combat, Peddicord and his assistant, Capt. Sam O'Regan, returned to Ceylon to establish the base of operations. The remaining six officers and thirty-two enlisted men finished their training in mid-1944. Due to the Normandy landings, which put a strain on all shipping requirements, the OG was put on a slow boat across the Pacific along with a shipment of mules and muleskinners. It took the men seventy-two days to get to Ceylon from California.[2]

Once the OG was reunited in Ceylon, they embarked on a strenuous training plan, including night landings on rocky shores, operations from submarines, and long-distance navigation. This demanding and dangerous training cost the life of one of the OG's officers. Capt. Dolan S. Ritchie, a man who had trained hundreds of OG personnel in the Washington area training centers, drowned in the surf during a landing practice on 25 November 1944.[3]

By the time the men entered into the final stages of their training, the mission changed. Japanese shipping disappeared from the Indian Ocean and the submarines which were to be the OG's primary means of transportation were pulled out of the British base at Trincomalee, Ceylon. Peddicord's OG, by now attached to OSS Detachment 404, Ceylon, had trained, in the best military tradition, for a mission which could no longer be executed. In place of submarines, Peddicord began training his men to work out of British motor-launches: 110-foot Fairmile boats with 40-mm. Bofors machine guns aft and Oerlikon machine guns on the small bridge. Only later did they manage to locate some U.S. PT boats to conduct their missions.

Instead of working on long-range submarine infiltration missions, the OG now began to focus on short, end-run type operations in support of the British XV Corps along the Arakan coast of Burma. The commander and staff of the XV Corps had requested a unit to perform reconnaissance along the coast, and in the troop-starved Burmese theater a unit without an active mission such as the OG was immediately snatched up. HQ OSS for the Southeast Asia Command organized the Arakan Field Unit for this mission. The Field Unit included a services section, an intelligence section (X–2, Counterintelligence and SI [Special Intelligence] collection), an Operations Section (which included Peddicord's OG, a separate Maritime Unit [MU], Morale Operations [MO], Special Operations [SO], and Air Transport) and a Communications Section.[4]

The plan was to use the skills of the Operational Group to perform reconnaissance of beaches for possible amphibious operations ahead of

XV Corps operations. They were also to find airstrips, gather intelligence on enemy troop locations and movements, capture prisoners, and generally keep the Burmese coast in an uproar to keep the Japanese guessing about Allied intentions.[5] On 6 December 1944, Peddicord's Operational Group was moved from Ceylon to Calcutta, Cox's Bazaar, and finally Chittagong for "temporary duty."[6] This "temporary duty" provided the Group with a jumping-off location for operations along the Burmese coast. Chittagong was the initial staging camp, but the Operational Sections eventually located at Teknaaf until forward bases were established on Akyab Island and Ramree Island.

The Arakan OG launched its first mission (Operation ZEBRA) from Camp Ritchie (named after the Captain Ritchie who drowned in the earlier training operation)[7] in Teknaaf, India, on 28 December 1944. It was a fairly straightforward reconnaissance mission of a village on the island of Akyab just south of the Burmese frontier along the coast. The two motor launches departed Teknaaf at 1635 on 28 December and were in position at 2345 to launch six landing craft ashore. Capt. George Bright commanded this first mission. Rocky reefs prevented a landing on the planned beach, but one of the boats acting in a scout mode diverted the teams 100 yards to the south. The forty-man team established a perimeter for security, left a security team in place to watch the boats, and began moving inland in two columns. The reconnaissance party itself consisted of twenty-four personnel, including Peddicord, who left the command of the team to Captain Bright but apparently could not resist the chance to go on the first mission.

The mission itself was generally uneventful, but served as an ideal "dress rehearsal" for later operations. Two local natives were encountered who provided the teams with the information that the Japanese had not been on that part of the island for over three months. The few Japanese who were left (around fifteen in number) were located in a small village on the north of the island. The reconnaissance elements collapsed onto their boats by 0240 and were picked up by the motor launch at 0322—mission accomplished.

The first mission of the Arakan Group set the standard for their future missions: meticulous planning, careful coordination between sea and land elements, and the conscientious placement of security elements to protect the stealthy reconnaissance elements. The first mission also served to point out the fact that local natives would be generally the best source of intelligence during their operations: Japanese prisoners were still quite rare. Later missions would provide them only a few chances to capture Japanese soldiers. In one instance, on mission number 4 (Operation

WEBFOOT), two Japanese soldiers blundered into one of the landing areas and the security element had to open up on them with their submachine guns. One was seriously wounded but had to be stabbed several times when he began groaning and moving, giving the men the impression he was only "playing possum." He died before reaching Teknaaf. The other wounded Japanese escaped.[8] As one of the members of the landing party later explained, the men were taken to task for killing the wounded Japanese since prisoners were so rare.[9]

By early January 1945 the Arakan Group had established a new Camp Ritchie farther south along the coast on Akyab Island, the scene of the first reconnaissance mission. From there they launched another mission, Operation VIRGIN ABLE, in support of the V-Force, a British intelligence-gathering force for which they capitalized on their knowledge of Burma. The OG provided security for a six-man interrogation squad which landed at the village of Agnu near Myebon in Hunter's Bay south of Akyab. The mission lasted from 9–14 January, made contact with a number of Burmese nationals, and departed without sighting any Japanese. Apparently the Japanese had left the area the previous month.[10]

Moving farther south in pursuit of the retreating Japanese, the Arakan Group, by now calling itself the First Operational Group, Southeast Asia Command (SEAC), established its forward headquarters on Ramree Island. Although part of the island was still occupied by the Japanese, they were moving to evacuate the island by the end of January. In a series of missions against Sagu, Cheduba, Foul, and Ramree Islands, the OG continued to locate enemy forces, contact natives for intelligence, and perform vital reconnaissance work. Close on their heels were the main British and Indian forces.

One particular operation against Cheduba Island illustrates the value of bluffing in special operations, and the suspicions of conventional forces about special operations units. The OG recon party slipped ashore on the island on a moonless night in January and ran into a party of Burmese coast watchers working for the Japanese. Exploiting the chance, the men of the Arakan Group revealed that they were Americans and that they were going to be landing shortly to reoccupy the island. They did this with the full knowledge that the coastwatchers would tell the Japanese everything the next day. As a result, the Japanese immediately evacuated the island. They swallowed the story. All the British had to do was send a small party ashore and reoccupy the island. The British, however, doubting the Arakan Group's report, launched a full-scale invasion the following week. They came in, in the words of one OG member, "with their battleships, with their guns blasting and everything else, blowing up cows and putting splinters in natives and all that sort of stuff, and there wasn't a Jap on the damn island."[11] As a corollary to that, the following night, Tokyo Rose announced the capture and execution of "Major Peddicord and his men" on Cheduba Island—fast information flow, if inaccurate.

Other operations followed—Operations ULCER, TARGET, RUGBY, and SNATCH. These missions proceeded on the whole successfully with a minimum of Japanese notice: reconnaissance forces should not be seen going about their jobs and the Arakan Group on the whole kept a low profile. This low profile was ruined during Operation SNATCH when one of their own BAR men tripped in the mud and set off his weapon. In another compromise during Operation YARDBIRD (9–10 January), barking dogs alerted the villagers who, it turned out, were loyal coastwatchers for the Japanese. They attempted to notify the Japanese of the landing party, but the OG intercepted the messengers, held them as temporary hostage, and made their way back to their boats.[12]

In the eleventh and final mission of the Arakan Group (Operation POPLIN), the OG was assigned to conduct a beach reconnaissance of the north bank of the Thanzit River east of Ramree Island to determine suitable landing areas for a possible British amphibious assault. The party left Kyaukpyu in broad daylight on 28 February and reached the mouth of the river at dusk. Paddling slowly upstream to avoid detection, the 15-man party stealthily located the proposed site. Suddenly hearing non-Burmese voices, the team pulled into the bank and hid in the mangrove swamps that abounded in the region. They were not spotted, and the commanding officer, Lieutenant O'Jibway, ordered the team to depart. Moving slowly down river and taking soundings every twenty-five yards with a seven-foot pole, the party returned to their motor launch shortly after 2100. Their mission was accomplished in a low-key fashion and they returned with important intelligence. This was a fairly typical mission, with stealth being emphasized over firepower and intelligence over combat operations.[13]

In all, the Arakan Group conducted eleven reconnaissance missions along the Burmese coast, making it possible for British forces to occupy the coast down as far as Ramree Island by February. Later, the British would move only as far south as Taungup in April before bypassing the entire region and conducting an airborne and seaborne attack directly on Rangoon on 2 and 3 May. Meanwhile, as the mission drew to a close in the Arakan region, the SEAC OSS commanders drew up plans for other missions for the Arakan operational group personnel. On 9 February the entire unit was transferred on paper from Detachment 404 Ceylon and placed under the command of Detachment 101, the principal OSS operating agency in Burma.[14] Detachment 101, under the command of Lt. Col. "Ray" Peers, directed the last few missions of the Arakan Group.

Finally, its missions completed, the members of the Arakan Group were transferred in the summer of 1945 to OG Command China, where Lt. Col. Alfred Cox was creating 20 Chinese Commando units of 100 men each for service against the Japanese. Major Peddicord and his men were broken up into various detachments and began training their commandos. At least one of the Arakan Group men was along on the attack against the Tanchuk Airfield (Operation BLACKBERRY) near Liuchow on 3 August 1945. In conjunction with the 265th Regiment of the 89th Chinese Division, this operation took the airfield from the Japanese at the cost of 22 men killed and 31 wounded. The operation, organized and led by the OSS, marked one of the few times in the war that Japanese troops lost territory to Chinese forces in China.[15]

In conclusion, we can say that despite changes in mission and the normal problems of new units, the Arakan Group accomplished its assigned tasks. Pioneering new techniques in amphibious reconnaissance, Peddicord and his men established an outstanding record of stealthy reconnaissance deep behind enemy lines. Using the exposed sea flank of the Japanese, the OG moved quietly behind Japanese lines at will, gathering intelligence and establishing contact with the local tribesmen. They provided the vanguard for the British and Indian troops during the Arakan campaign which, along with the main attacks in Central Burma around Mandalay and Yenangyaung, helped drive the Japanese back onto Rangoon. They were only a handful of men—amateurs in the Special Operations business—but their courage and zeal and their effective on-the-job training (in the best Special Forces tradition) turned them into a highly effective and successful fighting force.

NOTES

1. Interv, Dr. Richard W. Stewart, U.S. Army Special Operations Command (USASOC) historian, with Col (USA Ret.) Lloyd Peddicord and other members of the Arakan Group at the OSS Detachment 101 Reunion, Fort Bragg, N.C., 5 Oct 91. USASOC Historical Archives. Hereafter referred to as Peddicord Interv.

2. Ibid.

3. Monthly newsletter to the field on operational group activities covering Nov–Dec 44 and dated 9 Jan 45, published by Operational Group Command, 1st Lt Albert G. Lanier, entry 154, boxes 163–167, Record Group (RG) 226, National Archives and Records Administration (NARA).

4. HQ, OSS/SEAC Arakan Field Unit Plan, 6 Dec 44, sent to Lt Ray Peers, Commanding Officer Special Unit (SU) Detachment 101 by Lt Col Harry L. Berno, Acting Chief OSS/SEAC, in OSS Records, entry 154, boxes 2771–2778, RG 226, NARA.

5. Ibid.

6. Detachment 404 Special Order (SO) No. 75, 6 Dec 44, entries 117, 154, RG 226, NARA.

7. Interv, Stewart with Robert Abee of the Arakan Group, 4 Oct 91, Fort Bragg, N.C.

8. After-Action Rpt 4, Operation WEBFOOT, 15–16 Jan 45, Rpt by Capt George Bright, CO, and Capt Sam O'Regan, Beachhead Party, entry 154, boxes 163–167, RG 226, NARA.

9. Peddicord Interv.

10. Operations Order and After-Action Report for Field Operation No. 5, Operation: VIRGIN ABLE. Total of 16 personnel. Entry 154, boxes 163–167, RG 226, NARA.

11. Peddicord Interv.

12. After-Action Rpt, Operation YARDBIRD, 9–10 Jan 45; entry 154, boxes 162–167, RG 226, NARA.

13. Entry 154, boxes 162–167, RG 226, NARA.

14. HQ, OSS India-Burma Theater, SO No. 2, 9 Feb 45. It is apparent that Detachment 404 Ceylon, by now a long way from the fighting front, was being reduced to a small staff element, since all of the morale units, special intelligence personnel, and OG personnel were taken from Detachment 404 on this order and dispersed throughout the theater to Detachments 101, 303, and 505. Ibid.

15. HQ, OSS China Theater, sub: Report on Activities of Operational Group Commands, Office of Strategic Services, China Theater, 7 Oct 45, OSS Records, entry 154, boxes 162–164, RG 226, NARA.

Everything Old Is New Again
The American Military Effort in China, 1941–1945

Monroe M. Horn

The literature on America's involvement in China during World War II is replete with the theme of failure. Indeed, one has only to look at the titles historians have chosen to see that this opinion is generally shared in the historical community. *How the Far East Was Lost*, *Stilwell's Command Problems*, and *The American Failure in China* are all titles which reflect this dominant view.[1] However, the failure of the American military effort in the China-Burma-India (CBI) Theater cannot be solely attributed to strategic or tactical errors. This essay attempts to explain the failure in the context of traditional American-Chinese relations.

The problems which occurred in the CBI were the result of a unique combination of strategic and political mistakes that could only have been made in the context of American-Chinese relations.[2] The story of the CBI is the story of a breakdown in military leadership, but it is also part of the story of America's diplomatic and cultural relationship with China in the twentieth century. American military leaders were in China to win a war, but they were also diplomats. Moreover, Americans in China brought to their particular situation the accumulated baggage of over one hundred years of American-Chinese relations. With American generals came images that had come to dominate Americans' collective view of China— images of China as a land of nearly endless economic opportunity, a country ripe for political and religious evangelization, the home of the noble peasant and the wily Dr. Fu Manchu. These images of China shaped decisively the strategy chosen for CBI and the manner in which the American military interacted with the Chinese.

The military history of the China theater, therefore, cannot be treated in isolation. Any history of CBI must combine military, political, and even cultural history to create a picture of American-Chinese relations that explains not only how American military leaders failed, but also why. This essay begins with a narrative of the history of the CBI which highlights the way in which the theater was, from the very beginning, rife with division and intrigue. This is followed by a discussion of the nature of America's failure in China and its short-term causes. Finally, it concludes with an examination of the long-term causes of America's failure, setting American-Chinese relations during World War II within the context of the political and cultural relationship between the two countries.

America's involvement in China during World War II has been extensively chronicled by historians. The first attempts to tell the convoluted story of this period were made soon after the war by "official" historians. Herbert Feis, for example, while not employed by the government, made extensive use of his close ties to official Washington for his book, *The China Tangle*. Another effort is the official Army history of the war in China. This three-volume set written by Charles F. Romanus and Riley Sunderland remains the finest secondary source for purely narrative purposes.[3] Later works on the period are a more right-wing interpretation by Anthony Kubek, and Barbara Tuchman's more liberal *Stilwell and the American Experience in China*. More recently, Michael Schaller has attempted to analyze American wartime relations with China in his book *The U.S. Crusade in China*.[4]

The story of America's wartime relationship with China really begins not on 7 December 1941, but on 7 July 1937, when the Japanese attacked Southern China at the Marco Polo Bridge. That same month the Roosevelt administration provided China with a loan of $50 million for currency stabilization. A further $25 million followed in February 1939, $20 million in April 1940, and another $50 million on 4 February 1941. With the creation of the Lend-Lease Administration in March of that year, a second stage in aid to China began. T. V. Soong, Generalissimo Chiang Kai-shek's Harvard educated brother-in-law, established China Defense Supplies (CDS) on 29 April to get China's "fair share" of American supplies. A master at the game of influence peddling, Soong worked incessantly to ingratiate himself with the Washington establishment and Roosevelt's administration.

During 1941 most of Soong's efforts were devoted to building up the Chinese Air Force in the hope that air power could both protect China and roll back the Japanese invaders. The Chinese were aided in their efforts by an American, Claire Chennault, a man described by one observer as someone who "made his way through life at top speed, leaning on his horn."[5]

Never one to keep his opinions to himself, Chennault had resigned from the Army Air Corps in 1937 because he was frustrated by the Army's failure to adopt his ideas regarding the value of air power. An old friend soon got him a short-term contract as a consultant to the Chinese Air Force, and Chennault set out for what he thought would be a brief stay in

China. The Japanese attacked soon after he arrived, however, and Madame Chiang—the political head of the Chinese Air Force—hired him to supervise its development.[6] Though a colonel in the Chinese military, Chennault's stated employer became the Bank of China, thus allowing the Chinese to circumvent American neutrality laws.[7]

Chennault moved to China and soon established close friendships with nearly all the major figures in the Nationalist government. He was entranced by Madame Chiang, whom he referred to as "Princess," and became her confidante. She reciprocated his friendship and her brother, Soong, believed him to be an "outstanding military man." Chiang himself also considered Chennault a personal friend as well as a master strategist.[8]

Similar views on strategy accompanied these personal bonds. The Nationalists agreed completely with Chennault's emphasis on air power because their goal was to stop the Japanese without exhausting Chinese ground forces. Chiang knew he would need his armies after the war to destroy internal opposition and Chennault provided him with a strategic plan which could accomplish this goal. Thus, the two became allies in a quest to attain maximum assistance from the United States.[9]

In 1941 Chennault and Soong, with the help of administration officials such as Lauchlin Currie, worked to create a group of volunteers who would resign from the American military and go to China to fly planes purchased with American Lend-Lease funds. This was the genesis of the American Volunteer Group (AVG), the famous "Flying Tigers."

At the close of the year, as the AVG was beginning to mobilize and Soong was competing with Britain and the Soviet Union for American aid, the Chinese had a stroke of good luck; the Japanese Navy attacked Pearl Harbor, nearly scuttling the American Pacific Fleet and bringing the United States into the war. Now America needed China and the Chinese military could relax. America was going to take on Japan—or so Chiang hoped.

With American entry into the war came the necessity of establishing a military command in East Asia. Accordingly, the War Department created the China-Burma-India Theater with Maj. Gen. Joseph Warren Stilwell in command. Stilwell was the Army's foremost China expert. He had first traveled to China in 1920. This was followed by a second tour in 1926 and a third in 1932 as the military attaché to the U.S. Embassy.[10] As American commander, Stilwell wore three hats: he was the commander in chief of CBI and commanded American forces in the theater; he was the deputy commander of the Southeast Asia Command; and he was the chief of staff to Chiang, responsible for advising the generalissimo, controlling Lend-Lease, and—nominally—commanding Chinese troops in Burma.

When Stilwell arrived in China he quickly discovered his basic ideas of strategy were the opposite of Chiang's. Stilwell was eager to use the Chinese Army to attack the Japanese. Chiang, in order to maintain power in faction-ridden China, needed to have his best troops available to intimidate rival warlords and contain the Chinese Communists. This led the generalissimo to try to keep his best ground forces out of the fighting.[11] Stilwell, on the other hand, wanted to reorganize the Chinese Army by equipping and training thirty Chinese divisions to use American weapons and tactics.

Around the same time the situation in the theater worsened. The Japanese struck far into Burma, the lifeline between China and India. From March until May 1942, then, Stilwell worked to regroup Allied forces, a task made impossible by the attitudes of his allies. The British, nominally responsible for the defense of Burma, cared little for it and preferred instead to maintain a strong presence in India. Stilwell also had to fight constantly for control of the Chinese forces supposedly under his command. Both Soong and Chiang had assured the general that he would have operational control of Chinese troops in Burma. However, when it actually came to fighting, Chiang reserved for himself real power and frequently reversed or altered Stilwell's tactical directives.[12] Lack of troops, British reticence, and Chiang's desire not to risk his best armies—and thus a good deal of his power—combined with Japanese reinforcements to defeat Stilwell in Burma.

Stilwell's growing problems with Chennault augmented his frustrations with Chiang. Part of this friction was undoubtedly the result of their fundamentally different conceptions of strategy. Chennault believed Stilwell to be "indifferent" to the achievements of the AVG and backward in his notion that the "men in the trenches" win wars.[13] More important, however, was Stilwell's growing disenchantment with Chiang. Chennault believed Stilwell "poisoned" American relations with China by not fully supporting the generalissimo. He later wrote:

Friendly dignity and frankness were lacking from Stilwell's conduct of our partnership with China. He was in almost constant disagreement with. . .[Chiang] and seemed to regard him and other Chinese leaders not as colleagues but as obstacles to be overcome.[14]

Chennault was soon to join Chiang in numerous attempts to have Stilwell's authority restricted and, ultimately, to have him recalled.

A further point of conflict between the two was Chennault's role in the newly created CBI Theater. With the onset of hostilities, Chennault had been recommissioned in the U.S. Army as a brigadier general and made commander of the China Air Task Force (CATF). In this capacity, he became a subordinate of Clayton Bissell, an old enemy and the theater air commander. Chennault would have found it difficult to be second to anyone, but Bissell particularly upset him by planning to incorporate "his" AVG into the Regular Army. Chennault had gotten used to running the AVG his way and was bitterly opposed to losing absolute control.

Finally, in April 1942 the battle was joined. Chennault resisted induction with the powerful support of the Nationalists, who wanted to keep as many planes under their control as they could. They pressed instead for the creation of a separate air force under Chennault's command. Stilwell's disputes with Chennault, Chiang's favorite, combined with the conflicts over Burma to convince Chiang that Stilwell must be replaced by a more pliable officer.

The year 1942 also saw the arrival of two "special emissaries" from the president. These visits by Lauchlin Currie and Wendell Willkie saw the beginning of a systematic campaign by the Nationalists and their American supporters to have Stilwell removed.

Currie's visit to China in 1942 was his second. Hired by Roosevelt as an economic adviser, Currie quickly realized that China would become increasingly important to the president and labored to make himself the most knowledgeable of Roosevelt's assistants with regard to its problems. In 1941 Roosevelt took advantage of Currie's interest by sending him to study China's political and economic situation. Currie returned to Washington convinced that Chiang and the Nationalists were China's only hope and recommended that they receive more Lend-Lease equipment as well as a new loan. Currie was completely taken in by the Kuomintang leadership and declared that China was "an outpost of the world's present struggle for democracy."[15]

Currie's infatuation with the Nationalists was so pronounced that he quickly made enemies in Henry Morgenthau's Treasury Department. Morgenthau and his advisers believed that any Chinese loan should be dispersed gradually and with strings attached, thus reducing the possibility that a massive influx of American funds would precipitate widespread speculation. Currie, on the other hand, believed the loan had great "psychological" significance and should be granted in a lump sum without restrictions as to its use. Currie was so assiduous in his support of the Chinese agenda that Morgenthau wondered only half jokingly who was paying Currie's salary. "The trouble with Mr. Currie," he complained, "is that I don't know half the time whether he is working for Mr. Roosevelt or T. V. Soong. . . . Is he working for the Chinese Government or is he working for the United States Government?"[16]

In July 1942 Roosevelt again called on Currie to travel to China. Chiang, seeking more American aid, had presented the president with demands for three American combat divisions, the immediate creation of a 500-plane air force, and 5,000 tons of supplies monthly. If these "Three Demands" were not met, the generalissimo intimated, China might be forced to make a separate peace with the Japanese.[17]

Roosevelt sent Currie to smooth over relations with Chiang. He also instructed him to "support Stilwell's position," however, a directive which Currie proceeded to ignore. Instead, Currie chose to focus exclusively on a small part of his directive: "bolster Chinese morale and Chiang's position . . . by letting the impression be created that important developments are impending."[18] Once again demonstrating his divided loyalties, Currie told Chiang he "was not sure" when he was "speaking as the President's representative and when as his [Chiang's] friend and advisor, and didn't much care."[19] In spite of Roosevelt's instructions to "emphasize the importance of Stilwell . . . and the President's reluctance to intervene in strictly military operations," Currie did just the opposite. In his report to Roosevelt, therefore, Currie advocated every change in American policy Chiang desired.

First of all, Currie recommended Stilwell's recall. "I am convinced," he wrote, "that General Stilwell cannot function effectively as our chief military representative in China."[20] Indeed, Madame Chiang seems to have biased Currie against Stilwell even before he left for China. In a letter to her in May, Currie agreed with Chinese complaints that Stilwell had spent too much time fighting in Burma and not enough time securing American supplies for Chiang.[21] After listening to more complaints in Chungking, Currie was determined that Chiang should be rid of Stilwell. Currie's criticisms of Stilwell in his report were surpassed only by his praise of Chennault. "Our task force in China is the most brilliantly-led and at the same time the most poorly-equipped force," he reported. Currie also noted that Chiang had developed an esteem for Chennault which he did not have for Stilwell. He argued, therefore, that Roosevelt should support Chennault to please Chiang.

In the end, Roosevelt accepted only part of Currie's recommendation and ordered more supplies sent to the task force. Roosevelt did not, however, order Stilwell's recall. The general still had the adamant support of Marshall and, at least for the moment, Roosevelt was unwilling to override the opinion of his most trusted military adviser.

Much the same thing happened when Wendell Willkie visited in October. Willkie had been Roosevelt's Republican challenger in the election of 1940 and was traveling on a mission of bipartisan cooperation. Like Currie, Willkie paid little attention to Stilwell or embassy officials and was constantly shielded by the Nationalists from contact with anyone who might have supported Stilwell. Conversely, Willkie had many private talks with the Chiangs and was treated by them to lavish displays of hospitality. Not surprisingly, Willkie returned a strong supporter of Chiang and his strategic ideas.

Willkie also met privately with Chennault, who pressed upon the Republican both his strategic ideas and his growing dislike for Stilwell. Chennault protested so vehemently that Willkie asked him to write down his complaints in a letter to the president.[22] In the letter, Chennault said he had Chiang's support for his request for "full authority as the American military commander in China"—Stilwell's job. Given this, 147 new planes, and replacements, Chennault claimed, he could defeat the Japanese in China.[23]

At the outset of 1943, then, the forces arrayed against Stilwell were impressive indeed. The Nationalist leaders made it no secret that Stilwell was overstaying his welcome; and Chennault, one of America's first war heroes, had proposed himself for Stilwell's job. Additionally, FDR's two special emissaries had returned from Chungking advocating Chiang and Chennault. Only Stimson, the Secretary of War, and Marshall remained on Stilwell's side.

In February 1943 Roosevelt finally gave in to Chinese pressure and ordered the creation of the Fourteenth Air Force in China. Under the new arrangement Chennault would be the top air officer in China and the generalissimo's chief of staff for air. He was still, however, supposed to be subordinate to Stilwell.[24] Roosevelt also promised Chennault new planes and additional supplies to begin implementing his plan.

After this, Stilwell lamented, "Chennault . . . swelled up like a poisoned pup," and increased his maneuverings against both his commander and the War Department. Chennault and Chiang increasingly bypassed Stilwell and made decisions on their own. Complaining to the president, Stilwell "strongly recommended" that a statement to Chiang be made "explaining to him that the [M]ilitary [C]hannels must be maintained and that no independence of any portion of our military establishment will be countenanced."[25] The president, however, sent no such directive.

The months following the creation of the Fourteenth Air Force also saw a renewed effort to have Stilwell recalled. This time it was spearheaded by Joseph Alsop, the American Lend-Lease representative in Chungking. Alsop had long been a valuable ally of the Nationalists in their campaign to win American support. The scion of a wealthy and influential family, Alsop had all the credentials necessary to ingratiate himself with New Deal Washington. In addition to being distantly related to Roosevelt, Alsop had attended all of the right schools from Groton to Harvard. After graduation, Alsop's family acquired for him a position as a reporter for the

New York Herald Tribune.[26] In 1936 the paper sent Alsop to the capital where he quickly became a Washington insider with strong social ties to the government and a nationally syndicated newspaper column. Alsop's high school fascination with China was awakened in 1940 when he was introduced to T. V. Soong and the two quickly became close personal friends. His personal affection for Soong led Alsop to support Chiang and the Nationalists; from 1940 until the end of the war, he worked in various capacities to promote their cause.

In 1940 and 1941 Alsop used his excellent Washington connections to assist Soong and Chennault in acquiring American financial and military aid. He also served as an intermediary between his new friend, Chennault, and the White House. Soong praised Alsop's efforts in November 1940 when he wrote, "I know we can count on your continued active collaboration in our endeavors to obtain means for successful resistance."[27] Soong further acknowledged Alsop's effectiveness by hiring him as a public relations consultant for CDS. In this position Alsop devoted his time to securing the transfer of American military supplies to the Chinese.[28]

When Chiang created the AVG in 1941, Alsop left CDS and traveled to China as Chennault's personal aide and staff secretary.[29] In this capacity, he worked principally as a publicist and lobbyist for the AVG. Soong clearly sought to make use of the latter role when he cabled Alsop:

Suggest that you air mail letters to all your influential friends explaining picture of Col. Chennault unit and responsibility and urge immediate release [of] personnel and material [for the AVG]. This will help overcome administrative inertia.[30]

Alsop was only too happy to oblige. Like Soong and Chennault, he believed that America must support Chiang's government without hesitation and that an air strategy would best serve the Nationalists.

After America entered the war, Alsop continued to lobby for the Kuomintang as both an employee of CDS and Lend-Lease representative. After he was briefly interned by the Japanese in Hong Kong, Alsop was repatriated and immediately began looking for a way back to China. He therefore called upon his old friend, Harry Hopkins, Roosevelt's most trusted adviser.[31] In this case, Hopkins made provisions for Alsop to return to China as an agent of the Lend-Lease Administration. Some historians, however, believe that Alsop's appointment was merely a cover and that he went to China in order to open a direct line of communication between the Nationalists and the White House.[32]

Alsop returned to join Chennault in December 1942 and quickly entered the ranks of those hostile to Stilwell. He was later to argue that the arrival of Stilwell was "the beginning of the end of China."[33] His lobbying efforts intensified in 1943 as an employee of CDS and unofficial member of Chennault's staff. Alsop served as a covert link between Chennault's Fourteenth Air Force and the Nationalists and worked to coordinate their anti-Stilwell maneuverings. Because he had powerful friends in Washington and was outside of the military command structure, Alsop enjoyed a certain invulnerability. Stilwell's command was powerless to stop his subversive activities and could only complain ineffectually about the activities of "All-slop," as they called him.[34]

Alsop's most decisive lobbying victory was a furious 1943 letter campaign directed at Hopkins. Alsop wrote a total of seven letters to Hopkins in the first half of 1943, all anti-Stilwell, pro-Chiang, and apocalyptic in their vision of the disaster which would occur were Stilwell not relieved. In a 22-page letter on 1 March, Alsop (then Lend-Lease Administrator) gave Hopkins his amateur assessment of the military situation in China. He told Hopkins that "the only simple, easily available military opportunities in China are opportunities for the use of air power." Alsop also reiterated Chiang's line on Stilwell, saying,

General Stilwell's approach to the problem can only end in something very close to disaster for all of us. . . . If Stilwell is removed, and a properly instructed man sent out, that will clean the matter up entirely.[35]

Alsop hammered home these messages in subsequent letters. In late March he reported that "the only answer to our problem in China is to give General Chennault's air effort absolute, final and unchangeable priority over the ground effort." Another letter, written to Soong and passed on to Hopkins, concentrated on defaming Stilwell by presenting Alsop's "admittedly fragmentary but still depressing data on the character and quality of Stilwell's personal set-up." Pretending to be objective, Alsop alleged that Stilwell's command was poorly managed and "no more than a nest of private cronies."[36] In the end, Alsop's "Dear Harry" letters seem to have had the desired effect. Hopkins came to believe that Chennault was "remarkable" and supported him in later confrontations with Stilwell.[37]

Chiang and Chennault claimed another victory over Stilwell at the TRIDENT conference in May 1943. Roosevelt, at the prodding of the Chinese, had decided to bring Chennault to Washington to make his case personally. Only Marshall's insistence caused the president to bring Stilwell back as well. In Washington both men were to present their strategic plan to the commander in chief.

Chennault's invitation was a direct response to the efforts of Chiang and Soong, who pressed the president to give personal attention to Chennault's ideas.[38] Once this was accomplished, the Chinese set out to convince Roosevelt that Chennault's plans were superior. "On considering the matter further," Soong wrote, "he [Chiang] instructed me to re-emphasize the absolute necessity that the next three months be devoted entirely to carrying air supplies."[39] Soong also labored to convince Winston Churchill of the validity of Chennault's strategy by giving a copy of Chennault's plan to the prime minister, who was in Washington for the conference.[40]

Soong even went so far as to coach Chennault in his presentation. From Washington he sent the general a lengthy draft of what he should say to the president. The draft provided headings under which was a statement detailing what Chennault should insert. All that was left to the airman was to fill in the blanks. The telegram concluded:

It is of course intended that the foregoing should serve only as a sample for you. Nevertheless we believe you should definitely cover all points mentioned and even if suggested passages of argument and exposition do not suit you something similar should be substituted.[41]

In the end, though, Chennault's presentation closely followed Soong's draft.[42]

The plans Chennault and Stilwell presented at TRIDENT were nothing new. Chennault presented the plan he had worked out with the Chinese and supported Chiang in the face of Stilwell's criticisms.[43] He continued to argue that if he were given enough support he could single-handedly bomb the Japanese to their knees. Stilwell countered that any large-scale air offensive would bring swift Japanese retribution in the form of a ground attack to neutralize Chennault's airfields. This attack, he contended, could not yet be repulsed by the Chinese Army. Stilwell's counterproposal was to recapture Burma and open a land road to China which could support the restructuring and retraining of the Chinese Army.[44] Although Stilwell's presentation was not as effective as Chennault's, he enjoyed the vigorous support of both Marshall and Stimson, who pressed Roosevelt to accept it.[45]

It appears that the Nationalists' preparatory efforts were successful, however. Roosevelt gave Chennault superior consideration from the start. In the course of the conference Chennault had three private talks with Roosevelt, giving him ample opportunity to press his case. Stilwell had none. Roosevelt seemed to be treating Chennault, not as Stilwell's subordinate, but as Chiang's representative (which, of course, he really was). The president even went so far as to ask Chennault to report to him periodically outside of military channels.[46] Finally, Roosevelt ordered that Chennault's air force be expanded and that he receive first priority on supplies.[47]

Roosevelt's tacit approval of Chennault's maneuverings led the general to exercise even more independence from Stilwell in 1944, virtually ignor-

ing conventional military channels and instead cooperating nearly exclusively with Chiang. In April Chennault wrote a letter to Chiang accusing
Stilwell of blocking his attempts to hold off the Japanese. He did this in
spite of an order from Stilwell that any communications for the generalissimo be sent through Stilwell, Chiang's chief of staff. When asked why he
had disobeyed orders, Chennault snubbed his commanding officer, saying,

Again, my appointment as Chief of Staff for Air to the Generalissimo was made
by and with the approval of the President of the United States as well as by yourself. It was reasonable to assume that this appointment authorized his Excellency
to call upon me for advice on air matters at any time without reference to your
headquarters.[48]

Stilwell was furious at Chennault, but realized that he could take no
action because of Chennault's special relationship with the Nationalists.
"The issue seems to me to be that Chennault will obey the orders of the
theater commander only when it suits him," Stilwell complained to
Marshall. "The only reason Eye [I] have not already relieved him is
because of the political implications."[49] Stilwell realized that all of this was
an attempt by Chennault and the Chinese to decrease his power within his
own command. "There is a deliberate plan in the 14th A.F. to belittle
everything I do," Stilwell wrote in disgust.

Chennault's and Alsop's anti-Stilwell agitation reached its apex in the
spring of 1944 when Vice President Henry Wallace arrived in the theater.
As yet another of Roosevelt's private emissaries, Wallace was to pave the
way for the Army to send an observer group to Yenan, the Communist
stronghold.[50] Stilwell and his staff had long supported such a mission,
arguing that the United States should consider helping anyone engaged in
fighting the Japanese. Chiang, on the other had, was vehemently opposed
to American contact with Mao Tse-tung. Chennault and Alsop opposed
American aid to the Chinese Communists and worked along with Chiang
to get Wallace to torpedo the Yenan mission and intervene against Stilwell.
Like Currie and Willkie before him, Wallace's movements in China were
strictly constrained by Chiang and his American allies, who made sure he
had as little contact as possible with Stilwell's command.

When the vice president arrived in China, Chennault assigned Alsop to
be his "air aide."[51] Wallace, of course, had no need for a military aide of any
type. Alsop's real mission was to make sure Wallace saw what he was supposed to and left China an advocate of Chiang and Chennault. Since Alsop
had known Wallace professionally and socially before the war, he was the
perfect instrument with which to influence the vice president.[52] Stilwell
knew this and gave John Paton Davies, an embassy official assigned to his
command, the task of "tailing Wallace."[53] However, with Stilwell away con-

ducting a campaign in Burma, Chennault was successful in placing Alsop close to Wallace. Stilwell's staff in China feared they had been outflanked. "No friction to date but air show is bound to be emphasized," reported Brig. Gen. Benjamin Ferris, Stilwell's ranking officer in Chungking. Their fears were realized when Chennault and Chiang effectively blocked them from meeting with Wallace. "Jones and I were given the best job of run-around I have ever been up against," lamented Davies to Stilwell.[54]

The manipulation of Wallace was a coordinated effort by Chiang, Soong, Chennault, and Alsop, who all pressed upon him the same message. Chiang and Soong met first with Wallace in Chungking. During these meetings both men spoke out against Stilwell and intimated that they wanted him out. Wallace later recalled:

The generalissimo said to me very frankly that he lacked confidence in General Stilwell, while he had high confidence in General Chennault. . . . In any case, it was very clear to me, from the tone and language of the generalissimo, that he and Stilwell could not cooperate.[55]

Wallace traveled next to Kunming, Chennault's headquarters, where he spent three days. During this time the vice president spent a great deal of time with Chennault and even lived in his house. Chennault related to Wallace his appraisal of China's military situation and pressed Wallace to recommend Stilwell's recall. "It was at Kunming after talking with General Chennault," he was to write, "that I appreciated how terrifically serious the China situation was."[56]

Alsop was the most influential member of the team lobbying Wallace, however. From the moment the vice president arrived the new lieutenant rarely left his side. Alsop did more than anyone to convince Wallace that Chiang and Chennault were right in their assessment of the situation in China. Since Wallace "had not yet formed the opinion about China which his position required him to express," Alsop took it upon himself to mold it for him.[57] He told Wallace that "somebody had better do something drastic about the crisis without further delay," and, in the end, convinced Wallace to recommend drastic measures. Indeed, his own analysis of his role is quite accurate: "I thought at the time," Alsop has written, "and Wallace has since told me that I thought correctly, that my vehement plea served to crystallize the vice-president's decision."[58]

In the end, Wallace's "decision" was really a nondecision. He simply let Alsop report what he wanted in the vice president's name. Alsop even wrote Wallace's report for him. "I typed out the message to the President, Wallace signed it, and I filed it," he claimed.[59]

Not surprisingly, Wallace's report contained nearly all the recommendations for which Chennault and the Nationalists had pressed. First, it recommended that Stilwell be replaced by General Albert Wedemeyer. Stilwell did not enjoy the generalissimo's confidence, the report said, because of his "inability to grasp overall political considerations." Hence he should be replaced by Wedemeyer, who had been "strongly recommended" and was "persona grata" with the Chinese.[60] Wallace also asked Roosevelt to send a "personal representative" to China to act as a liaison between Roosevelt and Chiang. Such a representative would serve to smooth over the delicate "politico-military situation" in China.

In the end, then, Wallace's mission was a complete victory for those opposing Stilwell. The vice president had come to China ignorant and absorbed the opinions of his old friend Alsop. In fact, Wallace never even met with Stilwell before advocating his recall. After his meetings with Chennault and Alsop, the vice president decided it was unnecessary.[61]

By the time Wallace's report reached Washington, however, the China theater was in the midst of a crisis and Roosevelt had no time to consider changing his commander. As Stilwell had predicted at TRIDENT, Chennault's air offensive of 1943 had goaded the Japanese to attack. The launch of operation *ICHIGO* in the spring of 1944 soon placed the Chinese in grave peril and, though Stilwell agreed to shift even more supplies to Chennault, the airman's counteroffensive was ineffective. *ICHIGO* shook Roosevelt's faith in his pro-Chiang advisers enough to allow him to approve a War Department plan to place Stilwell in operational command of all Chinese troops.

Chiang was furious. He thought Stilwell was behind the American initiative, but could not bluntly reject it. Instead, the generalissimo stalled by cabling back that he intended to comply, but that he required a personal representative from Roosevelt to assist in the transition process. The president agreed and sent General Patrick Hurley.

Ironically, it was Stilwell's staunchest supporters, Marshall and Stimson, who originally recommended that Hurley be sent to China.[62] Hurley, "one of the wildest presidential envoys ever to enter a Foreign Service nightmare," has been described generously as an "ebullient and colorful character . . . not always long on tact," and less so as "the tragedy of a mind groping desperately at problems beyond its scope," and "senile."[63] The Oklahoman Hurley brought to East Asia a dynamic personality full of back-slaps and Indian war cries. He also brought what appears to have been a prerequisite for special emissaries—an encyclopedic ignorance of China's culture, history, and political situation. Hurley continually referred to Chiang as "Mr. Shek" and pronounced Mao's name "Moose Dung" with no sign he realized his errors.[64] A Republican, and thus good for bipartisan support, Hurley had undertaken other missions for

Roosevelt. Previous assignments as Roosevelt's minister to New Zealand and representative in the Middle East had inspired the president's trust and support. Hurley had first traveled to China in 1943 to arrange Chiang's travel to the Cairo Conference and the following year Roosevelt chose him as his special representative to the turbulent China theater.[65]

Hurley arrived in Chungking on 6 September 1944 and was greeted warmly. Chiang saw in Hurley his last chance to rid himself of Stilwell. He "cherished" Hurley and "flattered the American until he forgot his mission," American observers noted. Like every emissary before him, Hurley was treated royally by the Nationalists, who made sure he had minimal contact with those critical of Chiang. He was inundated by pro-Chiang propaganda and deliberately shielded from the American press, many of whom were critical of the Nationalist regime.[66] The treatment worked as well with Hurley as it had with those before him. After only a short time in Chungking he became a strong supporter of Chiang and began to consider himself the "counsel for the defense" in the case of Stilwell versus Chiang.[67]

As a result of his new-found allegiance, Hurley shifted the focus of his mission away from Roosevelt's instructions to "promote harmonious relations between General Chiang and General Stilwell and to facilitate the latter's exercise of command over Chinese armies."[68] Supporting Chiang became the cornerstone of Hurley's policy and all other considerations, including Stilwell, became secondary at best. In November 1944 Hurley told treasury officials in China that his directive was to "maintain the present government and work through the Generalissimo." Later, he was to tell Stimson that he was under direct orders to uphold Chiang.[69] Since there is no indication that Roosevelt explicitly changed Hurley's initial orders, it seems clear that this modification of American policy took place in Hurley's mind and developed as his relationship with Chiang improved.[70]

Chiang, with Hurley's support, immediately demanded that he be given personal control of all Lend-Lease supplies as a condition for placing Stilwell in command. This, of course, would have rendered Stilwell powerless. While negotiations continued, the military situation in East China worsened. Chiang demanded that Chinese troops engaged in Stilwell's successful offensive in Burma be transferred to China to stop the Japanese. He refused, though, to move inactive troops in China being used to blockade the Communists. Stilwell warned Marshall that the theater was in dire straits.

That warning reached Marshall and Roosevelt at the OCTAGON conference in Quebec. Marshall and his staff quickly prepared a sharp message to Chiang demanding he give Stilwell command immediately. Roosevelt, out of touch with his pro-Chinese advisers and in ill health, approved it, and this important message was sent on 16 September 1944. Stilwell delivered it on the nineteenth while Chiang was in conference with Hurley. The cable infuriated Chiang, and from that point forward even the facade of compromise was discarded by the generalissimo. He became adamant that Stilwell be recalled.

In the subsequent choice between Chiang and Stilwell, Hurley chose Chiang. He had come to believe that Stilwell was actively working to depose the generalissimo.[71] Taking his lead from Chiang, Hurley believed Stilwell had commissioned Roosevelt's demands of the sixteenth.[72] He also thought Stilwell had gone behind his back to Washington and undercut his authority. By this time Hurley "had secretly taken it upon himself to work with Chiang in ridding the generalissimo of the tiresome American general," Schaller argues.[73]

On 10 October Chiang sent a message to Roosevelt via Hurley in which he repeated his demand that Stilwell be sent home. Hurley also appended his own commentary calling for Stilwell's recall. He wrote,

There is no Chinese leader available who offers as good a basis of cooperation with you as Chiang Kai-shek. There is no other Chinese known to me who possesses as many of the elements of leadership as Chiang Kai-shek. Chiang Kai-shek and Stilwell are fundamentally incompatible. . . . There is no other issue between you and Chiang Kai-shek.[74]

This seems to have tipped the scales against Stilwell. The president accepted Hurley's opinions as fact. "Stilwell's protests, that Chiang's 'personal differences' were excuses to avoid fighting, were overwhelmed by reports from General Hurley," noted Roosevelt's son Elliott.[75] What was "true" according to Hurley and Chiang became accepted as such by the president. Consequently, he ordered Stilwell recalled.

After this, from Stilwell's recall until the Japanese surrender, the role of China in American military planning became nonexistent. General Albert Wedemeyer, Stilwell's replacement, labored mainly to smooth over relations with Chiang and institute new procedures for staff cooperation.

China remained important diplomatically, however. Following the Yalta conference, both Hurley and Wedemeyer returned to Washington for consultation. In Hurley's absence the staff of the American embassy prepared a telegram which argued that Hurley had forfeited any chance of compromise in China by refusing to deal with the Communists in good faith. These officials, silenced by Hurley while he was in China, insisted in his absence that Hurley and Wedemeyer's unflinching support for the Nationalists would inevitably lead to civil war. Hurley was furious when he heard of the cable and vowed to revenge himself on his staff. From this point on, the ambassador gave up any hope of compromise in favor of securing Chiang's position against those opposed to him.

In August the Japanese surrendered; by November Hurley had resigned as ambassador, blaming his "disloyal" subordinates for his failure to achieve harmony in China. With Hurley's resignation, wartime relations between America and China ended and postwar relations began. In the years to come, American troops would be committed to aid the Nationalists, and George Marshall would be sent in yet another attempt to avert a civil war. Marshall failed. And by 1949 Chungking had fallen to the Communists and Chiang had fled to Taiwan. Years of recrimination followed as endless debates over who had "lost" China plagued the American polity.

In light of the above history of CBI, it seems fair to say that American policy in China during World War II was a failure. Perhaps the best way to illustrate this is by comparing policy makers' hopes with the reality of CBI. At the outset of the war America had two primary goals for the China theater, one military and one political. Militarily, America sought to keep the Chinese in the war and, eventually, to use bases in China for the final assault on Japan. Politically, American policy makers envisioned a postwar order in which China would emerge as the preeminent power in Asia, thus serving as a check on the future ambitions of Japan.[76]

While the first aspect of America's military plan did prove successful, the second did not. Through cooperating with the Nationalists and supplying them with millions of dollars of American military and financial aid, America was able to keep the Chinese from negotiating a separate peace with Japan. The strategic result of this was that Japanese troops which might have been used against the Americans in the South Pacific were tied down occupying and, to a lesser extent, fighting in China.

The second aspect of the American strategic plan was not a success, however. There were few military gains in the theater and none that can be said to be strategically significant. Chennault's air war did a fair amount of damage to Japanese shipping in 1943, and in 1944 Burma was recaptured. The fact that the Japanese were quickly able to destroy the bases of the Fourteenth Air Force in Operation *ICHIGO*, however, is testimony to the failure of the Allies to make any real changes in the military situation in China. As a matter of fact, at the same time the Japanese were losing ground everywhere else, they were able to move virtually at will through eastern and central China. In the end, it proved impossible for the Americans and the Nationalists to regain any of the ground lost to the Japanese and this, combined with American success in the South Pacific, forced American military leaders to abandon earlier hopes of using China as a staging area for the assault against Japan.

American hopes for a strong postwar China also proved impossible to realize. The cornerstone of Roosevelt's vision for a postwar world was his belief that stability would rest not so much on the cooperation of all nations but on a few large nations acting as "sheriffs" to maintain world order. Roosevelt hoped that the United States, Britain, China, and the Soviet Union would work together as "four policemen," quarantining renegade nations in order to keep the peace.[77] Such a vision required two things with regard to China: first, China would have to be unified under one leader interested in cooperating with the United States, and second, it would have to emerge from the war a great power.

Neither of these things came to pass. Although Roosevelt continually sought to unify China by giving ever more American support to the Nationalists, Chiang's inability to compromise with the Communists—and vice versa—precluded any type of coalition government under the generalissimo. If there ever was any hope for a unified coalition government in China, the rising tensions of the war years stifled any possibility of Chiang and Mao coming to terms. Moreover, America's unqualified support of Chiang allowed him to harden his negotiating position in the belief that the United States would continue to support him no matter what. In the end, the ongoing civil war prevented China from emerging from the war united, let alone the dominant power in Asia.

The American policy seems a failure in retrospect as well. While it would be unrealistic to argue that the United States should have jettisoned the corrupt Nationalist regime and allied itself with the Communists, it is reasonable to question whether unqualified American support for Chiang was the most wise policy. In the first place, total support was probably detrimental to the Nationalist regime because American largesse encouraged corruption within the Kuomintang. The currency stabilization loans, for example, were immediately snapped up by inside speculators, thereby alienating many Chinese as well as influential members of the American press and military. One could also argue that absolute support for Chiang diminished any chance of him agreeing to meaningful power-sharing with the Communists. Chiang's stance toward negotiations hardened noticeably once he realized that he had Hurley in his pocket. Finally, America's unswerving support of the Nationalists destroyed any hope of amicable relations between the United States and the Chinese Communists.

Whether a different path would have produced better results is open to debate, but it is clear that the results of American policy were disastrous.

By 1949 Chiang had lost control of the mainland and any hope of civility with Mao's regime was lost. It is impossible to know what might have happened had America not followed the path it did. Perhaps things would have ended up the same. The point, however, is that by completely supporting Chiang the United States foreclosed any other options.

The short-term reasons for America's failure can be broken down into four general categories. First of all, CBI was, at all times, more of a political theater than a military one. While it would be unwise to draw too hard or fast a line between "military" and "political," it is fair to say that in CBI political considerations were given superior consideration from the start. To begin with, the command structure of CBI was far too convoluted for an effective military command. Those in the theater joked that in order to understand the command structure of CBI one needed a crystal ball and a copy of *Alice in Wonderland*; while Louis Mountbatten, commander of the Southeast Asia Theater, commented that "only the trinity" could fulfill Stilwell's duties and be in Delhi, Chungking, and Burma simultaneously.[78] CBI was a multilateral command with few resources allocated to it, the British and Chinese had fundamentally opposite goals and cordially hated one another, and America had few men to spare for the theater. In their history of CBI, Stilwell's staff realized well the nature of their theater. "The scene was dramatically set," they wrote, "for recriminations, differences of opinion, strategic deadlocks, inflammatory displays of diplomatic oratory, concessions, appeasement, bargains, and—in a small way—military battle."[79]

As the war progressed, any role the theater might have played militarily was obviated by a series of decisions on grand strategy. First, the Allies decided to defeat Hitler first, thus lowering the priority of the entire Pacific theater. Later, decisions to adopt an island-hopping strategy confirmed the lack of support of CBI and drew off precious supplies. Finally, China became superfluous with the capture of Guam and Saipan in July 1944. The United States could now launch bombing raids against Japan without having to capture bases in China. All of these combined to make the China theater more political than military.[80]

Roosevelt, the final arbiter on American policy decisions, clearly recognized the political nature of the theater. By the middle of 1943 he was openly speaking of the "importance of political and personal considerations in planning action in China." The president also told Stilwell that the fight in China was a "political fight."[81] CBI was thus thrown open to a degree of political intrigue that did not exist elsewhere. Certainly, there was politics everywhere, but nowhere did it achieve primacy over strategic considerations as it did in CBI. Roosevelt had written China off as a military theater. Thus it became an arena in which the Nationalists and their supporters tried to get him to make political decisions in their favor.

CBI was the victim of domestic political considerations as well. Roosevelt was very concerned that the American public not hold him responsible for the "collapse" of China. Thus public opinion, generally favorable to Chiang, came to play a role in his decisions.[82] By 1944 this element had grown in importance because of Roosevelt's reelection campaign. "All through 1944," historian Robert Dallek contends, "Roosevelt had tried to assure no foreign policy issue would undercut his reelection campaign." The president needed to attract independent voters and internationalist Republicans. "Losing" China by incurring Chiang's wrath would have made this impossible. Roosevelt was anxious to keep things as quiet as possible, especially during the recall crisis. The "quietest" option was to support Chiang because Stilwell could be—and was—silenced.[83]

A second short-term cause of America's failure was the way in which Roosevelt went about making policy. Enough has been written about Roosevelt's chaotic leadership style that it is unnecessary to elaborate upon it here. Suffice it to say that this style also pervaded his foreign policy, where he relied intensely upon trusted individuals and extra-bureaucratic channels for advice. His administration simply did not have an apparatus for making foreign policy. Policy making was reserved for Roosevelt alone. Those in the Departments of State and War frequently could only proffer advice in the hope that he would accept it. Often, though, he disregarded their opinions in favor of outside sources. Schaller argues that "policies of importance in all fields [were] frequently conceived and carried out by individuals and groups outside the regular bureaucratic structure, or by regular bureaucrats acting outside their official capacities."[84] Nowhere was this style more prevalent than in Roosevelt's formulation of China policy. He continually disregarded official advisers in the State and War Departments in favor of friends, relatives, friends of friends, and personal emissaries.

A third short-term cause was personalities. Stilwell, for example, did not get his nickname of "Vinegar Joe" for nothing. He was a fine leader of troops but never a diplomat. In a theater where political and diplomatic considerations quickly became paramount, Stilwell was ill equipped to succeed. Chennault, while more capable as a politician, shared Stilwell's knack for making enduring enemies. And, while both brought out almost fanatical loyalty among those who served under them, they had very different leadership styles: Chennault the renegade was a stark contrast to Stilwell, a soldier's soldier. When you added the unpredictable Hurley, Alsop, and others to this mix the result was predictably explosive. And yet it was not all about personal conflicts. "Given what Stilwell had to cope with," journalist Jack Fischer later wrote, "if Saint Francis of Assisi had been put in charge of the China-Burma-India theater he would now be known as Vinegar Frank."[85]

The situation in China was the final factor in America's failure. On the most fundamental level, American and Chinese wartime aims were diametrically opposed. Granted, both sides wanted to defeat Japan, but this was about as far as agreement went. The Nationalists knew that the Japanese were only the first enemy they would have to defeat to reunify their country. Therefore they had to plan a war effort which would allow them to expel the Japanese, destroy the Chinese Communists, and have resources left over to govern China when it was all over. The solution they came up with makes quite a bit of sense when looked at from their perspective. They felt that they had been fighting the Japanese for ten years by the time America entered the war and that they were due some rest. The Kuomintang wanted to let America take care of the first of their enemies, the Japanese. The Nationalists would then stockpile American aid in order to accomplish the second two. This is why they favored air power—not because they thought it would actually succeed in driving out the Japanese, but because it offered a way they could maintain good relations with the United States while at the same time protecting their own forces.

This is also the reason that Stilwell's plan to reorganize the Chinese Army on a "professional" model was so terrifying to Chiang and his supporters. Kuomintang power was based on Chiang's ability to maintain the loyalty of his generals, each of whom had nearly complete control over his troops. In a sense the relationship between the generals and the central government was almost feudal. Any move to make the army anything but this collection of private armies—even if it improved their fighting capabilities—would be utterly unacceptable to the generals and, therefore, to Chiang.

These, then, are four specific short-term reasons for the lack of success in CBI: the politicization of the theater, the highly personalized style of Roosevelt, conflicting personalities, and China's domestic situation. There are, however, broader issues to consider. For, in many ways, American policies and assumptions in its relationship with China during the war had their roots in the prewar era as far back as the nineteenth century.

The first theme that runs through American-Chinese relations is duality. Many Americans cared a great deal about China while at the same time knowing very little about it. This interest/ignorance duality was particularly evident during the war. Almost all of the individuals making policy for

CBI were intensely interested in the fate of China beyond simply allying with China to defeat Japan. "At Washington I had found the extraordinary significance of China in American minds, even at the top, strangely disproportionate," Churchill noted at the time.[86] Such an emphasis was rooted in the mid-nineteenth and early twentieth centuries, when China was seen as both the next great market for American manufactured goods and the next great Christian nation. As a result of their hopes for China Americans came to care very deeply about her fate. China came to occupy "a special place in a great many American minds," Harold Isaacs argues. It was "oddly familiar, full of sharp images and associations, and uniquely capable of arousing intense emotion."[87]

Stimson, Stilwell, and Alsop all had fascinations with China that predated the war. In this they reflected the concern of the American public. A Roper poll of July 1938 showed that Americans were more concerned over Japan's aggression in China than over Germany's seizure of Austria or events in Spain and Russia.[88] As the war progressed, organizations like United China Relief and the American Bureau for Medical Aid to China were very successful in raising money for Chinese relief efforts. Even Hollywood came out to help United China Relief when Madame Chiang toured the country in 1943. This theme was most clearly manifested, however, in Roosevelt's attempts to make China into a great power. Roosevelt and his advisers all shared a sense of what Michael Hunt has referred to as the "special relationship" between America and China.[89] Americans in general, and the Americans involved in China in particular, had an interest in China that extended beyond the common interest of defeating Japan.

And yet, all in all, Americans were ignorant of China. In fact, even after the outbreak of the war, most Americans could not locate China on a world map. Even a faithful reader of the *New York Times*, upon discovering that newsman Henry Lieberman had returned from China, responded, "Oh, isn't that nice. Did you drive?"[90] This general level of ignorance was apparent even in policy makers during the war. Stilwell was certainly the Army's leading expert on China, but he might also have been its only one. And even his knowledge of the country, its history, and its culture was fairly limited. The emissaries who paraded through CBI certainly had even less knowledge about the situation in China.

Even Roosevelt, who considered himself an old "China hand" because of Delano business interests in China, possessed little knowledge of what China was actually like during the war. Roosevelt's subsequent view of Chiang and the Kuomintang arose, not from observations or a close study of the situation, but out of his "policy" of making China a great power—a policy decisively influenced by his interest in and ignorance of China. He, in effect, stood policy making on its head, using a policy to formulate his vision of reality instead of devising a policy based on reality. The president's policy toward China was "rooted not so much in what existed as what should be," complained Davies.[91] He never made a concerted effort to discover what was really happening in China, preferring instead to make ad hoc decisions on the basis of his preconceptions. Thus American policy in CBI came to reflect the traditional interest/ignorance duality that had influenced American thinking on China for at least a hundred years.

A second general theme is that of amateurism. American China policy has always been characterized by a certain level of amateurism. In the nineteenth century American "diplomats" were generally drawn from the ranks of the American business or missionary communities in China.[92] While the State Department had changed by World War II, the amateurism with regard to China continued. It is significant that, despite the importance of political considerations in the theater, none of the career diplomats in the Far Eastern Section of the State Department played a major role in formulating policy for CBI. The American ambassador in Chungking, Clarence Gauss, was overshadowed first by the military and then by Roosevelt's personal emissaries who flew in for a couple of weeks, tried to do his job, failed, and then flew off. Gauss' superior in Washington, Stanley Hornbeck, also had little influence on China policy. The other foreign service officers in China, Gauss' junior officers, were sympathetic to Stilwell and suffered greatly when his protection was removed. Instead, the people who had real influence on American policy in CBI were men like Alsop, a journalist; Chennault, a brigadier general; and Currie, an economist.

Finally, there is the continuing importance of ideological/moral considerations in American opinions regarding China. Indeed, nearly everyone involved in CBI looked at China through a moral lens. For the minority, like Stilwell, it was a lens that magnified corruption and impurity in the Kuomintang leadership and made them unworthy of American support. For the majority, however, it was a lens shaped fundamentally by what James Reed has called the "missionary mind," a mindset with regard to China which focuses not on what it is but on what China might become.[93] Like the missionaries who sought to convert China in the late nineteenth century, supporters of Chiang during the war saw realized in him the myths of a Christian and Democratic China. Support for the Nationalists, then, was not simply a matter of prudent policy, but a moral necessity. The Kuomintang, led by nominally Christian and generally westernized men and women, were worthy of support because they were the hope of China. Through them the Chinese people would be redeemed, enfranchised, and merchandised. Alsop and Currie both saw the Kuomintang in this light. Roosevelt, too, succumbed to the temptation to see China as potentiality rather than reality. It led him to believe that China could become the fourth policeman. Even Stilwell, in his plans to recast the Chinese Army, fell victim to the temptation to see China as what he hoped it could be rather than what it was.

Policies based on such a distorted view could only fail. Chiang was not the George Washington or Abraham Lincoln of China and building him up as such meant that he could only disappoint in the end. No Chinese leader—and probably no human being—could have been all that Chiang's supporters made him out to be. In the end, the American failure in China during World War II was not caused by choosing the wrong strategy. It was not caused by the collisions of prickly personalities. And it was not caused by the often inexplicable policies of Franklin Roosevelt. The roots of America's failure in China during this period lie in the very nature of traditional American policy toward China, with its intensity, ignorance, amateurism, and moralism.

NOTES

1. It should be noted, however, that historians do not agree about the precise nature of America's failure. For example, Anthony Kubek argues that America failed by not supporting Chiang Kai-shek strongly enough, while Michael Schaller contends that America erred in not exploring the possibility of developing ties with the Chinese Communists.

2. Tang Tsou, in his book, *America's Failure in China, 1941–1950* (Chicago: University of Chicago Press, 1963), also discusses the American failure in light of long-term themes. His argument deals principally with the tradition of the open door, however.

3. Herbert Feis, *The China Tangle* (Princeton, N.J.: Princeton University Press, 1953); Charles F. Romanus and Riley Sunderland, *Stilwell's Mission to China*, United States Army in World War II (Washington, D.C.: U.S. Army Center of Military History, 1953); Romanus and Sunderland, *Stilwell's Command Problems*, United States Army in World War II (Washington, D.C.: U.S. Army Center of Military History, 1956); Romanus and Sunderland, *Time Runs Out In CBI*, United States Army in World War II (Washington, D.C.: U.S. Army Center of Military History, 1959).

4. Anthony Kubek, *How the Far East Was Lost* (New York: Twin Circle, 1972); Barbara Tuchman, *Stilwell and the American Experience in China, 1911–1945* (New York: Macmillan, 1970); Michael Schaller, *The U.S. Crusade in China, 1938–1945* (New York: Columbia University Press, 1979).

5. Sterling Seagrave, *The Soong Dynasty* (New York: Harper and Row, 1985), p. 359.

6. Jack Samson, *Chennault* (New York: Doubleday, 1987), pp. 5, 14.

7. Romanus and Sunderland, *Stilwell's Mission*, p. 10; Schaller, *Crusade*, p. 69; John Paton Davies, *Dragon by the Tail* (New York: Norton, 1972), p. 232.

8. Samson, *Chennault*, p. 13; Robert Sherwood, *Roosevelt and Hopkins* (New York: Harper and Brothers, 1948), p. 661; Memo of Conversation between Soong and Stanley Hornbeck, 28 Sep 43, box 103, Stanley K. Hornbeck Papers, Hoover Institution Archives, Stanford, California; Davies, *Dragon*, p. 232; Tuchman, *Stilwell*, p. 371.

9. Theodore White, *In Search of History* (New York: Harper and Row, 1978), p. 147; Tuchman, *Stilwell*, p. 335.

10. Eric Larrabee, *Commander in Chief: Franklin Delano Roosevelt, His Lieutenants, and Their War* (New York: Harper and Row, 1987), pp. 513–15; *Current Biography, 1942*, pp. 808–09.

11. What was true for his troops was also true for American lend-lease equipment. Gilbert Stuart, an Australian commissioned in the Chinese Army, verifies American accusations of Chiang's hoarding of American supplies. "They were accused of stowing it away in warehouses—which was true. We were very sure that directly after the war we would have a civil war on our hands," he said. Gilbert Stuart, transcription of tape-recorded autobiography, reel 24, p. 44, Gilbert Stuart Papers, Hoover Institution Archives.

12. Stuart, who was in Burma with the 5th Chinese Army, reports that "General Chiang Kai-shek had briefed his commanders in the field and General Tu [Li-ming] took his orders from the generalissimo in Chungking regardless of what Stilwell or anyone else suggested. . . . Stilwell was in the field more as a token of good will and a representative of lend-lease." Transcription of autobiography, reel 19, p. 28, Stuart Papers.

13. Claire Chennault, *Way of a Fighter* (New York: Putnam's Sons, 1949), p. 204.

14. Ibid., p. 309; "Stilwell's Bludgeon," *Washington Daily News*, 25 Mar 48.

15. *Current Biography*, 1941, p. 192.

16. "Group Meeting," 12 May 41, *Morgenthau Diary*, vol. 1 (Washington, D.C.: Government Printing Office, 1965), pp. 410–11.

17. Schaller, *Crusade*, pp. 109–10.

18. "Tentative Draft of Instructions to Lauchlin Currie," box 5, Currie Papers, Hoover Institution Archives. Initialed "OK, FDR."

19. "Report on Visit to China," 12 Aug 42, box 4, Currie Papers.
20. Ibid.
21. Currie to Madame Chiang, 26 May 42, box 1, Currie Papers.
22. Romanus and Sunderland, *Stilwell's Mission*, p. 252; Tuchman, *Stilwell*, p. 335.
23. Chennault, *Fighter*, pp. 112–13.
24. Notes on meeting with Chiang, Feb 43, box 38, Henry Arnold Papers, Library of Congress Manuscript Division, Washington, D.C.; Romanus and Sunderland, *Stilwell's Mission*, pp. 278–80.
25. Black and White Books, 18 Apr 43, box 18, and Memorandum, Stilwell for Roosevelt, 1 May 43, Career file, box 28a, Stilwell Papers, Hoover Institution.
26. Jonathan Seth Nichols, "Joseph Alsop and American Globalism" (AB thesis, Harvard College, 1987), pp. 4–7.
27. Soong to Alsop, 30 Nov 40, box 2, Alsop Papers, Library of Congress Manuscript Division; Schaller, Crusade, p. 71.
28. Schaller, *Crusade*, p. 76; Nichols, "Alsop," p. 18.
29. AVG files, box 13, Chennault Papers; copy of Chennault letter in Ludwik Rajchman [CDS] to Currie, 7 Oct 41, box 2, Currie Papers.
30. Cable, Soong to Alsop, 14 Nov 41, box 2, Chennault Papers.
31. Larrabee, *Commander*, p. 26; Sherwood, *Roosevelt and Hopkins* (New York: Harper and Brothers, 1948), p. 408; Romanus and Sunderland, *Stilwell's Command*, p. 385. For a contemporaneous profile of Hopkins' influence, see Clark Beach, "Harry Hopkins—The President's Right Hand," *Washington Post*, 20 Apr 41.
32. "Hopkins Files (RS notes)," box 122, Herbert Feis Papers, Library of Congress Manuscript Division; Personal Information, box 64, Alsop Papers. Sunderland apparently considered Alsop's Lend-Lease appointment a blind, though it is unclear who he believed set it up. See "Hopkins Files (RS notes)." Currie, too, seemed to realize the potentially subversive nature of Alsop's appointment and tried to distance himself from it in communications with State Department officials opposed to Chiang. He wrote John Davies: "The story back of [Alsop's] appointment to succeed Frank Ray is Harry Hopkins. You might just let this be known if you find I am being given the credit." Currie to Davies, 26 Nov 42, box 1, Currie Papers.
33. Joseph Alsop, "We Opened the Door for the Communists," *Saturday Evening Post*, 14 Jan 50, p. 26.
34. Frank Dorn, "After the Flag is Lowered," p. 572, TMs, Dorn Papers, Hoover Institution; Tuchman, *Stilwell*, p. 370. Dorn captures the opinion of the theater command in his description of Alsop: "He was a sort of gift bearing tooth fairy, winging his way in person or by letter between Roosevelt and Chennault with the magic wand of statements based on nothing more than opinionated superficiality and conceit."
35. Alsop to Hopkins, 1 Mar 43, box 64, Alsop Papers.
36. Alsop to Hopkins, 26 Mar 43 and Alsop to Soong, 12 Jul 43, box 64, Alsop Papers. It seems ironic that Alsop should complain so bitterly of Stilwell's cronyism to the friend who had got him his job in Lend-Lease.
37. Memorandum, Conversation between Davies and Hopkins, 4 Sep 44, in Romanus and Sunderland, *Stilwell's Command*, p. 421.
38. Black and White Books, 18 Apr 43, box 18, Stilwell Papers; Schaller, *Crusade*, p. 136.
39. Soong to Roosevelt, 18 May 43, box 32, Soong Papers, Hoover Institution; Kubek, *Far East*, p. 207; Romanus and Sunderland, *Stilwell's Mission*, p. 283.
40. Memo, Conversation between Soong and Churchill; Churchill to Soong, 25 May 43, box 23, Soong Papers.
41. Telg, Soong to Chennault, 20 Apr 43, box 2, Soong Papers.
42. Chennault, *Fighter*, pp. 221–22.
43. Ibid., p. 220.

44. "History of the China-Burma-India Theater," box 1, Stilwell Papers, p. 159; Minutes of White House Meeting, 14 May 43, box 182, Arnold Papers.

45. Diary entries, 1 and 21 May 43, reel 8, Henry Stimson Papers, Yale University, New Haven, Conn.

46. Chennault, *Fighter*, pp. 224–26. In recounting his final meeting with Roosevelt, Chennault reports, "He asked me if I had everything I wanted from the conference."

47. Schaller, *Crusade*, p. 136; Service, *State Department Duty* (Berkeley: University of California Press, 1981), p. 58; "Report of Conversation with the President," 18 May 43, box 32, Soong Papers.

48. Chennault to Stilwell, "China-Burma-India Command File," folder 31, box 6, Stilwell Papers.

49. Radio, CHC 123, Stilwell to Marshall, 30 May 44; Radio, CFB 17207, Brig Gen Benjamin Ferris to Stilwell, 11 May 44, folder 124, box 11, Stilwell Papers.

50. Wallace's negotiations with Chiang were of only secondary importance to the president, however. It was more important for Roosevelt to get Wallace out of the country during the Democratic convention so that he could nominate Harry Truman as his running mate in 1944. Wallace, though liked personally by the president, was opposed by more conservative members of the Democratic Party. To appease them it seems that Roosevelt sent Wallace as far away as possible. See Schaller, *Crusade*, p. 160.

51. Alsop had officially joined Chennault's command as a lieutenant in February 1944 after six months of effort. Stilwell initially refused to grant him the commission he wanted and relented only after seven months of badgering by Chennault and Alsop. Unfortunately, by this time the authority to commission civilians in the field had been restricted to the president and secretary of war. Since Alsop could hope for little from Stimson, he and Chennault went directly to Roosevelt, who ordered Alsop commissioned. See Schaller, *Crusade*, pp. 134–35; Larrabee, *Commander*, pp. 570–71; Romanus and Sunderland, *Stilwell's Command*, p. 374. For copies of their pleas to Roosevelt, see Chennault to Roosevelt, 27 Dec 43, Summary of letter, RS notes, box 122, Feis Papers; Chennault to Arnold, 28 Dec 43, box 10, Chennault Papers; Alsop to Soong [copy to Hopkins], 25 Sep 43, box 64, Alsop Papers.

52. Alsop testimony, U.S. Congress, Senate, *The Institute of Pacific Relations* (Washington, D.C.: Government Printing Office, 1951), p. 144; "Campaign at 14th A.F.," box 36, Stilwell Papers; Romanus and Sunderland, *Stilwell's Command*, p. 374.

53. Draft of radio, CHC 1200, Stilwell to Davies, 16 Jun 44, folder 120, box 11, Stilwell Papers.

54. Radio, CFB–18963, Ferris to Stilwell, 22 Jun 44, folder 121, box 11, Stilwell Papers; Davies to Stilwell, Jun 44, Stilwell numbered file 31, in Romanus and Sunderland, *Stilwell's Command*, p. 375.

55. Press release of Wallace's statement at IPR hearings, 9 Oct 51, box 80, Alsop Papers.

56. Wallace testimony, *Institute of Pacific Relations*, p. 1345; Alsop testimony, *Institute of Pacific Relations*, pp. 1444–45.

57. Ibid., p. 1445; Joseph Alsop, "The Strange Case of Louis Budenz," *The Atlantic Monthly* (April 1952): 31.

58. "Notes—U.S. Policy Toward China During World War II," 1951, box 65, Alsop Papers.

59. Alsop, "The Strange Case," p. 31; Joseph Alsop and Stewart Alsop, *The Reporter's Trade* (New York: Reynal and Co., 1958), p. 29; Tuchman, *Stilwell*, p. 465.

60. Wallace to Roosevelt, 28 June 1944, U.S. Department of State, *Foreign Relations of the United States: Diplomatic Papers, 1944*, (hereafter *FRUS*), vol. 6 (Washington, D.C.: Government Printing Office, 1966–1967), pp. 235–37. Alsop convinced Wallace to recommend Wedemeyer over Chennault, the vice president's initial choice, because he knew Marshall would never allow Chennault to command in China. See Gary May, *China*

Scapegoat: The Diplomatic Ordeal of John Carter Vincent (Washington, D.C.: New Republic Books, 1979), p. 106.

61. Davies, *Dragon*, p. 309; Romanus and Sunderland, *Stilwell's Command*, p. 376.

62. Diary entry, 3 Aug 44, Stimson Diary; Tuchman, *Stilwell*, p. 478; Romanus and Sunderland, *Stilwell's Command*, pp. 415–17.

63. Berry Rubin, *Secrets of State* (New York: Oxford University Press, 1985), p. 46; Albert C. Wedemeyer, *Wedemeyer Reports!* (New York: Henry Holt, 1958), p. 302; Theodore White and Annalee Jacoby, *Thunder Out of China* (New York: William Sloane, 1946), p. 246. At least three contemporary observers on both sides of the debate in China have specifically referred to Hurley as senile: Frank Dorn, "After the Flag is Lowered," p. 654, TMs, Dorn Papers; Wilbur J. Peterkin, "Dixie Mission Memoirs," p. 122, TMs, Peterkin Papers, Hoover Institution; Arthur N. Young, "An Oral History Interview with Dr. Arthur N. Young by James R. Fuchs," pp. 85–86, TMs, Harry S. Truman Presidential Library, Independence, Mo. (photocopy in Young Papers, Hoover Institution).

64. White and Jacoby, *Thunder*, p. 246; Russell D. Buhite, *Patrick J. Hurley and American Foreign Policy* (Ithaca, N.Y.: Cornell University Press, 1973), p. 246; Fred Eldridge, *Wrath in Burma* (New York: Doubleday, 1946), p. 302.

65. Romanus and Sunderland, *Stilwell's Command*, p. 415; Wedemeyer, *Wedemeyer*, p. 302; Testimony of Hurley, U.S. Congress, Senate, Committee on Foreign Relations, "Investigation of Far Eastern Policy," 1945, printer's copy, National Archives, Washington, D.C. (photocopy in Harvard University Library), pp. 102–07.

66. White and Jacoby, *Thunder*, p. 249; Eldridge, *Wrath*, p. 303.

67. "Facts Bearing on the Present Situation in China," Career file, box 28a, Stilwell Papers.

68. Copy of Hurley's instructions, Cordell Hull to Clarence Gauss, 22 Aug 44, vol. 6, *FRUS, 1944*, p. 251.

69. Harry Dexter White to Morgenthau, *Morgenthau Diary*, vol. 2, p. 1380; Diary entry, 8 Mar 45, Stimson Diaries.

70. John Stewart Service, *The Amerasia Papers: Some Problems in the History of U.S.-China Relations* (Berkeley, Calif.: University of California Press, 1971), p. 63.

71. Hurley later charged that the "record of General Stilwell in China is irrevocably coupled in history with the conspiracy to overthrow the Nationalist Government of China, and to set up in its place a Communist regime." As quoted in Lohbeck, *Hurley*, p. 305; Hurley Testimony, "Investigations of Far Eastern Policy," p. 47.

72. Romanus and Sunderland, *Stilwell's Command*, p. 447.

73. Schaller, *Crusade*, p. 170.

74. Hurley to Roosevelt, 10 Oct 44, vol. 6, *FRUS, 1944*, p. 170.

75. Elliott Roosevelt, *As He Saw It* (New York: Duell, Sloan, and Pearce, 1946), p. 148; Eldridge, *Wrath*, p. 303.

76. Tsou, *America's Failure*, p. 33.

77. John Lewis Gaddis, *The United States and the Origins of the Cold War* (New York: Columbia University Press, 1972), pp. 24–25.

78. White and Jacoby, *Thunder*, p. 149; Mountbatten quoted in Tuchman, *Stilwell*, p. 437.

79. "History of the China-Burma-India Theater," box 1, Stilwell Papers.

80. Koen, *The China Lobby in American Politics* (New York: Macmillan, 1960), p. 11; Romanus and Sunderland, *Stilwell's Command*, pp. 6–8; Larrabee, *Commander*, p. 553; Sherwood, *Roosevelt and Hopkins*, p. 809.

81. Minutes of White House meeting, 19 May 43, box 182, Arnold Papers; Stilwell quoted in Romanus and Sunderland, *Stilwell's Mission*, p. 324.

82. Memorandum, White House meeting, 14 May 43, box 182, Arnold Papers; Dallek, *Roosevelt*, p. 391.

83. Dallek, *Roosevelt*, pp. 481–82, 499; Sherwood, *Roosevelt and Hopkins*, pp. 822–25; Diary entry, 3 Nov 44, reel 9, Stimson Diaries. Stimson wrote in his diary: "At present we

are trying to keep [Stilwell] out of reach of all newspaper men and not give them an opportunity to catch and distort any runaway word just before Election."

84. Schaller, *Crusade*, p. 66. In addition to Schaller, the best recent works on Roosevelt's wartime policy are Larrabee, *Commander*, and Robert Dallek, *Franklin D. Roosevelt*. See also Rubin, *Secrets of State*, ch. 2. Most of the discussion of Roosevelt is derived from their work.

85. As quoted in Larrabee, *Commander*, p. 517.

86. As quoted in Tsou, *America's Failure*, p. 42.

87. Harold Isaacs, *Scratches on Our Minds: American Images of China and India* (New York: John Day Co., 1958), p. 66.

88. Isaacs, *Scratches*, p. 173.

89. Michael H. Hunt, *The Making of a Special Relationship: The United States and China to 1914* (New York: Columbia University Press, 1983), pp. 305–06.

90. Isaacs, *Scratches*, pp. 37, 47; Stephen R. MacKinnon and Oris Friesen, eds., *China Reporting: An Oral History of American Journalism in the 1930s and 1940s* (Berkeley: University of California Press, 1987), p. 170.

91. Davies, *Dragon*, p. 224.

92. See Hunt, *The Making of a Special Relationship*, for an extended discussion of this.

93. James Reed, *The Missionary Mind and American East Asian Policy, 1911–1915* (Cambridge, Mass.: Harvard University Press, 1983).

Army Advisers and Liaison Officers and the "Lessons" of America's Wartime Experience in China

Marc Gallicchio

When Dean Acheson became secretary of state in 1949, Chiang Kai-shek's Nationalist (Kuomintang) government was preparing to flee the mainland for the island of Taiwan. Chinese Communist armies were already advancing south of the Yangtze River and would soon reach the border of China and French Indochina. The Chinese Communist victory would give the Vietminh, a Communist-led coalition of anticolonial forces, sanctuary and a much needed source of supplies and technical advice in its struggle against the French. Worried by the implications of the Nationalists' defeat for anti-Communist forces elsewhere in Asia, Acheson cabled the following advice to the American consulate in Saigon: "Experience [of] China has shown [that] no amount [of] U.S. military aid can save [a] government . . . unless it can rally support [of its] people against Commies by affording representation [to] all important national groups manifesting devotion to national as opposed to personal or party interests." "Nationalists [in] China," Acheson explained, "came to present pass through [a] deficiency above qualities and [a] lack of [the] will to fight not because 'U.S. wrote it off.'"[1]

Acheson intended his message to be read as a warning to French colonial officials who thought they could thwart the Vietminh merely by creating a nominally independent colonial administration. But his synopsis of the failures of Chiang Kai-shek's regime also offered a preview of the main conclusions contained in the State Department's *U.S. Relations with China, 1938–1949*, published several months later. Known as the China White Paper, this narrative history with its supplemental documentary collection was the American government's first attempt to write an official history of its turbulent relationship with Chiang's regime. In highlighting Kuomintang corruption, resistance to American advice, military ineptitude, and factionalism, the White Paper placed the blame for the "loss of China" squarely on the Nationalists.

Although the White Paper sought to make clear the "lessons" of America's involvement with the Nationalist regime, Chiang's supporters in the Pentagon and Congress remained unconvinced that the United States had done all it could to aid its ally. The secretary was even less successful, however, in persuading his and subsequent presidents of the need to apply the lessons of China to the evolving American relationship with Vietnam. In the 1960s and 1970s, America's disastrous intervention in Vietnam refocused scholarly attention on the history of American contacts with East Asia. In particular, historians turned to studying America's earlier relations with China in an effort to find the roots of the United States' current predicament in Vietnam.[2] Like Acheson, they perceived a connection between America's experience in China and the Vietnam tragedy.

Among those tempted to make comparisons between the American role in China and the later intervention in Vietnam was Maj. Gen. Haydon Boatner, U.S. Army (retired). In December 1975 Boatner informed the librarians at the Hoover Institution on War, Revolution, and Peace in Stanford, California, that the recent defeat of the Republic of Vietnam convinced him that he should donate his personal papers to the institution's archives. During his thirty-year career Boatner spent nearly a decade in China, including four years as the chief of staff to the Chinese Army in India and chief of staff to the Chinese Combat Command. In both of these assignments he worked closely with Chinese officers and oversaw the operation of American liaison teams attached to Chinese forces. The general's papers contained a wealth of material of interest to military historians, most of which pertained to his experience in China in World War II. There was nothing, however, on Vietnam.

"I was not in the Viet Nam War, being retired in 1960 at age 60," Boatner admitted. "I don't pretend to know any details about that war." Nevertheless, he thought his papers would be useful to historians seeking the reasons for America's recent failure. "In retrospect, I believe some of [South Vietnam's defeat] might be due to the unbalanced literature and history on World War II on mainland Asia and also the Korean War." Specifically, Boatner believed that historians had failed to pay adequate attention to the methods employed by the Army in its successful collaboration with Chinese forces. The general regarded his wartime partnership with the Chinese as a model to be emulated and he blamed historians for the Army's failure to apply the lessons learned in China to the later experience in Vietnam.[3]

Few historians would quarrel with Boatner's suggestion that Americans and their Vietnamese allies never learned to work together. Most, however, would be surprised to learn that the general believed that

America's earlier military experience in China provided a model for successful cooperation between American and Asian soldiers. Historians, after all, are more accustomed to thinking of America's wartime relations with the Nationalist regime as a "failure" or at best a "tangle."[4] Following the pattern established in the China White Paper, traditional political and military histories of the wartime collaboration between China and the United States contain vivid descriptions of the incessant feuding between American leaders and Generalissimo Chiang Kai-shek. The overall impression is of a contentious partnership undermined by suspicion and intrigue. Boatner believed, however, that the Army's service in China could not be encompassed within a framework of high-level political and military interactions alone. What was needed was a more balanced appreciation of the American experience in China. Boatner wanted historians to shift their attention away from the wartime capital of Chungking and move out into the field where American Army officers and their Chinese counterparts worked on a daily basis to create a modern military force.

One need not accept uncritically Boatner's view of the Sino-American relationship to recognize that historians have much to gain by studying the conduct and perceptions of Army officers as they acted as liaisons and advisers to the Chinese. In their capacity as facilitators of Sino-American cooperation these officers necessarily became interpreters of Chinese military and civil customs for the several thousand American officers and enlisted men who came to the China theater. As the Army's "China hands," explained China to their colleagues, they simultaneously experimented with different ways to fulfill their mission. By the end of the war many of the Army's advisers believed that they had found the means by which China might be transformed into a unified and modernizing nation in the postwar era.

The U.S. Army's experience in China dates from the early 1900s, when the 15th Infantry regiment took up its station in Tientsin. Army officers also served as intelligence and language officers with the military attache's office for almost as long. During this period, American officers were mostly uninvolved observers of Chinese affairs. The Army's interest in China's military potential increased, however, after Japan's invasion in 1937. The Chinese resisted with only minimal outside aid for four years, but the United States enlarged its military role in China soon after Japan's attack on Pearl Harbor. In February 1942, as Japanese forces threatened to rout British and Chinese troops in Burma, the War Department sent a task force under Lt. Gen. Joseph Stilwell to China. Stilwell's directive made him the senior American commander in the newly formed China-Burma-India Theater and chief of staff to Generalissimo Chiang Kai-shek, the theater commander, and charged him with the task of improving the fighting efficiency of the Chinese Army. Army Chief of Staff General George C. Marshall chose his friend for this daunting task because of Stilwell's lengthy experience in China. Stilwell's China service included tours with the 15th Infantry and as an attache, during which time he became fluent in Chinese.[5]

Marshall hoped that Stilwell would be able to regroup Allied forces in Burma in time to halt the Japanese offensive. Instead the British and Chinese in Stilwell's words "took a hell of a beating" and retreated into India.[6] In the weeks after the fall of Burma, Stilwell moved between India and the Chinese capital of Chungking in an effort to create the basic organizations for rebuilding the Chinese Army. The first of these, the Chinese Army in India (CAI), was supervised by Brig. Gen. Haydon Boatner and located in Ramgarh, India. Boatner was a forty-year-old China hand who had moved from the 15th Infantry to the language school as an assistant attache in the late 1920s and early 1930s. During his six-year tour in China, Boatner had also found time to earn an M.A. in Chinese history.[7]

The second Training Center, under Brig. Gen. Frank Dorn, was located in Yunan Province in China. Like Boatner, Dorn was also a language student in China, having served as assistant attache to Stilwell in the late 1930s. A soldier-scholar, during the course of his military career Dorn produced the first syllabary of the Negritos dialect in the Philippines, wrote a monograph on the Negritos' life and customs, was offered a post as assistant professor of anthropology at the University of the Philippines, and published a novel based on his experiences with the tribe. He also published a cookbook of recipes collected during his travels in Asia. Dorn's appreciation of other cultures continued during his tour in China, where he developed an interest in Chinese art.[8]

In selecting Boatner and Dorn for these posts, Stilwell chose two officers who could be counted on to listen to the Chinese point of view and avoid bruising Chinese sensibilities while they undertook the task of constructing an Americanized Chinese Army. As Stilwell later explained to Chiang, "I know that [Boatner] is intensely interested in the Chinese troops and that he would do anything in his power for them. He is a very capable officer and was chosen for this position on this account and because of his sympathetic attitude towards the Chinese."[9]

From the outset, Boatner sought to build Chinese confidence and foster harmony between Americans and Chinese. As chief of staff to the CAI, he immediately decided to work with the existing Chinese staff system rather than adopt the standard American Army organization. To facilitate this process, Boatner enlisted his American subordinates in a crash course in Chinese. He also prepared a dictionary and phrase book that future liaison officers regarded as a valuable tool in communicating with their Chinese counterparts.[10] Several months later, in February 1943, Boatner could report: "We have completely broken the ice in reference to the distinction of two staffs. . . . We have a joint mess in operation, and all the American officers are assigned to specific Chinese staff branches."[11]

In building a functioning staff for the CAI, Boatner hoped that immersion in Chinese language and culture would make American officers more knowledgeable and respectful of their Chinese counterparts. His own experience had shown him how easily Americans could adopt an air of superiority toward the Chinese. During the retreat from Burma he threatened to court-martial an American lieutenant who refused supplies to a Chinese major. According to Boatner, the American was stunned. "Obviously it had never occurred to him that it was wrong for a U.S. lieutenant to lie to a Chinese major about official matters." In a second episode, Boatner dismissed and demoted a lieutenant colonel to captain because he objected to working with Chinese soldiers.[12]

With some practice, most American officers would learn to treat their Chinese colleagues with ritual politeness and courtesy by placing themselves in the other soldier's boots. The conformist nature of military service with its emphasis on measurable goal-oriented activities also encouraged a sense of shared purpose and perspective on the part of liaison officers and their counterparts. Boatner seemed to reflect this belief that the nature of military service reduced the cultural differences between the two peoples. "Be American," he told his officers, "but not too American, let the Chinese be Chinese, but not too Chinese."[13]

Learning to interact with Chinese officers, even at the professional level, was a significant challenge in itself, however, and some American officers learned the nuances of command relationships in the Chinese Army only through trial and error. According to the unofficial history of the CAI, the American instructors committed several errors that created problems once the army took to the field. The first of these was "the very great mistake of having American officers and enlisted men attempt to train Chinese enlisted men direct and not under the surveillance of their unit commanders. This was a tremendous loss of face to the Chinese officers and non-commissioned officers, and they did everything possible to block instruction." The unit history concluded that if the Americans involved the officers and passed information through them "much better instruction would have resulted, better feeling, and a better army."[14]

Although Boatner did not have direct control over training, he did exert greater influence over American-Chinese relations once the CAI began to move back into Burma in the fall of 1943. As chief of staff, Boatner oversaw the creation of special American liaison teams attached to Chinese units. These teams acted as advisers on tactical matters and provided special expertise on communications, supply, and medical problems. They also gave Boatner a reliable source of information on Chinese performance and overall compliance with orders. Before going into the field, however, the liaison officers received special training and instructions prepared by Boatner. As part of this "indoctrination" the liaison officers were constantly reminded that their duty was "liaison, not command." Officers were told to "Place yourself in the Chinese officer's situation—think how you would feel as a company or battalion commander, loyal and responsible to your own superior officer throughout many years of service, if a foreign officer assumed the right to give you direct orders."

"The most important feature of that training," Boatner recalled, was to "scrupulously respect the command authority, prestige, and dignity of the Chinese officer." Leaving nothing to chance, Boatner also made it clear that matters of face dictated that Americans were "never to get mad at Chinese officers in the presence of others." Eventually, as the teams gained field experience, Boatner assigned newer officers to the most successful teams to learn how to achieve their goals.[15]

When the Chinese 22d and 38th Divisions pushed off for Burma in the fall of 1943, General Stilwell could tell the Generalissimo that he kept his pledge to "stick as closely as possible to Chinese organization" and to "use American officers in command positions only when it was essential." "I am glad to say," Stilwell reported, "that in the divisions, as a result of thorough training it has been possible to use Chinese officers exclusively."[16]

In May 1944, several months after the CAI reentered Burma, a second, larger army, the Chinese Expeditionary Force, also known as the "Y" or "Yoke" Force, moved southwestward from Yunan province across the Salween River into Burma. Based in Kunming, Y Force began receiving American instruction in April of the previous year. Like Boatner, Dorn supervised the Americans assigned to the Y Force and made sure they understood the implications of their mission. To foster harmony, Dorn's staff prepared several memoranda on how to function smoothly with Chinese officers and enlisted men.

To officers reading these guidelines, the Chinese must have seemed a curious blend of the exotic and the familiar. Comparisons to American customs were frequent and references to the importance of preserving and saving face appeared throughout. As at Ramgarh, the Americans were asked to put themselves in the place of the Chinese officers who would be placing their units under the guidance of outsiders. To avoid friction, the

Americans were told to emulate the Chinese method of indirectness in communication and to avoid public displays of anger. Dorn also introduced American officers to the intricacies of Chinese etiquette on visits and other formal occasions, but here they were on more familiar ground given the U.S. Army's own attention to ceremony and custom. On this point the instructions sounded a reassuring note. "The most important thing to remember," the Americans were told, "is that if you live up to the standards of gentlemanly conduct, [with] which as an officer of the United States Army you are already familiar, you are certain to get along with your Chinese associates."[17]

Dorn's efforts to acquaint Americans with Chinese culture were designed to keep conflict to a minimum within Yoke Force, but there was probably little that he could do to soften the shock that the Americans experienced when they saw the wretched condition of the Chinese Army and the poor quality of its leadership.[18] Nevertheless, Dorn attempted to create a context for better understanding the deplorable condition of China's forces. Before anyone jumped to conclusions, they were asked to remember that the Chinese had been fighting for five and a half years against very heavy odds. Some of their practices may have seemed odd to Americans, but it was necessary to bear in mind that Chinese methods were probably "developed through experience during the long war period and adapted to the means at hand." Although Dorn and others lauded the courage and ingenuity of the average Chinese soldier, they nonetheless warned American officers that they could count on having disappointment and frustration as steady companions for much of their tour in China, especially since Chinese officers, particularly senior officers, were for the most part incompetent. Even here, however, Dorn asked the Americans to relate this information to their own experience. Most Chinese officers, he explained, held their posts through political influence, which was a practice not all that different from "our National Guard."[19]

As Dorn predicted, the plan to introduce American methods and instructors into the Yoke Force met with considerable resistance from the Chinese. According to a draft history of the program, some Chinese officers with other instructional backgrounds (Japanese, German, Russian, and Chinese) opposed any innovations that devalued their professional education. Others disliked foreign interference of any kind, and still others feared that their corruption might be uncovered.[20] American conduct also contributed to a sense of resentment among the Chinese. According to Eugene Wu, a Chinese interpreter for Y Force, the American officers ate in separate messes and interacted with the Chinese only on formal social occasions such as banquets. Wu also recalled how the Americans seemed unaware of the ill feeling created by their comparative material well-being. According to Wu, the American barracks were so well heated that the occupants wore undershirts and shorts to be comfortable, while Chinese officers shivered underneath three suits of clothing.[21]

Nevertheless, there is some evidence to indicate that Dorn's counseling of Y Force liaison officers made an impact. When illiterate Chinese soldiers showed up for instruction as artillery officers, the Americans did not send them back to their units for fear that the students would "lose face" with their comrades. Instead, the Americans gave them basic instruction which often qualified the students as noncommissioned officers.[22] It is less clear how well Dorn's guidelines helped the Americans deal with Chinese efforts to thwart significant reforms, but the unofficial chronicler of the program indicated that the Americans pursued an indirect course toward their objective. According to the draft history of the unit, little could be accomplished "until the active control had quietly been 'absorbed' by the Americans." But to "achieve this absorbing of authority without incurring ill will took time and care."[23]

The process of waiting out the Chinese was not without consequences, however. In March 1944, before the CEF joined the Burma campaign, Dorn polled some of his experienced officers to obtain their opinions of the Chinese armed forces. The results consisted of ten single-spaced pages of almost unrelieved criticism of the Chinese Army. Most of the seventeen respondents agreed with the officer who complained that "Many Chinese officers are absolutely incompetent to lead anything."[24]

None of this would have surprised Dorn and the men at his headquarters, but neither would the few positive themes sounded by the Americans have been unexpected. Most officers agreed with Dorn's earlier assessment of the abilities of the average Chinese soldier. The Americans commented favorably on the enlisted man's responsiveness to training, and they noted his doggedness and determination. The American officers' ability to see *any* possibility for real improvement testified to their self-confidence and to the high opinion most Americans had of the junior officers in the Chinese Army. Indeed, American references to the enthusiasm and discipline of Chinese junior officers appeared throughout the papers and reports of the Americans who served with the CAI and the CEF.[25] Americans found the contrast between the junior officers and their politically appointed superiors so stark that they placed much of their hope for the revitalization of the Chinese Army and even China itself on the patriotism exhibited by this cohort of young military professionals. "The officer that [*sic*] some day may make the Chinese Army into a real force," wrote Col. Reynolds Condon, "are those young officers who have been imbued with a sort of patriotism and who have not yet had all their initiative and desire to serve ground out of them by the deadening effect of example. We have found in the XX Group Army there is a considerable percentage of such officers up to the grade of Brig. General."[26]

As much as the Americans might have preferred to look ahead to better days, the present situation required their undivided attention. The real test of their efforts, they all knew, would take place in the field against Japanese troops. Here, despite the obvious grounds for pessimism, the results were mixed. Boatner's two divisions bogged down at first, but after some command problems were resolved, they began to push the Japanese back. In April Dorn's expeditionary force initially ignored American advice at a great cost in lives, but eventually began to advance with surprising results. Frequently Boatner's force closed with smaller Japanese units but permitted the enemy to escape. Nevertheless, the Chinese were at last beginning to retake ground and gain confidence in themselves. As one officer with the Y Force explained, the training periods were probably too short to be of much use, but the Americans did "gain valuable experience in dealing with the Chinese and made friends and acquaintances among them. This materially assisted the Americans when later they were sent on liaison detail."[27] By November Dorn was able to send a self-congratulatory report to Washington proclaiming that "the Y-Force staff discovered this year what they had long contended to be true: that the Chinese with training and modern equipment, can press an offensive—and win."[28]

Dorn issued his report shortly after Stilwell's recall from China, and he probably intended it to be read as a vindication of his chief's efforts in the theater. The circumstances surrounding Stilwell's recall have been ably told elsewhere, and we need not cover them here. For our purposes it is important to note, however, that although Stilwell's removal led to important changes in the American staff at the highest levels, including Dorn's recall, the system of liaison in the field remained relatively undisturbed. In large part this continuity is most readily explained by the decision of Stilwell's replacement, General Albert Wedemeyer, to assign Haydon Boatner as chief of staff to the newly formed Chinese Combat Command (CCC).

By keeping Boatner in the theater, Wedemeyer helped maintain some continuity in the American mission. Moreover, Wedemeyer's own programs tended to expand upon rather than depart from those established by his predecessor. At the heart of Wedemeyer's plan was the creation of thirty-six fully equipped American-trained divisions. Assigned to these "Alpha" divisions, as they were known, were teams of American liaison officers, all of whom served in Chinese Combat Command. Unlike the previous system of liaison, however, the Americans in the new teams had specific instructions for dealing with Chinese officers who consistently rejected American advice. All complaints would be sent up the chain of command, and if disagreements could not be resolved the liaison teams would be withdrawn and American supplies withheld from the offending Chinese unit.[29] The threat of cutting off supplies to uncooperative officers was always implicit in the earlier system, but Wedemeyer probably hoped that at least some disputes would be prevented by a forthright statement of policy. Wedemeyer's new instructions were also appreciated by those frustrated liaison officers who had come to believe that their Chinese counterparts looked upon them as supply officers rather than as advisers.[30] For their part, Chinese officials often resented what they perceived as American efforts to take charge of operations. Boatner took pains to remind Army officers that their role was to advise, but American control over Lend-Lease supplies blurred the lines of authority between the American liaison officers and the Chinese commanders. General Ho Ying-ching, Supreme Commander of the Chinese Army, called attention to this problem during an unprecedented press conference with foreign reporters. After Ho praised General Robert McClure, head of the Chinese Combat Command, by noting that the two men "had practically merged into one," he complained that "some Americans have misunderstood that every Chinese army unit with American officers participating is under the command of Americans. This is inaccurate information. The actual fact is that no matter whether the Chinese army units are supplied or trained by the Americans, or whether they have American advisors they are under the command of Chinese generals."[31]

The tensions that arose over command and control of Chinese units would persist for the remainder of the war, but Wedemeyer was able to ameliorate them somewhat by establishing a more cordial personal relationship with Chiang. It also seems clear that the Generalissimo became more cooperative as a result of the meeting of Soviet, American, and British leaders at Yalta in February 1945. The prospect of American reliance on Russian troops to hold down Japanese forces in China worried Chiang, as did the apparent shift in the internal balance of power toward his Communist enemies.

Japan's offensive in late 1944, code-named *ICHIGO*, severely weakened Nationalist forces, raised the specter of a Chinese collapse, and fueled skepticism about Chiang's ability to maintain power after the war. Thus although Chiang won the battle over Stilwell's recall, he was more willing to accept American advice once *ICHIGO* had run its course.[32]

In early 1945, while Wedemeyer was overhauling the Chinese Army and reequipping the Nationalist divisions, combined Chinese and British forces were continuing the reconquest of Burma. The sight of Chinese forces chasing the bedraggled Japanese out of the jungles proved an exhilarating experience even for the journalist Theodore White who by now had completely soured on the Nationalist regime. "Stilwell's training effort was now paying off," White recalled; "the thousands of Americans posted as liaison and training officers with Chinese troops, sleeping in hammocks in the jungle, in mud huts, in old Chinese temples, were now proud of the force they had created."[33]

Newsweek reporter Harold Isaacs also found evidence of swelling pride on the part of the Americans. "You can say anything you want about these people," declared one American, "but give me the infantry and give Colonel W. here the artillery and give us six months and we'll make an army that goes through Germany."[34] General Tojo Hideki, Japan's wartime premier, seemed to agree. "The Chinese Army in India," he observed, "is a highly trained crack army to which we should give our close attention." According to one assessment of the Burma campaign, by early spring the Japanese had suffered 72,000 men killed out of a force of approximately 100,000 men.[35]

In July of that year, Wedemeyer's forces began offensive operations in China. These were heady times. The Chinese "were fighting better each succeeding day" reported Wedemeyer's chief of staff, and they were "really enthusiastic about this business of attacking Japanese."[36] Wedemeyer was more restrained in his reports to Washington. He noted that the Japanese had been "cooperating" by withdrawing toward the coast, but he added that Sino-American cooperation was improving as was the combat effectiveness of the Chinese troops.[37] In order to build on this momentum, Wedemeyer requested additional American personnel to act as advisers to the American-trained and also the Chinese-sponsored divisions. The general also envisioned the use of American specialists to assist Chiang in reorganizing those government agencies most concerned with military affairs.[38] Confident that they had begun to transform China's Army, Wedemeyer's staff even produced a short-range plan for China's administrative and economic reorganization patterned after the liaison system. "Because the Government is more nearly a military dictatorship than a true democracy," read the report, "the same factors which have resulted in the strengthening of the Chinese army will accomplish the strengthening of the Chinese government."[39]

Thus, as the war ended, Wedemeyer and his staff had reached a verdict on the success of the training and liaison missions that would be echoed by Boatner thirty years later when he criticized historians for failing to instruct the next generation of military professionals in the lessons of the past. Following Japan's surrender, Wedemeyer's men thought well enough of their wartime role in China that they lobbied strenuously for the creation of a postwar military advisory group consisting of four thousand officers and enlisted men and modeled on the wartime liaison system. State Department critics led by John Carter Vincent, the head of the Office of Far Eastern Affairs, charged that the proposed advisory group would create a "de facto colonial army" in China. Vincent and others also feared that by providing assistance at the operational level the advisory mission would entangle the United States in China's growing civil conflicts. In early 1946 the State and War Departments finally compromised on a scaled-down mission of 900 officers and enlisted men who would be prohibited from offering operational advice or basic instruction to the Nationalists.[40]

In the years that followed, Wedemeyer and his supporters regularly advocated more military aid to the Nationalists.[41] In addition, they revised the course materials on China used at West Point and the National War College to comport with their view of Sino-American cooperation, and even prepared their own unpublished response to the State Department's White Paper on China.[42] The Army's critique of the White Paper contested the secretary of state's assertion that the United States had been unstinting in its support of Chiang's government and cataloged numerous instances, beginning with the military advisory group, in which recommendations for aid by the Joint Chiefs of Staff (JCS) were opposed or reduced by the State Department.[43]

In 1958 General Wedemeyer published his memoir, which among other things lamented that the United States had not followed through on "the success which even our limited effort had achieved during the war" in building up Chiang's forces. Wedemeyer maintained that the State Department's restrictions on the size of the postwar military advisory group and the prohibition against American officers accompanying Nationalist troops into the field deprived Chiang's men of crucial support against the Communists and undermined the Nationalists' ability to establish internal peace.[44] Taken together, these efforts can be seen as an informal attempt to write an alternative or dissenting history of the Army's China experience years before Boatner leveled his criticisms at historians.

It seems clear that for Army officers in China the success of Nationalist armies in the final months of the war encouraged a sense of guarded optimism about the postwar prospects for Chiang's government. Conversely, most foreign service officers and journalists serving in China at the end of the war saw little reason to hope that Chiang's regime could be revived without major political and economic reforms. Years later, historians writing in the aftermath of the Communist victory would echo the assessments of the civilian China watchers by ending their narratives of the American effort in China on a note of pessimism and foreboding.[45]

Most historians today, including this writer, would agree that in assessing China's prospects on the basis of the Nationalists' military progress at the end of the war, Boatner and other officers made the same mistake that later military historians would make in writing about the Vietnam War in the 1980s.[46] That is to say, the Army's China hands, like the later Vietnam revisionists, placed too much confidence in military remedies for what were essentially political, social, and economic problems.[47] Nevertheless, military historians should not allow this conclusion to obscure the larger point that Boatner sought to make. A reexamination of the American military experience in China and Burma may not serve the utilitarian purposes that Boatner intended, but it does remind historians of the need to balance descriptions of the fractious Chinese-American alliance with some appreciation of the more positive experiences of American officers in the field.

During World War II, after years as passive observers in China, American officers entered into a new and more active relationship with the Chinese. In their new role as military advisers, American officers often met with suspicion and resentment. For their part, many of the officers sent to China for the first time during the war exhibited little or no desire to serve in that theater. Nevertheless, American liaison officers came to the theater with the explicit assignment of working *with* the Chinese Army. Americans controlled the distribution of Lend-Lease aid in China, an important means of leverage to be sure, but they could not command the Chinese as if they were a colonial army, nor could they brush their allies aside and wage the war with American forces as was later done in Vietnam.[48] The officers sent to China could only advise and train their allies. For this they needed the cooperation of their Chinese counterparts. Faced with a frustrating distribution of power between host and outsider, Americans needed to make at least some effort to understand and cooperate with their allies if they hoped to succeed in their mission.

Within this context, the experience of educated and sympathetic officers like Dorn and Boatner played a vital role in reducing conflicts. In preparing their subordinates for the job of liaison officer, Dorn and Boatner acted as intermediaries, drawing on their experience and education to explain China and the Chinese to the American newcomers.[49] These efforts met with mixed success. Although many officers believed they formed relationships based on mutual respect, the degree to which Nationalist officers shared these perceptions is more problematic. Chinese resentment of the housing conditions in Kunming underscores how difficult it is for those with even the best of intentions to close the cultural gap that separated the Chinese and Americans. As mentioned, American officers at the Y Force training camps seemed unaware of how their comparative material abundance grated on their Chinese counterparts. Of course, most Americans probably regarded conditions in the camps as Spartan at best. In his memoirs, General Li Tsung-jen complained that the Americans displayed an imperious disregard for Chinese sensibilities. Moreover, it seems clear that other Chinese officers resented the American presence as a dangerous intrusion that threatened their own professional status and political influence.[50] Despite these obstacles, however, many American officers developed personal and professional friendships with their Chinese colleagues that lasted well beyond the war.[51]

In recalling how the Army's China hands perceived the results of their efforts, historians are reminded of a brief but important high point in what is most often remembered as a failed mission. This perception of success, which even Wedemeyer and Boatner conceded lay more in the realm of potential, sustained the Army's China hands during the period of China's civil war and shaped their response to subsequent American policies. In recognizing how the Army's China hands remembered their past and in understanding the lessons they drew from that experience, historians recapture a fleeting moment in the tumultuous relations between China and America. Equally important, scholars also gain a new perspective on Army efforts to aid the Nationalists after World War II.[52] For these and other insights they are indebted to Haydon Boatner, the unofficial historian of the Army's experience in China.

NOTES

1. Acheson to Gibson (Saigon), 20 May 49, *Foreign Relations of the United States: 1949*, vol. 7 (Washington, D.C.: Government Printing Office, 1977), pp. 29–30.
2. See, for example, Barbara Tuchman, *Stilwell and the American Experience in China, 1911–1945* (New York: Macmillan, 1971); Ernest R. May, *The Truman Administration and China, 1945–1949* (Philadelphia: J. B. Lippincott, 1976).
3. Haydon L. Boatner to the Hoover Institution on War, Revolution, and Peace, 12 Dec 75, Haydon L. Boatner Papers, Hoover Institution on War, Revolution, and Peace, Stanford, Calif. (hereafter cited as Hoover Institute).
4. Two of the earliest and most important histories on the subject are Tang Tsou, *America's Failure in China, 1941–1950* (Chicago: University of Chicago Press, 1963); and Herbert Feis, *The China Tangle: The American Effort in China from Pearl Harbor to the Marshall Mission* (Princeton: Princeton University Press, 1953).
5. Charles Romanus and Riley Sunderland, *Stilwell's Mission to China* (Washington, D.C.: U.S. Army Center of Military History, 1953), pp. 70–76; Tuchman, *Stilwell*, pp. 311–18.
6. The standard histories of the Army in the China-Burma-India Theater during World War II are Romanus and Sunderland, *Stilwell's Mission;* idem, *Stillwell's Command Problems* (Washington, D.C.: U.S. Army Center of Military History, 1956); idem, *Time Runs Out in CBI* (Washington, D.C.: U.S. Army Center of Military History, 1959). For a concise history of Stilwell's efforts, see David W. Hogan, *India-Burma: 1942–1945*, part of the U.S. Army Campaigns in World War II, a series of brief theater histories published by the U.S. Army Center of Military History (CMH).
7. Biographical resume of Haydon L. Boatner in Boatner Papers, Hoover Institute.
8. Dorn adapted Chinese brush techniques to his own painting. In his retirement he became a successful artist as well as an author. Brief Biography of General Frank Dorn, Dorn Papers, Hoover Institute.
9. Stilwell to Chiang, 27 Sep 43, Personnel file, box 4, Boatner Papers, Hoover Institute.
10. Comment of Col Trevor Dupuy, U.S. Army (Ret.), during a panel on Combined Warfare in the CBI, 14 Jun 94, Conference of Army Historians, Arlington, Va. Colonel Dupuy served as a liaison officer with the Chinese Army in India.
11. Boatner to Deputy Chief of Staff Siebert, 5 Feb 43, Troops folder, box 4; "Notes on Ramgarh," Campaigns and Strategy folder, box 2; Memorandum for Maj Gen Liao, 4 Nov 42, Personnel File, box 4, all in Boatner Papers, Hoover Institute.
12. "Command of Chinese Troops in WW II," Boatner's handwritten notes, ca. 1975, Troops file, box 4, Boatner Papers, Hoover Institute.
13. Boatner's notes, n.d. [c. 1973], Supplementary Documents file, box 2, Boatner Papers, Hoover Institute.
14. "Chinese Army in India" [unofficial history], pp. 17–18, box 1, Richard D. Weigle Papers, Hoover Institute; Romanus and Sunderland, *Stilwell's Command Problems*, pp. 306–12, 346.
15. "Instruction for Liaison Officers," n.d., Supplementary Documents file, box 2, Boatner Papers, Military History Institute (MHI); "Chinese Army in India" [unofficial history], p. 7, box 1, Weigle Papers, Hoover Institute; "Command of Chinese Troops in WWII," c. 1975, Troops file, box 4, Boatner Papers, Hoover Institute. For an account by one of the liaison officers, see Waldemar F. Breidster, To Whom It May Concern, 3 Oct 44, Troops file, box 5, Boatner Papers, Hoover Institute.
16. Stilwell to Chiang, 27 Sep 43, Personnel file, box 4, Boatner Papers, Hoover Institute.
17. "Notes to Bear in Mind When Dealing or Working with the Chinese," and "Notes for Officers Detailed to Serve with Units of the Chinese Army," and "Some Common Courtesies and Formalities," in file 83, box 8, Joseph W. Stilwell Papers, Hoover Institute.

18. On the glaring shortage of Chinese officers with adequate professional education and training see Hsi-Sheng Ch'i, "The Military Dimension, 1942–1945," in James C. Hsiung and Stevine I. Levine, eds., *China's Bitter Victory: The War With Japan, 1937–1945*, (Armonk, N.Y.: 1992), pp. 135–56.

19. Ibid. This remark about the National Guard caused Dorn some problems when he returned to the United States.

20. "Yoke Force Training Effort with Chinese Expeditionary Force," n.d., file 183, box 15, Stilwell Papers; Ibid.

21. Wu also served as an interpreter for a third training mission, the Z Force. Mr. Wu is now the director of Harvard University's Yenching Library. Interv, author with Eugene Wu, 8 Jun 94.

22. Historical Rpt of Y Force Operations Staff, 25 Nov 44, file 169, box 14, Stilwell Papers.

23. Ibid.

24. "Personal Opinion of the Chinese Army, 21 Mar 44, file 31, box 1, Dorn Papers.

25. Ibid., emphasis in the original.

26. Dorn to Commanding General, HQ, USAF in CBI, re: Observations of Col Reynolds Condon, 31 Dec 43, box 1, Dorn Papers.

27. "Yoke Force Training Effort with the Chinese Expeditionary Force," file 183, box 15, Stilwell Papers; Jonathan Spence, *To Change China: Western Advisers in China, 1620–1960* (Boston, Mass.: 1969), pp. 257–58.

28. Historical Rpt of Y Force Operations Staff, 25 Nov 44, file 169, box 14, Stilwell Papers.

29. Operational Directive No. 5 to Commanding General, Chinese Combat Command, 15 Feb 45; and Letter of Instruction to All U.S. Officers Serving With the Chinese Combat Command, n.d., both in file 1–A, Black Book–China, box 1548, Record Group (RG) 332, Records of the Commanding General, China-Burma-India Theater, National Archives and Records Administration, Suitland, Md. (hereafter cited as RG 332, CBI, NARA).

30. Comments by Col Dupuy, Conference of Army Historians.

31. William Langdon to the Secretary of State, enclosing translation from *The Morning Post,* 26 Jun 45, file # 800/891, China, Kunming Consulate, RG 84, General Records of the Department of State, NARA.

32. In November 1944, American fears about a Chinese collapse were such that George Elsey, a member of the White House staff, prepared a brief classified history of American wartime aid to the Nationalists to fend off possible criticism of the Roosevelt administration's policies toward Chiang's government. In effect, this was the first China White Paper. This history was later published as George Elsey, *Roosevelt and China: The White House Story*, with commentary by Riley Sunderland (Wilmington, Del.: Michael Glazier, Inc., 1979); Interv, author with George Elsey. For a discussion of Chiang's anxiety regarding American-Russian relations, see John W. Garver, *Chinese-Soviet Relations, 1937–1945: The Diplomacy of Chinese Nationalism* (New York: Oxford University Press, 1988), pp. 207–14. Tang Tsou has pointed out that Chiang became more cooperative because the Americans no longer asked him to make difficult choices. Tsou, *America's Failure*, p. 118.

33. Theodore H. White, *In Search of History: A Personal Adventure* (New York: Warner Books, 1978), pp. 222–23.

34. Harold Isaacs Notes, n.d., WW II Correspondent, box 21, Harold Isaacs Papers, Institute Archives, Massachusetts Institute of Technology, Cambridge, Mass.

35. Tojo quoted in Dick Wilson, *When Tigers Fight: The Story of the Sino-Japanese War, 1937–1945* (New York: 1982), p. 224. Casualty figures are from Hsi-Sheng Ch'i, *Nationalist China at War: Military Defeats and Political Collapse, 1937–1945* (Ann Arbor, Mich.: University Press, 1982), p. 81.

36. Caraway's report is considerably more positive than the later assessment of these Chinese operations made by the U.S. Army's official historians. Caraway to Col Devere

Armstrong, 2 Sep 45, Caraway Papers, MHI; Romanus and Sunderland, *Time Runs Out*, pp. 386–87.

37. Wedemeyer to General Thomas Handy, 13 Jul 45, Handy file, box 3–E, Wedemeyer Papers, Hoover Institute.

38. Ibid.

39. Brig Gen Olmsted to the Commanding General (Wedemeyer), 8 Aug 45, file: China, Misc. Information, China-Burma-India Theater, box 1555, RG 332, NARA.

40. Minutes of the State-War-Navy Coordinating Committee (SWNCC)–Far Eastern Subcommittee, 11 Sep 45, SWNCC Papers, RG 353, Interdepartmental and Intradepartmental Staffs, NARA; Lt Gen J. E. Hull to Secretary of War Robert Patterson, 17 Jan 46, Radios–Eyes Alone Book VII, box 1541, Records of CBI Theater, RG 332, NARA; F. F. Liu, *A Military History of Modern China, 1924–1949* (Princeton: University Press, 1956), pp. 236–40; James F. Schnabel, *The History of the Joint Chiefs of Staff: The JCS and National Policy, 1945–1947* (Wilmington, Del.: Michael Glazier, 1979), p. 419; Marc S. Gallicchio, *The Cold War Begins in Asia: American East Asian Policy and the Fall of the Japanese Empire* (New York: 1988), pp. 100–102.

41. For Wedemeyer's 1947 mission to China and Korea and his subsequent report to the president, see William Stueck, *The Wedemeyer Mission: American Politics and Foreign Policy During the Cold War*, (Athens, Ga.: University of Georgia Press, 1984). A copy of the general's report is printed in Albert C. Wedemeyer, *Wedemeyer Reports!* (New York: Holt, 1958), pp. 461–79.

42. Lawrence Lincoln, "Comments on 'China in War and Victory,'" n.d., Lawrence Lincoln Papers, MHI; Wedemeyer to Paul Caraway, 24 Oct 46, and Caraway to Gen Ernest Gruenther, 15 Apr 47, Paul Caraway Papers, MHI.

43. Memorandum for the Chief of Staff, 10 Aug 49, 091 China Section 1, Plans and Operations, box 152, RG 319, Army General and Special Staffs, Modern Military Branch, NARA.

44. Wedemeyer, *Wedemeyer Reports!*, pp. 400–401.

45. Compare Caraway's report on the last campaigns with Romanus and Sunderland, *Times Runs Out*, pp. 386–87. See also Spence, *To Change China*, pp. 228–78; Tuchman, *Stilwell*.

46. Gary R. Hess, "The Military Perspective on Strategy in Vietnam: Harry Summers' *On Strategy* and Bruce Palmer's *The 25-Year War*," *Diplomatic History* 10, no. 1 (Winter 1986): 91–106; Robert J. McMahon, "U.S. Vietnamese Relations: An Historiographical Survey," paper presented to the conference on "America and East Asia: A Research Agenda for the Twenty-First Century," Woodrow Wilson Center for Scholars, Washington, D.C., 6–10 Apr 94.

47. Hsi-Sheng Ch'i argues that the crushing political consequences of operation *ICHI-GO* gravely weakened the Nationalists' ability to survive. Ch'i, *Nationalist China at War*.

48. American perceptions of Vietnamese culture are described in George C. Herring, "'Peoples Quite Apart': Americans, South Vietnamese, and the War in Vietnam," *Diplomatic History* 14, no. 1 (Winter 1990): 1–25.

49. For a discussion of American civilians as communicators or intermediaries, see Akira Iriye, "The China Hands in History: American Diplomacy in Asia," in Paul Gordon Lauren, ed., *The China Hands Legacy: Ethics and Diplomacy* (Boulder, Colo.: 1987), pp. 81–96.

50. A study of how Chinese officers and enlisted men interacted with the Americans is beyond the capability of this author. Such a study would be a valuable addition to our understanding of the military relationship between China and the United States. Li Tsung-jen and Te Kong Tong, *The Memoirs of Li Tsung-jen* (Boulder, Colo.: University Press, 1979), p. 159.

51. Comments of Col Dupuy, 1994 Conference of Army Historians, and Interv, author with Dupuy, 12 Jul 94. See also Paul Caraway to the wife of General Cheng Chen, 7 Mar

65, Correspondence, 1965, Caraway Papers, MHI; Col Rothwell Brown to General Chen Yu Chao, 15 Dec 50, Correspondence, 1950, box 3, Rothwell Brown Papers, MHI; and the photographs and letters in the papers of Col John P. Lake, Hoover Institute. Eugene Wu also reports that at reunions of former Chinese interpreters now living in America, many of his associates have recounted the friendships they made with Americans.

52. For a discussion of JCS efforts to maintain support for the Kuomintang after 1945, see Ernest May, *The Truman Administration and China* (Philadelphia: Temple University Press, 1976); Dorothy Borg and Waldo Heinrichs, eds., *Uncertain Years: Chinese-American Relations, 1947–1950* (New York: 1979); Robert Blum, *Drawing the Line* (New York: 1982); William Whitney Stueck, *The Road to Confrontation* (Chapel Hill, N.C.: University Press, 1982); Michael Schaller, *The Origins of the Cold War in Asia: The American Occupation of Japan* (New York: Oxford University Press, 1985).

Nisei Linguists and New Perspectives on the Pacific War: Intelligence, Race, and Continuity

James McNaughton

What's left to say after half a century of writing about the Pacific War? Enormous amounts of ink have been spilled, especially on the war's dramatic beginning at Pearl Harbor and its dramatic ending. In between still lies a fertile field for research that academic and popular historians continue to till. Battle narratives and popular histories continue to pour forth from the presses. Meanwhile, a small group of distinguished historians has shown us over the past ten or fifteen years that there is still much to be said that is new about the Pacific War; not only new details, but new interpretations, and a broader context as well. The cultural and social context of evolving U.S.-Japan relations, and the long sweep of the history of the North Pacific, as one recent author has put it, "from Magellan to MacArthur," is still being explored. Over the past decade, the field has been reinvigorated in particular by two great works of synthesis: Christopher Thorne, *Allies of a Kind* (1978), and Ronald H. Spector, *Eagle Against the Sun* (1985).[1]

As every practicing historian will tell you, history advances based upon the questions you ask and the materials you work from. I would argue that there are still new questions to be answered and new materials to be worked. For example, historians still can learn a great deal from studying an unusual group of American soldiers; the several thousand Nisei (second generation Japanese-Americans) who served as translator-interpreters in the Military Intelligence Service during and immediately after the war.

In the summer of 1941, as America's relations with Imperial Japan approached a diplomatic impasse, the War Department Intelligence Division launched a secret effort to recruit and train West Coast Nisei to be Japanese-language interpreters and translators. By the outbreak of war, 60 students were in training at the Presidio of San Francisco. Within six months, the school had shipped its first 35 graduates to the field, just in time for Guadalcanal and the Buna-Gona campaign. It was the success of these first few Nisei linguists, by the way, that convinced the War Department to establish a Japanese-American combat unit, the famous 442d Regimental Combat Team that fought in Italy, France, and Germany. In 1942 the War Department moved the school, then named the Military Intelligence Service Language School, to Minnesota, and by the invasion of Saipan two years later, the school had graduated over 1,200 linguists. By the time U.S. forces landed on Iwo Jima and Okinawa in 1945, the school had graduated over 2,000 linguists, who fought in every battle and campaign. Three of these soldier-linguists earned the Distinguished Service Cross, and a number the Silver Star, some of them posthumously.

A purely descriptive account of the Nisei linguists' war experiences and their overall contributions would have a certain value and appeal. So far their story has only been told in the margins of history, and the pieces are fragmented. This has fed a certain resentment among many Nisei veterans, who believe that historians in general have neglected their contributions to the war effort, and thus in a way disenfranchised them. These veterans have a certain point, as much of what they did involved signals intelligence, and until the early 1970s this history was kept secret. Since then, however, historians have still been handicapped by fragmented records and the dominant weight of the by now established historiography. Also, the story of these soldiers is inextricably linked to a painful and tragic episode in the history of American race relations, the deep-rooted prejudice against Asian-Americans that culminated after Pearl Harbor in the internment camps.

Something more draws me to the story. As it turns out, the study of the Nisei linguists leads directly into the heart of several issues that are transforming the study of the Pacific War: intelligence, race, and the continuity of U.S. involvement in the Pacific, and promises to shed some useful light on each of these. What follows is only a preliminary sketch of the contributions a study of the Nisei linguists could make to each of these areas. What is left to say about the Pacific War? As it turns out, a lot.

Intelligence

The Army never published an official history of its military intelligence operations in World War II, nor did the other services. Of course, much was written at the time which never saw the light of day and is still being declassified. This material is slowly trickling out, such as two anthologies of historical documents on signals intelligence: Ronald H. Spector, ed., *Listening to the Enemy* (1988), and Jim Gilbert and Jack

Finnegan, *U.S. Army Signals Intelligence in World War II* (1993). But historians have yet to reach anything like a complete picture.[2]

Despite this shortfall, the most exciting new insights into the Pacific War in recent years have come as a direct result of historians exploiting revelations in the field of Allied intelligence. Historians have now begun to reconstruct the complex picture of theater intelligence activities and organizations and to delve into the role these various organizations played in the campaigns. Initial memoirs such as W. J. Holmes' *Double-Edged Secrets* (1979) and Ronald Lewin's *The American Magic* (1982) are being overtaken by careful historical studies such as Ed Drea's *MacArthur's Ultra* (1992).[3]

Reconstructing the story of the Nisei linguists promises to add to these insights and lend both breadth and depth to our understanding of the theater intelligence architecture that supported all commanders in the area. Since much intelligence information had to pass through the hands of interpreters or translators at some point, the Nisei linguists participated in virtually all aspects of theater intelligence.

A map of the Nisei linguist deployments in, let us say, 1944 would reveal much of the intelligence infrastructure: Indooroopilly Racetrack in Australia (Allied Translator and Interpreter Section [ATIS] and the Central Bureau); a former furniture store in Honolulu (Joint Intelligence Center, Pacific Ocean Areas [JICPOA]); Camp Ritchie, Maryland (Pacific Military Intelligence Research Section [PACMIRS]); Warrenton, Virginia (Vint Hill Farms Station); New Delhi, India (South East Asia Translation and Interrogation Center [SEATIC]); and an abandoned Civilian Conservation Corps camp in the Minnesota woods (Military Intelligence Service Language School [MISLS]). Nisei linguists also accompanied soldiers and marines in landing operations at regiment, division, and corps levels and flew missions with the Army Air Forces in B–17s, B–24s, and B–29s.

What do we learn by tracing the Nisei involvement in intelligence? Since they were pinch hitters, they served in a variety of intelligence functions and served under a variety of organizations and in every major campaign. We learn the overall scale and complexity of intelligence effort and organizations. We learn that intelligence required massive investment of talent, numbers, tenacity, and courage. It involved not just the big intelligence coups, such as shooting down Admiral Yamamoto, but also the grinding day-to-day work: interrogating prisoners, translating intercepts, evaluating and translating captured documents. Pacific-based intelligence operations also involved the war in Europe, such as the interception of cables from the Japanese ambassador in Berlin.[4]

Three incidents from the campaign for the Marianas can serve to illustrate this at the tactical, operational, and strategic levels. Before the battle, in late March 1944, Yamamoto's successor's plane crashed in the Philippines. By chance Admiral Fukudome was carrying the battle plans for the Japanese fleet. This document was spirited to ATIS by the Philippine resistance and translated with the help of two Hawaii-born Nisei, T3g. Yoshikazu Yamada and S. Sgt. George K. Yamashiro. MacArthur then sent the translation to JICPOA in Hawaii. This operational-level coup greatly aided Admiral Spruance a few weeks later as he met the Japanese at the Battle of the Philippine Sea, a major defeat for Japanese naval aviation.[5]

At the tactical level, linguist teams deployed with the 2d and 4th Marine Divisions and the 27th Army Division. Two of the Nisei, Ben Honda and George Matsui, won Silver Stars for their work during the battle. Another Nisei, Hawaii-born Bob Kubo, scored a major tactical coup while supporting the 27th Division. While interrogating a captured Japanese soldier one day, he learned of the timing for the last major suicide attack. He quickly relayed this to the division's leadership, who were thereby able to brace themselves for the blow.[6]

Saipan had strategic consequences for Allied intelligence as well. U.S. soldiers harvested some fifty tons of Japanese documents, which were crated up and shipped to JICPOA. Some crates were marked "no military value" and shipped to PACMIRS at Camp Ritchie. One of these documents, located and translated there, was the Imperial Army Ordnance Inventory. It was discovered by M. Sgt. Kazui E. Yamane, born in Hawaii and a graduate of Waseda University in Japan. This list was used in targeting the B–29 raids which were launched from Saipan later that fall, and greatly facilitated disarmament in the early months of the occupation.[7]

Much of the work on Allied intelligence in the Pacific focuses on the cryptographic battles, and rightly so. But as Edward Drea has pointed out, ULTRA does not explain everything, nor does it tell the whole story. The success of these translators in piecing together Japanese organizations, capabilities, and intentions was a great achievement in its own right. The perspective of the Nisei linguists could be the key that helps unlock the story of Allied intelligence in the Pacific War.

Race

A careful study of the Nisei linguists promises to shed some useful light on another sensitive, but absolutely critical aspect of the Pacific War: the matter of race and racism. Participants and historians have always known that racial hatred ran deep during the Pacific War, which in this aspect resembles the Russo-German War more than the campaigns in the Mediterranean and Northwestern Europe. Hatred on the battlefield was matched at home by the internment of over 100,000 Japanese-Americans for the duration of the war—the only ethnic group singled out for such treatment.

Harvard historian Akira Iriye has detailed the war's racial and cultural dimensions, and John W. Dower has compiled a disturbing catalog of prejudice in *War Without Mercy* (1986). Yet neither of these historians, and to my knowledge no one else who has examined this issue, has made use of the unique perspective of the Americans of Japanese ancestry who fought in the Pacific War.[8]

At the first level of analysis, all these young men were affected by the wave of prejudice and officially sanctioned discrimination that swept over the country in 1941 and 1942. They suffered the humiliation of seeing their families herded into internment camps and heard their commanding officer, Fourth Army Commanding General John L. DeWitt, explain the evacuation to West Coast newspapers by declaring that "a Jap is a Jap." In reaction, many mainland Nisei volunteered to serve their country straight out of the internment camps. In the Hawaiian Islands, Japanese-Americans, while not interned, were treated with great suspicion. Like other ethnic groups, these young Americans saw military service as a way to prove their patriotism. Many eagerly sought combat duty with the 442d Regimental Combat Team.

Of course, Nisei soldiers continued to face prejudice once in uniform. For example, while JICPOA found the services of these soldiers invaluable, they were not allowed to set foot inside the naval base at Pearl Harbor. Instead they worked at the JICPOA annex, a converted furniture store in downtown Honolulu. In the field, many Nisei experienced anxious moments when they were almost mistaken for enemy soldiers and nearly shot by their own side. For this reason, many Nisei linguists deployed into forward combat areas with their own Caucasian bodyguards. The American Nisei undoubtedly found the wartime racial stereotyping of the Japanese enemy undignified and personally offensive. To this day, Nisei veterans remain grateful to the officers they met who remained free of such prejudices and gave them a chance to prove themselves.

As evidence that Nisei linguists in training could keep their senses and maintain a sense of humor in this racially charged atmosphere, one need only look at the cartoon logo they adopted at the school. This fierce-looking, buck-toothed Minnesota gopher, wearing an all-American star-span-

gled Indian headdress, was a deliberate inversion of the then-current propaganda image of the rabid, buck-toothed Japanese foe.[9]

At a deeper level of analysis, for those who joined the Military
Intelligence Service to become linguists, the way they served was more
specific to their heritage, and thus psychologically more complex. While
translating captured diaries or radio messages and while interrogating prisoners of war, Nisei linguists had to confront issues of identity and heritage
in ways that most other American soldiers could not even imagine.
Although for most of them, learning the Japanese language was a major
challenge involving six months of hard work, the knowledge and appreciation of Japanese culture and society they had absorbed from their parents
and upbringing gave them a unique perspective on the enemy they faced.
They had a capacity, all too rare at that time, for seeing their opponents as
human beings, rather than animals.

The majority of Nisei linguists served in noncombat assignments in
JICPOA and ATIS. But several hundred linguists were sent forward to
serve in combat operations in New Guinea, Burma, the island-hopping
campaigns, and the Philippines. They served with the Army, Navy,
Marines, and Army Air Forces. Over a dozen were killed in action. Like
their fellow soldiers, they suffered the fear and stress of combat. But Nisei
soldiers experienced even more. In the typhoon of steel, they were in the
eye, grappling with the enemy, not with bayonet and bullet, but with their
eyes and ears and hearts. Some had the odd experience of having to
explain themselves to Japanese prisoners of war, and after the war in occupied Japan. These veterans can tell stories of the disbelief they met from
Japanese soldiers, who had been told by their own government that the
U.S. government had killed off all Japanese immigrants at the beginning of
the war.

A few Nisei linguists had chance encounters on the battlefield with
schoolmates, such as T3g. Takejiro Higa, who grew up on Okinawa and in
1943 volunteered from Hawaii. While interrogating prisoners on Okinawa
in 1945, he realized that two of them were former classmates from 7th and
8th grade. As he later recalled, at first they did not recognize him wearing
a U.S. Army uniform. "You idiots!" he yelled. "Don't you recognize your
own old classmate?" "They looked up at me in total disbelief and then
started crying . . . in happiness and relief. That hit me very hard and I, too,
could not help but shed some tears."[10]

The most difficult and dangerous role was reserved for those linguists
who became "cave flushers," using their ability to speak directly to enemy
soldiers. The best known was Hawaii-born Bob Kubo, who, while fighting
on Saipan in 1944, crawled into a large cave containing several Japanese

soldiers and over a hundred noncombatants to negotiate their release. He was armed only with his wits and a loaded .45 pistol stuck in the back of his belt. In the course of the lengthy negotiations, the trapped Japanese soldiers questioned how Kubo could fight on the American side. He psychologically disarmed them with a well-known saying from Japanese history: "If I am filial, I cannot serve the Emperor. If I serve the Emperor, I cannot be filial." They grasped his meaning at once, and realizing the futility of their position, released the women and children and surrendered. For this Kubo was awarded the Distinguished Service Cross.[11]

My sense is that the time is ripe for a more sophisticated study of the issue of race and culture in the Pacific War. In recent years historians have expanded the range of inquiry with provocative new books on such things as sex and gender in Hawaii under wartime conditions, encounters between Westerners and Pacific islanders, and the cultural impact of the flag-raising on Mount Suribachi.[12]

Perhaps the Nisei linguists can help historians find their way through this maze and tell a more nuanced story than one of just prejudice and racial hatred. The racial dimensions of the conflict should be the beginning point for analysis, not the end.

Continuity

A study of the Nisei linguists promises to shed light on a third and less well developed area, that of the essential continuity of U.S. military policy and experience in the Far East from World War II through the Korean War, and perhaps even beyond. Students of MacArthur have always made a case for this continuity. Indeed, one recent historian has labeled him "The Far Eastern General."[13]

But the continuity of U.S. military policy in the Far East involves more than an accident of one man's career. In the summer of 1945, the Military Intelligence Service Language School had over a thousand Nisei soldiers in Japanese-language classes at Fort Snelling, Minnesota. When Japan surrendered, these linguist soldiers were rushed into theater to fill key roles in the occupation. Indeed, of the six thousand students at the school during the war, over half graduated after August 1945. For them, as well as for the combat veterans, the occupation was simply the follow-on to the bloody campaigns that had just finished. ATIS, which had jumped to Manila in 1945 and Tokyo in 1946, redirected its work towards counterintelligence for the occupation. Although numerically reduced by demobilization, the Far East Command was able to civilianize large numbers of positions and entice several hundred Nisei to accept positions as War Department civilians. Many of them stayed on, almost to the present day. The multivolume official history of MacArthur's intelligence operations in the Southwest Pacific Areas, written in 1947–1948, is filled with glowing references to the Nisei linguists and their contributions which extended well beyond V–J Day.[14]

What surprised me in my preliminary research was to discover how quickly the extensive intelligence infrastructure built up by the theater commanders during the war was redirected toward a new threat, the Soviet Union. For example, in the spring of 1947 the Soviets began to return several hundred thousand Japanese soldiers through the northern port of Maizuru. The U.S. Army established the Maizuru Repatriation Center, which included about one hundred Nisei linguists with the mission of debriefing these repatriates about militarily significant information on the Soviets in the Far East. Soon afterward ATIS began to publish intelligence reports on the Soviet Union which had the same covers that they had used at the end of the war against Japan.[15]

In 1949 this same group turned its attention to the new People's Republic of China, and beginning in June 1950 ATIS became a principal intelligence center for the Korean War under the name of the 500th Military Intelligence Support Group, Far East. Many Nisei linguists were called back to active duty as reservists and served as linguists in Tokyo and on the battlefield. In fact, the FECOM G–2 was Col. Kai E. Rasmussen, one of the prewar Japanese language attaches and MISLS commandant during the war. In Washington, Brig. Gen. John Weckerling was named deputy assistant chief of staff for intelligence in July 1950. Weckerling was another of the prewar Japanese language attaches, and the real founding father of MISLS when he was Fourth Army G–2 in 1941.

On the battlefield, Nisei linguists were used to interrogate captured Korean soldiers, particularly officers, using their Japanese. In cases where the prisoner spoke no Japanese, the interrogations had to be carried out through two translators: from English to Japanese, then Japanese to Korean. And the answers came back through the reverse process.[16]

The end of occupation in Japan and the armistice in Korea did not end the story of the Nisei linguists. Dozens stayed on as civilians to work in intelligence and other assignments in the Far East. Harry Fukuhara, for example, who was recruited out of the Gila River, Arizona, internment camp in 1942, retired in 1991 from a senior intelligence position with the U.S. government in Japan and was recently inducted into the U.S. Army Military Intelligence Hall of Fame at Fort Huachuca, Arizona. Others stayed on active duty, such as Thomas T. Sakamoto, who stood on the deck of the USS *Missouri* in 1945 and went on to serve in Vietnam in

1967–1968 as chief of counterintelligence for MACV, retiring in 1970 as a full colonel.

So at an organizational, and in some cases a personal level, the American struggle against Imperial Japan and then against Communist Russia, the Chinese Communists, and perhaps even the Vietnamese Communists, had a certain continuity. The next assignment for historians of the Pacific War will be to trace this pattern.

A study of the Nisei linguists would bring into focus clear, strong elements of continuity, especially at that historic juncture where World War II became the Cold War in Asia. The criticality of this historic continuity will become increasingly clear as Americans come to see the importance of the U.S.–Japan strategic relationship. At a critical moment in this relationship these Americans served as a bridge between Japan and the United States.

Conclusion

So what's left to say about the Pacific War? As it turns out, quite a bit. My hope is that by following a new line of approach historians can shed some light on at least three areas of recent historical interest: the role of intelligence, the role of race, and the underlying continuity of American security policy in the Pacific during and after the war. It may turn out that the Nisei linguists have one more contribution yet to make, and that is to help historians and their readers reach a more accurate, and more complete, understanding of the tragic events that so convulsed the Pacific fifty years ago.

NOTES

1. Christopher Thorne, *Allies of a Kind: The United States, Britain, and the War Against Japan, 1941–1945* (New York: Oxford University Press, 1978); Ronald H. Spector, *Eagle Against the Sun: The American War With Japan* (New York: Free Press, 1985); and Walter A. MacDougall, *Let the Sea Make A Noise . . .: A History of the North Pacific From Magellan to MacArthur* (New York: Basic, 1993).

2. Ronald H. Spector, ed., *Listening to the Enemy: Key Documents on the Role of Communications Intelligence in the War With Japan* (Wilmington, Del.: Scholarly Resources, 1988); James L. Gilbert and John P. Finnegan, *U.S. Army Signals Intelligence in World War II: A Documentary History* (Washington, D.C.: U.S. Army Center of Military History, 1993).

3. W. J. Holmes, *Double-Edged Secrets* (Annapolis, Md.: U.S. Naval Institute Press, 1979); Ronald Lewin, *The American Magic: Codes, Ciphers, and the Defeat of Japan* (New York: Farrar, Straus, Giroux, 1982); and Edward J. Drea, *MacArthur's Ultra: Codebreaking and the War Against Japan, 1942–1945* (Lawrence, Kans.: University Press of Kansas, 1992).

4. Carl Boyd, *Hitler's Japanese Confidant: General Oshima Hiroshi and MAGIC Intelligence, 1941–1945* (Lawrence, Kans.: University Press of Kansas, 1992).

5. *Secret Valor: M.I.S. Personnel, World War II, Pacific Theater, Pre–Pearl Harbor to September 8, 1951* (Honolulu, Hawaii: MIS Veterans Club of Hawaii, 1993), pp. 55–57; Joseph D. Harrington, *Yankee Samurai: The Secret Role of the Nisei in America's Pacific Victory* (Detroit, Mich.: Pettigrew Enterprises, 1979), pp. 190–91, 195–97; Lewin, *The American Magic*, p. 254.

6. Interv with Hoichi Kubo and Ben Hazard, 30 Oct 87; Harrington, *Yankee Samurai*, p. 207. The story of the banzai attack is told in Philip A. Crowl, *Campaign in the Marianas, United States Army in World War II* (Washington, D.C.: U.S. Army Center of Military History, 1960), pp. 256–62.

7. *The Pacific War and Peace: Americans of Japanese Ancestry in Military Intelligence Service, 1941 to 1952* (San Francisco, Calif.: MIS Association of Northern California and National Japanese-American Historical Society, 1991), p. 68; *Secret Valor*, pp. 104–05; Harrington, *Yankee Samurai*, pp. 234–35, 358.

8. Akira Iriye, *Power and Culture: The Japanese-American War, 1941–1945* (Cambridge, Mass.: Harvard University Press, 1981) and John W. Dower, *War Without Mercy: Race and Power in the Pacific War* (New York: Pantheon, 1986). For a more recent treatment, see James J. Weingartner, "Trophies of War: U.S. Troops and the Mutilation of Japanese War Dead, 1941–1945," *Pacific Historical Review* (February 1992): 53–67.

9. The gopher logo was designed in 1943 by T. Sgt. Chris Ishii, who before the war had worked as an illustrator at Disney Studios. *MISLS Album* (Minneapolis, Minn.: 1946), p. 37. It is embossed on the album cover and appears to this day on the masthead of the *MIS Intelligencer*, the quarterly newsletter of the MIS Association of Northern California.

10. *Secret Valor*, p. 102.

11. Harrington, *Yankee Samurai*, pp. 209–10; *Pacific War and Peace*, p. 52; and Interv with Hoichi Kubo and Ben Hazard, 30 Oct 87.

12. Beth Bailey and David Farber, *The First Strange Place: The Alchemy of Race and Sex in World War II Hawaii* (New York: Free Press, 1992); Lamont Lindstrom and Geoffrey M. White, *Island Encounters: Black and White Memories of the Pacific War* (Washington, D.C.: Smithsonian Institution Press, 1990); Karal Ann Marling and John Wetenhall, *Iwo Jima: Monuments, Memories, and the American Hero* (Cambridge, Mass.: Harvard University Press, 1991).

13. Michael Schaller, *Douglas MacArthur: The Far Eastern General* (New York: Oxford University Press, 1989).

14. General Headquarters, Far East Command, Military Intelligence Section, General Staff, *A Brief History of the G–2 Section, GHQ, SWPA and Affiliated Units,* 10 vols., (Tokyo: Headquarters, U.S. Army Far East Command, 1947–1948).

15. See, for example, *ATIS Interrogation Reports, Far East Command,* vol. 2, 13 Jun 50, a tabular analysis of information in ATIS files on the Soviet armed forces and facilities in the Far East based on interrogation reports from January 1947–June 1950.

16. See Wesley Fishel, *Army Requirements for Language and Area Knowledge in Korea* (Operations Research Office, The Johns Hopkins University, HQ AFFE [Advance], ORO–S–91 [FEC], 15 Oct 53); the expanded version, Wesley R. Fishel and Alfred H. Hausrath, *Language Problems of the U.S. Army During Hostilities in Korea* (Operations Research Office, The Johns Hopkins University, ORO–T–356, Jan 58).

The Ultimate Dilemma of Psychological Warfare in the Pacific: Enemies Who Don't Surrender and GIs Who Don't Take Prisoners

Clayton D. Laurie

In a 1986 book entitled *War Without Mercy: Race and Power in the Pacific War*, historian John W. Dower cited numerous incidents from Japanese and Allied wartime accounts, postwar literature, government documents, and veterans' memoirs to establish the thesis "that the fighting [between the Allies and Japanese] in the Pacific was more savage than in the European theater," and was characterized by a high degree of brutality and frequent atrocities committed by the troops of both sides. "By the final years of the war against Japan," Dower wrote, "a truly vicious circle had developed in which the Japanese reluctance to surrender had meshed horrifically with Allied disinterest, on the battlefield and in decision-making circles, in taking prisoners.[1]

Numerous other articles, books, and memoirs published during the last fifty years support Dower's thesis. The harsh attitudes held by combatants on both sides of the Pacific conflict grew from generations of racial bigotry and stereotyping. Wartime atrocities, real and imagined, deliberate propaganda and military training programs aimed at dehumanizing the enemy created, in Dower's words, a war in which the standard was "Kill or be killed. No quarter, no surrender. Take no prisoners. Fight to the bitter end." Dower concluded that this "contributed to an orgy of bloodletting that neither side could conceive of avoiding, and made personal decisions about living or dying almost irrelevant for combatants on either side." Put simply, Japanese and Allied soldiers rarely surrendered voluntarily and neither side took significant numbers of prisoners between mid-1942 and V-J Day.[2]

Dower's findings provide one of many answers as to why the Allied psychological warfare campaigns against Japan, including those waged by American soldiers and civilians, were nearly complete failures. Charged with the task of undermining Japanese military and civilian morale by using the written and spoken word, with producing surrenders and POWs for intelligence purposes, and in general with destroying the Japanese will to resist, psychological warfare units dropped tens of millions of leaflets, made thousands of front-line tactical radio broadcasts and loudspeaker surrender appeals, and conducted hundreds of medium-and short-wave radio broadcasts, all without significant or practical effect. Even though propagandists had hoped to bring the Pacific War to a more rapid conclusion with less loss of life through the prevention of bloody last-ditch stands by the Japanese, they found that they faced many obstacles created both by their enemies and their own comrades.

Perhaps the most manifest obstacle faced by Allied propagandists was the lack of unity and coordination between agencies in the various operational theaters that included the Southwest Pacific Area under General Douglas MacArthur; the South Pacific under Admiral William Halsey; and the Central and North Pacific Theaters under Admiral Chester Nimitz. These theaters often overlapped and in places encroached on the British South East Asia Command and India Theater, as well as the China and the China-Burma-India Theaters under Chiang Kai-shek and his U.S. adviser, Lt. Gen. Joseph W. Stilwell.[3]

The inability to consolidate Allied propaganda efforts was peculiar to the Pacific. In Europe, between 1942 and 1945, all psychological warfare operations conducted by the Western Allies were controlled by two joint and combined military-civilian agencies: the Psychological Warfare Branch of Allied Force Headquarters, created in October 1942 in the Mediterranean, and the Psychological Warfare Division of SHAEF, founded in November 1943 in northwest Europe. These units were supported by radio and leaflet campaigns carried out by civilians belonging to the U.S. Office of War Information (OWI) and the British Ministry of Information (MOI); and by subversive propaganda activities implemented by the British Political Warfare Executive (PWE) and the American Office of Strategic Services Morale Operations Branch.[4]

A single umbrella agency never existed in the Pacific. By 1945, each theater had its own organization conducting its own combat propaganda campaigns while cooperating haphazardly with similar units elsewhere. Included among these agencies was the Australian-controlled Far Eastern Liaison Organization; the U.S. Army Psychological Warfare Branch–SWPA; the U.S. Navy–dominated Psychological Warfare Service of the Joint Intelligence Center, Pacific Ocean Area; the Psychological Warfare Service–China Theater; the Psychological Warfare Branch–CBI; and the Psychological Warfare Division–SEAC.

The inability to coordinate and consolidate Allied propaganda efforts was an outgrowth of the region's prewar colonial status and of wartime inter-Allied political disputes. Unlike Europe, which had in 1939 consisted wholly of sovereign states, most of Asia and the Pacific Ocean area were colonies of various European nations. After the crushing Allied defeats at the hands of the Imperial Japanese Army in 1941 and 1942, the perceptions of overwhelming western racial and military superiority previously held by indigenous peoples diminished. The European powers, as a result, not only had to evict the Japanese from areas of prior western control halfway around the globe, they also had to reestablish their supremacy in the region and reimpose colonial rule over peoples who were encouraged in their aspirations for independence by Japan.[5]

To further complicate the situation, President Franklin Roosevelt and many top policy makers in the Department of State and Office of War Information were ardent anti-imperialists who took the Atlantic Charter of August 1941 literally, publicly stating their hopes via American propaganda that the European powers would grant autonomy or outright independence to their colonies after the war.[6] This stance was contrary to the propaganda messages being disseminated by the British, French, Dutch, and Australians, each of which emphasized plans to return to their colonies after the war, and made it clear that they were not fighting wars of national liberation but were seeking a Japanese defeat and return to the prewar status quo, a theme which remained constant throughout the war. Inter-Allied disputes over propaganda messages and content which were not crucial in Europe, therefore, often delayed campaigns or diminished the effectiveness of propaganda in the Far East and affected both the tenor and composition of that propaganda, at times jeopardizing Allied unity and cooperation. From the very start, American psychological warfare in South and Southeast Asia encountered opposition from the British, who feared that the Americans would embarrass colonial authorities and fuel Indian and Burmese nationalism.[7] The Americans, in turn, resisted placing their psychological warfare personnel under British control, because, as one State Department official stated, "American psychological warfare operations are in part an expression of the political policy of the United States Government and as such cannot be subject to the control or direction of any foreign authority." The American desire not to be associated with British propaganda, especially in SEAC, which many Americans derisively claimed stood for "Save England's Asian Colonies," eventually reached such extremes that U.S. Army Air Forces crews were ordered not to drop British leaflets because recipients would begin to associate the offensive imperialistic messages with the United States due to the U.S. Army Air Forces emblems on the aircraft's wings.[8]

In the South and Southwest Pacific Theaters, U.S. Army and Navy commanders deliberately avoided using the propaganda offered by the Far

Eastern Liaison Organization, which many Americans considered a "British Imperialistic Agency" under Australian control. General MacArthur purposely waited until after the New Guinea campaign, when American forces were clear of the colonial areas of the Southwest Pacific and East Indies, to create a psychological warfare branch within SWPA. This prevented the inclusion of foreigners in any U.S. Army unit and at the same time avoided any inter-Allied political disputes. In the Central and Northern Pacific areas, U.S. Navy officials, in league with the Office of War Information, effectively blocked all Allied attempts to distribute or influence propaganda, even that dropped over the Japanese home islands.[9]

Even after psychological warfare agencies were set up and had surmounted political differences, the vast expanse of territory held by the Japanese which needed to be propagandized posed a further enormous obstacle. The U.S. Navy's proposed Central Pacific "island-hopping" route toward the mainland of Asia, for example, extended 8,000 miles from Hawaii to Japan and covered 6,000 miles from the Aleutians to Australia. This area contained thousands of islands occupied by a minimum of 145,000 Japanese troops manning hundreds of garrisons. General MacArthur's proposed route of advance in the Southwest Pacific, from Australia through New Guinea to the Philippines, also involved considerable island hopping and jungle fighting, and included 1,700 islands and 300,000 square kilometers of territory in the Philippines alone. MacArthur's route was defended by 140,000 Japanese troops in New Guinea, New Britain, and the Philippines, and if the SWPA commander had decided to liberate the East Indies as well, the Allies would have encountered a further 57,000 Japanese in Borneo, Sumatra, Java, and the Celebes. The task of locating and eventually reaching all of these enemy forces with airborne leaflets or even tactical or strategic radio propaganda was daunting, considering logistical difficulties and the manpower and equipment required. In 1943 supplying the needs of the U.S. Army and Allied conventional forces in the region was already proving to be a logistical nightmare of immense proportions. This meant that the printing presses, paper, and radio equipment needed to conduct large-scale psychological warfare campaigns would always be in short supply everywhere.[10]

In equally short supply were adequate numbers of civilian or military personnel familiar with the many Pacific and Asian peoples, their languages, and cultures. Unlike the relatively affluent, technologically advanced, urban, and literate populations of Europe, most of Asia, with few exceptions, was populated by semicivilized or premodern peoples who were illiterate and knew nothing of the outside world or Allied war aims. Most lacked access to modern forms of communication and many, especially in the East Indies, Southeast Asia, and the Philippines, inhabited remote areas that were nonetheless occupied by Japan. Maintaining the neutrality or gaining the support of these peoples required personnel fluent in little-known languages as well as individuals with a cultural and anthropological expertise which was virtually nonexistent in the United States and other western nations other than a few academics and missionaries. The Dutch East Indies, for example, contained 72 million people who spoke 25 languages with over 250 dialects, while neighboring Burma contained an additional 15 million people who spoke over 300 dialects. The problem was even worse when psychological warfare agencies attempted to find personnel familiar with New Guinea and the many Pacific islands. According to one OWI member, the number of Americans qualified to speak directly and effectively to these peoples at the beginning of the war could be "counted on the fingers of one thumb."[11]

Thus U.S. military propagandists had to prepare politically and grammatically correct messages for Japanese troops scattered over hundreds of thousands of square miles, find scarce transport to move it to some of the remotest points on the earth, deliver it to enemy garrisons hidden in mountains and jungles, and convince native peoples, many completely unknown in the west, not to cooperate with the enemy and to aid the Allies.

As if these problems did not pose great enough handicaps, propagandists also had to face the constant reluctance of Allied combat commanders, at all levels, in all operational areas, and in each military service, to use unconventional weapons such as propaganda. This hesitancy was due to a general lack of knowledge among combat soldiers about what psychological warfare was and what it could do, to the common military suspicion of civilians who made up a sizable portion of all psychological warfare units, and to the perpetual shortages of supplies and manpower in the combat theaters abroad.

The reluctance of field commanders to use psychological warfare was initially widespread. As Admiral Halsey's intelligence officer, Col. Julian P. Brown, USMC, recalled when he arrived in COMSOPAC in mid-October 1942, little was being done concerning the use of combat propaganda against the Japanese on Guadalcanal or elsewhere in the Solomons and only a few local and entirely spontaneous operations consisting of leaflets and loudspeakers were tried. This was due in part to the scarcity of resources and personnel. In addition, no staff-level agency controlled propaganda in Halsey's command, and the lack of personnel and the Japanese reluctance to surrender bolstered the general feeling that "any special effort by ground units of this nature would not be profitable." According to one member of the COMSOPAC staff, Halsey had dismissed psychological warfare at a very early date as "some impractical plaything of effete civilians."[12]

In the Southwest Pacific Theater, Col. J. Woodhall Greene, the founder of the Psychological Warfare Branch in that area, recalled that the idea of creating a propaganda unit existed as early as late 1943, but its actual formation was delayed repeatedly by staff officers such as Col. Charles Willoughby, who was hostile to the whole concept. This was confirmed by the later head of PWB/SWPA, Brig. Gen. Bonner Fellers, who remarked that he "ran into a number of unsympathetic officers" when forming a propaganda branch at MacArthur's GHQ.[13]

In the Central and Northern Pacific, U.S. Navy officials steadfastly maintained between 1942 and 1944 that there was no need for propaganda in a naval war against an enemy dug in on isolated islands or located within a mobile self-contained fleet. Although there had been some urging within CINCPAC to establish a propaganda unit for the November 1943 assault on Tarawa, such activities were dismissed as being of little value. Up until the middle of 1944, what little work was being done was accomplished by a team of fifteen to twenty U.S. Marine Corps language officers who prepared stock surrender leaflets and anti-morale materials. These efforts, according to one Marine Corps colonel, were "crude at best," and "brought negative results," because the attitude and training of the Japanese soldier provided a natural defense. "The early failures of this weapon, as well as the very nature of our island-hopping operations," he stated, "precluded its wide use." Naval and marine forces "did not care to disclose objectives by pre-invasion psychological warfare and once the invasion began the operation was usually of such short duration that there was hardly time for such measures."[14]

The hesitancy of commanders to use combat propaganda was often rooted in the fact that its main practioners were civilians of the OWI or the OSS who operated outside traditional military chains of command and control, and who were generally regarded as security breaches waiting to happen. Routinely, civilian propagandists were either excluded from combat theaters or were permitted to operate only under very restrictive military supervision. OWI Overseas Director Robert Sherwood, for example, was so alarmed at the prospect of being frozen out of the Southwest Pacific because of MacArthur's concerns that GHQ would become entangled in politics that he put OWI civilians under MacArthur's direct control in late 1943.[15]

In the Central Pacific OWI plans were repeatedly blocked because CINCPAC considered OWI "very dangerous to the security of our operations and intelligence." Those few naval officers who considered propaganda useful hesitated to allow civilians to practice it. Most were of the "opinion that psychological warfare in combat areas is a function of military command and should not be entrusted to civilian[s]." Even after OWI gained a toehold in the Central Pacific in March 1944, its efforts were hampered by Admiral Robert Ghormley of the 14th Naval District in Honolulu and Vice Adm. Charles E. "Soc" McMorris, Nimitz's Chief of Staff. It eventually took direct appeals to Nimitz and the intervention of both President Roosevelt and OWI Director Elmer Davis to force the CINCPAC staff to deal with OWI.[16]

William Donovan of the OSS was not so fortunate in establishing a niche for his psychological warfare unit, the Morale Operations Branch, and OSS men were generally excluded from the Pacific Theaters. General MacArthur had declared in early 1943 that "any OSS base in Australia would create [an] impossible situation and jeopardize [the] existing harmony." All psychological warfare in SWPA, MacArthur wrote the JCS, was currently being handled by GHQ and "due to security [concerns] and to avoid political questions" it was "inexpedient to send any organization for [further] participation." Donovan was also unsuccessful in establishing a foothold in either the South or Central Pacific, as U.S. Navy officials in both areas considered his plans and ideas nebulous and impractical, with Nimitz calling the OSS a "superfluous impracticality, whose value at present and for some time to come is not apparent."[17]

The ultimate, most nagging and persistent dilemma faced by Allied psychological warfare personnel, however, one that was never overcome and which seemed to avoid all efforts at solution, was the plain fact that Japanese soldiers did not readily surrender and that the Allies did not go out of their way to take prisoners. The tendency of Japanese soldiers to fight to the death was the result of strict social conditioning, thorough, yet specious, indoctrination about what to expect from their enemies, and rigid military discipline.

In basic training Japanese recruits were imbued with the idea that Occidentals, especially Americans, were soft and decadent, but were nonetheless cruel people who simply did not take prisoners. Even if Americans did capture a Japanese, recruits were told, the unfortunate individual was likely to be executed, usually by beheading, after first being subjected to hideous tortures. Through POW interrogations the Americans recorded a "number of references to apparently widespread fears that prisoners of the Allies are burned in oil, crushed while still alive by tanks and bulldozers, or otherwise tortured." Many were told that westerners routinely practiced cannibalism. Because Japanese soldiers were never instructed about the Geneva Conventions regarding the treatment of POWs, these beliefs in the certainty of encountering a horrible death in American captivity endured even beyond V–J Day.

The same fabrications were repeated by Japanese military officials to their Korean and Formosan auxiliaries and to civilians who often lived on islands garrisoned by Japan. Formosans, according to one interrogator's report, "fully expected on becoming American POWs, that we would cut off their ears, nose, arms, [and] legs. [That we would] Pour a coat of tar over the naked body and set fire to it. . . . [and] Leave them bound on the road and run tanks over their bodies. Even a college graduate believed this nonsense." Proof that such stories were taken to heart by the Japanese was seen in the thousands of suicides that took place on Saipan and from the large numbers of enemy "hold-outs" scattered across the Pacific who often took months, if not years, to capture.[18]

Another important factor in the refusal of Japanese soldiers to cease resistance, however, appears to have been the Japanese military's success in creating and maintaining *Seishin* or "spirit" within the ranks. This ideal supposedly produced such a high degree of loyalty and unit cohesion that surrender, an outrageous act of disloyalty and individualism, was unthinkable. When combined with high and unequivocal standards of self-discipline, the possession of fighting spirit supposedly made the average enemy soldier immune to propaganda. Social conditioning had also instilled the idea that to surrender was a shameful loss of face, a disgrace not only to one's self but to the soldier's unit, his family, home community, the Emperor, and the Japanese race. To escape the disgrace of capture and the torture that went with it, soldiers were "expected to commit suicide as the ultimate step in the spirit of aggressiveness."[19]

The reputed tenacious fighting abilities of the Japanese soldier and his penchant never to surrender were soon combined with a general disinterest on all levels of the Allied military services with even bothering to try and take Japanese soldiers captive. As was the case with the military training programs of the enemy, Americans also succeeded in thoroughly dehumanizing their adversaries to the point where taking prisoners or even winning the war soon seemed to many GIs to be secondary to just killing Japanese. The stress placed on killing as opposed to capturing was evident in the public statements of some of the highest Allied officials. Admiral Halsey was recorded soon after Pearl Harbor as vowing that "by the end of the war, Japanese would only be spoken in hell," and rallied his men thereafter under such slogans as "Kill Japs, kill Japs, kill more Japs." Even the former U.S. Ambassador to Japan, Joseph C. Grew, was recorded as saying that the Japanese would not "crack morally or psychologically," and would only be defeated through "utter physical destruction." Many of the Allies echoed these sentiments, with Australian General Sir Thomas Blamey stating in 1942 that Australian troops were "fighting a shrewd, cruel, merciless enemy, who knows how to kill and who knows how to die." Beneath the thin veneer of a few generations of civilization, Blamey claimed, the Japanese "is a subhuman beast, who has brought warfare back to the primeval, who fights by the jungle rule of tooth and claw, [and] who must be beaten by the jungle rule of tooth and claw." "Kill him," Blamey urged, "or he will kill you."[20]

Western stereotypes regarding the perfidious nature of the Japanese also proved extremely difficult if not impossible for those practicing combat propaganda to overcome. While Americans stood for all that was moral, upright, and good, the Japanese were allegedly just the opposite. In the ongoing effort to create home-front unity and boost front-line morale, Allied propaganda portrayed the Japanese as a diabolical, subhuman, simian-like race, prone to aggression, a people who were utterly untrustworthy, who lacked moral scruples or redeeming virtues.[21]

Thousands of Allied servicemen, for example, could recall having witnessed or heard of severely wounded or ill Japanese soldiers who under the guise of surrendering had taken advantage of the benign western attitude towards soldiers giving themselves up to close on Allied positions and inflict further casualties. As one Marine Corps officer noted on Guadalcanal in 1942, "when they [the Japanese] have indicated an intention to surrender, the Jap did so only in order to gain the advantage to kill his enemy by surprise." Thus, he admitted, "the Marines caught on very soon to these treacherous tactics, and now kill all Japs that are capable of causing them further trouble."[22]

The same pattern held true elsewhere. Numerous reports were received that natives throughout Asia and the Pacific refused to take prisoners, and acted on every opportunity to kill as many Japanese as possible. In China and the Burmese Northern Combat Command Area "surrender pass" leaflets that had proven very successful in Europe were not used because Chinese soldiers were reported as being more interested in exacting revenge for Japanese atrocities than in taking prisoners. The Psychological Warfare Service in China, unlike its counterparts elsewhere, could not, and would not, guarantee enemy soldiers good treatment if captured by the Chinese, nor assure them that their surrender would even be accepted. U.S. Army officials exercised little control over Chiang's troops, and while the Americans tried to get the Chinese to take prisoners, few ever did. Numerous reports noted the extremely low numbers of Japanese being taken prisoner and claimed that this was entirely due to enemy troops being "shot down by Allied combat soldiers, mainly the Chinese, but also by American forces who were ignorant of the psychological efforts to induce surrender." One American wrote that "it is obvious that successful surrender appeals cannot be made if Japanese soldiers become aware that no guarantee of safety can be given." Orders must "be issued by the highest possible authority in the theater indicating that prisoners shall be taken," and "that soldiers and officers be indoctrinated with the fact that the acceptance of prisoners yields vital information and saves lives." "Without the establishment of such a theater policy," the memo concluded, "no surrender appeal is likely to be more than fractionally successful."[23]

The Japanese themselves bore no little responsibility for the reluctance of Allied soldiers to take prisoners, for early in the war they established the practice of fighting to the last, of booby-trapping their dead and wounded, and of using fake surrenders to ambush unwary foes. Demonstrated and alleged instances of Japanese deceit, especially regarding false attempts to surrender, when combined with the belief that the Japanese were fanatics who would not surrender anyway, produced a definite reluctance on the part of American forces to take POWs or to use propaganda to encourage surrenders. As late as March 1945, for example, PWB/SWPA received "persistent reports that small groups of Japs in scattered locations" in the Philippines "have attempted to surrender, were allowed to come into the open with leaflets held up, and were then mowed down by our troops." One psychological warfare officer attached to X Corps in the Philippines wrote to General Fellers that U.S. troops appeared to "condone the merciless killing of helpless soldiers" and that "if something isn't done about the attitude of our men and officers toward taking prisoners and giving them a chance to be taken, we may as well pack up and quit trying."[24]

The cliché that seemed to predominate among Allied soldiers was that life to the Japanese was valueless, and enemy troops when cut off, surrounded, or defeated would commit suicide (*Seppuku*), die of starvation, or succumb to a myriad of otherwise treatable diseases before even considering the loss of face associated with the degrading and culturally disgraceful idea of surrender. In general, combat propaganda was useless when dealing with such peoples, and psychological warfare officers were often told by skeptics that the time, manpower, and resources expended on these activities were simply wasted.[25]

Thus, Allied propagandists soon found that the themes and messages that seemed so successful when used in Europe had no effect on the Japanese and that Allied forces were essentially unwilling to try psychological warfare against an enemy who was deemed impervious to it. Nonetheless, American personnel sought improved messages and propaganda techniques and worked to incorporate psychological warfare usage into the combat operations of Allied forces as early as 1943.

By early 1944 several goals were evident. First, psychological warfare units needed to educate and convince the armed forces, at all levels, everywhere, of the practical uses and effectiveness of propaganda as a weapon that could decrease resistance, produce intelligence-rich POWs, and save lives. They then needed to find out what themes were effective and why and convince the Japanese that they would be taken prisoner if they indicated a willingness to surrender. This all required a crash course in Japanese-language skills, history, and culture. Thus, in the spring of 1944 the OWI, in cooperation with the Military Intelligence Service of the War Department General Staff, created the Foreign Morale Analysis Division (FMAD) to provide information about Japanese morale and details about social conditions in Japan for the use of those conducting psychological warfare campaigns. Through detailed studies examining every aspect of the so-called Japanese national character FMAD hoped to enable propagandists to more closely tailor their output to uniquely Japanese traits, thereby, in theory, making it more effective.[26] In 1944 and 1945 the Foreign Morale Analysis Division produced numerous papers on topics such as "Japanese Morale in New Guinea," the "Effect of Bombing on Japanese Home Front Morale," "The Influence of Allied Propaganda" (as revealed in 1,025 interrogation reports), and the "Persistent and Changeable Attitudes of the Japanese Forces and Their Implications for Propaganda Purposes."[27] In PWB/SWPA, a Collation Section was created in August 1944 that essentially duplicated FMAD's efforts by gleaning intelligence from civilian and military agencies. This intelligence was studied and evaluated "in order to present enemy psychological vulnerabilities in the form of clear-cut objectives." As a final means of supporting field units, the Collation Section produced a periodic list of suggested propaganda themes and how to use intelligence in propaganda.[28]

Even after appropriate propaganda messages and themes were determined and produced in the form of colorful leaflets and attention-getting radio and loudspeaker programs, the job of obtaining enemy surrenders was only half complete. What was needed, according to psychological warfare officers, was a vast education effort directed toward Allied troops that focused on the need to take prisoners and treat them properly. To this end, a series of leaflets was developed for Allied troops throughout the region, informing them of what combat propaganda was and how it was used, and bringing to their attention the fact that Japanese soldiers may appear in their area with leaflets in their possession, and should be allowed to surrender. In addition, personnel at stateside military bases and in overseas rear areas were provided with information pamphlets and *Newsmap* and *Newstalk* broadsides explaining psychological warfare and its uses. Efforts were also made to publish articles about propaganda in military journals where combat officers were certain to notice them. Thus, as 1945 opened, a concerted effort was taking place, in the words of one psychological warfare officer, "to see that every unit of every front line organization becomes prisoner conscious."[29]

Despite the best efforts of psychological warfare personnel, however, progress was slow—much slower in fact than that being made by conventional Allied forces in destroying the Japanese Empire. Although combat propaganda was gaining acceptance by 1945, and was scoring some limited successes, most campaigns continued to produce only a handful of prisoners. A simple comparison between Europe and the Pacific makes clear the relative failure of the Far Eastern and Pacific psychological warfare campaign. In Europe, in July 1944, the U.S. Army revealed that 75 percent of German prisoners taken at Le Havre and 80 percent captured in the Brest Peninsula had Allied leaflets in their possession upon capture. Later that same month British Foreign Minister Anthony Eden reported to the House of Commons that well over 77 percent of the Axis prisoners captured in Normandy had leaflets when they surrendered and that Allied combat propaganda seems to have had an effect on enemy morale. These successes continued through the final year of the war in Europe. Over 50 percent of Germans taken prisoner at Aachen in October 1944 had leaflets in their possession, while between 70 to 90 percent of German soldiers captured between 1 January and 15 March 1945 had seen Allied leaflets and upwards of 75 to 80 percent indicated they were influenced to surrender by them. By V–E Day over 2.5 million Germans were in the custody of the Western Allies with combat propagandists claiming a good amount of the credit for putting them there.[30]

Meanwhile, by August 1944, a time when German POWs were arriving in the United States at the rate of 50,000 per month, a head count was taken by the Foreign Morale Analysis Division of Japanese prisoners captured by all U.S. forces operating in the Pacific between December 1941 and the conquest of Saipan in July 1944. The census takers were stunned to discover that only 1,990 Japanese had been captured in nearly three years, including the record 879 POWs taken during the Saipan operation.[31] Although Japanese military personnel captured by the Americans were routinely handed over to the Australians for incarceration, the number of POWs held by the Allies totaled just 4,400 in October 1944 and 3,400 of these were taken in New Guinea alone. During the remaining year of the war the totals of enemy personnel captured never dramatically increased, despite the optimistic reports of the various psychological warfare agencies. In the Philippines, for example, where a major emphasis was put on combat propaganda of all types, ratios of Japanese killed to those taken prisoner ran from a high of 100:1 in November 1944 to a low of 19:1 by 1 July 1945. The total number of POWs taken in the Philippines as of 20 August 1945 numbered fewer than 20,000—well over 350,000 Japanese military personnel were killed in ten months of intense combat. Totals coming in from CBI were even lower, and it was reported that fewer than 600 POWs were taken as of late August 1944, despite the efforts of the three propaganda agencies operating in the region.[32]

During the April 1945 invasion of Okinawa, the OWI and the U.S. Army and Navy launched their most comprehensive and technologically sophisticated propaganda campaign to date, gaining the praise of Under Secretary of War Robert P. Patterson for their efforts to obtain prisoners.[33] Yet, even in this self-proclaimed superlative psychological warfare campaign, of a Japanese garrison of approximately 120,000 men, only 11,000 prisoners had been taken by 25 July 1945. These consisted of 7,400 Japanese troops and 3,600 Korean and Formosan laborers. While many prisoners did come in due to psychological warfare efforts, and while many Americans claimed that this was the "greatest number and largest percentage of prisoners of war in any Pacific operation," the fact remained that the vast majority of Japanese, over 110,000, still refused to surrender and had either committed suicide or died in suicide charges such as those that had characterized nearly every other Pacific campaign.[34]

Thus, the problems associated with the backwardness of the region, the distances to be covered, communications difficulties, inter-Allied and interservice political disputes, transport and supply shortages, the task of educating Allied forces about the positive aspects of propaganda, and the inability of Allied psychological warfare personnel to clearly demonstrate the practical aspects of combat propaganda to front-line commanders were added to the difficult mission of convincing Japanese troops to surrender. Although most obstacles were surmounted by the 2,500 Allied personnel working with psychological warfare in the Far East, their campaigns never amounted to much more than a curious adjunct to conventional military operations and had, ultimately, little impact on the final Japanese defeat. Admiral William Leahy's assessment of psychological warfare seems to adequately sum up the attitudes most propagandists found in the Pacific. "Psychological warfare," Leahy stated, "was something new to the professional soldier and sailor. I am not certain as to what effect it ever had on the Japanese. The best psychological warfare to use on these barbarians was bombs, and we used bombs vigorously."[35]

NOTES

1. John W. Dower, *War Without Mercy: Race and Power in the Pacific War* (New York: Pantheon, 1986), p. 35.
2. Ibid., pp. 10–11, 62–65. See also Arnold Krammer, "Japanese Prisoners of War in America," *Pacific Historical Review* (1983): 67–91, especially 68–69; E. B. Sledge, *With the Old Breed at Peleliu and Okinawa* (Novato, Calif.: Presidio Press, 1981), p. 120; Richard Tregaskis, *Guadalcanal Diary* (New York: Random House, 1942), pp. 15–16; James J. Fahey, *Pacific War Diary, 1942–1945* (New York: Houghton Mifflin, 1963), pp. 68, 192; William Manchester, *Goodbye Darkness: A Memoir of the Pacific War* (New York: Dell, 1980), p. 439; John Toland, *The Rising Sun: The Decline and Fall of the Japanese Empire, 1936–1945* (New York: Random House, 1970), pp. 273, 290, 292; John Costello, *The Pacific War, 1941–1945* (New York: Quill, 1981), pp. 192, 200, 212, 227; Clay Blair, Jr., *Silent Victory: The U.S. Submarine War Against Japan* (New York: Lippincott, 1975), pp. 384–86; Samuel Eliot Morison, *History of Naval Operations in World War II* (Boston: Little, Brown, 1960), vol. 6, p. 62; Charles A. Lindbergh, *The Wartime Journals of Charles Lindbergh* (New York: Harcourt Brace Jovanovich, 1970), pp. 856–57; Russell Weigley, *The American Way of War: A History of United States Military Strategy and Policy* (Bloomington: Indiana University Press, 1973), pp. 127, 133–35, 149–52; J. Glenn Gray, *The Warriors: Reflections of Men in Battle* (New York: Harper and Row, 1959; reprint: 1970), pp. 178–79; S. E. Smith, ed., *The United States Marine Corps in World War II* (New York: Random House, 1969), pp. 662, 680; Meirion and Susie Harries, *Soldiers of the Sun: The Rise and Fall of the Imperial Japanese Army* (New York: Random House, 1991), pp. 424–25, 432, 437, 457–59, 461–62, 467, 481; and Allison B. Gilmore, "In the Wake of Winning Armies: Allied Psychological Warfare Against the Imperial Japanese Army in the Southwest Pacific Area During World War II," Ph.D. diss., Ohio State University, 1989, especially chs. 3 and 4.
3. Ltr, Davies to Hull, 15 Jun 44, file: China-Burma-India (CBI), box 2, Edward P. Lilly Papers, Record Group (RG) 218, Records of the United States Joint Chiefs of Staff, National Archives and Records Administration (NARA), Washington, D.C., hereafter Lilly Papers. See also Ray S. Cline, *Washington Command Post: The Operations Division* (Washington, D.C.: U.S. Army Center of Military History, 1985), ch. 5; and Maurice Matloff and Edwin M. Snell, *Strategic Planning for Coalition Warfare: 1941–1942* (Washington, D.C.: U.S. Army Center of Military History, 1986), chs. 3 and 5; Ronald Spector, *Eagle Against the Sun* (New York: Free Press, 1985), pp. 142–46; Louis Morton, *Strategy and Command: The First Two Years* (Washington, D.C.: U.S. Army Center of Military History, 1989); Charles D. Cook, Jr., "The Pacific Command Divided: The Most Unexplainable Decision," *U.S. Naval Institute Proceedings* 104 (September 1978): 55–61; Charles W. Florence, Jr., *Organization of the Southwest Pacific and Pacific Ocean Areas* (Washington, D.C.: n.p., 1946).
4. For psychological warfare operations in Europe, see Records of Allied Operational and Occupational Headquarters, World War II, Records of the Supreme Headquarters, Allied Expeditionary Force, 1942–1945, Psychological Warfare Division, SHAEF, and Records of the Allied Force Headquarters, 1942–1947, Psychological Warfare Branch, RG 331, NARA; see also Office of War Information, *Office of War Information in the European Theater of Operations: A Report on the Activities of the Office of War Information in the European Theater of Operations, January 1944 to January 1945* (London: n.p., 1945); Allied Force Headquarters, Psychological Warfare Branch, *Psychological Warfare in the Mediterranean Theater* (Washington, D.C.: Government Printing Office, 1945); SHAEF, *The Psychological Warfare Division, Supreme Headquarters Allied Expeditionary Force: An Account of Its Operations in the Western*

European Campaign, 1941–1945 (Bad Homburg, Germany: n.p., 1945), pp. 122–24; Clayton D. Laurie, "Black Games, Subversion, and Dirty Tricks: The OSS Morale Operations Branch in Europe, 1943–1945," *Prologue* 25 (Fall 1993): 259–71; Charles G. Cruickshank, *The Fourth Arm: Psychological Warfare, 1939–1945* (London: Davis-Poynter, 1977); William E. Daugherty and Morris Janowitz, eds., *A Psychological Warfare Casebook* (Baltimore: Johns Hopkins University Press, 1958); James Erdmann, *Leaflet Operations in the Second World War: The Story of the How and the Why of the 6,500,000 Propaganda Leaflets Dropped on the Axis Forces and Homelands in the Mediterranean and European Theaters of Operations* (Denver: University of Denver, 1969); Daniel Lerner, *Sykewar: Psychological Warfare Against Germany, D-Day to V–E Day* (New York: Stewart, 1949); idem, ed., *Propaganda in War and Crisis* (New York: Stewart, 1951); and Kermit Roosevelt, *The War Report of the OSS*, 2 vols. (New York: Walker, 1976).

5. For the effect of Japanese victories on European prestige, see B. H. Liddell Hart, *History of the Second World War* (Boston: Little, Brown, 1972), p. 233; Charles P. Romulo, "Japan Exploits Our Lost Face," *New York Times Magazine* (October 1943): 8; Joyce C. Lebra, ed., *Japan's Greater East Asia Co-Prosperity Sphere in World War II: Selected Readings and Documents* (London: Oxford University Press, 1975); Willard H. Elsbree, *Japan's Role in South-East Asian Nationalism* (Cambridge: Harvard University Press, 1953); Alfred W. McCoy, ed., *Southeast Asia Under Japanese Rule* (New Haven: Yale University Southeast Asia Studies, Monograph Ser. 22, 1980).

6. For inter-Allied political disputes, see William R. Louis, *Imperialism at Bay, 1941–1945: The United States and the Decolonization of the British Empire* (London: Oxford University Press, 1977); Christopher Thorne, *Allies of a Kind: The United States, Britain, and the War Against Japan, 1941–1945* (New York: Oxford University Press, 1978). For indicative U.S. attitudes regarding French Indochina, for example, see Gary R. Hess, "Franklin D. Roosevelt and Indochina," *Journal of American History* 59 (September 1972): 353–68; Walter LaFeber, "Roosevelt, Churchill, and Indochina, 1942–1945," *American Historical Review* 80 (December 1975): 1277–95; and George C. Herring, "The Truman Administration and the Restoration of French Sovereignty in Indochina," *Diplomatic History* 1 (Spring 1977): 97–117.

7. The Far Eastern Bureau of MOI and PWE were also severely restricted in their activities by GHQ/India and the Indian government, indicating that British concerns about the effect of propaganda on colonial peoples were not confined just to OWI. See Ltr, Davies to Hull, 15 Jun 44; Ltr, Davies to Pennoyer, 24 Apr 44, re: American PsyWar in CBI; Memorandum, Shulman for Hayne, 30 Aug 44, sub: PsyWar Operations; PsyWar in North Burma; all in file: CBI, box 2, Lilly Papers. On U.S. policy toward India, see Memorandum, Lane for Merrill, 5 Jan 45, file: Inter-Allied Relations, box 5, Lilly Papers, NARA.

8. See Cable, Stilwell to Marshall, 25 Oct 43, file: Chronology Oct–Dec 43, box 3; Memo, BCS, SEAC, 16 Aug 43, re: Coordination of American Agencies (OSS, OWI, FCB, FCC, BEW) with Comparable British Agencies, file: CBI, box 2; ch. 3, sec. 3, p. 40, box 16; and Ltr, Davies to Hull, 15 Jun 44, file: CBI, box 2, all in Lilly Papers. Finally, see Charles F. Romanus and Riley Sunderland, *Stilwell's Mission to China* (Washington, D.C.: U.S. Army Center of Military History, 1987), pp. 327–32.

9. For SWPA relations with FELO, see Memorandum, Fellers for Deputy Chief of Staff, 4 Jun 44, sub: Establishment of PWB, in ann. 1 of Rpt, Fellers to MacArthur, PW Against Japan in SWPA, RG 331, Records of Allied Operational and Occupational Headquarters, World War II, Records of the General Headquarters, Southwest Pacific Area, NARA; see also Interv, Lilly with Fellers, 26 Aug 46, Japan file, box 6; "Review of FELO Activities," Jul 42–Jun 45, Topical file, box 14; and Conference, Lilly with Col H. V. White (Sixth Army G–2), n.d., SWPA file, box 13; and ch. 3, sec. 3, box 16, Lilly Papers.

10. Japanese troop strengths, 20 Oct 43, notebook tab "Troops," box 2, Bonner Fellers Papers, Hoover Institution Archives.

11. Quote from Bill Davidson, "He Talked to Japan," *Collier's* (13 October 1945): 54; also see Clyde K. Kluckhorn, "Anthropologists Contributed to the Defeat of Japan," in Daugherty and Janowitz, eds., *A Psychological Warfare Casebook*, pp. 512–13; see also Indoctrination Course in Psychological Warfare file, FELO, box 31, entry: 283L, RG 331, Record of Allied Operational and Occupational Headquarters, World War II, Records of the Southeast Asia Command, 1943–1945, and Records of the Psychological Warfare Officer–China, both in NARA; and Federal Research Division, *Philippines: A Country Study* (Washington, D.C.: Library of Congress, 1993).

12. Interv, Lilly with Greene, 16 Oct 51, SWPA file, box 13; and ch. 3, sec. 3, box 16; Memo to Admiral King for C/S Sig, re: OSS in SWPA, 29 Sep 44, PWB/SWPA file, box 9, all in Lilly Papers. OWI Director Elmer Davis was especially concerned with MacArthur's hesitancy to employ OWI people and complained to U.S. Army Chief of Staff General George C. Marshall. Marshall's reply supported MacArthur's proposed PWB/SWPA organization and reaffirmed the theater commander principle. See Ltr, Marshall to Davis, 10 Jul 44, re: Information about SWPA, SWPA file, box 13, entry Lilly Papers, NARA; Memorandum, Willoughby, History of Relations of OWI with GHQ, 5 May 43, OWI Propaganda to NEI file, box 10, entry 283k, RG 331, NARA; and Memo, Stern for Director OWI, 27 Mar 43, box 11, entry 6G, RG 208, Records of the Office of War Information, NARA; see also Gilmore, "In the Wake of Winning Armies," pp. 23–24. For Halsey quote, see Ltr, Brown to Lilly, 25 Nov 46, COMSOPAC file, box 4, Lilly Papers.

13. For a history of the establishment of PWB/SWPA, an Organizational Chart, and a PWB Functions Chart, see anns. 1, 2, and 5, respectively, in Rpt, Fellers to MacArthur, "Psychological Warfare Against Japan, SWPA, 1944–45, PsyWar Against Japan file, Reference Copy, RG 331, NARA; see also "A Brief History of American Psychological War," hereafter "Brief APW"; Interv, Lilly with Fellers, 26 Aug 46, Japan file, box 6; ch. 3, sec. 3, box 16, all in Lilly Papers.

14. For quotes, see ch. 3, sec. 3, box 16; and Ltr, Col W. F. Coleman, USMC, to Lilly, 17 Dec 46, Theater Planning file, 1946, box 15; see also "Brief APW"; and Office of the Outpost Representative, 21 Mar 44 to 31 Oct 45, OWI file, box 9, all in Lilly Papers. The U.S. Marine unit was led by Capt. Earl Swisher, USMCR.

15. See Memo, E. A. W., re: History of Relations of OWI With GHQ, 5 May 43, OWI file, Propaganda to NEI, entry 283K, box 10; also Collation Section, GHQ/SWPA/PWB, G–5, Psychological Warfare Reactions and Developments, no. 2, 13 Oct 44, box 31, entry 283L, all in RG 331, NARA; and "Brief APW"; ch. 3, sec. 3, box 16, both in Lilly Papers.

16. Quotes from Memorandum for Comdr Cullinan, sub: PWS/JICPOA, 9 Mar 45, Theater Organization file, box 14; and Ltr, Coleman to Lilly, 17 Dec 46, Theater Planning file, 1946, box 15, respectively, both in Lilly Papers, NARA. See also ch. 3, sec. 3, box 16; "Brief APW"; Interv, Lilly with Twitty, 25 Nov 46, box 6; Office of the Outpost Representative Covering Central Pacific Operations, 21 Mar 44 to 31 Oct 45, OWI file, box 9; Conference, Lilly with Capt Waldo Drake, 19 May 45, Pacific Theater file, box 9; Pacific Fleet Confidential Letter 35CL–45 from Admiral Nimitz, COMINCH, U.S. Pacific Fleet, POA, to Pacific Fleet and Shore Activities, POA, 20 Jul 44, sub: Establishment of CINCPAC-CINCPOA PWB, Topical file, box 14, all in Lilly Papers. See Gilmore, "In the Wake of Winning Armies," p. 23.

17. Quote from Memorandum, MacArthur for JCS, 18 Jan 43; see also Memorandums, MacArthur for JCS, 22 Jun and 30 Jul 43; and Memorandum, Donovan for JCS, 12 Jun 43; all in Chronology Apr–Jun 1943 file, box 3; Interv, Lilly with Greene, 16 Oct 51, SWPA file, box 13; Memorandum to Admiral King for C/S Sig, re: OSS in SWPA, 29 Sep 44, PWB/SWPA file, box 9, all in Lilly Papers. Donovan visited

SWPA in April 1944. For Naval reaction to OWI and OSS, see Basic Military Plan for Psychological Warfare in the Pacific, JCS/403, 7 Jul 43; and Lawrence C. Soley, *Radio Warfare: OSS and CIA Subversive Propaganda* (Westport, Conn.: Praeger, 1989), pp. 183–89. For quotes see Roosevelt, *War Report OSS*, vol. 2, pp. 358, 365–67; and for Nimitz quote, see Ltr, Brown to Lilly, 25 Nov 46, COMSOPAC file, box 4, Lilly Papers.

18. First quote from Psychological Warfare Reactions and Developments, Collation Section, PWB/OMS/GHQ/SWPA, no. 6, 25 Jan 45, Reactions/F–3 file, box 15; second quote from Interrogation of Formosan POWs, HQ, Eighth Army, Assistant Chief of Staff, G–2, 30 May 45, Interrogation of Formosan POWs file, box 5; Interrogations by 170th Language Detachment of 25th Infantry Division, PW Interrogations, HQ, 25th Infantry, May–Jun 45 file, box 14; and FMAD Rpt no. 21, "Japanese Use of American Statements and Acts, Real or Alleged, in Propaganda to Create Fear," 15 Jun 45, OWI, BOI, FMAD file, box 9, all in entry 283k, RG 331, NARA; see also Warren J. Clear, "Close-Up of the Jap Fighting Man," *Reader's Digest* (November 1942): 124–30; Everett V. Stonequist, "How the Japs Got That Way," *Science Digest* (November 1942): 34–35. For Japanese military training, see Edward J. Drea, "In the Army Barracks of Imperial Japan," *Armed Forces and Society* 15 (Spring 1989): 330, 334–36, 344–45; Dower, *War Without Mercy*, pp. 35–36, 61–62, 68; Harries and Harries, *Soldiers of the Sun*, pp. 168–75, 319, 322, 343–44. For the high number of suicides on Saipan, see Paul C. Bosse, "Polling Civilian Japanese on Saipan," *Public Opinion Quarterly* 9 (1945): 176–82; Robert Sherrod, "Civilian Suicides on Saipan," *Reader's Digest* (October 1944): 83–84; Carl W. Hoffman, *Saipan: The Beginning of the End* (Washington, D.C.: Historical Division, HQ, U.S.M.C., 1950); Roy E. Appleman, James M. Burns, Russell A. Gugeler, and John Stevens, *Okinawa: The Last Battle* (Washington, D.C.: U.S. Army Center of Military History, 1948); and Harries and Harries, *Soldiers of the Sun*, pp. 432–33.

19. Quote from Psychological Warfare Reactions and Developments, Collation Section, PWB/OMS/GHQ/SWPA, no. 6, 25 Jan 45, Reactions/F–3 file, box 15, entry 283k, RG 331, NARA; see also Foreign Morale Analysis Division—OWI, Japan's Morale Under Bombs file, box 336, entry 172, RG 165, Records of the War Department General and Special Staffs, NARA. For "seishin," see Harries and Harries, *Soldiers of the Sun*, pp. 95–96, 101–02, 261–62, 322–26, 470–72.

20. Dower, *War Without Mercy*, pp. 36, 53, 113. For some of these stereotypical views, see Col Karl F. Baldwin, GSC (U.S. Military Attache to Australia), "Those Japanese: A Basic Psychological Study," 15 Jun 44, Those Japanese file, box 16, entry 283k; ann. 3, "Answer to Japan" from Rpt, Fellers to MacArthur, Mar 46, p. 20, Psychological Warfare Against Japan, Reference Copy; "Individual Research Study Submitted by Capt Bonner Fellers, CAC, to the CGSS, Ft. Leavenworth, Kans., 1934–35, in Rpt, Fellers to MacArthur, pp. 3–46, PW Against Japan, Reference Copy, all in RG 331, NARA; see also Psychological Warfare, Pacific file, box 329, entry 172, RG 165. For a detailed view of Allied and Japanese attitudes, see Dower, *War Without Mercy*; Stonequist, "How the Japs Got That Way," pp. 34–35; and Harries and Harries, *Soldiers of the Sun*, pp. 69–71, 95–98, 414–18, 424–25.

21. Dower, *War Without Mercy*, pp. 35–36, 45, 53, 56, 61–71. The American literature supporting the idea of the Japanese as being first invincible and then subhuman is vast; see George S. Andrew, Jr., "The 41st Didn't Take Prisoners," *Saturday Evening Post* (27 July 1946): 22; Clear, "Close-Up of the Jap Fighting Man," pp. 124–30; Stonequist, "How the Japs Got That Way," pp. 33–36; Col. A. G. Foxx, "Your Enemy: The Jap," *Infantry Journal* (March 1945): 23; "Why Are Japs Japs?" *Time* (7 August 1944): 66; Ford Wilkins, "Close-Up Report on the Japanese," *New York Times Magazine* (4 March 1945): 10–43; Sgt. Herman Kogan, "Those Nips Are Nuts," *The American Magazine* (February 1945): 88; Nathaniel Peffer, "Japanese Supermen? That, Too, Is a Fallacy," *New York Times Magazine* (22 March 1945): 14; Gonald

Gask, "Japs Do Surrender," *Newsweek* (30 October 1944): 32–33; William McGaffin, "What the Japanese Civilian Fears Most," *Saturday Evening Post* (14 October 1944): 35; John Beaufort and Clinton Green, "Japs Don't Want to Die," *Collier's* (21 October 1944): 14; Robert Sherrod, "Perhaps He Is Human," *Reader's Digest* (September 1943): 74.

22. Quotes from Notes on Guadalcanal by Col Roderick and Lt Col McDaniel, 27–28 Sep 42, Guadalcanal file, box 5, Lilly Papers. See also Dower, *War Without Mercy*, pp. 35–36, 45, 53, 56, 61–71.

23. Quotes from CBI/SEAC, ch. 3, sec. 3, box 16; and Memorandum, Hayne for Shulman, 30 Aug 44, sub: Memorandum on Psychological Warfare Operations, CBI file, box 2, respectively; and Weekly Reports (SWPA), no. 10, 10 Mar 45, A–2, PWB, SWPA/Untitled file, box 14, all in Lilly Papers. See also FMAD Rpt 21, "Japanese Use of American Statements and Acts, Real or Alleged, in Propaganda to Create Fear," 15 Jun 45, OWI, BOI, FMAD file, box 9; for natives' reprisals, see Significant Findings no. 257, 11 May 45, ATIS, SWPA–Significant Findings file, box 1, both in entry 283k, RG 331.

24. For quotes, see Ltr, Beard to Fellers, 3 Jan 45, SWPA/ Untitled file, box 14, Lilly Papers; also Dower, *War Without Mercy*, p. 64. Dower discusses the Goettge patrol, a group of twenty U.S. Marines on Guadalcanal who, while responding to a Japanese surrender attempt, were ambushed, shot, and bayonetted to a man on 12 Aug 42. Dower asserts that word of such incidents spread rapidly among American forces and produced a "shoot first and ask questions later" mentality among GIs.

25. For field commanders' attitudes, see Ltr, Hall to Hall, 19 May 45, X Corps file, box 16, entry 283k, RG 331; Ltr, Murphy to CG, 6th Army, Attn: Maj Paul F. Anderson, PWB, G–2, 11 Feb 45, sub: PWB Estimate Northern Luzon, Effectiveness file, box 5, Lilly Papers. For *Seppuku*, see Harries and Harries, *Soldiers of the Sun*, pp. 192, 400, 432, 437, 442, 458–60.

26. For FMAD and general sources on OWI, see Dower, *War Without Mercy*, pp. 55, 68, 137–38, 336–37; and Allen W. Winkler, *The Politics of Propaganda: The Office of War Information, 1942–1945* (New Haven: Yale University Press, 1978). For OWI Central Directives and Weekly Reports for the Pacific between April 1943 and April 1944, see OWI Analysis and Research Bureau file, box 9, entry 283k, RG 331; for OWI Overseas Branch Central Directives from August 1944 to July 1945, see Complete Set FMAD Rpts file, box 330, entry 172, RG 165. For a detailed discussion of the difficulties of Pacific propaganda, see Gilmore, "In the Wake of Winning Armies," chs. 3 and 4; and Richard H. Minear, "Cross-Cultural Perception and World War II," *International Studies Quarterly* 4 (December 1980): 555–80; and Shelia K. Johnson, *American Attitudes Toward Japan, 1941–1975* (Stanford, Calif.: American Enterprise Institute, 1975), pp. 4–7.

27. Included among the many surviving FMAD reports are "Japanese Home Morale Under Bombing," Japan's Morale Under Bombing file, box 336; "Biographies of Suzuki Cabinet and Other Persons in Important Roles as of 7 Apr 45," Complete Set FMAD Reports file, box 330; and Rpt 16, "The Japanese Domestic Audience," 15 Mar 45; Rpt 17, "Recent Trends in Japanese Military Morale as Revealed in the Interrogations of 251 Military POWs Captured in the Philippines, 15 Jan to 15 Mar 45," 9 Apr 45; Rpts 18, 19, and 20, "Aspects of Japanese Fighting Morale During the Papuan Phase of the New Guinea Campaign," 23 Apr 45; "Group and Individual Morale of the Japanese During the Lae–Salamaua Campaign," 12 May 45; "Factors Affecting Japanese Morale During the Aitape–Hollandia Campaign," 12 May 45, respectively; Rpt 25, "Japanese Behavior Patterns," 15 Sep 45; Rpt 26, "Principal Findings Regarding Japanese Morale During the War," 20 Sep 45; Rpt 28, "The Interrogation of Japanese POWs at Delhi," 29 Nov 45; Rpt 30, "Japanese Personality and Reactions as Seen in Soldiers Diaries," 19 Dec 45; Rpt 31, "The Attitudes of Japanese POWs: An Overall View," 29 Dec 45, all in OWI

FMAD Rpts file, box 335, in entry 172, RG 165; see also OWI FMAD Weekly Summaries nos. 1–9, 3 Aug–5 Oct 44; OWI FMAD Semi-Monthly Reports, Oct–Nov 44; OWI FMAD Rpts on Japanese Morale in New Guinea; and FMAD Rpt 21, "Japanese Use of American Statements and Acts, Real or Alleged, in Propaganda to Create Fear," 15 Jun 45, all in OWI Analysis and Research Bureau file, box 9, entry 283k, RG 331. See also ch. 3, sec. 3, box 16, Lilly Papers. In addition to the above, FMAD papers are a part of RG 208, NARA.

28. Memorandum, Fellers for Collation Section, 29 Aug 44; and Memorandum, Fellers for PWB Field Units, 13 Sep 44, re: Functions Collation Section, both in file: Collation Section, Aug–Nov 44, box 2, entry 283k, RG 331. For some examples of PWB/SWPA reports, see file: Psychological Warfare Pacific, box 329, entry 172, RG 165. Titles of Collation Section reports include "What the Japanese PW Thinks of Thought Warfare," 3 May 45, "Inside Japan–Food Crisis," 16 Jun 45, "Psychological Warfare: Reactions and Developments," published bimonthly as a progress report. For "Patterns, Trends, Current, and Prospective Developments Offering Opportunities for Exploitation and Implementation of Basic Military Plan," for 27 Aug 44, see file: Board, Agencies, box 2; also Organizational and PWB Functions Chart, anns. 2 and 5, Rpt, Fellers to MacArthur, "Psychological Warfare Against Japan, SWPA, 1944–1945, file: PsyWar Against Japan, Reference Copy, both in entry 283k; also Collation Section, G–5, GHQ/SWPA/PWB, Psychological Warfare Developments and Reactions, no. 8, Apr 45, box 31, entry 283l, all in RG 331; Interv, Lilly with Greene, file: SWPA, box 13; Fellers, 26 Aug 46, file: Japan, box 6, both in Lilly Papers.

29. See Ltr, Beard to Fellers, 3 Jan 45, file: SWPA/Untitled, box 14, Lilly Papers, NARA. Leaflets 1–A–8 and 1–A–1, produced by PWB/SWPA, entitled "Would You Take This Japanese Prisoner" and "Men of the Army! Why We Drop Leaflets; Why We Take Prisoners" were just two examples of this series, see leaflet nos. 1–A–1 to 1–H–6, box 23, entry 2832, RG 331; also Lt. G. B. Vail, FA, "Ideas Are Weapons," *Field Artillery Journal* (August 1945); and *Newsmap,* vol. 4, no. 7 B, Army Service Forces *Newsmap,* "Paper Bullets," OWI Area 3, vol. 1, 1945, file: Leaflet Newsletter, box 21, entry 283l, RG 331; and *What Is Propaganda* (EM 2–GI Roundtable), 46 pp., prepared for U.S. Armed Forces Institute by the American Historical Association, Jul 44, in Julius Schrieber Papers, box 1, Hoover Institution Archives.

30. See polls of POWs in *History of PWD/SHAEF*, pp. 122–24. For ETO POW figures, see Charles B. MacDonald, *The Last Offensive* (Washington, D.C.: U.S. Army Center of Military History, 1993), p. 478n8. This figure did not include over 4 million disarmed enemy personnel taken after V–E Day.

31. Exact figures for the number of Japanese prisoners taken in the Pacific vary widely and are contradictory, depending on the source. Some U.S. Army figures for July 1944 are higher than OWI's, although a War Department IG inspection of POW camps in April 1945 counted only 1,229 POWs (Korean, Formosans, and Japanese) in U.S. custody in the entire Pacific Ocean Area, see George G. Lewis and John Mehwa, *History of Prisoner of War Utilization by the United States Army, 1776–1945*, DA PAM 20–213 (Washington, D.C.: Department of the Army, 1955), p. 248. U.S. forces on Saipan, for example, claimed to have taken a total of 1,735 POWs, of which 879 were Japanese and 856 were Koreans, see FELO Information Review no. 10, 1 Nov 44, Camps file, box 33, entry 172, RG 165, NARA. For the OWI figures, see "Total POW's Captured by U.S. Forces by 1 Jul 44," in OWI–FMAD, Weekly Summary no. 5, 1–7 Sep 44, OWI Analysis and Research Bureau file, box 9, entry 283k, RG 331, NARA. Far fewer Japanese surrendered than was the case with Axis forces in Europe. The figures below represent another total for POWs held by the United States on the dates shown according to the U.S. Army Provost Marshal General's Office; see Place of Custody of Enemy POWs Held by U.S. Army From May 42–Jun 47, HRC file 383.6, POW Camps, U.S. Army Center of Military History:

	German	Italian	Japanese
May 42	31	0	1
Dec 42	512	1,317	52
Jun 43	34,161	19,212	62
Sep 43	115,358	48,253	95
Dec 43	123,643	62,784	297
Feb 44	133,874	70,296	592
May 44	139,034	99,080	1,584
Jul 44	209,193	124,325	1,785
Sep 44	274,103	173,433	3,988
Dec 44	563,812	117,437	4,534
Feb 45	589,210	117,999	5,458
Apr 45	883,326	117,361	7,337
Jul 45	1,527,181	126,481	16,429
Aug 45	1,538,837	123,807	24,138
Oct 45	1,465,579	43,583	50,141
Dec 45	1,334,786	25,696	113,151
Jan 46	1,335,801	25,696	84,748
Dec 46	971,72	330	6,955
Feb 47	964,314	22	2,877
Jun 47	915,204	18	0

For further information, see Krammer, "Japanese Prisoners of War in America," 68; file: ann. "A," sub: Information on OSS/OWI/USAF/GHQ/CBI, 20 Sep 44, file: CBI, box 2; and ch. 4, sec. 3, box 16, all in Lilly Papers, NARA.

32. For Philippines and New Guinea figures, see file: Japanese Statistical Trends, 1944–1945, box 5, entry 283k, RG 331; for China-Burma-India figures, see "Total POW's Captured by U.S. Forces by 1 Jul 44," in OWI-FMAD, Weekly Summary no. 5, 1–7 Sep 44, file: OWI Analysis and Research Bureau, box 9, entry 283k, RG 331; Lewis and Mewha, *History of Prisoner of War Utilization*, p. 260, claim that fewer than 100 POWs were taken in CBI. For the agreement between Australia and the United States regarding POW custody, see "Administrative History, Chief Provost Marshal, USAFP, 6 Apr 45 to 31 Dec 46" (mimeographed manuscript, U.S. Army Center of Military History, Washington, D.C.), p. 14. Following V–J Day over 260,000 Japanese were taken prisoner in the Philippines, see Lewis and Mewha, *History of Prisoner of War Utilization*, p. 253. New Zealand held a further 800 Japanese, see W. Wynne Mason, *Prisoners of War* (Wellington, N.Z.: War History Branch, Dept. of Internal Affairs, 1954), pp. 359, 520.

33. Patterson's praise in "The American Press on Your Work: A Round-up," file: Leaflet Newsletter, box 21, entry 283k, RG 331.

34. Quote from W. H. Lawrence, *New York Times*, 19 Jun 45, found in "The American Press on Your Work," Leaflet Newsletter file, box 21, entry 283k, RG 331, NARA; see also Intelligence monograph, Ryukyu Campaign, G–2, Tenth Army, pt. 4, PW and Morale, Sep 46, Okinawa file, box 8, and HQ, Tenth Army, Assistant Chief of Staff, G–2, "PW in the Ryukyus," CINCPOA/Okinawa file, both in box 4; and Rpt of PWS for Jul 45, JICPOA file, box 6; and Accomplishments file, box 2, all in Lilly Papers, NARA. See also Proceedings of OWI Chiefs, Area 3, OWI, 24 to 27 May 45 file, box 1, John Heistand Papers, Hoover Institution Archives; and Appleman et al., *Okinawa: The Last Battle*, pp. 465, 467, 473–74. The Okinawa Campaign produced many optimistic reports on the effects of propaganda, see Edgar L. Jones, "Fighting With Words: Psychological Warfare in the Pacific," *Atlantic Monthly* 176 (August 1945): 47–51; Hanson W. Baldwin, "This Is the Army We Have to Defeat," *New York Times Magazine* (29 July 1945): 5ff; "Jap Surrenders Are Increasing: Psychological War Proves Effective," (9 July 1945): 67–68.

35. For Leahy quote, see William D. Leahy, *I Was There: The Personal Story of the Chief of Staff to Presidents Roosevelt and Truman Based on His Notes and Diaries Made at the Time* (New York: McGraw Hill, 1950), p. 72; see also file: ch. 3, sec. 3, and file: ch. 4, sec. 3, both in box 16, Lilly Papers, NARA.

Generals, Admirals, and Atomic Bombs
Ending the War With Japan

Robert James Maddox

The dominant interpretation among diplomatic historians is that dropping atomic bombs on Japan in August 1945 was unnecessary.[1] The
Japanese probably would have surrendered earlier if only Washington had
signaled them that they could retain their emperor, according to this view,
and even without such assurance they would have had to give up before 1
November, target date for an invasion. The most extreme version is that
President Harry Truman knew the bombs were superfluous but *wanted* to
use them to intimidate the Soviet Union. More moderate critics tend to
regard intimidation as just one factor, but fault Truman for not exploring
alternatives. In reality, he acted as he did because he believed a bloodbath
lay in store.

Those who have argued that Truman knew, or should have known, that
the bombs were not needed to bring about capitulation before the invasion
date have relied largely on the following: Office of Strategic Services
(OSS) reports about Japanese "peace feelers"; decryption of Japanese
diplomatic messages through what became known as the MAGIC intercepts;
postwar reports such as the United States Strategic Bombing Survey; and
later assertions by a number of high-ranking admirals and generals that
they regarded the bombs as uncalled for.

Although this essay will deal with the last of these points, brief analyses of the others are relevant to the larger issue. The OSS did report
approaches by minor Japanese officials in Switzerland and elsewhere,
some of whom claimed to have important connections in Tokyo. *Not one*
ever produced evidence that he was authorized to speak for his government. This led to the understandable conclusion in Washington that they
were either well-meaning individuals acting on their own or, as one report
to the Combined Chiefs of Staff put it, they were part of an orchestrated
effort to "weaken the determination of the United Nations to fight to the
bitter end, or to create inter-allied dissension."[2]

A careful reading of the MAGIC intercepts reveals that while the Japanese foreign office was trying to attain a negotiated peace through Soviet mediation, it gave no indication that retention of the emperor was the sole obstacle to ending the war. On the contrary, it appeared to seek terms that no American official could even consider. As late as 11 July, the Japanese foreign minister instructed Ambassador Sato Naotaki in Moscow to inform the Soviets that Japan "has absolutely no idea of annexing or holding the territories occupied as a result of the war." Sato ridiculed the idea of offering to give up territories "we have already lost" and replied that it was useless to negotiate on the basis of "pretty little phrases devoid of all connection with reality."[3] From then until the end of the war, he pleaded with his superiors simply to ask Washington what terms would be acceptable. No such approach was ever made.

Exclusive reliance on diplomatic traffic to evaluate Japanese attitudes toward peace is misleading in any event. The foreign office did not control the situation in Tokyo, the military did. Intercepts of army and navy traffic, designated ULTRA, told a very different story. "ULTRA did portray a Japan in extremity," as Edward J. Drea has written, "but it also showed that its military leaders were blind to defeat and were bending all remaining national energy to smash an invasion of their home islands."[4] Even after both bombs had been dropped and the Japanese government had asked for terms, ULTRA produced from high military echelons messages such as: "The Imperial Army and Navy shall by no means return the sword to the scabbard, even though this should mean the total annihilation of the armed forces of the entire nation."[5]

The most often quoted sentence from the Strategic Bombing Survey of 1946 is that "Japan would have surrendered even if the atomic bombs had not been dropped, even if Russia had not entered the war, and even if no invasion had been planned or contemplated."[6] But this document and all others based on information available only after the war ended are completely irrelevant to what Truman could have known at the time.

Now to the admirals and generals. On 25 May 1945, the Joint Chiefs of Staff (JCS) had issued a preliminary directive for the invasion of Japan. The first phase, code-named OLYMPIC, provided for an assault on the southern island of Kyushu, scheduled for 1 November. Assuming success, it would be followed by CORONET, an invasion of the main island of Honshu on 1 March 1946.

In preparing for the Potsdam Conference, where he was scheduled to meet with British Prime Minister Winston Churchill and Soviet leader Joseph Stalin beginning on 15 July, Truman had to make the final determination of American strategy toward Japan because this in turn directly affected what he would seek from Stalin. The Soviet Union was not yet at war with Japan, but Stalin had promised President Franklin D. Roosevelt at the Yalta Conference (4–11 February 1945) to enter the conflict two or three months after V–E Day (8 May) in return for concessions in Manchuria and elsewhere. If an invasion proved necessary, Soviet forces could prevent Japanese troops in Manchuria and North China from returning to the homeland.

With the availability of atomic bombs uncertain, the president had to decide whether to approve the plans for invasion or to rely on conventional bombing and naval blockade as some of his advisers urged. Okinawa afforded a preview of coming attractions. Since 1 April the Japanese had fought with a ferocity that mocked any notion that their will to resist was diminishing. They had inflicted nearly 50,000 casualties, many resulting from the first large-scale use of kamikazes. The Japanese could be expected to defend their sacred homeland with even greater fervor, and kamikazes flying at short range promised to be more devastating.

On 14 June Truman had his personal chief of staff, Admiral William D. Leahy—who was also a member of the JCS—notify the other chiefs and the Secretaries of War and Navy that a meeting would be held at the White House on the afternoon of the eighteenth. The chiefs were asked to provide estimates of the time required and casualties expected in defeating Japan by invasion compared with relying on air bombardment and blockade. "He [Truman] desires to be informed," the memorandum concluded, "as to exactly what we want the Russians to do."[7] Truman called the meeting within the context of reports from Japan that a decision had been made at the highest level to fight the war to a finish. Only a week earlier, an imperial conference had adopted "The Fundamental Policy to be Followed Henceforth in the Conduct of the War," the key statement of which read that Japan would "prosecute the war to the bitter end in order to uphold the national polity, protect the imperial land, and accomplish the objectives for which we went to war."[8] On the evening before his session with the chiefs, Truman wrote in his diary: "I have to decide Japanese strategy—shall we invade Japan proper or shall we bomb and blockade? That is my hardest decision to date. But I'll make it when I have all the facts."[9]

The meeting began at 3:30 in the afternoon. Present were Army Chief of Staff George C. Marshall, Lt. Gen. Ira C. Eaker (sitting in for U.S. Army Air Forces Chief Henry H. Arnold who was on an inspection tour in the Pacific), Admiral Ernest J. King, Navy Chief of Staff, and Leahy. Secretary of the Navy James Forrestal, Secretary of War Henry L. Stimson, and Assistant Secretary of War John J. McCloy also attended.

Truman began by alluding to Leahy's memorandum stating the purpose of the meeting, then asked Marshall to state his views.

Marshall said that the chiefs believed that the invasion of southern Kyushu, southernmost of the main Japanese home islands, "appears to be the least costly worth-while operation following Okinawa." The two top commanders in the Pacific, General Douglas MacArthur and Admiral Chester W. Nimitz, concurred. Occupation of southern Kyushu, Marshall continued, was essential to tightening the blockade, providing additional airfields for bombers, and to serve as a staging area for the invasion of the main island of Honshu.

The chiefs advocated a target date of 1 November because by that time Japanese industry would be shattered, the navy rendered impotent, and American sea and air power would "have cut Jap reinforcement capabilities from the mainland to negligible proportions." Postponement beyond 1 November would give the Japanese more time to prepare, and bad weather might delay the invasion, "and hence the end of the war," for up to six months. Marshall said it would be "wrong" to try to estimate total casualty figures, but indicated that losses in the Kyushu operation during the first thirty days should not exceed those suffered in taking Luzon in the Philippines—31,000 men killed, wounded, or missing in action. He concluded by stating that in his opinion this was the only course to pursue. Air power had not been able to defeat Germany, and it would not be "sufficient to put the Japanese out of the war."

Admiral King said he fully endorsed Marshall's position. He regarded Kyushu as the "key to any siege operations" and a necessary acquisition for the invasion of Honshu. Preparations for the latter operation also should get under way because "they cannot be arranged for later." Once started, these preparations "can always be stopped if desired."

Admiral Leahy challenged Marshall's estimated casualty figures. He said that the Kyushu operation would be similar to Okinawa, and that the same percentage of casualties could be expected. He estimated that the first thirty days on Kyushu would incur about 49,000 casualties as opposed to Marshall's 31,000. King interjected to say that there would be more room to maneuver on Kyushu, and guessed that casualties probably would fall somewhere between those taken on Luzon and on Okinawa. Leahy insisted on the difficulties involved, at which point Truman complained that the proposed operation was "practically creating another Okinawa closer to Japan, to which the Chiefs of Staff agreed."

General Eaker made it unanimous among those who represented the services. He supported Marshall's proposal and said he had just received a message from Arnold that also "expressed complete agreement." Existing plans called for the use of an additional forty groups of heavy bombers, which "could not be deployed without the use of airfields in Kyushu." He concluded by saying that delay only favored the enemy, and "he urged that there be no delay." Secretaries Stimson and Forrestal agreed with the chiefs.

After discussion of other matters, Truman summed up: he considered "the Kyushu plan all right from the military standpoint" and directed the chiefs to "go ahead with it." He said he had hoped to avoid "an Okinawa from one end of Japan to the other," but that "he was clear on the situation now" and was "quite sure" that the operation should proceed.[10]

Truman later declared that dropping atomic bombs on Japan avoided an invasion that would have cost 500,000 American lives. Other administration officials such as Stimson cited similar or higher figures. Recent critics have attacked such claims as wildly unrealistic. Several have cited a report prepared by the Joint War Plans Committee (JWPC) for the chiefs' meeting with Truman. This report estimated that landings in southern Kyushu, followed by an invasion of Honshu (which is what the JCS proposed) would cost 40,000 dead and 150,000 wounded and missing in action, for a total of 193,500 casualties.[11]

That those who participate in a controversial decision should magnify the consequences of the alternative is commonplace. Some writers profess to see more sinister motives. The much lower JWPC estimates, they say, call into question the very idea that atomic bombs were dropped to avoid heavy casualties. By disparaging that justification as cover-up, they seek to strengthen the case that the bombs were dropped for political rather than for military reasons.[12]

The proposition that an estimated 193,500 casualties (far more actually, for this figure omitted nonbattle casualties for ground forces, and naval losses were expected to be much heavier than at Okinawa) were too inconsequential to have caused Truman to use the bomb can only have occurred to intellectuals sitting in the safety of their studies decades after the event. There is more. These critics have ignored the disclaimers sprinkled throughout the JWPC report: that casualties "are not subject to accurate estimate," and that the projection "is admittedly only an educated guess." Most importantly, they neglect to mention that these figures never were communicated to Truman, and in any event had become irrelevant by the time the atomic bombs were dropped.

When the JWPC paper was reviewed at the next higher level by the Joint Staff planners, the latter group excised the casualty estimates and stated that they "are not subject to accurate estimate." The amended document then went to Assistant Chief of Staff John E. Hull, who drew up a memorandum entitled "Amplifying Comments on Planners' Paper for Presentation to the President." Hull wrote that "it is considered wrong to give any estimate in numbers," and he merely listed the casualties taken in several previous campaigns. He went on to say that "There is reason to believe that the first 30 days in Kyushu should not exceed the price we paid for Luzon." It was Hull's memorandum from which Marshall read in his report to Truman during the 18 June meeting. Hull himself later said that casualty estimates had ranged "from a few hundred thousand to a million men to do the thing."[13]

Marshall's casualty estimate for the first thirty days on Kyushu was based on the assumption that there were about 350,000 Japanese troops stationed there and that American air and sea power "will have cut Jap reinforcement capabilities from the mainland to negligible proportions." That assumption proved unwarranted. By the time the first bomb was dropped, estimates of Japanese defenders had risen to 560,000, and projections for "X Day" (1 November) placed the number at 680,000—nearly double the original figure. MacArthur's G–2 reported on 29 July that "this threatening development, if not checked, may grow to a point where we attack on a ratio of one (1) to one (1) which is not the recipe for victory." A casualty estimate of 31 July predicted they might run as high as 394,859 *for the Kyushu operation alone*.[14] Truman may have exaggerated the cost of an invasion, but not on the scale which his critics have charged.

Regardless of what any of the chiefs might have *thought* at the time of the 18 June meeting, as a group they had informed Truman that air bombardment and naval blockade were insufficient, and that invasion would be necessary to end the war in the foreseeable future. Those who actually represented the services (Marshall, Eaker/Arnold, and King) had personally endorsed the operation. No one dissented when Truman stated that the proposed operation was "practically creating another Okinawa closer to Japan." As Marshall put it, "It is a grim fact that there is not an easy, bloodless way to win war."

Special mention must be made of Admiral Leahy, who is often cited as having protested to Truman on military and moral grounds against using the bombs. Leahy had retired from active duty in 1939. After a brief stint as governor of Puerto Rico, he was appointed ambassador to the Vichy government of France in 1940 and later became President Roosevelt's personal chief of staff. He became a member of the JCS for two reasons: to act as liaison between the chiefs and the president and to serve as a counterweight to the imbalance having the U.S. Army Air Forces represented would create (Arnold was technically Marshall's subordinate). Leahy had no constituency. Admiral King, as Navy Chief and Chief of Naval Operations, spoke for that service.

In his memoirs, published in 1950, Leahy wrote that he had favored bombing and blockade over invasion and that he had so informed both Roosevelt and Truman. He did not claim that this course would force Japan to capitulate before the projected invasion date, merely that it would do so eventually and was worth the wait. What has led to misunderstanding about his role is that in the last pages of his book he condemned using the bombs as "barbarous," and said they were of "no material assistance in our war against Japan."[15]

One creative author has made it appear that Leahy conveyed these sentiments to Truman by braiding together snippets from the end of the book with an earlier quotation about his preference for relying on conventional bombing and blockade.[16] Nowhere in the volume does Leahy himself make any such claim, and there is nothing in his detailed diaries (in which he mentioned the bombs freely) to support such a notion. Indeed, during the months before their use he had "as a munitions expert" predicted that they would not work, and still scoffed at them as a "professor's dream," even after one was successfully tested. Two days after Hiroshima, Truman told aides that "the admiral said up to the last that it wouldn't go off."[17]

No one yet has produced evidence that any of the service chiefs ever informed Truman that they had changed their minds about the need for invasion, or conveyed to him any moral reservations about using the bombs. As late as 10 July, less than a month before the first bomb was scheduled to be ready, the JCS considered the possibility that even a successful invasion would not compel the Japanese to surrender if they transferred their government to the mainland, where "the presence of large ground forces in Manchuria and China will permit continued resistance." To forestall such a move, they approved an operation code-named PASTEL. This was a scheme to deceive the Japanese into believing that because of the heavy losses suffered at Okinawa and other reasons there would be no invasion until the autumn of 1946.[18]

Neither MacArthur nor Nimitz ever questioned the need for invasion or expressed any reservations about the bomb. When asked for his opinion before the 18 June meeting, MacArthur had replied, "I most earnestly recommend no change in Olympic." About that time he told General Arnold in Manila that although bombing would help win the war, "in the final analysis, the doughboys would have to march into Tokyo."[19] He continued to urge that preparations go forward even after the first bomb had been dropped. When Nimitz was notified about the bomb in early 1945, he is supposed to have replied, "This sounds fine, but this is only February.

Can't we get one sooner?"[20] After Hiroshima and Nagasaki he recommended dropping a third on Tokyo.

Only one high-ranking officer, Dwight D. Eisenhower, claimed to have entered a protest against using the bombs. In his *Crusade in Europe*, published in 1948, he recalled that when Stimson told him about the bomb during the Potsdam Conference, he replied that he hoped "we would never have to use such a thing against any enemy," because he did not want the United States to be the first to use "something as horrible and destructive as this new weapon was described to be." He admitted, however, that "My views were merely personal and immediate reactions; they were not based on any analysis of the subject."[21]

Eisenhower's recollection ripened with the passage of time. In his 1963 *Mandate for Change*, he remembered telling a "deeply perturbed" Stimson that "dropping the bomb was completely unnecessary." That same year he provided an interviewer with an even more colorful account. "We'd had a nice evening at headquarters in Germany," he recalled. Then, after dinner, "Stimson got this cable saying the bomb had been perfected and was ready to be dropped. The cable was in code. . . . 'The lamb is born' or some damn thing like that."

After listening to Stimson outline the plans for use, Eisenhower claimed to have replied that he was "against it," because "the Japanese were ready to surrender and it wasn't necessary to hit them with that awful thing," and because he "hated to see our country be the first to use such a weapon. Well . . . the old gentleman got furious."[22] In this version he had gone from merely expressing dismay to delivering such a forceful protest on moral and military grounds as to infuriate the secretary. And he omitted his earlier qualifications that his views were "merely personal and immediate reactions" and were "not based on any analysis of the subject."

The best thing that can be said about Eisenhower's latter account is that it was imaginative. Part of it is demonstrably false, the rest of dubious authenticity. The first coded cable arrived in Potsdam on the evening of 16 July, the second on the morning of the eighteenth. Eisenhower was at his headquarters in Frankfurt at the time. Stimson first met with Eisenhower at a flag-raising ceremony in Berlin on the twentieth. General Omar Bradley also attended, and Stimson merely noted in his diary that "I had a pleasant chat with each of them after the show was over."[23] None of Eisenhower's several versions of his debate with Stimson has it occurring during this brief encounter.

Stimson next saw Eisenhower at the general's headquarters on 27 July. Stimson wrote in his diary that he tried to persuade a somewhat dejected Eisenhower how important his new job as military governor of Germany was, but said nothing about the bomb. Notes prepared by Stimson's aide, however, refer to a lunchtime conversation (with General Lucius D. Clay attending) about "civil affairs and General [Leslie R.] Groves' project [the bomb]." As Stimson had only two meetings with Eisenhower during the Potsdam Conference, this had to have been the one in question.[24]

Stimson's failure to mention talk about the bomb suggests two possibilities. One is that Eisenhower's protest was so strong and so obviously correct that Stimson was too embarrassed to record it. The other is that Eisenhower responded so mildly that Stimson saw no reason to allude to it. The latter is more likely and more closely fits with Eisenhower's first version of the conversation. Truman himself, after all, had referred to the bomb as "the most terrible thing ever discovered." That Eisenhower in the presence of Clay would have condemned as harshly as he later claimed a decision made by the president, Marshall, and the secretary, would have been totally out of character for this diplomatic general.

Several other factors must be kept in mind, regardless of what actually was said. Eisenhower had commanded Allied forces in Europe, after all, and possessed neither special expertise nor private sources of information on conditions in Japan. The discussion took place on 27 July, furthermore, three days after orders to drop the bomb had been issued. Finally, Stimson left for Washington immediately following the meeting, arriving back on the twenty-eighth, and did not speak with Truman until after Hiroshima. Using Eisenhower's alleged protest as evidence that Truman knew the bombs were unnecessary has no basis in fact. The claim put forward by some writers that Eisenhower personally broached Truman as well has been shown to be pure fiction.[25]

Whether the Japanese would have surrendered had Truman let them know that they might retain their emperor can never be known. Considering the bitter struggle that took place within the Japanese government even *after* both bombs had been dropped and the Soviet Union had entered the war, the idea that they would have accepted comparable terms even before these cataclysmic events seems farfetched.

Stimson and others had long contended that assuring the Japanese about the emperor might remove the last obstacle to capitulation. They also claimed that the only way to gain an orderly surrender was through an imperial rescript, without which Japanese troops everywhere might continue to fight regardless of what orders the government in Tokyo issued. Finally, perhaps as a constitutional monarch, the emperor would provide a stabilizing influence on a society in transition. The secretary included such a provision in his draft of what became known as the Potsdam Declaration, which called upon Japan to surrender or face utter destruction.

Those who opposed making an overture did so on several grounds. Japanese hard-liners were certain to contend that it represented a weakening of American resolve, and that continued resistance would wring further concessions. Some antiretentionists claimed that the emperorship was inextricably bound up with Japanese militarism, and that a premature armistice would betray both the sacrifices already made and future generations if a resurgent Japan again chose the path of aggression. The only way to assure lasting peace was to fight on until the United States and its allies could occupy Japan for as long as it took to achieve full democratization.

One State Department Soviet expert insisted that the Russians would interpret an offer to retain the emperor as an act of treachery. Stalin in May had told Truman envoy Harry Hopkins that he favored eliminating the emperorship as a means of crushing Japanese militarism, and said at Potsdam that there was "no change" in his views.[26] He would consider an American overture to the Japanese as an attempt to end the war before Soviet entry activated the Yalta agreement, and to use Japan as a counter to Soviet influence in the Far East.

Finally, there were domestic considerations. President Roosevelt had announced the "unconditional surrender" policy at the Casablanca Conference in 1943, and it since had become a slogan of the war. Regardless of his real role in the Japanese system, Hirohito was considered by most Americans to be as culpable for the war as Hitler and Mussolini. An offer to preserve his throne would provoke public outrage and constitute a betrayal of Roosevelt's legacy. Small wonder that although Truman on several occasions said he did not oppose retaining the emperor, he refused to tender a public offer.

The Joint Chiefs of Staff wanted to make it as easy as possible for Japan to surrender. When the chiefs reviewed Stimson's draft ultimatum at Potsdam on 17 July, it contained the provision that the Japanese might retain "a constitutional monarchy under the present dynasty." Relying on a report he had just received from the Joint Strategic Survey Committee, General Marshall pointed out that some Japanese might interpret this to mean the Allies meant to depose or execute Hirohito and replace him with another member of the royal family, while "radical elements" would oppose retaining the system in any form.

Marshall suggested and the chiefs endorsed a more general statement: "Subject to suitable guarantees against further acts of aggression, the Japanese people will be free to choose their own form of government." In his memorandum fowarding the proposal to Truman, Leahy wrote that "such a statement . . . would be more likely to appeal to all elements of the

Japanese populace."[27] The formula Marshall offered, though not his exact words, would appear in the Potsdam Declaration.

When the Potsdam ultimatum was issued on 26 July the order to drop the bombs already had been sent to the Pacific. Only the president could stop the machinery set in motion if he considered the Japanese reply satisfactory. It was not. Although Japanese moderates wished to withhold any comment, hard-liners succeeded in having the reply take the form of a flat rejection. One atomic bomb was dropped on Hiroshima on 6 August and another on Nagasaki three days later. After much wrangling the Japanese on 14 August accepted the American offer to retain the emperor provided his and the government's authority "shall be subject to the Supreme Commander of the Allied Powers."[28]

In view of subsequent statements by those such as Leahy, Eisenhower, and Curtis LeMay (who later claimed that atomic bombs "had nothing to do with the end of the war")—often cited on faith by approving authors—it is important to understand what was being said at the time.[29] Two days after Hiroshima, General Arnold in Washington delightedly informed Carl A. Spaatz, commander of United States Army Strategic Air Forces, that "Atomic bombing story received largest and heaviest smash play of the entire war with three deck banner headlines evening and morning papers." That same day Marshall rebuked Spaatz and bomber commander Curtis LeMay for telling reporters that because of the bomb "an invasion will not be necessary." "However good your intentions," Marshall warned, "you can do incalculable harm."[30]

On 9 August Spaatz and Maj. Gen. Nathan Twining, commander of Twentieth Air Force, urged dropping a third bomb on Tokyo. LeMay and Admiral Nimitz concurred. Spaatz explained on the tenth that "the psychological effect on the government officials still remaining in Tokyo is more important than destruction." The next day Arnold replied that the recommendation was "being considered on a high level."[31]

Spaatz also asked that a "hardstand" with hydraulic lift for loading atomic bombs into aircraft be installed at Okinawa "ready for use no later than 15 September," an odd request if he thought Japan would surrender any moment. On 13 August he pleaded that "every effort be made to expedite delivery of [the third] atomic bomb." A few days after Japan surrendered, Arnold lamented to Spaatz that while he was "naturally feeling very good," it was, "shall I say unfortunate that we were never able to launch the full power of our bombing attack with the B–29s" to convince "doubting Thomases" how devastating conventional bombing could be. Arnold obviously thought at the time that atomic bombs had ended the war and had denied the air force its opportunity to kill many more thousands of Japanese than had perished at Hiroshima and Nagasaki.[32]

General Marshall was afraid that an invasion still might be necessary even after the bombs were used. The day after Hiroshima, he sent an "eyes only" message to MacArthur. Because a Joint Military Intelligence Committee report indicated so large a buildup of ground and air forces in Kyushu and southern Honshu, Marshall asked MacArthur for his views on "possible alternate objectives to OLYMPIC" such as Tokyo or Sendai. Estimates as of 2 August placed the number of troops stationed in Kyushu at 545,000 (nearly 200,000 more than the 18 June figure), and the Japanese Navy recently had released 100,000 sailors to bolster the ground forces. As a result, defenses against invasion *already* were "in excess of that previously estimated as Japanese capability by OLYMPIC target date." MacArthur replied that he opposed the "slightest notion of changing the Olympic operation."[33]

If the Japanese did not surrender after several atomic bombs, Marshall told an acquaintance, "we must prepare to continue a prolonged struggle to compel such action."[34] On 13 August a member of his staff told one of Groves' assistants that "General Marshall feels we should consider now whether or not dropping them as originally planned [on cities], or [if] these we have should be held back for use in direct support of major operations."[35] In other words, as tactical weapons against enemy troop concentrations before and during the invasion. Japan's surrender the following day, of course, ended such speculation.

Until newly uncovered documents show otherwise, the available sources point to the unremarkable conclusion that Truman approved using the bombs for the reason he said he did: to end quickly a bloody war that would have become far bloodier had an invasion proved necessary. There is no real evidence that *any* admiral or general expressed to Truman opposition to using the bombs or indicated to him that Japan would surrender prior to the scheduled invasion.

What often goes unmentioned is that fighting still was going on in the Philippines, China, and elsewhere, and that thousands of prisoners of war were condemned to live and to die in unspeakable conditions every day the war continued. Fear also existed that the Japanese would slaughter their captives if the sacred homeland were invaded. Truman was Commander in Chief of American armed forces and had a duty to the men under his command not shared by those passing moral judgment years later. One can only imagine what would have happened had tens of thousands of young Americans been killed or wounded on Japanese soil, and then it became known that the president had chosen not to employ weapons that might have ended the war months earlier.

NOTES

1. J. Samuel Walker, "The Decision to Use the Bomb: A Historical Update," *Diplomatic History* 14, no. 1 (Winter 1990): 97–114.

2. Department of Defense Press Release, Sep 55, "The Entry of the Soviet Union Into the War Against Japan: Military Plans, 1941–45," p. 88, Hanson Baldwin Collection, George C. Marshall Library.

3. Togo Shigenori to Sato, 11 Jul 45; Sato to Togo, 12 Jul 45, both in folder 571, James F. Byrnes Papers, Clemson University.

4. Edward J. Drea, *MacArthur's Ultra: Codebreaking and the War Against Japan* (Lawrence: University Press of Kansas, 1992), p. 204.

5. Publication of Pacific Strategic Intelligence Section, SRH 90, 29 Aug 45, MAGIC collection, U.S. Army Military History Institute (MHI), Carlisle, Pa.

6. United States Strategic Bombing Survey, *Japan's Struggle to End the War* (Washington, D.C.: 1946), p. 13.

7. Memorandum, Admiral Leahy for Joint Chiefs of Staff, 14 Jun 45, attached to JCS 1388/1, xerox 1587, Marshall Library.

8. Cited in Robert J. C. Butow, *Japan's Decision to Surrender* (Stanford, Calif.: Stanford University Press, 1954), pp. 99–100.

9. Robert H. Ferrell, *Off the Record: The Private Papers of Harry S. Truman* (New York: Harper, 1980), p. 47.

10. All quotations from paragraphs above are from "Extracted From Minutes of Meeting Held at the White House 18 Jun 45 at 1530, attached to JCS 13881, "Details of the Campaign Against Japan," xerox 1567, Marshall Library.

11. The report is JWPC 369/1, "Details of the Campaign Against Japan," 15 Jun 45, ABC file 384, Record Group (RG) 319, National Archives and Records Administration (NARA).

12. See Gar Alperovitz, "Why the United States Dropped the Bomb," *Technology Review* (September/October 1990): 22–34; Barton Bernstein, in "A Postwar Myth: 500,000 Lives Saved," *Bulletin of the Atomic Scientists* (June/July 1986): 38–40, without making overt accusations, states that the "myth" helped deter Americans from asking "troubling questions" about use of the bomb and that destruction of the myth "should reopen these questions."

13. The Joint Planners Rpt of 16 Jun 45 and Hull's "Amplifying Comments" of 17 Jun 45 are in ABC file 384, RG 319, NARA. Hull's later estimate is from Interv, Hull Papers, MHI.

14. The 560,000 estimate is in Order of Battle Bulletin 74, 4 Aug 45, SRH, War Military Intelligence Division, MHI; the projection for X-Day is in Walter Krueger, *From Down Under to Nippon: The Story of Sixth Army in World War II* (Washington, D.C.: Combat Forces Press, 1953), p. 333; MacArthur's G–2's comment is in Drea, *MacArthur's Ultra,* p. 216; and the casualty estimate is in Lt Col D. B. Kendrick to Chief Surgeon, American Forces Western Pacific, 31 Jul 45, cited in "Medical Service in the Asiatic-Pacific Theater," ch. 15, p. 18, unpublished Ms, U.S. Army Center of Military History, Washington, D.C.

15. William D. Leahy, *I Was There* (New York: Whittlesey House, 1950), p. 441.

16. Gar Alperovitz, *Atomic Diplomacy: Hiroshima and Potsdam. The Use of the Atomic Bomb & The American Confrontation with Soviet Power* (New York: Updated and expanded version by Elizabeth Sifton Books, 1985), pp. 14–15; for the passage showing that Leahy was speaking in the context of naval blockade and bombing, rather than atomic weapons, see his *I Was There,* p. 385.

17. Leahy, *I Was There*; Truman quote from Eben Ayers diary entry for 8 Aug 45, in Robert H. Ferrell, *Truman in the White House: The Diary of Eben Ayers* (Columbia, Mo.: University of Missouri Press), p. 61.

18. Joint Staff Planners Rpt proposing "PASTEL" and JCS approval, box 24, Carl A. Spaatz Papers, Library of Congress (LC).

19. MacArthur's message to Marshall is in JCS 13881/1, "Details of the Campaign Against Japan," p. 3, xerox 1567, Marshall Library; his comment to Arnold is in the latter's *Global Mission* (New York: Harper and Brothers, 1949), p. 569.

20. Fletcher Knebel and C. W. Bailey, *No High Ground* (New York: Harper, 1960), p. 90.

21. Dwight D. Eisenhower, *Crusade in Europe* (Garden City, N.Y.: Doubleday, 1948), p. 443.

22. Dwight D. Eisenhower, *Mandate for Change* (Garden City, N.Y.: Doubleday, 1963), pp. 312–13; "Ike on Ike," *Newsweek* (11 Nov 63): 108.

23. Henry L. Stimson Diary, 20 Jul 45, Stimson Papers, Yale University Library.

24. Stimson diary entry, 27 Jul 45; Col W. H. Kyle, "Notes on the Trip of the Secretary of War," 6–28 Jul 45, reel 128, both in Stimson Papers, Yale University Library.

25. Barton Bernstein in "Ike and Hiroshima: Did He Oppose It?" *Journal of Strategic Studies* 10 (September 1987): 377–89, casts doubts on Eisenhower's claims and shows that the alleged confrontation with Truman was merely invented by the coauthor of Omar Bradley's autobiography.

26. Walter Brown's diary, 18 Jul 45, folder 602, James F. Byrnes Papers, Clemson University Library.

27. "Military Aspects of Unconditional Surrender Formula for Japan," JCS 1275/5 in CCS 334, Joint Chiefs of Staff, and Leahy Memorandum of 18 Jul, verifax folder 128, both in Marshall Library.

28. The American offer is reprinted in Michael B. Stoff, Jonathan F. Fanton, and R. Hal Williams, *The Manhattan Project* (New York: McGraw-Hill, Inc.), p. 247.

29. LeMay quotation is from Alperovitz, *Atomic Diplomacy*, p. 17.

30. Arnold quote from Knebel and Bailey, *No High Ground*, p. 221; Marshall to Spaatz, 8 Aug 45, box 85, folder 25, Marshall Papers, Marshall Library.

31. For Spaatz, Twining, LeMay, Nimitz recommendation, see Commanding General 313th Bomb Wing to Twining, 9 Aug 45, and Twining to Nimitz and Spaatz, same date; Spaatz quote from Spaatz to General Lauris Norstad (Arnold's chief of staff), 10 Aug 45, and Arnold's reply in Norstad to Spaatz, same date, all in box 24, Spaatz Papers, LC.

32. Spaatz to Arnold, 10 and 13 Aug 45, box 24, and Arnold to Spaatz, 19 Aug 45, box 21, Spaatz Papers, LC.

33. Marshall to MacArthur, 7 Aug 45, Operations and Plans Division, General Staff, xerox, Marshall Library; MacArthur's reply is in Drea, *MacArthur's Ultra*, p. 223. The Joint Intelligence Committee report is attached to Joint War Plans Committee 397, 4 Aug 45, CCSJ, Joint Chiefs of Staff, RG 218, NARA.

34. John Callan O'Laughlin to Herbert Hoover, 11 Aug 45, PPI, Herbert Hoover Presidential Library. O'Laughlin's five-page, single-spaced letter is based on a long talk he had with Marshall on 9 August 1945.

35. Transcript of Telecon between General John E. Hull and Col L. E. Seaman, 13 Aug 45, Atomic Bomb/Manhattan Project folder, Marshall Library; Marc Gallicchio, "After Nagasaki: General Marshall's Plan for the Use of Tactical Nuclear Weapons Against Japan," *Prologue: Quarterly of the National Archives* 23, no. 4 (Winter 1991): 396–404.

Contributors

Robert H. Bouilly served as historian at the U.S. Army Armament, Munitions, and Chemical Command at Rock Island, Illinois, from 1978 to 1990 and at the U.S. Army Sergeants Major Academy at Fort Bliss, Texas, from 1990 until 1997. He holds a Ph.D. degree from the University of Missouri.

Boyd Dastrup has been command historian at the U.S. Army Field Artillery Center and Fort Sill since 1984. He is the author of *U.S. Army Command and General Staff College: A Centennial History* (1981), *Crusade in Nuremberg: Military Occupation, 1945–1949* (1985), *King of Battle: A Branch History of the U.S. Army's Field Artillery* (1992), and *The Field Artillery: History and Sourcebook* (1994). He earned his doctorate at Kansas State University.

Christopher Gabel has been a historian at the Combat Studies Institute, U.S. Army Command and General Staff College, Fort Leavenworth, Kansas, since 1983. He is the author of *Seek, Strike, and Destroy: U.S. Army Tank Destroyer Doctrine in World War II* (1986) and *The U.S. Army GHQ Maneuvers of 1941* (1991). He holds a Ph.D. degree from Ohio State University.

Harry A. Gailey is a professor emeritus in the History Department at San Jose State University in California. He is the author of *Peleliu, 1944* (1983), *The Liberation of Guam* (1988), *Bougainville, 1943–1945: The Forgotten Campaign* (1991), and *The War in the Pacific, From Pearl Harbor to Tokyo Bay* (1995). He holds a Ph.D. degree from the University of California at Los Angeles.

Marc Gallicchio is an associate professor of history at Villanova University in Pennsylvania and holds a Ph.D. degree from Temple University. He is the author of *The Cold War Begins in Asia: American East Asian Policy and the Fall of the Japanese Empire* (1988).

Henry G. Gole was an Army colonel in the Special Forces. He taught at the U.S. Military Academy and the Army War College. He holds a Ph.D. degree from Temple University and is the author of articles on war planning, military morale, war literature, and NATO issues.

John T. Greenwood is chief of the Field Programs and Historical Services Division at the U.S. Army Center of Military History. He was chief of the Office of History at the U.S. Army Corps of Engineers from 1978 to 1988. He holds a Ph.D. degree from Kansas State University.

Charles Hendricks has been a historian with the Field and International Branch of the U.S. Army Center of Military History since 1995. He served with the Office of History of the U.S. Army Corps of Engineers from 1981 to 1995. He holds a Ph.D. degree from Cornell University.

Monroe M. Horn has taught American history at the Commonwealth School in Boston, Massachusetts, since 1993. He is also director of computing there. He is a doctoral candidate in history at Harvard University. His dissertation topic is "Vox Populi, Vox Dei? William Borah and Public Opinion on Foreign Policy, 1919–29."

David Horner is the research officer at the Strategic and Defence Studies Center of the Australian National University, where he earned his doctorate. A retired lieutenant colonel in the Australian Army, he is the author of numerous books on Australian military history, including *High Command: Australia and Allied Strategy, 1939–45* (1983, rev. ed. 1992), *General Vasey's War* (1992), and *Inside the War Cabinet: Directing Australia's War Effort, 1939–45* (1996).

Thomas M. Huber has been a historian at the Combat Studies Institute, U.S. Army Command and General Staff College, Fort Leavenworth, Kansas, since 1985. He has written *Pastel: Deception in the Invasion of Japan* (1988) and *Japan's Battle of Okinawa, April–June 1945* (1990). He holds a Ph.D. from the University of Chicago.

James A. Huston was a professor of history at Purdue University in Indiana. He received a Ph.D. degree from New York University. Huston is the author of *The Sinews of War: Army Logistics, 1775–1953* (1966), and *Out of the Blue: U.S. Army Airborne Operations in World War II* (1972).

Charles E. Kirkpatrick is command historian with V Corps in Germany. He is a retired Army major in Air Defense Artillery and the author of *Archie in the A.E.F.: The Creation of the Antiaircraft Service of the United States Army, 1917–1918* (1984), and *An Unknown Future and a Doubtful Present: Writing the Victory Plan of 1941* (1990).

Clayton D. Laurie has served as a historian in the Histories Division of the U.S. Army Center of Military History since 1986. He is the author of *The Propaganda Warriors: America's Crusade Against Nazi Germany* (1996) and coauthor of *the Role of Federal Military Forces in Domestic Disorders, 1877–1945* (1997). He holds a Ph.D. degree from the American University.

James McNaughton has been command historian at the Defense Language Institute Foreign Language Center at the Presidio of Monterey, California, since 1987. He holds a Ph.D. degree from Johns Hopkins University. He is currently writing the Army's official history of the service of Japanese-American (Nisei) linguists in World War II.

Robert James Maddox is a professor of history at the University Park campus of Pennsylvania State University. He is the author of *The New Left and the Origins of the Cold War* (1973), *The United States and World War II* (1992), and *Weapons for Victory: The Hiroshima Decision Fifty Years Later* (1995). He holds a Ph.D. degree from Rutgers University.

Frances Martin was a historian at the U.S. Army Chemical Research, Development, and Engineering Center at Aberdeen Proving Ground, Maryland, from 1988 to 1992 and at the U.S. Army Space and Strategic Defense Command at Huntsville, Alabama, from 1992 until 1997.

Patrick Murray is professor of history at Valley Forge Military Academy in Pennsylvania. He is the author of *Eisenhower Versus Montgomery: The Continuing Debate* (1996). He holds a Ph.D. degree from Temple University.

Mason Schaefer has been a historian at the Military Traffic Management Command in Falls Church, Virginia, since 1990. He holds a master's degree in history from the American University.

Keir B. Sterling has been the Army's Ordnance Branch historian since 1983. He is on the staff of the U.S. Army Combined Arms Support

Command at Fort Lee, Virginia. He is the author of *Last of the Naturalists: The Career of C. Hart Merriam* (1984) and editor of the *Biographical Dictionary of American and Canadian Naturalists and Environmentalists* (1997).

Richard W. Stewart has been director of history, archives, library, and museums at the U.S. Army Special Operations Command at Fort Bragg, North Carolina, since 1990. He is the author of *Staff Operations: The X Corps in Korea, December 1950* (1991), and *The English Ordnance Office, 1585–1625: A Case Study in Bureaucracy* (1996). He holds a Ph.D. degree from Yale University.

Theodore Wilson is a professor of history at the University of Kansas. He is the author of *The First Summit: Roosevelt and Churchill at Placentia Bay, 1941* (1969, rev. ed. 1991), and *The Marshall Plan, 1947–1951* (1977). He holds a Ph.D. degree from Indiana University.